NO TURNING BACK

NO TURNING BACK

A HISTORY OF AMERICAN PRESBYTERIAN INVOLVEMENT IN SUB-SAHARAN AFRICA, 1833-2000

"Write down for the coming generation
what the Lord has done,
so that people not yet born
will praise Him."

—Psalm 102:18 (Good News Bible)

JAMES A. COGSWELL

To order additional copies of this book, contact:
Xlibris Corporation
1-888-795-4274
www.Xlibris.com
Orders@Xlibris.com
38951

CONTENTS

FOREWORD

As coordinator for the work of the Presbyterian Church (USA) in Africa, I have had numerous opportunities to hear about God's faithfulness over the ages. I have heard the stories of church beginnings and have been reminded of the PC(USA)'s part in bringing the Good News to this part of the world. Cameroon, Congo, Sudan, Ethiopia have vibrant, growing churches that PC(USA) missionaries, with God's faithfulness, started so long ago. These partners and others are celebrating 50, 100, and 150 years of ministry. Too many people to mention from the PC(USA) and its predecessor denominations as well as our Africa Christian partners have leaned on God's faithfulness and served to spread the gospel in Africa over the past 170 years. What a witness to God's love through Jesus Christ!

The early missionaries went to Africa in response to Christ's call to "go and make disciples of all nations" and "As the Father has sent me so I send you." Many died while in service, and more buried their loved ones in foreign lands. I have heard our African brothers and sisters attest to the witness of earlier missionaries and how their presence and witness among them brought them to the Lord. Today we call them "mission co-workers" instead of "missionaries" to reflect the partnership nature with which we go to share the Good News. And yes, the PC(USA) is still sending out mission co-workers, fewer than we need to, but God is faithful and many are hearing God's call.

In this book, Jim Cogswell seeks to capture the amazing story of American Presbyterian mission involvement in sub-Saharan Africa over the past two centuries. While Jim's mission service was in Japan, through his subsequent years of service in mission administration as Asia Secretary, World Service and World Hunger Program Director, and Overseas Ministries Director for the National Council of Churches, he has been enabled to consider mission history from a broader perspective. Following retirement, Jim was appointed a Specialist in Mission History by the PC(USA) Global Mission Unit. He decided to focus his research on mission in sub-Saharan Africa, where the Christian movement is growing more rapidly than anywhere else in the world and where comparatively little work has been done to record this history.

Those of us engaged in the administration of the Worldwide Ministries of the Presbyterian Church (USA) are happy to endorse this history, with the prayer that it may not only increase our church's understanding of what God has wrought through our church's witness and work in sub-Saharan Africa, but also challenge us to greater support and involvement in this part of the mission which Christ has given His Church.

Elder Douglas M. Welch, Coordinator for Africa
General Assembly Council, Presbyterian Church (USA)

ACKNOWLEDGMENTS

This book has been some sixteen years in the making. There have been numerous interludes when it was impossible to focus on the research and writing, yet I could not leave the task unfinished. During my time of service as Director for the Division of Overseas Ministries of the National Council of Churches, U.S.A., I came to realize that, while the Christian movement is growing more rapidly in sub-Saharan Africa than anywhere else in the world, very little history has been written to trace the development of that phenomenon. Hence I decided that, upon retirement, this would be my primary project. After considering working on some type of ecumenical history, I came to realize that both time and resources dictated narrowing the focus. Naturally, it led me to think in terms of the American Presbyterian involvement in the Christian movement in sub-Saharan Africa.

There have been far too many who have assisted in this project for me to acknowledge them all. First and foremost, following my retirement in 1989, the Global Mission Unit of the Presbyterian Church (U.S.A.) graciously approved my appointment as a Specialist in Mission History and provided an initial grant to undertake the research and study. Their vote of confidence has been a long time in bearing fruit! During the period that my wife and I were retired in Atlanta (1989-1995), the Columbia Seminary Library very kindly provided not only the resources that were available in their excellent collection but also secured books and dissertations which it would have been impossible for me to obtain otherwise. My special thanks in this regard go to Dr. Christine Wenderoth, who was at that time Associate Librarian. A course on African Christianity at the Interdenominational Theological Center in Atlanta proved very helpful in providing an African-American perspective. Through the years, resources have been found in numerous other seminary libraries, especially Union Seminary, Richmond; Princeton Seminary; and Yale Divinity School. Of course, the Presbyterian Historical Society in both Philadelphia and Montreat has been a very valuable source of materials which could not have been found elsewhere. My special thanks go to Bill Washburn in Atlanta and Dan Reilly and Candy Williams in Black Mountain, who led me through the jungle of computer jargon and rescued my work when my first computer crashed. Personal correspondence with numerous missionaries, both active and retired, as well as Missionary Correspondence letters received through mission headquarters, have been most valuable in bringing facts to life. I would especially express thanks to those missionaries, mission board staff and African church leaders who were kind enough to read the first draft of sections relating to their areas of experience and offer valuable comments and suggested changes. Special thanks go to Doug Welch, missionary and later Coordinator for West and Central Africa, for his help in finalizing the text. And sincere gratitude to Cliff Kirkpatrick, who assisted in securing the initial grant and whose encouragement has brought this printing of the work.

Along with acknowledgments, apologies are in order. There are so many who devoted their lives to mission service in Africa whose names do not appear in this work. Needless to say, it would be impossible to name all those in the devoted Christian community in Africa, both national leaders and foot soldiers, who have been the primary agents of the advance of Christ's Kingdom in that continent. Hopefully later historians will provide a more complete history than can be afforded in this survey of the entire history of American Presbyterian involvement.

Finally, my wife Peggy has endured many hours of my being occupied in various libraries and at the computer, yet through it all she has encouraged me to complete the task. On my file cabinet stands a card which she gave me early in this undertaking, which reads, "Whatever you can do, or dream you can, begin it." I thank her as well as the Lord whom we serve that the task is completed.

James A. Cogswell
Black Mountain, North Carolina

INTRODUCTION

Where will the Christian movement be in the new millennium? Can we discern some signs as to what will be the situation of Christendom? How far will Christ's church have advanced in proclaiming the Good News to all nations? What impact will the Christian message have had on the life of the world? What will have happened in the tumultuous twentieth century that will provide direction for Christ's people as we enter this new era?

The purpose of this study is to help prepare the church (American Presbyterians in particular) for Christian mission in a new millennium, in light of the history of the Christian movement in a particular region of the world, sub-Saharan Africa, during the 19th and 20th centuries. American Presbyterians have had a significant role in that movement, primarily through their missionary representatives, but also in numerous other ways. As American Presbyterians, we have great cause to celebrate what God has wrought through our participation in Christian mission on that continent—the advance of the Gospel into the lives of peoples previously untouched by its redemptive power, the growth of Christ's Church as the redeemed and redeeming community, the impact of the Christian movement upon virtually every aspect of African society.

At the same time, the Christian movement has undergone more profound change during the past half of the twentieth century than at any previous period in its history. This is a reality which comparatively few Christians in our Western world realize. It is imperative that we assess the scope and nature of this change, and set our sails to catch the wind that is blowing as the Spirit moves in the life of the world.

With regard to the Christian movement in the Third World (that vast area which encompasses Africa, Asia, Latin America, and the islands of the Pacific and Caribbean), this is where the most profound and significant change has taken place. We in the churches of the West have usually heard that story from the perspective of those who represent the mission-sending agencies of the Western world. For this we can be thankful, for they have provided us with insights into the advance of the Christian movement among peoples largely ignored in secular histories and news media. Often this story has been told in terms that glorify the missionary ("hagiography" it is called by some Third World Church historians) with little if any consideration of the important role played by dedicated Christian leaders of the nations where the Gospel was planted, let alone of those times and ways in which mission policies and programs may have been a hindrance to the Christian movement. This study endeavors to be critical in the best sense of the word, evaluating the impact not only of particular policies of mission boards, missions and missionaries, but also of Western nations upon the life of the people of Africa. For this reason, every effort has been made to draw upon information and perceptions from those who represent the church within that world, for it is they who have experienced in their own lives and societies the impact of the Gospel.

We undertake this history in light of an astounding fact: *Within the past half century, the center of gravity for world Christendom has shifted from North to South, from the First and Second Worlds to the Third World.* It is hard for us in Europe and North America, who have traditionally thought of ourselves as the center of "Christendom", to comprehend that there are more professing Christians now in the nations which we have thought of as our "mission fields" than there are in those nations which have been the initiators of the modern missionary movement. While vast areas and large groups of people in the so-called Third World remain with little contact with or knowledge of the Gospel and without the presence of a Christian community, the fact remains that Third World Christians outnumber First and Second World Christians, and that the Third World is where the Christian movement is experiencing its most dramatic growth as the 21st century begins.

Catholic missiologist Walbert Buhlmann, in his seminal book, *The Coming of the Third Church*, puts it this way: The first millennium of the Christian era (from the time of Christ until about the year 1000) saw the predominance of Eastern Christendom, those ancient churches which emanated from the Holy Land and the Middle East and moved into Northern Africa and Eastern Europe, with strong autonomous patriarchates, which now are part of the Eastern and Oriental Orthodox traditions. The second millennium (from about the year 1000 to our own time) has been the era of Western Christendom, with the predominance of the Roman Catholic Church and then the explosion of Churches emerging from it—Protestant and Anglican churches following the Reformation and more recently Pentecostal churches in the past century. But the coming third millennium, Buhlmann contends, will see the predominance of Southern Christendom, those churches in the developing world, with some scattered roots which go back to the early Christian centuries but most of which have emerged as a result of the missionary movement of the 19th and 20th centuries.

How we ought to thank God for that! With all the failures and foibles of the modern missionary movement, look at what God has wrought! The body of Christ now is truly global with Christ's people in virtually every nation on the face of the earth. The late William Temple, Archbishop of Canterbury and one of the great Christian leaders of the past century, has called this "the great new fact of our time."

Now, that fundamental shift has great significance for us as we think of our role as American Presbyterians and First World Christians in mission in the years ahead.

1) We can no longer think of Christian mission as a one-way street, with those in the West as the active agents and "those people over there" as the objects of mission. We must rid ourselves of every vestige of the mentality of colonialism and paternalism, and see mission as the whole church proclaiming the whole

Gospel to the whole world. As one Korean Christian leader put it in addressing am American church audience, "Once you came to share the Gospel with us because you saw us as the ends of the earth. But because you came, we are no longer the ends of the earth. Now we want to join you in being Christ's witnesses to the ends of the earth."

2) The vitality, the vibrancy, the freshness of the faith of this Third World church needs to be injected into the bloodstream of the First World church. Certainly we have much to share out of our Christian heritage and our far greater resources. But we must be open also to receive from Third World Christians that fresh grasp of the Gospel and its relevance for the life of the world.

3) This brings us to one of the major themes which will emerge in this study: The Third World Church is much closer to the context of the church of the New Testament than are we; for it exists within the world of the poor and oppressed. We First World Christians find it difficult to realize that Scripture was written largely by the poor and for the poor, and that its meaning often comes through most powerfully to the poor. The Biblical message, "The Lord executes justice for all who are oppressed", leaps out to them with a relevance which our ears often have difficulty hearing.

The Gospel is loose in the Third World. It is ultimately more powerful than any two-edged sword, any MX missile, even any nuclear bomb. The ferment of the Gospel is being put into new wineskins, infusing ancient cultures with transforming power, and sometimes breaking them open and creating new cultural realities. We Western Christians need to set our antenna to hear the Gospel afresh as it thunders from the Third World, to recognize the mighty acts of God among those who were treated as no people but now are God's people, and to envision mission in partnership with that new reality.

*　　*　　*

To tell the story of American Presbyterian involvement in this amazing Christian movement in one area of the Third World is no small task. Certainly it will be impossible to tell the whole story—there is so much that deserves to be told, of committed people, of heroic deeds, of history-shaping events, that much will need to be reserved for more detailed histories by future historians. Wherever possible, reference is made to writings which tell particular parts of the story in detail. The purpose of this study is to enable the serious American Presbyterian to "see the big picture", in order to grasp major developments which have taken place and which have profoundly changed the direction of Christian mission, especially in those nations where American Presbyterians have been involved.

From the American Presbyterian perspective, with the reunion in 1983 which brought an end to 122 years of division in the American Presbyterian family and brought into being the Presbyterian Church (U.S.A.) or PC(USA), three major streams of missionary endeavor have now come together: that of the United Presbyterian Church in North America (UPNA); that of the Presbyterian Church in the U.S.A. (or PCUSA, which after merging with the UPNA in 1958 became the United Presbyterian Church in the U.S.A. or UPCUSA), and that of the Presbyterian Church in the United States (PCUS, popularly known as the Southern Presbyterian Church).[1] It is urgently important that our reunited church see the history of American Presbyterian engagement in mission as a unified whole, within the context of the total Christian movement, claiming it as our own and committing ourselves to its advancement.

We focus in this volume upon the region of sub-Saharan Africa. The very title indicates a basic reality: The African continent is pulled in two directions, with Islam the major faith system of those north of the southern edge of the Sahara, and Christianity rapidly becoming the predominant faith of those below it. Africa is often the last and least in our Western histories and news media, yet it is the area of the world where the Christian movement is growing so rapidly that by the year 2000 it has become the continent with the largest percentage of its population claiming the name Christian.

Africa, which has experienced such profound political change in the past half century as it has moved from colonialism into a period of struggle for nationhood. Africa, which contains a larger number of underdeveloped nations than any other continent and faces horrendous economic problems that affect every aspect of the lives of its people. Africa, whose people have suffered so intensely because of wars of liberation and inter-tribal conflict. Africa, which now is struggling with the plague of HIV/AIDS and other diseases which have been virtually eliminated in the developed world. Africa, where the struggle for a world free from the bondage of racism finds its most intense expression. The story of the Christian movement in Africa is one that both thrills and instructs us as we consider the prospects of the Christian movement in a new millennium.

Let an African church historian, Prof. Ogbu U. Kalu of Nigeria, give us a guiding word as we enter this study:

> The basic assumption of church history is that the Kingdom of God is here among us, offering enormous opportunities for renewing and reshaping the life of individuals and communities. Church history seeks to understand not only the shape and flow of this presence but also its intangible yet powerful effects. Church history is not just the study of an institution but also the process of interpreting history from a Christian standpoint. The essence of church history is to start with the assumption that the Kingdom of God is present like leaven in human history and, in the light of that, to study the complex process whereby societies have been transformed through time.[2]

ADDENDUM

In the years since the initiation of this project, the writer has become acutely aware of the limitations within which I am working:

1) Not having served in mission in Africa, I have no personal experience upon which to draw and must depend entirely upon written and oral resources.

2) I recognize that I cannot deal adequately with the relationship of the Gospel to African culture, which is so vital to an understanding of how the Christian mission succeeds or fails in its witness.

3) While seeking to place the American Presbyterian involvement within the setting of the overall political situation, inevitably it has been necessary to omit much that others may consider significant.

4) Most important, the documentation needed for writing the history of the Christian movement in general and the American Presbyterian mission involvement in particular since 1972 is extremely scattered and disorganized. It is evident that, with the demise of the organized "missions", the interest of mission agencies in keeping vital historical records, to say nothing of preparing histories of the Christian movement, has been given low priority. For this reason, as well as the lack of time to do the research needed, the history for the period from the year 1973 (when major reorganization of the boards of both the United Presbyterian Church, U.S.A. and the Presbyterian Church, U.S. took place) to the end of the century is episodic rather than complete.

Having said this, I do believe that this effort has some particular values:

1) It brings together the history of the three streams of American Presbyterian involvement in mission in sub-Saharan Africa, providing an opportunity to compare and contrast the strengths and weaknesses of the policies which each pursued.

2) It seeks to place the history of the Christian movement in individual countries within the context of an Africa-wide perspective.

3) It explores the relationship between the mission boards, the organized missions, and the indigenous churches, showing how each affects the other for good or for ill.

4) It makes an attempt to include as fully as possible both information about and insights of indigenous Christian leaders.

The writer expresses the earnest hope that more exhaustive histories are waiting to be written, especially by African church leaders, and hopefully with more adequate resources from both written and oral documentation. It is my prayer that this effort will provide some incentive for that undertaking.

What has become increasingly evident to the writer in the course of this study is that there is indeed "no turning back." For mission agencies and personnel, there is no way to return to the days when American Presbyterians controlled the policies and programs of the Christian movement in those countries in which we have been engaged in mission. With gratitude for what God has done through our efforts, we now must be willing to be "mission co-workers" with those who have responded to Christ's call to be His living church in each place. And for those in sub-Saharan Africa who have received Jesus as Savior and Lord, while there is much in traditional culture that is worthy to be redeemed and brought as a treasured contribution into the life of the Church Universal, there is no turning back to the life which they knew apart from Christ. For "if anyone is in Christ, there is a new creation; everything old has passed away; see, everything has become new." (II Corinthians 5:17—NRSV).

CHAPTER I

ENTERING AN UNKNOWN CONTINENT: PIONEER EVANGELIZATION (1833-1914)

In the early 19th century, Africa below the Sahara was known to the Western world simply as the "Dark Continent." True, there were trading posts established by European nations along the fringes of the continent, but the great interior regions were simply marked on the maps as "unexplored." The rich natural resources in minerals, lumber and agricultural products could only be guessed at, from those which had been brought to the coasts for trading. But the ignorance about the peoples of Africa was even greater. Little was known of their culture, nor of the existence of highly developed civilizations within the continent. The "darkness" in the heart of Africa waiting to be redeemed by the power of the Gospel was matched by a "darkness" in the minds of the general population of the Western world in their knowledge of and attitude toward the people of Africa. Hence it seems more appropriate to speak of Africa at this point in history as the "Unknown Continent."

The primary knowledge about the peoples of Africa was learned through the institution of slavery. Accepted by most as the basis for the agricultural economy of the New World and justified through a literal interpretation of selected passages of Scripture, only a few dared to raise their voices against it. However, soon after the opening of the 19th century public sentiment began to be strong enough to secure action on the part of some Western governments. Tiny Denmark led the way, in 1792 declaring that slavery in its territories must cease by the year 1801. Other European nations soon followed: Britain in 1807, Sweden in 1813, the Netherlands in 1814, and France in 1818.

As for the United States, in 1808 Congress declared an end to the African slave trade, prohibiting further transportation of slaves from Africa. However, the maintenance of the agricultural structure on the great plantations, especially in the southern states, was so dependent upon slave labor that the law proved to be ineffective. Vessels continued to smuggle slaves into hidden ports, especially along the Gulf Coast, and the buying and selling of African slaves continued unabated. Struggles continued through the ensuing years, as northern states sought to forbid slavery and southern states fought to retain the practice. It was not until the northern and southern states became embroiled in the Civil War in 1861 and President Lincoln issued the Emancipation Proclamation in 1862 that the practice of slavery was officially banned. But the complete abolition of slavery in the United States was not finally achieved until Constitutional Amendment 13 became law throughout the nation in December 1865.

Protestant missionary work had been begun in West Africa as early as 1736, when the British United Brethren sent a converted mulatto to the settlement Christiansburg, near present-day Accra, Ghana. He was followed by several others, but all died and in 1770 that mission was abandoned. Other efforts were made by missions sent from England and Scotland in the late 18th and early nineteenth centuries, but with meager success. The prospects for evangelization of Africa seemed very dim when American Presbyterians made their first attempt at Christian mission in Africa in 1833.

A. WEST AFRICA

THE CONTEXT

West Africa bulges out into the Atlantic Ocean, and immediately to the south of it the continent is drawn in as if with a tight belt. Across the southern coast of the bulge stretch a number of geographically small nations. Except for Liberia and Sierra Leone, they represent the varied colonial histories of these countries, as different colonial powers claimed their slices of this region as ports for trade in slaves and other precious commodities. From west to east, they are Sierra Leone (where Britain resettled its freed slaves), Liberia (the product of the American anti-slave movement), Ivory Coast (formerly a French colony), Ghana (formerly British), Togo (formerly German, then French), and Benin (formerly French). At the end of the chain is Nigeria (formerly British), by far the largest country geographically in West Africa, and the most populous nation in all of Africa.

At the juncture of West and Central Africa lies a triangular shaped country, slightly larger than the state of California, which now is known as **Cameroon**. It faces the Gulf of Guinea to the southwest, is bordered by Nigeria to the northwest, Chad to the northeast, the Central African Republic to the east, and Equatorial Guinea, Gabon, and Congo to the south. It contains four topographical regions. The southern region consists of coastal plains and a dense inland tropical rain forest; hot and humid, it contains some of the wettest places on earth. The central region rises progressively to a rugged plateau which forms a barrier between the north and the south. In the northern tip of the triangle, a savanna plain slopes downward toward the Lake Chad basin. And to the west is a mountain region which rises to the highest elevation in West Africa, Mount Cameroon.

Cameroon is one of Africa's most diverse countries not only in relation to its topography but also in relation to its peoples. With over 180 indigenous ethnic groups and some 24 major language groups, its diversity has perpetuated its lack of cohesiveness and helped to make it vulnerable to foreign conquest. Its very name reveals the checkered history which these peoples have experienced at the hands of European colonial powers over the past several centuries. When the Portuguese first visited the Gulf of Guinea in

1472 and sailed up the estuary of what is now called the Wouri River, they caught many small crayfish. Mistaking them for prawns, they named the river Rio dos Camaroes, "River of Prawns." Variations of the word "Camaroes" have given the country its name through succeeding periods: Kamerun (German), Cameroun (French), Cameroons (British), and today the Republic of Cameroon.

From the beginning of the 16th century to early in the 17th century, Cameroon's coast was a principal source of supply for European and American slave traders. Britain's attempt to put an end to the West African slave trade during the first half of the 19th century greatly increased British influence in the area. A British missionary station, the first permanent white settlement in the area, was established at Victoria at the foot of Mt. Cameroon in 1858. Although British interests had an advantage over French and German traders who were active in the area, Germany managed to sign a treaty with the chiefs of the Douala tribes along the coast in 1884 and established a German protectorate over what came to be called the Kamerun. The German protectorate lasted for 30 years, during which time the Germans developed the basic colonial economy of the country.

During World War I, Allied forces overwhelmed German resistance and in 1916 the Kamerun was divided between Britain and France. Under the terms of the peace settlement, the country was divided into two territories which became Trusteeships of Britain and France under the League of Nations. France received four fifths of the territory from the coastal plain eastward, while Britain received the remaining one fifth in the mountainous west. Both powers thus added to their existing colonial empires, with France holding the large area to the east adjacent to French Equatorial Africa, and Britain holding the area to the west adjacent to Nigeria. The ensuing years until World War II saw little visible progress in the British sector, while the French sector used forced African labor to clear lands, build roads and construct public projects, though doing little to improve social and political conditions.[3]

It is against this background that we must view the **Christian movement** in Cameroon. First, it is necessary to recognize the pressure of Islam from the north. Islam was introduced in the 18th century by Fulani Muslims who entered northern Cameroon from the areas of Mali and Nigeria. At the beginning of the 19th century, the Fulani chiefs in the north began to impose their authority on the tribal peoples, subduing some while many took refuge in the mountains and retained their traditional religions. The Fulani then set up a feudalistic system which has subsequently resisted the development efforts of both colonial and independent Cameroon. Christians in both the central and northern parts of the country have faced stiff resistance from Islam, with frequent cases of churches being destroyed and authorization to open new work refused.

Catholic mission efforts were effectively introduced in 1890 in the south by the German Order of Pallotins. German missionaries, both Catholic and Protestant, who were in Kamerun during slightly over a quarter of a century of German colonial administration, were not permitted to return following World War I. On the departure of the German Roman Catholic missionaries some defection among Catholic Christians took place, but the arrival of French mission orders with strong support from the French colonial administration brought renewed progress. In the 1930s a mass movement toward the Roman Catholic Church took place, so that by World War II Catholic membership in French Cameroun was nearly twice that of Protestants, numbering over half a million, with their strength especially in urban areas. The Catholic Church had its greatest success among the younger generation due to its extensive involvement in education and its strong emphasis on preparing African priests.

As for Protestant mission efforts, the first missionary to arrive in Kamerun was an English Baptist, Alfred Saker, who came to the coastal town of Douala in 1845. Saker and his colleagues confined their efforts to the area surrounding Douala, but when the Germans annexed the Kamerun in 1884, the English Baptist Missionary Society was forced to withdraw. Four Protestant missions initiated work in Kamerun during the period of German colonial rule, three of which were German with the fourth being American Presbyterian. Out of the work of the Basel Mission would emerge a significant Presbyterian community which later would figure in the history of the American Presbyterian story. In the years following World War I, the Paris Missionary Society, along with several Baptist and Lutheran missionary societies entered Cameroon. Such was the pattern of Protestant missionary involvement in Cameroon at the beginning of World War II.

Slightly north of the equator and below the bulge of West Africa lies a tiny rectangular region that resembles the buckle of the belt that draws in the southern half of the continent. Traditionally it has been known by the Spanish name of its major estuary, Rio Muni. Together with the island of Fernando Po, which lies to the north in the Gulf of Guinea, and the small islands which lie off the coast of Rio Muni (including Corisco), they form the second smallest country in Africa (about the size of Maryland) and the smallest in population. Through much of its modern history it has been known as **Spanish Guinea.** Since Spain under pressure from the United Nations granted it a degree of self-government in 1960, it has taken the name Equatorial Guinea.

Largely mountainous, Rio Muni resembles the southern section of Cameroon to its north. From a coastal plain extending inland ten to fifteen miles, the terrain rises to inland plateaus with dense tropical forests. Then toward the eastern frontier with Gabon, it peaks in the Crystal Mountains, which reach a height of 4,000 feet. The island of Fernando Po consists of volcanic cones, crater lakes and rich lava soils, the residual of an extinct volcano which soars to almost 10,000 feet.

The colonial era for this region began as early as 1469, when a Portuguese navigator Fernao do Po became the first European to set foot on the island which later would bear his name. Portugal claimed the island but after making no permanent settlement finally ceded it to Spain in 1778. As the Spanish also failed to establish a colony, in 1827 the British were permitted to found a base there to aid their anti-slavery activities, settling many freed slaves on the island. Spain resumed control in 1843, and the island became a dumping ground for political deportees and refugees, as well as a penal colony. It remained a backwater until the beginning of the 20th century, when Spain began the development of its colonial economy.

In the meantime, Spain had begun to occupy the coastal areas of Rio Muni, laying claim to it at the Berlin Conference in 1885. In 1900, there was a shuffle of colonial territory and France ceded to Spain its claim to Rio Muni. However, Spain did not effectively occupy the total mainland area until as late as 1926. The two regions, Fernando Po and Rio Muni, remained separate Spanish colonies until 1959 and 1960, when under pressure of anti-colonial sentiment at the United Nations, these colonies were converted into overseas provinces and the name of the region was changed from Spanish Guinea to Equatorial Guinea.

Throughout the colonial era, Spanish Guinea felt the heavy hand of a very conservative Roman Catholicism. Because of a Concordat with the Vatican, Spain declared that in its colonies the Roman Catholic Church would be the only official church. Thus Spanish Guinea came to have a higher proportion of baptized Catholics than any other country of continental Africa. Except for a brief period following the founding of the Spanish Republic (1932-1936), Protestant activity under Spanish rule was severely restricted.

BEGINNING OF AMERICAN PRESBYTERIAN WITNESS IN WEST AFRICA (1833-1894)

The involvement of American Presbyterians in missionary witness in Africa began with a period of trial and tribulation in searching for a place for effective service and for the best avenue through which such witness should be undertaken. During the first quarter of the 19th century, the attention of many Americans had been directed to the west coast of Africa. While slavery was still legally recognized in the United States, the movement for its abolition was growing. The number of slaves who had been freed was increasing, especially in the North, and the problem of their status was becoming serious. There was a strong movement in favor of sending these "freedmen" back to Africa. Toward this end Colonization Societies were formed to establish colonies of freed slaves on the southern edge of Africa's western bulge. The area where these colonies were formed was to become the Republic of **Liberia**.

Liberia grew out of the efforts of the American Colonization Society, organized in 1816. The society sent its first group of freedmen to Africa in 1822. These people settled at the mouth of the St. Paul River and named their town Monrovia in honor of then President James Monroe. The early settlers had to fight a number of wars with the local tribes people. Finally, by mutual agreement between the settlers and the Colonization Society, Liberia was declared a republic in 1847. In succeeding years, Liberia had to contend with neighboring French and British colonies who encroached upon the interior land claimed by Liberia. The United States Army helped to organize and train the soldiers of the Liberian Frontier Force to protect Liberia's claims. Liberia would become strongly attached to the United States, especially as a source for rubber.

The involvement of American Presbyterians in mission in Liberia began with the following action of the 1831 General Assembly:

> The General Assembly again calls the attention of the churches under its care to the efforts now making to colonize the free blacks of this country on the Western coast of Africa, and affectionately commend them to their earnest attention and zealous support; and it is particularly recommended that the Presbyterian Churches throughout the United States to take up collections in aid of the American Colonization Society on or about the fourth of July.[4]

In the following year, the appeal was expanded "to draw in a special manner, the attention of American Christians and of young men . . . to the cause of missions to that long neglected and interesting part of the globe. The climate of Africa, however, is terrific to the white man, and few, it is to be feared, will have the courage to face its dangers."[5]

Meanwhile, there were differing views regarding the best avenue through which the Presbyterian missionary enterprise should be undertaken. As early as 1810, the American Board of Commissioners for Foreign Missions (ABCFM) had been formed as the organization through which Congregationalists, Presbyterians, German Reformed, and Dutch Reformed churches might carry on their Foreign Mission work. Like numerous other such "benevolent societies", this was a voluntary organization, subject to no denominational control and appealing to all evangelical Christians for support. Several General Assemblies (1812, 1828, and 1831) had considered overtures to establish a Presbyterian Foreign Mission Board "for sending the gospel of Christ to the regions beyond", but each time the General Assembly declined to act, referring Presbyterians who wished to engage in such activities to the ABCFM. Finally advocates of a Presbyterian Board could wait no longer and asked the Synod of Pittsburgh to establish its own foreign mission agency. In 1831 the Synod constituted the Western Foreign Missionary Society which was accountable to and supported by the Synod.

The minutes of the Executive Committee of this Society for January 16, 1832 contain the following record:

> A communication was received from Mr. John Brooks Pinney, a student of the Theological Seminary at Princeton, stating his purpose to devote himself to the work of preaching the gospel among the heathen and submitting certain inquiries to the Committee in reference to the contemplated African Mission. [The names of other seminary students were mentioned as volunteers to be taken under the care and direction of the Society.] On motion, resolved that this Committee receive with great pleasure and sincere gratitude to God the expression of these sentiments and determinations on the part of these young brethren . . . and they hereby are taken under the care of the Committee with a view of their ultimate engagement in the work of Foreign Mission.[6]

Though the Society had planned to send a colleague to accompany Pinney on this first missionary venture to Africa, the man who had been appointed with Pinney died suddenly soon after his appointment. So it was that on January 1, 1833 Pinney sailed alone from Norfolk, Virginia. He arrived in Monrovia, Liberia on February 16. Not only was he the first American Presbyterian missionary to serve in Africa, but also the first Protestant missionary to serve in Liberia. Pinney soon would be followed by several other associates, including Mr. James Temple, "a young Negro who has been taken under the care of the Presbytery of Philadelphia as an assistant missionary."[7] Pinney served in Liberia for the next four years, during which time he was acting Agent and Governor of the Board of Managers of the American Colonization Society, "who had been favorably impressed by his character and ability."[8] However, he was forced to retire from the field in 1837, broken in health.

Meanwhile, The American Board of Commissioners for Foreign Missions was initiating work in several foreign lands. In 1833, the Synod of South Carolina and Georgia had organized a Southern Board of Missions, as an auxiliary society to the American Board of Commissioners. Under this Board, Southern Presbyterians sent out their earliest missionaries. Among them was the Rev. John Leighton Wilson, who was commissioned for service in Africa. The Maryland Colonization Society was about to plant a new colony of freedmen on the coast of West Africa, to be located at Cape Palmas, some 250 miles south of Monrovia. The society was anxious to have a mission started with the commencement of this colony. After an exploratory tour to Cape Palmas in 1833, Wilson returned to marry his betrothed Jane Elizabeth Bayard, and together they returned to Liberia in 1834, to serve there for the next seven years. This would be the beginning of an outstanding missionary career for Wilson, who would render notable service as linguist, evangelist, author, naturalist, humanitarian, and missionary statesman.[9]

The vision of these early missionaries was that Liberia would serve as a base from which to launch Christian witness into "the heart of Africa." From 1833 until 1891, American Presbyterian missionaries were sent to Liberia, with the purpose of working chiefly among the native African people rather than simply the colonists. By 1848 there were sufficient results to justify the formation of the Presbytery of West Africa, attached to the Synod of Philadelphia.

However, the experience of the missionaries serving in Liberia was tragic, with early death or shattered health for almost all those who ventured there in mission. Distressed by the repeated casualties in the staff of white missionaries, the Western Foreign Missionary Society decided to increase the number of American Negro missionaries until the total number would reach 59 of the missionary force of 75. One couple, Mr. and Mrs. James M. Priest, served for forty years. However, the results were meager. By 1892 there were but 332 communicant members of whom less than fifty were native Africans. Therefore in 1894, the Presbyterian Board of Foreign Missions (which had absorbed the work of the Western Foreign Missionary Society in 1838) decided officially to withdraw from Liberia. The Presbytery of West Africa persisted for some 37 more years, with meager support from the American Presbyterian Board. In 1931 the PCUSA General Assembly dissolved its relationship to the Presbytery of West Africa. A small Presbyterian Church has continued in Liberia.

To what can we attribute the failure of this first mission attempt of American Presbyterians in Africa? While the terrible cost in loss of missionary health and life was certainly a major factor, the chief reason why the effort in Liberia was abandoned lay in the relationships between the missionaries, the "freedmen" colonists and the native Africans. The colonists, who only recently had been freed from slavery themselves, set up rigid rules to control the African population. Further, they attempted to enlist those native teachers and students of the mission into their militia. Consequently, riots broke out between the colonists and the Africans. At one time the home of the John Leighton Wilsons became the refuge of a group of colonists, while some 500 Africans came to the gate "armed with guns, cutlasses and spears, intoxicated with revenge and intent on shedding blood, with fierce yells, war horns and bells."[10] Such incidents revealed that there was little hope of establishing a viable church on such a flawed foundation.[11]

Meanwhile, the way had opened for American Presbyterian involvement in the territory which would become **Gabon**. In 1842, missionaries of the American Board of Commissioners for Foreign Missions, led by J. Leighton Wilson,[12] transferred their work from Liberia, and opened work at the site of an old slave barracks near the French post at Libreville, fourteen miles from the mouth of the Gabon River. In 1871 this work was transferred from ABCFM to the Presbyterian Board and a Presbyterian Church was soon organized at Baraka. Further expansion of work would take place in the next two decades along both the Gabon and Ogowe Rivers.[13] However, the French government, which had claimed Gabon as a colony, began to enforce regulations which made the work of an American mission increasingly difficult. Therefore in 1892 the entire work in Gabon was transferred to the Paris Missionary Society.[14]

Meanwhile, a more stable and successful work was developing among the people on the tiny Spanish-held island of **Corisco**, within the Gulf of Guinea and just 15 miles from the mainland. Two missionary families were sent there in 1850, with the expectation that health conditions on the island would be more favorable than those on the mainland. Alas, the hope was soon shattered, with all but one missionary dying within the first year. Reenforcements arrived in 1855, and by 1856 a church was organized and a presbytery (Corisco) formed in 1860, attached to the Synod of New Jersey.

The missionaries on Corisco made frequent journeys to the mainland, and by 1865 the prospect of opening work there finally could be realized, as a solitary missionary, George Paull, settled at a site at the mouth of the Benito River in **Spanish Guinea**. He lived there but three months before his death, but his work opened the way for the organization of a church of 18 members in December 1865. In the next 20 years several churches were established along the coast, including one at Batanga, Kamerun (fifty miles beyond the Campo River border from Spanish Guinea into German-held Kamerun) in 1879. By 1875 it had become evident that the work on the mainland would prove more fruitful, and therefore the Mission changed its base from Corisco to the continent, turning over the work on Corisco to the leadership of the Rev. Ibia J. Tkenge, a remarkable man who had been the first convert to be baptized on Corisco. The work of American Presbyterians became the primary Protestant witness in Rio Muni, the mainland portion of Spanish Guinea.

However, as difficulties with the Spanish colonial government intensified in succeeding decades, the work in Spanish Guinea became peripheral and the focus shifted to stations established in neighboring territories, especially Kamerun.[15]

So it was that during the first 46 years of their witness in West Africa, American Presbyterian missionaries labored in four different areas before finding a base from which to develop a full-orbed mission: Liberia (1833-1894); Gabon (1843-1894). Corisco (1850-1875); and Spanish Guinea (1865—)

BEGINNING OF AMERICAN PRESBYTERIAN WITNESS IN GERMAN KAMERUN (1879-1914)

The country which would become the major focus of American Presbyterian involvement in West Africa was German-controlled Kamerun.[16] In a sense, this country was entered "by the back door." From the base at Benito in Spanish Guinea, there had been advances into southern Kamerun, leading to the establishment in 1879 of a church at **Batanga**, on the coast 93 miles north of Benito. It would be ten more years before the first resident missionaries, Mr. and Mrs. B.B. Brier, were assigned to Batanga station in 1889. It was the Rev. Adolphus C. Good who, after valuable experience in Gabon, determined to explore the hinterland of southern Kamerun. Beginning in the year 1892, Good penetrated the jungles of Southern Kamerun and undertook exhaustive journeys of exploration hundreds of miles into the interior.[17] As a result of his pioneering work, in the succeeding years missionaries opened several new stations:

—   In 1893 at **Efulan**, 52 miles from the coast, where the first church was established among the Bulu people. The church was organized with six charter members and one elder. American Presbyterian missionary Mary Johnson described the event:

    May 13 of the year 1900 was a day long looked forward to and long to be remembered. On that day the first Bulu were baptized and formed into the first church of Christ in this part of Kamerun, and for the first time the Lord's Supper was celebrated by members of the Bulu race.[18]

—   In 1895 at **Elat**, 56 miles still further east, which in time would become the center of the work of the West Africa Mission. The original name of this site was Ebolewo'o, meaning Rotten Chimpanzee, a name retained by the German government post. However, the name Elat, meaning *covenant* or *uniting* "was chosen as more befitting a center dedicated to the proclamation of the Gospel that was to cement the tribes together as brothers in a new pact of peace, and to make them partakers in the new covenant of God."[19]

—   In 1897 at **Lolodorf**, 75 miles northeast of Batanga, a military post of the German colonial government. The American Presbyterian Mission later would give its work here the name, MacLean Memorial Station, and still later the African name Bibia.

— In 1909 at **Metet**, 73 miles northeast of Elat, expanding the Mission's work into the area of the Bene people. This station was established as the result of the visit of a site committee of the Mission, which set out in May 1905 "to explore the jungles toward the east in search of a suitable location for another station." Since the Mission at first did not have adequate personnel to staff this new station, the young church at Elat was challenged to send workers to this region. Two church elders, Ako'o Ze and Osom, "the Bulu John the Baptist", pioneered the work among the Bene people.[20] The other places visited by the site committee were also to be occupied in later years. "All along the trails they explored, there are chapels and schools and churches today, where the tribes, having laid aside their old animosities, worship together the Great Chief whose tribe they have become."[21]

Thus American Presbyterians were the first to bear Christian witness in the interior of southern Kamerun. Among the great pioneers of this period were missionary doctor Dr. Silas F. Johnson[22] and missionary evangelist the Rev. Dr. William Dager. Dr. Evelyn Adams, who would serve as a medical missionary in Cameroun for 40 years, recalls how her uncle, Dr. Dager, made a trip by bicycle in 1911, to the border of Kamerun and Oubangi Chari, later a part of French Equatorial Africa. The trip took him three months and over 1000 miles, over jungle paths "into the utterly unknown regions beyond—the great forest which is haunted by pygmies and supposed unclean spirits, . . . until he had crossed the watershed, beyond which all the streams flow in a new direction toward the Congo."[23] It would be some 22 years later that American Presbyterian missionaries would be stationed at Momjepom to follow up the pioneer visit of Dr. Dager.

However, the early years of work in Kamerun saw slow progress. By 1903, there were 1,800 converts, chiefly concentrated in Batanga and the coastal area. In light of the past experience in West Africa and with demands for missionaries coming from numerous other fields, the PCUSA Board of Foreign Missions faced the question of the advisability of withdrawing from the field and turning the work over to the Basel Mission. Finally, the Board approved a ten-year trial "with a careful policy to be marked out in the prosecution of the work and this policy to be consistently carried through." The policy called for (a) an average force at each station of three missionaries, one to be a physician; (b) regular and systematic itineration; (c) a native pastor to be in charge of each local church; (d) self-support to be emphasized and introduced; (e) educational work to be developed, with boarding schools and industrial training.

In the fall of 1904, the Board's Executive Secretary A.W. Halsey visited the West African mission stations, including Corisco, Gabon, Benito and Kamerun, to discuss with them the new policy and to "bring words of cheer to the lonely missionaries and the African Christians."[24]

The ensuing years saw remarkable progress in several dimensions of mission endeavor:

— EVANGELISTIC WORK: By 1914, 16 organized self-supporting churches could be reported. But that was only the beginning. For example, Elat station reported that in addition to its thriving church at Elat, there were two outposts at Fulasi and Endenge, which were ready to be occupied as stations because of the "unparalleled development of the work" but which could not be staffed because of lack of missionary personnel. In addition to these three points (Elat, Fulasi and Endenge), "there are ten other centres in charge of native evangelists . . . . Tributary to these thirteen central points there are 70 others where native evangelists are settled for all or part of the year as we may be able to secure the evangelists."[25]

By the year 1914, the West Africa Mission would report 5,121 communicants and 15,257 catechumens, with 6 ordained African pastors and 403 evangelists, teachers and assistants.

The stories which emerged concerning new Christians were equally remarkable. Efulan station reported the following:

This has been another year of great things in the Kingdom of God; not only have we had the numbers but some of these have been remarkable conversions. Several notable characters have taken the stand for Christ. There is Zo'o Ango, a headman in Nemeyon, who had at least thirteen wives. Formerly he had persecuted the Christians, but now he himself is an earnest Christian. Only the other Sabbath we could hardly believe our eyes when Mekulu, a headman with twenty-one wives, and one of the worst characters in the neighborhood, stood up before over three thousand people, thus signifying his intention to follow Christ. A visit to his town showed us that he meant business, for he immediately began to dispose of his wives. One day a polygamist came in whose face showed the hard life he had lived and one wondered at the grace of God that could touch such a heart. Again and again one hears how "The men are coming." Formerly in many places there were only women and they were despised and persecuted, but now in some of these places some of the worst cases among the men have taken a stand for Christ.[26]

— EDUCATIONAL WORK. Alongside the churches and outposts, schools were emerging for the education of boys and girls. By 1914, 144 schools were reported, with a total enrollment in both boarding and day-schools of 10,827. "Each week there come requests from some interior towns to send them a teacher, and we are supplying these places as fast as possible."[27] For the mission station schools, it was necessary to conduct classes in both Bulu and German. However, the vast majority of the village schools were taught in Bulu, enabling the pupils for the first time to become literate in their own language.[28]

— MEDICAL WORK. With the presence of six medical missionaries, dispensaries had been established at each of the stations. Efulan station reported, "About the beginning of February of this year, the new Schauffler dispensary was begun . . . It is divided into three rooms, one a dispensary and examination room, the middle a drug room and the end, an operating room. The medical work has been somewhat restricted because of two circumstances, viz: space and time, especially the latter, as the doctor has had to superintend the building operations."[29]

— INDUSTRIAL WORK. Alongside the burgeoning advance in evangelistic, educational and medical work, the Mission had developed the Frank James Industrial School at Elat. The school served several distinct purposes: (1) It prepared students for the daunting task of building churches, schools, dispensaries, and other buildings needed for the growing work. Its carpenter class turned out young men who were employed by the mission at the different stations, as well as being in great demand for government and business contracts. (2) It prepared students for several other vocations. There was a tailor class, a furniture class, a shoe class, and a printing class. These graduates also were highly employable in Kamerun's growing economy. (3) It provided a large part of the support needed for the work of the emerging church.

It is impossible to estimate the good the school is doing in the lives of the natives about. It is changing their idea of life and their mode of living. Their old way was a low house without windows and only a small hole to crawl through in place of a door. Now many of them are being built higher, you walk in at a door, a window lets in light and you see instead of a bed of poles a real bed and in some cases a table and chairs. Instead of doing cooking in the house where there is no outlet for the smoke, you find them doing it in an open kitchen, keeping their houses clean.[30]

— STEWARDSHIP. One of the most remarkable aspects of this ten-year period of growth was the development of a strong program of stewardship. The mission had taken seriously the Board's injunction to work toward a self-supporting church. Toward this end, church members were encouraged in regular systematic giving. "Along with the growth in numbers, there has been a corresponding growth in giving, especially for people who have so little and yet have a [government] head tax of $2.50 each year." Monthly contributions were received at each of the villages where native evangelists were serving, to be spent for the support of evangelists, the improvement of village chapels and current church expenses. Tuition was received at the station schools to pay for the salaries of native teachers. Food produced in the station gardens was sold to care for other expenses.

Medicines and medical services at the dispensaries were paid for, except in emergency cases; the treatment of Europeans was especially beneficial in the support of the medical work. Items produced at the Industrial School provided income needed for its support: garments made by the tailor class, rattan furniture produced by the furniture class; shoe repairs by the shoe class.

Little wonder that by 1914, the 62 American Presbyterian missionaries serving in Kamerun viewed the future with tremendous optimism. With enthusiasm they met with the other Protestant missions operating in Kamerun[31] to reach an agreement regarding occupation and division of responsibilities for evangelization of Kamerun, and to plan strategies for major advance, agreeing that all were to press toward Yaounde, the geographical center of the colony.

B. CENTRAL AFRICA

THE CONTEXT

The story goes that, when representatives of the European colonial powers gathered around the table in Berlin in 1885 to carve up Africa, King Leopold of Belgium placed his hand on the heart of Africa and said, "This is mine." The imprint of that hand remains on the political map of Africa today in the boundaries of the nation now known as the **Democratic Republic of Congo.**[32]

Although its frontiers were drawn up around a conference table, Congo has more logical boundaries than most other African states. The largest country geographically within sub-Saharan Africa, its most defining characteristic is the Congo River, which cuts a giant arc through the heart of the African continent—"an enormous snake uncoiled," Joseph Conrad wrote, "with its head in the sea . . . and its tail lost in the depth of the land." Lying almost entirely within the country of Congo, the river flows 2,700 miles from the headwaters of the Lualaba, crossing the equator twice, draining the vast rain forest nestled in the Congo Basin. Countless tributaries lace the forest, feeding the waters that make the Congo, at ten million gallons a second, the most powerful river, after the Amazon, in the world. This river system offers more than 8,500 miles of navigable waterways, an unparalleled network of virtually maintenance-free highways reaching into every corner of the country and beyond.

The river curves around a central basin, a major depression in the northwestern quarter of the country. Plateaus rise in every direction from the central basin. To the east, they merge with the mountains at the western rim of the Rift Valley, and rise above 16,000 feet in the mountains outside the Ugandan border in the northeast. To the south and southeast, the plateaus culminate in the mountain peaks of Shaba (Katanga) bordering Tanzania and Zambia. At Congo's narrow strip of Atlantic coast, the river empties its vast supply of water into the sea.

The central basin contains one of the world's most extensive rain forests, which merges into savannas to the east and south in the higher plateau areas. Despite its vast area, less than three percent of Congo's land is arable, which makes for a high concentration of its people in the fertile areas. However, the mountains contain some of the world's most important reserves of copper ore, cobalt, industrial diamonds, zinc, cadmium, silver and uranium. A country of vast and varied natural resources, Congo probably has the greatest potential for economic growth in all sub-Saharan Africa.

No country has a better claim to be called the geopolitical key to Africa. Congo has common boundaries with more countries or territories than any other African state, making it a bridge between various countries and sections of tropical Africa. Conversely, it is also susceptible to being used by outside powers as a base for subversion from neighboring territories.

Ethnically, Congo is more homogeneous than most countries of Africa. Despite its fractured society of more than 250 tribal groups, all of its inhabitants, except for the Pygmies and a small Nilotic population across the border from Sudan, belong to the general category of Bantu people, and 90% fall into the subgroup known as "Congolese." While more than 200 languages and dialects are in use, four have become national languages—Swahili, Tshiluba, Lingala, and Kikongo. In the years since its colonization, the French language of Belgium has become its official language, providing a link between Congo and other countries of Francophone Africa.

While traditional African religions have shaped the life and thought of almost all the peoples of this nation, the past century has brought about profound change in the religious faith of most of its peoples. Islam has had only limited influence, especially in northeastern Zaire bordering the Sudan and Uganda. But it is the Christian faith which has claimed the hearts of most of Congo's people.

Christianity reached this part of Africa in 1482, when the Portuguese explorer Diogo Cao discovered the estuary of the mighty Congo River. Two years later he had made contact with the Kingdom of Kongo and opened the way for trade with Portugal. The first Roman Catholic missionary party, which arrived in 1491, had amazing success. Before long they had baptized the King and built a large stone church at the royal capital (in present-day northern Angola) which they renamed San Salvador. The monarch invited Portuguese trade and technical assistance, and exchanged ambassadors with the courts of Lisbon and the Vatican. Between 1506 and 1543 one of the most remarkable Christians of African history, Afonso I, ruled the Kongo kingdom. His son Henry studied in Portugal and was the first Black African to be appointed a Catholic bishop, in 1518. During the next three centuries, Portuguese traders and missionaries attempted to penetrate the interior by ascending the river, but seldom progressed beyond the site of present-day Kinshasa.

However, other factors were at work. The growth of the Portuguese slave trade had an increasingly negative impact, sapping the vitality of the Christian movement. For 200 years the regions of present-day Angola and Congo were the main sources for the slaves demanded by plantations in Brazil and Cuba. By 1850, some 150,000 slaves were being shipped from this area each year. Also, the focus of Catholic mission effort was shifting elsewhere, with the island of Sao Tome chosen as the see for western Africa under a Portuguese bishop in Lisbon. When the modern era of Christian mission dawned for Congo with the arrival of Holy Ghost priests at Boma in 1865 and British Baptist missionaries as the first Protestants in 1878, there was little left of the church which had flourished there nearly four centuries before.

It was not until after 1850 that the vast reaches of the Congo Basin began to be known to the Western world. European explorers such as David Livingstone reached the periphery of the Congo Basin and made their amazing discoveries known to a fascinated European audience. But it was Henry Stanley who, on his 999-day trek across the African continent from 1874 to 1877, navigated the Congo River from its upper course to the Atlantic Ocean. His explorations fascinated Leopold II, king of Belgium, who hired Stanley to set up posts along the river and to sign protectorate treaties with local chiefs along the way. Dreaming of claiming a large colony in Africa for his small country, Leopold organized the International Association for the Exploration and Civilization of Central Africa in 1878. Yet other European powers were at the same time making advances in their claims upon this vast unexplored area. In an attempt to settle these colonial rivalries, fourteen Western powers, including the United States, met in Berlin in 1884-1885. In November 1885, a treaty was signed which carved Africa into regions under the control of the various Western powers. Africa's colonial era had officially begun.

While the Berlin Treaty assured equal navigation and trading rights to all participating nations in a carefully defined Congo Basin, Leopold was recognized as sovereign of the Congo Free State, which he presented to the world as a federation of African tribes for which he himself was the European representative. Actually, however, the territory was divided into fifteen districts which completely disregarded tribal distributions and reduced or eliminated the authority of local chiefs. The Congo Free State was primarily an economic venture and had no institutional links with Belgium. However, financial difficulties and the growing world demand for rubber soon led to harsh economic exploitation of the people of the region and mounting criticism from outraged Western nations. Finally Leopold was forced to grant the Free State a colonial charter in 1908, and Belgium itself was prodded into taking over the region as the Belgian Congo, a land eighty times the size of Belgium itself, presumed to be rich in resources but totally undeveloped.

Belgian colonial rule continued in much the same manner as that of the Congo Free State. Traditional chiefs were incorporated into the administrative system as auxiliaries of Belgian officials, and local government institutions were totally lacking. Belgium attempted to insulate Congo from Belgian political life as well as from the currents of African nationalism. Rather, a policy of outspoken paternalism was promoted, with the colonial administration, business interests and the favored missionary community concurring.

Without question, the "favored missionary community" was Belgian Catholic. King Leopold II had obtained agreement from the Vatican that the evangelization of Congo should be essentially a Belgian affair and that only Belgian national missions (i.e. those having their headquarters in Belgium, directed by Belgians and counting a fair number of Belgians among their missionaries) should be involved. Since Belgium itself was predominantly Roman Catholic, the Catholic Church enjoyed a very privileged status. From the creation of the Congo Free State, King Leopold controlled placement of missionaries who in return received large concessions of property, subsidies, the right to carry out certain state functions, and a virtual monopoly over education and medical service. When Belgium assumed control of the colony in 1908, the "trinity of power" (colonial administration, the business world, and Catholic missions) continued to exercise their respective roles. Thus Protestant missions were placed at a severe disadvantage, which would not be overcome until after the Second World War.

As for the Protestant witness, British Baptist missionaries were the first Protestants to arrive in 1878, building a series of stations following the course of the Congo River. Later joined by American Baptists, the work would eventually bear fruit in the Baptist Community of the River Congo. American Southern Presbyterians were the next major missionary force to arrive, reaching Luebo (near the juncture of the Kasai and Lulua Rivers) in 1891, and henceforth concentrating their work in the region known as the Kasai. We shall return to tell this story more fully later.

The following years found missions of many Protestant groups coming to this "field ripe unto harvest": the Disciples of Christ in 1899; the African Inland Mission in 1912; American Methodists, both northern and southern, in 1913; British and American Pentecostals in 1915; and others too numerous to mention in the years that followed. By the year 1940, some 43 Protestant missions were at work in the Belgian Congo, coming from the United States, the British Isles, Scandinavia and other parts of Europe. By and large they sought to work on the basis of a comity agreement whereby each sought to evangelize and establish churches within its assigned region, though some of the more conservative missions refused to abide by such limitations.

Recognizing the need for cooperation among the various missions, the Protestant missions began as early as 1902 to meet in the Congo General Conference. Basic steps taken toward greater unity included cooperation in transport and translation; a united front against government abuses and injustice; and the beginnings of agreement on comity (i.e. delineation of territory to be served by each mission). This cooperation became formally organized into the Congo Protestant Council (CPC) in 1924. In the mid-1930s a common name was adopted by several of the missions for the churches which had come into being, *L'Eglise du Christ au Congo* (the Church of Christ in the Congo), assuring that church members would be accepted wherever they may go in the colony. It was the first step toward a major uniting of the churches in the years ahead.

The full story of the Christian movement in the Belgian Congo during the first four decades of the twentieth century would require many volumes. Suffice it to say that the growth of the church after 1914 was among the most impressive in all of Africa, or indeed in the world. By 1940 the population of the Belgian Congo was estimated at some 12 million. Of that number, some two million were reported to be Roman Catholic, a growth of some thirtyfold in a quarter of a century. Baptized Protestants were estimated to number about half a million. Together they represented about 20 percent of the population.

Yet the full story of the Christian movement in the Belgian Congo cannot be contained within traditional Western categories. Here, as in much of the rest of tropical Africa, significant indigenous churches emerged. The largest of these in the Belgian Congo, and indeed in the whole of Africa, would be the Church of Jesus Christ on Earth through the Prophet Simon Kimbangu, popularly known as the Kimbanguist Church. The church was founded by a Baptist catechist Simon Kimbangu from the Bakongo or Lower Congo, an area which had seen waves of European intervention since the fifteenth century. Kimbangu began an extensive preaching and healing ministry in 1921 which attracted immense crowds and a large following, including many from the Catholic and Protestant churches. While taking the New Testament as its standard, the movement was generally antagonistic to missionaries and to foreign domination. This alarmed the Belgian authorities who feared the movement as potentially a political insurrection with nationalistic objectives. Kimbangu was brought to trial and condemned to death, a sentence which later, upon the appeal of Baptist missionaries, was reduced to life imprisonment in Elizabethville in distant Shaba Province. The movement which Kimbangu had begun came under severe persecution and many of the followers were exiled. However, this only contributed to the spread of Kimbanguism throughout the country, often as an underground movement. The story of the Kimbanguist Church as well as other indigenous Christian movements would be interwoven with that of the total Christian movement and the nation in the years ahead.[33]

BEGINNINGS OF AMERICAN PRESBYTERIAN WITNESS IN BELGIAN CONGO (1891-1914)

American Presbyterian witness in Central Africa was initiated through the work of the **Presbyterian Church in the United States (PCUS)**, popularly known as the Southern Presbyterian Church. Soon after it came into being with the onset of the Civil War, the PCUS General Assembly in 1865 expressed its determination to start its own mission work in Africa, seeing it as a field of missionary labor "peculiarly appropriate to this Church, and with this view to secure as soon as practicable missionaries from among the African race on this continent who may bear the Gospel of the grace of God to the homes of their ancestors."[34] It was the Rev. Dr. J. Leighton Wilson who inspired the General Assembly to undertake this goal. Dr. Wilson had rendered distinguished service as a pioneer missionary in West Africa and had returned to America to serve as one of the secretaries of the Board of Foreign Missions in New York. When the Civil War broke out, he resigned his position in order to throw in his lot with the Confederacy. He soon was chosen as the Secretary of the Committee on Foreign Missions of the new Southern Presbyterian Church. It was Dr. Wilson who had written the ringing missionary declaration adopted by the 1861 General Assembly, and who would persevere in his efforts to arouse the PCUS, in spite of its monumental adversities, to assume its global mission responsibility. He kept the needs of Africa constantly before the Church until his death in 1886.[35]

This call was laid especially on the heart of Dr. C.A. Stillman, pastor of the Presbyterian Church in Tuscaloosa, Alabama. Prior to the Civil War, he had helped to educate a slave bought at his instigation by the Synod of Alabama to go to Africa as a missionary and had gone to New Orleans to see him embark. Convinced that the most effective way to reach Africans would be through an educated ministry of their own race, Dr. Stillman persuaded the General Assembly of 1876 to establish the Institute for the Training of Colored Ministers at Tuscaloosa, to train black ministers for service in Africa and the United States. From this school (later to become Stillman College) would come the first Presbyterian volunteer for work in Central Africa, the Rev. William Henry Sheppard from Waynesboro, Virginia.[36]

At last, on January 14, 1890, the PCUS Executive Committee of Foreign Missions officially commissioned two ministers, Sheppard and the Rev. Samuel Norvell Lapsley of Selma, Alabama, to establish the Presbyterian Mission in Central Africa. Lapsley, a young white minister, had worked in the black community of the Washertown Mission in Anniston, Alabama, where "for the first time in the lives of the poor people of that spiritually neglected locality there came into their homes, ate at their tables and walked with them on their streets one who bore the manifest image of the Lord Jesus."[37]

It was in May 1890 that Sheppard and Lapsley[38] landed at Banana Point in the mouth of the Congo river and began seeking a suitable field for Presbyterian missionary work in the Congo Free State. Their quest eventually led them almost a thousand miles inland to **Luebo**, a small Belgian trading post on the banks of the Lulua River, where they arrived on April 18, 1991.[39] This was the first Protestant mission to depart from the beaten trail up the Congo River and to venture inland. Providentially, they had reached the Kasai Valley, a high and comparatively healthful plateau between the Kasai and Sankuru rivers. It was an area inhabited by nearly two million people, of five major tribes: Bena Lulua, Baluba, Bakete, Bakuba, and Basonge or Zappo-Zaps. All five used one trade language, Tshiluba.

Early on, Sheppard and Lapsley decided to ransom several slave children, most of them Baluba, and bring them to Luebo. The first Sunday School and day schools opened in the Kasai were attended by these freed slave children. "With smooth sand for slates, sharp sticks for pencils, a class in writing and reading was begun."[40]

In January 1892, Lapsley undertook the long journey back to Boma at the mouth of the Congo River, in order to seek legal recognition (*personalite civile)* for the mission from the colonial authorities. He succeeded in registering the mission as the American Presbyterian Congo Mission (APCM), the name which it would bear throughout the remainder of its existence, until 1970. However, the journey ended tragically: on his return trip to Luebo, Lapsley suddenly fell ill with malarial fever and died near Matadi on March 26, 1892, the first of a noble army of martyrs in the Presbyterian witness in the Congo. Fortunately, missionary reenforcements had begun to arrive, six in 1892 in response to Lapsley's death and by 1895 six others, including five black missionaries whom Sheppard had recruited on his furlough in 1894, including his own fiancee, Lucy Gantt, who had been waiting for him ever since his graduation from Stillman. The teamwork of black and white Americans in the evangelization of the Congo would remain an outstanding characteristic of Southern Presbyterian witness for years to come.[41]

The first twenty years of APCM were a twofold struggle: one to obtain and maintain a foothold for its work in the Congo; the other to secure the sustained interest and support of the church at home, despite meager results. The problems presented were tremendous. There was the personal struggle to contend with loneliness, illness and physical hardships, and possibly most difficult of all to maintain spiritual strength to rise above discouragement in face of unyielding paganism.

There was the barrier of an unknown language to be learned in order to reach the minds and hearts of these people with the Gospel story. As curious onlookers came from nearby villages, the missionaries listened intently to their chatter, and recorded each word whose meaning they caught. With amazing rapidity the notes grew and a language pattern began to emerge. Soon the missionaries dared to venture to hold Christian services among those who would gather for worship. Presently homes for boys and for girls were opened, the boarders being orphans sent by the colonial government to the mission for care or children redeemed by the missionaries from passing slave raiders. A first reader was prepared, a few hymns and scripture verses translated.

At last, after almost four years, the first response of faith came on March 8, 1895, when four children and three adults stood up in the little mud and stick Luebo church and confessed their faith in Jesus Christ as Lord and Savior. The first Presbyterian community of what was later to be called the Church of Christ in the Congo was born. Significantly all seven of those baptized that day were from the Bena Lulua and Baluba people. "These were peoples who had suffered oppression and to them the Christian message of liberation and salvation was relevant and attractive."[42]

In the case of the Baluba, they had fled their original homelands in face of Arab slave traders and of the cannibalistic Zappo-Zaps. The Bena Lulua had lost their tribal unity because of civil wars. Both were ready for a new beginning and were quick to accept the leadership of the missionaries. Gradually the new believers and their families moved to the station compound at Luebo and formed the nucleus of a new community. Missionaries found themselves making the laws and assuming the role of judges and policemen of this new society. "Africans were not kept by force on the Protestant station or its dependent village, but if they elected to remain there, they had to obey the rules of the mission."[43]

The little group of believers soon became witnesses to their neighbors. Prayer bands were formed, out of which young Christians were sent out two by two to tell others of the love of Christ. Some were trained and sent as evangelists to nearby villages; others became voluntary teachers. Missionaries traveled constantly to supervise, encourage, advise, and open new work. By 1904, there were as many as forty outstations within a four-mile radius of Luebo, and a few others which were farther away. Church membership stood at 3000 and many more villages were pleading for evangelists and teachers. By 1907, some of the over forty evangelists were far enough advanced in training to be ordained, and the election of five elders and six deacons marked the first step toward the organization of an indigenous church.

In the meantime, as the work at Luebo began to expand, it was decided that a renewed attempt should be made to enter the region of the dominant Bakuba people, who occupied and controlled the territory lying between the Sankuru, Kasai and Lulua rivers north of Luebo.[44] Appointed for this task were the pioneer missionary, Dr. Sheppard, and also the Rev. William M. Morrison, who had arrived in 1896 and who would become in many ways the senior statesman during this early period of the work of the American Presbyterian Congo Mission.[45] In 1897 Sheppard and Morrison ventured northward but were halted at the Bakuba border town of **Ibanche**, 40 miles north of Luebo, and told that the Bakuba king would receive them at his convenience. With no royal invitation forthcoming, Morrison returned to Luebo, while Dr. and Mrs. Sheppard took up permanent residence at Ibanche. The Sheppards would persist in their valiant efforts to reach the Bakubas, achieving remarkable success before their retirement in 1910.[46] Another African American missionary couple, the Rev. and Mrs. Alonzo L. Edmiston, would devote their 35 years of missionary service primarily to work among the Bakuba people. Among Mrs. (Althea Brown) Edmiston's accomplishments was the preparation of a grammar and dictionary of the Bakuba language.

Yet it was the native evangelists who would bear the primary responsibility as pioneers of the Gospel. In fact, the APCM was recognized as the outstanding example among Protestant missions in the use of African evangelists. "It was in the Kasai that the system of native evangelism and missionary visitation won its most striking successes . . . . Luebo and Ibanche became training centers from which increasing numbers of evangelists were sent out to the villages, and the outward movement spread in everwidening circles."[47]

But the witness of the American Presbyterian Congo Mission during this period would take on quite a different and unexpected form. Mention has been made of the cruelties and injustice with which the Congo Free State exacted quotas of rubber and ivory from the people. As early as 1898, Presbyterian missionaries had complained to local authorities that state officials had embarked on a policy of forcibly moving several thousand Baluba people to the State post at Luluabourg to supply forced labor, imposing a heavy food-tax upon them. For the collection of this tax the State had made use of soldiers of the Zappo-Zaps, who engaged in slave-raiding, cannibalism and other atrocities against the people of the Kasai.[48]

When William Morrison left on furlough in 1903, he stopped first in Belgium, seeking an audience with King Leopold II, in order to report to him personally the abuses existing in the Congo. The audience was refused, and Morrison went on to England and America, determined to add his testimony to that of others trying to arouse public sentiment for reform in the Congo Free State administration. What resulted was the formation of the "Congo Reform Association" in England in 1903 and in America the following year. The Association would work assiduously for the welfare of the Congo people over the next ten years, playing a significant part in bringing about not only reforms in the practices of the regime but also the transferring of power from King Leopold's Congo Free State to the colonial administration of Belgium.

In pursuing the relentless campaign against these injustices, Morrison, as editor of the APCM's *The Kasai Herald*, published an account written by Sheppard regarding the deteriorating conditions among the Bakuba people caused by the forced labor extorted by the *Companie du Kasai* (Kasai Rubber Company). In response, the company in 1909 brought a libel suit against Morrison and Sheppard. The trial brought international attention to the Congo and support from many quarters in England, the United States and Belgium for the cause which the missionaries represented. The trial finally took place in Brussels in September 1909 and the missionaries were completely vindicated. In many ways it marked the end of an epoch for the Congo, as the Belgian Parliament in October 1909 announced projected reforms in the new Belgian Congo that would eventually stamp out many of the previous abuses. For the mission itself, it brought a new respect and response from the people for the message and work of the APCM, even among the Bakuba. As missionary William Crane later would observe, "There is no doubt that the missionaries' espousal of the cause of human rights during this period did more than anything else to open the door to the Gospel in the years that followed."[49]

By 1912 the body of believers resulting from American Presbyterian witness had grown to over seven thousand members. Some two hundred teachers and evangelists were scattered through an area of roughly four hundred square miles which constituted the field of the mission. To carry out Christ's mission of preaching, teaching and healing, each of the two mission stations built its work around a church, a school, and a dispensary.[50] Also, the mission boasted its own printing press, named the J. Leighton Wilson Press as a memorial to Dr. Wilson who had worked so diligently for the establishment of Southern Presbyterian work in Africa. Problems of communications and supplies had been greatly helped by the securing of a steamer, the Lapsley, which plied the rivers between the stations and served as the connecting link with the outside world.[51] The scene was set for a period of growth seldom equaled and perhaps never surpassed on any mission field.

C. THE HORN OF AFRICA

Across the continent from West and Central Africa where American Presbyterians pioneered in mission in Cameroon and Congo, another branch of the American Presbyterian family, the **United Presbyterian Church in North America (UPNA)**[52] was pioneering in evangelization in two major countries of northeastern Africa, Sudan and Ethiopia. That story is a fascinating one, which begins with entry into the Sudan in 1900, and leads later to entry into Ethiopia in 1919.

THE CONTEXT

The lifeline of northeast Africa is the Nile. From its many sources in east Africa and the southern Sudan which flow into the White Nile; and from its sources in the mountains of western Ethiopia that flow into the Blue Nile, the Nile, the world's longest river, meanders northward. At its sources it creates a lush tropical forest, then a marshy plain. But from the point of its convergence at Khartoum, it cuts its way through desert at the eastern edge of the Sahara until it reaches its fertile delta in northern Egypt and empties into the Mediterranean Sea.

The Nile has been the birthplace of some of the world's oldest civilizations, the source of life for many generations who have lived along its banks. The Lower Nile (to the north) has been the heart of Egypt through the centuries. The Upper Nile (to the south) has seen the rise and fall of numerous civilizations and empires, yet never have its peoples attained a sense of unity.

This Upper Nile region is the Sudan. It is Africa's largest nation geographically, comprising an area roughly equivalent to one third the size of the United States. Prior to 1820, many small kingdoms rose and fell in the region now known as the Sudan. Then Egypt conquered the region, capturing thousands of Nilotic Sudanese and selling them as slaves. In 1881, a Sudanese Moslem leader, Mohammed Ahmed, rose in revolt. Great Britain, which had occupied Egypt by this time, sensed the threat of the Mahdist revolt to control of the Nile River. After the vain attempt of General Charles Gordon to defend Khartoum ended in his assassination, British and Egyptian troops launched a successful campaign for the reconquest of the Sudan, and in 1898 set up a condominium government under which the Sudan was to be governed jointly by Great Britain and Egypt. Succeeding years saw revolts and mutinies, but Great Britain and Egypt continued in an uneasy alliance, with Britain providing the higher officials and Egypt the subordinate office-holders.

The fundamental reality in the life and history of the Sudan is that two worlds collide within its borders: in the north, the culture of North Africa; and in the south, traditional African culture. In the north the people are Arabized Hamites, Islamic in religion, with Arabic predominating over numerous tribal languages. In the south, on the other hand, the people are divided into many tribal groups of Nilotic and Bantu origin, speaking distinct languages and with varied African traditional faiths. Here the clash of Africa's faiths and cultures is felt most painfully, and through the years the peoples in the south have experienced oppression and exploitation from the governing powers in the north.

BEGINNINGS OF AMERICAN PRESBYTERIAN WITNESS IN THE SUDAN (1900-1914)

The Christian presence in the Sudan dates back to at least the third century when Coptic Christians held sway in the kingdom of Merowe in Nubia (now northern Sudan).[53] About AD 1000, a Nubian bishop introduced the Orthodox Melkite tradition, provoking a split between the Church in Nubia and the Copts in Egypt. Christianity continued to flourish up to the 14th century, when Islam increasingly gained ascendency and ultimately extinguished all Christian presence. The modern era of Christian mission began with the entry of Catholic missionaries in 1842. The Catholic work was virtually destroyed during the Mahdist insurrection in 1881 but was begun again by Catholic missionaries in 1898.

Anglican missionaries of the Church Missionary Society entered about the same year, followed shortly thereafter by American Presbyterians.

The pioneer American Presbyterian missionary to Sudan was the Rev. J. Kelly Giffen of the **United Presbyterian Church of North America (UPNA).** Dr. Giffen had already served with distinction for seventeen years as a missionary to Egypt. After the British successfully quelled a Sudanese revolt in 1898, the time seemed ripe for an expansion of the American Presbyterian missionary thrust from Egypt into the Sudan. With a missionary colleague, Dr. Andrew Watson, Giffen took an exploratory trip from Egypt into the Sudan in January 1900.[54] From the outset they received the cooperation of missionaries of the Church Missionary Society of England, a partnership which would be an important feature of American Presbyterian work in the years ahead. On their return to Cairo, they reported on the need for an immediate forward move into the Sudan, and suggested that the Arabic-speaking Evangelical Church of Egypt adopt the Muslim Sudan as its sphere of missionary enterprise.

In 1900 the Rev. and Mrs. Giffen and Dr. and Mrs. H.T. McLaughlin, along with an Egyptian Evangelical pastor, the Rev. Gebra Hanna, were appointed to serve in the Sudan. As they were about to leave, the Anglo-Egyptian administration of the Sudan refused to grant permission for the foreigners to work in the north, but promised to grant them facilities for work beyond, in "the pagan Sudan." However, as missionaries are prone to do, they "proceeded in faith" with their families from Egypt to **Omdurman**, near the capital city of Khartoum, where they began to gather the Egyptian members of the Evangelical Church of Egypt who were working in the Sudan. Soon a small congregation was gathered, and the first Communion service was celebrated on March 17, 1901.[55]

When the time was ripe, the missionary families left Mr. Hanna to serve the small Evangelical Church in Omdurman, and pressed up the White Nile for a survey of a possible site for the location of a mission station in south Sudan.

> Two sailboats were hired to transport all the equipment necessary to establish a base of operations, and after several aggravating delays the little party set off. Three weeks later, on March 27, 1902, they landed near a little hill crowned with doleib palm trees which gave the site its name, **Doleib Hill.** On shore to meet them was a silent crowd of Shilluk warriors armed with clubs and spears, a rather chilling reception when you recall that the only white men these people knew were the hated slavers. Yet nothing was done to harm the newcomers, and finally all the luggage on the two ships was landed and the missionaries were left there alone. It was imperative that houses be built at once, because the rainy season was almost upon them . . . . By the time the rains came, three small native-style thatched huts had been erected. The problems, though, had only begun. White ants and beetles burrowed in the house, the roofs leaked, and Mrs. Giffen became ill, but somehow they managed to survive. This was the first time the Mission had undertaken work with a completely primitive people, and the tasks were endless.[56]

Their station at Doleib Hill was fortuitously located at the convergence of the White Nile and the Sobat River, near the city of Malakal. While the work began among the Shilluk people, the location afforded an avenue for future expansion among other tribal groups living along the Sobat and White Nile. Thus the Giffens and the McLaughlins "ventured for God as the first Evangelical missionaries ever to bear Him witness in the basin of the Upper Nile."[57]

From these two beginnings grew the American Presbyterian involvement in North and South Sudan. In the North, the evangelistic work was being undertaken officially by the Evangelical Church of Egypt, since foreign mission agencies were not allowed at first to engage in such work. By 1907 the number of evangelical Christians in the North Sudan had grown to the place where a Protestant congregation could be organized. Evangelistic work was also begun in Khartoum North, Atbara, Wadi Halfa, Wad Medani, and Port Sudan. The growth of the work was not spectacular, but it was steady.

The American Presbyterian Mission finally secured permission to undertake education and medical work under the auspices of the Evangelical Church, providing Arabic schools for Egyptian Christians but seeking also to reach out to the larger non-Christian community. The Mission initiated several ventures in educational work: a boys' home in **Khartoum** in 1905, in connection with which a boys' school was developed in 1911; a boys' day and boarding school in Omdurman, founded in 1905, providing elementary and intermediate education; a girls' boarding school at **Khartoum North** in 1908 (the first girls' school in the Sudan), in connection with which a welfare center later developed.

In addition to this institutional work, a strong program of Bible Women's work was initiated in the "three towns" (Khartoum, Khartoum North, and Omdurman), as well as in **Wad Medani** further up the Blue Nile. This work was supported primarily by the UPNA Women's General Missionary Society, which since 1883 had been very active in the UPNA foreign mission program. To promote this work, a Christian Training School for Bible Women would later be established in 1927. "The Bible Women give weekly lessons in reading and writing, with the Bible as the textbook, to Sudanese women . . . . They know, of course, that the women can never become Christians, but they hope to influence their home life and bring some measure of hope to lives condemned otherwise to the narrow boundaries of the *harim* outlook."[58] The witness among women would become a strong feature of American Presbyterian work in the North Sudan, as it had been in Egypt.

Meanwhile, the Evangelical Church of Egypt continued to grow with the influx of members from Egypt into clerical posts in the Sudan. Urban congregations were organized, pastors were called and churches were built not only in "the three towns" but also in Wad Medani, **Atbara** (on the Nile north of Khartoum), and **Port Sudan** on the Red Sea coast. These six churches were organized into the Presbytery of the Sudan in 1912, joining the four presbyteries in Egypt that formed the Synod of the Nile. The work remained closely tied to the witness in Egypt and shared the context of a largely hostile Muslim environment.

The relationship of Christian work in northern Sudan to the Anglo-Egyptian government was a strained one. Administrative regulations enacted in 1905 and renewed in

1933 read: "No Mission station may be formed north of the 10th parallel of North Latitude in any part of the Sudan which is recognized by the Government as Moslem." However, the absolute character of the restrictions was relaxed in the case of the two mission societies with long experience in work among Muslims, i.e. the Church Missionary Society of England and the American Presbyterian Mission. They were allowed to undertake medical and educational work in certain towns where there were Christians, but were not allowed to talk openly to Muslims about religion. "Yet within these limitations the Societies have greater freedom to do Christian evangelistic work than in almost any other Near Eastern Muslim land."[59] Further, Orthodox Islam did not recognize conversion from Islam and conversion was considered apostasy punishable by death. However, Sudan was the first Muslim country which issued a procedure for the registration of conversion, though it required renouncing all one's rights within the Islamic community.[60]

In the southern Sudan, the Presbyterian work among the Nilotic tribes scattered through the forests and marshy plains seemed to progress much more slowly. Working in extremely primitive areas of the Upper Nile Province and under the most difficult conditions, missionaries expanded the ministry among the Shilluk people at Doleib Hill begun in 1902. The missionaries worked hard to learn the Shilluk language. Since no study had ever been made of the Shilluk tongue, the missionaries contrived their own grammar, syntax and vocabulary tools, devising a script to reduce the language to writing.

The first school was opened in 1903 with two boys as students; slowly the number rose to 16. In time "bush" schools were created in the surrounding villages, with the village chief providing a hut for the school, and the Mission providing a native teacher. These schools became feeders for the school at the Mission station and thus were the first link in an educational system.

In 1903 the first church building was completed. "It was a native building of mud and grass, and the services had to be given through an interpreter, but as soon as the missionaries had mastered the language, they led the services. This was a great improvement."[61] Though a number of persons had expressed an interest in the Gospel, it was not until July 1913 that the first Shilluk convert was ready for baptism.

It was very fitting that Dr. J. Kelly Giffen should baptize Nyidok, for it was he, who in connection with Dr. H.T. McLaughlin, began the work on the Sobat thirteen years ago. At one time Nyidok leaned much toward Mohammedanism and was very generally known by the Arabic name 'Abdulla', but he requested that his Shulla name be used in the baptismal service as a bond to his own people. The service was very impressive and was witnessed by all the missionaries, who had gathered for the annual meeting of Association, and by thirty-five natives.[62]

Soon after the Doleib Hill station was opened, medical work was begun on a small scale. By 1911 a small hospital building of concrete block was erected, and several *tukls* (huts) for the patients were built around it. While the patients waited for medical care, they were given the gospel message.

Progress also was made in preparing literature for the people. "Half the Gospel of John has been revised and thus its usefulness has been increased. Four of the Psalms have been translated and set to music and are used in the church services . . . . The people are fond of music. The little boys especially are very ready to sing and often remain after service to practice. The favorite Psalm is the twenty-third."[63]

Meanwhile, the missionaries used the rivers as highways of travel, fitting out a sailboat "The Elliott" to do itinerating work among the villages of the Shilluk, Dinka, Nuer and Anuak peoples along the Sobat and Pibor rivers.[64] With the boat having living accommodations for only two persons, an evangelistic missionary and a medical doctor undertook these journeys, seeking to minister to the great needs of both body and spirit. In 1912, Rev. Elbert Creery and Dr. Tom Lambie were posted at the military and trading station of **Nasir** on the upper Sobat River, not far from the Ethiopian border, to begin work among the Nuer people.

While there was much greater freedom for evangelistic outreach in the southern as compared to the northern Sudan, results seemed meager, with few organized congregations and no ordained African ministers. Educational work was limited to village schools for boys teaching basic literacy skills, and medical work to meeting most critical needs through rudimentary clinics. The years of harvest were still ahead.[65]

CHAPTER II

WORKING BETWEEN WORLD WARS: MISSION EXPANSION (1914-1940)

The period from the beginning of the First World War until the beginning of the Second World War found almost all of Sub-Saharan Africa under colonial rule. With the exception of South Africa, Liberia and Ethiopia, Africa south of the Sahara lay under the heavy hand of European colonial powers. The "independence" of South Africa, attained in 1910 by the union of four British colonies to form the Union of South Africa, was actually the rule of a small white minority which dominated the lives of the black majority. The Berlin Conference of 1885 had sliced up the continent among the participating European empires, cutting across the intricate pattern of tribal and linguistic groups so as to create a crazy-quilt of national boundaries that would remain with Africa far beyond the colonial era.

The legacy of colonialism profoundly affected the life of every African, bringing both bane and blessing. The structures created by colonial regimes to draw the wealth of natural resources out of Africa for the benefit of the empires reached into every corner of the continent, creating burgeoning cities, introducing modern transportation and communication, penetrating ever more deeply into traditional tribal life, creating a new class of educated elite, planting seeds of Western ideas that would inevitably disrupt the status quo.

As a result of Germany's defeat in the First World War, that nation was stripped of all its colonies in Africa. They became mandates of the League of Nations in 1919, but were parceled out to the victorious allies, particularly Great Britain and France. European rule varied from colony to colony. France pursued a policy of assimilation and direct rule. The objective was to acquaint its African subjects as fully as possible with French institutions, language, and culture, the ultimate goal being complete assimilation of the colonies to the home country. In the case of Great Britain, the theory of "indirect rule" was the basis for government administration. British officers governed through the traditional chiefs, seeking to preserve as much as possible the power and prestige of those leaders, while adapting the customary methods to meet the needs of modern society. However, it soon became clear that this system left no place for the young, educated Africans to share in local administration.

Portuguese policy, to a greater degree than that of France, was based on full assimilation. Administratively its colonies were regarded as overseas provinces of Portugal. But Portuguese rule was characterized by abuse of authority, a low level of African education, and severe limitations on economic development. Spain pursued much the same policy in its small colonial holdings.

In the Belgian Congo, the home country pursued a policy of strong paternalism. Africans were prepared by widespread primary education for low-level technical positions, but virtually no attempt was made to create African political representation, nor were political parties allowed to organize.

Whatever the system, racial discrimination was common throughout the colonies. The lack of opportunities for political and economic advancement for Africans would create a situation in which the yeast of democratic ideas which were being introduced, primarily through missionary efforts, would eventually explode in strong independence movements.

A. WEST AFRICA

THE DISRUPTION OF THE FIRST WORLD WAR (1914-1919)

While the outbreak of World War I had catastrophic impact upon the nations of Europe, it also had devastating repercussions in Africa. In Kamerun, the Germans armed the Bulu tribemen, among whom the American Presbyterian work was especially strong. The British attacked these forces with Senegalese troops from the north and the French with Fang tribesman from the south. It was a time of great suffering for the people of Kamerun. An estimated 200,000 people were killed and countless thousands of refugees fled their homes, many dying along the road from starvation or dysentery. Other thousands languished in detention camps hundreds of miles from their homes. The mission station at Batanga had been occupied by the Germans and was heavily shelled by British and French gunboats, forcing missionaries to evacuate to Benito in nearby Spanish Guinea.[66]

Much damage had been done to the mission properties. The industrial school at Elat had been used as a munitions factory. Both government and mission schools were closed from August 1914, with few being opened again until 1918.

Far more serious than the physical damage was the devastating effect of all this upon the spirit of the people, as they experienced on their own soil the death and destruction brought about by warfare between foreign empires. "For twenty years missionaries had been preaching to these Africans the Gospel of Peace. In response to the mandates of the Prince of Peace they had laid down their crossbows, their knives and poisoned spears, ceased their tribal wars and had begun learning to value human life. Suddenly they were confronted with the bewildering spectacle of white men who, although exposed for centuries to that same Gospel of Love, were at one another's throats, and black men who had been taught to lay down their arms were commanded to take them up again in the white man's defense."[67]

NEW BEGINNINGS IN FRENCH CAMEROUN (1916-1940)

The withdrawal of German forces to Spanish Guinea in early 1916 and the Allied occupation of the country made for a return to a degree of normalcy in mission activity. But the period following the war had its special problems. Returning African soldiers brought with them the experiences of war and the influences of Western life, for good and for ill. The horrendous gap between Western lifestyles and the abject poverty of their own people created a deep unrest and determination for change. The situation was further complicated by the attitude of the new French colonial government of what would now be called "French Cameroun". All the stations of the German missions were closed and it was insisted that all instruction in a language other than the vernacular must now be in French. Returning American missionaries found themselves under careful scrutiny to determine whether they might have German ancestry or sympathies.[68]

Still the work of the American Presbyterian mission persisted in spite of all adversities. A year after the hostilities had ceased, the largest additions to the Church in the history of the Mission were recorded. The work at the central station of Elat especially showed remarkable growth, reporting an increase of 25 percent in the immediate postwar years.[69] The inability of the home board to get money into the country during the war was compensated by increased African generosity in the doubling of local contributions. In 1916 a new station was opened at **Foulassi**, seventy miles east of Elat, the farthest inland point thus far occupied.[70]

A major question facing the Protestant witness in the French Cameroun was what would become of the work which had been established by the German missions. In 1920 a survey was undertaken of the territory to the west and northwest formerly occupied by the Basel Mission. As a result of consultation between the headquarters of the various missions, the Paris Missionary Society and the American Presbyterian Mission divided the work of the Basel Mission, the Paris Society occupying the coastal region surrounding the seaport of Douala, and American Presbyterians assuming responsibility for the work further north at **Edea** and **Sakbayeme** in 1920, and still further north at **Bafia** in 1921.[71] Thus began the involvement of American Presbyterians in work among the Bassa people, a major new dimension of Christian witness.[72] These new centers also brought the mission for the first time into direct contact with the southern advance of Islam, as Muslim villages were scattered through the vicinity of these mission stations.

In 1922 missionaries were stationed in the colonial capital **Yaounde.** And in 1928 missionaries were located at the most distant interior field in the Abong Mbang region, some 150 miles east of Yaounde and 350 miles from the coast. As with several other stations, the Africans gave the location a new name, **Nkol Mvolan,** "Hill of Help." The opening of additional stations at **Momjepom** in the southeastern region in 1933, and at **Ilanga** near Edea in 1940 brought the total number of American Presbyterian mission stations in Cameroun to twelve.[73] The French colonial project of road building greatly improved transportation and communication with the interior of Cameroun, thus facilitating all this expansion.[74]

Along with the opening of mission stations there was the expansion of the work out of each station in villages all along the newly opened roads. The Rev. Frank D. Emerson became especially noted for his zeal and determination in such pioneer work, plotting sites for new "evangelistic outposts" and locating evangelists at each place. He would "set out on his bicycle, and when the speedometer read five miles from the last outpost, he located the next outpost, whether it was in a town or in the open bush. Thus no one would have more than two and a half miles to walk to services." The amazing growth of the Camerounian Church during the 1930s was due in large extent to such intrepid outreach.[75]

The expansion of the mission's field of service was accompanied by a steady growth in the size and strength of the Camerounian Church. By the year 1940 it was reported that the American Presbyterian witness had borne fruit in 178 organized churches, 1,556 other groups of believers, 52,477 Christian communicants, served by 814 ordained pastors and some 1,799 evangelists. There was much pride in the development of a "self-governing, self-supporting, self-propagating church." However, the missionaries continued to have final responsibility for the church budget, a factor which in time would prove to be an Achilles' heel.[76]

Down to the year 1936, the churches in the "West Africa field" were organized as the Presbytery of Corisco, the name under which the work was organized in 1860 and attached to the Synod of New Jersey. However, the growth of the churches in numbers and membership and the development of competent African ministers and elders, as well as the wide distribution of the churches over an extensive territory, had made it impossible for the Presbytery to function efficiently. Therefore in 1935 the Presbytery asked the Synod of New Jersey to petition the General Assembly for a separate Synod, to be known as the Synod of Cameroun, which would be divided into three presbyteries: the Presbytery of Corisco, consisting of those churches in the southernmost section of Cameroun from Elat westward, as well as in Corisco and Spanish Guinea; the Presbytery of Metet, consisting of churches in the middle section of the mission's territory, east of Elat; and the Presbytery of Sanaga, consisting of the churches in the northern area inherited from the Basel Mission. The PCUSA General Assembly's approval of that request in 1936 laid the foundations for a strong Synod in which African church leaders would take a greater leadership role.

Along with the expansion of the church, there developed an extensive system of educational work overseen by the mission. By 1940 it included 1,194 primary schools, 8 middle and high schools, a Normal Training School at Foulassi, the Dager Biblical Seminary at Lolodorf, a Bible Institute at Sakbayeme, and the Frank James Industrial School at Elat. The whole system included some 32,056 students. Needless to say, this required a large corps of African teachers and administrators, to say nothing of missionary personnel. The French colonial government continued the German policy of assisting mission schools financially, gradually increasing its assistance to Protestant institutions. While there was some ambivalence among Presbyterian missionaries about this tie to the colonial government, the practice was continued, "because of the liberal regulations of non-interference with school programs, and the fear that the Roman Catholics would swell their enrollment in an attempt to squeeze out the Protestants."[77]

The importance of this educational undertaking in the future development of Cameroun (as well as the rest of sub-Saharan Africa) cannot be exaggerated. Though the French colonial government in 1920 seemed to be about to take the same position in Cameroun as it had in Gabon (i.e. requiring that all instruction be carried out in French), it subsequently modified its policy and allowed instruction in the vernacular languages in the village primary schools. "The only schools in which the natives of Cameroun learn their own language are the Mission schools, and their familiarity with the Scriptures and with Christian hymns, and with Christian literature from abroad, have come through the service of these schools and through the emphasis consistently maintained from the beginning of the work upon the use of the vernacular."[78]

Equally extensive was the mission's medical work, since "in no other part of the world are serious diseases more prevalent or more deadly in their effects."[79] At the heart of the mission's medical network was the Central Hospital at Enongal near Elat. Established in 1925, by 1928 it was recognized as one of the finest hospitals on the West Coast of Africa. Scattered through the area served by the mission were, by 1940, nine "bush" hospitals, five leper colonies and twelve dispensary clinics, most with only basic equipment. In the year 1940 these facilities served 114,408 patients, afflicted with every manner of disease from sleeping sickness to leprosy.

The burden placed upon medical missionary personnel was enormous. "The medical missionary must do everything himself, perform unaided every kind of operation from the simplest to the most severe, combine the duties of hospital superintendent, medical staff, surgical staff and chaplain, and concern himself with scores of details which no hospital surgeon in America would think of touching."[80] Yet the witness of the medical work was in many ways at the heart of the evangelization process, drawing people out of age-old beliefs centered around the "medicine man" and into faith that used the best of modern medical practice activated by Christian compassion.[81]

The provision of Christian literature in the numerous languages of Cameroun presented a monumental task. This work was greatly aided by the effective cooperative effort of the International Committee on Christian Literature for Africa, formed in 1929 as a sub-committee of the International Missionary Council, in which American Presbyterians fully participated. Through the work of American Presbyterians, several spoken dialects were transformed into written languages, grammars and dictionaries were compiled, tracts and teaching materials prepared, and the ultimate goal of translation of the Bible undertaken. By 1940 portions of Scripture translated by Presbyterian missionaries were available in the Bulu, Bassa, Bakele, Benga, and Mpongwe languages.

The task of translation involved not only putting the Gospel into the vernacular but also into African thought patterns. "The lost coin rolls under the bamboo bed of that village, and the lost sheep strays off into that forest, and the prodigal son goes away by the tribal path to the beach and is lost. And the Son of Man comes down by the trail from the town of Zambe, the Creator, to seek and to save the things that are lost."[82]

The establishment of the Halsey Memorial Press[83] in 1921 became a tremendous resource for the publication of Christian literature for the Camerounian Christian community, as well as a quarterly magazine *The Drum Call* for interpreting and promoting the work of the mission to the church in America.

By 1940, with well over a century of missionary witness in West Africa, American Presbyterians had been represented by a noble army of missionary evangelists, educators, and medical workers, many of whom had laid down their lives in Africa. The fruit of their labor was enormous, in a strong Christian community in southern Cameroun and nearby areas, as well as in significant institutions and systems for education and medicine. The benefits of their work were shared by literally hundreds of thousands beyond the bounds of the organized church. Yet the impact of the western imperialism under which they labored was destined to be a formidable force confronting them in the period ahead.

WORKING AGAINST THE ODDS IN SPANISH GUINEA (1915-1940)

The story of the beginnings of American Presbyterian witness in Rio Muni (the mainland portion of Spanish Guinea) has been told in the previous chapter. Though at the outset the work of the PCUSA missionaries at Benito in 1865 was auspicious, the focus soon shifted to stations established in neighboring Gabon in 1871, and then Kamerun in 1879. In Rio Muni the work of American Presbyterians was the primary Protestant witness. However, they were not officially recognized by the Spanish authorities until 1906, when the colonial government decreed that all Protestant work must be carried out in Spanish.

Difficulties with the Spanish colonial government intensified in succeeding decades. All Protestant missionaries were forced to withdraw from Spanish Guinea between 1924 and 1932 due to government opposition. Henceforward all Protestant schools and hospitals were officially forbidden. The Presbyterian mission hospital at Benito (later known as Bolondo) was the only Protestant mission hospital in Rio Muni when it was forced to close in 1924. While all mission-related schools were officially closed, some schools continued to operate unofficially.

After 1932, Presbyterian mission work was extended along the roads into the interior. By 1940, the West Africa Mission reported only one missionary family serving in Spanish Guinea, the Rev. and Mrs. Joseph McNeill, with only one ordained African pastor in that area, the Rev. Bodumba Ibia. These, along with an unnamed number of evangelists, served eight churches, 55 preaching points and 47 Sunday Schools.[84]

Relationships with the Spanish colonial government were continually tenuous. Schools in Spanish and the vernacular were carried on in a number of villages, even though not officially permitted. To seek better relationships with Spanish authorities, a Spanish Evangelical pastor, the Rev. Ramon Ruiz Valera, was invited to join the work in Rio Muni and to take responsibility for all the educational work. "He made a favorable impression upon his colleagues, is well received by the Spanish officials, and the work has taken on a new lease of life."[85]

Under a relationship of benign neglect with a Spanish government in turmoil in Spain, the mission pressed forward its work in the interior of Rio Muni, establishing a church at Ngon, an outpost of an older church at Bijabijan. One of the missionaries wrote: "In this group I found a type of Christianity that I had lost sight of for some years, that early, primitive, whole-souled belief that may be pretty weak in technical knowledge, but is long on unshakable faith. The kind that comes from a town with no evangelist anywhere to teach or help, but which holds on to what little it has with a tenacity that can not be beaten. It was most refreshing to meet such people again."[86]

B. CENTRAL AFRICA

YEARS OF EXPANSION IN THE BELGIAN CONGO (1912-1919)

The years 1912-1919 were to see an advance in the work of APCM which found both the home church and the mission trying "to keep pace with the work as it expands of its own force."[87] Up to this point, the Belgian colonial government had refused to grant the mission concession for any new stations or even permits for temporary occupancy. In a way this was a blessing in disguise, for it was necessary to depend almost entirely on African workers for sustained evangelistic work beyond the two stations of Luebo and Ibanche and their immediate environs.

But 1912 was a turning point. In the home church, the Laymen's Missionary Convention in Chattanooga, Tennessee in early 1912 brought a flood of volunteers for missionary service in the Belgian Congo. And in the Congo, the government at last opened long-closed doors, so that missionaries could follow into those territories opened by African evangelists. With the necessary personnel and the permission of the government, four new stations were opened:

— In 1912, at **Mutoto**[88], some 100 miles east of Luebo, deep in Bena Lulua territory;
— In 1913, at **Lusambo**[89], the capital city of the Kasai District;
— In 1915, at **Bulape**, north of Luebo, in the heart of the Bakuba kingdom;[90]
— In 1917, at **Bibanga**, far to the southeast and deep in Baluba country.

The story of Bulape deserves special mention. Dr. Sheppard's dream of winning the great Bakuba people had never been realized before his retirement. Ibanche Station, which had been opened for that purpose, had been absorbed by work with the Baluba and Bena Lulua. Bulape, only thirty miles from the Bakuba capital Mushenge, was given ten years in which to make a significant entry into the Bakuba Kingdom. Therefore the Mission decided that Ibanche should be abandoned as a mission station and its work turned over to evangelists working from Luebo. To Mr. and Mrs. H.M. Washburn was given the double duty of dismantling Ibanche and opening Bulape. For 35 years they were to give themselves to work among the Bakuba. Within three years sixteen evangelists were teaching in 53 outstations. Further, the Bulape Christians were to take the lead among all the Kasai Christians in achieving self-support. "In the fullness of time God was opening the hearts of the Bakuba to the Gospel."[91]

Recognizing the need for better training for the growing number of evangelists, elders and deacons, the APCM voted in 1913 to open a Bible school at Luebo to provide the beginnings of theological training. When the first session opened on July 1, 1914, twelve African students gathered from the various APCM stations. The institution grew rapidly; in 1917 its location was transferred to Mutoto. And in 1918, following the sudden death of Dr. William Morrison, the school was named Morrison Bible School in his memory.

For those who were not able to attend the Bible School, regular conferences were organized at each station. At the first such conference held at Luebo in 1914, there were 225 participants. "The conferences drew closer together not only African workers and missionaries, but also Africans of different tribes . . . . The various churches or parishes were introduced to each other and a denominational infrastructure was being born."[92]

In 1916 further trust was expressed in African leadership through the ordination of three elders to the ordained ministry. These first three pastors, Kabeya Lukengu, Musonguela, and Kachunga, "were given authority to baptize, discipline, administer the Lord's Supper and arrange all church questions."[93] More and more to these pastors and their successors was turned over the work of itineration previously done by missionaries, especially since they could go into places almost inaccessible to the missionary.

By 1919, church membership resulting from APCM work had reached 17,268 communicants. Statistical reports from the 15 Protestant mission groups working in the Belgian Congo revealed "the almost incredible fact that, while the APCM missionaries composed only about eleven percent of all Protestant missionaries in the colony, over thirty-five percent of all Protestant Christians were communicants of the Presbyterian Mission."[94]

Meanwhile the institutional work of the mission was beginning to take shape. With the opening of new stations came the need for builders. In 1915, Mr. C.R. Stegall, a graduate of Georgia Tech, arrived to open the Carson Industrial School, which during its fifteen years of operation trained about 750 young men in carpentry, brickmaking and masonry, then tailoring, shoemaking, tanning, and blacksmithing. While the school had to be closed in 1930 due to the great depression, it proved to be of lasting value both in the development of the mission and the church, and in the industrial life of the Congo.

The healing ministry of the mission saw a major advance in the arrival of the first trained nurse in 1913 and the second doctor in 1914. Soon after, the McKowen Hospital at Luebo was begun, to be completed in 1916. With an operating room whose window opened on the hospital lawn, curious crowds had an unobstructed view of the operating theater. "That there was nothing occult in the work of the Mission medical staff must be clearly demonstrated."[95] Not only did the medical work serve to break down barriers of superstition among the Africans, it also served to remove barriers of misunderstanding and opposition between the mission and European officials. As early as 1914 the State recognized the value of the mission medical work by making a grant for medicines, a practice which would be continued as new hospitals and dispensaries were opened.

By 1919 the mission had established two industrial schools, two hospitals and two dispensaries, one Bible School and 428 elementary schools. Yet there was an aspect of this institutional growth which in time would raise new problems. The rapidly growing institutions absorbed an ever increasing number of new missionary recruits, until they outnumbered those in work directly related to building up the church. The tensions between church and mission institutions had begun.

As the APCM became firmly established in the Kasai and had more to do than they themselves could handle, they encouraged the entry of other Protestant missions. In 1911, the Mennonite Church of America established its mission some seventy miles southwest of Luebo, inheriting work begun by APCM. And in 1914 the Southern Methodist Episcopal Mission entered the Kasai region, organizing its work around two evangelists and thirteen members received from APCM work at Luebo. APCM cordially received the newcomers and helped them to get started, providing both material and spiritual assistance. Also, as the fame of the APCM spread as "one of the most successful missionary enterprises in Africa," representatives of other churches, as well as persons working for the government and trade companies, cast in their lot with this enterprise. In fact, in 1918, a Catholic priest who was the Father Superior at Lusambo, Joseph Savels, joined the APCM staff, producing "a profound sensation in Belgium and in the Congo."[96]

YEARS OF TESTING (1920-1931)

The years 1920-1931 would see a profound change in the Belgian Congo which in turn would have far-reaching effect upon the Christian movement as a whole and upon the American Presbyterian work in particular. Recovering from the impact of the First World War, Belgium looked toward its vast colonial holding in the Congo with a new attitude. The discovery of vast, hitherto unsuspected, mineral resources and agricultural possibilities gave her a new pride in *Notre Colonie*. By 1923 the Katanga district was the world's third largest supplier of copper, its thriving provincial capital of Elizabethville tied in with the Copper Belt to the south. A wealth of diamonds had been found in the Kasai, and the mines at Bakwanga came in time to lead the world in the production of industrial diamonds. Further, the addition of the rich Ruanda-Urundi district, formerly a colony of Germany, to the Belgian colonial mandate stirred a new sense of opportunity as well as responsibility.

Some immediate steps were taken "for African welfare": an African police force was established; Belgian doctors and health agents were sent out; agriculturists taught new farming techniques that would move farmers from subsistence to cash-crop farming. Priority was given to solving the overwhelming problem of transportation. As new enterprises were opened in the colony, the narrow-gauge railroad around the cataracts of the Lower Congo proved utterly inadequate; a new wide-gauge railroad was projected, and was completed in 1927. Further, to bring the tremendous mineral wealth out of the southern Katanga area, a railroad line was built from the Katanga mining towns to Port Francqui on the Kasai River, straight through the heart of the Kasai, the territory for which APCM had assumed evangelistic responsibility. "Each small [railroad] station along the line was to open new evangelistic opportunities, and the larger stations were to grow into thriving centers whose spiritual needs challenged the best the Mission could offer."[97]

However, along with the new opportunities came tremendous new problems: "The Presbyterian's work was no longer limited to winning the Kasai people to Christ and organizing them in a church. Their work would also include finding answers to the challenges of modernization, urbanization, materialism, and changes in the traditional African lifestyle."[98]

Even more rapidly than the railroad, quite passable motor roads spread across the district in a network connecting the more important state, company, and mining posts. Hundreds of villages were moved onto the highways, each village responsible for the building and maintenance of a section of the road. New enterprises ranging from mining centers and plantations to trading posts were being developed. All these undertakings were dependent on African labor to carry them to success. In ever-increasing numbers, the people were drawn from the quiet of village life into the bewildering complexity of modern civilization. Further, most of the able-bodied men were uprooted to work in railroad camps, at the mines, or as low-level employees of government and trading companies, leaving villages made up chiefly of women, children and older men. The men who left the village stepped into a new world, with new wealth, new culture, as well as new temptations and new vices. It was remarkable that many a Christian went into this new life carrying the Gospel with him, remaining strong in faith and conduct despite his modern pagan surroundings.

These tremendous changes in the life of the Congo and its people inevitably affected the work of the APCM. Along with and often ahead of the colonial engineers, missionaries participated in the surveying and building of the roads joining the stations and outstations. Concurrently bicycles were exchanged for motorcycles, later with sidecars added. In 1925 the first Ford cars made their appearance, soon followed by small trucks to take the place of human portage. Perhaps nothing so emphasized the changed conditions under which the Mission was working as did the sale of the river steamer, the Lapsley. For over 25 years it had served as virtually the sole means of transporting cargo and passengers into the Kasai area, as well as the means of ministering to Christian groups along the river. Now with both railroad and motor transportation available, the Lapsley's services were no longer needed.

With the sale of the Lapsley, Lusambo was no longer needed as a transport station. In 1925 the decision was made to transfer the work at that station to the English Plymouth Brethren Mission, and to open a new station at **Lubondai**, some 100 miles south of Mutoto. "Apparently the Mission considered that this station . . . completed the occupation of the field for which it was responsible."[99] From this time forward for a considerable number of years, missionary personnel would be concentrated at these five stations: Luebo,

Mutoto, Bulape, Bibanga, and Lubondai, serving a geographical area larger than North and South Carolina combined.

The institutional work at these stations grew. Well-equipped permanent or semi-permanent hospitals or dispensaries were built on each of the five stations, with an increasing number of highly trained missionary doctors and nurses. The age-old diseases which plagued the people of the Congo—malaria, sleeping sickness, leprosy, and yaws—were treated with increasing effectiveness by modern medical injections. This drew people from a wide area to the mission hospitals to receive "the medicine of the needle." Likewise, the schools at the mission stations became better staffed and equipped, though far from being as modern as the medical institutions. Hence the responsibility for the evangelistic outreach through some 600 outstations fell more and more to African workers.[100]

Yet all was not well. Judging by statistics alone, this was a discouraging period. In 1924 a drop of over six thousand in church membership was recorded and school attendance had decreased by nearly ten thousand. Much of the loss was due to the disruptions caused by the rapid development of the colony as people were uprooted, voluntarily and involuntarily, and relocated. Also, hundreds had died in the epidemics of influenza and dysentery following the First World War, as well as the outbreaks of sleeping sickness and smallpox in the early twenties. Still another factor was the fragmentation of the Christian community throughout the Congo by the rise in the number of African indigenous sects, such as the Kimbanguist Church. It was not until 1928 that statistics again began to record a steady increase in all departments of work.

In the Congolese church which had come into being as a result of APCM work, there was slow progress toward indigenization. In 1920 the mission discussed the possibility of giving more power to the church by organizing a "native" presbytery. This came about as a result of the first "general conference" of African church leaders held at Luebo in 1919. For the first time African pastors, elders, evangelists, deacons and teachers of all the APCM stations in the Kasai had gathered, discovered their Christian unity and shown signs of their potential for governing their own affairs. Yet this large and growing church had only two African pastors, [101] and no organization, authority or budget of its own.

There were signs that the mission was being strongly intimidated at this time by the pressure of the Belgian colonial authorities. Around 1921, the new Governor General of the Belgian Congo called representatives of Protestant missions together and insisted that the African "tribes" be kept separate in the churches, that Africans not be ordained as pastors, and that no additional black missionaries be sent to the Congo. During the next five years in the work of the APCM, no new pastors were ordained, no new black missionaries came, and the organization of a "native presbytery" was delayed. Undoubtedly, the rise of the Kimbanguist and other indigenous Christian movements had profoundly affected the attitudes of both the government and the missions.[102]

But the tide seemed to turn with the calling of the first international conference of the churches working in Africa south of the Sahara in 1926 in Le Zoute, Belgium. The APCM was well represented by the Rev. and Mrs. Hezekiah Washburn and Ms. Althea

Edmiston, a black missionary. The conference gave strong emphasis to adapting the methods of mission work to the African context, strengthening African church leadership, and greater cooperation in education and literature development. It was a turning point for the APCM, as well as other Protestant work in Africa.[103]

With this renewed impetus, steps were taken toward strengthening the organization of the church in the Kasai. Five "provisional" presbyteries were formed, corresponding roughly to the areas for which each mission station was responsible; thus each presbytery included members predominantly from a particular tribe of people. The nuclei of the provisional presbyteries already were present in the ordained pastors and elders in each station. These, together with the missionaries of the area for which a given station assumed responsibility, constituted the provisional presbytery. Later representatives from each presbytery were elected annually to represent the presbytery at the level of the next highest court, the provisional synod. In 1931 a Book of Church Order, based roughly upon that of the Presbyterian Church in the United States, was adopted by the church courts and by the Mission, and published in both French and Tshiluba. The levels of ecclesiastical authority from bottom to top were the local church session, the provisional presbytery, the provisional synod, and (here an additional level departing from the PCUS Book of Church Order) the Mission.

While these steps toward church structure were significant in providing a larger opportunity for African participation in church affairs, the emphasis on the "provisional" nature of the organization was not especially appreciated by the African church leadership. "The word *tshidi-kisha* ("provisional" or "trial") was much used in reference to the presbytery and synod particularly. However, the inference was made that if the church courts were provisional, then logically the Congolese pastors and elders could be regarded also as being provisional, not ordained leaders in the same sense as the missionaries. The rift became wider and wider between Church and Mission as the leaders brooded about these things."[104]

Meanwhile, the Mission itself was becoming more and more highly structured. During this period, as mission hospitals, schools, buildings and modes of transportation and communication were being modernized, the mission found it necessary to appoint more and more standing committees to oversee its work. Likewise each mission station became "a government within a government." Depending upon the size and its work, each station might have a business department, a legal department, an industrial department, a printing department, an educational department, a medical department and an evangelistic department (composed of the presbytery made up of missionaries and African pastors). While there was one legal representative for the mission as a whole in its relation to the national government, each station had its chairman who would serve as its spokesman before local government authorities. Kiantandu observed, "The Mission of the period seemed to focus its attention upon institutions and because of this the APCM was becoming more and more a big business, administering large institutions with large funds in its hands."[105] And Crane commented, "It is safe to say that the growth of the Mission as a power structure was a contributing factor, of great importance, to the spiritual anemia that sapped the vitality of the indigenous power structure of the Church."[106]

Yet at the same time, one of the most important steps toward the development of an indigenous church was taken during this period, i.e. the completion of the Bible in the Tshiluba language. Building upon the work done so ably by Dr. Morrison, the Rev. T.C. Vinson carried on the work of translation virtually alone after Dr. Morrison's untimely death in 1918. Upon Vinson's completion of the work in 1923, both the American Bible Society and the British And Foreign Bible Society published editions of the book in 1926. Copies of the treasured Bible quickly spread across the Kasai as well as other centers where Tshiluba speaking people had moved. By producing the Bible in Tshiluba, the APCM had provided the basic tool not only for its own work and that of other Protestant missions working in the Kasai, but also for the Kimbanguist Church and other indigenous churches for whom Tshiluba was the common language.[107]

YEARS OF ECONOMIC DEPRESSION YET CONTINUING GROWTH (1932-1939)

The world-wide economic depression of 1931 had its impact on both the Mission and the Church in the Kasai. For the Mission it meant a significant reduction in missionary force as serious illnesses, emergency furloughs and retirements were compensated for by very few new missionary reenforcements. "The burden of increased responsibilities fell on the shoulders of the few."[108] As for financial resources, the APCM's budget was cut by one-third, making it increasingly difficult to support the expanded work.

Yet these adversities seemed to work together for good in the advancement of the Church. Thousands of unemployed returned from the large cities to their own villages, many of them reentering the life of the church. Hundreds went back to the mission schools, requiring that schools be expanded and developed. While primary school work continued to be carried out in every village where there was an evangelist, regional schools were established for groups of villages, giving higher and more specialized instruction.[109] Many graduates from these schools later would be accepted for entrance into the State's medical schools and specialized railroad schools, as well as for positions in government service, commerce and with the mining companies. Those who left home often became Christian leaders in their new communities. Among those graduates who remained were many who entered Christian work with a genuine sense of call, receiving salaries from three to thirty times less than that offered by lucrative government and business positions. Yet all this moving about of people would have a serious effect upon the continuity of church life, as many church officers and teachers moved on to larger communities for more remunerative employment.

Two major new developments took place as a result of the visit of Dr. Egbert M. Smith, General Secretary of the PCUS Executive Committee of Foreign Missions, in 1932. Concerned by the slow and limited response of women and girls to the Gospel as contrasted with the eager response of men and boys, Dr. Smith urged that this become a focus of the Mission's attention. As a result, and through resources made available by the PCUS Women's Auxiliary Birthday Offering, girls' boarding schools were established on every mission station. These would in time become the source of strong leadership for the women's work of the church in the Kasai, training outstanding Christian women for home and community life. Concurrently a Women's School was developed at the Morrison Bible School, preparing ministers' wives for their important role in church and community.

Also, Dr. Smith suggested that the Mission reevaluate its "five stations" policy and consider establishing small evangelistic centers in areas not adequately covered by existing mission stations. Accordingly, in 1935 a new station was opened at **Mboi**, eighty miles southeast of Lubondai, serving the Babindi, Bena Ngoshi and Balualua peoples, in the most thickly populated region of the whole mission area. Then in 1937 a station was begun along the Kasai railroad at **Kasha**, to work among the Bena Kanyoka people. The work at these two stations met with limited response "among a very conservative people who were deeply attached to their tribal ways."[110] Also the original intention of keeping these stations as "small evangelistic outposts" was soon obscured as each soon developed the same institutions and programs that were found on the larger stations.

As for the church in the Kasai as a whole, these were years of steady growth. Faithful teaching and preaching by missionaries, pastors and evangelists resulted in additions of over three thousand a year to the church by profession of faith. As missionary ranks were depleted, pastors and elders took on new duties, and for the most part measured up to their new responsibilities. Even when the Mission faced the painful alternative of reducing the number of paid workers or cutting the subsidy which each worker received from the Mission by half, the reaction of the church leaders was unanimous: "*Kosa bintu, kadi kukoshi bantu*" ("Cut off money, but don't cut off people").

By 1938, among the 281,000 Protestant communicants in the Belgian Congo, 45,124 were Presbyterians. The APCM recorded the largest Protestant community in the Belgian Congo, numbering 94,579 adherents.

Yet, strangely, growth in membership was not paralleled by an increase in the number of organized congregations. The twenty particular churches organized so hopefully and reported so triumphantly in 1931 had not fulfilled their promise. Instead, one by one they were dissolved until only nine were left by 1944. Most of these were station churches where the missionaries had been at hand to advise and direct. Numerous factors were involved. First, the organization of particular churches coincided almost exactly with the time when many members were thrown out of work by the depression, and the cash income of many Christians was cut off entirely. Also, there were few trained lay leaders, and pastors knew little about how to develop leaders. Clan and tribal jealousies were still a stumbling block. Undoubtedly there was also the sense that, since the Mission had ultimate control over the church, there was no need for church members to strive to develop self-governing, self-supporting churches. Yet while the first venture in organizing particular churches was a disappointing one, "the Church had come far in fifty years. One could trust the power that had led them thus far to bring them into complete fulness of God's purpose for them in His Church and His Kingdom."[111]

C. THE HORN OF AFRICA

WORKING AGAINST THE ODDS IN THE SUDAN (1915-1940)

The Anglo-Egyptian condominium government of the Sudan continued on shaky ground during the years between the World Wars. Egyptian resentment against the part Britain played both in their own country and in the Sudan reached a climax in 1924 when an Egyptian nationalistic revolt broke out, resulting in the murder of the British Governor-General of the Sudan. The Egyptian troops were immediately withdrawn from the Sudan and Egyptian officials were increasingly replaced by Sudanese. For the next 12 years, British and Sudanese officials governed the Sudan without Egyptian help. In 1936 Great Britain and Egypt signed a new agreement that restored Egypt's participation in the government of Sudan. However, by this time the Sudanese had tasted the prospect of self-government and there would be no peace until that goal was achieved.

The American Presbyterian witness in both North and South Sudan continued with only a few signs of progress during this period. In the north, in 1917 a Christian Bible Woman, Sitt Faruza Girgis, was brought from Egypt to begin home visitation with Mrs. Giffen in the harems of Omdurman and Khartoum.

> It was very discouraging work at first, with many rebuffs from the men in the homes, but persistence gradually won out. At first in the homes of the lower social classes among the women who made native beer, and then in the homes of the more respectable and wealthy, the Bible Women became familiar figures.[112]

To promote this work, a Christian Training School was established in 1927 to prepare Bible Women for this important service. When enough of them were trained, Bible Women were assigned to Atbara, Wad Medani, and Port Sudan.

One of the most significant projects of the mission during this period was the J. Kelly Giffen School of Agriculture which was opened in 1924 at Gereif. Thanks to a special grant, land was purchased on the Blue Nile, a few miles south of Khartoum. Here a number of buildings were erected and pure-blooded stock was procured to teach young Sudanese the latest methods in scientific cattle-raising (since most of them were nomadic cattle herders). Unfortunately, the cost of maintaining the school proved too great, so that the program had to be discontinued in 1939.

Meanwhile, the church in the north Sudan continued to grow at a slow but steady pace. By 1936 there were six ordained pastors serving nine established congregations, with a number of preaching points not yet organized. The Evangelical Church in the north Sudan, although numbering only a few hundred members, shared extensively in almost every phase of the Mission's work. "The initiative in evangelism among non-Christians from church centers has been taken by Sudanese, Egyptian and Ethiopian members of the congregations in many instances."[113]

In the southern Sudan, the Presbyterian work among the Nilotic tribes scattered through the forests and marshy plains progressed more slowly. While there was much greater freedom for evangelistic outreach in the southern as compared to the northern Sudan, results were meager, with few organized congregations and no ordained African ministers by the year 1940. However, by 1935 about 200 persons had been baptized.

At first, educational work was limited to village schools for boys, teaching basic literacy skills. However, in 1925, at Doleib Hill a boarding school for boys was begun, and eight years later a girls' school was started. The bush schools became feeders for the schools at the Mission stations.

At Nasir, where work had been begun in 1912 among the Nuer tribes people, work was begun to reduce the language to writing. By 1919 a school was built, with a missionary assigned to this particular task. "As long as the British government controlled the Sudan, it favored the mission schools and even subsidized their operation. English rather than Arabic became the language of the schools. It was an incomparable opportunity and was of immense benefit to the Mission."[114]

Medical work was generally limited to meeting the most critical needs through rudimentary clinics. However, in 1923, a small hospital was built at Nasir, providing medical care not only for the native population, but also for the British assigned to the military post at Nasir, as well as Arab traders.

Even though the Sudan government had invited the Mission to open a school among the Anuak people as early as 1903, it was not until 1935 that the prospect could be explored:

> A preliminary trip into the Anuak country was taken by Dr. Paul J. Smith in February [1935]. He spent three weeks up in that region. Previous to this journey, he had sent on an Anuak named Gila who had become a Christian at Nasir and who was, of course, familiar with all the territory. On the arrival of Dr. Smith at Akobo he found that Gila had started a school and had surrounded himself with twenty-two boys about thirteen years old and younger, and was teaching them in a temporary house. On Sabbath, Gila conducted a service, which really marks the opening of Christian work in Anuak territory.[115]

In 1938 missionary personnel and funds could be spared for this work, and Don and Lyda McClure opened a station at **Akobo** near the Ethiopian border. This would be the base for a major thrust among the Anuaks, who inhabited an area overlapping the border between the Sudan and Ethiopia.

Fellowship with other mission bodies in southern Sudan resulted in cooperative evangelistic endeavor in several places. In **Malakal**, the largest city in the southern Sudan, the Mission shared with six other communions, including three of the ancient Eastern Churches, in the erection of a beautiful church building for worship. "In this church our Christian people from the pagan tribes can gain a new conception of the spiritual unity of all believers in Jesus Christ including themselves."[116]

BEGINNING OF AMERICAN PRESBYTERIAN WITNESS IN ETHIOPIA (1918-1936)

The second American Presbyterian involvement in northeast Africa was an outgrowth of its work in the Sudan, across the border into Ethiopia. To understand the setting for this missionary venture, it is necessary first to consider the context.

THE CONTEXT

The Horn of Africa protrudes out of the northeastern edge of the African continent like the snout of a rhinoceros. In the center of the snout rises a vast block of rugged mountains, unique in beauty with towering peaks, vast plateaus with fertile fields, forest-covered hills, and mountain streams. Here is the heart of Ethiopia. To the west lie the valleys of the Upper Nile which is the lifeline of the Sudan. To the east are the hot desert plains of Somalia, and to the north facing the Red Sea the shores of Eritrea.

On the mountain top land is a unique civilization, one of the oldest in the world. Originally of Hamitic origin, its people have been modified through the centuries by the infiltration of peoples from the Upper Nile and Semitic people from across the Red Sea, yet have maintained a remarkable ethnic and cultural integrity. Legends trace the ancestry of the imperial line back to Solomon and the Queen of Sheba.[117] In language and racial characteristics, these people are different and apart. Cut off by mountain barriers from the great trade routes, they have developed a unique culture, which until the twentieth century existed independently of the rest of the world. The mountain barriers have made it difficult for rulers to maintain their hold on outlying provinces or to subdue independent governors and local officials. Rebellions and civil wars have been common. Yet throughout the centuries, the people as a whole have maintained a substantial unity.

At the heart of this unity is the Ethiopian Orthodox Church. It has its roots in the Coptic Church of Egypt which in turn traces its origin to the Church of Alexandria, one of the three original patriarchates of the ancient church. In the great Christological schism of the fifth century, Egypt was unable to accept the Council of Chalcedon, a theological divide which reflected an underlying cultural divide between the Greek-Latin imperial world on the one hand and that of Africa and Asia on the other. Thus the Coptic Church became the core of so-called "monophysite" Christianity, believing in the single nature of Christ, as opposed to belief in the divine-human nature of Christ which characterized western Christendom. It was through the Coptic Church of Egypt that the Ethiopian Orthodox Church was founded in the fourth century, and to which it remained subject through the ages until the 1940s. From the See of Alexandria it received its *Abuna* or Archbishop, its creed, its liturgy, its monastic spirituality.

Nevertheless, its practical isolation for so many centuries has permitted the development of a unique tradition. One of the most distinctive elements of Ethiopian Orthodoxy is its Hebraic substructure. It seems undeniable that in some way the ancient Aksumite kingdom, from which Ethiopia has grown, had been profoundly influenced by

Judaism before the coming of Christianity. This pre-existing Judaism both made Christian conversion easier and in an extraordinary way controlled its institutional evolution so that the resulting pattern of worship and religious life is as much reflective of the Old Testament as of the New. Its priests, for example, are chosen from traditional priestly families and form a caste similar to the Levites of the Old Testament. Worship centers around the ark, which is kept in the inner shrine, or holy of holies, in each church. The rituals of worship are conducted in the ancient Ethiopian language Geez, no longer understood by most of the priests themselves. Here then was a Christianity which seemed "frozen in time."[118]

At the heart of Ethiopian Orthodox Christianity through the centuries has been the Emperor, acclaimed as "King of Kings," "Elect of God," "Conquering Lion of Judah." The Ethiopian Church and State were seen as one, the Emperor being the head of the Church because he is the head of the State. Traditionally, to be an Ethiopian of Amharic lineage was to be a Coptic Orthodox Christian.[119]

And here it is necessary to distinguish between the several peoples which inhabit the Horn of Africa. There are three great ethnic groups within the traditional political boundaries of Ethiopia: (1) Peoples of Cushitic (i.e. Hamitic Ethiopian) stock who have, over a long period, received Semitic admixtures originating from the Arabian shores of the Red Sea. These form the core of Ethiopia, speaking several related languages, all related to the ancient language Geez. Chief among them is the Amharic language, which in time dominated Ethiopia and was imposed upon all the inhabitants. (2) Cushitic groups who have remained comparatively free from the influx of such outside elements, e.g. the Oromo, Beja, and Sidama. These largely inhabit the arid plains surrounding the central mountain area, especially to the north and east. Here are the strongholds of Islam which through the centuries have challenged the Ethiopian Empire. (3) Peoples of Nilotic origin, who are the principal inhabitants of the tropical lowlands in the western and southern parts of Ethiopia. These people constitute the scattered groups who have entered Ethiopia from the upper reaches of the Nile Valley in the Sudan and other neighboring countries, their cultures based upon African traditional religions.[120]

Over this empire reigned one of the most colorful emperors of the twentieth century, Haile Selassie I. Appointed as regent in 1916, he was crowned emperor in 1930. He soon gained an international reputation by shouldering the monumental task of combining the ancient Ethiopian tradition of the divine right of kings with the modernization of his poor and inaccessible kingdom. To assist him in the gigantic task of reforming the educational, medical and cultural life of his people, the emperor enlisted the aid of scores of foreign experts, including missionaries.

AMERICAN PRESBYTERIAN BEGINNINGS

Christian witness from the Western world came to Ethiopia with the first Catholic missionaries who arrived in the 16th century. The first Protestant missionary, Ludwig Krapf of the Church Missionary Society (British) was sent to Ethiopia in 1837 but was able to serve only briefly.[121] Swedish Lutherans came in 1866, to be followed in later years by Lutherans from Germany, Norway and the United States, providing a strong Lutheran base to the Protestant community. Presbyterian work was initiated in 1918, and herein begins a fascinating story which gives evidence of God "working His purpose out" beyond anything that those participating in it could ask or think.

Toward the end of 1918, a terrible flu epidemic hit western Ethiopia, causing an overwhelming number of deaths. An Ethiopian chieftain, who was also serving as provincial governor of the Sayo region, appealed to the British District Commissioner at Gambeila for help. The Commissioner in turn relayed the message to Dr. Tom Lambie, UPNA medical missionary serving at Nasir, about 200 miles down the Sobat River. Lambie was thrilled at the prospect, since up to that time the Ethiopian government had given very little encouragement to the establishment of new mission stations. Lambie cabled the Board for permission to go. Making a quick trip across the border, Lambie began medical treatments in the flu area. His work so delighted the governor that he asked Lambie to set up a permanent station and gave him a tract of land near Sayo. Soon a clinic was begun among the Oromo people near the village of **Dembi Dollo.**

After two years, with the permission of the Board, Lambie was joined by Mr. and Mrs. Fred Russell and Ruth Beatty, R.N. As Mr. Russell supervised the construction of a two-story stone house which would be used for the clinic, the other missionaries preached to day laborers, clinic patients and those who brought them. Soon a church and a school were constructed nearby and the first Presbyterian mission station in Ethiopia was established.

In 1922, when the time came for the Lambies to leave on furlough, instead of going back by way of the Sudan, they crossed Ethiopia. Stopping off at Gorei for a week, the Lambies were urged by the governor there to set up a medical station; Lambie purchased a house and a piece of land for future use. Going on to Addis Ababa, the Lambies were courteously received by the Regent, Haile Selassie, who had heard of the successful work of the Dembi Dollo Clinic. The Regent invited the Presbyterian Mission to erect a hospital in the capital city, Addis Ababa, giving them a twelve-acre tract of land outside the city. Arriving in the States, the Lambies were on fire for the establishment of a new mission in Ethiopia. While the Foreign Mission Board was sympathetic, additional funds and missionary personnel were not available at the time. Undaunted, Lambie went directly to the Church with his appeal. A generous layman, Mr. W.S. George of East Palestine, Ohio, donated the large sum needed to build the hospital in Addis Ababa. Thus came into being the renowned George Memorial Hospital in **Addis Ababa.**[122]

Meanwhile, new missionaries came to swell the ranks of the first pioneers, and in 1923 evangelistic work was begun at **Gorei**, about fifty miles southeast of Sayo. In 1924 all the Mission staff were called to Sayo to organize the Ethiopia Missionary Association. Then in 1933 the Jean R. Orr Memorial Hospital was completed at Sayo. Thus by 1936 the United Presbyterian Mission had established three strong center of work—Dembi Dollo (at Sayo), Gorei, and Addis Ababa. In Addis Ababa, in addition to the hospital, there was the Gulelei Church and the Annie Campbell George Girls School. Dembi Dollo in the Sayo area had become the center of the evangelistic work in the region, along with the hospital and an elementary school. And in nearby Gorei a medical clinic and another school were underway, accompanying the evangelistic witness. While the growth of this Christian community was slow, small groups of believers had sprung up here and there, giving hope of a future spiritual harvest.

The Mission was fortunate in having excellent relations with other Protestant missions working in the country, especially the Swedish Lutheran Mission. Before housing was available in Addis Ababa, the Swedish missionaries housed and fed the Americans until they could procure shelter elsewhere. Most prized of all, the Swedish Mission made available to the Americans the Galla translation of the Bible which had been done by one of their Oromo converts. Thus the missionaries at Dembi Dollo and Gorei could undertake their work with the Scriptures in the native language of the Oromo people.

CHAPTER III

THE CLOSING OF THE COLONIAL ERA: STRENGTHENING THE CHURCH (1940-1957)

The very shape of Africa, said Ghanaian Christian leader James E.K. Aggrey, is that of a question mark and indicates the veil of uncertainty that overhangs its future.[123] Certainly the Africa which entered the 1940s was a continent whose future was filled with uncertainty.

It was upon this colonial-controlled Africa that World War II burst with a vengeance. Africa was much more deeply affected by the Second World War than by the First. Some of the major battles of the war between the Allied and Axis powers were fought on African soil. But far more profoundly, from the outbreak of the war almost all African territories were involved because, with the exception of Spain and Portugal, all the European colonial powers in Africa were at war. The French, Belgian and British territories, together with the Dominion of South Africa, took up arms on the side of the Allies, while the Italian territories, including recently invaded Ethiopia, were brought in on the Axis side. Germany had been stripped of its colonies in Africa after World War I, but with the collapse of France to the Germans in June 1940 and the setting up of a German-dominated French state based at Vichy, North Africa and French West Africa fell under Vichy control. However, French Equatorial Africa aligned itself with Free France under General DeGaulle, and for all intents and purposes became the landbase from which Free France operated. In Sub-Saharan Africa the major theatre of war was Italian East Africa, where British and African troops dislodged the Italians in 1941.

But the war brought profound change in other ways. Most African airports became vital to the Allies as a staging route for air offensives. African seaports became increasingly important as the difficulty of getting supply convoys through the Mediterranean increased. As the war continued and Japan gained control of British Malaya and the Dutch East Indies, the Allies depended more and more on their African colonies for the supply of raw materials needed for war—rubber, tin, palm products.

What would be of most lasting effect, Africa supplied soldiers who fought not only in the East and North African campaigns, but also made significant contributions in campaigns in Asia. Thus they were made aware of the world beyond their traditional tribal cultures, the world both within and beyond Africa. The remark of an able African from Nyasaland (later Malawi), a Christian leader in the armed forces, was significant of a growing sense of racial solidarity: "Men of many tribes have lived and worked together happily—Bemba, Tumbuka, Angoni, Kikuyu, Achewa, and others. In the future we must still help one another."[124]

The war forced a radical change in the attitude of the European colonial powers toward their colonies, due to pressure of liberal opinion in their own countries and from their wartime allies, America and Russia. Even more they were strongly influenced by the growing demands of the educated African elite for greater participation in their own governments. The British and the French especially made promises of political liberalization in their colonies, and pledged a devolution of power to Africans along with rapid economic and social development. As African historian J.F.A. Ajayi put it, "In effect, the Second World War marked a watershed in African colonial history; it was a prelude to the post-war political awakening, the emergence of organized parties agitating for African political emancipation which culminated in the achievement of independence in the greater part of Africa during the next three decades."[125]

The Second World War made it plain to Africans, as to colonized peoples throughout the Afro-Asian block, that their colonial masters were not really capable of defending their colonies and subjecting people to their dominance indefinitely. The Christian Gospel itself had planted the seeds of this spirit of liberation, in declaring that every person is equally precious in the sight of God and that these subjected peoples were bound together beyond their tribes and countries in their struggle for independence.

It is against this background that we consider the story of the Christian movement in Sub-Saharan Africa during the period from the beginning of World War II (1940) to the surge toward independence (1957), and our American Presbyterian participation in it. The missionary movement which had begun in the nineteenth century out of Europe and America had borne amazing fruit by the 1940s. Statistics can be only rough estimates at best,[126] but according to those which are available, the progress between 1925 and 1938 was nothing short of phenomenal: Protestant communicants increased from 996,000 to 2,131,000; Roman Catholics from 2,294,000 to 4,613,000. The size of the Orthodox and indigenous church communities is more difficult to measure, but in the whole of Africa was probably in the neighborhood of two million. Needless to say, the growth varied from area to area; yet taking the region as a whole, no comparable growth in the Christian community was taking place in any other part of the world.

The impact of the Christian missionary movement up to this point had been profound. In the whole of Africa, Protestant missionary forces grew during the period between 1925 and 1938 from 5,556 to 7,514, while Roman Catholic foreign workers expanded from 7,006 to 10,384. Most formal modern education was being carried out through Christian schools, with approximately 85% of all education (elementary and secondary) in West Africa being done under Protestant and Catholic mission auspices. Protestant elementary school enrollment had grown from 882,000 to 1,452,000 and secondary school enrollment from 14,000 to 17,000.[127] The lives and resources poured into the healing of the myriad diseases and infirmities which plagued the people of Africa had brought into being a network of hundreds of hospitals and thousands of clinics and dispensaries.

Here then was the strange paradox: the white civilizations of the West were extending two hands into this continent so rich in natural and human potential, one hand to exploit in the name of empire, another hand to bless in the name of Christ. The story of this period is largely one of the interplay of these forces, and of the growing determination of African leadership, largely Christian, to achieve political independence.

A. WEST AFRICA

IMPACT OF THE SECOND WORLD WAR IN FRENCH CAMEROUN (1940-1945)

The onset of the Second World War had immediate repercussions on Christian mission work in the French Cameroun. With the collapse of France to the Germans in June 1940 and the setting up of a German-dominated French state at Vichy, the strong work of the Paris Missionary Society in Cameroun as well as French Equatorial Africa was severed from its base. The International Missionary Council, based in New York at this point, set up an "orphaned missions" fund to provide help for those European missionaries cut off from their home bases. The fund assisted the French missionaries in Cameroun, and American Presbyterians provided additional assistance.

But the war struck close to home for American missionaries as well. With the setting up of the Free French regime of General De Gaulle in French Equatorial Africa and Cameroun with its capital at Yaounde, the government in exile asked for the use of mission property as quarters for soldiers and bases for military equipment. Willy nilly, American missionaries found themselves involved in the war effort. While relations with the colonial government improved for American Protestant missionaries, this relationship would in time prove to be a bone of contention in relationships with the national church, as well as the Camerounian people.

The PCUSA West Africa Mission "felt the effects of war in almost every phase of its work."[128] The danger of the Atlantic crossing led to drastic reduction in the number of new missionaries arriving as reenforcements. Needed supplies became more and more expensive and difficult to secure.[129] Also, the cutback in funds from America meant that necessary repairs and improvements in mission buildings had to be postponed, leading to considerable deterioration. The result was a very evident increase in "the strain and tension under which the remaining missionaries have been laboring as . . . they overstayed their regular furloughs and tried to assume responsibilities of those who were absent."[130] The sixty missionaries who remained on the field (down from over one hundred at the outbreak of the war) found themselves stretched to the limit, "from Batanga on the coast, far into the jungle fastnesses of Momjepom on the eastern border of Cameroun,"[131] serving a territory which in the last ten years had increased one-third in size, with a third greater church constituency.

Most important was the effect of the war upon the Camerounian people themselves. After DeGaulle began to organize the Free French fighting forces, "Africans by the thousands enlisted and went off to war to fight *pour la gloire de la France.* But somewhere in the heart of battle the illusion exploded. "What am I doing here?," many African soldiers began to ask themselves. "This is a white man's war. I should go home and fight for the independence of my own country."[132] Further, there was a growing distrust in the ability of the French to control their colonies. "Once considered by many of the Africans to be invincible and permanent, they now appear defeated, lacking in power, and totally undependable."[133]

Although the work of the schools and hospitals of the American Presbyterian mission in Cameroun was badly crippled, the work of the churches proceeded full speed ahead with increasing leadership being taken by Camerounian Christians. Of immeasurable worth to the growing church was the publication of the first complete edition of the Bible in the Bulu language.[134]

"For years, the Bulu churches had been nourished on the New Testament message, and for several years all the Christians looked forward eagerly to the arrival of the entire Bible. Finally, word was received from the American Bible Society in New York that the first shipment of two thousand Bulu Bibles was on the seas . . . . But Hitler's U-boats did not discriminate between Bibles and bombs. The two thousand Bulu Bibles . . . . went to the bottom . . . . I wondered truly if we would ever come out of this African night."[135]

Fortunately, another shipment of 300 Bulu Bibles arrived shortly thereafter. While only a minuscule supply for over 100,000 Christians, "the joy on the faces of those who receive them is a sight worth seeing . . . . As one passed along the street . . . , a word was constantly being heard,—the word *Kalate*, the Book. It was on everyone's tongue and here and there under the eaves of a house could be seen a group gathered about something, and one knew that there was a Bible in the hands of some fortunate one."[136]

With reduced resources from abroad, the stewardship of the Camerounian Christians rose to the challenge. Beyond the congregations themselves, missionary societies were formed. "Missionary interest has been greatly quickened, and in almost all instances the offerings of the missionary societies this year exceeded that of last year, which had also been a banner year . . . . One pastor writes, 'when we see our Christians sacrificing new clothes and other much desired articles of civilization that they may pay their church pledges and even give extra to make up the deficit, we are impressed by the loyalty to Christ and his cause."[137]

Much of the parish work was now carried out by the approximately sixty ordained ministers and licentiates of the Synod, and evangelists were reaching out into the many village preaching places. "A full-time African evangelist has been working . . . among the pygmies of the region around MacLean Memorial Station. White missionaries could not reach these little people, for their lives are nomadic, and their fear of outsiders deep, so that they simply disappear into the depths of the jungle when strangers attempt to make any enduring contacts with them. The African evangelist has gone along with them, learning their language and their customs. As a result of his efforts, twenty-nine of them . . . have confessed Christ."[138]

Under the pressure of the growing nationalist spirit, the Camerounian pastors grew increasingly dissatisfied with the relationship of Church and Mission. In December 1940, a long letter from a number of pastors was delivered formally into the hands of the Executive Secretary of the Mission, registering fifteen complaints against the control exercised by missionary pastors over the life of the church. The initiative taken by the pastors brought many issues to a head. The Mission set to work preparing a "supplementary constitution" to be added to the constitution which the Church in Cameroun had received from the Presbyterian Church in the U.S.A. Approved by the Mission in December 1942 and by the National Church Synod in January 1943, the "supplementary constitution" spelled out in detail a new relationship between missionaries and national church leaders, "virtually giving complete control of finances and church government into the hands of the national Christians." Ordained missionaries still remained members of Presbytery but completely on a par with their national colleagues. Thus it could be reported, "the church is now completely autonomous, although retaining its relationship to the [Presbyterian U.S.A.] General Assembly."[139]

In December 1945, a Mission-Synod Committee was formed "to discuss all questions of policy and administration overlapping in the present Mission-Synod plan which may be referred to it by Synod or Mission." While many areas of practical difficulty remained, there was a marked improvement in the strained relationship of Church and Mission.[140]

Meanwhile, the pressure of wartime conditions led the various Protestant missions to recognize the importance of strengthening their cooperation. In 1940 the Federation of Protestant Missions in Cameroun was formed, with four missions as charter members. Then in January 1941, at a meeting held at the Presbyterian station in Elat, the organization was expanded to include two new societies working in Rio Muni and French Equatorial Africa, and given the new name: The Federation of Evangelical Missions in Cameroun and Equatorial Africa.

The importance of the Federation for future Protestant work in Cameroun can scarcely be exaggerated. With regard to mission-government relations, it gave the Protestant community visibility and influence in this predominantly Roman Catholic country. Also, it created a sense of unity among Evangelical missions and in time among churches which were the fruit of their work. As its constitution declared, "This Federation has as its aim to work for the propagation and defense of Evangelical Christianity in facilitating the task of each of the missionary societies which are members thereof, and in developing amongst them the greatest and most brotherly collaboration possible."[141] Inter-communion was a determined policy of the Federation from the beginning. Further, the Federation would pave the way for significant cooperation in the many educational efforts of the various missions, and eventually to the establishment of a united Christian college, the *Institut des Missions Evangeliques* at Libamba.

While the object of the Federation was to develop the greatest possible cooperation among the member missions, its fundamental weakness was that no national church representatives took part in its deliberations or decisions. While this might be excused because of temporary wartime conditions, it also was evidence of the lack of autonomy in those churches founded by the cooperating missions. It was not until 1950 that this omission would be rectified, when representatives from the African churches would be invited to participate in drawing up a new constitution for the formation of the Protestant Council of Cameroun and Equatorial Africa.

POSTWAR POLITICAL CHANGES (1945-1957)

It is impossible to understand the postwar changes in the Christian movement in Cameroun without considering the political developments which were taking place. As the cause of Free France advanced in Africa, Cameroun took on increasing importance as the locale where General DeGaulle held talks with African leaders. The new political spirit found expression at the Brazzaville Conference of 1944, convoked by the Free French and gathering representatives from the various French African territories. Great promises were made by the former and great hopes raised for the latter: the territories would have a voice in the construction of a new constitution for the French Republic, and be represented in its assembly; there would be some type of colonial parliament representing the interest of the various colonies; local assemblies in each colony would have wide powers of decision in economic matters; all forms of forced labor would be abolished, and trade union activity would be legalized.

With the end of the war in 1945, the French government adopted a new constitution for its Fourth Republic in 1946, which retreated somewhat from the Brazzaville promises but for the first time gave Africans in the French territories a share in formulating political policies. The high hopes of eventual independence were further raised as the newly-formed United Nations in 1946 assigned to France and Great Britain the trusteeship for the eastern and western territories of the Cameroons.

The genie was out of the bottle, and a period of intense organized political activity would now begin in Cameroun. The end of the war signaled the resumption of political struggle in France, which would be reflected in the political struggles in Cameroun as well. Two groups had emerged in France untainted by Vichy collaboration: the Communists and the Catholic left. These two would struggle for dominance in the new Africa. In Africa itself, there emerged the *Rassemblement Democratique Africain (RDA)* seeking greater political rights for French-speaking Africans. The Camerounian branch of this inter-territorial party, the *Union des Populations de Cameroun (UPC)* was formed in 1948, led by two former students of Presbyterian schools, Charles Assale (Bulu) and Ruben um Nyobe (Bassa).[142] Both had been active in the emerging labor movement which was strongly influenced by the French Communist party. The UPC, which soon became "by all odds the best organized political party in the Cameroun," announced a two-point program: the unification of the two Cameroons and rapid progress toward complete independence under the terms of the United Nations Charter.

On the opposite end of the spectrum were such leaders as Dr. Louis Aujoulat, a physician and Catholic lay missionary, founder of the *Bloc Democratique Camerounais (BDC)*, which took a more moderate position seeking legislative and administrative reform while remaining within the French Union. Between these two poles there emerged parties of every description, coalescing and re-forming around various political leaders.

As the political climate became more and more intense as well as confused, the UPC engaged in more aggressive propaganda campaigns coupled with local incidents of violence until it took on the appearance of a communist-inspired movement. Attacking the missions as "disguised colonialists," UPC followers systematically terrorized and destroyed numerous mission stations.

On Easter Sunday, 1955, the Catholic bishops in the Cameroun circulated a pastoral letter that warned the faithful against Communism and its influence within the UPC.[143] The letter, read from Catholic pulpits throughout the territory, provoked an almost immediate response from the UPC, triggering a series of strikes, demonstrations and riots in every major city of Cameroun that resulted in much loss of life and destruction of property. The country became virtually paralyzed, as bridges crossing the innumerable small streams on the motor roads leading from the capital Yaounde to the South and West were burned or torn down, effectively blocking all traffic.

The response of the French colonial government was almost immediate: a decree was issued dissolving and outlawing the UPC. The government brought in highly trained guerrilla fighters from Senegal and other parts of French colonial Africa to patrol the streets in virtually every city and town, and to make "sweeps" through the forest with orders to "seek and kill" the terrorists.[144] Some of the UPC leaders crossed the border into British Cameroons to continue plotting their strategy; others went underground to engage in a guerrilla struggle that would last until 1970.

In the meantime, in France the government recognized that time was running out. A series of constitutional reforms was being drafted in Paris, and in July 1956 a Statute of the Camerouns was issued giving the Cameroun a wide measure of autonomy under a new Assembly. As a result of elections conducted in December 1956, the new Assembly was formed in January 1957, and in May chose as the first Prime Minister Andre-Marie Mbida, a former Catholic seminarian. While the UPC had been driven from official political activity, its agenda had become the common ground for the new Assembly: the unification and independence of the Cameroun.[145]

POSTWAR WORK OF AMERICAN PRESBYTERIANS (1945-1957)

It is within this context of intense political ferment that the postwar work of American Presbyterians, as well as other mission agencies in Cameroun, must be seen. At the close of the war, the Presbyterian Church, U.S.A. initiated a Restoration Fund to help with the much needed rehabilitation of church and mission properties in mission areas which had been partially or totally destroyed by the war. This proved to be of tremendous help to the work in Cameroun, especially to mission schools and hospitals.

However, the resources available for ongoing activities were not commensurate with the expanding program and rapidly rising postwar inflation. A major bone of contention was the low wages paid to African workers in church, school and medical work. "Most Africans who were ardent believers in the faith quietly received the low pay, and were critical of their colleagues who quit their jobs to cultivate cocoa farms or engaged in other businesses for higher wages." But as nationalist awareness combined with strong anti-colonialist sentiment and opposition against exploitation of African labor, the issue became increasingly explosive. With the organization of labor unions in the mid-forties,[146] the demand for higher wages and better conditions of service increased tremendously. Although the finance committee of the Mission considered the workers' grievances legitimate, no immediate action was taken to redress them. "The African staff was instead blamed and accused of greediness and materialism."[147] The relationship between the Mission and its workers took a turn for the worse in the fifties, when dissatisfied workers sought redress at the Labour Court to reclaim what they called "back pay." Such conditions intensified the demand for an independent church in Cameroun.

Another area of controversy was the failure of the PCUSA Board to appoint black American missionaries to serve in Cameroun. It was not until 1928 that the first black American couple, the Rev. and Mrs. Irvin Underhill, was appointed to serve in Cameroun. While their appointment was received with great joy by the black constituency of the PCUSA, "the Underhills were treated with indifference by the white missionaries." In the 1940s, as the nationalistic sentiments of Africans was causing the French colonial government increasing anxiety, the Underhills became the scapegoats. "The attitude of the government hardened against the presence of Rev. Underhill in the territory and his influence on the Africans. It would appear that the Mission and the Board negotiated for the withdrawal of Rev. [and Mrs.] Underhill based on the accusations of the colonial government that he had an undue influence over the Africans. Without giving Rev. Underhill a hearing the executive committee of the Mission approved his withdrawal."[148] No other black American missionaries were appointed during the remainder of the French colonial era.

A focal point for much of the church-mission tension was the **Dager Biblical Seminary.** Established in 1922 and named in honor of William M. Dager whose pioneer work in theological education had laid the foundation for the school, the seminary struggled with very inadequate facilities until 1939 when classrooms, library, chapel and dormitory facilities were built. Yet the staff for the seminary remained woefully inadequate, usually with only one missionary and one African pastor assigned to the task. In 1943, a dispute arose out of a personality conflict between an African staff member of the catechists class and a relief missionary staff member of the theological class.[149] The dispute intensified and became interwoven with other issues until both men were removed, and the seminary was temporarily closed "because no leadership was available to assume the administration of the institution."[150]

In 1945, a deputation of the Board visited Cameroun, and after studying the ill-feeling at the Seminary, declared: "A great deal of the trouble would have been avoided if there had been an adequate staff at the Seminary, and it has been recommended to the Mission and Synod that there be at least two missionaries giving full time to the work of the Seminary in association with two national pastors. This cradle of National Church leadership was found to be in a sadly inadequate state both in equipment and in student body."[151]

Within the next few years, the curriculum was overhauled[152] and adequate staff assigned to serve in this important work of strengthening African church leadership. In 1948, two Camerounian ministers, the Rev. Francois Akoa Abomo and the Rev. Joseph Tjega, both of whom had studied at Princeton Theological Seminary for one year, were appointed to the staff of Dager Seminary and began the succession of competent African professors on this faculty. By 1956, it could be reported, "Practically every tribe of importance is represented in the student body of Dager Biblical Seminary . . . . By training these ministers, lay evangelists, and their wives to be the leaders in an indigenous, self-supporting and self-propagating African Church, the Seminary is effectively serving the Christian Church in the Cameroun."[153]

Tensions would arise also in the **general educational work** initiated by the American Presbyterian Mission. To begin with, the Mission had developed through the years a well-integrated system of lower schools, with a policy of teaching in the Bulu and Bassa languages. However, the French government decided to restrict the use of these languages to the first two or three grades, requiring the use of French from that point, thus reducing the proficiency of students in the reading of their own language and the use of Bibles and other Christian materials published in the vernacular. Further, the marked increase in the cost of living in postwar Cameroun made it difficult for the Mission to keep pace with salaries in comparable government and commercial occupations, so that "mission educational institutions are having trouble retaining the better educated teachers and instructors who are offered so much more by other concerns."[154]

More serious still was the growing disparity in resources available for Protestant mission schools in comparison to those being invested by the Roman Catholic Church. Limited and deteriorating accommodations, lack of educational missionaries, and the paucity of trained national teachers led most Protestant schools to sense they were falling further and further behind. "Everybody wants to go to school. The French government is responding by rapidly enlarging its educational program. The Roman Catholic Church is bringing trained educators in large numbers into the Colony. Our Mission, which has played such an important part in the education of the people in this part of Africa, has fallen from first to third place in this important branch of its service."[155]

Topping it off was the growing fear of the advance of the ideology of Communism both without and within the school system. "While the missionary stays at the station repairing, building, teaching, all about him the young men and women are reading a half dozen or more periodicals, originating in Bucharest and printed in France, calling on all Africa to rise up and overthrow capitalism and accept the only hope of the world—Communism."[156] Newspapers edited by Africans highlighted interracial disturbances in the United States and South Africa, creating still further anti-colonial and anti-Western sentiment. Union organizers, spurred on by the nationalist movement, sought to organize the teachers and "militantly attack Mission and Church as enemies of progress." In 1956, a group of teachers in American Presbyterian schools formed an organization of their own, outside the national labor union, "still loyal to the Church but indicating their desire to be free from ecclesiastical control. The unsettling atmosphere created by much of this activity has impaired the effectiveness of classroom work."[157]

Despite these ominous trends, there was a significant advance in the American Presbyterian involvement in education during these years. Outstanding among them was the establishment of the *Institut des Missions Evangeliques* (IME, better known in the United States as **Cameroun Christian College**[158]). The American Presbyterian Mission and the Paris Missionary Society took a major role in this cooperative project of numerous missions, to address the critical need for higher education of promising young men and women from across French Equatorial Africa. Though plans had been initiated as early as 1942 and the first classes were held at Ilanga in 1944, the problem of a suitable location still remained. "It would have to be some central place easily accessible to all the tribes of South Cameroun where our Mission had established schools as well as for the students who might be recruited from other French speaking areas of West Africa."[159] An ideal location at **Libamba** was offered by the people of the Bassa tribe, about 2000 acres on the Nyong River and bordering the Douala-Yaounde railroad, about 150 miles from the coast and fifty miles from the Capital, near the junction of three major tribal regions.

It was not until August 1946 that the first building at Libamba could be dedicated. "A most gratifying and enjoyable occasion was celebrated on Wednesday, the 21st of August, 1946, when a small party of missionaries from Yaounde station journeyed to Libamba, the site of the *Institut des Missions Evangeliques* (Cameroun Christian College), upon the invitation of S.P. Njock Bot, the very efficient African teacher who was chosen to begin this work . . . . On the day noted above he was able to move his class of 40 pupils to the buildings, constructed on the college site. With banners flying and happy songs ringing in the air, two large schools from the adjacent towns of Minka and Makak converged upon the college site at Libamba while hundreds of the local citizenry joined in the march and accompanied the crowd along the path deep into the forest where the gala opening of the school was celebrated."[160]

The college's first buildings were of a temporary nature, thatch and clay, plus a war-surplus psychiatric portable hospital converted into residences for missionary teachers. Further developments faltered until 1951, when the Opportunity Gifts of the women of the PCUSA enabled an extensive building campaign to get underway. By 1957, it could be boasted that Cameroun Christian College (now known in French as *College Evangelique de Libamba*) was the only Protestant Christian college in French Equatorial Africa, with an international faculty of African, Swiss, French, German, Italian and American professors, and with a student body drawn from at least 27 different tribes of Cameroun and French Equatorial Africa. In due time graduates of "Libamba", as it was popularly called, would be providing leadership for all aspects of Cameroun's life—provincial governors, business leaders, doctors, lawyers, educators and pastors.[161]

The other aspects of the educational program of the American Presbyterian Mission continued with little change, except for the constant struggle to maintain both staff and facilities. The **Ecole Camille Chazeaud** (also known as the French Normal School) at Foulassi struggled to provide teachers for the expanding number of primary and secondary schools, which by 1957 enrolled over 25,000 pupils.[162] The Frank James Industrial School of Elat, a four-year technical training school, helped to prepare young men for the skills needed in the increasingly modernized society of Cameroun.[163] The Agricultural and Rural Training School at Metet endeavored to enable young men to improve rural life with basic modern agricultural techniques; however, in 1954 it was found necessary to close this school and move this work to the college site of Libamba.

Even more than the educational work, the Mission's **medical work** felt the impact of the tumult of the times. Perhaps the work most severely curtailed during the war, the Mission's medical program had but one lone missionary doctor left on the field at the war's end. This placed a heavy burden upon the corps of African medical assistants who were expected to perform medical procedures far beyond the level of their formal training. True, these medical assistants had received training and internship at the Central Hospital in Elat, followed by residency at one of the hospitals in the field—Efulan, Metet, Foulassi, Sakbayeme, Bafia, Nkol Mvolan and Yaounde.[164] Later they might serve at one of the many dispensaries, leper settlements or orphanages established to supplement the work done at the hospitals. Yet the colonial government refused to recognize this training, and the status and compensation for medical assistants was hardly commensurate with the responsibility which they carried.

As the labor movement gained momentum, a number of the medical assistants joined the labor unions or "syndicates." The Mission sought to ease the unrest by raising salaries to provide a living wage. Yet the activities of the syndicates continued to be a disturbing factor, frequently interrupting the work at the nine hospitals. It was the hospital at Sakbayeme which suffered the most serious disruptions. In June 1954, the Mission found it necessary to close this, the mission's second largest hospital as the syndicate called a general strike for better wages and living conditions, also demanding "that the employees of the hospital be free from any disciplinary control of either Mission or Church." After two months of negotiations, the hospital was reopened "with each employee signing a declaration and contract that he was entering the work of the hospital as a Christian service in a joint effort to alleviate suffering and to win men and women to Jesus Christ."[165] Far from hindering the work of the hospital, "public reaction to that disturbance was so strong and the union's efforts to destroy the Christian control of the hospital raised such a storm of protest that the ministry of the hospital has become more effective than ever. Never before have the hospitals been as crowded as they were this year."[166]

Despite these constant hindrances, the medical work continued to expand. In 1950 the Central Hospital at Elat added to its program the Weber Dental Clinic, a program unique for West Africa, through which skilled dentists were trained for service in towns and villages throughout the region. A new program was initiated in the leper colonies, in cooperation with the American Leprosy Mission. A major leprosy work was initiated at Ndjazeng, a remote village 45 miles south of Elat, not far from the Spanish Guinea border. Through new methods of treatment the dread disease was being arrested, and eventually some afflicted with it were able to return to their own villages.[167] To help in rehabilitating the victims of leprosy, in 1957 an artificial limb clinic was added at Central Hospital, another first in West Africa.[168]

By 1954, the nine hospitals and eight dispensaries of the American Presbyterian Mission were staffed by 10 missionary doctors, 10 missionary nurses, and 155 medical assistants, with 1,092 hospital beds, serving some 71,513 patients.[169] While the medical work expanded to meet the enormous needs of the people, the Mission found it very difficult to train Camerounian doctors or senior administrative staff to assume positions of leadership. To begin with, the French colonial government strictly controlled the training of African professional and supervisory personnel, reserving the few who were trained for positions in government medical facilities. Further, the French educational system required seven years for medical training, beyond the college degree. Now time had caught up with the Mission. Though a plan to train and educate Africans as physicians and surgeons was developed in 1954, by 1957 there was not a single African Presbyterian medical doctor with a recognized degree.[170]

GROWTH OF THE CAMEROUNIAN CHURCH (1946-1957)

In the midst of such political unrest and anti-Western sentiment, it is truly a wonder that the church continued to grow. Significant increases in missionary personnel enabled the Mission to expand its evangelistic field in 1948 to include two additional stations: at **Ibong** north of Sakbayeme among the Bassa people, and at **Batouri** in the jungle of central Cameroun close to the eastern border.[171] Such expansion stretched Mission resources to the limit. Yet the well-developed churches in the older fields came to the rescue. "It became apparent that some of the advance into the untouched areas would have to be arrested for lack of funds. With true spiritual insight it was decided that the best way to meet the emergency was to call upon every church member of the community to rededicate his life in service and in gifts. An ambitious program was drawn up by the national Church . . . , in cooperation with members of the Mission, which aimed at reaching every tribe, every village and every individual with the message of a Christian's duty as a steward of God's gifts . . . . The response has been most gratifying."[172]

An area of work of particular significance was **women's work.** A Women's Missionary Society had been formed in 1922 among the Bulu people of Corisco Presbytery as a result of the work of women missionaries. A weekly women's gathering at Efulan for prayer and Bible study had ignited a missionary zeal to preach the Gospel and to help the sick. Suddenly similar groups mushroomed in other villages, and within a few years the women's prayer groups were building chapels, paying the wages of evangelists and then pastors, and organizing women's societies in every congregation. By 1944 the Women's

Society had become such a strong element within the life of the church that one of its founders, Martha Nyangon, was named treasurer of Corisco Presbytery. About the same year, the women's work among the Bassa people was begun in Sanaga Presbytery under the leadership of missionary Martha Peirce and Bassa leader Marie Gwate.

In 1946, women missionaries aided the African women in forming a well-planned adaptation of the Presbyterian women's societies in America. In 1947 a Council of Women's Work was established and thus became an integral part of the life of the church. During these years, it was the women's organizations which united in campaigns against polygamy, child marriage, bride price, prostitution, and alcoholism. In many ways the women's work "was decidedly the most active part of the Cameroun Church", linking it with the larger Christian world through its partnership with the women's work of the Presbyterian Church in the U.S.A.[173]

The **work among youth** was equally significant during this period. French colonial policy was encouraging the development of an elite class (known as *evolues*) among Camerounian young adults, who through their educational development would be partially Europeanized and therefore no longer bound to traditional village society. The separation of these youth from the land and from village life led to a secular attitude which the Camerounian Church found it difficult to deal with. Some of the *evolues* became bitter against the church, accusing the pastors of exploiting their people on behalf of Western imperialism.

Fortunately, however, there were those in the churches and missions who saw this as a critical evangelistic opportunity. A young Presbyterian missionary, appointed by the Federation of Missions as director of youth work, initiated Youth Conferences across the churches. He was joined by a young Camerounian graduate of Dager Seminary who had participated in the International Conference of Christian Youth in Norway in the summer of 1947. Together they travelled across the country, sharing a message of a vital worldwide Christian fellowship. Out of their work emerged the organization of a large and active *Jeunnese Evangelique* which enrolled as many as 10,000 young Camerounians. This youth organization became a Christian counterpart to the secular *evolue* movement, and a saving factor for youth in this crucial moment in the Church's development.[174]

Other features of the work of the church were inaugurated during this period: Bible Conferences, Elders' Conferences, Preaching Missions, Audio-Visual Education and Evangelism. Not only did these efforts strengthen the church's witness but they also served to bind together the various tribal groups within which the Christian community had come into being.

Yet tribal tensions persisted and caused serious disruptions. In the Bibia area, Pastor Simon Ngiamba Ngalli of the Ngoumba people (a comparatively small ethnic group among whom the Presbyterians had worked since 1897) strongly objected to the Mission's policy of using the Bulu language exclusively for evangelistic and educational work among the Ngoumba. In 1934 he had led a group of fellow Ngoumba pastors to withdraw from the Presbyterian Church and establish the *Eglise Protestante Africaine* (African Protestant Church). As years passed the tensions cooled and some of the disenchanted members returned to the main Presbyterian body. However, the Corisco Presbytery in 1945 declined to receive the Ngoumba pastors because of their inadequate training for the ministry. The Mission later did review its policy, and vernacular schools were established for Ngoumba children with literature prepared in Ngoumba.[175]

TENSIONS BETWEEN MISSION AND CHURCH

But it was the tension between Mission and Church which was the most troubling issue. Beyond the persistent problem of adequate wages, there was the matter of control of the vast range of work in which the Mission was engaged. The Mission sought to put its position in the best light, stating that "the Church . . . is entirely in the hands and under the direction of the Africans," and that "the Mission has wisely planned a program of intense training for those Africans who could replace the missionary in some of the less essential routines of mission procedure and administration . . . . These trained men and women, however, have not kept pace, numerically speaking, with the rapid expansion of the Church and Mission."[176]

Finally tensions reached a point where in 1951 missionaries and pastors converged at the Dager Seminary for a three-week conference on current problems. "The pastors pleaded with the missionaries to (1) inform the government and the people that the church was an entity in its own right, though not divorced from the mission; (2) set them apart for full time work in the church; (3) petition the Board for more missionaries qualified in diverse fields; (4) do all in their power to increase Christian testimony in the French schools; (5) aid 'bush' churches by giving them loans of money and building equipment; and (6) hold similar institutes for pastors annually."[177]

In 1952 the PCUSA Board of Foreign Missions, responding to this and similar expressions from the "younger churches," completely overhauled its Manual, instituting changes which would have far-reaching effect on the work of the church in Cameroun as well as other areas where PCUSA was involved in mission: (1) Henceforth the term "fraternal worker" would replace the title "missionary."[178] (2) Churches in the various fields were asked to appoint committees and boards to run agencies and institutions. (3) Churches were asked to give field training to missionaries and to supervise their work; to make requests for appointment of new missionaries or for withdrawal of old ones. (4) Finally and most far reaching, plans were to be made for the transferral of official ownership of all property, except that related to the maintenance of the missionary, from the Mission to the Church.[179]

Thus a monumental task was laid upon Church and Mission in Cameroun for the years immediately ahead. A joint planning committee of the Church and the Mission was named in 1953, with the assignment of devolving authority from Mission to Church with the ultimate goal (remarkably similar to that of the nation of Cameroun) of an independent church which would unify the total Presbyterian work within Cameroun. The following year, the Synod of Cameroun was divided into the Cameroun and Bassa Synods, thereby taking an additional step toward the creation of an independent self-governing General

Assembly. In July 1954, Government recognition was granted to the Administrative Council of the Cameroun Presbyterian Church, thus making it a legal holding body which could take over property rights for church buildings amd manses. In the same year, several "mission stations" became officially known as "church stations," with leadership turned over to African staff.

The most difficult part of the task, of course, would be the transfer of responsibility for all educational and medical institutions which up to this point had been under the control of the Mission. Toward this end, certain long-closed doors had to be opened. "For the first time in the history of the Mission, church-appointed African delegates attended all sessions of the annual meeting of the Mission, and sat in on committee meetings."[180] Further, each major institution appointed an African as co-director to assist the missionary in charge. The new idea of church-controlled boards of directors of mission hospitals and schools was initiated, with varying degrees of success. A Church-Mission Educational Committee was appointed to take responsibility for the vast system of primary schools.

As the intensity of political agitation increased after the UPC rebellion in May 1955, the work of missions and churches felt the impact keenly. Most of the Presbyterian stations were located in the areas affected by the riots.[181] The Presbyterian station at Ibong was invaded several times, one building burned and important papers destroyed.[182] Missionaries were under great suspicion of conniving with the aspirations of the nationalists against the colonial administration.[183] Prior to the elections of 1956, signs were printed in red paint on the school and church buildings warning the people against voting. A train was wrecked near the Cameroun Christian College and bridges blown up along the road. Most tragically, Bernard Kopf, a missionary of the Paris Missionary Society, was gunned down at a shopping center at Douala. Several local pastors and evangelists also were terrorized or murdered.

The political turmoil forced both Board and Mission to realize that, in order to prevent chaos, autonomy must be granted to the Camerounian Church as quickly as possible. At the historic Lake Mohonk Conference called by the PCUSA Board of Foreign Missions April 22 to May 1, 1956, the Camerounian representative, Pastor Meye Me Nkpwele, urged that as soon as possible the Board dissolve the Mission as an administrative body and have all the personnel and activities integrated into the church. The conference and the Board concurred, and an international team was despatched to Cameroun to study Mission-Church relationships and make a proposal for the transition. The proposal was forwarded to the meeting of the Mission in August 1956, and with Camerounian church leadership present, plans were made for the "new day" in the history of the Presbyterian Church of Cameroun.[184]

THE MISSION YIELDS TO THE CHURCH

So it was that at the 169th General Assembly of the Presbyterian Church, USA, held in June 1957, approval was granted for the formation of the *Eglise Presbyterienne Camerounaise (EPC)* and the dissolution of the West Africa Mission, with all its work integrated into the life of the Church. A Planning Conference in July brought together representatives of Church and Mission to work out the mechanics of integration and to plan for the meeting of the EPC General Assembly in December.

What happened then can best be described in the words of Mary Hunter, in an article appearing in *The Drum Call*, April 1958:

> The date was December 11, 1957. All roads led to Elat. People in all walks of life came from many parts of the world to witness the occasion. Among them were high French and African civil servants, the American Consul, a minister from Ghana, a minister from Zaire, and from the United States, the Stated Clerk, a member of the Board of Ecumenical Mission, the Portfolio Secretary for Africa and the Near East, and a Secretary of the National Mission's Board for Women's Work, and several church leaders. Over ten thousand people attended the celebrations. The Rev. Francois Akoa Abomo, later elected Stated Clerk, read the history of the Mission . . . . During the election of church officials, the Rev. Simon Mvodo Atyam was elected moderator . . . . The Mission was terminated andi integrated in the Church. The American Presbyterian Mission became the Presbyterian Church of Cameroun.[185]

The EPC General Assembly, as constituted at that historic meeting, was composed of three synods, with 74,908 communicants, 86 ordained ministers, 1,561 evangelists, 184 churches and 1,490 preaching points, reaching a total church community of over 200,000 persons. Its schools served 24,014 students, its hospitals and dispensaries 15,075 patients. Serving this vast missionary outreach were 120 American Presbyterian fraternal workers.[186]

The spirit of this new church at its best was expressed in the following statement prepared by the African ministers at the July 1957 Planning Conference:

> . . . the goal envisioned by the Mission has been reached, that is, the establishment of an independent, autonomous Church. We give thanks to God. But what does one mean in saying that the Mission is no more? Does it mean that those whom we now call missionaries should leave us? Far from it . . . . It is the time when the responsibility and powers pass from the missionary to the people of this land. We still need the missionaries at our side and back of us. They stand back of us to encourage, to help us develop leaders here and abroad, to help us carry the Gospel to the regions beyond, to help us reach out to Christians of other countries, thus to help us assume our legitimate place in the world-wide fellowship of Christian people and to help us to preach the Gospel without any compromise . . . . To this end it may be well to reaffirm the qualities necessary in these fraternal collaborators: they should be the outstanding members of our Church, specialists well qualified and well equipped, colleagues with a progressive spirit and able to identify themselves with our life.[187]

THE CHURCH TAKES SHAPE IN SPANISH GUINEA (1940-1957)

The bloody civil war which gripped Spain from 1936 through 1939 left little time for that country to be concerned about its tiny colony, Spanish Guinea. Though the military rebellion led by General Francisco Franco finally resulted in the defeat of the Republican forces, Spain lay ravaged and desolate, having suffered over a million casualties. While remaining officially neutral during World War II, Spain sent some 40,000 "volunteer" troops to fight beside German and Italian forces on the Russian front. The turmoil within Spain left the Protestant witness in Spanish Guinea unhindered for the period from 1940 until 1952.

By 1947 the American Presbyterian work in Rio Muni had grown strong enough to justify the organization of a presbytery.

> This was a very happy occasion for the people of that country, especially for those tribes living along the coast. They came in considerable numbers from the coast churches to the town of Bolondo where all the meetings were held. From far away Corisco Island two canoe loads of Christians came with quantities of food to join the gala crowd, rejoicing greatly to be able once again to gather with God's people to celebrate this historic occasion. From all nine of the churches from Spanish Guinea, representatives journeyed to Bolondo and there was quite a debate as to the most appropriate name for the new Presbytery. Finally sentiment prevailed and the much-loved name of Corisco was retained, though coupled with the official name of the colony, which results in the name CORISCO-RIO MUNI.[188]

One important phase of the church's development in Spanish Guinea was the vitality of the **women's organizations.** "For enthusiasm the women's group far outshines any other activities in Spanish Guinea. This is the first group in our West Africa Mission to reach the status of a Presbyterial." Leaders of the Presbyterial traveled extensively visiting women in the remote churches, "entering into almost every house, preaching and witnessing to the power of the Gospel in their lives." The officers and leaders of all the women's societies within the borders of Corisco-Rio Muni Presbytery met for a week of prayer, fellowship and leadership training, receiving an offering of nearly $600. "They requested that this money be paid out through the church sessions to evangelists serving in newly established outposts. As a result, five new centers have been opened in addition to the two outposts pioneered by the women last year."[189]

One of the women in particular, Senora Rebecca Oko, became an outstanding leader among the women not only in Spanish Guinea but also in Cameroun. Chosen to represent the women of the churches in Cameroun and Spanish Guinea at the Presbyterian Quadrennial Women's Conference in the United States, "not only did she captivate the hearts of many in America, but she has returned unspoiled, humble and terribly in earnest, to her own home church. She knows full well the deadness of the older churches of this country, for she comes from one of the oldest. Probably the success of the women's movement in this Church is the reaction to the routine deadness of many of its congregations."[190]

The women also took leadership in the literacy campaign which had been initiated by the Mission. "Under the tutelage of presbyterial secretary-treasurer Enriqueta Makongo, scores of women have graduated from the company of Rio Muni's illiterates into the fellowship of those who can read the Laubach primer. The women of the interior marvel at this consecrated beach woman, the friend and companion of the old Benito missionaries, volunteering to travel 150 miles inland to teach her bush sisters."[191]

But the window of opportunity for Protestant witness in Spanish Guinea was short-lived. As General Francisco Franco tightened his control in Spain, the restrictions on religious liberty in the mother country carried over to its colonies. The tremendous strides which the Protestant community had been making, especially in the interior villages, came to a sudden halt in 1952. "A change in personnel in government circles seems to have been the occasion for invoking a law of 1938 by which all chapels, in order to operate, must have written authorization by the Government . . . . So over twenty chapels opened by the Protestant Church and built by the villagers were ordered closed."[192]

As the government tightened restrictions, all Presbyterian chapels in newly evangelized areas, some 38 of them, were officially closed, leaving open only those established before 1939.[193] The government refused to issue passports to any new missionaries, thus leaving the Rev. and Mrs. Joseph McNeil again as the only resident Protestant missionaries in Rio Muni. Fortunately one outstanding national Christian leader had been ordained in 1952, the Rev. Gustavo Envela. A national of the coastal Kombe tribe, he was the first native of Rio Muni to be ordained since Rev. Ibia's death. The Rev. Envela served as pastor of the six coastal churches from 1952 to 1969.

By 1957, the 15 congregations[194] of Corisco-Rio Muni Presbytery with some 2500 members were struggling for survival under the severe restrictions and opposition of a hostile government. Yet the Presbyterian Church had a tremendous reservoir of good will among the African people within its territory, as it proclaimed the Good News and sought to meet the needs of the people.[195]

B. CENTRAL AFRICA

YEARS OF WAR AND STRUGGLE IN BELGIAN CONGO (1940-1944)

The Second World War had its effect on the Belgian Congo, though not as directly as on many other parts of Africa. When Germany attacked Belgium without warning on May 10, 1940, King Leopold III soon surrendered. However the Belgian cabinet refused to give up; moving its headquarters to London, it became the Free Belgian Government-in-exile. The Minister of the Colonies was given authority to administer all affairs related to the Congo. From the London base, the colonial minister organized resistance of the colony in collaboration with Great Britain. By September 1940, the Belgian National Army began to be reenforced by troops from the Belgian Congo "to defend the cause of the Allies in Africa." Thus Congolese found themselves drawn into a foreign war of which they had little comprehension.

Because of the demands of war, raw materials from the Belgian colony became increasingly important, especially since sources in Asia were cut off. Rubber was particularly crucial. Food supplies were needed for the troops fighting in Africa and Europe. Most crucial were the mineral supplies from Shaba Province, such as copper, zinc, cassiterite, cobalt, manganese and uranium. (The first atomic bomb was made with Congolese uranium.) As these industries were called on to increase their production, they needed more local and foreign workers. The local ones were found, of course, in the villages. The colony witnessed another mass migration, as young men were drawn into the war industries. Once again the African traditional lifestyle was disrupted abruptly by a mass movement of people into urban and industrial situations.

The impact of these developments was soon felt by both the Mission and the Church. During the war years, the APCM suffered a critical missionary shortage. Not only were few new recruits sent to the field, which kept growing in size and responsibilities, but those who were in the United States on furlough had great difficulty returning, since travel was seriously interrupted by war conditions. In 1940 the APCM recorded that the Church in the Kasai had a membership of 51,429, with twelve organized congregations. However, there were only 26 ordained missionaries and less than 25 African pastors.

Despite the adversities brought about by war, the mission institutions continued to serve to meet increasing critical needs. In 1940, for example, the five APCM hospitals and five dispensaries treated more than 52,000 patients. This despite the fact that four of the six medical doctors were at home either on furlough or sick leave during much of this period.[196] Yet the work was carried on with the service of missionary nurses and medical orderlies (*aides-infirmiers*) who had been trained at the hospitals.[197]

Included in the work of each of the hospitals was a colony for leprosy patients, located at a discreet distance from the hospital. Great interest was shown by the Government in the production of chaulmoogra oil, used in treatment of leprosy, from trees grown in the vicinity of the hospitals. Soon patients were being discharged from the colonies as the disease was arrested. The outstanding work of a veteran Presbyterian missionary doctor, Dr. Eugene Kellersberger, had led to his appointment in 1940 as director of American Leprosy Missions, Inc., an American organization which has led the way in the treatment and eradication of this dread disease in many countries around the world.[198]

Meanwhile the Mission's educational department in 1940 recorded 869 lower elementary schools, forty-two higher elementary (regional) schools, four training industrial schools and one theological school. In all, more than 34,000 Congolese were under instruction.

The consequence of all this, observed William Crane, was that "increased workloads, longer terms on the field, and the advancing age of a few key people, coupled with the hazards of malaria and the debilitating climate took a heavy toll of the missionary force."[199]

Yet missionary annals of the period reveal that the spirit was high and missionaries showed remarkable courage in facing the difficulties.

Other Protestant missions showed the same spirit. Determined to implant a united church in the Belgian Congo, missionaries found that the most effective way to face the ordeal of the war was to join hands in helping one another. In October 1940, the Congo Protestant Council reported: "After Denmark, Norway, Holland and Belgium had been occupied by the Germans, the Congo Protestant Council quickly organized a Missionary Relief War Fund in order to try to help those missions and missionaries in Belgian Congo and Ruanda-Urundi that were thereby cut off from their usual sources of supply."[200] Soon generous gifts were received from the Orphaned Missions Fund of the International Missionary Council, as well as from missionaries and African Christians all over the colony, to provide assistance to those "orphaned missions" from Belgium, Denmark, and Norway. "Helping one another" was also seen in the establishment in 1941 of a united Protestant Chaplaincy for the soldiers of the *Force Publique* (National Army). Missionaries were called to work as Chaplains accompanying the Congolese troops in the battlefields of West and North Africa and as far away as Palestine.

As the Protestant missions found themselves drawn into the defense of the cause of Belgium, the Belgian colonial government seemed to be changing its attitude toward them. In 1941, the Governor General granted the Congo Protestant Council (CPC) a *personnalite civile* (legal recognition). Then, when the Allies asked the Belgian Congo to produce more rubber for the war effort, the Governor General approached CPC officials, asking for the help of the missionaries in support of this campaign wherever possible. The CPC dutifully passed the message on to all the missions, and most missions agreed to help the effort. Kiantandu comments that at this time, "an expression which became popular in the Kasai was that 'love had died with Kuonyi Nahila.' This was the African name of William H. Morrison and the saying illustrates that missionaries of the time were tempted to become allies of colonialists at the expense of the rights of the colonized people."[201]

The APCM, even under the duress of shortages of personnel and resources due to the war, found itself drawn into expanding its work into a new area. In 1942 the Belgian colonial government asked the Presbyterian mission to take over the work in the area of **Moma**, some 85 miles south of Lubondai. The Protestant work in this area among the primitive, cannibalistic Basala Mpasu people had been founded originally by the Four Square Gospel Mission, but the colonial government had found it necessary to expel these missionaries because of "gross misbehavior." Although the Presbyterian Mission was not sufficiently well staffed to undertake this new work, it appeared to be a matter of dire necessity that Moma be occupied, "lest the station be turned over to the Roman Catholic priests." The occupation of Moma was carried out by two missionary families and twenty trained evangelists from Lubondai, relocated in strategic places throughout the area. Also two large regional schools, the result of the work of the former mission, were taken over and revived. This act of faith proved to be "well justified by the subsequent history of the work in this most primitive region of all."[202] With the addition of Moma, the APCM now organized its work around eight stations, scattered over an area comprising about one-tenth of the Belgian Congo, inhabited by about two million people.

The growth of Church membership in the Kasai continued remarkably despite the war. Statistical reports show that, from the 1940 figure of 51,429 members, by 1944 church membership numbered 62,436, with a constituency of about 122,000. It was the largest Protestant Christian constituency in the Belgian Congo, making up about ten percent of the total Protestant community of about one million.[203]

Yet strangely the Church had made little progress in autonomy or organization. With no *personnalite civile* of its own, it did not exist in the eyes of the government. All Mission and Church properties were registered in the name of the APCM, and the church, legally speaking, did not own anything. Meanwhile, despite its shortage of personnel, the Mission continued to expand its work until even the "evangelistic centers" at Kasha, Mboi and Moma became big stations with schools, dispensaries, Boys' and Girls' Boarding Schools, and evangelistic schools. "In time, the Mission ceased talking about the idea of 'small stations' and resigned herself to the fact that any post that was opened would develop into a large station as the work progressed."[204]

While missionaries generally took on the problems of administration of the schools, hospitals, Mission and Church budget, mission personnel, and relations with the State, the task of overseeing the work of the Church was left in the hands of some 37 African pastors (in 1944), who had neither the authority nor sufficient training for such an undertaking. Since few of the missionaries had time to travel among the village churches, their contact with the Christians was mostly through the pastors and evangelists[205] who came to the Mission stations to report activities, such as number of villages visited, amount of offerings collected, number of new members and number of those under church discipline. Consequently local Christians felt more comfortable giving their ultimate loyalty to the Mission rather than to the Church; "it was much more fashionable to be regarded as the 'people of the Mission.'"[206]

Yet there were developments that later would lay the groundwork for the emergence of a self-governing church. One of the occasions for thanksgiving was the completion of the revised Buluba-Lulua New Testament, after nine years of painstaking labor on the part of five missionaries and their co-workers. The revision had become necessary by many changes and discoveries in the language as new territory was opened, and was an attempt to produce the Bible in a language that "will be better understood over the whole territory covered by our own Mission and by several sister missionary societies."[207] Actually, the use of one Bible had much to do with the welding together of the varying dialects in the Kasai area.

Also, with more and better educational institutions, the Mission's program of leadership training was greatly strengthened. The Morrison Bible School was graduating classes of forty and fifty new ministers for the growing Church each year, drawn from all eight of the mission stations. "The training these men received in Bible, church history, pastoral theology, the larger catechism (systematic theology) and homiletics was a vast improvement over what the early catechists had been taught."[208] At five of the stations there were Evangelistic or Gospel Schools, training men for the ministry who were not qualified to take regular courses at the Morrison Bible School. Refresher courses were provided on several stations, giving both evangelists and their wives an opportunity for further study.

The J. Leighton Wilson Press was rapidly increasing the printed resources available to this growing church. Among the more than two million pages of material produced each year were Bible commentaries and dictionaries, hymn books, Sunday School lessons, religious helps of many kinds, a Tshiluba monthly periodical "News of the Kasai People", as well as all the school books in the Tshiluba language used in the hundreds of schools across the Kasai Province. Not only in the Kasai, but also in the whole of Africa, "despite the mounting difficulties of the times, the emerging church slowly was becoming rooted in African soil."[209]

RENEWED PROGRESS AND GROWING PROBLEMS (1945-1953)

With the end of the Second World War, Belgium looked at its large African colony with new eyes. Not only did the Belgian Congo's tremendous resources have new appeal, but there was a recognition that the Belgian government's paternalistic colonial policy would have to change. The election of Robert Godding as Belgium's Minister of Colonies in mid-1945 marked a turning point. Godding, a representative of the liberal-socialist wing of the Belgian Parliament, was determined to decrease the influence which the Catholic Church had in the "trinity of power" (government, business,[210] Catholic Church), and to increase the role which the Congolese themselves would have. "Planned political change" was the watchword, beginning with a "Ten Year Plan for Economic and Social Development of the Belgian Congo."

Borrowing a concept from French colonial policy, the Belgian colonial government had begun to encourage the development of an elite class of *evolues*, young Congolese who because of their educational development would be regarded as "Europeanized" and therefore eligible for special privileges. Immediately after the war, the *evolues* demanded that the colonial administration consult with them before enforcing important decisions concerning Africans. In early 1946, Jean Bolikango, leader of the *evolues*, helped to found the *Union des interets Sociaux Congolais* (an association for the social interests of the Congolese), with the objective of "elimination of practices of racial discrimination, . . . the amelioration of the social conditions of Congolese . . . and the protection of the rights of the *evolues*." Joseph Kasavubu, a former Catholic priest who later would become the first President of Zaire, was named spokesman for the association. Congolese nationalism thus started in the circles of the *evolues*, and "because of mission monopoly of education all or nearly all of the *evolues* had at some point in their lives attended mission-operated schools." Thus the mission educational system, without realizing it, was to be the mother of African nationalism.[211]

With the end of the war, the Belgian Congo experienced an economic upsurge, with its raw materials in great demand in war-ravaged Europe. The need for labor in the mines and factories continued to increase. At the demand of the *evolue*s, the colonial government permitted the establishment of Congolese trade unions in which African workers' representatives could play an active role. Still another element was thus added to the volatile political mix. A corollary effect was an increasing mass movement toward the big cities and mining centers. This rapid urbanization would profoundly affect the program of the APCM, as well as the other Protestant missions.

The new Colonial Minister, concerned for the social improvement of the people of the Belgian Congo, made several other significant reforms. He founded the *Fonds du Bien Etre Indigene* (Native Welfare Fund) and the *Office des Cites Africaines* (Office of Housing Development in African Cities), both of which would be drawn upon by the various missions for health, educational and civic improvements. Most significantly, he was firm about his determination to end the Catholic monopoly on government funds for education. In February 1946 he announced officially that the "Belgian Government had decided that from now on all Christian missions in the Colony would be placed on the same footing, under similar conditions and with equal guarantees."[212] Protestant missions had gained a new status in the Belgian Congo.

The Protestant missions eagerly responded to this new opportunity for cooperation with the State in a vital aspect of their work, thus securing for graduates from their schools the advantage of recognized diplomas. But the recognition of Protestant schools and the extension of government subsidies would be on the condition that the missions adopt the government's educational program. This would necessitate several significant changes: (1) All educational missionaries would be required to undergo a period of residential study in Belgium, "in the study of language and in the pursuit of 'normal' and 'colonial' courses."[213] (2) The curriculum would have to be brought into conformity with the requirements of the colonial government, as to both content and quality. (3) Protestant schools would be subject to governmental inspection and certification. (4) There would need to be a central agency through which every Protestant mission would deal with the government concerning education. To fulfil the last requirement, the Congo Protestant Council (representing most of the Protestant missions) set up an Educational Secretariat, which would become the most important unifying service of the Protestant community.

Possibly the most significant change in post-war Belgian Congo was in the attitudes of the people about themselves. They had gone to war for and beside the white man; under his directions they had worked with him to produce needed war materials; now they heard themselves publicly commended, and were told that they had helped him win the war. They felt a new sense of personal worth, and perhaps for the first time they were stirred with some consciousness of their importance and power as a people regardless of clan or tribe. They wanted more for their own people than they had ever had before, and many saw in education the one hope of advancement. It was the beginning of a new awakening.

To the APCM, the greatest promise in the cessation of war lay in the prospect of receiving new recruits for their long depleted forces. Early in 1945 a steady stream of new missionaries began coming to the field, a stream that would increase the number of missionaries from 81 to 156 by 1953, making the APCM the strongest of Protestant societies in the Belgian Congo. Spurred on by a visit from Dr. C. Darby Fulton, Executive Secretary of the PCUS Executive Committee of Foreign Missions, in November 1945, the Mission dreamed great dreams of new beginnings, to be funded through the denomination's five-year Program of Progress.

Foremost in its plans was the strengthening of every aspect of its educational program. At its annual meeting in November 1946, the APCM voted to begin a Normal School at Bibanga, to train primary school teachers and to prepare candidates for higher education. Further, each station was urged to bring its schools up to government standards. Plans were made for the beginnings of a medical school, later to be supplemented with a dental department. All this required a surge of building; the next few years would see major building programs on each station, carried out primarily through funds secured from the colonial government and the PCUS Program of Progress, and done largely by Belgian colonial contractors.

Along with most of the large Protestant missionary societies in the Belgian Congo, the APCM now focused much of its attention upon preparing its schools for government recognition and consequent subsidization. Since most of the village schools were in poor shape, new school buildings were built. "Thousands of standard school desks were made in the various mission carpentry shops, for most of the schools were equipped with the simplest sort of benches with no writing desks. Hundreds of thousands of text-books were bought to provide every child with the required text in each subject; until then only the teachers of classes possessed textbooks."[214] The primary schools gradually took on a new look. The first government inspections took place in 1948; "while they showed that a great deal of improvement was still called for, [they] gave evidence of sympathetic understanding on the part of the majority of government inspectors."[215] The first government subsidies were granted the same year.

As the government became more and more insistent that classes in the mission primary schools be taught by competent Congolese teachers, the importance of improved teacher training became evident. The *Ecole de Moniteurs* (Normal School) begun at Bibanga in 1946 was moved to Mutoto in 1949, where the Morrison Bible School had been located for the past 33 years. But then a grander scheme was envisioned: the Mission decided to combine the two schools into one Morrison Institute, with a Bible School Division and a Normal School Division, and to relocate this new venture at a new station, **Kakinda**, at the southeastern edge of the mission's area. In 1951 the new institute moved to its new campus, "wonderfully equipped with new stone buildings financed by the Presbyterian Program of Progress funds, and to a lesser extent by government funds."[216]

However, the life of the combined schools was "doomed from the start." The students in the state-accredited Normal School were promised the security and status that accompanied state accreditation, while the students in the Bible School were promised little or no security and prestige in their future positions in the church. Consequently enrollment in the Normal School increased over the years, while at the same time enrollment for the

Bible School decreased in inverse proportion. Within a few years, the Mission would recognize the necessity for restructuring the whole program of ministerial training.

The tension between teacher training and ministerial training developed at a lower level at the same time that it became so acute at Kakinda. After the war the Mission had organized five schools at the elementary school level for the purpose of training village catechists; these were called *Ecoles Evangeliques* (evangelistic schools). Then, shortly after the Mission signed the agreement accepting government subsidy and accreditation, the decision was made to develop several schools for training village school teachers, called *Ecole d'Apprentissage Pedagogique* (EAP). However, as years passed, the Mission came to see that the relationship of the two functions of teaching and preaching at the village level was becoming more and more ambiguous. "There was no need to maintain two different workers in a village, one to carry on the functions of evangelism and the other to carry on the function of Christian education, when one man adequately trained could do both tasks."[217] For this reason it was decided to correlate the work of the two separate schools, making each a distinct and necessary part of a four year course which would train village catechist-teachers. A further advantage would be that graduates would receive their salaries in large measure from the state subsidy as accredited village schoolteachers, releasing church funds to pay full-time church leaders more adequate salaries.

In the insatiable thirst of Congolese youth for education, there was a growing demand for schools for medical training. To strengthen its program for training medical orderlies for the various mission hospitals, the decision was made to develop a school for training *infirmiers diplomes*, a higher grade of medical assistant that the government alone had been training until this time. Toward this end the APCM at its meeting in 1953 decided to initiate a medical school at Lubondai, to be called the *Institut Medical Chretien du Kasai* (IMCK), and to appoint two missionary doctors and a nurse as the initial faculty. Connected with this school there would be initiated in 1955 a school for training Congolese dental assistants, the only school of its kind in all of Central Africa. Later a third teaching program, a school for laboratory assistants, would be added to the Institute.

Two schools for training carpenters and masons were developed, one at Lubondai and one at Kasha, called *Ateliers d'Apprentissage*. In addition, three domestic science schools (*Ecoles Menageres*) were organized at Lubondai, Bibanga and Moma, to train Congolese young women in the arts of homemaking, cooking and sewing. Thus the Mission sought in every way possible to respond to the clamor of the Congolese, and especially the Christians, for education to prepare them for the new day.

Unfortunately the Mission assumed this responsibility to a large extent *for* the Church rather than *along with* the Church. "The tortuous decisions regarding the location of training institutions; the debate over the financial problems arising out of the differential between state-subsidized teachers' salaries and church-supported leaders' salaries; questions regarding the motivation of a church vocation, all of these topics have been central concerns of the annual mission meetings. On the other hand they are concerns that have not been shared in a real way with the church courts."[218] Some beginning steps were being taken by bringing Congolese church leaders into the boards of trustees of the various training institutions, and by the organization of school councils on each station. Also, by 1950, some Africans were named to the Faculty of Morrison Institute at Kakinda. Yet the final decisions on all important matters were reserved for the Mission itself.[219]

Responding to the rapid urbanization taking place in the Kasai, the Mission in 1946 initiated its first urban work in **Luluabourg.** At the end of the war, Luluabourg had been an insignificant trading post on the Bas-Congo Katanga Railroad. Then the colonial government transferred the capital of the Kasai Province from Lusambo to Luluabourg and the city took on all the complexities of a "boom-town," drawing thousands of workers from all over the Kasai.[220] "In this growing population it could always be estimated that at least ten percent would be Protestant church members, while another large proportion would express sympathy for Protestantism, although they were not church members."[221]

The churches which would emerge in this and other urban settings would be quite distinct from those which had been established in the villages, with a cross-section of people from various tribal groups, a larger number of *evolues* in government civil service, and a much stronger sense of autonomy. Indeed the composition of the Luluabourg city church would be called "a microcosm of the 'New Tribe.'"[222] It would also mark the beginning of a new pattern of missionary work, with missionaries moving into residences in the native city, rather than living in mission station compounds. With Luluabourg now becoming the center of railroad and airplane transport and communication for the Kasai, the Mission made the decision to transfer its business and legal departments from its oldest station at Luebo to the capital city of Luluabourg.[223]

These were indeed years of amazing progress. Yet along with this progress there were growing problems, especially in the relationship of Mission and Church. Ecumenical mission events in the postwar period were giving a greater and greater role to representatives from the "younger churches." The first regional missionary conference to be held in Africa after World War II was the West Central Africa Conference that met at Leopoldville (later Kinshasa) in July 1946. The 200 delegates, of whom 35 were Africans, represented no fewer than 75 missionary organizations, covering the region including Angola, the Belgian Congo, French Equatorial Africa, and the Cameroons. The conference strongly emphasized the new responsibilities devolving upon the missions in relation to the emerging churches, in light of the rapidly changing conditions in the Belgian, French and Portuguese colonial territories.

Of even greater impact was the conference of the International Missionary Council, held at Whitby, Ontario in July 1947, which insisted that the older and younger churches were called to be "partners in obedience to our Lord's Commission." Influenced by the Whitby meeting, a group of missionaries at the APCM annual meeting in November 1947 proposed that Congolese be invited to future mission meetings. But the Mission rejected the idea: "In answer to the overture regarding native representation in the Mission Meeting, we feel that the common meeting place for missionaries and natives is in the already established Mpungilu [Synod]."[224] At the same meeting, decision was made regarding the urgent task of completing the revision of the Tshiluba translation of the Old Testament; yet only missionaries were assigned to this task, with no thought of including competent African pastors.[225]

Other Mission actions in succeeding years reenforced the tensions between the Mission and the Church. In 1948, the APCM forbade individual correspondence between members of the Church in America and Kasai Christians, advising the Mission Board that African Christians lacked "financial responsibility."[226] In the same year, the APCM warned the Board about the "government's critical and suspicious attitude towards the negro Americans" and advised it against appointing black missionaries,[227] thus going against what had been one of the distinguishing characteristics of the APCM, its interracial fellowship.

Most serious of all were the implications of the tremendous expansion of the educational program upon the life of the Church. Since most missionaries were tied up in school administration, there would be less missionary itineration among the village churches than there had ever been before. There would be no significant increase in the mission subsidy of church leaders' salaries, the amount from overseas funds remaining substantially the same as it was in 1945. While the Mission continued to provide funds for church buildings on the mission stations and in a few urban centers, the rural churches that were in direst economic straits were not helped at all. When these facts sank into the consciousness of the church leaders, their morale suffered greatly. Recruiting for the ministry fell off until there were very few candidates presenting themselves for ministerial training at the higher levels. "Those who stayed in the work carried on their ministries under the sheer momentum of the past, more often than not with no vision or ambition for the Church . . . . The Church came more and more to be a static society, rather than a living organism, and those who were responsible for this situation became more and more apathetic."[228]

Yet at the same time, American Presbyterians were making remarkable contributions to the future development of the Church in the Kasai. Missionaries produced commentaries in the vernacular on every book of the Bible, as well as materials on church polity, church history, pastoral counseling, catechism and worship. "They were far ahead of their [missionary] colleagues in the Kasai" and other missions requested permission to translate the Presbyterian books into their local languages. "In this way, the APCM contributed much to the Africanization of Christianity in the colony."[229]

To express their respect for local values, the Mission meeting of 1951 insisted that both missionaries and Africans make use of the African names for the American Presbyterians. Henceforward the indigenous names for the missionaries were inserted in the record of the Mission's minutes, and most African Christians referred to the missionaries only by their "native" names. "This helped the Africans understand that the new faith brought by the missionaries would not destroy all their cultural values," and that "missionaries were attempting to become integral parts of the African society."[230]

Yet, even as the APCM became increasingly aware of "the rise of a strong nationalism among the people of the Congo", there was also recognition of the importance of "the maintaining of a friendly and cooperative relationship with the

Colonial Government in its highly difficult task of administration.[231] Hence no voice was raised when the Colonial Government refused religious liberty to Kimbanguists and adherents of other indigenous Christian movements. With the government increasing its subsidies to the Mission schools and medical work every year, as well as making grants of land for the expansion of the Mission's work, it was difficult to press for the "selfhood" of the Church which might be interpreted by the Colonial Government as yielding to the spirit of nationalism.

But external forces were at work to move the APCM toward facing the radical changes that were taking place in the Belgian Congo. Spurred on by the meeting of the International Missionary Council at Willingen, Germany in July 1952, the Congo Protestant Council insisted to its member missions that the time had come for missionaries to transfer responsibility to African church leaders. With this impetus, the APCM invited Dr. C. Darby Fulton, Executive Secretary of the PCUS Board of World Missions,[232] and Dr. James A. Jones, the Board's Chairman, to come to the Kasai and "plan with the missionaries and the African leaders for the future, with a view to preparing the Church for whatever eventualities lay ahead."[233]

The two emissaries arrived in September 1952, and held regional conferences of missionaries and Africans at six places across the Kasai. These integrated conferences were followed by a conference that involved only the missionaries and the two delegates of the Board. The conclusions reached would shape the work of the Mission for the years ahead:

(1) The Mission had over-extended itself in the Kasai. Therefore no new mission stations should be initiated, though witness might be extended into some of the growing urban centers.

(2) Pastors, evangelists and lay leaders of the church had not received sufficient training. Therefore, "let there now come a period of intensive work in training the Christians in churchmanship, stewardship, and responsibility as leaders and as lay Christians."

(3) The Mission had pursued an ineffective church polity toward the establishment of an indigenous Christian community. Therefore the APCM should move deliberately toward organizing autonomous presbyteries (replacing the "provisional presbyteries" which had been in operation since 1931) in which African pastors would have "a position of dignity and leadership."

(4) Instead of encouraging a separation between Mission and Church, the APCM should make "provision for representatives of the African Church, elected by the Africans, to be present for a period during the Mission Meeting when major matters concerning the Church are under consideration."[234]

It was a turning point in the history of the American Presbyterian Congo Mission. Reporting to the PCUS Board of World Missions, Dr. Fulton stated that the Church of the Kasai was now a reality: "It stands as a vigorous and growing body of believers, a true ecclesiastical organization."[235] Despite the vicissitudes of this period, the Church in the Kasai had grown from a communicant membership of 59,971 in 1946 to 71,486 in 1953. Working with the 156 missionaries were 71 pastors, though the total number of "native workers" (evangelistic, educational, medical) came to 3,179.[236]

Doubtless it was out of the experience of his visit to the Belgian Congo that Dr. Fulton wrote his memorable description of the situation of Africa in this time of transition:

> A complex situation has developed in which it might be said that there are actually three Africas reflecting the strangely conflicting influences that are shaping the life of the people.
>
> One Africa is primitive and pagan, stark and wild. It is the 'dark continent', still in spiritual midnight. Hundreds of villages are there, where all the degradations of heathenism are apparent. This is Africa unimproved and unredeemed, with its mud huts, naked people, witchcraft, sorcery, ignorance and fear. This is still the principal Africa.
>
> Another Africa is modern and progressive. It displays the gadgets of civilization. Its people adorn themselves with the tawdry trinkets of superficiality and assume an air of sophistication. This Africa, too, is largely pagan. Its interests are secular. Money is its god. A price is on everything, and even virtue can be bought and sold. There are saloons, gambling dens, cheap moving pictures and cheap women. This new Africa is encroaching rapidly upon the old.
>
> Another Africa is Christian. It is like a psalm of reverence in the midst of a Babel of blasphemy. There is the African Christian community, worshipping in its own little houses of praise, led by its own national pastors, singing the hymns of the Church, joining in the reading of the Scriptures. There amid all the darkness and fear and despair is a fellowship numbering thousands of souls, bright with hope and confident in faith. This Africa, too, is growing.
>
> These are not descriptions of different areas of the continent. The three Africas are superimposed one on the other, making their impact concurrently upon a bewildered people.[237]

THE PACE QUICKENS TOWARDS INDEPENDENCE (1954-1957)

The year 1954 marked a quickening of the pace toward independence for both the government and the Church. Both Belgian colonialists and Christian missionaries recognized that the day was not too far off when the Congolese would take destiny into their own hands, and therefore began to prepare for eventual transfer of power.

In Belgium, the elections of 1954 saw the defeat of the Catholic party and the coming into power of a liberal-socialist coalition government. A liberal colonial Minister, M. Petillon, decided not only to continue the progressive program started by Godding more than eight years earlier but to institute many new administrative reforms. This meant that in the Belgian Congo, greater freedom of speech and publication was allowed, and Africans were given a fuller share in the various institutions that directly concerned them. Such phrases as "Belgian-Congolese community" became fashionable.

A leading Belgian political figure, Van Bilsen, proposed that within thirty years the Congo should be independent, opening "a Pandora's Box for the Europeans: once raised the issue was there for good."[238] Joseph Kasavubu was elected president of ABAKO in 1954, an organization begun in 1950 in Leopoldville for the "unification, preservation, perfection and expansion" of the Kongo culture. Under Kasavubu's leadership, ABAKO became a dynamic political organization.[239] In August 1956, the ABAKO leaders published a manifesto in the *Conscience Africaine* (a paper for the *evolues*) in which they demanded preparation of the colony for eventual independence. Other leaders went further in their demand: Patrice Lumumba, a young postal clerk and leader of the *evolue* circle in Stanleyville, insisted on immediate independence under the aegis of a provisional government. Still other political organizations emerged in other parts of the Congo: the Lulua-Freres Association, started in 1950 in Luluabourg, sought to revive Lulua traditions under the leadership of Kalamba Mangole, the direct heir to the traditional throne of the old Lulua Kingdom.[240]

The changes in colonial policy had a significant effect upon the growth of the various indigenous Christian movements, especially the Kimbanguists. Following the death of Simon Kimbangu in prison in 1951, his followers, who had suffered severe persecution over the past three decades, took on new life. There were reports that Kimbangu had risen again and visited his incredulous disciples banished in detention camps in eastern Congo. From about 1954 Kimbangu's youngest son, Joseph Diangienda, a well-educated and competent government official, assumed a directive role in the movement, gaining legal toleration from the new colonial government, drawing together the unorganized network of believers into a recognizable body, and establishing a coherent doctrine and organization quite distinctive from the Catholic and Protestant mission churches. No longer simply a movement, the *Eglise du Jesus Christ sur la terre par le prophete Simon Kimbangu* (EJCSK) would in time become the largest and best organized independent church on the whole African continent.

In the field of education, the year 1954 marked the establishment of the first public schools operated by the government itself, *ecoles officielles*. The Roman Catholic missions at first opposed the public schools, fearing the competition with their own institutions. However, "the Protestants gave them their blessing and regarded their establishment as an answer to prayer. Some missionaries even counted on turning over the whole irksome school program to the State." In accordance with Belgian law, all pupils in government schools had to take a course in religion or morals. Missionaries were invited and urged to give or supervise this religious instruction, providing "an added opportunity to teach God's Word of which the missionaries gladly avail[ed] themselves."[241]

The year also brought the opening of the first full-scale university, Lovanium, a Roman Catholic institution at Leopoldville, linked to the University of Louvain in Belgium. Soon would follow a "free" government university at Elisabethville in 1956. Both brought together European and African students as had not been experienced before, thus increasing among bright young Africans a sense of the disparity between the status of Europeans and their own Congolese people.

In the same year of 1954, the Colonial Minister announced that Africans would be selected to serve in the government council. Three among those chosen were Protestants, one of them a Presbyterian, Kalondji Isaac. By late 1956, the Colonial Minister had named the first African, Antoine Bolamba, to his Cabinet. And in 1957, the government authorized the free election of Mayors, first in the capital city of Leopoldville, and soon in other cities such as Luluabourg. It was among these Congolese mayors that the demand for "immediate and total" independence for their nation was made. As there were as yet no official African political parties, the voting largely followed tribal lines, awakening in tribal groups around the country the determination to fight for their political rights.

Within Protestant circles, significant steps were taken in moving toward turning over greater authority to the Church. The Congo Protestant Council (CPC), which had been wrestling for years with how to move the Church toward autonomy and unity, made two important decisions at its meeting in February 1954. First, it was agreed that the methods and practices of the various mission groups be brought into greater conformity so that they might provide the basis for a single Congo Protestant Church: "We would not want our sectarian differences to prove an obstacle to the establishment of the Church of Christ in Congo." Next, the Council recommended that a Conference of selected Congolese representatives be held in September 1954, with a view to creating a Central Consultative Church Council: "Such a Council would be invited to send representatives to confer annually with the CPC on church matters."[242] Before the end of 1954, the Conference of the Consultative Council of the Church of Christ in Congo had been formed with seven churches participating: the Presbyterians, the American and British Baptists, the Salvation Army, the Disciples, the Methodists, and the Swedish Covenant. The Rev. Tshisungu Daniel[243] represented the Presbyterian Church in the Kasai. A significant step had been taken toward the formation of what would in time become the Church of Christ in the Congo.

Other important decisions were made by the 1954 conference: A Central Fund of the Church of Christ in Congo was established, to which contributions would be made from the various African churches. Also, in light of the critical need for improvement in theological education that would prepare African pastors for the new era of independence, it was recommended that a Central Theological School be established. Further, the Conference recognized the growing membership and influence of "the subversive movements" of Kimbanguism and other indigenous Christian groups and called on all believers to "unite in prayer that the movements not lead people astray". Finally, six delegates were chosen to meet with the Congo Protestant Council (representing the missions) at the next CPC meeting.

The annual meeting of the CPC in 1955 received for the first time African delegates from the Consultative Church Council. The joint session recommended that regional conferences be organized in which the various churches would discuss the formation of an integrated Congo Protestant Council. At the 1956 meeting, it was voted that the integration take place, and the CPC constitution was changed to make it a council of both Churches and Missions, representing the fruit of the work of forty-six participating Protestant missionary organizations in the Congo.

Similar developments were taking place within the Roman Catholic community, which now numbered some four million communicants. In the summer of 1956, it was announced that Pierre Kimbondo was to be ordained as Bishop of the Congo, the first Congolese to hold that office since the sixteenth century.[244]

Within the APCM, 1954 marked an increase of missionary trust in the African church leaders. At the annual Mission meeting, five Congolese church delegates were received for discussion regarding matters relating to the life of the Church. The APCM recorded its appreciation for the constructive spirit of the African delegates, and "the valuable contribution that they made to the discussions."[245] From this point, the mission's minutes and other official documents ceased to use the term "provisional" in relation to the synod and presbyteries. Actions which the Mission had heretofore taken without consideration of the opinions of church leaders were sent to the appropriate church courts for confirmation, recognizing that their decisions on matters concerning the church should be regarded as final. Also, it was decided to appoint African church representatives to the Board of Trustees of each mission institution for the training of Africans. Further, a plan was developed to organize a *Caisse Centrale* or Central Synod Treasury, which would receive seven per cent of all presbytery funds, in addition to mission funds that were designated for the subsidization of church workers' salaries and pensions. And in response to the call for a more adequately trained ministry, it was decided to open the *Ecole de Theologie* at Kakinda the following year, providing a higher level of theological education than had been available previously.

Other ventures were initiated which brought Congolese church leaders into work that previously had been the prerogative of the Mission. In 1956 a Christian Education Committee was set up, composed of both missionaries and Africans, with a full-time Director of Christian Education. Training classes were held throughout the Kasai training teachers in Sunday Schools and government schools, as well as leaders for work among women and youth. This coincided with the holding of Africa-wide conferences in 1955-1956, for the planning of an All-Africa Sunday School Curriculum, to be prepared by writers both African and missionary. And in 1957, the APCM joined the Mennonites and Brethren in the Kasai in forming a Tshiluba Literature Committee composed of both African and missionary representatives. A catalogue of all available Tshiluba literature was compiled, and a book store established in Luluabourg. A long-time dream was realized in the publication of the original literary efforts of three Congolese church leaders.

In the midst of the ferment of change, the Mission launched two new ventures in urban work. The first was far removed from the Kasai, in the capital of the Belgian Congo, **Leopoldville**, where, upon the urgent invitation of the British and American Baptist missionary societies, two senior evangelistic couples were assigned in 1954. Technically this was a new Mission, for the government recognized its *personnalite civile* under the name *"Mission Presbyterienne de Leopoldville"* (MPL). Leopoldville had become a sprawling, modern city of a third of a million inhabitants and burgeoning cites or subdivisions, housing the large influx of Congolese attracted to the booming colonial capital. Three such subdivisions became the principal responsibility for the new MPL. Temporary church buildings were quickly erected, with meager funds and much volunteer labor. One congregation soon became fully organized, with a pastor from the Kasai and a substantial group of Baluba members who were already acquainted with the Presbyterian form of church government. From the outset this and the other congregations that would follow saw themselves as self-supporting and self-governing, breaking the pattern of dependence on the Mission which prevailed in most of the churches in the Kasai.

The second urban venture was in **Bakwanga**, east of Luluabourg, and location of the world's largest commercial diamond mining center. Although many Protestant Christians were among the employees, the Forminiere Mining Company for years had opposed any Protestant work being admitted to the mining camp. However, in 1956 there was change in the official attitude of the Company, and not only did they permit Protestant mission work to be done but also presented a beautiful church edifice to the newly organized Protestant congregation.

Still another location was opened for APCM involvement in 1957 at **Katubwe,** southeast of Luluabourg. This would become the home of the *Ecole Secondaire*, a Union High School sponsored by the APCM and two Methodist missions. Made possible by generous grants from the Belgian Government and the various home churches, this was the highest institute of learning in the Kasai, preparing students who would be eligible to attend university, and later would be among the leaders of the emerging church and nation.

Another indication of growing confidence in Congolese church leadership was the visit of the first official representatives of the Kasai Church to the Presbyterian Church in the United States. In 1957, Pastor and Mrs. Isaac Kanyinda of the First Presbyterian Church at Luluabourg not only visited the "home base" at the Board of World Missions in Nashville, but spoke at numerous churches and conferences across the General Assembly. "Many in our homeland saw their radiant faces, heard their simple, stirring witness for Christ, and went away saying, 'What wonders God hath wrought.'" They returned to the Congo "with fresh zeal and a new concept of what the church is and should be."[246]

Thus by the end of the year 1957, the American Presbyterian Congo Mission had come a long way in enabling an autonomous church to come into being in the Kasai. From the point of view of staff, it was making an enormous investment in personnel; by 1957, there were 183 missionaries, making it by far the largest of the American Presbyterian missions not only in Africa but around the world. Working alongside this missionary force were 67 Congolese pastors and 1224 unordained evangelists, serving a communicant membership of approximately 70,000 and a total Christian constituency of more than 123,000.[247] There were congregations in hundreds of communities throughout the Kasai, as well as over 1400 preaching points. The church in the Kasai was now organized into ten presbyteries with one synod, which had become the final court in the governance of the church.

Still, it was recognized that the church had a long way to go: "The Church of the Congo has come to a critical period in its life, when it must be weaned from its dependence upon missionary personnel and financial help and establish itself on its own resources of men, money and faith. This is not an easy task; for along with the spirit of nationalistic self-reliance and self-assertion, there is still to be found an almost child-like dependence on the missionary both for leadership and for financial aid. The former stems from the prevailing mood of subject peoples throughout the world; and the latter from the colonial mentality that has developed out of a long-dependent status. The transition from dependence to autonomy involves a major psychological adjustment for a people who have only recently been introduced to the idea of self-support and self-government . . . . It is easier for the church to accept the implications of self-government than to shoulder the responsibility of self-support."[248]

Alongside the church, the APCM had developed a large institutional program for which the mission bore full responsibility. Its 1,068 schools reported a total of 36,844 students in 1957, and its seven hospitals and numerous dispensaries treated a total 50,034 patients. In 1957, the Christian Medical Institute of the Kasai graduated its first class of students and sent them to the mission's hospitals to serve two years of internship. The Dental School graduated its first class of nine students, and the first young women were received into the nursing school at the McKowen Memorial Hospital at Luebo.

But the dilemma confronting the Mission was evident: "The APCM has become big business. How is all of this to be transferred to the African Church? Will it want it? Will it need it? Is big business its business?"[249] As the missionaries wrestled with these questions, one answer seemed to emerge: "Our unity must lie at the deepest possible level, that level at which our individual differences are lost in our common devotion to Christ and to Him alone. Just here lies the very crux of our personal dilemmas—the staring fact that the only way we can serve Him in Africa today is in ABSOLUTE HUMILITY. Only in this spirit can we successfully relinquish the role of director and become the understanding, sympathetic counselor."[250]

C. THE HORN OF AFRICA

ETHIOPIA'S COLONIAL INTERLUDE AND MIRACULOUS EVANGELIZATION (1935-1941)

Five years before the Second World War thrust most of Africa into the struggle of European colonial powers, Ethiopia had suffered a devastating interruption to its sovereignty by the unprovoked invasion of Italian armed forces. Italy had gotten its foothold on the Horn of Africa by its occupation of the coastal area Eritrea and southern Somaliland in 1889. Suddenly in October 1935, the Fascist forces of Italian dictator Benito Mussolini invaded northeast Ethiopia from Eritrea and soon afterward southeast Ethiopia from Somaliland. Italian bombs made ruins of Ethiopian towns. Despite the condemnation of the League of Nations and the protests of the civilized world, the Italian invaders employed poison gas as well as incendiary and high-explosive bombs, indiscriminately machine-gunning the common people. Emperor Haile Selassie felt it was hopeless to continue the war against an enemy equipped with such modern weapons, and fled into exile in Great Britain. During the conflict, Ethiopia lost seven percent of her population, suffering some 760,000 casualties. In May 1936 Italian forces took control of Ethiopia's capital, Addis Ababa, and Mussolini declared Ethiopia, Eritrea and Italian Somaliland to be Italian East Africa.[251]

The Italian invasion and occupation of Ethiopia was a devastating blow to the budding Protestant Christian community. Italy strongly favored the Catholic missionary presence.[252] Almost all Protestant missionaries were forced to leave the country and a few were imprisoned. Only one American Presbyterian missionary family was allowed to stay: the Rev. Duncan C. Henry and his family continued their residence in Addis Ababa, "residing on property generously placed at the disposal of Mr. Henry for the Mission's use by Mr. Daniel Alexander, an aged American negro who has made his home in Ethiopia for a number of years."[253] Dr. Henry and his son would suffer several months imprisonment before the liberation of Ethiopia in 1941. Strict travel limitations made it impossible for Dr. Henry to visit the remote region of western Ethiopia, where American Presbyterians had made their strongest witness. It appeared that virtually all Protestant work and witness had come to a halt.

But what was happening among the Ethiopian Protestant (or Evangelical, as they preferred to be called) community was "like reading the Book of Acts in a new setting."[254] Cut off from missionary contacts, they found for themselves the power of Christ's spirit at work among them. A few humble dedicated Ethiopian Christians became the instruments through whom an awakening swept through those areas where Protestant missionaries had been at work. "Thousands of pagan Ethiopians, living under the heel of Italian dictatorship, turned to Christ as their Saviour and Lord, finding in Him new freedom in spite of their political slavery."

What took place in western Ethiopia where American Presbyterians had been at work is largely the story of two remarkable men—Gidada Solon and Mamo Chorqa. It was the epidemic which first brought Presbyterian missionaries to Ethiopia that also blinded the boy Gidada at the age of five. Gidada's parents saw their children die one after another until all were dead except Gidada, whose life was spared but whose eyesight was lost. Until the age of twenty, Gidada, like most of those blinded in poverty-stricken lands, lived as a beggar. Hearing that missionaries had come to Sayo and were holding meetings for beggars, he went to Sayo seeking some handout of money or bread. What he found was the Gospel. Recognizing the unusual mind and spirit of the man, missionaries enabled Gidada to learn Braille and to read the Bible for himself. He soon received Christ as his living Lord, and became an outstanding Christian among his people.

When the Italians invaded Ethiopia and forced the missionaries to leave, it was Gidada who gathered a few faithful Christians about him, and under the very eyes of the occupiers, they began to travel from house to house and village to village, preaching the Gospel and strengthening the Christian community. The response was electric and hundreds began to turn to Christ. In time the Italian authorities caught up with Gidada and his little group of itinerant preachers. When they found Gidada preaching from his Braille Bible, not knowing what it was, they suspected that it was a secret document, branded the whole group as spies and had them thrown into prison. But their witness continued. In prison, like Paul and Silas, the little band sang their hymns, offered their prayers and shared their Good News, until hundreds of political prisoners heard and received their message. As prisoners were freed, they returned to their own villages to relate their experience and share the liberating Word. The fire was lit and spread in ever-widening circles.[255]

Learning that Dr. Henry was still in Addis Ababa, Gidada sent word of the amazing growth of the Christian community and an urgent request for help. Henry sent his reply, "Gather the church members and tell them to elect a spiritual man who knows the Word of God well, one who can lead the church according to the gospel."[256] The church members were gathered and elected Gidada Solon and his colleague Mamo Chorqa and sent them off one at a time to Addis Ababa, where after two months of tutelage by Dr. Henry, each was ordained to the gospel ministry. After his ordination, on his return trip to his home province of Wollaga, Gidada celebrated Holy Communion with congregations in two places where new churches had come into being. "It was . . . the first time that an Ethiopian without Orthodox ordination served Holy Communion in the evangelical congregations in Wollaga."[257]

Through Dr. Henry, the request was sent to the UPNA Board of Foreign Missions and to the 1940 UPNA General Assembly for the organization of a Presbytery in Ethiopia, composed of 500 baptized members and four times that number of adherents. With the General Assembly's approval, "ecclesiastical standing is given to a group of Christian believers who truly are the fruitage of our missionary work in the land of Ethiopia, but who are, in a deeper sense, the fruitage of the working of God's Holy Spirit." This new branch of the United Presbyterian Church was given the name Bethel Evangelical, with the prayerful hope that it "may be used of God in gathering all evangelical Christians in Ethiopia into one communion, able to sever its ecclesiastical ties with churches outside its native land and to continue in its own life a vital witness to Christ's love and power."[258]

After five years of gruelling guerrilla warfare and the heroic liberation campaign of Ethiopian and British troops, the Italian troops were driven from Ethiopia and Eritrea in 1941 and Haile Selassie returned to the throne.in February 1942. A select group of missionaries were allowed to return to the devastated nation. One of the earliest American Presbyterians to return was Dr. V.F. Dougherty, who after a trip to western Ethiopia reported:

Instead of one organized congregation and the few preaching places we had five years ago, the native Evangelical Church now has seven organized congregations and some 28 preaching places. That the Church in Sayo belongs to the living body of Christ in this world is amply borne out by its work during these years that it has had to stand alone without financial aid from abroad and practically without encouragement and advice from without. One wonders whether God is not graciously rebuking us for our too frequent assumption that unless His ark is constantly upheld by our hands it may fall. God has amply vindicated the faith that He can make it to stand.[259]

A NEW ERA FOR THE ETHIOPIAN EVANGELICAL MOVEMENT (1942-1950)

Liberty from the Fascist occupation meant the beginning of a new era for the evangelical movement throughout Ethiopia. The war years had forced Evangelical Christians to cooperate as never before. Feeling the urgency of continuing that cooperation, representatives of the various Evangelical communities came together in December 1944 to constitute the Ethiopian Evangelical Church (EEC) "as a nation-wide organization for promoting spiritual fellowship, mutual counsel and uniform practice." Actually, the name indicated more of an intention than a reality; yet the EEC annual conferences were important instruments for the development of national evangelical leaders.

As missionaries returned in increasing numbers, especially following the end of the Second World War, they sent thankful and jubilant reports to their home boards, asking for more reenforcements. Yet many "did not seem to have fully understood the indigenous ecumenical character of the movement and the leadership capacity of those in charge. They came in with their great resources in funds and educated staff and sometimes took over as if nothing had happened since they left." The Ethiopia Inter-Mission Council (organized in 1943) "discussed comity matters and divided the areas among themselves like colonial powers, without consulting those concerned."[260]

The victory over the Italian occupation soon led to a strong resurgence of Ethiopian nationalism, and with it a sense of pride in the ancient church tradition. Seeking to protect its people from further incursion by the rapidly growing Evangelical churches, the government in 1944 issued a decree to regulate foreign missionary societies by dividing the country into "Christian" (or "closed") areas and "non-Christian" (or "open") areas, the "Christian" areas being those in which the population were predominantly members of the Ethiopian Orthodox Church, and the "non-Christian" areas those in which a high percentage of the population was not related to the ancient church in profession or practice. In "non-Christian" areas missionary activity on the part of mission societies already established within the country prior to the Italian invasion would be welcomed. In the "Christian" areas mission activities could be conducted on a broad philanthropic basis only, without any evangelistic activities. (The capital city Addis Ababa was excluded from designation as either, to remain an open area in which the activities of all religious groups could be carried on under well-defined conditions.) Further, all mission groups would be required to promote the learning of the Amharic language in spoken and written form, with the goal that this *lingua franca* might work toward the unification of the Ethiopian people.

Within the "non-Christian" or "open" areas various geographical spheres were assigned to the mission groups permitted by the Government. Through the advocacy of its representatives, the United Presbyterian mission (in addition to having freedom to work in the capital city) was assigned to work within a territory of about 40,000 square miles lying south of the Blue Nile and west of the the 36th parallel longitude, "a territory contiguous with the area for which the United Presbyterian Church carries exclusive responsibility in the Sudan; also, the people of the area are, like those of our Sudan field, principally pagan or Moslem."[261]

Thus began a period of intense planning by the United Presbyterian Mission for expanded witness in southwest Ethiopia. In November 1947, a missionary survey party undertook an expedition into the more primitive area south of Gorei. They returned with enthusiastic reports regarding the unusual opportunities that were presented by the areas around the two towns of Maji and Ghimeera. Indeed, government officials at Maji had welcomed the survey party enthusiastically and offered them an excellent site of land for their work. (The prospect of the beginning of medical work seems to have been especially attractive.) While the area around Ghimeera seemed to present even greater opportunities, definite land grants and permission for work evidently would not be as readily forthcoming.

With Mission approval, a party of one missionary family and a nurse set out in early 1948 for **Maji**, with two trucks and a jeep carrying basic supplies. The rugged mountain roads and swollen unbridged streams took their toll as both trucks broke down and the party proceeded in one jeep until they reached Maji. "There they were welcomed by government officials who sent out hundreds of natives to go back over the road with them to pick up the abandoned equipment and trucks." Temporary native type houses were constructed, though they "leaked so badly that the missionaries had to pitch their tents beside the houses to keep warm and dry." Sickness and discouragement followed, but the party hung on. Soon a dispensary was opened to care for the sick, and small meetings were held and the Gospel preached. By 1951 it could be reported that the work included an organized girls' school, a medical clinic and weekly services. Here was but one example of how missionary pioneers opened new areas where the first formal education was provided, the sick were healed and the poor had the Gospel preached to them.[262]

By 1951, similar work had been begun in **Ghimeera**, so that by the end of that year it could be reported that the Mission was maintaining five centers of work:

— Addis Ababa, with the American Presbyterian School for Girls and the Gulelei congregation.
— Sayo (or Dembi Dollo), in Wollega Province, with the Jean R. Orr Memorial Hospital, an elementary school receiving pupils from the numerous village schools in the district, and a school for training the blind.

— Gore', capital of Illubabor Province, with a primary school, village schools, a dispensary, and missionaries teaching in the government school.

— Maji, in Kaffa Province, with a dispensary and a small school for girls.

— Ghimeera, also in Kaffa Province, with the beginnings of evangelistic and educational work.

Alongside this mission-related work was the rapidly growing Bethel Evangelical Church (declared independent of the UPNA in 1947[263]), now numbering sixteen congregations, six organized Christian groups and numerous evangelistic points, and more than 16,000 communicants.[264]

Yet relationships with the Ethiopian Government became increasingly tense. A particular bone of contention after 1946 was the property rights to the George Memorial Hospital in Addis Ababa. The government contended that, since this property had passed into Italian hands by expropriation during the war, after the defeat of Italy, it became the lawful possession of the Ethiopian Government. After several years of legal dispute and appeal directly to the Emperor, a settlement finally was reached in 1950, relinquishing claim to the hospital in exchange for property across the road, which would provide a very desirable location for the Girls' School, as well as the mission office and several missionary residences. The home board confidently declared, "With the settlement of our property discussions at Addis Ababa, which had been unsettled since the Italian war, we are now in position to advance."[265]

THE BEGINNING OF PERSECUTION (1951-1957)

But such was not to be the case. In the spring of 1951, persecutions began to break out against evangelical groups in various parts of Ethiopia. It was fostered by a new sense of the status of the Ethiopian Orthodox Church, which in 1948 had signed an agreement with the Coptic Church of Egypt, providing that the EOC become an autocephalous church, with its own indigenous leadership. The consecration of Abune Basilios as Metropolitan of Ethiopia on January 13, 1951 gave strong impetus to this new self-confidence. "The Ethiopianization of the leadership of the (Ethiopian Orthodox) Church strengthened its critical attitude towards the evangelical churches, non-Orthodox and missionary dominated as they were."[266] Then in the revised Constitution of 1955, the Ethiopian Orthodox Church was recognized as the established church of the empire and as such was supported by the state.

Thus from 1951 on, persecution began to break out in the so-called "open" areas where most of the evangelical churches were located. In the Sayo area, evangelists and teachers were thrown into prison for preaching the Gospel and were told that they would not be released until they promised not to preach. Evangelical leaders appealed to the emperor and were time and again assured that religious freedom prevailed in the country. However, somehow these orders did not seem to penetrate into the distant provinces, where local authorities found themselves under pressure from the Orthodox Church leadership.

As persecution mounted and resentment toward the foreign presence increased, missionaries came to realize the critical importance of training leadership for the young evangelical church. Up to this point, virtually all the evangelistic work had been done by a large number of evangelists with minimal training, working under the supervision of missionaries and of the few ordained Ethiopian pastors. A modest effort at theological education had been begun in 1947 at Dembi Dollo (Sayo) as Dr. Carl J. Kissling gathered some 36 evangelists for training. By 1950, three men had been ordained and assigned to work among more than a dozen congregations in the surrounding area. Eight more would be ordained in 1951. In ensuing years, the critical importance of training church leadership would become increasingly urgent.

In 1952, the persecution moved a step further: In the Sayo area, local officials closed the churches of the Bethel Evangelical Church. Only the church on the Mission compound remained open, and became a gathering place for Evangelical Christians from the surrounding area, "crowded at every service."[267] Now the wisdom of having initiated work in the Maji and Ghimeera areas became apparent: in these more remote areas, opposition was virtually absent; the people of the surrounding tribes showed a growing friendliness and an increase of confidence in the missionaries, coming in increasing numbers to the clinics, the schools and the religious services.

By 1955, the pressure had become still more intense: the Government declared the areas around Sayo, Gorei, and Addis Ababa to be "closed", meaning that missionaries would not be allowed to work outside their compounds. Still, the medical and educational work on the compounds drew in so many that "our workers still have plenty of opportunity to bear their witness." The areas around Maji and Ghimeera continued to present a great evangelistic opportunity, beyond the human resources available to the missionary community. There was great rejoicing in 1955 when the Rev. Tarfa Tiba with his wife and family were sent as the first missionaries from the Bethel Evangelical Church to serve in Maji. When another volunteer was sought to go to Ghimeera, it was blind Gidada Solon who stepped forward. ". . . [T]hat little church is now overflowing. Made of sticks and sheets of iron, the walls can be pushed out at any time to enlarge its seating capacity."[268]

By 1957, it had become evident that the role of the foreign missionary in Ethiopia would be increasingly restricted and that the burden of witness must be placed upon the shoulders of the young church. Within the short span of less than two decades, there had come into being a new kind of community. The evangelical Christian movement offered the peoples of southwest Ethiopia the Gospel within their own tribal contexts, and yet with a new unity across age-old tribal barriers. Indeed, "the Christians were forced to form a new community, a society in which they could have spiritual fellowship as well as a substitute for the lost tribal relationship and its many institutions of aid and assistance. The group of believers had to care for its members in all matters of life."[269] The pastors and evangelists, though limited in training, courageously confronted the traditional leaders of the religious, political and tribal communities. "They, possibly more than anybody else, are the heralds of a new community, a community, though related to the traditional society, still signifying the inception of something completely new."[270]

IMPACT OF THE ETHIOPIAN STRUGGLE ON THE SUDAN (1940-1942)

The impact of the Italian invasion of Ethiopia began to break in upon the Sudan in 1940, as British forces engaged the Italians in battle along the Sudan/Ethiopian border. Port Sudan, the port of entry for most supplies (as well as missionaries) coming to the Sudan, was bombed repeatedly and eventually closed. Other cities in the Sudan also were bombed. For a brief period most missionaries were evacuated from the trading town of Nasir.

The serious shortage of missionary staff on the field led to a significant change in strategy. In the north, Evangelical Church members, while only a few hundred, took an increasing share of leadership in almost every phase of Christian work, becoming teachers then heads of the various schools. By 1943, the Church proposed to the Mission that it would support all established congregations and preaching centers, as well as an evangelist among non-Christians, "thus releasing funds originating in America for new work." [271]

In the south, with the mission station at Akobo unoccupied and with Nasir under repeated attack, the work at Doleib Hill took on an increasing sense of urgency. In the midst of this time of extremity, "Doleib Hill has experienced its greatest spiritual awakening . . . . A significant result has been the ordination by the Presbytery of the Sudan of an outstanding [Shilluk] leader as a minister of the Gospel. La Amoleker, for many years an able teacher in the boys' school, has earnestly entered upon this new service. He is the first man of the Southern tribes to accept this holy calling.[272]

EXPANSION IN SOUTH SUDAN (1943-1951)

The period following the Ethiopian War saw new doors opening for expansion of mission work and witness. To begin with, the British-dominated government realized as never before the importance and urgency of preparing the peoples of the southern Sudan for their place in an eventually independent nation. Recognizing that the missions were virtually the only providers of education in this vast area, they turned to them asking that they take over responsibility for education in the south, assisted by government subsidies. Since the American Presbyterian mission had not developed an intermediate school (grades 5-8), the government did so, opening the Atar Intermediate School at Abwong (halfway between Doleib Hill and Nasir on the Sobat River) in 1944, but granting to the Presbyterian mission the task of providing a chaplain and a Bible teacher. Although the Atar School was moved to a new location 25 miles south of Malakal in 1945, it became a center around which the mission developed its work among the Ngok Dinka people. In time, the Atar School would become an important source of leadership for numerous tribal groups in the South, in church, education and government.[273]

The same year 1944 saw the outbreak of serious famine in the South, especially in the isolated area of the Anuak people. Nevertheless, through the relief efforts initiated by the American Presbyterians, the work at Akobo was begun again. Within the course of the next year, "there was the Christmas ingathering at Akobo when 25 souls, the firstfruits among the Anuaks, were baptized from pagan animism into the Christian faith."[274] The first Anuak church was organized in 1945, with the ordination of three elders.

With opportunities opening on every hand, the American Presbyterian mission decided to begin work in several new stations as soon as possible: in 1945 at **Abwong** (on the Sobat River between Doleib Hill and Nasir) among the Ngok Dinka people; in 1948 at **Obel** where a proposed Elementary-Vernacular Teachers' Training School was to be located, "the direction of which Government wants our Mission to take"[275]; and in 1948 at the busy river port **Malakal**, government headquarters of the Upper Nile Province, which in time would become an important link between the work in the North and the South Sudan.

A few years later, in 1952, still another new work was begun at the lonely outpost **Pibor,** south of Akobo on the Pibor River, among the Murle people, "the last remaining [tribe] in the Sudan to come under government administration[276]. Dr. Albert Roode, the medical missionary who pioneered this work, would later write, "When we began to clear the mission site we had as our evangelist Lado Lukerngoli. Every morning he talked to the workmen before the days work began and every morning he spoke about Christ to the patients awaiting treatment. Lado . . . had memorized the entire book of John so he knew the Gospel story well." [277] It was an Anuak evangelist and his wife who saw the first fruit of witness among the Murle people. "After a year of work a service of baptism was held. The little grass church was too small for the group that came together that night, so they met under a big tree. The moon was nearly full as the service began. Thirty-five of the Murle tribe stepped forward to receive baptism. Later they all partook of the Lord's Supper. Dry bread and tea were used—the tea sipped from an old tumbler—but the redeeming Christ was vividly present as the congregation, made up of African tribesmen, shared in His Holy Feast."[278]

By 1948 the Christian community among the tribal people evangelized by the UPNA missionary effort had grown to the extent that the Presbytery of the Upper Nile was formed, though officially a presbytery of the United Presbyterian Church in North America. The necessity of fostering strong local government among the Christian communities founded by the mission was early recognized. These councils exercised a steadily growing influence not merely in purely religious matters but in the total life of the community as well. "It is these local governing bodies of Sudanese Christians which deal with such problems as arise through the conflict of native custom with the Christian outlook on life and with other social problems which may arise . . . . The growth of local church government is leading to a harmonizing of the differences, whether it means elimination or adaptation or assimilation between Christian standards and their former life into a new social structure which is essentially indigenous, but whose heart's core is Christian."[279]

With opportunities in the South Sudan developing so rapidly, it was most welcome news to learn that the Reformed Church in America (RCA) had decided to cooperate with the UPNA in the evangelization of the South Sudan.[280] The first three missionaries appointed by the RCA in 1947 were assigned to Akobo for the work among the Anuak people. It was the beginning of a mission partnership that would continue through succeeding decades.

Still another type of partnership manifested itself in this heyday of expansion. The Church Missionary Society (CMS) of the Church of England, in light of limited resources available from its home church in postwar Great Britain, had decided to confine its efforts in the southern Sudan to the tribal people of the Province of Equatoria in southernmost Sudan. Therefore CMS turned to their American Presbyterian colleagues to assume responsibility for their evangelistic, educational and medical work among the Central Nuer people at Wang Lel, on the Bahr el Zeraf River some distance west of Doleib Hill and in 1947 two UPNA missionary families were assigned to this station. In 1953 still another CMS station at Ler, among the Western Nuer people, was turned over to the American Presbyterians. The partnership with CMS was deepened still further in 1953 when the first ministerial candidates from the tribal churches evangelized by the American Presbyterians were sent to Bishop Gwynne College, the Anglican theological school in **Maridi,** Equatoria Province.[281] In 1955 the college became a partnership between CMS and the American Presbyterian mission, when the first Presbyterian missionary, Rev. William B. Anderson, was assigned to teach there and Presbyterians participated in construction of new buildings.

It was during these comparatively unimpeded years that a daring missionary couple dreamed a great dream, called "the Anuak Project." Don and Lyda McClure, after having pioneered the work among the Anuaks at Akobo in 1938, conceived a plan to evangelize the Anuak people as a whole within the next 15 years. One evident problem was that the Sudan-Ethiopian border ran straight through the Anuak area. While some 20,000 Anuaks lived in the southeast corner of the Sudan, approximately 40,000 lived in Ethiopia along the Gilo and Baro Rivers. "Thus when an Anuak gets in trouble with one government, he simply crosses the border to his friends on the other side and cannot be touched."[282] The Anuak Plan involved concentrating a staff of fifteen missionary units in three different areas of Anuak territory, with five missionary units at each point "with a combined expertise in evangelism, medicine, agriculture, and education." Thus there would be "a concentrated presentation of the gospel in a context of genuine concern for improving the overall quality of human life and a respectful understanding of the indigenous culture."[283]

The McClures pursued the plan with all the vigor and dedication that characterized their missionary careers. They went so far as to secure an audience with His Imperial Majesty, Haile Selassie, who made a significant grant of land along the Baro River for the establishment of a mission station, to be called **Pokwo,** "Village of Light." Later another station would be established on the Gilo River, with school and clinic accompanying the evangelistic work. The McClures and their colleagues devoted themselves to the Anuak Plan from 1950 to 1962. The plan was never fully realized as it was originally conceived, primarily because of lack of adequate resources and personnel. Yet the impact of the concept was great upon those planning mission, and the result was the birth of a strong Christian community among the Anuak people living on both sides of the Sudan—Ethiopian border.[284]

In the midst of such activism, a quiet work was taking place that would have far-reaching consequence. A few veteran missionaries were "partially freed from other duties" to engage in translation of Scriptures and to "teach selected natives how to apply the principles of phonetics to the analysis of their own language." [285] Eventually the translation of Scripture into the various tribal languages (Anuak, Shilluk, Nuer, Dinka, Murle) would have an impact on the growth of the Christian community in the southern Sudan far beyond the bounds of other missionary effort.

EXPANSION IN NORTH SUDAN (1943-1951)

Meanwhile significant developments were taking place in the work in the North Sudan as well. In addition to the Presbyterian mission schools already in existence, American Presbyterian missionaries in 1947 were called upon "to stretch their efforts to embrace the conduct of two girls' schools in the great railway center at **Atbara** [on the Nile north of Khartoum]. These schools, with a history of splendid Christian service under the direction of the Church Missionary Society, would have ceased to exist had not our Mission undertaken their continuance in conjunction with Christian work already carried on through a local congregation of the Evangelical Church."[286] In 1952 CMS asked the American Presbyterians to assume responsibility for the girls' school at Wad Medani: "The Sudan Presbytery has been concerned to save the school from falling into Muslim hands and has contributed a large sum from its funds for the initial cost."[287]

Another significant joint venture in mission with CMS was the establishment of a Christian Center in **Omdurman** in 1949 "for the building up of a Sudanese Christian community upon which all existing work could be based." The center served as a church, a meeting hall, a club and hostel for southerners, a pastor's house, a literary center and a sports area. While the Anglican and Evangelical churches followed their separate traditions regarding the sacraments, every opportunity was taken for joint worship and ministry of the Word. "In work amongst Muslims what we need to ensure is that the small Christian communities are living a common life so far as they can with their Muslim brethren and ministering to them through the activities of the Church in educational and social welfare work. Thus only can they influence the life of the community and draw others into their fellowship."[288]

American Presbyterian missionaries also were assigned to begin work in two other important cities in the North Sudan in 1948: in **El Obeid** to the west, capital of Kordofan Province "on the old slave trail from the South"[289]; and in **Gedaref** to the east, a commercial center near the border of Ethiopia. "El Obeid is the scene of a special effort to integrate the work among South Sudanese and North Sudanese, though this is receiving emphasis in every station in view of the ever growing number of people, some baptized, coming from the pagan south to live in the Muslim north." In Gedaref, "a beginning has been made among the large Ethiopian population by the use of Gospel recordings in Amharic."[290] The geographic base of American Presbyterian mission involvement in the North Sudan also was expanding rapidly.

A little noticed but significant development during this period was the opening of hostels or "clubs" in several large cities of the North Sudan, to provide facilities for education, recreation and fellowship among the young men from the South Sudan who were converging on the cities for education and employment. In time these would become the seeds for congregations of southern Sudanese Christians living in the north. [291]

Thus by the close of this period in 1957, the fruit of the American Presbyterian witness in the Sudan had progressed far beyond what any could have imagined at its beginning in 1940. In the North Sudan, the Sudan Presbytery of the Coptic Evangelical Church had grown to 364 communicant members in seven congregations, with the strongest center in the tri-city area of Khartoum, Khartoum North, and Omdurman, and other congregations in Port Sudan, Atbara, Gedaref, and Wad Medani. Missionary co-workers were also at work at El Obeid and Gereif.

However, the greatest expansion in this predominantly Muslim context was in institutional work. Eight primary schools enrolled 2,296 pupils, and four secondary schools had an enrollment of 287. More than 1100 were registered in Bible institutes, literacy classes, industrial and night schools. A Children's Home at Khartoum North cared for children orphaned by the loss of one or both parents. In Omdurman, American Presbyterians participated in a hospital of the Church Missionary Society of England. The Christian Literature Center in Khartoum published a magazine for new literates and offered a library, reading room and literacy classes for inquiring young minds. Along with these efforts aimed at North Sudanese, the surge of young people from the South had led to establishment of numerous shelters and centers providing basic care and assistance to these who had come from a more primitive tribal environment.

But it was in the South Sudan that the Christian movement had grown most remarkably. The Church of Christ in the Upper Nile, which had become an independent ecclesiastical body in 1956, now consisted of 1013 communicant members and a large unnumbered body of inquirers, gathered in five organized congregations and 24 outpost groups, served by eight ordained pastors and 17 unordained evangelists. This Christian community was spread among five of the tribes in the Province of the Upper Nile, and increasingly served as a unifying force among them. In addition to the evangelistic outreach from these bases, basic educational and medical ministry was being provided in areas where previously they had been non-existent. The beginnings of theological education had been launched in cooperation with the Church Missionary Society through Bishop Gwynne College. Agricultural work had been begun at Akobo, with both basic training and experimental work in farming and animal husbandry. Significant literature work had been initiated through the Spearhead Press in Malakal, "the only mission press in the entire Sudan," and off its presses rolled translations of the Gospels, hymnbooks, and tracts in the various tribal languages, as well as a monthly magazine Light, in English, published on behalf of the South Sudan Christian Council. The introduction of air travel through the arrival of the Mission Aviation Fellowship in August 1950 greatly accelerated the advance of every aspect of the work in this region where transportation had been a formidable obstacle: "The trip by the Sobat River from Malakal to Akobo, which formerly required nine days, can now be flown in one and a half hours." [292]

Meanwhile cooperation among the various Christian missions in the southern Sudan was progressing rapidly. In 1945 the American Presbyterian South Sudan Mission became a cooperating member of the South Sudan Intermission Council. Three years later this Council was reorganized to include Sudanese Christians and became known as the South Sudan Christian Council. In many ways, the future seemed remarkably bright.

CHANGING POLITICAL CONTEXT IN THE SUDAN (1952-1957)

But the political context in the Sudan was changing rapidly. After the Second World War, the uneasy alliance between Great Britain and Egypt in the governance of the Sudan was deteriorating. In 1951, Egypt proclaimed Farouk to be King of Egypt and the Sudan. When the Egyptian Army seized control of its government in 1952, it became evident that Great Britain would need to relinquish its hold on the Sudan as well. Thus as the result of the Anglo-Egyptian agreement in February 1953, elections were held for the Sudanese parliament in November looking toward independence. From the outset it was evident that tensions would be high between the pro-Egyptian party (Khatmiya) and the anti-Egyptian party (Ansar). When Parliament was scheduled to convene on March 1, 1954, with Egypt's President Mohammed Naguib attending, riots broke out leading to massacres on the streets of Khartoum. The bloody history of Sudanese independence had begun.

Concurrently, the people of the southern Sudan were becoming restive under government controlled by the Muslim North. Southerners were promised that independence would mean that they would have a major role in ruling themselves. Instead, by 1954 they found that they were to be ruled, taught, policed and traded with by Northerners. As British officials in the South were replaced by Northern Sudanese administrators, the smoldering hatred erupted in revolt. In August 1955, Southern rebellion in the province of Equatoria led to the massacre of over 400 Northern Sudanese administrators and traders posted in the South, and the flight of many thousands of southern Sudanese across the borders into neighboring countries. The struggle between the North and the South Sudan had begun.

Thus when the flag of the independent Republic of Sudan was raised on January 1, 1956, a very different and troubled era in the life of the peoples of the Sudan had begun. Soon after the Sudanese Parliament was formed in 1953, though religious freedom was "guaranteed", the tide began to turn in the relationship of government to the Christian movement, especially in the South Sudan. In 1955, the government decided that Arabic (which had been a required subject in Junior and Senior Secondary Schools in South Sudan) be the medium for all education. By 1955, permits and visas for new missionaries had become very difficult to secure. Suspicion of the missionary effort as a tool of opposition to the Muslim-dominated government was widespread. "The radical newspapers in the Sudan have insisted that the problems all root in mission education.

They claim that the preaching of Christ in the South has caused an antagonism against the Muslim North which can only be righted when the missionaries are sent home."[293]

On February 13, 1957, all mission leaders and educational workers were called to Khartoum. The newly independent Sudanese government issued an order which would radically affect the future of all Christian work in the southern Sudan: All schools were to be taken over by the Ministry of Education and were required to provide religious instruction for Muslims. With Christian missions no longer in charge of those schools that they had brought into being, the best that they could do was to cooperate wherever possible by providing teachers and headmasters where requested. A glimmer of hope emerged in 1957 as the government requested cooperation of the American Presbyterian Mission in the establishment of a new intermediate school at Obel, financed by government but with the Mission providing the headmaster. It would prove to be one of the last positive experiences in the relation of American Presbyterians with the Sudanese government for years to come.

When the takeover was announced, there were about 300,000 Christians in the South out of a population of four million. Of these, two hundred thousand were Roman Catholic and 90,000 were Protestant, the fruit of the work of five Protestant missions: the Church Missionary Society, the American Presbyterian Mission, the Sudan United Mission, the Africa Inland Mission, and the Sudan Interior Mission. When the action was completed, the government had taken over 51 boys' elementary schools, 350 village or 'bush' schools, and 6 vernacular teacher training centers. For a brief period, the missions continued to operate the schools for girls.[294]

Many missionary teachers had orginally entered the southern Sudan to do pastoral and evangelistic work. When the schools were nationalized, they returned to their pastoral duties. But letters began to arrive from the Ministry of the Interior: "We have taken over the schools. Your services are no longer required. You have two weeks to leave the country." There would follow protests and explanations: "Teaching is not our principal work. We are working with the church." But the expulsion orders were irrevocable. One by one missionaries began to be forced to leave. As the missionary cadre decreased, those remaining increasingly wondered how such a small young church could be prepared for the difficult years ahead.

CHAPTER IV

THE SURGE TOWARD INDEPENDENCE: ECUMENICAL EXPLOSION (1958-1972)

As the various colonial territories in Africa stood poised by the mid-fifties on the brink of independence, American Presbyterians joined other Christian mission agencies in seeking to discern their role in a new Africa.

A. THE RADICALLY CHANGING POLITICAL CONTEXT

Little could they anticipate the rapid pace of change that would be taking place. Between 1957 and 1972, the map of Africa was altered radically, not so much with regard to national borders, which remained substantially the same, but with regard to the status of the territories enclosed by them. By 1972, with the exception of the Portuguese colonies of Angola, Mozambique and several small countries in West Africa, and the last bastions of white supremacy in southern Africa (South Africa, Rhodesia and Southwest Africa), all other colonies in Sub-Saharan Africa had become independent under black African governments.

This period of rapid decolonization and independence was accompanied by several attempts at federation or loose union, with varying degrees of success: British and French Camerouns became Cameroun in 1960; Tanganyika and Zanzibar became Tanzania in 1963; Ethiopia swallowed former Italian-held Eritrea in 1962.

Also, bloody wars ensued as particular regions within nations sought unsuccessfully to secede: Katanga seceded from Congo from 1960 to 1964; and Biafra seceded from Nigeria from 1967 to 1970. Yet the boundaries that had been set by the colonial powers remained very much intact as the era of independence began.

It was Great Britain and France who led the way in moving their colonies toward independence, as well they might, being in control of the largest colonial territories in sub-Saharan Africa. Following the Second World War, both colonial powers undertook a definite liberalization of their colonial policies, though independence in some territories was achieved only after bitter struggle between nationalists and colonial forces. The British colonies in sub-Saharan Africa gained their independence during this period as follows: Sudan (1956); Ghana (1957); Nigeria (1960); Sierra Leone and Tanzanika (1961); Uganda and Gambia (1962); Kenya (1963); Malawi and Zambia (1964); Lesotho, Botswana, and Mauritius (1966); Swaziland (1968). Yet all but Sudan remained members of the British Commonwealth, united by a common allegiance to the Crown, a common language and colonial heritage, and preferential economic and trade agreements.

France sought to integrate her African colonies into a greater French Union. However, widespread independence movements during the 1950s forced France to give up many of its colonies and loosen its control over other possessions. In 1960, the French parliament decided to grant independence to most of its colonies in sub-Saharan Africa, while allowing them to remain in the French Community, a loose economic association that sought to work together in trade, economic aid, and educational and industrial development. Thus strong ties developed drawing together the countries within Anglophone Africa and within Francophone Africa. Belgian Congo, being part of French-speaking Africa, felt the winds of change in its neighboring nations that had been under French control. Yet Belgium did little to prepare the people of its massive colony for the change that inevitably would come. When independence was granted in 1960, the new Republic of the Congo was plunged into a period of chaos and civil war that would plague it for years to come.

Portugal and Spain remained largely indifferent to the changed climate of world opinion and the clamor of their colonial subjects for independence. Spain finally granted independence to its small colony Equatorial Guinea in 1968. It would be 1975 before the will to resist the nationalist forces in Angola and Mozambique collapsed and Portugal reluctantly granted them independence.

Another important feature of the map of independent Africa was a decolonization of nomenclature, as most new nations determined to break their ties to the colonial past by giving new African names not only to the nation itself but also to major cities and other geographic terminology.[295] Still another manifestation of the new political reality was the establishment of the Organization of African Unity (OAU) in 1963, which sought to forge a unity among the new African nations across the differences of tribes, cultures and colonial heritage, and to be an instrument of the new order in Africa. Yet tensions between neighboring nations and tribes plagued the new states, and the OAU struggled with little success to find its own identity and proper place in this new political climate.

Despite the radical changes in the political situation, the newly independent nations found themselves still caught in the web of the colonial economy. The monocultures developed during the colonial period (i.e. cash crops, raw materials and natural resources produced primarily for the benefit of the colonial powers) continued to dominate the economies of most of these nations. Colonial patterns of labor mobility continued, with urbanization growing apace and rural areas suffering the loss of their most promising youth. The rapid growth of cities placed increasing demands on the food crop sector, but with the emphasis being placed on production of export crops, agriculture for domestic needs began to decline, necessitating an increasing dependence on food imports.

While the United States and the Western European community provided some food aid and development assistance, it often seemed that the primary objective was to protect American and European interests rather than to aid African development. The prosperity or poverty of each nation was heavily dependent on the foreign trade terms granted by the former colonial powers. While income received for basic exports fluctuated wildly but seldom increased substantially, the cost of imported manufactured goods climbed steadily, resulting in the new nations having to pay more and more to buy less and less. With the political restrictions of the colonial powers out of the way, transnational corporations increasingly entered the picture, making agreements with inexperienced government leaders that were tremendously profitable to the corporations but often devastating to the people themselves. Little wonder that soon the new nations began to cry out against "neo-colonialism."[296]

CHALLENGES FACING THE CHURCH

Within this revolutionary context, the Christian movement faced the challenge of other strong movements seeking to claim the mind and spirit of the newly independent Africa.[297]

Nationalism—Many names have been given to this new life force which began surging through the African continent in this generation: African Nationalism, Black Nationalism, Negritude, African Socialism. Under whatever term it is known, it was an overpowering force that brought a tremendous release of energy, a sense of purpose and opportunity, a conviction among the common people that a new age had begun. This spirit was given expression in different ways country by country, within the boundaries inherited from the partition of the continent during the colonial era.

The first duty of the various independent governments was to ensure the unity of the nation, to form a common allegiance from the many different tribal groups, with their different languages and levels of economic development. When the cohesive strength of the colonial power vanished overnight, some new symbols of national unity and identity needed to be found that would bind together each nation's fragmented people. The new flags that were raised had behind them at first little more than the negative opposition to colonial rule. Those who rose to leadership found it necessary to develop the "cult of the leader", with all the trappings of power.

Within this context, the Church found itself in a very ambiguous situation. It could not help but rejoice in the movement of the spirit that brought about the liberation of oppressed people from foreign domination. It saw for itself a special role as a reconciling influence within the nation, bringing together the peoples of many tribes into the "New Tribe" of God's people. Yet it could not help but be in tension with the aggrandizement of power by those who stepped into positions of leadership, sometimes with brutal force. In the face of the growing demand for unquestioning loyalty to the new African state, the Church in humility was compelled to address the issues of human rights and of larger loyalties that transcended national boundaries.

Islam—Along with Christianity, another world faith was pressing for allegiance in the new Africa. Having become firmly established in the countries north of the Sahara and within the Sahara itself, Islam was penetrating into sub-Saharan Africa in various ways.

Muslim traders and laborers had come south over the past century, and were to be found in most cities and towns stretching across the arid Saharan belt of Africa and along the eastern and western coasts. In those countries where Islam was predominant, the protective religious neutrality of the European colonial powers had added the authority of colonial government to that of Muslim rulers, thus making resistance to Islam more difficult.

For some leaders of newly independent nations, Islam seemed to provide the institutional basis for national self-expression. It made less demand for change than Christianity in regard to polygamy and the practices of traditional African religions. It offered a more readily evident brotherhood crossing tribal boundaries, without the legacy of attachment to Western colonialism that burdened Christianity. Perhaps the most immediately potent advantage lay in the doctrine of the Islamic State, rather than one neutral toward religion. Not only did this provide a strict legal code to be rigidly enforced, but also a strong political tie to neighboring nations in North Africa and the Middle East.

For the Church in Africa, the encounter with Islam presented a peculiar challenge. How to hold to the conviction that in Jesus Christ God had spoken uniquely to all people and that the salvation He wrought is meant for all, and yet seek genuinely to understand the faith of Muslims, to discern the large amount of common ground shared, and to learn the things that belong to peace? The shadow of the Crusades still lay darkly across the path of mutual understanding, and often that spirit had been reflected on the part of Christian missionaries as well as African preachers. Those places in independent Africa where Muslim-controlled governments made life increasingly difficult for Christian minorities presented especially critical problems. Conflict frequently arose in the frontier zone between areas of Islamic and Christian dominance, as was the case with the civil wars in the Sudan and Nigeria, and the ethnic conflicts in Chad and Mauritania.

This period would find the African churches struggling with the encounter with Islam, and seeking to learn the hard lesson that "the attitude of Christians towards Islam largely determines the attitude of Muslims towards Christianity."[298]

Communism—Within the soil of newly independent Africa, the missionaries of Communism found a receptive seedbed, offering what seemed to be a quick path to the achievement of equality in the face of racial discrimination and economic poverty. Often the followers of Marx manifested a spirit of solidarity with the African people that was lacking among some Christian missionaries. Chief Albert Luthuli, noted Christian leader in South Africa, expressed the feeling of many Africans in responding to the accusation of having been an associate of Communists: "Now we don't know Communism; all we know is that these men and women came to us to help us. I don't deny that some might have ulterior motives; all I am concerned about is that they came to assist us in fighting racial oppression; and they have no trace of racialism or of being patronising—just no trace of it at all."[299]

From a distance, the major Communist countries presented a model that was very attractive to new African nations, as they struggled to deliver their people from illiteracy and widespread poverty toward universal education and industrialization. Both the Soviet

Union and China sought to increase their spheres of influence in the new Africa through diplomatic and economic means, as well as by building up the military might of their African allies. The dividing up of newly independent Africa into two armed camps, with the allies of Western Europe and America on one side and the allies of the Soviet Union and China on the other, bode ill for the future and prepared the way for numerous "proxy wars" both between and within African nations.

The Christian Church in Africa faced a serious challenge in confronting Communism. While the Christian movement had enabled the beginnings of a middle class to emerge, it could ill afford to ally itself solely with that segment of African society. As Dr. A. Aluko of Nigeria contended, "Christians should recognize that it is the revolt of the people against injustice which gives Communism much of its strength. They should seek to recapture for the Churches the original Christian solidarity with the distressed peoples."[300]

African Traditional Religions—Outwardly it would appear that the traditional religions of Africa were rapidly eroding under the onslaught of the faiths and ideologies now contending for the hearts of the African people. This would seem to be especially true with the break-up of village life, where traditional religion regulated the pattern of life for both the individual and the community. The statistics gathered by missionary societies indicated that the number of "animists" was steadily decreasing as the followers of both Christianity and Islam were increasing.

Yet in most of sub-Saharan Africa, beneath the surface of radical political change there continued the steady current of the worldview and social customs created by the traditional religions. As Trimingham commented, "The break-up of traditional religions is apparent everywhere, as is the fact that abandonment of their African religious heritage is only partial and that the springs of conduct of those who have joined one or other of the two available world religions is still that of the old animistic heritage."[301]

In time, the leaders of some of the newly independent African nations would use this African religious heritage as an instrument to call their people to "authenticity" and to throwing off the influences of their Western colonial past. It would be the task of the young African church to deepen its roots in the context of African life and culture, redeeming the best of traditional religious belief so that the Gospel would be clothed in African garb.

Secularism—Over, under, around and through all other forces at work in the new Africa was the irresistible tide of secularism. While few if any Africans would claim secularism as their operative faith (for Africans, "atheism has no meaning and no appeal"[302]), it impinged directly or indirectly upon the lives of all. Suddenly they found themselves caught up in the industrial and technological revolution that had developed in the West over the course of more than a century, welcoming the good that it brought with it, but also experiencing its corrosive power upon traditional society.

Rena Karefa-Smart, Christian leader in Sierra Leone, spoke of secular materialism as "the unconscious missionary faith of the West."[303] Certainly the films, advertisements, literature and broadcasts from the West often were the purveyors of a secular lifestyle that undercut the Christian missionary witness. The task would fall upon the young

African churches to enter into the developing technological society so as to offer spiritual resources that would not only resist the temptations of secularism but also develop a sense of community in the face of the disintegration of traditional tribal life.

THE CHURCH FACING THE CHALLENGES

In this period that saw the surge toward independence, Christianity south of the Sahara was characterized by several common features.

Growth of the Church—The number of Christians continued to mount. The most conservative statistics pointed to a movement claiming adherents in every country in sub-Saharan Africa; in most a significant minority, in some a majority, in the aggregate somewhere near a fifth of the total population. In the overall statistics, the increase of Roman Catholics was greater than that of Protestants. In 1962, it was reported that the number of African Roman Catholics had grown from 5 million in 1931 to some 23 million in 1961.[304] In the same year, Protestants were estimated to total some 11,873,000.[305] Much depended upon the Christian tradition of the former colonial power. Most remarkable was the very rapid growth of the Roman Catholic constituency in the former Belgian Congo, where 6,299,000 Catholics surpassed the number of Catholics in Belgium itself.[306]

Development of African Leadership—Among both Roman Catholics and Protestants rapid progress was being made in raising up an indigenous leadership and in transferring responsibility to it. While this may be attributed to some extent to the pressure of the spirit of nationalism, there was a growing determination on the part of mission agencies to move their work from a mission-based to a church-based approach. In numerous places, various Protestant churches became constitutionally autonomous well before national independence.

The relative place of missionaries in the life of the Church was a critical factor that underwent change, sometimes willingly, sometimes with great stress. There was a marked tendency to maintain the Mission as a corporate entity apart from the Church, with responsibility for the major institutional work such as schools and hospitals. Thus many missionaries related to institutions continued their work as members of the Mission without being an integral part of the life and work of the Church. A factor which delayed the process of devolution from missionary control was the presence of white settlers, especially in Central, Eastern and Southern Africa, where the pressures of settler-paternalism made it more difficult to accept the idea of African leadership. In several places, the continuation of missionary control would prove to be one of the major factors in the birth of Independent African Churches.

In many cases, African church leaders were ill prepared to take on such responsibilities. Only a few had received sufficient theological training to assume leadership in the church and its institutions. Thus with the high-speed revolution which accompanied national independence, churches were often compelled to mark time while African church leaders got the training and experience needed. Meanwhile, the cream of Christian secondary school graduates were being drawn into the ever-multiplying positions of leadership in government and public administration, and the Christian ministry with its meager compensation had become one of the last professions to be considered. That a select group of university graduates did enter the ministry was a tribute to the sense of vocation not only of themselves but of their families.

However, the relative scarcity of ordained clergy did have a beneficial effect in the development of a strong lay witness within the African churches. The multitude of village congregations required lay leadership on a day-to-day and week-to-week basis. A by-product was experience in democratic decision-making by local leaders and elders. In the interval between the old tribal council decisions and those of more recently elected local and regional councils, "the Church was often the only element in African life in which Africans were free to discuss, to reach compromise, to reflect common agreement."[307]

All in all, the Christian church played a very important role in the development of leadership for the new Africa. As *The Ashanti Pioneer*, a newspaper which was in the vanguard of the self-government movement in Ghana, commented: "While we cry ourselves hoarse after self-government and africanisation, the Churches silently but surely are laying solid foundations for these; that is, while we labour and trouble ourselves, africanisation and self-government come smoothly and naturally to the Churches. It is the gift of God."[308]

The Provision of Education—Undoubtedly one of the most significant ways in which the Christian movement impacted the new Africa was through the provision of education. At the time of the meeting of the All-Africa Ministers of Education Conference at Addis Ababa in May 1961, it was estimated that 68 percent of children in school were in schools that were church-managed or church-related. Approximately 33 percent were in Protestant schools, and 35 percent in Catholic schools.

It goes without saying that an enterprise of this magnitude was a heavy tax on the resources of the missions and churches, both in staff and finance. "What had begun in the village church as a bush school with an untrained village catechist teaching a handful of boys to read, write and work sums, with the aid of a cast-off reader from a school in Paris or London and a piece of chalk and the end of a packing-case blackened with charcoal, had become a full school with its own purpose-built classrooms, up-to-date equipment and trained teachers, with fees and government grant to account for."[309]

The rapid and phenomenal growth of the church school system had several consequences. There was an increasing demand for the service of expatriate missionary staff, sometimes at the expense of those services that would strengthen the church itself. There was an increasing reliance on government funding to maintain and expand the schools, making the churches more and more subservient to government regulations and less and less likely to voice criticism of government policies. "A bigger danger . . . was the possibility of the Church becoming so dependent on Government, in the name of cooperation, that it might lose that clarity of perception which was its best gift to the good life of the people." There was a growing tendency to rely upon the church schools, rather than the churches, to be the primary avenue of transmitting the Christian faith. This led at times to mounting pressures of local Christian communities for schools of their own denominations, and then to competition between church schools within the same town or region.

Yet with all these criticisms, it must be recognized that the church schools made an overwhelming contribution to the new Africa. Not only did they plant the seeds of the movement toward independence, but also provided the mental discipline and moral integrity which would be so desperately needed as African nations entered this uncharted new era.

THE MOVEMENT TOWARD ECUMENICAL COOPERATION

At first glance, it would appear that Christianity in sub-Saharan Africa at this point in history was hopelessly fragmented. Four main streams seemed not only separated but often in tension and conflict with one another: the ancient Orthodox Church in Ethiopia and parts of Sudan; the Roman Catholic Church established out of the witness of mission orders and especially strong in those countries where the colonial power had been predominantly Catholic; the plethora of Protestant churches, established by missionaries representing virtually every denomination and mission agency in Europe, Britain and America; and the growing number of indigenous churches, usually offshoots from the mission-established churches.[310]

Yet during this period (1958-1972) there would emerge a strong movement toward closer cooperation among the churches in Sub-Saharan Africa. Several factors can account for this development.

(1) This period saw a peak in the global tidal wave of the spirit of ecumenism. The World Council of Churches Assembly in New Delhi in 1961 brought the full integration of the International Missionary Council into the WCC, as well as the entry into the WCC of four large Eastern European Orthodox churches. Further, the calling of the Second Vatican Council by Pope John XXIII (1961-1965) opened the door for the Roman Catholic Church around the world to consider seriously a much closer relationship and cooperation with the "separated brethren" in other Christian communions.

(2) Another factor that entered into the picture was the surge toward independence among the various African states. This new spirit led the churches, especially the Protestant constituency, to seek a closer cooperation with other Christians within their own nation, as a counterbalance to their relationship with the expatriate mission agencies.

(3) Then there were critical external pressures that would lead to the sense of the urgency of Christian cooperation. For example, Christians in the "frontline" states in southern Africa were faced with the impact of the apartheid regime in South Africa, as well as with the serious refugee problem of persons fleeing from that country. The churches in Sudan and other countries where the Muslim majority gained control of the government made Christian work and witness extremely difficult. Throughout Africa, critical social needs brought about through the drastic change from colonialism to independence necessitated the churches responding in some common manner.

The principal manifestation of this movement toward cooperation was the emergence of Christian Councils at the national and continental level. By the end of this period, National Christian Councils would have come into being in 22 of the countries of Sub-Saharan Africa.[311] True, some 12 of these had come into existence prior to this time; yet all found new life and energy in the wake of independence. Among the 22, there were five in which the Roman Catholic Church was a full participant: three "frontline" states in southern Africa—Botswana, Lesotho and Swaziland; and two in Muslim-dominated countries—Sudan and Uganda.

The range of activities of these councils varied greatly. One common feature was serving as an avenue for the churches to relate to government and thereby to seek peace and justice within the nation. This would be especially needed in Muslim-dominated countries such as the Sudan, where the Christian Council would give the churches a common voice helping them stand against the Muslim tide, while at the same time serving as an avenue through which international ecumenical agencies could work towards some peaceful settlement between north and south Sudan.

Then there were the numerous service programs that could best be accomplished together, with the National Christian Councils providing the avenue through which both denominational and ecumenical mission and development agencies abroad could channel much-needed resources. These would include relief and reconstruction; ministry with refugees; urban and rural development; joint participation in educational, social and medical work; as well as nation-wide programs focusing on evangelism, the family, youth, literature in the new Africa.

The crowning achievement in ecumenical cooperation would be the founding of the All-Africa Conference of Churches. Conceived at a regional gathering of West African church leaders in Ibadan, Nigeria in 1958, the AACC became a reality at its inaugural meeting in Kampala, Uganda, in 1963. Sir Francis Ibiam,[312] the first Chairman of the AACC, referring to the Ibadan meeting, said:

> For the first time in known history, the Churches in Africa had an opportunity to 'discover and love one another, to speak to one another, and to learn something from one another.' In that atmosphere, charged with vision, and inspired by high ideals for Christian service, the Church in Africa woke up from its slumber, so to speak, and realized with great force and intensity the tremendous tasks and responsibilities which were hers in the evangelization of the peoples of Africa.[313]

At the Ibadan meeting, a Provisional Committee was set up to consult with Christian councils and agencies in Africa, with a view to organizing a permanent body. Dr. Donald M'Timkulu[314] was elected the first General Secretary. Between the Ibadan meeting and the Kampala Assembly, M'Timkulu traveled widely throughout Africa, conferring with church leaders and enlisting support for the new Africa-wide ecumenical organization. The movement was greatly strengthened by the support of the newly formed Commission on

Ecumenical Mission and Relations (COEMAR), which came into being after the merger of the Presbyterian Church, U.S.A. and the United Presbyterian Church in North America in 1958. Dr. Clinton Marsh, African-American Presbyterian pastor, was appointed to serve as the organizational secretary for the AACC, and from August 1962 until the Assembly itself in 1963 served at the Mindolo Ecumenical Center in Kitwe, Northern Rhodesia in setting up the structure and program for the first AACC assembly.[315]

The Inaugural Assembly brought together 350 delegates from one hundred churches in forty countries, the most representative gathering of African Christians ever held up to that time. The theme of the Assembly was "Freedom and Unity in Christ." Dr. John Mbiti later would comment:

> There was a frank facing of realities as delegates . . . recognized that after centuries of Christianity in the continent, the churches had not attained selfhood. The pattern of establishing missions had followed largely the colonization pattern of the European powers, control being exercised from the home base. Fettered by the shackles of foreign forms, traditions, and patterns, the church has not yet developed an intelligent recognition of her tasks. She deals in foreign, prefabricated theology. She is a personality that has not yet begun to do her own creative thinking.[316]

By the end of 1964, 56 churches and councils from 20 countries had become members of the All Africa Conference of Churches. Among them were Presbyterian churches in South Africa, East Africa, Ghana, West Cameroun, Rwanda, and Equatorial Guinea. In 1965 the AACC office was moved from Kitwe to Nairobi, Kenya, where it has continued to the present. A strong organization emerged, with Commissions on the Life and Selfhood of the Church; Social, National and International Responsibility of the Church; Literature and Mass Communication; Refugee and Emergency Response; and Economic and Social Development.

Other expressions of the ecumenical spirit in Africa during this period are almost too numerous to mention. As a result of their togetherness in the various councils, church union discussions were begun. Some were successful, as with the United Church of Zambia formed in 1965; others failed, as was the case in Ghana and Nigeria. Then there were the Bible societies, Christian medical associations, ecumenical study groups, Christian literature associations.

The establishment of joint or united theological colleges was especially significant, for the spirit of ecumenism was fostered through training together persons for service in different denominations. Then there were the associations of theological schools, which encompassed Protestant and Roman Catholic seminaries, Bible institutes, university departments of religion and other programs of theological studies. Such associations sponsored conferences and institutes and published Bible commentaries and studies in Christian education and church history. By bringing together African Christian theologians and scholars from across the spectrum of nations and communions, denominational barriers began to erode, the African context was taken seriously and a distinctive African Christian theology began to emerge.

An ecumenical project deserving special mention was the Islam in Africa Project, later termed the Project for Christian-Muslim Relations in Africa. Founded in 1960 with an American Presbyterian missionary, Dr. Donald Bobb, as its first Director, the project began as a channel for expressing the concerns of churches in Africa in their relationships with Muslims. In time it would develop to include dialogue between Christian and Muslim leaders to engage in mutual sharing of ideas and ideals, and to work toward solutions to the deep-seated problems confronting Christians and Muslims in their communal and international relations.

Mention needs to be made of other continent-wide cooperative bodies that came into being during this period. Those churches that were the outgrowth of the so-called "evangelical" missions founded the Association of Evangelicals of Africa and Madagascar (AEAM) in 1966. While limiting its constituency to "evangelical" churches that often were uncooperative with "non-evangelicals" at the local level, the AEAM did become a sounding board for these churches to find their own identity in relation to their founding missions. Then there was the pan-African Roman Catholic organization, known as the Symposium of Episcopal Conferences of Africa and Madagascar (SECAM), which was inaugurated by Pope Paul VI in 1969, with its secretariat in Accra, Ghana. Bringing together Roman Catholic bishops from across Africa, it often joined the predominantly Protestant Christian councils in dealing with such ecumenical themes as human rights in various African countries.

An African Christian leader, John Pobee of Ghana, comments:

> African ecumenism is fragile and has shortcomings. Nevertheless, the ecumenical efforts are an index of the growing consciousness of the church in Africa, of a shared identity as Christians, despite differences of language and denomination, and of the celebration of unity, common faith and commitment in spite of diversity.[317]

AMERICAN PRESBYTERIANS PREPARE FOR THE NEW DAY

The dramatic changes taking place in the churches in Africa were matched by equally dramatic changes in the mission structures of the churches and mission agencies in the United States and Europe. In the forefront of those churches that sought to prepare for the new day was the **United Presbyterian Church, U.S.A. (UPCUSA)**. This church was the fruit of the merger in 1958 of the Presbyterian Church, U.S.A. (PCUSA) and the United Presbyterian Church in North America (UPNA).[318]

The Board of Foreign Missions of the PCUSA had been preparing for an overhaul of its mission structures for some time. The World Consultation called by the Board and held at Lake Mohonk, New York from April 22 to May 1, 1956 was seen as "a notable milestone in the life of the Church. It marked the fruition of 120 years of its sending mission. It also marked the clear recognition that the ecumenical mission is an accomplished fact."[319] With representatives of sixteen related Churches overseas, chosen by those Churches themselves to advise the Board as to how it could best cooperate with them in the future, the Consultation agreed "that ecumenical mission must be pressed at every point", and that every effort must be made to integrate Church and Mission as soon as possible. In keeping with the Lake Mohonk recommendations, several ecumenical mission teams were appointed to visit various areas in order to consummate this integration. As previously noted, one of the first places where such integration would take place was the Cameroun, where in December 1957 the West Africa Mission was dissolved and its work absorbed by the newly formed *Eglise Presbyterienne Camerounaise (EPC)*.

But the major changes would take place with the constituting of the **Commission on Ecumenical Mission and Relations (COEMAR)** by the General Assembly of the newly formed United Presbyterian Church, U.S.A. in May 1958. Actually COEMAR would bring together five former bodies from the uniting churches: the Board of Foreign Missions of the UPNA[320]; the Board of Foreign Missions of the PCUSA; the Permanent Committee on Inter-Church Relations of the UPNA; the Committee on Ecumenical Affairs of the UPNA; and the Permanent Committee on Inter-Church Relations of the PCUSA.

The basic concept for COEMAR would be "mission in unity and unity in mission." Among its objectives would be:

1) participating in a more effective thrust in evangelism from an ecumenical base;
2) helping to prepare leadership for partner churches overseas, e.g. through providing scholarships for study in the U.S.A.;
3) appointing missionaries to serve as "fraternal workers" with partner churches;
4) assisting partner churches in the appointment of personnel for mission service in other countries;
5) receiving persons from partner churches to serve in mission in the United States.

The rationale for these new initiatives was stated as follows: "that mature and independent Churches of Jesus Christ, to many of which our Church is related by historic and fraternal ties, continue to need each other and can assist one another, both materially and spiritually, in a mission which is ecumenical in scope."[321] "Recognizing that history and habit can confine and blind," the Commission established an Advisory Study Committee of which at least two-thirds were overseas churchmen; "over a two-year period this team will assess the present work of the two former denominations, will evaluate the responsibilities, and suggest opportunities which the United Presbyterian Church in the U.S.A. should meet through the Commission on Ecumenical Mission and Relations."[322] The product of the committee's work would be published in 1961 as *An Advisory Study*, and would assist in shaping COEMAR's policies for coming years.

The impact of these new concepts would be felt not only throughout those places where the Commission had inherited mission involvements (some 28 countries around the world) but also in numerous new areas to which COEMAR would become related through ecumenical ties. John Coventry Smith, COEMAR General Secretary, later would recall, ". . . our conception of Africa was enlarged. The U.S.A. church had had missionaries only in the Cameroon and Spanish Guinea, which did not begin to acquaint us with the whole continent. Now Ethiopia and the Southern Sudan had been added in Mission; and in Relations, we were now becoming acquainted with Christians all over the continent, many of whom were Presbyterians whose churches were founded by missionaries from Europe and Great Britain. All this was a mind-expanding experience for the new church."[323]

Recognizing the crucial importance of Africa in this new approach to mission, COEMAR designated 1960 as Africa Emphasis Year and began a review of all contacts with that area. A special Moderator's Conference on Africa was convened, followed by a Moderator's Deputation to West Africa "to carry greetings to churches and to open new contacts."[324] Dr. Edler Hawkins, African-American Presbyterian pastor and Vice-Moderator of the General Assembly, was named the deputation leader; "his presence reflected the American black community's growing interest in Africa."[325] The delegation's travels included not only the traditional mission field of Cameroun, but also Liberia, Ghana and Nigeria, opening the way for the UPCUSA to enter into partnership with churches in these nations.

Probably the greatest impact would be upon the way in which Western churches would conceptualize mission in the future. Sooner or later, most mainline denominational mission agencies in North America and Europe would be following the path pioneered by COEMAR.[326]

Less dramatic but equally significant were the changes taking place in the mission policies of the **Presbyterian Church, U.S**. During the 1940s, the PCUS had experienced a changing climate which was shown in a new enthusiasm for the ecumenical movement. It shared in the formation of the National Council of the Churches of Christ in the U.S.A. in 1950 and accepted membership in the World Council of Churches at the time of its formation in 1948. These changes gradually influenced the policies of the Board of World Missions (which succeeded the Executive Committee of Foreign Missions in 1950), and led to the appointment in 1960 of an ecumenically minded Executive Secretary, Dr. T. Watson Street.

Under Street's leadership, the way was prepared for a major Consultation on World Missions, held in October 1962 in Montreat, North Carolina. "Representatives of our church, our missionaries, Christians from other lands and leaders of the world missionary enterprise met there to advise the Board of World Missions about today's crucial frontiers, about elements of strategy, program and organization. This advice has been taken seriously."[327]

While the PCUSA Lake Mohonk Consultation had placed major emphasis on policies and strategies, the PCUS Montreat Consultation gave particular emphasis to motivation. The Consultation report declared:

We confess that the measure of our discipleship, as demonstrated by our missionary outreach, is unworthy of our Lord. If our church aspires to fulfill its responsibility for meeting the needs of the world in Christ, an increasing missionary corps and increasing financial support will be required.[328]

Nevertheless, the critical question of church-mission relations was thoroughly debated. The outcome was that, instead of adopting a single plan of merging the Missions into the National Churches (as appeared to be the case with COEMAR), joint mission-church committees in each land would work out a plan suited to the particular church. As Watson Street would comment:

The growth of autonomous independent Churches raised questions, faced by all Mission Boards, of Church-Mission relationships. In the "new day" in missions, some boards placed all missionaries under the National Church. The Southern Board adopted no single policy. Affirming the belief that the guidance of the Holy Spirit comes through the national Churches as well as through the Southern Church, it had sought when the issue arose to work out, in cooperation with national Church leaders, what appeared to be the best solution. On the basis of past experience, encouragement was not given to merging of mission and national Church, lest autonomy and self-support be undermined, but was given to the co-operation of mission and Church through co-ordinate committees.[329]

Following up on this approach, consultations would be held with each of the churches which had come into being through the missionary endeavor of the PCUS, and mutual agreements worked out as to how the PCUS could best assist in the strengthening of the life and witness of the partner church.

With regard to its work in Africa, the PCUS would be more than fully occupied with the revolutionary changes that were taking place in the former Belgian Congo. However, it gradually would be drawn into the policy set by UPCUSA/COEMAR and begin to participate in partnership with churches in other African nations, beginning with Ghana.

With this broad perspective on Africa in mind, let us look more specifically at the involvement of American Presbyterians in Christian mission in particular African nations during this critical period.

B. WEST AFRICA

POLITICAL DEVELOPMENTS LEADING TO THE UNITED REPUBLIC OF CAMEROON[330]

Cameroun has been called the hinge between West and Central Africa, connecting the nations to the west, north, east and south, especially those which had been under

French colonial rule and which were now surging toward independence.[331] This placed it in the vortex of the political forces swirling through Africa. Its internal diversity made it subject to the interaction and conflict of numerous pressures: its over 200 tribal groups; its religious diversity, with Islam predominant in the north, Catholicism in the central area, Protestantism in the south, all mingled with African indigenous religions; combined with its troubled colonial history, first under Germany, and then divided between Britain and France. All these factors made for a very volatile mix as Cameroun moved steadily and at an accelerating pace toward national independence.

In addition to these internal forces, external forces were also at work from power groups within emerging Africa seeking to draw Cameroun into their orbit: the pro-Islamic bloc, in which President Nasser of Egypt was the predominant force; the pro-Communist bloc, led by the left-leaning governments of Guinea and Ghana; and the French-speaking bloc, which sought to guard the benefits of the colonial heritage against outside influences.

The story of Cameroun's march to independence is too complex to be told in detail here.[332] Yet it is important to see those aspects that affected the Christian movement generally and the Presbyterian community in particular.

As was noted in Chapter III, new governmental institutions had come into being in May 1957. Cameroun had become an autonomous state under French trusteeship, with its legislative assembly elected by direct universal suffrage, but with its Prime Minister, Andre-Marie Mbida, appointed by the French High Commissioner. The nation chose its own flag, its own seal, and its own national anthem. (The anthem bore a distinctly Presbyterian imprint, since it had been adapted from the school song of the Presbyterian-established normal school, *Ecole Camille Chazeaud*.) French continued as the official language of the new state, assuring its continued participation in the sizable community of nations in Francophone Africa.

However, the government of Prime Minister Mbida (a Catholic) had its troubles from the start. Mbida made the error of maintaining that Cameroun was not ripe for independence, proposing a ten-year program of economic, social and political development at the end of which the situation could be reconsidered. As if this were not enough, his party decided not to include reunification with British Cameroons in its proposal. The Assembly refused to go along with such a plan, and to avoid the Assembly's vote of censure Mbida resigned in February 1958.

Mbida was succeeded by his deputy prime minister, Ahmadou Ahidjo, a Muslim and an adroit politician. Ahidjo formed a government more representative of the numerous political parties in Cameroun. The new Prime Minister's program could not help but please most of the legislators, as it incorporated demands for full internal autonomy, establishing a timetable for independence and reunification with British Cameroons, along with cooperation with France in international matters. Through Ahidjo's skillful negotiation, the French government recognized the Cameroun's option for independence, and the Cameroun Assembly proposed and the United Nations approved the termination of the French trusteeship of Cameroun, to take place on January 1, 1960.

Meanwhile, the proclamation of the coming of independence did not end the terrorism that for years had caused much bloodshed throughout the country. The left-leaning *Union des Populations Camerounaises* (UPC), which had been banned by the French colonial government in 1955, set up its headquarters in Conakry, Guinea, where its leaders had taken refuge, and from that base planned numerous forays into Cameroun. "The UPC wanted nothing to do with leaders appointed by the French. Terrorism spread from the Bassa to the congested Bamileke tribes, the major commercial people of the Cameroun. Killings mounted at an alarming rate. The terrorists were determined to cripple the economy to the point where the French would flee and the other political parties would collapse."[333] Douala and its outskirts, as well as the Bamileke tribal country, were continually attacked during the first nine months of 1960, with more than 3000 people killed. The attacks often were aimed directly at the missions and churches. "In north central Cameroun the radio reported that an African pastor had been beheaded and his head put at the polling place to intimidate those who came to vote. It seemed that his fault was that he had encouraged his people to vote although he did not tell them which way to vote."[334] It was said that in one district, about one out a hundred of the population were killed, and that 3/4ths of Protestant churches, schools, and manses were destroyed.[335] Presbyterians in particular were distressed when, in July 1960, the remote Ibong station was attacked during the absence of the American Presbyterian fraternal worker, and much damage was done by burning and looting. Throughout the country, church activities were greatly hindered when curfew and other restrictions were enforced due to terrorist activity. The UPC revolt continued to flare up especially in the southern and western parts of the country until 1962, when it finally was put down by the government.[336]

Nevertheless, at last, the long-awaited Day of Independence arrived on January 1, 1960. "The Cameroun Army of some three-hundred strong, wearing jaunty green berets, paraded in Yaounde along with the visiting delegations from other countries. Cameroun school and college students also paraded. Overnight the consulates became embassies including the United States."[337] During the Independence Day ceremonies, a choir of 100 students of the Presbyterian teachers' training school, *Ecole Camille Chazeaud*, sang a special rendition of their school's class hymn, which had now become the national anthem of Cameroun. Congratulations from the United Presbyterian Church in the U.S.A. to Cameroun's Prime Minister were read to the assembled crowd:

> United Presbyterian Church in the United States of America congratulates you and your government on the occasion of its independence. We pray God's blessing upon your citizens as they build their new nation and make their contribution to a free world. Having through these years developed friendly relations with the people of Cameroun through a program of Christian mission, we pledge our continued cooperation through the *Eglise Presbyterienne Camerounaise.*"[338]

It was no coincidence that this day on which Cameroun proclaimed its independence was also the day on which the United Nations inaugurated its "Decade of Africa," a decade within which some 31 African nations would achieve their independence.

The Cameroun Presbyterian Church had no small role in the beginnings of Cameroun's new government. Rev. Francois Akoa, Stated Clerk of the Presbyterian Church, was the Protestant representative on the special Government Consultative Committee, which had been asked to assist in the writing of the new Cameroun Constitution. "Partly as a result of Mr. Akoa's work, the Cameroun Constitution recognizes the existence of God by placing the country under his protection. The constitution also declares that the state is to be 'lay,' or neutral, in religious matters . . . . Roman Catholics, Muslims, and Protestants agreed on the inclusion of the name of God in order to have a stronger position against Communist infiltration. Later, under the new Constitution, when 100 members were elected to form a National Assembly, one third were nominal Protestants; in comparison, the highest estimates put the Protestant population of Cameroun at only twenty per cent."[339]

The new Constitution of the Cameroun Republic was adopted by national referendum on February 21, 1960, and general elections to the first National Assembly of independent Cameroun took place on April 10, with Ahmadou Ahidjo elected as first President on May 5. The new nation was admitted to the United Nations on September 20, affirming its place among the family of nations.

Meanwhile, steps were taken to fulfil the second goal of Ahidjo's platform, reunification of the former French Cameroun with the British Cameroons. On February 11, 1961, a United Nations plebiscite was held in the British Cameroons to ascertain the will of the people. In a strange twist, the people of the British Southern Cameroons voted to join the Cameroun Republic in a federal union; however, those in the predominantly Muslim British Northern Cameroons elected to join Nigeria and subsequently became a province of Northern Nigeria. On June 1, when the Northern Cameroon became a part of Nigeria, President Ahidjo proclaimed the day a Day of National Mourning. However, he moved quickly to call a conference to outline the terms for reunification, and on August 14, the National Assembly adopted the revised Constitution of the Cameroon Federal Republic, with Ahidjo as its Federal President. For the time being, regional assemblies served as the basic legislative machinery, with the former British Southern Cameroons becoming West Cameroun, and the former French Cameroun designated as East Cameroun.

However, these welcome political changes were taking place against the backdrop of a rapidly deteriorating economic situation. With about 75% of its economic activity agricultural, Cameroun was dependent upon its export of agricultural products as its major source of foreign exchange. While large plantations produced such export items as bananas and rubber, cocoa was the crop produced by small farmers for their livelihood. As independence was approaching, the foreign market for cocoa fell. "The cocoa-based economy, strong and growing in 1957, turned suddenly downward in 1958. Farmers, for fear of being slain, stayed away from their plantations. Cocoa pods rotted on the trees, and plantations were burned . . . . The weakened economy meant a scarcity of markets and an absence of cash. The old problem of 'no money' was back with a political vengeance."[340] The disastrous state of the economy played a significant part in the later financial problems that arose in the Cameroun Presbyterian Church. Despite all obstacles, President Ahidjo moved steadily toward the consolidation of political power. In September 1966, he accomplished the fusion of the principal political parties of East and West Cameroun into a single national party, the Cameroun National Union (CNU). In October 1969, the three principal trade union organizations merged to become the trade union arm of the CNU. In March 1970, federal presidential elections were held, and Ahidjo was re-elected President, winning 97% of the vote. Then in May 1972, a national referendum was held on the creation of a unitary state; the proposed Constitution received an overwhelming majority. Thus East and West Cameroun, their governments and separate institutions, ceased to exist, a unicameral national legislature replaced the previous regional ones, and the Cameroun Federal Republic formally became the United Republic of Cameroon. Ahidjo had accomplished for Cameroun what few African nations had been able to do during this surge toward independence, a stable government with the beginnings of democracy. With the support of the populace, Ahidjo remained president from independence until he resigned in 1982.

THE FIRST YEARS OF THE AUTONOMOUS *EGLISE PRESBYTERIENNE CAMEROUNAISE* (1958-1963)

The *Eglise Presbyterienne Camerounaise* (EPC, known in the United States as the Presbyterian Church in Cameroun) began its life as an autonomous church with some 83,000 members, 190 churches, 1,250 evangelistic outposts, 92 ordained ministers, and 1,400 evangelists. Its General Assembly was composed of three synods and nine presbyteries. Working with the EPC were some 123 American Presbyterian fraternal workers (making it the largest mission group among the five Protestant mission agencies working in Cameroun), at work in 18 places.[341]

The Church inherited from the Mission a highly developed system of institutions. In the educational field, there were the following:

> 235 Primary Schools, with an enrollment of 28,500;
> 4 Middle and High Schools, with an enrollment of 231;
> A Normal School (*Ecole Camille Chazeaud*), with 187 students;
> Cameroun Christian College, with 291 students;
> Dager Biblical Institute, with 62 students.

In the medical field, there were:

> 6 hospitals and 12 dispensaries, with a total of 1,561 beds;
> 1 leprosarium, and 3 other leper colonies; 1 dental clinic.

With all this responsibility thrust upon it, the church immediately felt the need of a stronger central organization. To help meet this need, the UPCUSA made a gift to the General Assembly of the Cameroun Church that enabled it to build "an adequate and very attractive central office" in Yaounde. "The new building, dedicated on November 15, 1958, has accommodations for the stated clerk's office, with a room for his secretarial staff and filing department, offices for the church treasurer and heads of the Department of Christian Education and Publicity, and a large room for meetings and committees."[342] However, fears were expressed about "the ever present danger of bureaucracy. Patterned as the Church is after the Church in America, it has a tendency to attempt the creation of the many agencies and committees necessary for a large communion of over three million members. The less that 90,000 members of the Cameroun Church cannot afford this top heavy organization."[343]

Also, it was recognized that the long-held missionary insistence on self-support simply no longer could be maintained. "In the concept of ecumenical relations the former idea of complete self-support as a prerequisite to autonomous control is irrelevant. At the same time there is a danger in making the new Church wholly dependent on outside help, cutting it off from the blessings inherent in Christian stewardship. The problem in relations, then, arises in this delicate adjustment of financial aid and control. One can hardly envision the American Church, with its comparatively unlimited resources, standing aloof to immediate and insistent calls for help on the thesis that self-help is salutary and necessary . . . . The self-sacrificing, dedicated Christian, conscious of his responsibilities as a steward of the mysteries of God as well as of His bounty, is the hope of the Presbyterian Church in Cameroun."[344]

Despite these concerns, the *Eglise Presbyterriene Camerounaise*, with the encouragement and assistance of the UPCUSA/COEMAR, was energetically preparing itself for the new day. The change in relationship to the American church was most clearly expressed by the coming of a Commission Representative:

> The new Commission Representative . . . is symbolic of the recently accomplished integration of Church and Mission. No longer the director of the Mission, the present Commission representative introduces himself by explaining, "I am not the director of the Mission, for the Mission no longer exists. You cannot ask me for money, or for missionaries. I can only transmit the requests of your Church.[345]

The most notable evidence of this effort to prepare for a new day was the increasing number of young Camerounians sent abroad for study and experience. They returned to Cameroun with exciting new ideas for the life and work of the church. In relation to the work of the Women's Missionary Society, "The women have organized presbyterials and synodicals with Mrs. Suzanne Tjega holding huge crowds of men as well as women spellbound by the story of her trip to Chile, Brazil, and the United States." In relation to youth work, "Two young pastors have come back from the study of youth programs in France, Switzerland, and America all agog with enthusiasm and plans for the future of youth work in the Cameroun Presbyterian Church."[346] A young pastor, returning from training in Brazil, inaugurated the Audio-Visual Department, so that the church could take full advantage of the free time granted to the Church on government radio, as well as supply the churches with films and filmstrips.[347]

The number of Camerounian students studying at seminaries in France and the United States increased dramatically. Church leaders were sent as delegates to international ecumenical meetings, such as the World Alliance of Reformed Churches and the All Africa Conference of Churches. Teachers from primary school through college went on trips abroad to observe methods that would make them more effective in their work. COEMAR's enthusiasm for these developments was expressed in its 1960 report:

> Asia, Africa, Europe, North America, and South America, were all visited by Cameroun Presbyterians in one year; certainly this will some day help to give this Church a great vision of "the whole inhabited earth." Yet, it soon becomes apparent that these men and women returning from other countries need the advice of fraternal workers who will talk over with them the problems of adapting what they have seen and heard to the needs of their own Church and people.[348]

Meanwhile, the church continued its steady thrust into the hinterlands, primarily through the work of its rural pastors and evangelists. "Across the forests far into the interior of the Cameroun, the good news of the Christian way spread. They carried it down rivers, across hills, over jungle trails. They preached it and sang it, and the drums boomed it through the tropical air like a thunderous celestial anthem."[349] With the majority of its membership in the rural villages and the majority of its ministers having limited theological training, the gap between the grassroots of the church and the national leadership was becoming increasingly strained.

Nevertheless, there was a pervasive enthusiasm in the leadership of the church about the church's life and ministry in the years ahead:

> "God has given our Church so much, so much! This I must mention in my report to the General Assembly." So ran the comments of Moderator Jean Andjongo who returned late in November [1960] from a trip to Nigeria and a visit to the Presbyterian Church in [southern Cameroons], under British Trusteeship until February 1961. Moderator Andjongo recognized the great responsibility of the Cameroun Presbyterian Church to its sister Presbyterian and Reformed Churches. "I don't know how, yet, but I must report at Efulan, in January 1961, to our General Assembly, that we must learn to serve the other Churches of Africa."[350]

Meanwhile, the **institutional work** established by the American Presbyterian mission struggled to adapt itself to the new day. Problems related to the load of hospital and school administration placed upon the church led to the establishment of a Council of Institutional Administration "as an attempt to handle these problems outside the courts of the church."[351] However, this still did not relieve the church of its heavy responsibility.

> The church's first generation of converts—they memorized the hymns, the catechism, and the Scriptures—found Christianity to be deeply meaningful. The second generation asked the inevitable . . . question: What is the church's usefulness? The answer was obvious—the school and the hospital.

> This development—it is basically similar from one end of Africa to the other— was bound eventually to lead the Christian church to ponder its own *raison d'etre*. These humanitarian services of the church, legitimate and necessary in their own right, would grow into elephantine proportions before independent African nations could take them under wing. Consequently, that which was never the primary message of the church was to become the grounds upon which the church was to be judged.[352]

The **medical work** especially felt the urgency of training Camerounaise personnel to take responsibility for the extensive medical program that American Presbyterians had developed to serve the critical health needs of the people of the southern part of Cameroun.

> United Presbyterians had built an extensive hospital network in the Cameroun. In addition to the Elat Hospital and its unique (for Africa) Weber Dental Clinic, the Medical Council of the Cameroun Church administers work at Njazeng, Sakbayeme, Ibong, Bafia, Metet, and Nkol Mvolan. These hospitals are not only centers to which persons come for healing, but are also places from which an outreach in preventive medicine, sanitation and medication is mounted. The jeeps of doctors and nurses go bumping regularly along roads of surrounding villages.

> [However these medical institutions] had no Camerounaise doctors or senior administrative workers. During the colonial period, Camerounaise were not allowed by government to be trained for professional and supervisory positions. Though young men all over the country hastened to equip themselves for entrance into medical schools, there is an inescapable time-lag in which qualified medical practitioners are not available.[353]

The UPCUSA Leadership Development Program enabled a select group of young people to study medicine in France, with a view to their taking positions of leadership in the hospital network. Meanwhile, those who had received training as *infirmiers* were called upon to fill the urgent need for administrative leadership, along with EPC pastors.[354] The UPCUSA's Fifty Million Fund was called upon for construction and badly needed repair of the six hospitals and twelve dispensaries, as well as for housing for Camerounaise staff.

The doctors serving as medical fraternal workers found themselves in the difficult position of seeking to apply their advanced medical training and experience, while working under the administration of inadequately trained medical personnel. Nevertheless, their accomplishments were remarkable.

> Dr. Frank W. Newman, veteran missionary doctor in the Cameroun, has written: "In recent years, a chapter of medical history has been written on the eradication of sleeping sickness, the disease that only generations ago was wiping out whole villages but now is on the way to becoming a medical curiosity. Credit for this belongs to the French government doctors, Presbyterian medical missionaries and their African medical assistants, all working together. Another chapter well started is on the control of yaws, a disease that once covered so many thousands of children with sores, leaving many permanently crippled; again by the same team, with their bright new tool, penicillin. The next chapters, it is hoped, will be on leprosy, or the control of fecal-borne diseases, or both."[355]

Particular mention needs to be made regarding the work of Dr. Evelyn Adams, who was serving as Director of the hospital in remote Nkol Mvolan. As the only modern hospital in a wide area, it found itself waging war on all the diseases that plagued tropical Africa. Yet under Dr. Adams' leadership, it added to its ministry as a 130-bed hospital a school for training medical assistants and a school for training nurses' aides. Clinics were conducted in the bush country around Nkol Mvolan, with special attention to pre-school clinics providing regular treatment for malaria, intestinal parasites, and childhood virus diseases.

Dr. Adams' special commitment was to her work with mothers. After many years of planning and hoping, her long-held dream became reality.

> October 10, 1962 was a red-letter day. Our beautiful modern maternity hospital was finally finished and dedicated. It had a modern delivery room, four private rooms with plastic cribs, a large ward with ten beds and also plastic cribs for the babies, and an incubator (run by kerosene) for use when we had a premature baby delivered . . . . The beds were soon filled. One reason was that we had had a great increase in the number coming to our prenatal clinic, which had become even more popular due to the fact that we were giving preventive immunizations against tetanus. Previously we had had a number of cases of tetanus in newborn babies who had been born in the village and had had mud smeared on the umbilical cord. Now, even though the mother did not come to the hospital for delivery, the baby was protected.[356]

In relation to **educational work**, primary education presented some of the most urgent challenges and opportunities. While the country as a whole faced a 90 percent illiteracy rate, in southern Cameroun where the Presbyterian work had been concentrated an estimated fifty percent of the population under forty was literate. The Central School Office of the EPC General Assembly, with a Comerounian director and staff, supervised a rural primary and elementary school system employing more than 400 teachers, instructing more than 30,000 students.[357]

Keeping these schools provided with competent teachers was a formidable task, to say nothing of the funding. The Camille Chazeaud Normal School at Foulassi, which in 1960 was turned over to a Camerounian Director, Simon Ngo'o, sought as best it could to respond to this need. "Our students come from all the regions of Southern Cameroun in which our Church works . . . . Some have also come from Northern Cameroun where the Norwegian and Sudan Missions are working." Most courses by now were being taught by African teachers, though the teaching of the French language was done primarily by French-speaking professors from France and Switzerland. "Most of the students coming out of our school after a more or less thorough education go and work as State employees, generally as teachers, which is understandable. But they can be found everywhere: commerce, municipal staff, National Assembly, central administration, from Assistant Administrator to Minister. Our former students were the pioneers of independence and unification of Cameroun."[358] Thus, while the school was fulfilling a very important function by providing leadership to meet the needs in the life of the nation, it had difficulty providing enough teachers for the church's primary school system, since its graduates were paid more elsewhere than in the EPC schools.

In addition to primary education, the church's educational system also sought to equip young people for occupations that would better their livelihood in this rapidly changing society. The Rural Training Center at Libamba drew young people from the ten Presbyteries of the EPC, training them in agriculture, as well as poultry raising and animal husbandry. The Frank James Industrial School at Elat was training village youth in carpentry, masonry, mechanics, and other skills, "constantly adapting its program to meet the needs of modern Africa."[359]

Along with these institutions, the Cameroun Presbyterian Church, with the assistance of United Presbyterian personnel and funding, sought to prepare persons to meet the critical need for administrative and professional positions in the new Cameroun. Chief among these efforts was the Cameroun Christian College at Libamba, at this time the only Christian college in French-speaking West Africa. Several missions and churches cooperated in support of this ecumenical secondary school that prepared students for entrance to university. In 1963, the college installed its first Camerounian principal, who had obtained his Master's degree abroad under the sponsorship of the United Presbyterian Leadership Development program.

As was the case with the medical work, the capital needs of this vast educational system were enormous, as buildings were needed for new ventures and those at the older institutions were deteriorating or had "never been adequately built nor equipped completely." In remote outposts such as Momjepom, "the long distance over which materials must be transported, over bad roads and across flooded rivers, adds to building costs."[360] Little wonder, then, that there was an urgent call for funding from the UPCUSA's Fifty Million Fund.

Theological education for the training of ministers and other professional church workers continued to be a top priority for the EPC. Dager Biblical Seminary at Bibia continued to be the primary instrument for this purpose. Its entrance requirements were on a par with those of most seminaries in Africa, enrolling students with a high school education. With approximately sixty students studying under a seven-member faculty (both African and American), Dager prepared the majority of those ministers who would be serving the EPC churches. The capital fund request for Dager Seminary was the largest among those made by the EPC to the UPCUSA's Fifty Million Fund.

There continued to be a need for evangelists to serve the small Christian communities scattered through rural Cameroun, as well as to reach into new villages. To meet this need, the church maintained several presbytery Bible Institutes, training persons who were not equipped with the basic education necessary for study at Dager Seminary.

But there soon was recognized the need for church leadership with a higher education that would equip the church for the challenge of the new day in Africa. The first All-Africa Conference held at Ibadan, Nigeria in January 1958 lifted the horizons of African church leaders from local concerns to the larger African Christian community. There emerged the plan for a Faculty of Theology at university level for ministerial students from across French-speaking Africa, "from Dakar to Brazzaville, from Donaky to Bangui."[361] "When independent republics within the French Community of Nations, covering huge areas of West Africa, are coming into being, the importance and timeliness of this move can well be imagined."[362] The idea was given additional impetus with help from the Theological Education Fund, established at the Ghana Assembly of the International Missionary Council (1957-58) to advance theological education among the churches of Asia, Africa and Latin America.

At last, the dream became reality as the United Theological Faculty was opened in Cameroun's capital city Yaounde in February 1962. The new faculty was formed of teachers representing the six nations in the Federation of Churches in West Africa, as well as missionary co-workers. Serving on the faculty was UPCUSA fraternal worker Dr. William D. Reyburn, who taught in the seminary's Africa Studies Department.

> In a questionnaire sent to seminary teachers and African specialists relative to the creation of an African Studies Department in this seminary, the opinion was nearly uniformly expressed that the African church should consider African studies as an essential phase of seminary training to enable young African pastors to view more systematically the nature of African society and life. The results of this survey also generally maintained that the African church should relate itself more dynamically to its own cultural heritage in such aspects of ethics, church government, and methods of evangelization.[363]

Still other **ecumenical ventures** were initiated at this creative time in the life of the churches of West Africa, aided by COEMAR. In 1960, a Protestant school of nursing was opened at Douala, offering a regular R.N. degree, the first in Cameroun. In 1961, a Protestant bi-weekly newspaper, *La Semaine Camerounaise*, was founded, and soon was expanding its circulation beyond Cameroun to the rest of French-speaking West Africa.[364] Then, in August 1963, the EPC, affirming the vision of its young leaders, joined the World Council of Churches. The spirit of ecumenism appeared to have carried the day.

While COEMAR was assisting in all these developments in the life of the Camerounian church, still other **special initiatives** were being taken by COEMAR itself. Interracial youth work camps to Africa were undertaken under the leadership of Dr. James H. Robinson, pastor of the Church of the Master in New York City. One such work camp in Cameroun brought together 15 young Americans and a like number of African youth to build a schoolhouse in a remote village in East Cameroun, Beul.

> It was rugged at first. The villagers were too shy or too unbelieving to cooperate, but after some days of doubt the enthusiasm, sacrifice, and hard work of the campers broke down all opposition. The local people, united as never before, joined forces with the visitors. The school was completed and used as a dormitory. The old mud and thatch church was demolished. A month later, there was a new permanent church built from the foundation to the roof at Beul, the isolated village in the African bush. Not complete, but adequate, the building was dedicated the final Sunday of the work camp. During an impressive service attended by hundreds of interested people of the community, several of the young campers and their African associates publicly dedicated their lives to the service of Jesus Christ. One of the campers, a nurse, decided to stay as a short-term fraternal worker, filling an important post in a Church hospital.[365]

COEMAR also took the initiative in sending special advisors to assist the EPC in particular aspects of its work. In 1959, Dr. Henry Jones visited Cameroun to assist in strengthening an Industrial Evangelism program in the rapidly developing industrial city of Edea. In 1960 Dr. Frank T. Wilson, Education Secretary for the Commission, visited Cameroun to provide advice and counsel regarding the educational problems from primary schools through theological education and "revealed that adjustments to new situations do not come automatically." In the same year another African-American UPCUSA leader, Mrs. Thomas E. Wilson, a member of the National Executive Committee of United Presbyterian Women, "charmed the hearts of Cameroun Presbyterians . . . [as] she went from place to place, encouraging with her quiet smile the women's growing work." Also in 1960 the Rev. Paul R. Lindholm, stewardship education specialist, spent five months in Cameroun, assisting the EPC in making 1961 a special Stewardship Emphasis Year.[366]

Despite all the problems of developing nationhood and increasing administrative responsibility in the church, COEMAR was entering this strategic and critical period in the life of the EPC "in full hope and Christian love, knowing that God is at work, building his Church in Cameroun and 'the gates of hell shall not prevail against it.'"[367]

A TIME OF TRIAL (1964-1967)

By 1964, the numerous points of tension that underlay the changes taking place in the *Eglise Presbyterienne Camerounaise* began to take on serious proportions. "Any progress in the Cameroun Presbyterian Church has almost been overshadowed by its crises in 1964."[368]

The first crisis was **within the EPC itself**. The younger leadership of the church, with the encouragement of COEMAR, pressed ahead in its ecumenical approach. In 1964 church union discussions were begun with two neighboring churches of the Presbyterian-Reformed family in the former British Cameroons (which now had become West Cameroun): the Presbyterian Church in Cameroon, the fruit of the work of the Basel Mission of Switzerland; and the Evangelical Church of Cameroon, the fruit of the work of the Paris Mission of France. "Although early indications were of a hasty union, it now becomes evident that considerable time will be spent in studying the situation. In the meantime, definite plans are being made for uniting seminaries of these three Churches. The combination of student body and staff should produce one strong seminary at the undergraduate level."[369]

COEMAR also encouraged the EPC in the development of other cooperative ventures in such areas as audiovisual programming, literature, medical education, and agricultural program. However, it was acknowledged that "the proper relation of these to the program of the *Eglise Presbyterienne Camerounaise* has not yet been developed."[370]

Meanwhile, there was a growing element within the EPC expressing dissatisfaction with the ecumenical movement and suggesting withdrawal from the World Council of Churches. The communication gap widened between Church leaders who attended the ecumenical conferences and the mass of Christians, both lay and clerical, who were not aware of the forces that were transforming the Christian movement in Cameroun and across Africa. Numerous meetings were held in the Bulu area to win elders and ordinary church members to the anti-ecumenical side. The mood of the dissident group was strongly expressed in a letter to COEMAR from a Camerounian minister, the Rev. J.C. Obam Eteme, dated February 1, 1966:

> Ever since ecumenicity interfered with our church in January 1963, the work that went on in harmony between us is now becoming faulty and despicable . . . .
> The General Assembly is becoming secular. It is letting itself be torn apart by two opposing parties. The party supported by the white man is often victorious because the Moderator becomes his puppet and he forgets he was elected by the whole Assembly . . . .
>
> Ecumenism is a neo-colonial movement in our church and is the instrument with which the mother church is taking away the young church's personality

in order to subject it to the inter-ecclesiastical movement . . . . Ecumenism has already given birth to an asexual child in the name of church union . . . .

Even our Dager Seminary is mortally bitten by this viper called fusion which at the moment is advancing, mouth open, jaws threatening the EPC herself, so-called mother of the Seminary. After having had her Presbyterian personality swallowed up, she will have nothing of her own anymore. Woe to the future generation of our dear church which will have no more fine theologians coming from this fusion of seminaries.[371]

Finally, the dissension led to division, and schism took place at the 1967 EPC General Assembly. Dr. Evelyn Adams was present and records the experience:

In January, now accepted as a member of the church council, I went to Elat for General Assembly. It was a sad meeting, for there was discord, and on the morning of January 12, 1967, seven pastors and thirteen elders left the Assembly and formed a new church, the Cameroun Orthodox Presbyterian Church. Among those leaving were Martha Ebutu, the big leader of the Women's Association, and her husband, who had long been a pastor at Batanga. This was a great blow, as many of the faithful members of the Women's Association joined the new church, but those remaining fell together with a will, vowing to keep alive the Cameroun Presbyterian Church, and they succeeded. True, there was a sharp decrease in membership in the Elat, Batanga, and Metet regions, but the church survived.[372]

The pastors and elders withdrawing from the General Assembly soon were joined by others until approximately 12 pastors and several thousand members had left the EPC to form the Cameroun Orthodox Presbyterian Church. However, they took the point of view that they were the true and original EPC, and their Stated Clerk sent letters and circulars to Government officials and others, seeking to gain their official recognition. Banks were advised by the COPC Stated Clerk not to honor checks signed by the EPC Treasurer. The regularly elected officials of the EPC were obliged to defend themselves in court against these false charges.

Eventually the COPC strategy backfired. Government authorities, seeking to promote unity in the nation and interpreting disunity of any kind as a subversive movement, forbade the COPC congregations to meet for worship. For over a year, hundreds of their constituents had no public church services. Unfortunately, about the same time a conspiracy to overthrow the government was being rumored. Some high government officials came to the conclusion that the COPC movement was part of the same plot, and the dissident pastors were arrested for subversion. They were accused of having sent false telegrams announcing that they had won the court case, when actually the case had been decided in favor of the EPC. Their imprisonment, which in some cases included brutal beatings, created a legacy of bitterness between the two churches and their leaders that would linger for years to come.[373]

As far as the EPC was concerned, the withdrawal of the separatist group had little effect on the structure, administration and ongoing work of the Church. "Leaders of the Church at Presbytery, Synod and the General Assembly meetings all remarked on the peace and unity within the Church since the dissidents had withdrawn."[374] However, at the local level, in the pockets of resistance where the churches had split, concentrated around the older fields of mission activity such as Elat, Foulassi and Metet, the results were tragic. Pastors in the same clan would be found on opposing sides of the controversy. In one case a father, one of the oldest active ministers in the EPC, remained in the Church, while his son, one of the most active in the separatist movement, would not have anything to do with his father. When the division first took place and the majority in a village congregation withdrew, there were cases where the church furniture was destroyed and those remaining loyal to the church were forcibly detained from entering the place of worship. In retaliation the minority would report the incident to local authorities, resulting in more imprisonments and endless legal procedures, all interpreted as persecution.

With the lapse of all church activity in those places where the dissident group was predominant and the Government had forbidden all gatherings for worship, many of the church members fell into laxness not only in their religious life but also in their personal conduct. "One wonders whether the withdrawal from the Church was, in some cases at least, an excuse to return to the old way of life . . . . A generation is growing up without spiritual guidance, nothing but hate and animosity to demonstrate Protestant Christianity, to the amazement of their Roman Catholic and pagan fellow villagers."[375]

Fed by the hope that a new independent Presbyterian Church would soon be recognized by the government, and with promises of new church buildings, new missionaries, and new sources of funding from the McIntyre group in the United States ("promises [which] have resulted in nothing but disillusionment and heartache"[376]), the dissident Presbyterian pastors remained firm in their decision to continue apart. However, gradually some of the disaffected members returned to their former churches. As one former elder said, "Our bodies, souls and minds are sick and weary of being away from the Lord's house with no food for our souls. We long for the fellowship of believers in Jesus Christ."[377]

By 1967, largely as a result of the withdrawal of members who joined the Cameroun Orthodox Presbyterian Church as well as disillusionment with both sides, the membership of the EPC had declined to approximately 72,000.

*   *   *

Concurrently crises were arising **between the EPC and the UPCUSA**. Early in 1964, it became evident that there was a financial crisis in the Church, revealed through the misuse of the considerable funds transmitted from the UPCUSA to the EPC. The EPC Treasurer implicated certain Church leaders. Immediate investigation, the request of an audit, and the appointment of a special commission to deal with particular problems straightened out some aspects of the crisis, but the integrity of the Church leaders involved remained unresolved.[378]

COEMAR developed some new financial practices supporting certain activities directly through special bank accounts and transferring funds with clear designation. A new financial structure which would reduce the amount of subsidy to the central structure of the Church was established, and certain aspects of the work of the Church were "set free" from funding from the U.S.

COEMAR developed some new financial practices supporting certain activities directly through special bank accounts and transferring funds with clear designation. A new financial structure which would reduce the amount of subsidy to the central structure of the Church was established, and certain aspects of the work of the Church were "set free" from funding from the U.S.

At the same time, a crisis arose in the **medical work**. Reyburn comments:

> Among the many committees created was the medical committee, a group of pastors, medical assistants, and two missionary doctors. The church was not long in awakening to the fact that the mission, like a rich uncle, had died and the inheritance was waiting.
>
> Salaries began to zoom, and the union leaders, now gaining more control within the [Central] hospital, began to defy the church . . . . Having boosted salaries without considering other expenses, the medical committee had put Central Hospital four million francs in the red. In order to cover the debt, the medical committee decided to reduce the budget by dismissing fifteen more staff members. This time nine of the fifteen sued Central Hospital for a total of nine million francs ($36,000).[379]

In an effort to salvage the situation, early in 1964, the post of Medical Director for Cameroun was established by COEMAR and a UPCUSA fraternal worker doctor was appointed to the post. This office established contact with the government ministries and clarified some administrative rules of procedure for the hospitals. However, resenting this move, the Camerounian medical workers (*infirmiers*) began accusations against the American doctors, a problem complicated by the fact that there were not as yet any Camerounian doctors prepared to work in the church hospitals. Accusations against the fraternal worker doctors were sent to the government and to the General Assembly of the Cameroun Church.

The problems reached a peak in November 1964, when the Commission's Associate Medical Secretary visited Cameroun. COEMAR notified the EPC that administrative changes for the medical work were necessary and requested that the Church share with the Commission in appointing a special committee to resolve these administrative problems, to prepare plans, and to see that they were properly implemented. Also, a letter of resignation was signed by all fraternal worker doctors, unless some changes were made in hospital administration.

During 1965, a special Administrative Council for Medical Work was established, with three representatives appointed by EPC and three by COEMAR. The Council included two members not employed by the EPC nor related to the UPCUSA: an African physician Dr. Samuel Abane, and an African Hospital Administrator Mr. Samuel Mabom, both EPC laymen. The report to COEMAR of the work of the Administrative Council included the following:

> I cannot emphasize enough the importance of having on this committee the two African laymen and the contributions they made. The EPC has never used its laymen on church boards or committees before and I think the employees of EPC, Pastor Meye [EPC General Secretary] and Francois Yinda [*Infirmier-chef*], were very much aware of the contribution their fellow Africans were making. I would consider this an excellent precedent for the Commission to urge EPC to use more of its excellent laymen on its Church Councils.[380]

Members of the Administrative Council visited with several government officials, who "seemed very anxious to maintain good rapport with all mission work in the country and were very cognizant of the contribution of missions to the Health Department's work."[381] From these officials the Council learned that there were 27 government hospitals throughout the Cameroun providing a total of 6,500 beds, while there were 4,300 beds in private hospitals, the majority of these in mission hospitals. Also, there was a total of 139 doctors, 53 of these African, 36 missionary doctors and 50 French military doctors. Further, the government was planning a medical school to be established in Yaounde, sponsored by four African countries, Cameroun, Chad, Gabon and the Central African Republic. What was becoming apparent was that the day when mission hospitals provided the basic health care for Cameroun would soon come to a close.

The Administrative Council also visited several of the mission hospitals: at Enongal (Central Hospital), at Bafia, and at Sakbayeme. At Central Hospital, "the *infirmiers* had requested a meeting with us and this was done. The spokesman for the *infirmiers* apologized for the bad mistakes of *infirmiers* since the church had become independent and he spent many words and minutes assuring us that this particular group of *infirmiers* wanted their fraternal worker doctors and additional nurses. They also assured us that they would do everything they could to cooperate with the new Administrative Council."[382]

The result of the work of the Administrative Council was the proposal for a new constitution for the medical work "follow[ing] the form for French constitutions and hav[ing] the wording in proper French form." The medical work would be under a Council for Administration of Medical Work in the Cameroun, with a majority of the members from the medical profession ("there is still a big question as to what will happen among the pastors for whom the new council means some loss of power").[383]

By 1966, the EPC Medical Department, under the leadership of fraternal worker Dr. H. Wallace Greig, would report to the EPC General Assembly: "… the period of dependence on the Presbyterian Church in the United States has finished not only with regard to finances but also to the unique kind of dependence on the USA for state doctors and nurses."[384]

The arrival of an American hospital administrator in 1966 "with extensive knowledge of the subject . . . makes us hope that we will now see the end of disorder and have a well organized program." At the same time, the number of doctors and nurses sent from America would plunge to an all-time low, with only Dr. Jack Payne at the Central Hospital in Enangal and Dr. Evelyn Adams at Nkol Mvolan. The training programs for nurses and nurses' aides would come to an end. Since supervision of all the hospitals and dispensaries was no longer possible, several dispensaries were forced to close, and personnel at several hospitals was sharply reduced. The hope for well-trained African doctors seemed far away: "There are students in the Medical Faculties at Dakar, in France and in America, but we can't know when they'll come back and indeed if they will accept to work for the Cameroun Presbyterian Church at all."[385] All in all, the outstanding record of medical work that had been established in Cameroun by American Presbyterians now seemed to be in shambles.

While the **educational work** established by American Presbyterians did not undergo as traumatic an experience during this period as did the medical work, it felt keenly the strains of this time of transition. Especially stressful was the struggle between primary and secondary education. The vast network of primary schools that had grown up around the EPC churches scattered across southern Cameroun drew heavily on the limited resources of the church. From the viewpoint of COEMAR, the greatest need was for stronger emphasis on secondary education, and even within this field, to concentrate on specific institutions.

> Seeking to assist the church in making the difficult decisions necessary, in 1966 COEMAR sent to Cameroun an Evaluation Team to study and report on the whole educational system related to the EPC. The team's report to COEMAR included the following:
>
> There were many similarities in the conditions that were observed at various institutions. In all of them there were evidences of inadequacy in teaching staffs and insufficiency of financial and material resources . . . .
>
> The Church is attempting to carry on an educational program in a setting where government and various private agencies are at work also. It is important to have an understanding of the capability of the Church to maintain educational institutions and to help in meeting the educational needs of the nation and, at the same time, to fulfill the unique objectives of the Church without lowering the standards of its distinctively educational efforts . . . .

The matter of most serious urgency is the unsatisfactory relationship between the Directions for Primary Schools and Secondary Schools and the local schools and colleges . . . . The condition cannot be corrected by minor changes or superficial patchwork. It requires a fundamental change in philosophy of work and a reorganization of structures and procedures so as to deal with local institutions helpfully through a national secretariat.[386]

It was evident that the educational system established through the American Presbyterian mission effort and now under the supervision of the Cameroun Presbyterian Church was falling behind the system established by the Camerounian government, and that the Church was not certain as to its role in education for the future.

*   *   *

A third area of crisis which arose during this time of trial was **within the American Presbyterian family** itself, specifically in the relationship of the Commission on Ecumenical Mission and Relations with its missionary personnel serving in Cameroun. The first signs were appearing in the early 60s. The 1961 COEMAR report to the General Assembly stated:

Some frustrations among fraternal workers resulted in the resignation of two couples. This together with retirements and the untimely death of Miss Valentine Rochat, girls' high school teacher, depleted the ranks of fraternal workers more than they were filled by replacements. The Cameroun Presbyterian Church still calls for men and women determined to join the battle for Christ in Africa.[387]

In 1964, a delegation from the UPCUSA met with the General Council of the Cameroun Church and agreed that there should be a program for a cutting back in fraternal worker personnel and the introduction of a crash program for development of leadership in the Cameroun Church. By 1965, the situation of fraternal workers in Cameroun had become critical. The COEMAR Report for that year stated:

The relationship of the fraternal workers in the Church presents a difficulty in itself . . . . It becomes evident that the Church has not found the way in which it can establish its rapport with the American group, and the latter have felt great uncertainty in their relationships with the Church. Fraternal worker morale has reached a low point over a number of circumstances. It has been the intention of the Commission to reduce the number of personnel, but the way in which this can be done with study, with understanding, and with some sense of strategy, has not yet been discovered. Therefore, there has been a depletion of personnel through reassignment, through resignation, and without any new appointments, until the situation begins to clarify.[388]

The situation of fraternal workers in Cameroun was but a reflection of what was happening in numerous places across Africa, and indeed around the world. The assumption of more responsibility by younger churches, combined with inflation in the West, increased cost of missionary maintenance and rising living standards overseas, was bringing a steady reduction of missionary personnel. In light of the changed circumstances, in 1966 COEMAR began a new system of missionary appointments: personnel were appointed for specific periods of years for particular assignments agreed upon with the inviting Church, the length of the appointment geared to each situation. The "career service" concept was possible only through a series of appointments. Also, a personnel development interview program was introduced for those already overseas, involving self-evaluation, evaluation by others, and an interview with a counselor. "It was felt that this would make for a more flexible and efficient use of personnel in a fast-changing world."[389]

As a result of all these external and internal factors, the number of UPCUSA fraternal workers serving in Cameroun declined dramatically during this period. Whereas there had been 123 persons under appointment in 1958, by 1967 the number had declined to 62, and by 1972, to 30.[390]

Truly, the mid-sixties were a time of trial for the *Eglise Presbyterienne Camerounaise*, as well as for the UPCUSA in its efforts to find the most effective way of cooperating for the advancement of the Christian movement. The 1967 COEMAR Report reflected:

> The problems which face the Cameroun Presbyterian Church will not be resolved easily. Part of them root in the particular problems which face Africa today, part of them root in the structure of the Church, but the great majority of them root in the method by which the integration of Church and mission was undertaken.[391]

Veteran missionary Dr. Robert Peirce, reflecting on the first decade of the Cameroun Presbyterian Church (1957-1967), would write:

> There were plenty of occasions when one with vestigial remnants of paternalism might have taken an I-told-you-so attitude. Unqualified personnel were frequently elected to important positions or given scholarships abroad. Relations with fraternal workers were strained at times. There was mismanagement of funds. And surely a delegation from COEMAR will not soon forget two days of deadlock with the General Council of the EPC over the question of transfer of properties! . . .
>
> [Yet] as the EPC enters its second decade it does so with much promise and confidence, "for building up the body of Christ, until we all attain to the unity of the faith and of the knowledge of the son of God" (Ephesians 4:12-13).[392]

THE BEGINNING OF HEALING (1968-1972)

As the tensions of the past several years began to subside, there were signs of healing both within the *Eglise Presbyterienne Camerounaise* and in its relations with the American Church. Robert Peirce noted several of these in his report on the First Decade of the Church (1957-1967):

> An encouraging sign of strength is the growth at Dager Seminary. Although the entrance requirements were tightened a few years ago to include the High School diploma instead of merely attending school for four years at this level, enrollment has steadily increased, with fifty-five students now in attendance, plus seven at the Union Seminary in Yaounde, where the Bachelor Degree is required.

> Although a few sporadic evangelistic campaigns have been held during these ten years, it is only now that a serious effort is being made to return to the primary business of the church.

> The Bassa Synod is planning an Evangelism-in-Depth Campaign to start in July, patterned after the lines of this worldwide movement so greatly used especially in Latin America on a national scale. Another effort will be launched in the Bulu area weakened by the present division . . . .

> Still more encouraging is an increasing use of qualified and consecrated laymen in important posts, such as the Assistant Stated Clerk of the General Assembly and the recently elected Director of Primary Schools.[393]

Though the EPC suffered a serious loss of members as a result of the withdrawal of the Cameroun Orthodox Presbyterian Church (the EPC membership reported for 1967 was 71,939), by the year 1972, there was a resurgence, with a reported membership of 80,997.

While COEMAR had stated in its 1967 report to the UPCUSA General Assembly that its policy was to "put itself out of business" in Cameroun[394], personnel provided by the UPCUSA continued to make effective contributions to the mission of the EPC as they worked in close association with African colleagues in many different types of activities: pastoral work, developing Christian education programs, working with schools and hospitals, administrative roles, maintenance, agricultural projects, industrial evangelism, home and family life. When Dr. L.K. Anderson visited Cameroun in 1969, he noted another very significant contribution by American Presbyterian personnel:

> The presence on the field of Fraternal Workers of the United Presbyterian Church of the U.S.A. is a great blessing. Carrying on their duties in school and hospital without any discrimination between loyal Presbyterian and dissident members, they demonstrate the reconciling spirit of Christ.[395]

Of special note was the work being done by missionary personnel in the translation of Scripture. In the November 1969 issue of *The Drum Call*, Dr. Robert Peirce wrote a moving account of the completion of the translation of the entire Bible into the Bassa language, a task to which he had dedicated himself since 1940 and for which he had served as secretary of the translation committee:

> Yes, "The Bible has come". Finally. The entire Bible in the Bassa language. No more fielding the "When?" question with progress reports ("The committee has finished its work"; "I'm typing the manuscript"; "I'm reading proof now.") The book was really in Douala, clearing customs, and the local Bible Society set Sunday, September 14, as the day of dedication and rejoicing through the Bassa field.

> Finally. After more than thirty years . . . . Two of the missionary participants have since died, and one has retired. The Bassa members of the committee remained faithful through these many years, meeting three or four times a year, eight to ten days each session.

> Finally. Can you imagine the joy of the Bassa people? Two hundred thousand more Camerounians now have access to the entire Word of God in their own tongue, the fourth tribe in this country to be thus blessed.[396]

Fraternal workers also had a key role in strengthening the work of the women in the Camerounian Church. Dr. Evelyn Adams, in addition to her significant contribution to the church's medical program, was instrumental in the formation of the Congress of the Cameroun Presbyterian Women, the first national organization of Presbyterian church women. She tells the story of their first national meeting:

> The long awaited day finally arrived, and our first session was held July 12, 1972, in the Elat Church. There had been a long drawn out greeting ceremony with songs, drums, and dances. We—the two official delegates from the USA and I—saw that the pulpit was full with twelve pastors and that the Cameroun Women's Association officers were seated at a table on the floor level. The pastors thought the women were not capable of conducting such a large meeting, and some were still bitterly opposed to women standing in the pulpit. However, I did stand in the pulpit when I read my paper on the History of the Women's Association of the Cameroun Presbyterian Church . . . .

> There was a tremendous parade into Ebolowa on Sunday with over two thousand women, all wearing the official Congress dress. One of the delegates gave birth to a little girl, and she was called Congres.[397]

The "Evangelism in Depth" Program mentioned earlier began to take more concrete shape as an ecumenical undertaking. A national committee was formed in September 1969, with ten national churches and missions participating, representing almost the entire Protestant force working in the country. A three-year calendar was approved, starting in 1970, seeking to reach the entire nation. Translation of handbooks and teaching guides in five languages was undertaken. Then followed pastors retreats, regional retreats for evangelists, the organization of prayer groups, training classes for personal workers, house-to-house visitation. An EPC pastor who was serving as one of the national coordinators placed the challenge before the Cameroun Christian community in a message based on II Kings 7:3-9:

> This day is a day of good tidings and we hold our peace! If we tarry till the morning light some mischief will come upon us. We have the news of a Saviour to bring. Let us go and tell the Good Tidings to all men![398]

This joint endeavor undoubtedly had much to do in preparing the way for the formation in 1970 of the Federation of Protestant Churches and Missions in Cameroun, replacing the wider regional federation formed in 1943 among missions and churches in Cameroun, Rio Muni, Gabon and Congo-Brazzaville.[399]

As the UPCUSA missionary presence decreased and responsibilities were passed to trained and qualified Camerounians, the decision was finally made to conclude the publication of *The Drum Call*, which had been the primary avenue of communication with the home church for UPCUSA personnel in Cameroun since 1922. The final issue in November 1969 concluded with the following prayer:

> Forgive us, O God, our illusions of being indispensable. We are aware of the power of your Spirit in our midst, but we forget the same Spirit is with our brothers in other lands. We have learned lessons of faith and experience, but we find it hard to let our brothers learn without our control. We have thought our mission was always to give and we do not know how to receive. We have felt it was our task to speak and we have not learned how to listen. Forgive us for getting in your way, for suffocating our brother's initiative, for being slow to accept a servant role. Have mercy upon us and teach us the disciplines of true brotherhood, for the sake of Jesus Christ our Lord. Amen.[400]

WANING SPANISH COLONIAL RULE IN EQUATORIAL GUINEA (1958-1968)

1960 marked the centennial of the founding of Corisco Presbytery, "the cradle of Presbyterianism in Gabon, Rio Muni, and Cameroun." On December 2, 1960, a group of forty Christians, including four UPCUSA fraternal workers and the COEMAR

Representative, made their way to this tiny island to celebrate the occasion. Mrs. Jane Strange describes her experience:

> A solemn yet happy group of forty Christians sang hymns in the bright moonlight as their chartered trawler from the mainland anchored in sight of Corisco beach, famous for its snow-white sand. The last hurdle of our 13-hour traveling day to Corisco was a ride by poled boat from the ocean-going motor launch to shore, eight people at a time. Then each passenger was carried in two islanders' arms across the sliding surf to greet the church community gathered on the beach in the moonlight. We were shown our houses before we had a midnight supper.

> Corisco had been host to presbytery meeting 100 years ago, so the church members and many other volunteers gladly served the 40 delegates and guests. Women carried wood and water, cooked quantities of fish with hot pepper sauce, and washed clothes . . . .

> Gathered in the lamplight, on Saturday evening, five pastors and thirteen elders gave their "Ya, ya" as they adopted the new Constitution of the Rio Muni Presbyterian Church. They renewed, before God, the pledge which had been taken by five missionaries and three African elders when the presbytery was originally formed and had but a single church . . . .

> At daybreak on Monday, pastors, elders, and many believers walked to the grave where a pioneer missionary, George Paull of Fayette County, Pennsylvania, lies buried. He had sailed from Corisco Island in 1965 to Benito, Rio Muni, but he lived on the mainland only three months after he wrote: "To go and live among the mainland tribes and declare unto them the Gospel—is not this high honor?" And in 1960 honor came again, as men from the mainland bowed in prayer around this final resting place, determined that the preaching of the Gospel will continue.[401]

Just south of Cameroun, in the tiny country of Spanish Guinea,[402] Spain was much more reluctant than other European colonial powers to relinquish its control over its only colony in sub-Saharan Africa. In 1959-1960, under pressure of anti-colonial sentiment in the United Nations, Spain converted its colonies into overseas provinces. Spanish Guinea was renamed Equatorial Guinea and divided into the provinces of Fernando Po (the main offshore island) and Rio Muni (on the mainland). The first popular elections in the two areas took place in 1960. Four years later, in July 1964, both provinces were granted limited internal autonomy, with Africans serving as President, Ministers, members of the Chamber of Deputies, and regional administrators, all subject to Spanish approval. The new administrators were "exceptionally sympathetic to the Protestants".[403] Further, the Second Vatican Council that was being held in Rome during 1962-65 contributed to a more favorable political and religious climate, with Catholics for the first time expressing an openness to fellowship with Protestants. Finally, in 1968, reluctant Spain granted independence to the nation of Equatorial Guinea and it joined the family of newly independent nations of Africa.

These shifts in Spain's administrative policy, along with the rapid changes taking place in neighboring Cameroun, brought changes in the status of the church in Equatorial Guinea. Recognizing that the Presbytery of Corisco-Rio Muni should no longer be part of the Presbyterian Church in politically independent Cameroun, in May 1959, the second General Assembly of the Cameroun Presbyterian Church released that presbytery so that it might become directly related to the United Presbyterian Church in the U.S.A. through membership in the Synod of New Jersey. However, the 1959 UPCUSA General Assembly voted to grant full independence to the Rio Muni Church.

Then in December 1959, "great joy and great surprise came to the small group of Presbyterian Christians who gathered around their five ordained pastors at the yearly meeting of Rio Muni Presbytery, the first meeting held since the independence of the Spanish Guinea Church. God wonderfully answered prayers: a visa to attend the historic meeting was granted to the Rev. Eugene Carson Blake, Stated Clerk of the General Assembly of the big mother-Church. The Commission representative for Cameroun also was permitted to accompany Dr. Blake . . . . For the people of Rio Muni Presbytery, . . . it was thrilling . . . to know that their Church, with just one presbytery, was considered as important in the eyes of the American Church as the elder sister-Church in Cameroun with ten presbyteries and three synods."[404]

The Corisco-Rio Muni Presbytery chose for itself the name *Iglesia Evangelica Presbiteriana en Rio Muni* (The Evangelical Presbyterian Church in Rio Muni). At this point, the membership of the newly-formed Church was reported as approximately 2,500, with a Christian constituency of about 5,000, in 14 congregations (six along the coast and eight in the interior) and 60 preaching points, served by five pastors and some fifty-five unordained evangelists, assisted by one American Presbyterian missionary couple. Small as it was, the church rejoiced in its new status and in the new freedom which it had under the changed political situation, after long years of restrictions and occasional persecution under the Roman Catholic-dominated Spanish colonial government. "That it has not long ago been stifled is probably due to the fact that the Presbytery has been there longer than the Spanish colonizers."[405]

The young Church wasted no time in allying itself with the larger Christian community, voting to join the Federation of Evangelical Churches of Cameroun and Equatorial Africa, the All Africa Conference of Churches, then the World Presbyterian Alliance.

Of course, the tiny Church looked with envy at its big sister-Church in Cameroun. "There are times when they wish they, too, could have schools and hospitals like the Church in Cameroun. Yet, there has been a steady growth in communicant membership during recent years. Might it be that growth is due partly to the fact that here the Church is the Church, and is not burdened with institutions?"[406]

By the close of 1960, the outlook seemed bright, with "continued growth in communicant membership, growth in giving, and growth in understanding of the Christian task through the leadership conferences for elders conducted by a fraternal worker couple." Four young men were in training for the ministry (most of them at Dager Seminary in Cameroun), and four more were candidates under the care of presbytery. Also encouraging was the arrival in November of a second fraternal worker couple with full government permission, Mr. & Mrs. Roy Strange. This would be the first time in 25 years that the Rio Muni Church had the aid of more than one missionary family. Further, the influence of the church on the country's political life was becoming evident, with the election in June 1960 of two evangelical Christians to government office, Jose Nsue Argue Osa and Jorge Oma. With all these favorable signs, the Rio Muni Church voted to join COEMAR in making 1961 "Evangelism Emphasis Year."[407]

By 1964, membership had increased to 2,767 and an additional congregation had been formed at Ocong, bringing the total to 15. "Open doors are everywhere in the country. There are three specific districts where the Gospel is spreading like a brush fire and urban centers are increasingly important in the life and witness of the Church . . . . With illiteracy at 85%, and among women 95%, there is a tremendous educational need. The Presbyterian Church has received official government recognition of its one primary school." Regarding health conditions, "the common tropical diseases continue to call for a ministry of healing; infant mortality is 50%. So far the Presbyterian Church has not had the personnel to reopen medical work which was closed many years ago."[408] Nevertheless, the fraternal workers, though with no formal training in medicine, engaged in simple first aid including the treatment of malaria, worms, infections and other common illnesses. "This limited amount of medical work has been thrust upon us by the daily requests at our doors."[409]

The most exciting growth was in the interior eastern regions. The dense forests were being opened up by Spanish lumber companies, who began to build a system of lumbering highways in order to exploit the apparently inexhaustible supply of tropical hardwoods. The highways provided much easier access for pastors and evangelists in their evangelistic work in the area. "Churches that formerly have been closed and destroyed have now been rebuilt, and four new chapels have been erected. An area which was formerly closed has now been opened and regular Gospel meetings are held."[410]

With so few pastors and ordained fraternal workers to serve the congregations and preaching points spread across the country, a special plan had to be devised to provide the necessary pastoral services. The churches and preaching points were divided into fifteen areas with a center for each area. Three times a year the Christians in each area would gather for what was called "The Big Worshipping."

> Each [pastor] goes to the center of his area for fellowship, Bible study conferences, and talks with the Session. All of the activity culminates in morning worship and Communion on Sunday.

During each of these three Big Worshippings, there are, in addition, marriages performed, baptisms, new members received, and new believers who confess their faith.

One of the things enjoyed at this time are the choirs, which usually are good ones. Children from six or seven years to young married couples sing in the choir. The choir often starts to practice after the evening session, at 9 p.m. perhaps, and sings until the middle of the night.[411]

The work in the urban centers also was developing significantly. In Bata, the capital city and major port for commerce and shipping, the Presbyterian Church (*Mision Evangelica*) provided the only Protestant witness in a city of about 20,000. Its pastor, the Rev. Gustavo Envela, fluent in English, French, and Spanish, as well as the African tribal languages of Bulu and Kombe, would conduct services in several languages each Sunday to serve the diverse populations of the city. "Well-known by nearly everyone in town", he also served on the faculty of the Catholic-run government high school, the only high school in Rio Muni.[412] In Bolondo (formerly Benito), some 25 miles south of Bata, where the oldest Presbyterian church in Rio Muni as well as Cameroun was located (founded in 1865), the William W. Ainley family served as directors for a conference center and training center for lay leaders.—In Mengo, some 38 miles east of Bata along the main east-west paved highway, the church had enabled COEMAR to secure ownership of about 65 acres of property, to serve as a focal point for future medical and educational work.—In Ebibiyin, in the northeast corner of Rio Muni on the main highway between Cameroun and Gabon, the Roy P. Strange family worked with the pastor of the largest Presbyterian Church in Rio Muni, the Rev. Pablo Mba Nchama, in evangelistic work in smaller towns and villages along the highway.

Meanwhile, the Rio Muni Church was strengthening its relations with the Evangelical Church in Spain. In 1965, the Evangelical Theological School in Barcelona began granting scholarships to cover all expenses of lodging and tuition for several theological students from Equatorial Guinea to study in Spain. In the same year, representatives of the Presbyterian Church in Equatorial Guinea, on their way to a World Presbyterian Alliance meeting in Frankfurt, Germany, visited the Spanish Evangelical Church and presented a request for a fraternal worker, seeking especially a doctor to undertake medical work. "They have established an understanding with the new government hospital [in Bata] whereby the Church-related clinics can be associated with these fine medical programs when clinic patients need special care."[413] As plans developed, COEMAR agreed to participate in this project, sharing in the support of a Spanish evangelical doctor, Dr. Javier Llobell, to begin service in 1967.[414] The plans called for a mobile clinic run by the doctor, his nurse-wife, and an African anesthetist-nurse, Miss Elvira Muanache, "who is even now training in Barcelona."

Along with these favorable trends within the Rio Muni Church, there came improved relations with the majority Roman Catholic population. "When the Youth Presbytery was meeting, the local Catholic priest and a group of nine Catholic women visited and brought gifts of food. The occasion became one of establishing good fellowship, with a spirited exchange of hymns and songs by both groups."[415]

Still further marking the change in the political climate, in 1965 The Rev. Gustavo Envela, pastor of the Bata Church, was selected by the President of Equatorial Guinea, Bonifacio Ondo Edu (himself a former Catholic catechist), to accompany him as official counselor and translator to the United Nations where the case of Rio Muni was being discussed before the Trusteeship Council. Pastor Envela relates the following incident which happened at the U.N.:

> The Spanish Ambassador to the U.N., Don Maniel Aznar, invited the Equatorial Guinea delegation to a special banquet at the Spanish Embassy. I was asked by the ambassador, a Roman Catholic, to give the prayer of blessing before the dinner. I closed the prayer of blessing with the Lord's Prayer and sat down. During the dinner the Spanish ambassador made a toast and spoke these words: "Who says that Spain never changes. Who would have ever imagined that a Protestant pastor would ever give a prayer of blessing at a Spanish Embassy!" Ambassador Aznar later would become the Prime Minister of Spain.[416]

Despite numerous problems facing the young Church (such as lack of funds to support more than the present force of national pastors and difficulty in securing authorization to reopen or rebuild the chapels which had been closed in 1952), the future looked very promising: "In the next several years as Rio Muni gains greater internal autonomy and probably independence there will undoubtedly be much greater freedom to preach the gospel."[417]

THE BEGINNING OF A DECADE OF TERROR (1968-1972)

The bright hopes that the Rio Muni Church had entertained were soon dashed when the nation of Equatorial Guinea gained its independence. To begin with, there was some opposition to independence within the country itself, as the indigenous Bubi people on Fernando Po feared possible domination by the more populous, less developed mainland territory of Rio Muni. To reassure this element of the population, the Spanish Cortes (parliament) on July 24, 1968 approved a draft constitution embodying certain guarantees for the future rights of the Fernando Po inhabitants in relation to the state as a whole. The constitution was accepted by a majority of the Guinean voters in a national referendum held on August 11.

Elections to the presidency, the new 35-member National Assembly, and local councils took place on September 22. In a run-off election a week later, Francisco Macias Nguema was chosen as the republic's first president. On October 12, 1968, Equatorial Guinea was declared an independent nation.

Soon after gaining its independence, Equatorial Guinea ran into serious economic difficulties. The production of cacao (cocoa), its major export, had fallen precipitously, bringing a sizable drop in foreign exchange and balance of trade. Even though Spain, the major importer of Guinean products, had given Equatorial Guinea preferential treatment in both purchase price and custom duties, President Macias soon began demanding greater economic independence from Spain.

When tension between the Spanish community and the inhabitants of Rio Muni exploded into rioting in February 1969, the Spanish ambassador mobilized a civil guard, which seized communication and transportation centers. Macias complained to the Spanish chief of state (Francisco Franco) and to the United Nations Secretary General (U Thant) that the Spanish ambassador was plotting to overthrow his government, whereupon the Spanish government advised Spanish citizens to seek protection. On March 5, it was reported that there had been an unsuccessful attempt to overthrow the government and shortly thereafter several of the supposed leaders of the abortive coup (mostly members of the Bubi people native to the island of Fernando Po) were found dead.

From this point, Macias assumed dictatorial powers amid economic chaos. He accused Spain of having supported the attempted coup, which the Spanish government firmly denied. By April 5, 1969, of the 7000 Spaniards who had lived in the country, all but about 600 had fled, leaving most of the country's commercial activity without technically trained leadership. Macias suspended the constitution and launched a reign of terror that was among the most brutal and destructive in post-colonial Africa. Calling himself the "Unique Miracle", Macias spent his eleven years in office waging the equivalent of war on his own people. Thousands, mostly Bubi people, were killed and other thousands were enslaved on government plantations. Eventually an estimated 100,000 Guinean people had fled the country, most of them fleeing into Cameroun and other neighboring African nations. The rich cocoa plantations were nationalized and eventually destroyed. Schools were closed and fishermen were forbidden to use their canoes. By 1971, a U.S. State Department report concluded that Macias' regime was "characterized by abandonment of all government functions except internal security, which was accomplished by terror; this led to the death or exile of up to one-third of the population."[418]

The Macias years were a time of terrible persecution for the church in Equatorial Guinea, both Catholic and Protestant. Macias instituted a regime of militant atheism and anti-Christian propaganda was openly encouraged. Most Spanish priests and nuns were expelled, and most of those remaining were imprisoned or placed under house arrest. By 1973, only 20 Catholic priests were actively in service. Protestant churches were confiscated, missionaries were expelled, and national clergy suffered increasing persecution, including imprisonment and torture. Guineans studying abroad found it impossible to return, while church leaders were refused permission to leave the country. All meetings of more than 10 persons were banned, limiting the work of the church to personal contacts and officially recognized worship services. In 1974 a presidential decree was announced requiring priests and pastors to read at each worship service a message of praise to President Macias: "Never without Macias, all for Macias. Down with colonialism and those who are ambitious."[419]

On July 14, 1972, Francisco Macias Nguema was appointed "president for life" at the second National Congress of his "Party of National Unity". The future for the church in Equatorial Guinea appeared dark indeed.

Nevertheless, in the midst of this oppressive situation, there was one hopeful development for the Protestant community. After considerable negotiation, on February 6, 1970, the two Protestant churches in Rio Muni, *the Iglesia Evangelica Presbiteriana en Rio Muni* and the *Mision Evangelica Cruzada* (growing out of the work of the Worldwide Evangelistic Crusade of Great Britain), united to form the *Iglesia Evangelica en la Guinea Ecuatorial*. A letter from the new Church's Stated Clerk, Rev. Pablo Mba Nchama, to COEMAR presented a poignant appeal for continued cooperation:

> For some time there was been a wall of silence between us with only intermittent correspondence between our two sister churches. With this letter we hope to break this wall of silence and enter into correspondence once again as brothers of the same Lord and Saviour.

> Engraved in our hearts is an undimmed memory of you, of the impact caused by your presence among us and the evangelistic work which you carried out in our country. God has allowed this to grow inasmuch as we have come to be a national independent church as the fruit of your work and the result of your sacrifices and sufferings.

> Moved by Christian love within the ecumenical orbit, inspired particularly by the World Council of Churches and the other interchurch organisms, we have achieved the unification of the two Protestant Churches in our Province of Rio Muni, the Worldwide Evangelistic Crusade and the Evangelical Presbyterian Church . . . . We believe that with this act we have fulfilled the Lord's will that all of us should be one . . . .

> As you know, our union has been accomplished in difficult times. The transitional period from being a colony to an independent state, the peaceful and voluntary withdrawal of our missionaries, the lack of workers and the great demand of the population, all of these factors make difficult the tasks of evangelisation, social work, and education. In spite of all of these difficulties, the Church has been motivated by the warmth that independence has brought to our country. This is the propitious moment to develop ourselves freely and without the limitations of the colonial period. People want the Gospel and it is an embarrassment to us not to be able to satisfy their desire.

... With gratitude we hope for the assistance which our brothers of other churches in the world can provide. We have one strong bond which unites us, Jesus Christ, who broke down all the discriminatory barriers of separation which have always been an obstacle to progress in this world . . . .

Cordial greetings of your brethren in Christ. Pablo Mba Nchama, Stated Clerk.[420]

BEGINNING OF INVOLVEMENT IN OTHER NATIONS OF WEST AFRICA

The impact of new concepts of mission in response to the new day in Africa were soon evident, as both American Presbyterian churches became related to African churches and involved in work which up to this time had not been a part of their mission history. The intention was threefold: first, to establish partnerships with churches in other areas of Africa; second, to experiment in programs and projects, "using a different style than that we had developed through our mission history"[421]; third, to reduce the missionary force and resources invested in those places where the American churches previously had been involved: "We did not intend to have so many personnel or so much money in any one area that we could determine the churches' program in that area."[422]

This was especially evident in West Africa. After the Commission on Ecumenical Mission and Relations (COEMAR) had designated 1960 as Africa Emphasis Year and a special Moderator's Conference on Africa had been convened, a Moderator's Deputation visited West Africa to carry greetings to churches in that area and to open new contacts. Out of these visits there emerged new programs and projects in partnership with various churches in West Africa, some of which were more lasting than others.

The situation of the Christian churches in these nations differed according to their colonial heritage, with Protestants being strong in those nations that had been British, and Catholics in those nations which had been French. It is understandable then that, as American Presbyterians felt their way into new church relationships in Africa, their first initiatives would be in former British colonies, especially where Presbyterian or Reformed church communities had been established, and where there was the advantage of English being the national language. Also, it was usually through acquaintance with outstanding Christian leadership in those countries, primarily through ecumenical relations.

*　*　*

LIBERIA, we recall, had been the place where American Presbyterian missionary work in West Africa had its beginning in 1833. The work had suffered monumental missionary casualties with meager results that had led to the withdrawal of remaining missionaries in 1894, and the conclusion of any official relationship and support in

1931. However, there remained a small Presbyterian Church with 960 members in 11 congregations.

With COEMAR's new mission policies in the 1960s, an attempt was made to renew the relationship with the Presbyterian Church of Liberia. A gift of $5,000 was made to assist in the building of a much-needed school. (Liberia had only a five percent literacy rate, and that primarily among the ruling class of 15-20 thousand Americo-Liberians descended from the first settlers.) A fraternal worker was assigned to teach at a church-operated grade school. A retired school teacher came to Liberia in 1961 to establish a Christian literature and audio-visual aid center in Monrovia. And assistance was given for the conducting of In-Service Pastors' Training Seminars, as well as Christian Education seminars. It was hoped that this would be a "mutual rediscovery" between United Presbyterians and Liberian Presbyterians.[423] However, the attempt to renew relations with the Presbyterian Church of Liberia proved to be futile.

*　　*　　*

GHANA (known as the Gold Coast prior to its independence) claimed a noble history. As far back as 300 A.D., an empire called Ghana had flourished in western Africa. However, in its conflict with neighboring kingdoms in the 1000s and 1200s, its capital was destroyed. In succeeding centuries, other peoples founded strong states within the area now known as Ghana: the Akan; the Mande and the Hausa in the north; the Ga and the Ewe in the southeast; and the Ashanti in the central forest region. All these continue to exert a strong influence within the modern state of Ghana.

European exploration of what is now Ghana began early in the 15th century when the Portuguese landed on the Gold Coast (so named because of its rich gold deposits). Along with their exploitation of the area's rich natural resources, the Portuguese established a headquarters for the slave trade. By the 17th century, the Portuguese slave monopoly had given way to traders from the Netherlands, England, Denmark, Sweden and Prussia, who established forts along the coast, primarily as gathering points for the shipping of slaves. Eventually most of the slaves who were brought to America came from the Gold Coast. Britain made the Gold Coast a crown colony in 1874, and in 1901 established protectorates over the Ashanti and the Northern Territories.

Recognizing the history of self-government within the various groups composing the approximately seven million people living in the Gold Coast, in 1946 Great Britain granted the colony a new constitution that gave Africans a majority of seats in the colony's legislature. After riots broke out in 1948 and 1950, still further freedoms were granted. During this period, a strong leader emerged: Kwame Nkrumah, a powerful advocate of African nationalism, often arrested and imprisoned, nevertheless elected to parliament in 1951 and in 1952 chosen as prime minister. Through Nkrumah's leadership, on March 6, 1957 Ghana became the first former colony in "black" sub-Saharan Africa to achieve independence, "one of the most significant dates in modern African history."[424] On July 1,

1960, the legislature voted to make Ghana a republic within the British Commonwealth and Nkrumah became the country's first president.

Nkrumah's popularity in the country rose, as new roads, schools, and health facilities were built and as the policy of Africanization created better career opportunities for Ghanaians. Also, his reputation as a spokesperson for African independence spread across the continent, and he became the leading advocate for a pan-African federation, which eventually led to the formation of the Organization for African Unity in 1963.

However, the relationship of Nkrumah to the churches soon became strained. Although he had been educated in Roman Catholic schools in Ghana and had studied at universities of Protestant origin in the United States, he publicly attended not only Christian services but also Moslem and pagan rites. Further, Protestant leaders felt it their duty to protest against some of his government's measures, especially the arrest and imprisonment without trial of his political opponents. Many Christians were also unhappy because Nkrumah seemed to be seeking to create a political religion with himself as *Osageyfo* (Savior), and the pedestal of his statue which he had erected in Accra bore the words: "Seek ye first the political kingdom and all else will be added."[425]

Meanwhile, the country's economy remained essentially controlled by foreign interests (which Nkrumah resisted) and its development plans incurred increasing deficits. In response, Nkrumah began to evolve a much more rigorous apparatus of political control, and in 1964 had himself elected "president for life" of both the nation and its one political party. Turning increasingly to Communist countries for support, he was visiting the People's Republic of China in 1966 when the army in Ghana seized power. Though a new president was elected in 1969, he was dislodged by another coup in 1972, which dissolved the National Assembly. Thus began a period of repeated coups that brought this proud nation to its knees both politically and economically.

Within this political context, there had emerged in Ghana a strong Christian community that has had a significant influence on the nation and on the whole of Africa. By the mid-1970s, within its total population of some 8,500,000, Protestants numbered about two million, and Roman Catholics approximately 1,350,000. Among the Protestants, Presbyterians were the largest constituency, with approximately 12% of the population, and Methodists followed close behind, with approximately 11%.[426]

The Presbyterian community is divided between two denominations. The Presbyterian Church of Ghana is the oldest and largest, growing out of the work of the Swiss Basel Mission, which had come to Ghana as early as 1828. This work was greatly strengthened by the coming of Moravian Christians from Jamaica in 1843. During World War I, the Basel Mission was forced to withdraw, and was replaced by representatives of the United Free Church of Scotland. By 1931, out of the work of the Basel and Scottish missions, there had arisen an autonomous, self-supporting Presbyterian Church of the Gold Coast. By 1957 it was reported to have a membership of some 36,000 and a Christian community of 110,000.[427]

The second Presbyterian church, the Evangelical Presbyterian Church of Ghana, grew out of the work of the Bremen Mission from northern Germany, which began work in 1847 among the Ewe peoples thus far unreached by the Basel Mission. This area, also known as the Volta region, was at first a German colony and later a British trusteeship. When the Bremen Mission was expelled in 1914 at the outset of World War I, the Evangelical Presbyterian Church gained its autonomy. Thus there had developed in both churches a strong sense of self-government, with administrative responsibility for a significant network of educational and medical institutions.

Along with self-government there emerged a conviction of the importance of ecumenical cooperation. The Christian Council of the Gold Coast was founded in 1929. With Ghana's achievement of independence in 1957, the name of the organization was changed to the Christian Council of Ghana. From its earliest years, the Council provided its member churches with opportunity to participate in a united ministry of service and outreach, including literature production, family planning clinics, preparation of religious education material, united theological education, and a Christian Service Committee conducting relief, agricultural and development programs. Ecumenical relations between the Roman Catholic Church and the Christian Council of Ghana were greatly strengthened following the Second Vatican Council, and in 1966 a Committee of Cooperation was established to coordinate the activities of the Christian Council and the National Catholic Secretariat.

With such a strong and cooperative Christian community, it is little wonder that Ghana became a leading participant in world ecumenical affairs. In 1957-58, the International Missionary Council held its Assembly in Ghana. It was a pivotal meeting, at which the old terminology of "sending and receiving countries" and "older and younger churches" was discarded, and a new theme accepted, "one Church sent with the whole Gospel to the whole world in obedience to Christ." Recommendations were hammered out which would lead to the integration of the International Missionary Council into the World Council of Churches at New Delhi in 1961.[428]

At the same time that the older, established churches were moving toward greater cooperation, from about 1960 on there was an outburst of new evangelical missions beginning work in Ghana, as well as small indigenous churches. Unfortunately, the splintering of the Christian community took place within the Presbyterian Church of Ghana as well, as a former Presbyterian, Charles Yeboa, led a seceding group to form the Feden Church.[429]

With COEMAR's strong emphasis on ecumenical mission, Ghana soon became a focus of attention. Contacts between United Presbyterians and Presbyterians in Ghana widened quickly after July 1, 1960, when the United Presbyterian Church, USA sent its greetings to the Ghana government and churches upon the proclamation of the Republic. Subsequently COEMAR funds were contributed for numerous ecumenical projects, such as Bible translation and the granting of scholarships for promising theological students. Conversely, American students were sent to Ghanaian institutions, for study both at universities and at the outstanding ecumenical seminary, Trinity Theological College. Also COEMAR, working with the Mennonites, sought to build bridges to the many independent African churches in both Ghana and Nigeria, meeting them at their points of need in education and leadership development. Further, Ghanaian church leaders were invited to the United States to bring "their insights . . . to our own tormented racial relationships in the U.S.A."[430]

As for American personnel, these were sent by COEMAR primarily on a short-term basis. Culver Williams, a California architect employed on the massive Volta River Dam Project, designed church buildings for congregations in the towns of Tamale and Akosombo. Under Operation Crossroads Africa, youth work camps from the United States constructed school buildings in Ghanaian villages.[431]

In time, the Presbyterian U.S. Board of World Missions would also become involved in partnership with the churches in Ghana. In 1968, the Rev. and Mrs. Harry F. Petersen were sent to Ghana to establish the first full-time Protestant chaplaincy on the campus of the University College of Cape Coast. The college, established under Nkrumah's regime, had as its principal purpose the preparation of teachers for Ghana's secondary schools and training colleges. In reporting on their experience, the Petersens wrote:

> Most of [the students] are nominally Christian having come from Christian families and/or church-related secondary schools . . . . All students in Cape Coast are pulled by the lure of city life, far removed from the village, rural life which comprises most of Africa . . . . Bright, energetic Ghanaians freshly back from doctoral studies abroad are slowly replacing expatriate faculty members, giving new impetus and an African-oriented approach to studies . . . .

> Trying to broaden Christian students' horizons poses a continual challenge, especially in terms of "africanizing" their faith. New forms of worship—a departure from inherited European forms—featuring African hymns and drumming provoked discussion and thought. The campus church, though having no membership roles of participating students and faculty, encourages strong ties between students and the churches of their respective denominations . . . .

> A few visible aspects of growth can be glimpsed occasionally: Through students taking on leadership in both church-related and academic groups. Through a Moslem who wants to become a Christian and join the church. Through students who want to know how can they express their love for Christ tangibly in a Ghanaian society.[432]

Through the Petersens, opportunities were opened for U.S. college students to participate in Summer Service Programs both on campus and in the surrounding villages. Also a seminary intern devoted a year to work with the Ghana Student Christian Movement, making contact with the many chapters of SCM in colleges and secondary schools scattered throughout Ghana, and offering leadership support and assistance in conference planning and editing the SCM student magazine.

Ghana would become a major partner in mission for American Presbyterians in years to come.

* * *

NIGERIA stood as a colossus among the new nations of Africa. With a population estimated in 1959 to be 35 million, occupying a land area larger than any other Sub-Saharan African nation except Sudan and Congo, it is one of the most densely populated countries of Africa. While there are more than 250 distinct ethnic peoples, three major language groups determine the predominant culture of the three areas of Nigeria: Hausa in the Northern Region, Ibo in the Eastern Region, and Yoruba in the Western Region.

Its history closely parallels that of Ghana. From an early date, African kingdoms rose and fell. The colonial era began with Portuguese sailors exploring Nigeria in the late 1480s and developing a slave trade along the coast. Then for the next 300 years, British, Dutch and other European traders competed for slaves, until Nigeria became known as the "Slave Coast." The British gradually became the predominant colonial power, creating separate protectorates over Southern and Northern Nigeria in 1900. These became British mandates under the League of Nations in 1922, and United Nations Trust Territories in 1946. Then in 1954, a new constitution created the Federation of Nigeria. Nigeria became an independent member of the British Commonwealth on October 1, 1960, and its Prime Minister, Sir Abubakar Tafawa Balewa, became president of the new nation. In February 1961, neighboring Northern Cameroon voted to join Nigeria. The Federal Republic of Nigeria was made up of three regions: Western, with its capital at Ibadan; Eastern, with its capital at Enugu; and Northern, its capital at Kaduna.

Religiously, Nigeria is divided between Islam, Christianity and indigenous African religions. In the latter part of the 19th and the first half of the 20th century, Islam spread rapidly in Northern Nigeria, its progress facilitated by the growing trade with Moslem North Africa across the Sahara. Conversely, Christianity was strongest in the coastal regions, since this was the area where European influence was strongest. By the 1960s, approximately one-half of Nigeria's people were Muslim (primarily in the Northern Region), one-third were Christian (primarily in the Eastern and Western Regions), and participants in African traditional religions were scattered throughout the rural areas.

Christianity first came to Nigeria late in the first half of the 19th century, with the Church Missionary Society of England leading the way, chiefly through freed slaves who had been in contact with the Society in Sierra Leone and then returned to their homes in the Western Region. In 1864 an African, Samuel Adjai Crowther, who in his boyhood had been rescued from a slave ship by a British cruiser and had been educated in Sierra Leone and England, was consecrated in Canterbury Cathedral as Anglican Bishop of the Niger Territories.

In 1846, the United Presbyterians of Scotland began a mission east of the Niger River, the dividing line between Western and Eastern Nigeria. Some of the early missionaries had served in Jamaica and were assisted by Jamaican Christians in the work in Nigeria. Among the outstanding missionary pioneers was Mary Slessor, for whom a hospital in Itu in the Eastern Region is named.

Between the outbreak of World War I and Nigerian independence in 1960, Christianity had a remarkable numerical growth and also became more deeply rooted in African leadership. The total Protestant membership had reached 287,000, with an estimated Protestant Christian community of 1,370,000; Roman Catholics reported their total constituency at 1,676,000. Both Protestants and Catholics had recruited and trained a strong African clergy. In 1954, the Scottish Presbyterians transferred their responsibilities to the national church, and the autonomous Presbyterian Church of Nigeria came into being.

The impact of the Christian community, though a minority, on the nation has been profound. The large majority of the children receiving elementary education were in schools maintained by either churches or missions, most of them in the Eastern and Western Regions. Almost all who went on to secondary and university education were from Christian schools, and about four-fifths were Christians. Christian bodies also have provided a major part of Nigeria's basic medical facilities.

The Christian community soon learned the importance of ecumenical cooperation. The Christian Council of Nigeria, founded in 1930, brought together the efforts of nine Protestant bodies in ministries of witness and service. Out of its initiative several ecumenical institutes have been established. The Institute of Church and Society, founded in 1964, has engaged the churches in study and dialogue on critical issues in the life of the nation. The National Institute for Religious Sciences, founded in 1971, is involved in the training of secondary school teachers of religion. The Christian Health Association oversees the Christian commitment to health services. The Christian Education Research Council discusses with the government issues related to the church's involvement in education. The National Institute of Moral and Religious Education, founded in 1971, seeks to inspire moral ideals among the nation's leaders.

In this nation where the relation of Christians and Muslims is of such critical importance, churches took the initiative in forming the Islam in Africa Project in 1959. The project seeks to prepare Christians for their relationship with Muslims in Africa south of the Sahara. It soon had personnel working in Sierra Leone, Liberia, Ghana, Nigeria, Cameroon, Ethiopia, Kenya, Upper Volta and Malawi. The project eventually would lead to the establishment of the Study Center for Islam and Christianity in Ibadan.

One of Nigeria's renowned Christian leaders was Dr. Akunu Ibiam (later known as Sir Francis Ibiam), a physician who with his wife had so devoted himself to his own rural people that he was known as the "black Schweitzer." In 1960 he was named the first governor of Eastern Nigeria. He also had served as chairman of the Christian Council of Nigeria and as the first president of the All Africa Church Conference.[433]

It was through the visit of Sir Francis and Lady Eudora Ibiam to the United States in 1961 that United Presbyterians became acquainted with the Christian community in Nigeria. Both had been invited to speak to major conferences sponsored by the UPCUSA Moderator and by United Presbyterian Women. From that time, United Presbyterian involvement with the Presbyterian Church of Nigeria developed on numerous fronts. In 1964, a American Presbyterian pastor was called to serve with the Student Christian

Movement in Nigeria. Another was assigned to provide pastoral services for a number of schools, and an interdenominational congregation.

> These fraternal workers serve in a beautiful country where lush forests and grasslands surround you but food shortage is a major problem, where great rivers flow through the land . . . but water supplies for drinking are scarce, where there is an intense spirit of nationalism but . . . an equally intense spirit of tribal loyalty.[434]

COEMAR worked with the Christian Council of Nigeria in an urban experiment at Port Harcourt in Eastern Nigeria. It also provided numerous scholarships for potential leaders selected by the Nigerian church for training abroad. And United Presbyterian students were sent to study at the University of Ibadan under the Junior Year Abroad program.

Beneath the hopeful signs that prevailed following independence, there persisted intertribal rivalries. In 1966, there erupted clashes between the predominant Muslim people and the Ibo (primarily Christian) people in the Northern Region, which led to the mass killing of thousands of Ibo living in that region. This sparked a migration of masses of Ibo people to the Eastern Region, leaving many Northern areas with hardly any Christian community.[435] Estimates as to the total massacred range from 10,000 to 30,000, and the migration affected about one million people.

The crisis brought about the formation of a military government for Nigeria, and a year later, civil war broke out when the former Eastern Region declared itself the Republic of Biafra. The siege tactics of the Nigerian military led to the cutting off of food supplies to the new nation, and mass starvation ensued. The worldwide Christian community sought to bring aid to the starving nation, but many died. By 1969 Nigerian troops had captured much of Biafra, and in January 1970 the Biafrans surrendered. The Nigerian government had before it the enormous task of reconciliation with the defeated Ibo.

The defeat and collapse of the attempted Biafran nation resulted in a serious interruption in the development of what was formerly the most dynamic part of the country. Needless to say, the effect on the Christian community was profound. At the end of the civil war, most foreign missionaries were expelled from the region and Christian primary and secondary schools were nationalized. Nevertheless, the Nigerian church rallied to the situation and sought to train needed leadership for the monumental task before the wounded nation.

C. CENTRAL AFRICA

> *The Sunday after Christmas [1959], it was the turn of Kasonga Paul, the head teacher in our primary school at Lubondai, to conduct the worship service in the big station church. He found his text in I Corinthians1: "I hear there are divisions among you . . . . IS CHRIST DIVIDED?" and suggested that, in this*

time when the church seemed to be going forward with such hope, Satan had been busy once again as he had in Job's day, to try to prove that a little trouble in the lives of Christians so-called would show up the fact in a hurry that they were really not God's people at all. The way Kasonga put it was that Satan got God's permission to throw a scare among the Christians . . . and they turned into Baluba and Lulua istead of Christians. Finally this Lulua preacher challenged his congregation, all of his own tribe except for some twenty Baluba Mission employees who have remained here in spite of unpleasantries and threats from various ones of the local folk, some of them members of the congregation that Sunday. (It's the custom for our preachers to require answers from their listeners from time to time during the sermon).

THE PREACHER:　　　*Suppose we were having Communion in this church today. Would you people eat the bread?*
THE CONGREGATION: We'd eat it.
THE PREACHER:　　　*And the cup, would you drink it?*
THE CONGREGATION: We'd drink it.
THE PREACHER:　　　*One cup?*
THE CONGREGATION: ONE CUP!

Kasonga closed with this word of dismissal: "Today I don't want a single Baluba to walk out of this church. I don't want a single Lulua to leave this building. I want Christians to get up, walk out, and to be Christians one with the other even after they get outside."
And that's the way they left.[436]

THE GATHERING STORM (1958-1959)

The surge toward African independence which was sweeping down the continent would find its most difficult challenge as it reached Belgian Congo. By the end of 1960 most of West and Equatorial Africa had won its independence, with some eighteen states having gained their freedom from colonialism. But, as a consequence of Congolese developments, a hard core of resistance to African independence was consolidated, particularly in Southern Africa—South Africa, Rhodesia and the Portuguese colonies of Angola and Mozambique. Indeed, the crises which gripped Congo during this period would transform the political life of the African continent from this time forward.[437]

By 1958, the drastic changes which were taking place in other nations of Africa began to be felt in the Belgian Congo. In that year, French President Charles de Gaulle, in a speech in neighboring Brazzaville, offered autonomy to France's sixteen colonies in Africa, within a French Community patterned after the British Commonwealth. Also, an All-Africa People's Conference was held in December 1958 in newly independent Ghana. Several Congolese leaders attended the Accra conference and learned firsthand of the independence movements in other parts of Africa. Upon their return they began calling openly for independence. Among these was a fiery orator named Patrice Lumumba, leader of the left-wing National Congolese Movement (MNC), a political party in eastern Congo centered in Stanleyville, which was attempting to be broadly based and national in scope.

Pressures built rapidly jolting Belgium into announcing far-reaching political reform. But such announcements came too late to forestall turmoil. At a rally in Leopoldville on January 3, 1959, Lumumba called for immediate independence. A confrontation with police erupted into violence that led to two weeks of rioting in the capital. The crowds looted public buildings and invaded mission schools and churches, concentrating their fury on Roman Catholic more than Protestant institutions. By the time the riots had ended, more than 175 people had been killed. "The word *independence* became coin-of-the-realm in every one of the hundreds of dailects spoken throughout the colony; people far out in the forests or deep in the 'bush' who had no idea of the true meaning of the word were nevertheless talking avidly of the day when they would GET it."[438] In April, a congress of political parties was held in the capital city of the province of Kasai, Luluabourg, an assembly of political groups which had come into being for the most part since the first of the year. By the end of the year, there were well over 100 political parties in the Congo, basically tribal in their orientation and composition.

In August the visit of Lumumba to Luluabourg led to riots and the arrest of several political leaders. Soon the unrest brought on the outbreak of tribal warfare, starting in Luluabourg and spreading out into the province. Unfortunately the most severe conflict was between the two largest tribal groups with whom the APCM was working, the Lulua and the Baluba. While the Lulua backed Lumumba, the Baluba were united into a tribal party led by Albert Kalondji. Since the city of Luluabourg was in Lulua country, the Lulua demanded that all the Baluba leave their city. Besides those driven from Lulua territories, some 70,000 more were soon added coming from Elizabethville where "authentic Katangese" wanted to rid themselves of the "foreign" Baluba. By October 1959, the hostilities between the tribes had taken a toll of some 300 killed.

> It is apparently inevitable that such differences arise among peoples in the present circumstances. As tribes who have been living more or less peaceably side by side through the decades, while a strong force of government has kept law and order, see the approach of the day when that strong force is to be replaced by some new and indigenous authority, those tribes become suspicious of one another and jealous of having the best places . . . and thus, the tribal warfare, to settle the question of who's to be the new boss.[439]

In the area in which the APCM was working, the approximately two million people represented as many as ten distinct tribes. However, the Lulua and Baluba made up the overwhelming majority of that population, as well as of church leadership and constituency. While they had lived peacefully alongside one another under the Belgian government, the prospect of independence brought to light something which was happening under the surface.

> The simple fact is that the Baluba (many of whom had been bought as slaves [from Arab slave traders during the 18th century] by the Lulua and then given their freedom and lands upon which to settle), living in large numbers in an area claimed by the Lulua as their national heritage, have gotten off to a better start than have their hosts, and as of now have the better education, the better salaries, the more influential and important jobs; and the Lulua do not want an immediate independence which will put the control of their land into the hands of this other tribe.[440]

As a result of the ensuing tribal warfare, major problems arose in relation to the approximately 200,000 displaced Baluba people. Basic was the problem of food. People who lived on the products of their fields were forced to move to new areas before harvesting their crops. A time of famine for many seemed inevitable. Through Church World Service, the relief arm of the U.S. National Council of Churches, the Congo Protestant Council was able to aid many of the displaced people in the years ahead.

Meanwhile, the Belgian government, in an effort to calm the tense situation, offered to move toward limited forms of self-government in the colony and election for local councils were held in December of that year. However, some of the most influential political parties which were emerging boycotted the elections. In the face of continued unrest, the Belgian government agreed to hold a Round Table Conference in Brussels in January 1960 to discuss some form of autonomy for the colony.

These political developments were accompanied by ecumenical events which would influence the situation of the churches in the Congo. The International Missionary Council held its Assembly at Accra, Ghana from December 28, 1957 through January 8, 1958. The Assembly adopted a statement which described the distinction between older and younger churches as no longer "valid or helpful." The most important issue discussed was the plan for the integration of the IMC and the World Council of Churches. Some conservative mission societies working in the Congo (most from America) threatened to create another council if the Congo Protestant Council joined the WCC. The Ghana Assembly also dealt seriously with the question of theological training for the ministry of the emerging churches. It established the Theological Education Fund which in later years would provide funds and books for African seminaries and the training of African theologians.

Following the IMC Ghana Assembly, the first All-Africa Christian Conference was held in Ibadan, Nigeria, January 10-19, 1958. The main theme was "The Church in Changing Africa." Those attending from the Congo learned of the development of the indigenous churches across the African continent. Soon afterward the Congo Protestant Council met at Leopoldville, February 23-March 2. The CPC voted to withdraw from the International Missionary Council, saying that their action was "justified in order to preserve the unity of action and spirit which has always characterized the work of Missions in the Belgian Congo."[441] Nevertheless, the CPC and other ecumenical bodies kept pushing the American Presbyterian Congo Mission to begin transferring authority to the Congolese church.

Despite this climate of political ferment, the Christian movement continued to advance. By 1959, about 36 percent of the Congolese were Roman Catholics and 9 percent Protestants, thus making about 45 percent of the population counted as Christian. The 1959 report of the Congo Protestant Council indicated the presence of 45 mission groups from at least ten different countries of Europe, America, and South Africa, with 2,608 missionaries on 345 stations, laboring together with 645 ordained Congolese pastors and 11,200 non-ordained evangelists. Protestant communicants numbered 821,025, with 345,473 catechumens. In the educational field, there were some 469,667 pupils in 11,170 primary schools, 1,228 students in 10 Protestant secondary schools and some 4,000 certified school teachers. And in the medical work, there were some 186 hospitals and dispensaries, with more than 700 medical assistants.[442]

Within this context, the American Presbyterian Congo Mission carried out its work with a sense of urgency. At this point, eleven stations in the Kasai provided the centers of activity from which the program of the Mission was directed. In predominantly Lulua country were the following:

LULUABOURG, the capital of Kasai Province. Here was located the business headquarters of the Mission, and in the center of the city a growing self-supporting church.

MUTOTO. Inhabited by the Lulua and the Bakua Luntu people, here were located one of the three evangelist schools, one of the two teachers' training schools, and one of the finest hospital plants in the Kasai.

KATUBUE. Here in 1957 was established a large secondary school, a cooperative enterprise with two neighboring Methodist Missions.

LUBONDAI. Here were one of the Mission's two manual training schools and a new home economics school for girls established in 1959. Also, the Christian Medical Institute of the Kasai (IMCK) which trained both nurses and dental assistants. And, very important for missionary families, the Central School for Missionaries' Children, a union institution with Methodist and Baptist Missions.

LUEBO. This, the oldest of the Mission stations, while originally inhabited by the Bakete, was now on the borders of the Lulua "nation", and had become the center of a large multi-tribal city. Here were located the Mission Press, a hospital, and an intermediate training school for pastors.

Located in Baluba country were the following stations:

BIBANGA. Here were a hospital, the Mission's second teachers' training school and one of the home economics schools for girls. Also, close by was the city of Bakwanga, the world's largest commercial diamond-mining center, where four churches had been built with money from the Birthday Offering of the Women of the PCUS.

KASHA. Though inhabited by a large number of Baluba, the land was claimed by another tribe, the Bena Kanyoka. Many of the Baluba peoples driven from their homes among the Lulua moved into the area between Bibanga and Kasha. The Mission's work here included a manual training school.

KANKINDA. Inhabited by both the Baluba and the Kanyoka peoples, this was the location of Morrison Institute, which comprised both a normal school for the training of teachers and the principal theological school for the Kasai. The theological school graduated its first class in 1959.

Three other stations were located in the territory of still other tribal groups:

MBOI. In the territory of the Babindi, here was located another of the three evangelist schools.

BULAPE. In the territory of the Bakuba and the Bakete, here was the third of the evangelist schools, as well as a school for the training of the wives of the student evangelists.

MOMA. Located in the territory of the Basala Mpasu people, here was one of the home economic schools.

In addition to this extensive mission program in the Kasai, there was the emerging work in the capital city of Belgian Congo, LEOPOLDVILLE. In this burgeoning city a small missionary force was assisting Presbyterian Christians largely from the Kasai in establishing self-supporting Presbyterian churches in three districts of the city.

Along with the programs within these particular stations, there were numerous programs which were carried out across the Mission area, drawing the churches together across divisions and reaching out into untouched areas:

WOMEN'S WORK was being organized at the local and regional levels, with Women's Schools conducted at each station and a Women's Conference drawing together women from across the Kasai, both the educated and the illiterate, learning not only how to teach the Bible and conduct meetings, but "the three R's and such skills as sewing, knitting and crocheting."[443]

YOUTH WORK was being given greater emphasis, with a region-wide Youth Fellowship Organization and an Annual Youth Conference in which young people actively participated in all phases of the planning. "As these young people gradually but eagerly break away from their strong tribal ties and venture out, their loyalties can be claimed for [Christ]."[444] In time, Youth Centers would be opened designed primarily to help school drop-outs learn trades and skills which would help them earn a living in the newly industrialized economy.

LAY TRAINING was being implemented through Bible Conferences and Leadership Schools, training churchmen for their eventual acceptance of church leadership responsibilities.

LITERARY WORK was advancing, with a Christian monthy magazine *Sankai* being published in Tshiluba and more advanced Christians—pastors, teachers, nurses, dentists—being encouraged to write for this publication. "Never before have there been any publications other than the Bible, textbooks and tracts in this language which is spoken by approximately three million people."[445] Also, a small bookstore was established in Luluabourg, the crossroads of the Kasai Province.

RURAL EVANGELISM continued to reach out into the "bush" areas, with the itinerant missionary travelling with members of an established church Session, both sharing the Gospel and explaining the workings of Presbyterian democratic church government. "The sharing of the old but still excellent film, THE KING OF KINGS, by means of a portable generator in numerous villages has brought about a renewal of great spiritual interest."[446]

  To fill all the responsibilities related to such an extensive program, the APCM at this point had 161 missionaries. This would be the largest missionary staff that the Mission would ever have, but even with such a number, the tasks to be done would stretch the personnel to the limit.

  In the midst of all its work, a major concern which absorbed the attention of Mission and Board alike was the relationship between the Mission and the indigenous church. As the 1958 World Missions Report stated:

> The vexing problem of church-mission relationships to which our missionaries have already given much earnest study will likely become more and more acute. The need to accelerate the independence and autonomy of the African church becomes daily more apparent. Yet, the solution is not easy. Is the church ready? Does it really want to go it alone? Is it mature enough spiritually to assume the responsibilities of self-government? Is it conscious of the responsibilities, as well as the privileges, which full autonomy implies? Does it have the resources with which to support its own program of work? And would the government of the Congo permit the existence of a native autonomous church in the present circumstances of political uncertainty?[447]

Complicating the process was the disruption of various phases of the Mission program, as key personnel found it necessary to leave their work simply because they belonged to the "wrong" tribe. Further, there was the difficulty of carrying forward the educational program when particular institutions meant to serve the whole Mission area could no longer offer their services to students from all tribes. Most serious of all was the threat that this divisive spirit would enter the life of the church to such an extent that it would be split into two or more basically tribal churches.

Confronting these developments, the Mission began to take definite steps towards the self-government of the church. In February 1959, an Executive Council was formed composed of representatives from both the Church and the Mission. The Council's function was "to seek legal status for itself and to administer the existing church until such time as the Congo Church is able to acquire this status for itself."[448]

Building on the work of the Executive Council, on November 2, 1959, a special meeting of the Church Synod was called, meeting in Luluabourg.[449] After deliberation, they declared that the Church had become "a separate and self-governing entity, free of any veto or other overriding control from the outside." As evidence of the existence of this new body, it was resolved that "funds provided by the Board of World Missions to assist the African Church to pay its workers were now to be sent directly to that Church rather than be administered through the Mission." Also, the Synod resolved to apply for *personalite civile* by which the government would recognize the Church as an independent organization with all legal rights and privileges. Thus the Presbyterian Church in Kasai would become the first Protestant body to arrive at such a status in Congo.[450]

Against the background of the bloodbath of tribal warfare that had taken place in October, the November 1959 Kasai Synod meeting in Luluabourg marked a new sense of the unity of the church.

Although the atmosphere of the city was charged with hate and distrust, the members of Synod manfully overcame their own deep feelings and met together for several days. Lulua delegates stayed in Baluba homes and Baluba delegates stayed in Lulua homes; they ate together, discussed affairs of the Church together and finally sat down to the Lord's Supper together. The success of this meeting not only presaged great hope for the unity of the Church in face of tribal jealousies, but it became symbolic of the dramatic reality of the church as the New Tribe.[451]

Sadly, after the November 1959 Synod, it became practically impossible for the Kasai Church leaders to sit down together and discuss the implications of the decisions made concerning the autonomy of the church. The Kasai Church was ill-prepared to assume the responsibilities of autonomy. With a total membership of some 70,000, it had less than sixty ordained pastors. There was no university graduate among all its leaders. The theological school of Kakinda had graduated its first class in that year (1959), yet there were only four members in the class and their degree was equivalent to only two years of college.

The Mission realized that, however much or little time was left, the supreme emphasis now must be upon the preparation of the leadership of the Christian community in the

Congo. With this in mind, the Mission devoted itself with new vigor to the whole program of leadership training.

> Throughout the whole educational system . . . standards are being raised. Ministers are being prepared to serve the increasingly well-educated and sophisticated congregations which are developing in the urban areas. Educators are being readied to take over the tasks of school administration heretofore handled almost entirely by missionaries. Classes are being held in the training of church officers. The supreme emphasis now is upon the development of a leadership competent for the responsibilities of the new day which cannot be too far ahead.[452]

THE FIRST CONGO CRISIS (1960-1963)

The year 1960 began with high hopes. In January the Belgian government organized a Round Table Conference, grouping 81 African political leaders, including 45 Congolese delegates from various parties, with Belgian officials. The key resolution stated: "As of June 30 next the Congo, within its present frontiers, shall become an independent state whose inhabitants have the same nationality and shall be free to move about and establish themselves within the confines of the said State, and in which goods and merchandise may also circulate freely." Elections for the two houses, Chamber of Deputies and Senate, were scheduled for May 1960.

In anticipation of independence, political activity blossomed and more than one hundred political parties were formed. While most parties remained basically ethnic, three parties emerged as striving for national power: the right-wing party of Moise Tshombe in Elizabethville, the left-wing party of Lumumba in Stanleyville, and a centrist party led by Joseph Kasavubu in Leopoldville. In May elections took place and on June 25 Kasavubu was named president and Lumumba Prime Minister.[453]

On June 30, Congo became an independent nation.

> There was a tumult of joy that swept the length and breadth of the Congo, but the demonstrations were the expressions of a natural enthusiasm, without violence or threat. Letters from the field, written as late as July 6, told of the peaceful and orderly transition; but by the time these were received [at the Board of World Missions] in Nashville five days later the whole Congo was suddenly threatened by serious outbreaks of rioting and terrorism.[454]

Elements of the Congolese army, angry over low pay and the declared intention of their Belgian officers to remain in power, mutinied. The rioting, looting and atrocities that followed caused the complete breakdown of law and order and placed the whole population, especially the foreign residents of every nationality, in imminent danger. Added to this was the increased ethnic fighting, especially in the Kasai and Katanga

Provinces. A large exodus of most of the remaining foreigners in the Congo followed, including the APCM missionaries.

> On the urgent insistence of our diplomatic representatives, all our stations in the
> Kasai were evacuated, and missionaries found refuge in the adjoining territory
> of Rhodesia in the South. Many returned to the United States, especially those
> whose furloughs were near due, and families with small children.[455]

Some of those who fled to Rhodesia, especially the men, began a gradual trek back to the Kasai in the following months, and at the end of 1960 there were 45 missionaries on the field as compared with 102 on June 30.[456] Thus independence not only closed a chapter in the history of Congo, the era of Belgian control, but also closed a chapter in the history of the American Presbyterian Congo Mission. "The Congo to which we returned after a brief evacuation period in Southern Rhodesia is strikingly different from the Congo of pre-independence days."[457]

Meanwhile, conditions continued to deteriorate. The rioting, looting and atrocities led to the occupation by Belgian paratroopers of a number of cities. But the worst was yet to come. On July 11, Moise Tshombe, whose party had swept the provincial elections in Katanga but who had been omitted from leadership in the new Congo government, led Katanga into secession, saying that he was "seceding from chaos." Aided and encouraged by foreign commercial interests in Katanga's rich mineral deposits, Tshombe declared Katanga an independent state and called for Belgian troops to put down the Force Publique mutiny in the Katanga. Soon afterward, Albert Kalonji, a political leader in southern Kasai, declared South Kasai (the "homeland" of the Baluba people) an independent state.

Fearful that the Belgian government intended to retake control of the country, on July 12, the Congolese government made an urgent appeal to the United Nations for military and administrative assistance. On July 14, the U.N. Security Council authorized the sending to the Congo of a peacekeeping force drawn from small neutral nations. By July 23, the Belgian army had withdrawn to its bases and the United Nations was established in the Congo, its first "police action" in Africa.

> In ten tragic days the Belgians lost what they had spent fifty years achieving
> in the Congo. In the first two weeks of nationhood the Congo saw its military
> and police forces disintegrate, its richest territories break away, its integrity
> threatened by foreign intervention, its technical assistants gone. The African
> continent and the world beyond [were] caught up in a crisis of the first
> magnitude, intrinsic in the explosive Congo situation.[458]

The departure of virtually all foreign merchants and technicians from the Congo led to a time of extreme economic disruption. "The cities were deserted and dead. Utilities did not function. Communications were disrupted. Offices of administration and commerce were empty . . . . The European population of the Congo, which had reached a high of 110,000 in 1959, dropped to an estimated 20,000, with the greatest number of those remaining in the Katanga."[459] The problem of securing basic supplies became very difficult and thousands of unemployed were left in the large centers of population.

The central government was finding it more and more difficult to function. When Lumumba threatened to seek military aid from Soviet-bloc countries to put down the secessions, on September 5 Kasavubu dismissed Lumumba. However, Lumumba refused to accept the dismissal and his cabinet voted to "dismiss" Kasavubu. The constitutional crisis led Army Chief-of-Staff Joseph-Desire Mobutu to "neutralize" all political activity and to form a provisional caretaker government composed of young intellectuals and technocrats. Lumumba was placed under house arrest, but escaped and was heading to join his supporters in Stanleyville when he was captured by Congolese army troops and taken to Elizabethville where, under mysterious circumstances, he was killed on January 17, 1961. Lumumba's assassination provoked an international outcry and led to the secession of two other provinces, Orientale and Kivu.

By August 1961, Parliament had reconvened and the constitutional confusion seemed to be resolved. Mobutu's provisional government handed power back to a civilian government with Kasavubu remaining President and Cyrille Adoula invested as Prime Minister. Adoula proved to be an able negotiator; "by compromise and statesmanlike tactics he succeeded in establishing in Leopoldville the parliamentary coalition government that no previous leader had provided."[460] With the apparent return of some degree of order, Kalonji ended the South Kasai secession and joined in the central government. A measure of stability had been restored by the beginning of 1962.

However, the Katanga secession continued. When negotiations failed time and again, Adoula at last persuaded the UN to commit its troops to break the Katanga secession. This military intervention so troubled UN General Secretary Dag Hammarskjold that he personally came to the Congo to use his influence for peace. Sadly his plane crashed just south of the Congo border. His death had worldwide impact and made Tshombe's recalcitrance ever more conspicuous. When U.N. troops took military action against the Katanga militia, the Katanga secession was finally brought to an end on January 14, 1963.

However, political fragmentation continued to take place. The original six provinces, whose boundaries had been arbitrarily set by the former Belgian colonial government, had broken up into 25 tribal states. Within the larger tribal units there were divisions into smaller groupings around clans fighting for power, and even fighting between rival chiefs within the same clan. All this brought about a rapid economic decline, accompanied by shortages of needed articles and foods along with inflation and every-increasing prices. The privileged few with government jobs were receiving salaries far out of proportion to the rest of the economy, while the masses of people, particularly those away from the urban centers, were "poor, discouraged and really hungry."[461] All this was accompanied by an appalling growth in corruption, of which diamond smuggling was the most flagrant example.

Within this situation of political instability, the Church along with every other institution, suffered serious disruption of its life and work. "Christians have been and are being subjected for the first time to large-scale persecution and testing, arising out of the necessity to make a choice between tribal loyalties and the atrocities often associated with them, and loyalty to Jesus Christ."[462] In numerous places mission property was destroyed. In the area served by the APCM, Kasha and Kankinda stations were pillaged and much personal property was stolen. For a while the station of Luebo was occupied by the secessionist government of South Kasai, with one missionary residence used as a prison, another as the courthouse and other buildings for various offices. The assembly grounds at Lake Munkamba, located in a "no man's land" between two warring tribes, was destroyed and looted, leaving only gaping walls.

Yet, in many ways the Church was the major stabilizing influence within these chaotic conditions. And, to the amazement of returning missionaries, the local pastors, elders, evangelists, teachers, medical helpers, and others had picked up and carried on the work which the missionaries had laid down when they were forced to leave their posts.

Providentially, preparations had already been made by the mission and church in Kasai that would prepare the way for such a time as this. In March 1960, at a historic meeting of the Synod, that body ratified the proposals made by the called Synod meeting of November 1959, and the Church became in fact an autonomous body, choosing for itself the name *Eglise Presbyterienne du Kasai.* A Joint Church-Mission Committee, composed of 25 Congolese Church leaders and ten missionaries, was given the task of working out the division of responsibilities to be carried by the Church, those to be borne by the Mission and those to be borne jointly by both bodies. The Committee met at Moma in July 1960 and drew up what would be called "the Moma plan": (1) The church would be responsible for all ecclesiastical business and some institutions, such as the primary schools, girls' homes, and ministerial training schools on the lower levels. (2) A joint board made up of representatives of both Church and Mission would function in the areas of budgeting, finance, use of properties, equipment; it would also assume responsibility for administration of hospitals, secondary education, higher ministerial training and the Mission Press, as well as the assignment of available missionary personnel. (3) The Mission would be responsible for "housekeeping" details related to missionary personnel, including schooling for missionary children, housing and transportation for missionaries and their families. The Committee of 35 proposed that this plan operate for five years (1960-1965). While the plan was far from perfect and left a number of areas of work in an ambiguous situation, at least there was a basis for church and mission to work together in an extremely chaotic situation.

Accompanying these developments, there was a great groundswell of church-consciousness. This was especially evident among the better-educated laity, who expressed "a discontent with the 'clericalism' that seeks to inherit the authority-image once represented by the mission, a censuring those who jealously seek to withstand the rising tide of younger, better trained men coming out of ministerial schools."[463] Indicative of this initiative on the part of the laity was a new impetus for the establishment of particular churches, organized congregations that were self-governing and self-supporting. While tribal dissensions and communication problems brought the 1963 synod meeting to divide themselves into three synods, "by the gracious alchemy of God this very breakdown has led the Congo church to organize a General Assembly of all synods, that the oneness of the Body of Christ might be proclaimed in the diversity of its members!"[464]

An encouraging factor in the Kasai was the favor which Protestantism enjoyed. There were Protestant Christians in places of responsibility at every level of authority. Missionaries found opportunities for service as interpreters, mediators of tribal wars, and advisors to the new government. During the visit to the Kasai in November 1961 of two representatives of the Board of World Missions, Executive Secretary Dr. T. Watson Street and Board member Dr. J. McDowell Richards, the provincial president of the Kasai expressed his profound gratitude for the work of the Presbyterian missionaries and the desire of the government for their continued help in the development of the country.

As missionaries returned to the Kasai, they found themselves in a totally reshaped program of work.

RELIEF WORK. The plight of the refugees from among all tribes who had been driven out of their homes and into new areas demanded a compassionate response. The APCM along with neighboring missions had requested early in the year supplies of food and clothing from Church World Service. Following the initial upheaval after independence, a relief organization of all Protestant missions was set up, the Congo Protestant Relief Agency, and was given the responsibility of distribution of these supplies and carrying the burden of feeding and clothing the thousands of homeless people. As the crisis became more acute, the United Nations and International Red Cross took over the procurement of supplies, but the task of distributing food and medical supplies to the famine stricken areas was left with the Congo Protestant Relief Agency. After the critical phase of the food program was over, the CPRA turned its attention to a rehabilitation program including setting up temporary tent cities for the incoming refugees until they could provide themselves housing, and giving technical assistance to those who were ready to build houses.

EMERGENCY MEDICAL WORK. One of the most critical problems following independence was the disruption of medical services throughout the land. With the departure of most of the European medical personnel who had served under the colonial administration, large hospitals were left unstaffed and unstocked, with an elaborate public health service completely disintegrated. In response to this critical need, a medical relief organization entitled "Operation Doctor" was formed to coordinate the efforts of all Protestant missions in the medical field. Under the leadership of Presbyterian missionary Dr. William Rule, some fifty missionary doctors cooperated in developing an emergency medical program, and an effort was made to recruit an additional 100 medical missionaries and to provide them with drugs and medical supplies.[465]

A RESHAPED EDUCATIONAL PROGRAM. The tribal divisions following independence necessitated a duplication of several of the major educational institutions. Since the *Ecole Secondaire* was located at Katabue, in what was regarded as "Lulua country," it became necessary to provide the personnel and assistance to establish a school of similar academic level at Bibanga, in "Balubaland." The *Ecole de Moniteurs* (Morrison Institute), closed at Kankinda as a result of tribal war, was transferred to Bibanga. The relocation of several other schools was also necessary, leading to a concentration of trained leadership in a small area and a serious lack of adequate staff in others.

A RESHAPED THEOLOGICAL EDUCATION PROGRAM. With the lower level of ministerial training, the *Ecoles Evangelique* (evangelist schools), now the full responsibility of the church, the mission could focus its attention on training pastors with a higher level of education. The *Ecole de Predicateurs* (school for pastors) at Luebo, while under the direction of the church, was staffed with a number of missionary professors. Meanwhile, there was recognition that emphasis must be placed on a higher level of theological training. The Morrison Institute experiment in joint training of preachers and teachers had not proven to be satisfactory. "At the stage of training that had now been reached in all departments of the work, it was manifest that the Presbyterian Mission alone could never expect to have sufficient funds or personnel for the quality institutions of superior and specialized preparation that the times required."[466] Therefore in 1962 the *Ecole de Theologie* (higher theological school) was moved from Kankinda to Ndesha, a suburb of Luluabourg, and became a cooperative effort with the Disciples of Christ Congo Mission. In 1964 the Belgian Protestant Mission in Ruanda also became a participant. In this location, the school would draw students not only from the Presbyterian Church in the Kasai but from neighboring provinces and even other French-speaking African countries.

A RESHAPED EVANGELISTIC PROGRAM. With the assumption of the direction of many schools and other administrative tasks by Congolese leaders, evangelistic missionaries were released from such duties and given a mobility to pursue their evangelistic calling more fully than they had been able for some years. Evangelistic teams were formed with three or four missionaries each, none of whom was assigned permanently to any one station. The teams were invited by presbyteries for specific periods and for specific purposes, outlined in the invitation. Their work included (1) the establishment and training of leadership for particular churches and regions; (2) leadership training for churches wishing to invigorate their workers; (3) evangelistic conferences; (4) pioneer evangelistic work in unreached areas.

AVIATION. With the disruption of surface travel by tribal warfare and the general deterioration of roads, the mission's two planes plus two missionary-owned planes became the primary means of communication between the various centers of work. The doctors were able to visit hospitals and dispensaries which were without resident medical personnel, committees were able to function, evangelistic missionaries were able to travel as teams to various localities and supplies could be moved where needed.[467]

A NEW EMPHASIS ON LITERATURE. The 1961 Birthday Offering of the Presbyterian U.S. Women of the Church presented one of the most promising aspects of the work in this new era. With greatly improved equipment for the J. Leighton Wilson Press, new manuscripts by Congolese church writers began to come off the press in rapid succession. The publication of a new Tshiluba-language periodical *Tuyaya Kunji?* (Where are we going?) seemed to speak to the Congolese situation with special relevance. The Protestant Bookstore of the Kasai, now known all over the Congo as LIPROKA (acronym for *Librarie Protestante du Kasai),* saw phenomenal growth.

> Each of the three cooperating missions working in the Tshiluba-speaking area, Mennonite, Brethren and Presbyterian, has contributed a missionary couple to full-time literature work, making possible for the first time a full-scale program that begins with writer-training and goes on through every phase of literature production and circulation.[468]

RADIO. The mission radio network, with a daily transmission station by station and more frequent schedules as needed, linked together all the mission posts. With telephone communication totally lacking, the radio network enabled missionaries to coordinate plans with much more efficiency than would be possible by slow, uncertain postal routes. "Pilots obtain weather reports, doctors listen to descriptions of symptoms and prescribe remedies, industrial workers advise concerning repairs for broken-down light plants or water pumps or cars, hostesses learn how many travelers to expect for the next meal."[469]

LEADERSHIP DEVELOPMENT. With the increasing responsibility being placed on Congolese church leaders, the training of both lay and clergy for positions of leadership in church and society became urgently important. By 1961 there were twelve students studying abroad who were sponsored by the American mission board: five students in Switzerland taking courses in theology and education, seven in America studying theology and general college courses, one of them looking forward to medical training. In addition to these, a number of graduates of mission schools were studying abroad through grants offered by the American, Belgian, French and Swiss governments. Also, there were a number of unusual opportunities for outstanding Christian leaders to participate in ecumenical and international meetings, such as an All-Africa Presbyterian Alliance meeting in Ibadan, Nigeria, a theological training conference in the Cameroun, the PCUS Consultation of World Missions in Montreat, and the historic constituting meeting of the All-Africa Conference of Churches in Kampala, Uganda.

In face of all the disruptions of work established through years of devoted service, how were individual missionaries adapting to the new situation? The answer given by a particular missionary was very revealing:

> In spite of the inefficiencies and the 'not-to-be-founds,' I much prefer working after independence to before! The black-white tension is much less now. The foreigner can more easily crack the barrier of prejudice against him as a white man and be a real brother. There is more fraternization across racial lines. There is a real desire for help and a realization of this need which can be met by a cautious, human-relations-conscious foreigner, who puts the bond of love into every contact and places more emphasis on this than on getting his own ideas

across. Now the foreigner must step into the background more, which goes against the grain of some natures but renders the role of a servant of Jesus Christ more accessible and more joyous.[470]

THE SECOND CONGO CRISIS (1964-1965)

By the close of 1963 the Christian community in Congo had breathed a sigh of relief and hoped that the political storm had passed. But "as the calm of the eye of the hurricane means only a brief respite from the storm before fresh gales assail"[471], so the storm which was to follow would unleash destructive forces which could not have been anticipated. In July 1964 the United Nations, thinking that the worst was over, withdrew its forces from the Congo. In the same month, when the four-year term of the precarious central government expired, President Kasavubu turned to Moise Tshombe to form a transitional government charged with maintaining national unity. Tshombe formed a southern-dominated coalition and the country's first constitution was adopted in August.

Tshombe recalled the white mercenary units that had formed the backbone of the Katanga secession, and with substantial U.S. and Belgian military aid, recaptured many rebel-held towns and established at least nominal control over most of the nation.

However, in the meantime, leftist forces who were capitalizing on massive discontent and economic chaos were fomenting rebellion. In the southwest Pierre Mulele, after returning from training in Communist China, had organized youth groups into forces that took on the tactics of Maoism with African adaptations, including witchcraft, war dress, and war paint. In the northeast General Nicholas Olenga had organized his *Simba* (lions) army and was rapidly overrunning Stanleyville. The Mulelists were pushing northeastward while the Simbas moved in a southwest direction, effectively threatening to cut the Republic of Congo in two. Establishing headquarters in Stanleyville, on September 7, 1964 the Mulelist/Simba rebellion proclaimed their government the People's Republic of Congo and received recognition from thirteen left-leaning nations. The mid-point between the two advancing forces was the Kasai, with a spearhead column coming within 40 miles of Luluabourg.[472] By the end of September a large part of the Congo was under rebel domination. Thousands of Congolese had been tortured or killed, as well as many foreigners including 150 Catholic and 29 Protestant missionaries.

As Prime Minister Tshombe's army, aided by foreign mercenaries, began to push back the rebel forces toward Stanleyville, the rebels began to gather foreign hostages in that city from a widespread area, in hopes of bargaining for military concessions. Reports of atrocities by Stanleyville-based troops against Congolese and foreign hostages led to a rescue operation by Belgian paratroopers in U.S. military transport planes, dropping on Stanleyville on November 24. They recaptured the city but not before several hundred foreigners and several thousand Congolese had been killed. The intervention prompted further indignation among supporters of the Stanleyville government and placed all Americans in Congo, most of whom were missionaries, in a dangerous position.

With the successful suppression of the Stanleyville rebellion which at one point held approximately two-thirds of the country in its grip, the National Army of the Congo reduced the pockets of rebellion to small groups of guerillas hiding out in the forests. Once again the spotlight shifted from the military to the politicians. In keeping with the Constitution of 1964, elections were held in March 1965 and Tshombe's party made significant gains. Once again a power struggle emerged between the two men at the top posts in government. In October 1965 President Kasavubu dismissed Prime Minister Tshombe from office. However, like Lumumba before him, Tshombe and his supporters in parliament refused to accept the dismissal, precipitating a build-up of tension and threatening another outbreak of intermural hostilities.

In the face of the political standoff, on the night of November 24, General Mobutu and 14 senior military commanders decided to take over the government. The coup d'etat was carried out without bloodshed and Mobutu was named head-of-state with the power of decree. Mobutu began what he proclaimed would be a regime to put an end to division within the country, bringing real unification to the fragmented Congo and a "five-year period of peace and prosperity." Only within a few years did it became apparent what price would be paid for this superimposed unity.

Remarkably the Presbyterian Church of the Congo and the American Presbyterian Congo Mission escaped the major brunt of this period of trial and suffering. However, the turmoil of the times was brought home to them as Luluabourg became a refuge for missionaries from several neighboring provinces who had been forced to abandon their work and their homes as the rebels advanced. Their presence in Luluabourg "added a real spirit of ecumenism, and their helping hands are already strengthening the Protestant work in this area. At present we have missionaries from other denominations working in Luluabourg in literature distribution, radio, Bible translation, women's work, theological education and medical work."[473]

The urgency of developing and strengthening the church became paramount. In April 1964, the first official meeting of the new General Assembly of the Presbyterian Church in Congo was held at Bibanga, bringing together representatives from the three synods. "It was a meeting full of promise for the church, as the Congolese leaders demonstrated initiative, responsibility and judgment in the midst of the developing complexities of a young church."[474] The influence of the church leaders who had studied abroad became evident, as well as the increasing role being played by the laity.

Particular aspects of the reshaped mission programs received greater emphasis. The new frontier of radio was greatly strengthened with the opening of *Studiproka*, the first religious radio programming studio in the Kasai, a joint project with the Mennonite Congo Inland Mission. Producing programs of music, drama, sermons, and Bible stories, the broadcasts reached transistor sets everywhere through the government radio stations at Luluabourg, Mbuji-Mayi and Leopoldville.—A Youth Center in the metropolitan center of Luluabourg was begun in September 1964, with the youth of the church doing most of the actual planning and supervision of activities.—The literature program continued to expand; a system of 44 literature outlets was set up and divided into six circuits, with these points visited, inventoried and restocked every two months by a literature van.—And, wonder of wonders, a Protestant-Catholic translation of the New Testament in Tshiluba was proposed by some Catholic leaders, indicating the impact of the recent Second Vatican Council as well as the sense of urgency in both Protestant and Catholic circles.

Meanwhile, education was recognized as one of the greatest long-term needs for the new Congo. A project long envisioned by the Protestant community was the Free University of the Congo, to give a genuine university education to the brightest and best of Congo's youth. A preparatory year was opened in Stanleyville in October 1963, but in 1964 it was unable to continue when that city fell to rebel forces. After a period of waiting, the university's board voted to open in Leopoldville, accepting the invitation of the Roman Catholic Lovanium University to share its facilities. A Faculty of Theology was envisioned as part of the university, but could not be initiated for several years due to lack of adequate faculty. In time it would become the capstone for Protestant theological education in the Congo, supplementing the Preachers School at Luebo and the United School of Theology at Ndesha near Luluabourg.

This was a difficult but dramatic period for the medical work. With their frontiers of responsibility greatly increased by the political turmoil, the original group of eight missionary doctors had been reduced to three. "This 'thin line' has been able to cover the various hospitals and dispensaries only because all three are experienced pilots with planes at their disposal."[475] Despite these limitations, the APCM was moving ahead with its plans for strengthening and centralizing medical education. The provincial government at Luluabourg offered the *Institut Medical Chretien du Kasai* (IMCK) a concession of land and buildings at Tshikaji, eight miles from downtown Luluabourg, "property which could not be duplicated for a half million dollars."[476] Built two years before independence, the buildings were originally used by the Belgian government as a school for training Congolese in government administration. Classes at IMCK were begun in October 1964, with 38 students enrolled. The school was officially inaugurated on December 12, 1964, with the PCUS General Assembly Moderator, Dr. Felix B. Gear present. In time the institute would become the major center for medical education in the Kasai.[477]

The increasing centralization of the work in the city of Luluabourg, coupled with a lack of adequate hotel accommodations for visiting missionaries and others, led to the decision to purchase an old hotel in the heart of the city. This would become the *Centre Protestant,* providing not only living quarters for visitors but space for mission and church offices, accommodations for church-wide conferences and for church and mission committees, and in time for nationals from other countries who were coming to Luluabourg in increasing numbers to work in United Nations programs.

As the five-year period set for the "Moma Plan" (1960-1965) was drawing to a close, it became increasingly apparent that a new plan was needed that would place increased responsibility in the hands of the church.

> This was not a bad plan, and under it Congolese leadership has emerged and tried its wings. On the other hand, it has permitted both church and mission to blame failures on the other, and some aspects of the work have suffered greatly from the lack of any clear sense of responsibility on either side. Furthermore, it

was hard to maintain the posture of equal partnership when one of the partners had superior technical know-how, the support of a constituency enjoying unprecedented prosperity, and as a result, considerable self-confidence, while the other was in the throes of political turmoil, economic disaster, and was consequently feeling anything but self-confident. While these facts of life produce tensions which no re-shuffling of organizations will quickly remedy, the existence of the APCM as a legal entity and a separate organization became the abrasive factor around which irritation centered.[478]

Hence a church-mission committee was named to draw up a plan for the integration of the mission into the church. This committee's report, called the "Mboi Plan" after its place of meeting, was approved by the 1964 General Assembly of the Congolese church and referred to both the presbyteries and the PCUS Board of World Missions for study. The plan of integration sought (1) to allow the church to be "master in its own house", (2) to avoid smothering the young church under a mass of institutions and services she did not create but from which she could not extricate herself, and (3) to safeguard the institutions and services from destruction by inexperienced leadership.

The plan of integration sought to accomplish these aims by entrusting the functions heretofore fulfilled by the mission to "semi-autonomous councils" which would include, so long as necessary, both missionary and Congolese members, but which would be entirely and solely named by and answerable to the General Assembly of the church. There would be four such councils: secondary and higher education, primary education, medical work, and property.

> The highly technical nature of medicine and the unhappy experience in church-controlled medical work elsewhere in Africa make this one of the most sensitive points in the new plan. However, the EPC has asked that the constitution for this semi-autonomous council be drafted by a committee composed of all missionary medical doctors.[479]

It would be several years before the Mboi Plan could be put into full effect, as guidelines for the various semi-autonomous councils were being worked out. However, it was apparent that the APCM was in the process of devolution as responsibilities were being transferred to the church.

By the end of 1965, the spirit of the mission and church was upbeat.

> In the midst of this fluid situation, 1965 has been a constructive year. Organizationally the church is better equipped for its task. The *esprit de corps* is the best it has been since independence. Signs of personal and institutional maturity are abundantly evident . . . (W)e can join with the Congolese Christians in thanking God for his bounty so richly bestowed.[480]

There was also a profound sense of gratitude to the PCUS Board of World Missions for its support during these trying times:

> The Board of World Missions policy regarding missionary commitment in these trying times had displayed a very careful respect for individual conscience and a desire not to impose on any one or any family obligations beyond what each considered right in his own case. Decisions have been honored. Losses have been recompensed. Missionaries have known the undergirding of the daily prayers of Christians in the home Church for ourselves, for our Congolese brethren and for the Church of Christ in Congo.[481]

THE BEGINNING OF ORDER—AND DICTATORSHIP (1966-1972)

Mobutu lost no time in establishing absolute control of the Congolese government. In April 1966, the *Mouvement Populaire de la Revolution (MPR)* was launched and eventually was proclaimed the sole legal party. Mobutu easily resisted a plot of some of the displaced politicians, four of whom were publicly hanged on June 2, 1966. Others either accepted the new regime, went into exile or were imprisoned.

However, there was one last spasm of opposition, this time from the opposite camp. White mercenaries, said to represent High Finance seeking to control and profit from the Congo's wealth of natural resources, defied the government that had hired them. On July 4, 1967, mercenaries attached to the National Army revolted and staged a dramatic takeover of Stanleyville.

> Suddenly, all white foreigners in the country became suspect of complicity in a massive plot to overthrow the established authority. Missionaries were caught in the overall restriction of movement. They felt the backlash of a wave of hysteria whipped up by inflammatory radio oratory condemning "Western economic imperialism." This even had disturbing anti-Christian overtones—"See the way the so-called Christian nations act!"[482]

Several battles were waged between the mercenaries and the Congolese army, but finally the mercenaries quit the country and the emergency subsided. However, the ill will created by the episode remained.

Political power was gradually centralized by decree in the presidency and codified in the second Constitution, promulgated on June 24, 1967. Provincial governments were streamlined in order to conform to the new national control. In 1966 the Kasai province was divided along ethnic lines, with the Baluba province becoming East Kasai with its capital at Bakwanga (soon to become Mbuji-Mayi), and the Lulua province becoming West Kasai, with its capital at Luluabourg (soon to become Kananga).

A program was begun aimed at abolishing tribalism and regionalism and developing a sense of nationalism among the people. The program became known as "authenticity" Under this theme, the names of major cities were "Africanized": Leopoldville became Kinshasa, Luluabourg became Kananga, Elizabethville became Lubumbashi, and Stanleyville became Kisangani. Citizens were encouraged to change their Christian names for African ones. Mobutu himself dropped his Christian name and became Mobutu Sese Seko. European-style dress was discouraged, and Congolese fashions came into vogue. Mobutu also announced a policy of economic nationalism, beginning with the country's largest mining operation, the *Union Miniere du Haut-Kananga (UMHK)*. This led to conflict with the Belgian corporations which had kept control of Congo's major industries and gradually led to the flight of foreign capital. Seeking confirmation for his strong-armed tactics, Mobutu invited the Organization of African Unity to meet in Kinshasa in 1967, and Mobutu himself became the OAU Chairman.

As the projected "five-year period of peace and prosperity" drew to a close, Mobutu's control became even more absolute. When elections were held in November 1970, Mobutu was the sole candidate for the presidency and the MPR was declared the sole political party and supreme institution of the country. On October 27, 1971 even the name of the nation was changed to the Republic of Zaire.

The impact of these developments on the economy of the nation was disastrous. The nation sank ever deeper into bankruptcy, with dwindling support for schools, the health care system, and all aspects of infrastructure such as transport. The nation's currency came to have no value outside national boundaries. Worst of all, Mobutu systematically and continuously drew his personal wealth from the potential riches of this country rich in natural resources, sucking the means of livelihood from a poverty-stricken people until Mobutu amassed a fortune making him one of the wealthiest people in the world. "This conduct has inspired and encouraged a system of corruption in Zaire that can hardly be equaled anywhere else in the world. Services of any sort must be bought with 'money under the table' so to speak . . . This is Mobutuism!"[483]

The impact of this political situation upon the Christian community was profound. Under government pressure, at the March 1970 assembly of the Congo Protestant Council, all the various Protestant churches in the country were united into one recognized church, the *Eglise du Christ au Zaire (ECZ)*. The union was unique in that, even though the assembly's vote was not unanimous, there was no reference back to the member churches for approval.[484] Henceforth the member churches became known as "communities". The Presbyterian Church in the Kasai became the *Communaute Presbyterienne de Zaire (CPZ)* and the Presbyterian Church in Kinshasa became the *Communaute Presbyterienne de Kinshasa (CPK)*. The ECZ permitted these communities to maintain their previous ecclesiastical traditions, structures and fraternal ties with churches outside Zaire, building its unity principally through national co-ordination and oversight. At the time of its establishment, the ECZ was composed of some 53 Protestant communities.

Since the MPR party was now to be recognized as "the supreme institution of the Republic," all other institutions including religious groups were to be subordinate. An ordinance promulgated in 1971 declared that every church or sect "has the obligation to inculcate in its members a civic spirit conforming to the principle of this Manifesto." This was to be applied not only in the churches but also in all educational establishments, including theological schools.

The increasing application of the politics of authenticity was further evidenced in August 1971, when the three existing universities—Lovanium University in Kinshasa (Catholic), the Free University of Kisangani ((Protestant), and the Official University of Lubumbashi (State)—were amalgamated into the National University of Zaire (UNAZA), with three campuses under direct government control. In December 1971, a presidential decree abolished as national holidays any Christian celebrations which fell on weekdays. In February 1972 the churches were placed under surveillance by members of the MPR's youth organization to "denounce subversive actions" by pastors and priests in any form, including prayers. In the same month a directive was issued requiring that all infants born after this date be baptized with only Zairian names. In succeeding months numerous foreign missionaries were expelled from Zaire. And on November 29, 1972 all religious youth organizations were suppressed, and the MPR youth organization (JMPR) became the only authorized youth organization in the country. By the end of 1972, it appeared that no aspect of the life of the Zairian people was exempt from the strict control of Mobutu's MPR party.[485]

In the early stages of Mobutu's regime, the Christian community rejoiced in the stability which had been brought to the life of the nation. With a sense of new opportunity, in 1966 the Congo Protestant Council launched a nation-wide evangelistic campaign under the theme, "Christ for All!" "The deliberate effort is to be made by the churches of the Congo to reach the entire nation, over 15 million people, with the Good News of Jesus Christ during 1967-68; already local campaigns are being directed toward this end in the various sectors of this huge area in Central Africa."[486] The coordinated campaign included the formation of prayer cells, organization of lay visitation programs, distribution of literature and mass evangelistic rallies. Working together, the various Protestant communities "were drawn closer together in the unity of faith as they seek to bring others to Christ."[487]

Within the work of the Mission in the Kasai, the urgency of training Congolese leadership became still more critical. In medical work, the transition from the direct healing ministrations of the missionary doctor to the development of a medical school was not an easy task. With only three missionary doctors on the field, they commuted by plane to maintain medical services as best they could at the scattered hospitals and dispensaries at Bulape, Bibanga, Mutoto, Moma and Lubondai, and at the same time supervised the students at IMCK. Finally, despite voluble resistance from church leaders and the people at large, missionary doctors, nurses and technicians would have to be withdrawn from other hospitals and located at IMCK. The school carried on its work effectively and graduated its first class in 1966 and its first girl nurses in 1968. The announcement in 1968 that the Women of the Church of the Presbyterian Church U.S. had chosen the medical center at Tshikaji as the objective for their special Birthday Offering in 1969 rekindled the dream of building a modern 200-bed hospital "to complete a quality institution to give Christian medical training and to serve as a witness in the heart of the Congo as to what 20th century Christian medical service can really be."[488] Until the Good Shepherd

Hospital was completed and opened in 1975, clinical training for the student nurses was provided at the Bulape and Lubondai hospitals.

Meanwhile, the Congolese were clamoring for more opportunities for higher general education. "Congolese governments, central and provincial, encouraged the opening of new secondary schools everywhere, whether these could be adequately staffed and equipped or not."[489] The Presbyterian Church of the Congo added numerous new junior high schools to its system, entirely staffed and directed by Congolese. The Mission saw its most valuable contribution to be in strengthening the three established senior high schools at Katubue, Bibanga and Kinshasa, all of which adhered to the highest academic requirements. "These are all university-preparatory and feed a stream of well-qualified Protestant Christian students into the universities and on into the professional and public life of the nation."[490]

The Free University of the Congo, of "Protestant inspiration", after two years in its temporary home at the Lovanium Catholic University in Kinshasa, was preparing to return to its Kisangani campus in 1966 when the mutiny of mercenaries there made that impossible. The university found a second temporary home at Kananga (Luluabourg) during 1966-1967. "This sojourn in Luluabourg enriched the life of the Protestant community there and helped the Kasai students to know the university better."[491] However, at the insistence of the central government, the Free University moved back to Kisangani for the school year 1967-1968, and found its permanent location there. Its fields of special emphasis were agriculture, education and theology. A preparatory year and extension courses continued from a small affiliated campus in Kananga.

As the Mobutu regime exerted increasing control over all aspects of the life of the people, education at all levels was nationalized with a uniform program and standards, along with some government financing. However, among schools at all levels, six out of seven were church-related. The strain between government and church/mission related schools became increasingly pronounced:

> The educational difficulties which plague the country as a whole loom large in our church-related institutions: more schools, more children, more classes. A constant necessity to upgrade is felt . . . find better teachers . . . modify the program so graduates can teach in primary schools . . . add a fifth grade . . . add a sixth grade . . . stretch to get accreditation as a high school. Stretch, too, to cultivate that precious sense of responsibility in students, parents, principals and teachers. Stretch to provide education to meet basic needs of Africans in 1972. Stretch to improve the spiritual as well as physical aspects of education.[492]

What was becoming apparent in the work of the APCM was the increasing concentration of its effort in urban areas. Until the 1950s, the work had been predominantly rural, concentrating on reaching out into the unreached villages. However, with the coming of the 60s, the program became increasingly urban. "Four rural stations have been completely turned over to the Church, with no missionaries in residence: Kasha and Kankinda in the wake of tribal fighting, Mutoto in 1965 and Mboi in 1966 because of higher priority needs for the limited missionary personnel."[493] Missionaries continued to live and work at the rural stations of Luebo, Bulape, Bibanga, Lubondai and Moma, but the major focus centered on work in the cities, which were growing rapidly as political and financial centers and drawing increasing numbers out of the rural areas.

Luluabourg (now Kananga) had become the central city in the heart of the nation, growing in importance as a transportation center on the railroad and new network of airways. "By 1958 Luluabourg was a proud, pleasant little city with broad avenues, handsome homes and public buildings, busy railroad station and air terminal, and a population of some 115,000 Congolese and 3,800 Europeans."[494] Missionaries lived not only at the "station" of Ndesha on the city's outskirts but also scattered throughout the city in polyglot neighborhoods of Congolese, Belgians and other Europeans, Pakistanis, Haitians, as well as other Americans. "The consequent social mingling presents manifold and diverse opportunities for Christian witness."[495] The presence of missionaries of other denominations who had taken refuge in Luluabourg during the times of tribal warfare opened the door for numerous opportunities for ecumenical undertakings: Mennonite missionaries worked in the literature and radio programs, since their former constituents had also used the Tshiluba language; Methodist missionaries collaborated in medical and educational work. And during this period, as has been mentioned earlier, numerous other aspects of the work of mission and church had been drawn to Kananga: the mission business office, the church headquarters, the higher theological school, the IMCK, a bookstore, a youth center, an extension of the Protestant Free University.

As Kananga had become the capital city for West Kasai Province, Mbuji-Mayi (formerly Bakwanga) had become the capital for the East Kasai. In contrast to Kananga, Mbuji-Mayi was a "boom-town" which had grown up overnight, with thousands of Baluba refugees. The presence of the mining company which had become the world's largest supplier of industrial diamonds offered a solid core of economic stability, but along with it came all the vices and problems of such a frontier town. Among the Baluba refugees were many outstanding business and professional persons, including many excellent church leaders. Under their leadership new congregations began to form in all parts of the city, always with schools alongside. However, the Baluba resented the fact that so many missionary personnel were serving in Kananga and its environs, while only a very few were located in Mbuji-Mayi. The fact that the Church's central office, especially the central treasury, was located at Kananga, became a sore point for the proud Baluba. At the 1968 General Assembly, a substantial splinter group of Baluba churches broke away from the Church as centered at Kananga, hoping still to retain the Presbyterian name and the fraternal ties with the Presbyterian Church in the United States. The split inserted a deepening wedge into the unity of the Presbyterian Church in the Congo.

In addition to the two large cities of the Kasai, smaller urban centers along the railroad became increasingly important places in program and planning—Mweka, Muena Ditu. But the major focus of urban work was in Congo's troubled capital, Kinshasa. As the city grew to over a million people, the two Baptist missions which had been assigned to this area by early comity agreements, finding themselves unable to keep up with the pace of its needs and challenges, invited the Presbyterians to come to the capital and help them.

In 1955 the Presbyterian Mission of Leopoldville was opened and given four communities of the city as its particular charge. In 1959, the Presbyterian Mission in Leopoldville ceased to exist, merging into the Presbyterian Church of the city. As new missionaries were assigned to this location, they learned the languages of the Lower Congo region, so that their witness could extend beyond those persons from the Kasai who had gravitated to Kinshasa. Alongside the Presbyterian churches in the capital city, the Presbyterians carried a big educational load, with a primary school system of more than 6000 students and one full six-year high school. The Presbyterians also took the initiative in efforts toward church unity and the formation of a citywide council of churches.

> Congolese pastors and church officers from different parts of the city, who had scarcely been acquainted with each other before, began to have regular meetings in one church after another, sometimes having meals together. School directors and other key laymen were included on occasion. Every such friendly encounter in the Christian context helped to heal old hurts . . . . The Presbyterians took all the initiative.[496]

It was out of this ministerial council of Kinshasa that there came the inspiration and drive for a National Evangelistic Campaign in 1966-1968.

As the church advanced, the call for missionaries became all the more insistent. In addition to the demand for more co-workers in the fields of evangelism, education and medicine, numerous needs arose for specialized ministries.

> In the complex of modern adjuncts to the original preaching-teaching-healing ministries, many present-day missionaries are specialists in some particular field. We have pilots and printers, electricians and architects, broadcasters and editors, business managers and a hospital administrator, chemistry teachers and Latin teachers, gynecologists and ophthalmologists. Visiting doctors come to devote some weeks or months within the field of their specialties. Short-term appointees, summer volunteers, medical and seminary interns come to lend a hand in whatever special ways they may. Young men assist with construction jobs, transport, mechanical repairs, sports and recreation; young women with secretarial chores, sewing classes, English classes, sorting and shelving of drugs and other supplies.[497]

Architects and builders were especially required. The Presbyterian Development Fund which was being raised in the Presbyterian Church, U.S. for postwar building needs in mission around the world would make resources available to build and rebuild churches, schools, medical facilities, and numerous other centers of ministry.

> Bob Gould was asked by the General Assembly to serve as church architect.
> With his skilled assistance, a beautiful new chapel has been erected at Luebo

and another is underway at Mweka. For some structures elsewhere, he helped with plans and procurement. He has conducted some classes in drafting and plan-reading that have enabled others to go out and build on their own.[498]

Other new ventures in mission were undertaken. Elijah Barnes, an African-American missionary, initiated a program in community development in Kinshasa, including training in setting up cooperatives.—A gift from the Preston Hollow Presbyterian Church in Dallas, Texas provided for a well-digging machine, to provide cleaner and more abundant water for the health and convenience of remote villages.—A program to encourage the economic and nutritional development found expression in four herds of cattle sprinkled over the Kasai area. A specialist missionary Joe Spooner, along with Peace Corps workers and Zairois helpers cared for the herds and trained others in animal husbandry.—Nutrition clinics for small children were developed under the leadership of missionary doctor John K. Miller, with a specially equipped trailer traveling from village to village. About 3,000 children were examined each month by missionary doctors and Zairois nurses. "In many clinics a package of soya flour is given to each mother when she pays the 30 cent registration fee. She is taught how to prepare and feed her children soya flour-and-corn meal cereal mixed with a variety of other high protein foods such as powdered caterpillars."[499]—Along with the baby clinics, classes in family planning were being provided. "Traditional methods of spacing children required the wife to return to her home for several months with the new baby, leaving the husband alone or with another wife. Modern methods provide an alternative which is more conducive to family unity."[500]

Meanwhile, the Plan of Integration proposed by the "Mboi Plan" was slowly making its way toward implementation. After being enthusiastically endorsed by the General Assembly of the Congolese church in 1964, it was referred for study to the Presbyteries and to the Board of World Missions. The 1965 General Assembly invited a delegation from the Board to come to the Congo to discuss these matters face to face with representatives of the Church. Dr. T. Watson Street, the BWM Executive Secretary; Dr. David L. Stitt, the Board Chairperson; and Dr. Walter D. Shepard, Africa Secretary met in November 1965 in Luluabourg with a committee of twelve Congolese leaders named by the Church, and seven missionary observers. The resulting paper, now called "the Luluabourg Plan", called for the transfer of all mission properties and almost all Mission responsibilities from the American Presbyterian Congo Mission (APCM) to the Presbyterian Church of Congo (EPC). It was agreed that the APCM should give up its separate legal status as soon as mutually acceptable arrangements could be made to assure the continuity of its vast complex of activities. The Plan of Integration was submitted to the Board of World Mission at its January 1966 meeting and approved in principle.

The next three years were fraught with much debate over the implementation of the Plan. Points of particular strain included the uses of money, property and machinery, and the placement of missionary personnel. The transfer of mission properties to the juridical foundation of the church was especially tedious. "Not until 1968, after long legal delays, has the first actual transfer of property been accomplished, certain church and school sites being ceded to the Presbyterian Church of the Congo."[501] Finally, at the meeting of the EPC General Assembly in 1969, "decisive action was taken to proceed forthwith to seek prompt implementation of the integration of APCM into the EPC, and accordingly the dissolution of APCM."[502] A committee appointed by the General Assembly met at Bulape in May 1969 to work out the final report; the resulting document was 35 pages long! At its July 1969 meeting, the Board of World Missions voted "that the Board approve the constitutions, by-laws and related organizational agreements drawn up at Bulape, May 26 through June 6, 1969, to implement the integration of the American Presbyterian Congo Mission into the *Eglise Presbyterienne au Congo*."[503]

At last, after much preparation, the long-awaited time for the formal ceremonies of integration had come. On March 15, 1970, thousands gathered in Kananga to recognize the "coming of age" of the Presbyterian Church in Congo/Zaire. Among those attending were representatives of the Presbyterian Church, U.S.: Dr. R. Matthew Lynn, moderator of the General Assembly; Dr. T. Watson Street, Executive Secretary of the Board of World Missions; and John Pritchard, Africa Secretary of the Board. Representing the Presbyterian Church in Congo were the Rev. Joseph Nsenda, stated clerk, the Rev. Mikobi Jacques, General Assembly Moderator, and Mr. Jacques Pierre Bakatushipa, legal representative. Other dignitaries included representatives of the American Ambassador and of the provincial government. "The parade was to begin at 9:30—but Nzenda and Bakatushipa were not there yet! At 9:50 they drove up in a flower-bedecked car right to the tent [where dignitaries were seated] and were deposited right in front of their chairs! They were fully robed. Then the parade started, and I must say that it was VERY impressive. All the different groups: choirs, classes, women's groups, etc. were dressed alike and they all passed by the tent in front of the visitors . . . . The parade lasted for about an hour. The program got off to a late start, and even with cutting out a lot, we finished at 2:00 p.m. to go the [Protestant] Centre for lunch. The signing took place toward the end . . . . It was 4:00 p.m. before the meal was over."[504] A second ceremony took place on the following day at Mbuji-Mayi, and a third on March 17 at the founding point of Presbyterian work in the Congo, Luebo. Later Moderator Lynn commented, "The ceremonies were characterized by enthusiasm and real joy. The fact that so many people—there were thousands in each place—would give so much time spoke to me of the importance they placed upon this event."[505]

The new fraternal relationship between the Presbyterian Church U.S. and the Presbyterian Church in the Congo was expressed in the following statement:

In the complete integration of the APCM and the EPC we do not tie the EPC only to the Presbyterian Church U.S., nor the Presbyterian Church only to the EPC. Each Church is autonomous. The EPC can request help anywhere she desires and can refuse help that she sees will harm her independence. The Presbyterian Church U.S. can refuse the actions and requests of the EPC if she sees that such will not help the EPC and if she does not have what is requested. In the will of God, these Churches have walked together for many years and still feel responsibility to each other in the work of God in Congo.[506]

At this point in its life, the Presbyterian Church in the Congo (or Presbyterian Community in Zaire, as it had become known) was composed of some 130,000 members, in over a hundred organized congregations (although "some weak ones, prematurely born into the organizational life of presbytery, synod and general assembly waver on the sick-list.")[507] Stretching out beyond these congregations were some 1,540 non-organized churches where evangelists faithfully labored.[508] The church had organized its work in five departments: Evangelism, Education, Medical Services, Property and Finance. Within this structure, some 95 Presbyterian U.S. missionaries were serving, meeting as best they could those needs which had been identified by the church.

Virginia Pruitt well summarized the changed attitude which was needed for mission service in the new nation:

> The old we-they concepts must be cast away. We share alike in the failures and in the triumphs. We must pool our human and material resources to the glory of God and the bringing of His reign in the hearts of men. We must be able to humble ourselves, each considering the other better than himself. But WE together are THE CHURCH, and there is neither missionary nor national, neither American nor African, neither white nor black, but WE, THE CHURCH, one in faith, one in hope, one in the Lordship of Jesus the Christ.[509]

D. THE HORN OF AFRICA

Malcolm Forsberg of the Sudan Interior Mission describes a poignant scene when all missionaries were ordered to leave southern Sudan in February 1964:

> It was difficult for the missionaries to gather together all the last bits of equipment and clothing. Finally they moved toward their trucks. They were surrounded by Christians and unbelievers. All wanted to shake hands for the last time. The police shouted. The crowd was delaying the departure. Then the people began to sing. In the last year a little chorus had drifted into the Sudan almost unnoticed. It had been translated into Arabic and into several tribal languages. Perhaps the Lord had sent it for such a time. The Christians sang it with deep feeling:
>
> *I have decided to follow Jesus,*
> *No turning back, no turning back.*
> *The cross before me, the world behind me,*
> *No turning back, no turning back.*

The missionaries climbed into their trucks. The police pushed the people back. The cars moved slowly through the waving crowd. Then they were on the open road. As they increased their speed, the singing faded. The last words the missionaries heard were, "No turning back, no turning back."[510]

POLITICAL CONTEXT IN THE NEW SUDAN

The spirit of nationalism that swept Africa at the opening of this period expressed itself with particular force in the Sudan. Soon after the independent republic of the Sudan was proclaimed in 1956, the new government exerted every effort to bring the rebellious peoples of southern Sudan under its control. Sporadic guerrilla warfare had erupted in 1955, and only increased in intensity with the coming years. With the parliamentary government proving ineffective, a bloodless coup in November 1958 installed General Ibrahim Abbud as leader of a military government. His period of power was short-lived, and in 1964 another ineffective period of parliamentary government followed. Once more the military took matters into their own hands; in May 1969 a group of young military officers, led by Colonel Gaafar Mohamed el-Nimeiri seized power. In July 1971, a Communist-backed coup sought to overthrow Nimeiri, but within three days he was back in charge; at once he cut ties with the Soviet Union and Eastern Europe and became a strong ally of the United States, managing to stay in control of the Sudanese government through the tumultuous events until 1985. Thus, within this 15-year period (1958-1972) the government of the Sudan had changed hands five times, usually accompanied by considerable violence.

Throughout this period, the underlying reality was the growing conflict between northern and southern Sudan. During their years of colonial control, the British had maintained separate policies for northern and southern Sudan. The focus of economic and political development had been on the north and the south was virtually ignored. What attention was given in southern Sudan in the way of health care, education and community development came through missionary efforts.

By the time Sudan had gained its independence, the seeds of civil war had already taken root. The north was no more interested in the needs of the south than the British had been, nor were northern officials willing to incorporate more southerners into the administration of the country. To add insult to injury, the Sudanese government attempted to exploit southern resources for its own gain, seeking to place the South's rich agricultural potential within the northern sphere of influence without proper compensation or recognition of southern claims.

As resistance to government policies broke out, the Sudanese military responded with increasing harshness and severity. Villages in the south were destroyed, with large populations decimated. Refugees from these villages fled, both to the larger cities of the Sudan and across borders into the neighboring nations of Ethiopia, Kenya, Uganda and Zaire. The people of southern Sudan entered a long night of suffering for years to come.

IMPACT UPON THE CHRISTIAN MOVEMENT

Needless to say, the Christian churches increasingly felt the pressure of the Muslim-dominated government. Following the takeover of all mission related schools in 1957, the government used every means possible to bring Christian medical work to a close.

> "It is our duty to provide social services for all our people," government officials said. "We must provide government medical facilities for all." Some of these "medical facilities" brought ours to a close. In each place the announcement was made: "We are going to build a clinic here." . . . There were many places where there was no medical work but the government built its first clinics next to ours.[511]

In March 1960, suddenly and without warning Christians working in government offices in the South were told that Sunday as a Christian day of rest was to be no more. The Christians were to join the Moslems in having Friday as the weekly day of rest. Everybody was to work on Sunday. Thus the rights of Christian Sudanese were being taken away one by one, and it had become illegal to protest government actions.

Then in 1962 came the "Missionary Societies Act," which made it illegal for any church or missionary society to "perform in the Sudan any missionary act except in accordance with the terms of the license granted by the Council of Ministers." Although licenses were repeatedly applied for, the authorities never issued them. According to the new law, the purely Sudanese churches were considered "missionary societies," making it very difficult for them to carry out any overtly Christian witness. The one redeeming feature was that the government found the law virtually impossible to enforce.

But the crowning blow was still to come. The government found provocation for more aggressive action in the activities of some of the southern students and youth.

> [Southern] students and young people, restless under the military jurisdiction in the southern provinces, distrustful of the government leadership, have been escaping over the borders and joining in an exile revolutionary movement. In early 1964, this group felt that it gained enough strength to make an open attack upon a town near the southern border of the Sudan. This proved to be abortive, and the government expelled all missionaries, making the accusation that they had aided and abetted this revolutionary movement.[512]

Thus, on February 27, 1964, all missionaries working in the southern Sudan (some 300 altogether) were ordered to leave.

> The Minister of the Interior stated that British imperialists and missionaries had alienated the Southern tribespeople from their Northern Arab brothers.

> The British had left the country but the missionaries remained to deepen
> the gulf between the South and the North. Were it not for this outside
> interference [the Minister said], the Sudan would have been a united
> country.[513]

With missionaries gone from the South, the government was able to begin in earnest its military operations there unobserved by the outside world. However, the expulsion of the missionaries only strengthened the resolve of the people in the South to separate from the North.

> Some Southerners demanded secession from the North. They would not discuss
> any other solution. Others thought they might have a chance of coming to
> an agreement with the North if they asked for federation. But the North was
> willing to consider neither proposal.[514]

From 1964, as the army stepped up its campaign in the South, those Southerners who escaped jail or execution fled to the bush. Guns were brought out of hiding. The civil war was on. The people in the former Presbyterian, Anglican and Africa Inland Mission areas suffered most. Many in the rural areas were killed if they did not succeed in escaping into the forests or across the border into neighboring countries. Many churches and mission stations were destroyed.

> By mid-1965 chaos in the South was complete. Medical help was available in
> the three provincial capitals only. No schools were open. Roads were not safe.
> People who had lived along the roads had fled.[515]

During the next eight years, the outside world knew little of what was going on in southern Sudan. Mission agencies that had been working there waited anxiously and prayerfully to know what was happening to their Sudanese colleagues. What information was available came through the church offices in Malakal, where evangelists from the rural areas would come to report on the situation in their villages.

In northern Sudan, Christian witness continued though under many new constraints. Restrictions on the travel of all foreigners began in 1967, and in 1970 all church-owned periodicals were suspended. Accusations against churches and missionary organizations, fanned by the mass media, created an atmosphere of suspicion around Christians in general and church leaders in particular. On the other hand, there were a few gestures of tolerance on the part of the government, especially in response to relief and press campaigns abroad regarding the Sudanese refugees. In 1969, the government created an Office for Christian Education within the Ministry of Education, and provided for the secondment of a number of teachers to be trained for teaching Christianity in some government elementary schools.

In face of the increasing government pressure, the churches in northern Sudan determined to stand together through the establishment of the Sudan Council of Churches in 1965.[516] Its membership included churches of eight communions, covering a wide spectrum—Catholic, Orthodox, Anglican and Protestant (the churches established by the more conservative faith missions declined to join until later). The Council gave the churches a common voice helping them to stand together in their relationship with the government. Later it would provide an avenue through which international ecumenical agencies could work to relieve the suffering of the multitude of southern Sudanese refugees who had fled to the cities of northern Sudan.

THE STATUS OF AMERICAN PRESBYTERIAN WORK FOLLOWING INDEPENDENCE

To fully comprehend the impact of these developments upon the work in which American Presbyterians had been engaged, it is necessary to review the scope of that work at the outset of this period. The Church of Christ in the Upper Nile (later to be known as the Presbyterian Church in Sudan (PCIS)), which had been officially established in 1956, had brought together the fruit of the American Presbyterian work in southern Sudan, as well as a few other groups of believers. In 1957 it consisted of one presbytery with three ordained pastors and five organized congregations, covering five tribal groups: the work among the Shilluk people, centered at Doleib Hill; the work among the Ngok Dinka, centered at Abwong; the work among the Gajaak Nuer, centered at Nasir; the Anuak work centered in Akobo; and the work among the Murle tribe, centered in Pibor.

In addition, there were other places where significant witness was being given. In the sleepy provincial capital Malakal there was a remarkable union church with Presbyterian and Anglican members from five different tribes, each meeting separately for worship in its own language. And to the southwest of Doleib Hill, there was missionary witness among the Central Nuer people at Wang Lel, and among the Western Nuer people at Ler.

The outlook seemed bright. As Margaret Crawford wrote in her report to COEMAR in early 1958,

> The Church of Christ in the Upper Nile is definitely growing in many ways—in the number of its members, in its spiritual interests and outreach. This growth is accompanied by an increasing hunger for the Word of God.[517]

In addition, the relationship of this young church with the larger Christian community was also growing.

> Last year in 1957 for the first time, the church sent delegates to conferences outside their land. A young man has been sent to the Alexandria Youth

Conference, and two others to the All-Africa Church Conference. Through such contacts our Church got a wider vision of Christendom.[518]

These ecumenical ties would be of tremendous value in following years, in eliciting the concern and support of the larger Christian community in the time of trial for the church in southern Sudan.

The Christian witness in the southern Sudan was being greatly strengthened through the mission printing press at Malakal, the only Mission press in the entire Sudan.

> As a means of evangelism, the United Presbyterian Mission has set up a printing press at Malakal. It is well named, "The Spearhead Press", for it has pioneered in the use of the small photo-offset printing unit in Africa . . . . Four years ago the training of the first three men began—men with from four to six years of schooling, and with no experience whatsoever of machinery . . . . Today the staff numbers about 12—each one with some degree of special skill.[519]

In the vast area covered by the work of the American Presbyterian Mission in southern Sudan, where only a small percentage of the people were literate but where there was a great hunger for the written word, the production of printed materials in the vernacular, as well as in English and Arabic, was eagerly received.

The mission continued to conduct small elementary schools, sometimes called "bush schools", in little one-room school houses, located usually in places near enough to the mission station for missionary oversight.

With regard to medical work, two small hospitals had been built through an American Presbyterian endowment fund in areas of particular need, at Pibor and Wang Lel. Also a small hospital at Ler had been inherited from the Church Missionary Society when it transferred its work there to the American Presbyterian Mission. Small clinics were operated at Doleib Hill, Nasir, and Akobo.

> When the Nuer pastor was asked, "Why is the mission hospital so much busier than ever?", he answered, "Because in the villages people are giving up witch doctors. They're turning to the Christian doctor."[520]

The work among people from the southern Sudan extended also into the north. As Southerners gained in education, they often found their way to Northern cities in search of work. Also, as the civil war intensified, the number of Southern refugees in the camps surrounding the larger cities increased.

> Since their background is primitive African, they find themselves in a difficult cultural and racial atmosphere among the Arab Muslims in the North. Because they have been trained in mission schools, and many of them are Christians, the

Mission in the North has a definite responsibility for assisting these young men as they try to make their way in what is really a strange land. The Mission must assist in such adjustments. One of the best ways is to establish hostels in which the young men of the South are given Christian fellowship, an opportunity to learn Arabic, and some help in adjusting to the new life. Two such hostels have already been established and this very vital program will be expanded by the National Youth Project of 1958.[521]

In the North Sudan, congregations that were the fruit of the evangelistic work of the American Presbyterian Mission had been organized into a presbytery of the Coptic Evangelical Church in Egypt. Congregations had been organized in nine major cities, in each of which "there is an Egyptian pastor carrying on the usual pastoral activities and also some that are not so usual."[522] Also, in each of these cities, the Mission was engaged in the "important job of educational evangelism . . . . It is done in several different ways with one fixed purpose—to introduce the students, whether they are children or adults, to Christ and His message of love."[523]

Among the most effective avenues were the schools for girls in Khartoum North, Atbara and Wad Medani, which offered courses beginning with kindergarten and continuing through high school. "The influence for good which [these institutions] through [their] former pupils has exerted on the country cannot be estimated. Among its alumnae are to be found the best educated women some of whom hold important positions in government and commerce."[524]

In all nine of the major cities, there were teams of women missionary teachers who held regular classes for women and older girls in their homes. Most of these women and girls had little opportunity to leave the confinement of their homes. "Many of these pupils learn to read and continue their learning until they become well educated, relatively speaking, and have a knowledge of the way of salvation through their study of the Bible. There have been some who have confessed their faith in Christ as their Saviour, but this confession has been only to their teacher."[525]

Two schools for boys in Omdurman continued, one a grade school with a boarding department, which became known as "the Boys' Home"; the other a commercial high school, preparing student for service in government and business offices. In Khartoum North there was a home for orphans "and other unfortunate children"; and in Khartoum, the Christian Literature Center which provided a lending library and a reading room "which are proving of great value to the members of the congregations and others in each community."[526] All in all, at the beginning of this period the future seemed bright as "the Sudan moves into its New Day."[527]

IMPACT OF CIVIL WAR ON AMERICAN PRESBYTERIAN WORK

But the bright future for which American Presbyterians had hoped turned rather into stark tragedy. The 17-year guerrilla war (1955-1972) brought devastation to the

American Presbyterian related work in the South, as it did to the Christian movement as a whole. Virtually every mission station was destroyed, beginning with the center at Doleib Hill. Schools and clinics were no longer operating. Churches were burned down, and Christians scattered. Theological education ground to a halt, as the only theological institute in the South, the Bishop Gwynne College, was destroyed, and faculty as well as students fled for their lives.

Pastors and evangelists were especially targeted by the government forces. A later visitor would write,

> I heard of the struggles and the near-martyrdom of evangelists of the Presbyterian Church in Sudan during the 17-year war . . . . I met Reverend Moses Makuat who was placed in cell number one (next in line to be executed) in the mid-1960s because of his work as an evangelist . . . . I am sure that many workers of PCIS lost their lives because of who and what they were in those days.[528]

As the civil war intensified, American Presbyterian missionary Don McClure wrote movingly from Addis Ababa about what was happening in southern Sudan:

> The fighting in Sudan gets worse and worse, and many of our friends have been killed. Nearly every day we hear of another of our old boys who has been shot by Sudanese troops. From the reports we have received, they are being tortured and even elementary schools are being machine-gunned to break the resistance. The Sudan army began to move after the rains, and one company of over a hundred soldiers was surrounded and ambushed by Nuer rebels. They fought for three days, and the soldiers were not able to break out. However, a couple of soldiers did manage to slip away during the night and get back to Akobo. They wired to Nasir for reinforcements, and another company of about one hundred men were sent out from Nasir. Before they reached Akobo they, too, had been ambushed and most of them killed by the Nuers. The government then sent out planes and dropped five-gallon tins of benzene on villages everywhere and sent word that they were going to annihilate all the Nuers in the Lau area. So now there are thousands of women and children fleeing to Ethiopia.[529]

It was the Nuers and the Anuaks who especially felt the brunt of the attack of the government army forces, with many of their people, especially older men, women and children, fleeing across the border into Ethiopia. (The younger men usually had joined the rebels.) The Sudanese army followed them in hot pursuit. Ethiopia could do little to object or even give assistance to the refugees, since it could ill afford hostilities with Sudan in the west, in addition to its internal conflicts.

Recognizing the desperate plight of some five thousand Anuak refugees, American Presbyterians in Ethiopia initiated a program called the Anuak Resettlement Project.

It is our desire to move these people back from the troubled border and get them settled as quickly as possible in new villages of their own. Once they are settled they can become self-sufficient within three or four months, which is the time required to plant and harvest a crop . . . . Thus we have decided on a pilot project to lead about 240 families away from the border area to a site on the Gilo River.[530]

The Ethiopian government gave semi-official approval to the pilot project, and the governor of Gambela province, in which all the refugees resided, enthusiastically endorsed the plan. The plan proceeded with remarkable success.

The situation of the Nuer refugees was even more desperate. Because of the vast number of their people killed and their villages razed by the Sudan army, some three thousand Nuers had crossed over into Ethiopia. However, they could not move deeper into Ethiopia, because the Anuaks stoutly defended their tribal lands. Thus the Nuers were unable to go forward or backward, yet also could not stay where they were. Their presence was an open invitation for the Sudanese army to attack across the border. Trapped in a no-man's-land, without shelter or food supply, these people suffered terribly in the months ahead.

As soon as Don McClure learned of the Nuers' plight, he chartered a plane from the Ethiopian Air Lines and began dropping food, blankets, and mosquito nets to the refugees. Then, receiving permission from the Ethiopian government to grant refugee status to the Nuers, he began to work toward moving them to a permanent site away from the border and the territory of the hostile Anuaks. When a suitable location was found, Don McClure Jr., who had just graduated from Pittsburgh Seminary and returned to Ethiopia, accompanied 22 Nuer clan leaders on an eighty-mile trek by foot to survey the relocation site. After a harrowing seven days that came close to claiming their lives, the location was reached and the Nuer leaders agreed that the land was suitable for their people. One of the Christian Nuers had named the site "Kadesh", remembering how the Israelites had camped at Kadesh on their way to the promised land (Numbers 20).[531]

When the Nuers arrived in Kadesh (a place previously known as Adura), they promptly constructed homes, schools and stores and restored some semblance of their village life. American Presbyterian missionaries Don McClure, Jr. and his wife Ginny lived with the refugees at Kadesh and "according to a United Nations observer, their mere presence did more to stabilize the situation than anything he could do or suggest."[532] The Nuer settlement at Kadesh quickly grew from three thousand to nine thousand refugees. Because of his leadership in the resettlement, Don Jr. was accused by the Sudanese government of training guerrillas. "He was declared to be an enemy of Sudan, and a Sudanese army unit came across the Ethiopian border to murder him. By mistake the soldiers destroyed the wrong village and killed the wrong people."[533]

Despite the best efforts of the missionaries, the situation in the refugee villages was constantly desperate. In June 1966 an observer reported that staple food was almost exhausted throughout the Gambela district and about 15,000 people, a third of them refugees from Sudan, had entered a famine situation that would continue until January.

> People are traveling throughout the region to see if friends or relatives in other areas have food. Women are going out at night to hunt for wild onions and to dig roots. The price of corn has quadrupled, and even those workers who receive wages cannot find corn to buy . . . . Thus at least 50% and perhaps 75% of the 75,000 people will be without food in July and August and again in October through December.[534]

In response, missionaries planned airdrops of grain in the most needy areas, though this could only begin to meet the need. The threat of famine continued to hang over the refugee villages for years to come.

In the midst of these desperate circumstances, the impact of the Gospel grew even stronger.

> All the Christian churches in the South Sudan have been living through a nightmare of church destruction, seizure, and burning of publications, travel bans, razing of villages, and burning and trampling of crops. And yet, instead of dying, the church lives on, and in some places it is even growing. After military forces destroy a church, its congregation, instead of going underground or fleeing, will petition the central government for permission to build anew. Although many pastors have fled, there are those who are stubbornly remaining and who persist in asking for permission to hold meetings of the judicatories bodies of their churches. Thousands of church members and leaders have also fled, but the churches that remain are well attended.[535]

By 1967, it was reported that "the Church of Christ in the Upper Nile reports about 4,000 members and a worshiping community of some 25,000."[536]

Despite these adversities, various members of the American Presbyterian Mission had been at work translating the New Testament into the Nuer language. The work was completed in 1968 by Mac Roy, who had been expelled from southern Sudan and was working in Kenya. The Scriptures became a bulwark of strength for Nuer Christians during the coming years of trial and suffering.

Meanwhile, in northern Sudan, the American Presbyterian missionary presence worked under increasing difficulty. In face of the uncertainties and a growing anti-Americanism, by 1964 the Presbyterian-established churches in northern Sudan were organized into the Presbytery of North Sudan, completely independent of the Synod the Nile (Egypt); and by 1966 all administrative responsibility for the various phases of work formerly under the American Mission were turned over to the Evangelical Church of the Sudan (the successor to the former Presbytery of the North Sudan), with the missionaries "staying on to work as partners and friends." By 1967, this church was reported to have about 600 members, in six congregations, with 11 pastors.[537]

The political instability of the government took its toll. In December 1964, as the military government of General Abbud was being toppled, riots broke out in Khartoum. An American Presbyterian missionary, Mary Ann Bode, who had been relocated in Cairo, wrote:

> In Egypt many of us sat together and listened intently to accounts of rioting and of the complete destruction by fire of our Khartoum compound—five houses—the large literature and audio-visual center, and the offices. We gave thanks for the safety of our people through that strange night.[538]

Actually two missionaries, Bob Meloy and Bill Philips, had been beaten as they tried to help men from the south Sudan. More than a hundred displaced southerners were killed in the riots.[539]

The missionary force in southern Sudan, which had begun this period with such high hopes, now was scattered, some transferred to work in neighboring countries, others returning to the United States. A significant number took up work in Ethiopia. For compelling political reasons, Ethiopia generally refused to accept missionaries who were exiled by the civil war in southern Sudan. However, through the intercession of Don McClure with Emperor Haile Selassie, an exception was made in the case of American Presbyterian missionaries, and a significant number of missionaries with experience in work among the tribal communities were relocated to similar work in southwest Ethiopia.[540]

Others accepted work in educational institutions in places where they could be involved in training of young Sudanese refugees, in the fond hope that the day would come that these might return to be leaders in a new southern Sudan. William B. Anderson, who had been teaching southern Sudanese ministerial candidates at the Bishop Gwynne College in Maridi, Equatoria Province, now took up work at St. Paul's United Theological College in Limuru, Kenya, where a number of refugee students from southern Sudan had come. In a letter dated July 8, 1964 to Glenn Reed, COEMAR Field Representative, Anderson wrote:

> . . . we see a situation of both danger and opportunity. From the side of the Church itself, we see that there is a marvelous upsurge of new strength everywhere because of the removal of missionaries. And even those who have fled the Sudan, many of them are quite outstanding Christian men. The very fact that they haven't listened to us is a sign of hope: they are men, and acting like men. They do need help . . . .
>
> The most obvious way we can help out is in that of education and training. I personally feel the chances of them returning to Sudan are good. But even if

their chances were only one in ten, I still believe we should gamble on them. For if the South Sudan does get "federation" or "separation" in the near or not-so-near future, the burden of making it a success will inevitably fall upon the educated. Therefore I say—and so do the fellows here—that (1) we should of course train Christian in the Sudan. We must do this to the limit, in any way we can. But this is admittedly a problem. Can even Bishop Gwynne keep operating? Can men be sent out of the Sudan? (2) We should by all means also train those outside. Those who are deserving of overseas scholarships and worthy of them, for goodness sake let's get them into schools. Even if they never get back to the Sudan, they can be useful citizens and Christians elsewhere. (3) Even further, we should set aside money—and a man or two—to help provide education more generally for refugees. I think we could make arrangements to work them into secondary schools already established in Kenya, by contributing a dorm and a teacher. I cannot think of any investment which would be better. It would give these students something good to do besides rot as refugees. It would put them close to people of a progressive African country. If nothing else, it will make them useful citizens.[541]

PEACE AT LAST—FOR A WHILE

The civil war dragged on, with the Sudanese government controlling the main towns in the South, but the Anyanya (as the rebel forces became known) controlling most of the bush. The long conflict drained the resources of what was already a very poor country, and the government army was manifestly proving unable to achieve a military solution. In the meantime, on the government side, General Nimeiri, after the aborted Communist coup of 1971, had shown himself anxious to offer the South a new deal. The time was ripe for a major compromise.

While this was by no means a strictly religious war, the leadership of the South was largely Christian, and the government's unification policy, to which the South so strongly objected, had so many Islamic overtones to it that Christianity had become increasingly a part of the southern cause. The churches and mission agencies outside of the Sudan sought some means of aiding the peacemaking process. Finally in July 1970 a massacre of some fifty Protestants in a little refugee church just over the Zairian border was brought to the world's attention by the eyewitness reports of survivors. From that point there was an increasingly vocal church and humanitarian lobby for the southern cause.

The breakthrough came in 1971, following the aborted Communist coup. Through the initiative of Canon Burgess Carr, Executive Secretary of the All Africa Conference of Churches, the approval of the Sudanese government was secured for the AACC and the World Council of Churches to act as intermediaries between the Khartoum government and the umbrella organization of the southern rebel forces, the South Sudan Liberation Movement. The negotiations took place in Addis Ababa, Ethiopia, and led to an agreement that was signed on February 28, 1972. The main features of the agreement were the termination of the conflict; the integration of the rebel forces into the Sudanese army; and the establishment of new political structures granting a large measure of self-government to the three southern provinces grouped together into a single region.

During the next six months, an effort was made to restore order out of the chaos in southern Sudan. Six thousand members of the Anyanya military were integrated with an equal number of regular soldiers from the north to form a balanced force in the South. The new regional government had the enormous task of assisting the resettlement of an estimated half million people who had fled from their villages into the countryside during the years of fighting. The estimated 200,000 southern refugees who had fled to the North and to neighboring countries slowly began to return to their homeland.

To create the necessary economic and social conditions for their return, the Sudan government asked the world community for help. The United Nations High Commissioner for Refugees coordinated the relief program. Estranged from the Soviet Union and Eastern Europe since the abortive pro-Communist coup attempt, Sudan obtained little development aid from those countries, and very little from the Confederation of Arab Republics, which Nimeiri had decided not to join. However, with diplomatic relations reestablished with the United States and Western Europe, those countries responded to Sudan's desperate need with relief, loans and credits. By the end of 1972 $14 million had been raised toward the $17.7 million target for the massive task of restoring a livable situation for the people in the South.

With peace restored, the churches, assisted by mission agencies, faced the enormous task of rebuilding virtually every church structure, while missions cooperated with the regional government in the rebuilding of schools and hospitals. The resumption of training of leadership for the church would be an enormous task, since pastors and evangelists had especially been affected by the civil war. The desperate conditions during the war had brought about a large movement to Christian faith, so that there were now many flocks with few shepherds. The global Christian community faced an especially challenging task in helping to build new foundations upon the peace that it had assisted in bringing about.

THE CHANGING POLITICAL CLIMATE IN ETHIOPIA

Gidada Solon was invited to represent the Bethel Evangelical Church of Ethiopia at the General Assembly that united the Presbyterian Church U.S.A. and the United Presbyterian Church of North America, held in Pittsburgh in May 1958. In his memoirs Gidada writes:

> On Monday morning, we, from all over the world, gathered together to take the Lord's Supper. At an appointed time, the delegates from the Presbyterian Assembly started from their church, and we started from our church marching to each other. When we came together all shook hands and mixed together. On that most wonderful day, the whole group walked together to plan for the work of Christ in the world.

That night I, Gidada, the "one who weeps for people" wept. I had known tears many times: in my despairing times when I was a beggar; in my lonely times when I languished in prison; and in my sad times when I mourned the deaths of my children and mother. And now I wept again, but not in despair, or loneliness, or sadness. I wept in joy for what the blind eyes of Gidada, the former beggar, had seen: the joys and sorrows of my own life, the birth and growth of the Ethiopian church, and the outreach of Christ into the Ghimeera and Maji and Anuak peoples. And now, as in a vision, with sightless eyes furnished light by Christ, I saw the church in all the world—his followers everywhere joining hands, mixing together, praying and planning for Christ's work in the world.[542]

The beginning of the new age in sub-Saharan Africa found its expression in Ethiopia in the strengthening of the sense of its distinctive African heritage. According to the revised constitution of November 1955, the Ethiopian Orthodox Church was recognized as the established church of the empire and as such was supported by the state. By a formal agreement reached in 1959 between the Coptic Church in Egypt and the Ethiopian Orthodox Church, the abuna of the "established Orthodox Church of Ethiopia" was raised to the rank of Patriarch Catholicos. Henceforth he was to be chosen from among the Ethiopian monks, his election to be confirmed by the Emperor of Ethiopia, and his consecration and investiture to be affirmed by the Coptic Patriarch. While the strength of the church would continue to be among the Amhara and Tigrai populations in the northern and central highlands, it would continue to exert a strong influence over the policies of the government in the surrounding areas inhabited by other ethnic groups.

The emperor Haile Selassie, recognizing the quasi-feudal attachment of the Orthodox Church to the past and its lack of trained priests, sought to improve the quality of the Orthodox clergy by inaugurating two theological schools in Addis Ababa, and by sending the most promising young men to study in Greek Orthodox seminaries in Athens and Istanbul. Yet the obstacles to lasting improvement in the Ethiopian Church were formidable. Although priests and monks were numerous and about one-third of the land of the country was said to be owned by the Church, the training given by the seminaries and monasteries still did not prepare the candidates for priesthood to deal with the problems which came with this new revolutionary age. "On the whole the educated despised the clergy and the Church. The pagans in Ethiopia were being converted either to Christianity or to Islam, but in the 1950s, because of a differential in the birth rates, Moslems were increasing more rapidly than Christians."[543]

Secure in his backing by the conservative Ethiopian Orthodox Church and a wealthy land-owning class intent on preserving feudal ways, Haile Selassie ruled in a largely autocratic manner. A bicameral parliament, introduced under the 1955 constitution, made no provisions for minority representation and was granted few powers. Social unrest, growing from demands to end government corruption and institute land and other reforms, accelerated after an abortive coup attempt in 1960. Social and political conditions worsened as famine and rising prices, together with reported government efforts to cover up an estimated 200,000 deaths from starvation in 1972, added to the unrest.

Meanwhile, the Ethiopian government's control over territories on its borders began to erode. To the northeast in Eritrea, which the United Nations General Assembly of 1950 had declared "an autonomous unit federated with Ethiopia under the sovereignty of the Ethiopian Crown", guerrilla warfare began in 1960, led by the Muslim-dominated Front for the Liberation of Eritrea (FLE). In May 1971 the fighting intensified as a new group called the Popular Liberation Force (PLF) joined the conflict. The PLF included in its number Christians who were more radical ideologically than the leaders of the FLE.

To the southeast, strained relations developed with the newly constituted Somali Republic. The Ogaden Region, which had been administered since 1941 by British Somaliland, was transferred to Ethiopian administration in 1955. However, grazing rights in that area, secured to Somali tribesmen by an Anglo-Egyptian agreement in 1897, led to disputes over the national frontiers. During the 1960s there was often conflict between Ethiopian and Somali forces in the Ogaden.

In 1966, when the French government declared its intention to hold a plebiscite in French Somaliland to enable the people to decide their own future, Emperor Haile Selassie claimed Ethiopia's right to the territory in the event of the people opting for independence. In so doing he countered a similar claim put forward by the Somali Republic. However, the plebiscite held in March 1967 decided for continuation of the territory's association with France.

Despite all these strains both internal and external, Haile Selassie intensified his efforts in the international field. After strengthening his ties with other African states, he sponsored the establishment of the Organization of African Unity (OAU), with the objective that the independent states in Africa achieve unity of purpose and action. The OAU organizing conference, held in Addis Ababa in May 1963, brought together for the first time representatives of 31 independent African states, who signed the OAU charter. Addis Ababa was designated the seat of the permanent secretariat of the OAU. Addis Ababa was also chosen as the seat of the newly constituted United Nations Economic Commission for Africa, as well as other UN agencies. Thus Ethiopia was fulfilling a unique role of leadership among the newly independent nations on the continent.

MOVEMENT TOWARD CHURCH INDEPENDENCE AND PROTESTANT UNITY

With the spirit of national independence pervading the African continent, the urgency of establishing self-governing national churches increased dramatically. For the Ethiopian Evangelical Church Bethel (which had been recognized by the United Presbyterian Board and Mission as an independent church since 1947), it was a matter of becoming more than an aggregate of loosely related congregations. The question of drawing up a formal constitution for the church was first raised at the meeting of the Church-Mission

Committee in December 1961. A committee was appointed to draft a constitution, and after two years of work, the Constitution was approved at a meeting of church delegates in November 1963.

With the Constitution in place, the next step was to bring together all Bethel-related churches into official presbyteries and synods to form the Ethiopian Evangelical Church Bethel. At the first official church-wide meeting in 1964, it was agreed that the Ethiopian Evangelical Church Bethel would be composed of seven presbyteries: i.e. Dhae, Anfillo, Alaku and Saddi in Qellem; Addis Ababa-Gore; Maji-Ghimeera; and Pokwo. Addis Ababa was chosen to be the location of the Church's headquarters, while Gore was chosen as the location for annual meetings. In 1965, the response of the Ethiopian government to the application for official registration of the Church was received, and the Ethiopian Evangelical Church Bethel at last was recognized as a legal body. "This was a great breakthrough and an occasion of praise to God because this Church had lived through a whole generation without any recognition of the right to exist as a Church."[544]

At the third official church-wide meeting in 1966, after lengthy discussion it was voted that the Qellem presbyteries (which had been functioning as a Synod for a number of years) remain as a Synod in itself; and that Addis Ababa-Gore, Maji-Ghimeera, and Pokwo together form their own Synod, to be called the Eastern Bethel Synod. The two Synods thus would constitute the General Assembly of the Ethiopian Evangelical Church Bethel. The COEMAR report to the 1967 UPCUSA General Assembly noted:

> The year 1966 marked the coming of age of the Bethel Evangelical Church, which further expanded its ministry to tribal people outside the Galla (*sic*) community it had served almost exclusively for many years. It reconstituted itself into two synods, with ten (*sic*) presbyteries embracing all the frontier churches for tribal groups, churches that previously had operated independently as mission stations. Now all are part of one church under the care of the General Assembly of the Bethel Evangelical Church.[545]

Meanwhile, similar movement toward independence was taking place among the evangelical churches established by the various Lutheran missions. The Lutheran World Federation (LWF) sought to consolidate world Lutheranism by encouraging the formation of national Lutheran churches in those areas where Lutheran missions had been working. At the Third LWF Assembly in 1957, a representative of the Lutheran community in Ethiopia, Ato Emmanual Abraham, was elected to be a member of the LWF Executive Committee. Following this initiative, the movement toward a national Lutheran church in Ethiopia gained momentum, and on January 21, 1959 the Ethiopian Evangelical Church Mekane Yesus (ECMY) was constituted.[546] The Church was comprised of four synods: The Western Wollega Synod, the Eastern Wollega and Shoa Synod, the Wollo-Tigre Synod, and the Sidamo and Gamo-Gola Synod; thus bringing together the work of Swedish, Norwegian, German and American Lutheran missions. By 1960 the Mekane Yesus Church had established a seminary in Addis Ababa that would become the heart of theological training for future pastors of numerous evangelical churches in Ethiopia.

Despite the fact that realization of the earlier dream of a United Evangelical Church in Ethiopia had failed[547], the two independent national Evangelical Churches (the Bethel Evangelical Church organized in 1947 and the Mekane Yesus Church constituted in 1959) continued to seek ways of cooperating while keeping their historical relationships intact. Representatives of the two churches continued to meet annually, and in 1963 appointed a committee to study ways whereby the two churches could cooperate more closely than they had done in the past. This Study Committee continued its work over the next decade, presenting various plans to the annual assemblies of the two churches, ranging from Federation in which each Church would maintain its own doctrine, tradition, liturgy, and administration; to full absorption of the Bethel Church into the larger Mekane Yesus Church.

By 1972 the Bethel Church was ready to apply to the Mekane Yesus Church for membership as a separate synod, and at last in 1974 agreement was reached that the churches which were part of the Bethel Church become two Synods of the Mekane Yesus Church: the Qellam Bethel Synod (later to become the Western Wollega Bethel Synod) and the Eastern Bethel Synod (which would become the Kaffa-Illubabor Bethel Synod). The covering letter by which the action of the ECMY Executive Committee was communicated to the two Bethel Synods made it clear that "the merger of the two Churches was the fulfillment of many years dream for which God was to be praised," and expressed "faith in the strength of God to overcome any obstacle the united Church may face as it discharged its responsibility as a Church."[548]

DEVELOPMENTS WITHIN THE ETHIOPIAN EVANGELICAL CHURCH BETHEL

During this period, numerous significant developments were taking place within the Evangelical Church Bethel. As government pressure on the evangelical Christian community continued and the missionary presence became more and more difficult, the importance of training leadership for the church became increasingly urgent. By September 1965, three levels of pastoral training had been initiated: (1) The first secondary school graduate, Debela Birri, was sent to the Mekane Yesus Seminary by the American Mission in cooperation with the Qellem Synod.[549] (2) A four-year pastoral training course for those below the 8th grade of formal education was started at the Sayo Training Institute. The candidates were chosen on the basis of their experience as spiritual leaders in their congregations. Agreement was reached between the Mission and the Church to share equally in covering their living expenses. By the time that the first class of seven candidates was ready to graduate in 1970, Debela Birri had assumed leadership of the Institute. The Sayo Training Institute would prove to be a significant resource for providing teacher-evangelists who could respond to the calls coming from many villages for the establishment of churches and schools.

(3) Another pastoral training course at a very low level was started for candidates chosen by the Anuak Church in the Pokwo area, where work had been begun in 1951. American Presbyterian missionary Harold Kurtz explained the program for the training of Anuak candidates for ministry:

> Missionary Niles Reimer discussed the situation at length with the leaders of the church, and it was decided that the church herself should choose those best qualified for spiritual leadership. Niles would then train them in a "tent-making" type of ministry where the men would continue their farming along with their instruction and parish work. The men chosen for training spent six months of each year studying with Niles Reimer in a modified classroom situation at the Pokwo mission station. The other half of each year the men returned to their villages and farms where they put into practice what they had learned. During this time, Niles visited them often to encourage them and to give them additional help out of the day-by-day experiences of their ministry as lay pastors.[550]

Alongside the male leadership of the church, a strong **women's movement** was developing in the Evangelical Church Bethel. Actually its history could be traced back to the earliest days of American Presbyterian witness in Ethiopia. In 1923, when the budding Mission School at Sayo was closed by order of the abuna of the Ethiopian Orthodox Church, the missionary wives, believing that the order did not apply to women, started a Women's Sewing Circle, which in time would become the foundation for the Women's Association in Sayo. Meeting every Thursday, the group engaged in prayer, Bible study, sewing, knitting, and all kinds of handcraft, as well as enjoying Christian fellowship. As the church developed, particular women became prominent evangelists in outreach to women in surrounding villages. When missionaries were forced to leave because of the Italian invasion, it was a woman leader Silge who, along with Gidada Solon, inspired the believers to carry on, pointing out that the departure of the missionaries would not change the presence of Christ among His people.[551]

After the liberation, the UPNA Women's Missionary Society assigned Miss Hazel J. McGeary to Sayo in 1947 to start the school for the blind. Miss McGeary greatly strengthened the women's organization, and by 1948 it was reported that 68 women workers were conducting prayer meetings and doing evangelistic work among women. In 1956, the women took full responsibility for their work, organizing themselves under the name "Women's Association." A Women's Association was established in every congregation, with regular monthly meetings at the local level and quarterly meetings at the presbytery level. By 1959, the Association was recognized as an integral part of the official church structure and given a seat as a voting member in the meetings of presbytery.

The accomplishments of the Women's Association were numerous. It employed women evangelists to travel from presbytery to presbytery to strengthen the women in their faith. It opened two primary schools, covering all the running expenses, including the salaries of the teachers. It provided both material and spiritual support for the total work of the church, sometimes remaining the major stabilizing influence in times of trouble.[552]

Equally important was the development of the **youth movement** in the Evangelical Church Bethel. The Ethiopian Youth Christian Association was established in 1954 upon the initiative of the students at the Training Institute in Sayo. The objective of the Association was to gather the youth of the Church under one organization so that they would be able to contribute their share to the ongoing ministry of the Church alongside their mothers and fathers. Branches were established in every congregation and meetings were held once a month. Later the Youth Association was organized at the presbytery and synod levels, and a representative of the Youth Association was given membership in these bodies.

The Youth Association made several significant contributions to the life of the Church. In 1961 the leaders of the Youth Association made the startling request to the Synod that the administration of all the Church-established schools be transferred to the Youth Association. The Synod leaders found the request very ambitious but finally agreed that the Association would take over the responsibility of running three schools, at Kara Jenno, Leqa Golbo and Garjeda Warro. Further, the Association provided financial support for needy students to enable them to continue their education at the Training Institute in Sayo.

Probably the greatest contribution made by the Youth Association came during the 1960s at a time of internal division among church leaders in Qellem Synod. Debela Birri writes:

> The days of enthusiasm were over. The period of stagnation had set in. Personal grudges had begun to raise their ugly heads. Exercise of power and authority took the place of Christian love and forgiveness.[553]

It appears that the strife arose between pastors and elders in independent congregations and those that continued to maintain some administrative relationship with the Mission. A so-called Masadas or "Renewal Meeting" was held in December 1962 to assert the authority of the Synod officers and to "punish the guilty."[554] Rather than solving the problem, serious division ensued. The pastors and elders of the two oldest congregations refused to be "put under discipline", leading to four congregations breaking away from Dhae Presbytery and organizing their own presbytery. Debela Birri refers to this as "the darkest moment in the history of the Evangelical Church Bethel."[555]

After various attempts were made by other church leaders to bring about reconciliation but without success, in October 1969 the Youth Association requested the elders of the two congregations which were at the heart of the controversy to turn over the administration of both congregations to the Youth Association for a period of six months, after which a new election of elders would be held and the responsibility handed back. This proved agreeable to both sides and a way of reconciliation was opened. The next step was to reunite the divided presbyteries. Both sides agreed to turning over administration of a reunited presbytery to the Youth Association for six months, after which responsibility would be returned to newly elected officers. Debela Birri comments: "The division was healed and reconciliation was effected. This was a landmark in the history of Bethel Youth Christian Association."[556]

By 1967, it was reported that the Ethiopian Evangelical Church Bethel had some 4,047 members, 55 congregations and 13 pastors, working with some 97 American Presbyterian missionaries.[557]

DEVELOPMENTS IN THE WORK OF THE AMERICAN PRESBYTERIAN MISSION

While the majority of American Presbyterian missionaries were engaged in institutional work (educational, medical, literature) alongside but separate from the Evangelical Church Bethel, there were those who felt strongly that the Mission must reach out into tribal areas of Southwest Ethiopia yet untouched by the Gospel.[558] In the early 1960s, the Mission conceived a program under the title of the **Untouched Tribes Project**[559], to begin work among tribes in the Illubabur and Kaffa provinces that had never been reached by any mission or government program. Conceived by Don and Lyda McClure, who had initiated the innovative Anuak Project, the plan involved several young missionary families who would make a commitment to devote their full careers to these untouched people. "The people [in these tribes] lived in primitive conditions, and the tribes were contained in definite locations. The Emperor encouraged the Mission to start such a program. The plan was to establish simple mission posts (in contrast to the elaborate mission stations of a past era), to start a school, a clinic and a worship center. In one tribe, the converts were to be directed to the Orthodox parish that was not far away, but in the other places an Evangelical congregation would be founded. The Evangelical Church was asked to assign evangelists to the project."[560]

As the Untouched Tribes Project was getting underway, the South Sudan was closed to mission activity by the increasingly repressive Sudanese government. Consequently, three missionary couples from the Reformed Church in America who had been working with the Presbyterian Church in South Sudan were relocated to Ethiopia, and two of these were assigned to the Untouched Tribes Project. The Project was also greatly benefited by the assistance of the Missionary Aviation Fellowship, which provided air service into areas where roads were hardly passable by jeep, so that travel between stations could be made in hours instead of days by mule.

The outreach of the Project was significantly increased when the Ethiopian government offered to turn over to the Mission the direction of all medical work in Ilubabor Province. Working out of the new government hospital in the provincial capital at Gore, a public health program was developed for the entire province, with mission doctors and nurses staffing government-built clinics. This mission-government cooperation opened doors of opportunity that were rarely given to a missionary body in the past.

Certainly one of the landmark accomplishments of this period was the establishment of the first secondary school in the area served by the American Presbyterian Mission. As early as 1947 church leaders had urgently requested that the Mission establish a secondary school for their youth. However, because of disagreement among the missionaries regarding priorities, implementation of the plan was indefinitely delayed. At last, first steps were taken and classes initiated in 1964, and in 1968 there was the groundbreaking ceremony for the Bethel Evangelical Secondary School (BESS). The first buildings were built with a grant of $200,000 from the Fifty Million Dollar Fund of the United Presbyterian Church, U.S.A., the largest grant made to any project in Africa.

On the occasion of the 25th anniversary of the founding of BESS, American Presbyterian missionary Harold Kurtz recalled:

> At the groundbreaking ceremony for the school in 1968 three of us spoke. I represented the Mission; Yen Whitney spoke representing the United Presbyterian Church; and Pastor Keis Gidada spoke representing not only the Bethel church as a denomination but the beginning of that church dating back to the 1920s . . . . [The school] has played a crucial role in training leadership for the Ethiopian Evangelical Church Mekane Yesus, which now has a Christian community of over one and a half million people! BESS has graduates spread all over the world in many areas of responsibility.[561]

The Bethel Evangelical Secondary School would prove to be one of the finest in the country, and a stalwart bulwark of Christian witness during the years of the Marxist revolution that engulfed Ethiopia from 1974 to 1991.

Even as these advancements were taking place, the strains between the Commission on Ecumenical Mission and Relations (COEMAR) and the American Presbyterian Mission in Ethiopia were steadily increasing. Those missionaries who had been appointed by the United Presbyterian Church in North America (UPNA) chafed under the new policies instituted by COEMAR. For its part, COEMAR seemed to feel that the Mission was stunting the initiative of the emerging Bethel Evangelical Church. Finally, in the late 1960s, COEMAR disbanded the Mission organization. New missionaries appointed to serve in Ethiopia were advised that this was a new era and that their work must be under the administration of the Ethiopian Church. Older missionaries strongly protested the move, threatening to go around COEMAR in an appeal to the church at large. Eventually a conference was held in New York, with representatives of the Ethiopian Church who had been chosen by COEMAR.[562] The result was that henceforth all American Presbyterian personnel and funding for work in Ethiopia was under the administration of the Ethiopian church.

CHANGING RELATIONS WITH THE ETHIOPIAN ORTHODOX CHURCH

During this period, the relationship of the Commission on Ecumenical Mission and Relations (COEMAR) with the Ethiopian Orthodox Church underwent significant change. As COEMAR sought to widen its ecumenical relationships around the world, it attempted to establish better relations with the Orthodox churches, including the Orthodox Church in Ethiopia. At the New Delhi Assembly of the World Council of Churches in 1961, COEMAR's General Secretary John Coventry Smith made a special effort to befriend the head of the Ethiopian Orthodox Church, Abuna Theophilus[563], sponsoring a banquet in his honor. The gesture cemented the personal friendship between the two leaders and opened the way for better relations in Ethiopia.

A new channel of communication opened through the COEMAR Office of Youth Relations, which set in motion an interchurch youth caravan to Ethiopia. The youth and their leaders were introduced to the head of the church, Abuna Theophilus, and to the chief priest of the Emperor's church, Holy Trinity. The UPCUSA Youth Secretary was asked to preach in the Orthodox Church at Dembi Dollo, the center of the American Presbyterian work in the western area of the country.

As might be expected, this event was not without tensions within the COEMAR family. The American Presbyterian missionaries in Ethiopia, as well as the COEMAR Area Representative, felt that they had been bypassed in the planning and that both the missionaries and the Evangelical Church Bethel were overlooked by the caravan.[564] The Evangelical Church Bethel remembered only too clearly the years of harassment and persecution which it had suffered at the hands of the Ethiopian Orthodox Church, especially in those areas which had been subjugated by the Ethiopian government and kept under its control through the collaboration of the Orthodox Church.

After some time and with considerable consultation, the work of American Presbyterian missionaries was drawn into a new relationship with the Orthodox Church. The work among the Teshima tribal people was done in cooperation with the Holy Trinity Cathedral of Addis Ababa. Also, a summer Bible training course for Orthodox Theological College students was conducted cooperatively, with theological students teaching in daily vacation Bible schools throughout Addis Ababa. However, the Evangelical Church Bethel found this Orthodox-Presbyterian cooperation to be one more strain on its relationship with American Presbyterian colleagues.

OTHER ECUMENICAL DEVELOPMENTS

Along with developments within the Evangelical Church Bethel and the American Presbyterian Mission, this period saw two major ecumenical developments taking place. The first was the establishment of a Christian radio station in Addis Ababa, called The Voice of the Gospel. Long a dream of Christian mission agencies working in the Middle East, the station received a franchise from the Imperial Government of Ethiopia in 1959 and began transmitting in early 1963. One of the strongest church-owned and operated stations in the world, its 100,000 watt transmitters broadcast the Christian message past political, national and lingual barriers to reach millions of people in the Middle East and Africa. Programs were prepared locally by Christians in particular countries, pre-taped at recording studios in those countries and then beamed directly from the Addis Ababa station to those countries.

While the Lutheran World Federation was the official owner and operator of the station, several American denominational mission agencies, including COEMAR, participated in supporting the project. Since the new UPCUSA had the most extensive mission involvement in the Muslim world of any Protestant denomination, extending from the Sudan in Africa to Indonesia in Asia, the Voice of the Gospel provided a means for evangelistic outreach across the entire region. It was a grand concept, which came to an unfortunate end with the advent of the Marxist revolution in 1974.

The second ecumenical development arose from within the youth movements in the Ethiopia evangelical churches. A **charismatic renewal** began in 1963 among Christian youth, especially university students. They met in informal groups across denominational lines. Evangelization was a hallmark of the movement from its beginning. The groups grew and multiplied and soon started to send out evangelists supported by the young believers. While some of the youth remained loyal to their particular denominations, a large number organized themselves into *the Mulu Wongel* (Full Gospel) Church.

The movement soon received strong opposition from the Ethiopian Orthodox Church. In 1971, the abuna publicly stated that he would "exert all my energy against every teaching and movement that may battle against the Ethiopian Church." He managed to secure the assistance of government agencies in a campaign against those who had abandoned Orthodoxy, alleging that membership in Mulu Wongel was essentially treasonous. A significant number of the youth were arrested and incurred heavy fines and long jail terms.

Although the "Pentes", as the youth were termed, incurred considerable opposition from the older leadership of the established churches, they represented a new spirit breathing through the evangelical Christian movement in Ethiopia, a spirit that would strengthen the churches to stand strong in the face of the even more difficult years which were before them.[565]

E. EAST AFRICA

BEGINNING OF INVOLVEMENT IN KENYA

On the eastern side of the African continent, south of Ethiopia and Sudan, is the country that is known as Kenya. With its beautiful coastline and its pleasant mountain region, it has been a favorite area for foreign settlement. Arab traders settled in the coastal regions as early as the Middle Ages, and Islam spread along the East African coast from the 7th century. At the same time a new culture evolved among the Africans who accepted Islam, with a distinct language and identity. One of the lasting consequences of the contact between Arabia and East Africa was the development of Kiswahili, a language combining elements of both Bantu and Arabic, which is now widely spoken all over Eastern Africa. By the year 1500, the East African coast was dotted with Islamic towns that were largely independent from one another, yet which linked East Africa with the outside world.

Christianity first came to Kenya in 1498, when Vasco da Gama set anchor off Malindi Bay. Contacts were made with the local population, followed by the work of Catholic missionary priests at various points along the coast. Other Portuguese explorers would visit the coast, building a fortress at present-day Mombasa called Fort Jesus. However, "the Portuguese, when they came to East Africa, were not interested in spreading Christianity. They were not even primarily interested in Africa—their main interest was trading with Asia, and Africa happened to have been 'discovered' while the new sea-route via Southern Africa was being explored."[566] The east coast of Africa provided calling ports for the ships destined for India and the Far East, and while in these ports the merchants collected cargo, including African slaves, to enhance their trade in Asia.

The Church Missionary Society (CMS) sponsored the first Protestant missionary to East Africa, Dr. Ludwig Krapf, who arrived in Mombasa in 1844. During the next several decades CMS missionary work (Anglican) concentrated mainly on abolishing the slave trade, which was controlled by the Arabs, and the rehabilitation of former slaves through the establishment of colonies along the East African coast. Some of the former slaves who were instructed in the Christian faith became the first missionaries to the people in the interior of East Africa.

British occupation of East Africa did not effectively begin until after the Berlin Conference of 1884-1885, which partitioned Africa among the European powers. Participating powers increasingly asserted their control and influence over the territories that they had claimed. In East Africa, Tanganyika fell under German control, being called German East Africa. Kenya and Uganda came under British control, and were called British East Africa.

The Berlin Treaty provided for free movement of missionary societies across territorial boundaries, irrespective of the colonial powers that ruled the territories. However, each colonial power tended to accord preferential treatment to missionary societies originating in its own country. Consequently, the territories falling under British control received a majority of British Protestant missionaries. In 1862, British Methodists appeared on the scene, and Scottish Presbyterians entered in 1891. The opening of a railway from Mombasa to Kisumu in 1902 resulted in a Protestant influx into the interior.

The response to Christianity in British East Africa was instantaneous and immense, with the number of converts doubling and even trebling every year. By 1916 a mass movement into all the churches, Anglican, Protestant and Catholic, had begun. By 1948, 30% of the population professed to be Christian, this figure rising to 54% in 1962. 206 denominations had been begun, 154 of which were independent indigenous churches.

However, the interpretation by African scholars of the significance of this rapid growth has become more critical in recent years. Professor J.N.K. Mugambi, of the University of Nairobi Department of Religious Studies, writes:

> The missionaries served as the link between the rulers and the ruled, between
> the powerful and the powerless. They provided literacy and other skills to the
> people who were later to become interpreters, clerks, teachers, evangelists and

artisans when colonial administration became established. The mission stations became centers of westernization . . . . The converts became like extension officers in the process of Europeanization. Evangelization was defined in terms of acculturation. The degree of conversion to Christianity was determined in terms of the extent to which the convert had absorbed and adopted the culture of the resident missionary.[567]

One of the important churches emerging out of this period of rapid expansion was the Presbyterian Church of East Africa (PCEA), which became an autonomous body in 1943. The greatest strength of the PCEA was among the Kikuyu. The Kikuyu lived nearest to the "white highlands", an area of about 12,000 square miles in the most pleasant mountain region that had been reserved for European settlement. It is little wonder that the Kikuyu especially resented the land policy which had favored "settler colonialism", and that they took the lead in the struggle for independence.

Following World War II (when many East Africans had been conscripted to fight on the side of Britain, and learned of other countries in Asia and Africa which were struggling for liberation from colonial rule), the struggle for independence accelerated. Along with the demand for the land that had been forcibly expropriated, African leadership called for political, economic, cultural and religious independence. When these demands were rejected by colonial authorities, a liberation movement called *Mau Mau* broke out among the Kikuyu in 1952. The government arrested Jomo Kenyatta, president of the Kenya Africa National Union party, charged him with leading the rebellion, and sentenced him to seven years in prison. Through the next four years, a state of emergency was declared. In the conflict between the liberationists and the security forces, some eleven thousand Africans were killed, along with some 95 Europeans and 29 Asians.

The *Mau Mau* brought a crisis to the African Christians:

> Christians were divided. There were those who sided with the colonial administration and some missionaries, on the one hand. There were others who identified themselves with the struggle for liberation. Many of these belonged to the independent churches, which had been banned. In between there were others who claimed to support neither side, because they were followers of Jesus. Some of these suffered persecution from both sides.[568]

Despite the dissension within the Christian community, there could be no denying that the ideological leaven behind the struggle for independence had been planted by both missionary and African Christian leaders who realized that white domination of this African country was a contradiction to Christianity.

In 1955, the colonial government adopted a land reform plan, and by 1956, the *Mau Mau* rebellion had been suppressed. Many of the leaders of the uprising were put in prison or detention camps. The Christian community made a deliberate effort to visit the imprisoned rebels, and some of them were won to Christian faith.[569]

During the next several years, the British adopted a program for the participation of African, as well as Asian and Arab, representation in the government, with the prospect of eventual independence. At last independence was granted on December 12, 1963. The aging but still formidable Jomo Kenyatta, released from prison in 1961, became the first premier of the new nation, Kenya.

Declaring itself officially a secular state, Kenya nevertheless guaranteed freedom of religion in its 1969 constitution. Although in 1968 the government took over management of all church-related schools, the churches were allowed to continue participation in education. Government cooperation and aid was also provided to other church-sponsored institutions including hospitals, dispensaries, and socio-economic development programs.

By the mid-1970s, this nation of some eleven million people claimed over seven million Christians (63% of the total population), with 2,700,000 Roman Catholics, 1,800,000 Protestants and 1,600,000 indigenous church members. Within the Protestant community, the Presbyterian Church of East Africa (which extended into neighboring Uganda and Tanzania) was oomparatively small, with some 62,000 members and a constituency of approximately 100,000. However, its leadership, both clergy and lay, was making a marked contribution in both ecumenical and national affairs.

Early on, Kenya's Protestants displayed a remarkable ecumenical spirit. Thirty-four churches of almost every theological position had come together in the National Christian Council of Kenya in 1943. With independence, the Council greatly expanded its work, through eight regional branches and six departments. With 120 full-time employees, it became one of the largest such national councils in the world, administering over 100 social service projects and assisting some 50 others belonging to its member churches.

The ecumenical approach was carried into the area of theological training as well. In 1955, the Anglican, Presbyterian and Methodist churches joined in establishing St. Paul's United Theological College in Limuru. It would become a center for training for the ministry not only for students of various communions in Kenya, but also for those coming from neighboring countries. It would prove to be of tremendous assistance in training leadership for the persecuted churches of southern Sudan.

Kenya also provided the center for the Africa-wide ecumenical movement. The All Africa Conference of Churches (AACC), formed in 1963, has been based in Nairobi. With over 100 member churches and councils from throughout the continent as members, the AACC brought together Protestant, Anglican and Orthodox church representatives to consider crucial issues facing the new Africa.

It was in the field of leadership development that **the United Presbyterian Church USA** would seek to make its distinctive contribution to the Kenya church following independence. After establishing relations with the Presbyterian Church of East Africa,[570] COEMAR's Office for Leadership Development opened the way for some 18 students from Kenya—"the next generation's pastors and educational leaders"[571]—to study in Europe and the United States. Also, it provided a grant for the Reverend John Gatu, general secretary of the Presbyterian Church of East Africa, to study Church Administration in Britain and the United States. In time, Gatu would become a strong spokesperson for the full "selfhood" of the churches of Africa.

The new relationship with the church in Kenya was further strengthened by the assignment of United Presbyterian personnel to various areas of work in Kenya: the development of nursery schools, urban and industrial work in Mombasa and Nairobi, and teaching at St. Paul's Theological College. Also, assistance was provided to enable an Egyptian physician to serve at a Kenyan hospital.

Assessing the situation in Kenya in the mid-1960s, Gittings would comment:

> Ahead for Kenya are difficult times of adjustment to the day-in, day-out workings of a mixed society in which all must learn to cherish the political and racial diversity of their country. Indian merchants—70,000 of them—and white settlers [some 11,000] must keep their confidence in the good faith of the African majority lest Kenya's commercial life be disrupted by their sudden exodus. Kenya's future horizon is bright, though certain threatening clouds are in the sky.[572]

F. SOUTHERN AFRICA

AMERICAN PRESBYTERIAN SUPPORT FOR CHANGE IN SOUTHERN AFRICA

The involvement of American Presbyterians in southern Africa had a very different beginning than that in other regions of Africa. As the surge toward independence was sweeping across nations in Western, Eastern, and Central Africa, there emerged a concerted determination on the part of the newly-independent African states to combine forces with liberation movements in southern Africa and to work toward the liberation of those nations in southern Africa which were under colonial or minority-white control. At the same time, there was a determination on the part of white-dominated governments in southern Africa that such an initiative should not succeed. As the situation became increasingly critical, American Presbyterians expressed support for the liberation effort, not only through more traditional mission strategies but also through exerting political and economic influence on the struggle for justice in southern Africa.

The problems of racism and colonialism in southern Africa had long been a matter of deep concern to the Presbyterian Church in the U.S.A. The 1954 General Assembly had taken an action "that the United States affirm its determination to support all sincere movements toward independence by colonial lands and peoples."[573] While the focus of this action was Asia, especially Indochina, it served as the basis for future actions regarding Africa as well.

In 1960, following the infamous massacre in Sharpeville, South Africa on March 21[574], the United Presbyterian Church U.S.A. General Assembly took the following action:

Speaking out of a sense of profound contrition in confession of our own guilt before God in the realm of race relations in our country, the 172nd General Assembly

Expresses its horror at the dangerous conditions in South Africa which the inconsistencies and moral absurdities of apartheid have brought upon that country;

Declares its deep concern about the course of events which seem to move with relentless logic toward a bloody conclusion;

Calls upon our Government to continue to use its influence, both directly and through the United Nations, to persuade the Union of South Africa to turn from the policies that bring only despair; and

Prays that the churches of South Africa be faithful instruments of God's grace for reconciliation among all men.[575]

By 1965, as the brutal implications of the South African policy of apartheid became still more evident, the General Assembly took a much more definitive action:

— It appealed to the United States Government to "take vigorous action, both directly and through the United Nations, to persuade the South African Government to consider the national convention proposal" [recommended by prominent South African Christians and by the Security Council of the United Nations].

— It called upon "the boards and agencies of the United Presbyterian Church, the National Council of Churches, and all other Christian and religious bodies to review investments and commercial dealings in order to persuade all banks and corporations with which we deal and which operate in any way with South Africa to use their relationships with South Africa to encourage and support the elimination of the apartheid system."

— It directed "the Commission on Religion and Race to convene a group of United Presbyterian businessmen and bankers to consider the moral implication of economic relationships with South Africa."

— It called upon "The Board of Christian Education, in cooperation with the Commission on Ecumenical Mission and Relations and the Commission on Religion and Race, to devise a program to interpret to the church the nature and significance of the South African situation and to report to the 178th (1966) General Assembly."

— And it "earnestly implore[d] all fellow Christians, including our brothers in South Africa, to join us in repentance for the sin of racism, to the end that we might be given by God's grace the new humanity in Christ . . . ; and that we might work with unflinching courage and obedience for racial justice and reconciliation in our respective countries . . . ."[576]

The 1967 General Assembly reiterated the call for the United States government, as well as industry and banking, to take specific actions in relation to the apartheid situation in the Republic of South Africa, but expanded its concern to include a call for racial justice in Southwest Africa and Southern Rhodesia.[577]

Then by 1969, the concern expressed by the General Assembly was broadened to include all of southern Africa, addressing "the blatant injustices south of the Zambezi River which continue to be supported by the tolerance, if not the tacit approval, of the United States and by the economic input of American business and industry." Quoting an article appearing in the July 1968 issue of *Foreign Affairs*, the General Assembly action asserted, "The policies of Portugal in her African colonies, of the rebel regime in Rhodesia and of the South African government in the area as a whole tend to be mutually supportive while they flow toward a common disaster." It recognized that "the hardcore of the problem" was the Union of South Africa, whose regime "has been forced to extend itself beyond its borders", illegally controlling the territory of Southwest Africa and placing troops and military equipment in Mozambique, Angola and Malawi.

In light of the above realities, the General Assembly directed the Council on Church and Race, in cooperation with the Commission on Ecumenical Mission and Relations and the Council on Church and Society, to form an Interagency Task Force on Southern Africa, with the following responsibilities:

— to explore the implications of the struggle against racism in the United States for the struggle against racism in southern Africa;
— to plan a long-range, coordinated United Presbyterian response to racism in southern Africa;
— to seek practical ways in which the churches can give immediate material and moral support to those engaged in the struggle to secure justice and freedom for the people of southern Africa;
— to coordinate efforts in Washington and the United Nations to bring the policies and pronouncements of the United Presbyterian Church with respect to southern Africa emphatically to the attention of government;
— to examine the corporations and banks from which boards, agencies and institutions now purchase goods and service or in which they have investments to ascertain what if any connections these firms and banks have in southern Africa.

The General Assembly also called upon COEMAR and the other boards and agencies of the church to make "greater utilization of black United Presbyterian leadership in the church's relationships and involvements in Africa."[578]

Thus by the end of this period, the United Presbyterian Church had made a strong commitment to call upon the church as a whole to become involved in the struggle for justice in southern Africa.

What was the history of the Christian movement in the countries of southern Africa to which American Presbyterians addressed these bold commitments? It is necessary to consider briefly the historical background of the Christian movement in each of these countries, in which American Presbyterians would have increasing involvement in the years ahead.

BEGINNING OF INVOLVEMENT IN SOUTH AFRICA

South Africa presents a history of such complexity that only a brief outline can be given here. Native to the region were the Bushmen and the Hottentots. Bantu peoples of various ethnic groups (including Zulu, Swazi, Sotho, Matabele and Xhosa) began to move into the region about the 17th century, and in time would constitute the majority population. Though Portuguese explorers had touched the coast in the 15th century, they made no effort to settle because of the hostility of the native Hottentots. The first European settlers were the Dutch in 1652, and for some years the major concern of the Dutch churches was simply securing clergy for the Dutch settlers. The first missionary to the Hottentots was George Schmidt, sent by Moravians in 1737.

Britain gained control of the Cape of Good Hope in 1795, and in 1799 the London Missionary Society founded Bethelsdorp near the southeast coast. Because of dissatisfaction with British rule and the British abolition of slavery in 1833, the Dutch settlers (known as Boers or Afrikaners) trekked north to the Orange Free State, Natal and the Transvaal between 1835 and 1848, leading to wars with the Zulus, Matabele and other Bantu states. In 1843 Britain gained control of Natal. Then, after the discovery of gold and diamonds in the interior in the 1870s and 1880s, there was a tremendous migration of people, both European and African, into this area; Britain annexed the Orange Free State in 1871 and the Transvaal in 1877. The Boers fought to regain their independence in 1899 but lost to the British in 1902, contributing to a bitterness which chronic political and economic tensions has perpetuated. In 1910 the four states became the **Union of South Africa**. In 1948 the Dutch Afrikaners gained control of the government and began to legalize the system known as *apartheid* (apartness) to maintain segregation between the races and to protect domination by the white one-fifth of the population.

Christianity had made steady progress since the 19th century. By 1970, 77% of the population were professing Christians, including 95% of whites, 90% of coloureds (i.e. those of Asian or mixed racial heritage), and 70% of blacks. Almost all Afrikaners belonged to one of the Dutch Reformed churches. Most English-speaking Europeans were members of the Anglican, Methodist, Presbyterian or Catholic churches, living mainly in Natal and the east coast. Among the coloureds, 31% belonged to the Dutch Reformed Churches, 43% to English-speaking churches. Among the blacks, indigenous churches (which are more prolific in South Africa than in any other country in the world[579]) claimed the allegiance of 18%, while 52% remained attached to the historic mission churches. Only 8% of the Asian population claimed Christian faith, and these were scattered among the various major denominational groups.

The Dutch Reformed Church (*Nederduitse Gereformeerde Kirk*, or NGK) began upon the arrival of the first Dutch settlers. The needs of the indigenous peoples were largely ignored until the end of the 18th century, the first Dutch missionary to blacks being commissioned in 1836. Between 1853 and 1866, 5 schisms took place within the NGK, due largely to opposition to native missions and the desire for complete independence from British control. However, in 1963 four of these separated churches reunited with the mother church to form the General Synod NGK. Though the members of all these churches were of European descent, their missions have resulted in the creation of separate churches for the various racial groups: the Dutch Reformed Church in Africa (for blacks); the Dutch Reformed Mission Church (for coloureds); and the Indian Reformed Church in Africa (for Asians).

The first Presbyterian church was formed in 1813 to serve whites at the Cape. In 1820 the first Scottish Presbyterian missionaries arrived, sent by the Glasgow Missionary Society. In subsequent years several other Presbyterian mission societies sent mission personnel. An outstanding product of this early Presbyterian work was the Lovedale School and University College at Fort Hare, with its comprehensive educational and community development programs. Out of this early work there emerged the following denominations:

— The Presbyterian Church of Southern Africa, established in 1829 and constituted as a church in 1897; this denomination is 65 percent white.
— The Reformed Presbyterian Church in Southern Africa (originally known as the Bantu Presbyterian Church), established in 1820 by the Scottish Presbyterian mission and becoming autonomous in 1923; this is a black denomination. Both the above denominations reach across the borders of South Africa into neighboring nations.
— The Evangelical Presbyterian Church in South Africa, begun by the Swiss mission in 1875, and becoming independent in 1962; this also is a black denomination.
— The Presbyterian Church in Africa, formed as a result of a Zulu schism which took place in 1898; this also is a black denomination.

The relation of church and state in South Africa has been a matter of international concern. The Dutch Reformed churches in general were supportive of the government's policy of apartheid, and frequently sought scriptural or theological justification for it.

In 1961 the NGK withdrew from the World Council of Churches after the WCC, at the Cottesloe Consultation, condemned apartheid following the Sharpeville massacre in 1960. The Dutch Reformed churches defended the idea that the historic role of the Afrikaner people is to protect Christian civilization from anti-Christian forces, in particular Communism. However, in 1963 an active left wing of the NGK under the leadership of the Rev. Beyers Naude formed the Christian Institute of South Africa, condemning the theory and practice of apartheid. The English-speaking churches for the most part officially opposed apartheid, although their protestations generally were made in theoretical terms.[580]

It was in the predominantly black churches that there emerged the strong voice for racial justice and equality. The leaders of that movement are too numerous to mention, except for a few outstanding examples. Z.K. Matthews was a pre-eminent figure among them. Professor of African Studies at the University College of Fort Hare and later its principal, he joined the African National Congress[581] in 1940, and in 1953 proposed a national convention of all races "to draw up a Freedom Charter for the democratic South Africa of the future." This became official policy of the ANC in 1956. From the perspective of the government, the Freedom Charter was seen as a communist revolution, and those involved in drafting and approving it (some 156 persons) were charged with high treason. The treason trials would drag on for five years, until in March 1961 the last person was acquitted. Matthews would later serve as visiting professor at Union Theological Seminary in New York, and in that capacity would have great influence on the leadership of the Presbyterian Church (USA), as well as other major American denominations. He was a key figure in the WCC Cottesloe Consultation in 1960, which, in response to the Sharpeville massacre, issued a statement that had far reaching implications for church and society in South Africa.[582]

Equally prominent in the Christian leadership for racial justice was Albert Luthuli. A Zulu tribal chief, he became a prominent Christian educator at Adams College in Natal, and a leader in the South African Council of Churches. After pursuing the path of moderation for many years in seeking to reconcile white and black South Africa, "knocking in vain patiently, moderately and modestly at a closed and barred door", Luthuli joined the African National Congress in 1950 and in 1952 was elected its president. In his acceptance of this position, he said, "It is inevitable that in working for Freedom some individuals and some families must take the lead and suffer: The road to Freedom is via the Cross." Adrian Hastings later would comment, "It was in a very real way Christianity as taught and practiced in the best liberal missionary institutions such as Fort Hare and Adams College which stimulated and even unified African nationalism up to this time."[583]

Under Luthuli's leadership, the African National Congress called a "Congress of the People" in 1955 that drew up the Freedom Charter proposed earlier by Z.K. Matthews. The Charter proposed a comprehensive alternative to apartheid, stating "South Africa belongs to all who live in it, black and white, and no government can justly claim authority unless it is based on the will of all the people." The Freedom Charter was too inter-racial for some, and shortly thereafter the Pan-Africanist Congress, led by Robert Sobukwe, broke away to form its own liberation movement.[584] Luthuli continued as ANC president until 1967, when he was assassinated.

It was the South African Council of Churches (SACC) that took up the cause of racial justice and equality on behalf of the churches, under the leadership of such pioneers as Matthews and Luthuli. Established in 1936, it built upon the foundation of the South African General Missionary Conference begun in 1904. At first it brought together virtually all the Christian denominations in South Africa. However, as the SACC took an increasingly firm stand against apartheid, not only the Dutch Reformed churches but also the Baptist Union and the Salvation Army withdrew. In 1968, the SACC published a "Message to the people of South Africa", describing the policy of apartheid as anti-Christian. Signed by 78 leading South African theologians, it became the rallying point for those seeking an end to the apartheid system.

In 1970, when the World Council of Churches decided to allocate the first grants from its Program to Combat Racism to assist anti-racist organizations throughout the world for humanitarian work, many of the South African churches criticized the implied support thus given to "terrorism". Among the beneficiaries was the African National Congress of South Africa and several liberation movements in Rhodesia and the Portuguese colonies. In 1971, the SACC elected for the first time a black churchman as its president. In 1972, the Christian Institute published details of 408 instances of state action against churchmen, including refusals of reentry or residence permits, withdrawals of passports, police raids, bannings, deportations and imprisonments. As a result, government repression became more acute for the leaders of the Christian Institute, as well as the South Africa Council of Churches.

In and through all these crises, the plight of blacks in South Africa continued to be desperate. Moving from their native villages to the mines and cities, the men as laborers, the women as domestics, they inhabited detribalized festering slums. The young men who made their way back to their villages after a period of work in the mines often contributed to the demoralization and disintegration of hereditary customs. With the growth of black population in the cities, the government adopted a policy of relocating whole populations of common ethnic groups to *bantustans*, arid regions where agricultural soil was exhausted and people were impoverished.

Many attempts were made by mission agencies, both in and outside of South Africa, to aid in the solution of the problems posed by the desperate situation of black Africans. Some programs were carried out with government assistance, others with only the support of the churches. Most of the education of the African population had long been carried out by Christian mission efforts. In 1953 the Bantu Education Act authorized the transfer of mission primary and secondary schools to local and regional authorities, withdrawing government subsidies to any mission schools that were not transferred. While implementation of the act brought a significant increase in the number of black children in school, the quality of the schools deteriorated significantly, especially when compared to schools for white children. A similar experience prevailed in relation to medical work provided by mission hospitals and clinics.

It was into this critical and complex situation that the **United Presbyterian Church in the U.S.A.** entered through its Commission on Ecumenical Mission and Relations. At first its involvement was through support of those agencies in South Africa working for racial justice, such as the Christian Institute. The involvement deepened through exchange of visitors with some of the South African churches, "in order to discuss racial issues that were of concern to our churches."[585] Then some of the youth assigned as Frontier Interns served in southern Africa, and these contacts did much to sensitize the American church to the issues.

Controversy arose within the UPCUSA as COEMAR sought to implement the General Assembly's mandate regarding the economic involvement of American banks and corporations in South Africa. Donald Black, COEMAR's Associate General Secretary, would later write: "We developed two lines of activity related to economic concerns. One was a series of dialogues with a consortium of banks that extended credit to the South African government . . . . The other line of activity was to file shareholder resolutions with companies doing business there . . . . Our most difficult series of discussions were with Gulf Oil. Major stockholders in Gulf Oil were a number of Presbyterian families in the Pittsburgh area where their head offices were located."[586]

The controversy became still more intense when COEMAR reported to the 1972 General Assembly that it had made a $10,000 grant to the World Council of Churches' Program to Combat Racism (PCR). In the 1960s, eminent Christians such as Martin Luther King, Jr. from the United States and Albert Luthuli from South Africa had deeply influenced the racism debate in the WCC. Luthuli's assassination in 1967 and King's assassination in 1968 gave the matter an urgent focus, especially since King's assassination came only weeks before he was to address the WCC's Assembly in Uppsala, Sweden. The Assembly urged the WCC to "embark on a vigorous campaign against racism" and to undertake "a crash program to guide the Council and member churches in the matter of racism."

As a result, the WCC Central Committee[587] at its meeting in Canterbury in the summer of 1969, after heated and emotional debate, set up the Program to Combat Racism, giving it a five-year mandate. The program had numerous emphases, including such aspects as those adopted by the UPCUSA General Assembly of 1969 regarding withdrawal of investments and bank loans in South Africa, and initiation of a comprehensive embargo against South Africa. However, the most controversial initiative was the WCC Special Fund to Combat Racism[588], from which annual grants were made to racially oppressed groups and organizations supporting the victims of racism. From 1970 to 1990, a total of more than U.S. 9.2 million dollars was distributed, to be used for humanitarian purposes such as education and medical work.

Looking back on the impact of the Program to Combat Racism, its first director, Baldwin Sjollema of the Netherlands Reformed Church, would write:

> PCR, from its beginning, has been one of the most controversial among WCC initiatives. While there was strong support from many member churches, there was also criticism, especially over its support of liberation movements in Southern Africa. Some of those movements are now legitimate governments,

and the WCC and PCR's vision and commitment have been vindicated. Indeed PCR is now often pointed to as one of the ecumenical success stories . . . . Member churches were challenged in an unprecedented way to take a stand and to become actively involved in racial issues. The WCC would never be the same again: it had taken sides with the racially oppressed. Charity was being replaced by solidarity. The WCC became more relevant to the majority of Christians and even to people of other faiths.[589]

BEGINNING OF INVOLVEMENT IN ZIMBABWE

The nations now known as Zimbabwe, Zambia, and Malawi each have their distinctive histories and yet have been inextricably tied to one another and to South Africa.

Zimbabwe traces its history back to the 12th century, when the Shona people came from the north and settled Mashonaland (now east Zimbabwe) and erected stone buildings (the word "zimbabwe" means "stone house"). By the 15th century the Shona empire had expanded to include most of what is now Zimbabwe. In 1837 the Ndebele people, in retreat from the advancing Boers from the Transvaal of South Africa, settled in southwest Zimbabwe, which became known as Matabeleland. Gradually the Ndebele king subdued the Shona people, gaining control of Mashonaland as well.

The way was prepared for penetration of the Western world by the famous Scottish explorer-missionary David Livingstone. He reached the Zambezi River in 1851, Victoria Falls in 1855, and Lake Nyasa in 1859. Soon afterward, precious minerals were discovered in the area, with gold in the south and copper in the north. The British became involved in mining operations. In 1888 the Ndebele king granted exclusive mineral rights south of the Zambezi River to British financier and empire-builder, Cecil Rhodes, who chartered his British South Africa Company. In the following year, Rhodes secured mineral rights north of the Zambezi, and British settlers began to occupy both territories. Then in 1893, after a series of tribal uprisings had been crushed, the British South Africa Company took control of the country, and brought together Mashonaland, Matabeleland and Zambia, naming it Rhodesia for Cecil Rhodes. By 1923, Southern Rhodesia (now Zimbabwe) had become a self-governing British colony under a minority white government, while Northern Rhodesia (now Zambia) became a British protectorate.

For the next 30 years, Southern Rhodesia pursued a policy of racial segregation, with some 175,000 Rhodesian whites controlling the government and maintaining dominance over almost three million black Africans. While at one time there had been consideration of union with South Africa, it was rejected since the British wanted to maintain clear control without the necessity of cooperation with South Africa's Boers. Yet the two nations pursued very similar policies so far as white minority rule was concerned. Black nationalists began to campaign for full democracy, joining the efforts of the African National Congress (ANC) in South Africa.

Seeking to solidify its control over the entire area, in 1953 Great Britain established the Federation of Rhodesia and Nyasaland (now Malawi), looking toward the establishment of a Union of Central Africa. The black African opposition intensified, since whites continued to maintain complete control of the government. A long series of political clashes ensued. After the ANC was banned in 1959, two separate liberation movements emerged: the Zimbabwe African People's Union (ZAPU) under the leadership of Joshua Nkomo, and the Zimbabwe African National Union (ZANU), with Robert Mugabe as its secretary-general. Both ZAPU and ZANU were declared illegal.

In 1963 Britain's attempt to maintain the Federation collapsed, and Northern Rhodesia and Nyasaland moved toward independence, becoming the black-governed nations Zambia and Malawi in 1964. Meanwhile, Southern Rhodesia under its Prime Minister Ian Smith rejected terms for independence proposed by Britain that required progress toward majority rule, and made a unilateral declaration of independence (UDI) in 1965. There followed years of struggle and guerrilla warfare. Both ZAPU leader Nkomo and ZANU leader Mugabe were imprisoned. Though Britain broke off all formal relations with Southern Rhodesia and the United Nations imposed economic sanctions, the Smith regime proceeded to declare the nation the Republic of Rhodesia in 1969, with white majority rule delineated in its constitution. Rhodesia received the help of both South Africa and Portugal (which maintained its colonial control over Angola and Mozambique) in its effort to suppress the ZAPU and ZANU liberation movements. With both ZAPU and ZANU now ineffective, a new body was formed in 1971 to engage in a non-violent struggle on behalf of black Africans—the African National Council presided over by the Methodist Bishop Abel Muzorewa. For the next several years, this would be the public voice for black African interests.

Christianity was introduced in the area of Zimbabwe as early as the 16th century, when the Portuguese Jesuit Gonzalo da Silveira made contact with the Shona people in 1561. However, by the 19th century all traces of this Catholic witness had disappeared. Following in the steps of Livingstone, the pioneer Protestant missionary Robert Moffat (Livingstone's father-in-law) founded the first Protestant mission in Zimbabwe in 1859, receiving permission from the Ndebele chief to open a London Missionary Society station at Inyati. Several missions tried to follow in the footsteps of the LMS but were unsuccessful, and it was not until 1888 that new groups were able to commence work in the country. Among these were Presbyterian missionaries from the Church of Scotland and the Free Church of Scotland, as well as Dutch Reformed missionaries from South Africa.

In the decades that followed, Christianity displayed a marked growth in the Zimbabwe area. By 1957, there were 207,000 members in Protestant churches and some 678,000 in the total Protestant community. White and black Christians formed their own communities, largely separated from each other. White Christianity was urban and bore the imprint of the whites' country of origin: England for Anglicans and Methodists, Scotland for Presbyterians, Ireland for Catholics, and South Africa for Dutch Reformed. Black Christianity, on the other hand, was mainly rural, characterized by personalistic piety and conservative theology. Zimbabwe is primarily a Protestant country, though there is no single predominant church. The Presbyterian community is comparatively small, with the South Africa-based Presbyterian Church of Southern Africa (PCSA) slightly larger than the Malawi-based Church of Central Africa Presbyterian (CCAP).

Many of the African conversions to Christianity came through mission schools, for the British administration depended upon the mission schools to prepare non-whites to be the clerks and interpreters in government offices. At the same time, it was the mission schools which would prepare the future political leaders for the new Africa—Nkomo had been trained as a Methodist lay preacher, and Mugabe was a product of a Catholic school. Although in the 1950's several hundred thousand were in schools of primary grade, only a few hundred were enrolled in secondary schools. Not until 1957 was instruction on a university level begun in the government-financed University College of Rhodesia and Nyasaland at Salisbury. As a result the institutions for preparing for the Protestant ministry had small teaching staffs, and enrollments were small.

For the most part, up to about 1970, white church leadership raised little protest to the policies of the Rhodesian government. While criticizing individual injustices and urging racial harmony, it hardly questioned the basic presuppositions and structures of white political dominance. However, with the adoption of the new constitution in 1969, which in many ways was more racist and oppressive than its predecessor, both Protestant and Catholic leaders raised their voices in protest. The Catholic bishops declared that they had to "reject and publicly condemn" the constitution, while Protestant leaders united to affirm that "these proposals to entrench separation and discrimination are a direct contradiction of the New Testament."

At this critical moment, the issue of the World Council of Churches' grants to liberation movements burst into prominence as a catalyst for polarization. The Rhodesian Council of Churches, which had been founded in 1964 and which had a black church majority, had been active in race relations, taking positions that had been opposed by most white Protestant churches. Now the Council openly supported the WCC grants. White Christians of all denominations began denouncing the Marxist influence in the World Council of Churches and in the Rhodesian Council's leadership. Meanwhile the political situation was steadily deteriorating, with guerrilla warfare beginning anew and in earnest. Regarding the apparent ineffectiveness of the church's witness, Hastings would comment: "the overall achievement remained limited, both on account of the ambiguity of the church's own internal practice, and because of a basic inability of [church leaders] to face up to the inherent moral rights of a liberation movement challenging a ruthless and oppressive minority government which had refused for years all peaceful change. They really had little meaningful advice to give Africans, while increasingly Africans were looking for deeds not words, for a major change of law not a well worded protest."[590]

During this period, contacts between the **United Presbyterian Church, U.S.A.** and Protestants in Zimbabwe/Southern Rhodesia/Rhodesia were quite limited, except for the presence of several frontier interns working among students at the University College of Rhodesia and Nyasaland.

However, the policy which the UPCUSA General Assembly was supporting in relation to the WCC Program to Combat Racism, and the effort to influence political and economic policies of the U.S. government and business would have long-range impact on the future of Zimbabwe as it did on the rest of Southern Africa.

BEGINNING OF INVOLVEMENT IN ZAMBIA

Zambia takes its name from the mighty Zambezi River, which flows through it and also helps to form its southern border. It is a butterfly-shaped nation of high plateaus, rich in minerals and fertile farmlands. As many as 73 ethnic groups and 80 languages have been identified in this landlocked nation.

Among this region's earliest inhabitants were peoples immigrating from the Luba and Lunda Empires of Congo in the 16th century, who set up small kingdoms. In the 18th century, Ngoni people immigrated from the west, and the Bemba kingdom was established in the north. Also in the 18th century, both Portuguese and Arab explorers engaged in slave trading from East Africa.

From this point, the history of Zambia closely parallels that of the region now known as Zimbabwe. The intrepid Scottish missionary-explorer David Livingstone reached the Zambezi River in 1851 and journeyed through what is now Zambia on his trek eastward. Abortive attempts were made to open work in the region by both Protestant and Catholic missionaries over the next three decades, but it was not until 1885 that the first permanent Christian work was established by the Paris Missionary Society.

Meanwhile, the British financier and empire-builder Cecil Rhodes was advancing British imperial authority in southern Africa. In 1889 he obtained mineral rights to the area north of the Zambezi River from the Barotse tribe. By 1895 all tribal uprisings had been crushed, and the territory came under the administration of Rhodes' British South Africa Company, to be named Northern Rhodesia. The mining of the rich deposits of copper began, and soon several thriving mining towns emerged. The region became known as the Copperbelt, drawing people both black and white into this area which previously had been vast uninhabited bush. In 1924 Northern Rhodesia became a British protectorate. Then in 1953 this country, along with Southern Rhodesia (later Zimbabwe) and Nyasaland (later Malawi), became part of Britain's Central African Federation.

At this point, the policies of the government of Northern Rhodesia were much the same as those in South Africa and Southern Rhodesia. A white European population of some 56,000 occupied prime grazing and farmland, controlled the mining industry and the government, and gave little heed to the rights of the two million majority black population. But rudimentary black political organization was emerging. The Northern Rhodesia African Congress (NRAC) was formed in 1948. "It had as yet little strength though it may be noted that in March 1950 a small group of men led by Kenneth Kaunda, a part-time teacher, set up a local branch in the remote rural centre of Chinsali. He already spoke clearly of racial oppression as a 'great burden of evil' and was seeking a way to combat it."[591] Imprisoned in 1958-1960 for his support of NRAC, in 1960, Kaunda broke away from the NRAC to form the United National Independence Party (UNIP) to campaign for independence and dissolution of the Federation, which was dominated by the white minority of Southern Rhodesia.

By 1963, Britain belatedly recognized the overwhelming opposition to the Federation from the black African population in Northern Rhodesia and Nyasaland, and opened the way for internal self-government in both countries. In 1964, the independence of the Republic of Zambia was achieved within the British Commonwealth, and Kaunda was elected its first president. "With Zambia's independence in October 1964 black rule had reached the Zambezi and the whole political map of Africa had changed almost unbelievably from what could have been anticipated only ten years earlier."[592]

The first years of the new republic were troubled with frequent outbreaks of violence because of disputes within the governing party and conflicts between the country's more than seventy ethnic groups. In response, in 1972 Zambia was declared a one-party state, and UNIP declared the only legal party. Under Kaunda, the government nationalized key enterprises and much privately-held land, and took control of 51 percent of the country's copper mines.

A word needs to be said at this point regarding Kenneth Kaunda. The product of Presbyterian mission work, Kaunda remained an active Presbyterian churchman during most of his life (though for a period he changed to the African Methodist Episcopal Church, which was very active in the black struggle). He sought in every way possible to work with the churches in the development of the new nation Zambia, in turn expecting their close cooperation. Hastings commented, "Kaunda's very real Christian values and moderate policies, which make it possible for the churches to work with him so enthusiastically, are balanced by his acute sense of the realities of power." Along with his Catholic counterpart in Tanzania, Julius Nyerere, and despite numerous failures along the way, Kaunda became a symbol of the kind of Christian leadership needed for the new Africa.[593]

The history of Christianity in Zambia closely parallels that in the area now known as Zimbabwe. Though early contacts were made in the 18th century by Portuguese priests, Catholic mission efforts were virtually fruitless until the arrival of the White Fathers in 1891. In like manner, early Protestant attempts to open work were made by the London Missionary Society in 1859 and the Paris Mission in 1878, but it was not until 1885 that the first permanent station was established by the Paris Mission. The London Missionary Society, Scottish Presbyterians and British Methodists soon followed. By 1959 about 19 percent of the population of Northern Rhodesia were Roman Catholics, and about 15 percent were Protestants.

The development of the copper mines posed serious problems for black Africans and thence for Christian missions. Young Africans recruited as laborers from the scattered villages came to crowded urban slums, weakening life in the villages and placing all the temptations of urban life in the path of these young men. To meet the challenge, some of the Protestant churches joined in cooperative efforts to minister in the mining areas, forming the United Missions of the Copperbelt, later to become the African Copperbelt United Church. Since the mineral deposits spanned the boundary between Northern

Rhodesia and the Congo, the Christian programs were carried out on both sides of the national boundary.[594]

From this beginning, unity negotiations among the numerous regional Protestant missions and churches proceeded step by step. In 1945, the Presbyterians in the northeast united with the London Missionary Society and the African Copperbelt United Church.[595] Then in 1958 there was a union of this group with some white congregations in the Copperbelt to form the United Church of Central Africa in Rhodesia (UCCAR). Finally, in 1965, with the encouragement of Kaunda, a very considerable further step was taken, as the UCCAR was joined by both Methodists and the Church of Barotseland to form the United Church of Zambia (UCZ). "The UCZ brought together Presbyterian, Congregationalist and Methodist traditions in what was certainly a wise, fairly broad-based, move to create a middle-sized church . . . . It came into being on a crest of popular excitement at a moment when 'One Zambia, one nation' was the great political cry . . . . The inauguration day of the United Church of Zambia . . . seemed in some way the culminating moment, not just for some rather troublesome local unity negotiations but for Zambian nationalism, and—on a longer view—the whole Protestant missionary movement in Central Africa."[596]

It was within this context of cooperation that there emerged one of the strongest ecumenical institutions in the new Africa, the Mindolo Ecumenical Foundation Center in Kitwe, Zambia. Founded in 1958, the Center had as its purpose the training of African leaders, both clergy and lay, as well as research on problems and issues common to all the churches of Africa. It has also been the location for the Africa Literacy and Writing Center, whose purpose was to stimulate the creation of Christian literature for African readers, written by African authors. While officially affiliated with the Christian Council of Zambia (which was founded in 1945 and has 13 member churches), the Center has had on its board of governors both Catholic and government representatives. It served as the center for planning the initiation of the All-Africa Conference of Churches and was the location for the first AACC office from 1963 to 1965.

Despite the spirit of cooperation which was generated among numerous Protestant churches during this period, there was a dark side as well, especially in relation to what may be called "marginal" Christian churches. Jehovah's Witnesses first entered the area of Zambia from Nyasaland in 1911, and had extraordinary success. Over 25 percent of Zambia's population is estimated to have been involved in Jehovah's Witnesses at one time or another in their lives, either as members or regular attenders or strong sympathizers. At various times in their history, the governments of Zambia have acted against the Witnesses. In 1969, they encountered serious persecution from supporters of the ruling United National Independence Party when they refused to vote or take part in political life. Many worship halls were seized or burned and many Witnesses fled across the border to Zaire. Although missionaries attached to Jehovah's Witnesses were expelled, Zambian Witnesses have continued their activities despite the conflict between their views and those of the state.

Similar was the experience of the Lumpa Church, founded by Alice Mulenga Lenshina among the Bemba people in northern Zambia. Lenshina had been a Presbyterian, but following a profound spiritual experience in 1953, she established her own church that combined missionary Christianity, witchcraft eradication, and black frustration with the political situation of the 1950s. "By late 1956 the Presbyterian and Catholic churches in the area seemed almost deserted while pilgrims were arriving at Alice's home . . . at the rate of a thousand a week."[597] Soon a segregated Lumpa community was constituting itself with whole villages completely committed to this charismatic woman. But this aggressive isolation did not fare well as the new Zambia came into being and every Zambian was required to participate in the new state. In July 1964 catastrophe ensued, and conflict escalated into pitched battles when government troops were ordered to bring the segregated Lumpa villages to an end. Lumpa villages were burned, over 700 people lost their lives, and the Lumpa Church was banned. It was the darkest day for the new government of Zambia.

It was into this volatile situation that the **United Presbyterian Church in the U.S.A.** initiated its involvement in the Christian movement in Zambia. Its initial ventures were in relation to the Mindolo Ecumenical Foundation Center in Kitwe, providing scholarships for Christian leaders from Zambia and surrounding nations to participate in conferences on community development as well as larger political issues. Also, it will be recalled, the UPCUSA provided the services of Dr. Clinton Marsh at the Mindolo Center during the formative years of the All-Africa Conference of Churches. In time American Presbyterians would be cooperating with the United Church of Zambia, as well as two smaller Presbyterian churches, the Church of Central Africa Presbyterian (CCAP) based in Malawi, and the Presbyterian Church of Southern Africa (PCSA) based in South Africa.

BEGINNING OF INVOLVEMENT IN MALAWI

Known before its independence as Nyasaland (meaning Lake Land) for the large lake that occupies one-fifth of its territory, Malawi had been inhabited by Bantu-speaking peoples since the first century A.D. By the 15th century, the various ethnic groups had come together in the Malawi Confederacy, which covered much of what is now central and southern Malawi. In the 16th century, Ngoni people immigrated from Tanzania and founded a strong kingdom in northern Malawi. The 17th century brought the Portuguese to pursue their slave trade, in cooperation with Arab settlers who introduced Islam. The Portuguese had hoped to annex Malawi into its colonial empire, thus linking the Portuguese colonies of Angola and Mozambique. However, Britain intervened in the mid-19th century, laying claim to what was as yet unexplored territory. The difficulty of the mountainous terrain, as well as the constant warfare between the Ngoni and Yao peoples, had prevented successful penetration of the area by outsiders. However, after the valiant David Livingstone had reached Lake Nyasa in 1859, exploration of the region began.

From this point, the history of Malawi is closely linked with that of the countries now known as Zimbabwe and Zambia. However, lacking the rich mineral resources of Zimbabwe and Zambia, Malawi was not considered as rich a prize as the latter two countries. It became the British protectorate of Nyasaland in 1891, valued primarily for the cash crops (coffee, tea, sugar, tobacco, rubber) grown on its fertile plains along the western and southern coast of Lake Nyasa. The small white population (less than ten thousand) maintained control of vast plantations, despite periodic violent uprisings from the displaced local population (numbering close to three million).

Between 1953 and 1963, Nyasaland became part of the white-dominated Central African Federation, along with Southern Rhodesia (Zimbabwe) and Northern Rhodesia (Zambia). However, African opposition had not lessened, ineffectual as it seemed at the time. In 1958, Dr. Hastings Kamuzu Banda returned to his native land of Malawi, after decades of absence in America, Britain and Ghana, to lead the African nationalist cause. He became head of the Malawi Congress Party (MCP), a conservative nationalist party that spearheaded the campaign for independence. "'To Hell with federation,' he cried. 'Let us fill their prisons with our thousands, singing Hallelujah.'"[598] Wide disturbances were followed by arrests, and Banda was to be in prison for the next year. But Britain, finally recognizing the overwhelming opposition to the Federation from the African population, dissolved the Federation in 1963, opening the way for Malawi's independence in 1964, with Banda as prime minister.

In 1966, Malawi became a one-party republic, with Banda as its first president. However, he soon followed a path very different from that of the leaders of other newly independent African nations. In 1967, he astonished his black African colleagues by officially recognizing the racist white-dominated Republic of South Africa, and in 1971 became the first black African head of state to visit that country. By accepting South Africa's offer of economic aid, Banda enlarged the network of power of the apartheid regime in South Africa.

After having himself elected as "president for life" in 1971, Banda ruled Malawi with an iron hand for the next 23 years. Saying that his opponents would become "food for crocodiles", he ruled the country with increasing severity, and reports were ever more frequent of murders, disappearances and other serious human rights violations, even against those who had worked with him to gain independence. He organized Malawian youth into the Young Pioneers and trained them as secret agents to spy on those who did not support his regime. While his presidency did have some positive aspects, such as the modernizing of major cities and the building of well-maintained roads, Banda's regime was experienced by many Malawians as bringing poverty, repression, detention without trial, torture, exile and all too often execution.[599] Within this political context, and often despite it, the Christian movement thrived in Malawi. Following in the footsteps of Livingstone, Scottish Presbyterians were the Protestant pioneers, with the Free Church of Scotland beginning work in northern Malawi in 1875 and the Church of Scotland beginning work in southern Malawi in 1876. The former concentrated its work at the renowned Livingstonia Mission headquartered at Khondowe. Help was asked from the students at the Lovedale School in South Africa, and five black South African evangelists joined Dr. Robert Laws in pioneer work in the region. One in particular, William Koyi, left his mark on the work as the peacemaker between the fierce Ngoni and the more docile

Tonga people. A far-reaching development was the establishment in 1894 of the Overtoun Institution that "grew into one of the best educational institutions in modern missions."[600] Meanwhile, in the southern area, the Church of Scotland was actively at work, its main location being at Blantyre. "Eventually Blantyre entered upon a course of development under wise and devoted leaders such as Rev. Dr. H. Hetherwick, which made it ultimately one of the greatest mission forces in the non-Christian world."[601]

In 1888, these two missions were joined by Dutch Reformed missionaries from South Africa, who concentrated their work in central Malawi around Mkhoma. As the work of the three missions prospered, indigenous presbyteries were organized—the Presbytery of Livingstonia in 1899, and the Presbyteries of Blantyre and Mkhoma soon afterward. Eventually the three presbyteries joined in 1926 to form the Church of Central Africa Presbyterian (CCAP). As the church continued to grow at a rapid rate, in 1956, the three presbyteries became synods with several presbyteries within each, joined together in the CCAP General Synod.

The evangelistic spirit of the CCAP could not be contained within the bounds of Malawi. The Livingstonia Mission expanded its work across the border into neighboring Zambia, and by 1945 the churches in this area were brought together in the Presbytery of Chasefu (later to be known as the Presbytery of Zambia). As the Central and Southern Presbyterian streams began to converge in Zambia, efforts were made to cooperate and to work toward union into one Presbyterian Church of Zambia.

While other Protestant groups have entered Malawi, the Presbyterian constituency is by far the strongest. By the 1970s, of the total population of some four million, approximately 1,250,000 were Protestants, with some 700,000 Presbyterians. Catholic constituency was approximately one million. Thus approximately 59 percent of the population claimed the name of Christian. The ecumenical movement has been very active in Malawi. The Christian Council of Malawi was formed in 1939, building on foundations laid earlier by the Consultative Board of Federative Missions of Nyasaland. Churches belonging to the Christian Council have been heavily involved in education, medical and social service, operating some 22 hospitals, 36 clinics, 5 teacher-training colleges, 3 lay training centers, 4 printing presses, in addition to two theological colleges and 8 Bible Schools.

Into this politically repressive but spiritually vibrant nation, **The Presbyterian Church in the U.S.A.** entered with limited partnership in ministry with the Church of Central Africa Presbyterian (CCAP). In time Malawi would become a nation where American Presbyterians would be major partners in Christian witness and service.

CHAPTER V

A CONTINENT IN CRISIS: PARTNERSHIP IN MISSION (1973-2000)

To attempt to summarize this period of 28 years of American Presbyterian involvement in the Christian movement in sub-Saharan Africa within one brief chapter would appear to be a foolish endeavor. Yet the story would be incomplete without attempting to do so. Both the lack of time and the difficulty of obtaining the necessary resources make it necessary to deal briefly with matters that deserve much more thorough treatment. The story will be more anecdotal than comprehensive.

A. POST-INDEPENDENCE AFRICA AND THE CHRISTIAN MOVEMENT

By the beginning of this period, almost all of sub-Saharan Africa had attained independence, except for the region of southern Africa. The young African states faced a variety of major problems. One of the most important was the creation of nation-states in societies that had been basically tribal. Most African nations retained the frontiers arbitrarily drawn by the late 19th-century colonial powers. Often ethnic groups would be divided by national boundaries. Loyalties to the ethnic group usually were stronger than those to the newly-established state. When the new states attained independence, the dominant nationalist movements and their leaders found it necessary to exercise strong control and sometimes installed themselves in virtually permanent power. They called for national unity and urged that multi-party systems be discarded in favor of a single-party state. When these governments proved unable or unwilling to fulfil popular expectations, those in control often resorted to military intervention. Military leaders would emerge as national power figures, sometimes becoming more dictatorial than their colonial predecessors. Unfortunately, during the Cold War era, donor countries, especially the United States and the Soviet Union, were the enablers of the militarization of many of the most dictatorial regimes.

Yet in the midst of all the struggle and suffering that has prevailed in most African nations, the 1990s has brought a renewed determination to move toward a more democratic multi-party system of government. Samuel Kobia of Kenya, who has staffed the Africa program of the World Council of Churches, has said, "After years as the battleground of the Cold War, Africa is on the verge of a renaissance. What is finally emerging now is the reality that African people have rich experiences and ideas that they want to put into practice. The cycle of coups and civil wars should be approaching its end. From Ghana to South Africa, we are seeing countries adopting democratic governance, and there is far more talk of a new society in Africa."[602]

Economically, the young African nations face formidable problems. Although a number of African states have considerable natural resources, few have had finances or the trained personnel to develop their economies. Further, they inherited economies geared to benefit the former colonial powers, with their products produced primarily for export rather than for the good of their own people. Foreign private enterprise has been spasmodic in its involvement, often regarding investment in such underdeveloped areas as too risky. The major alternative sources of financing have been national and international aid and lending institutions. These have had many strings attached, and easily subject to misuse and diversion on the part of corrupt political leaders. While the expectations of the people for a better living standard have increased, the prices of consumer and manufactured goods have soared, while the income from most African primary products have lagged far behind on the world market. The oil price increase in the 1970s and the subsequent worldwide recession in the 1980s hit the poorest nations hardest. Serious foreign exchange problems and ballooning foreign debt have created a downward spiral, with African governments able to spend less and less on basic human services such as health, education, and development of much-needed infrastructure.

Famine and drought have plagued vast regions of the continent. Millions of refugees have left their homes in search of food, increasing the problems of the countries to which they have fled. Medical resources, already inadequate, have been overwhelmed by epidemics of malaria, cholera, and other endemic diseases. In more recent years, the pandemic of AIDS has devastated the population of many countries, creating a situation in which millions of children are left orphaned and having to make their own way in poverty-stricken societies.[603]

In and through this tragic situation, the leadership of African nations has sought to find ways of working together toward peace and development. The Organization of African Unity (OAU), established in 1963, became a symbol of unity and mutuality for the new order in Africa, seeking to forge a unity of Africans across national and tribal differences. In 1975 the OAU became divided between Marxist and non-Marxist political alliances and approaches to issues, beginning with the Angolan Civil War and continuing during a series of subsequent wars between African nations. However, the OAU scored a number of successes in mediating border disputes, channeling financial support to movements seeking to defeat colonial rule, and supporting movements against white minority rule in Southern Africa. By raising public awareness and putting pressure on their governments throughout the 1980s and early 1990s, Pan-African groups succeeded in focusing the world's attention on the injustices of white minority rule in southern Africa, bringing that system to an end in one country after another and finally in South Africa itself. South

Africa became a member of the OAU in 1994, and since then has been a major force for peace, democracy, and economic development in Africa. Also, regional cooperative groups have emerged, notably the Economic Community of West African States (ECOWAS) and the Southern African Development Community (SADC), working toward regional economic cooperation and integration.

The Protestant Christian community has reflected this movement toward continent-wide cooperation through the All-Africa Conference of Churches (AACC), also inaugurated in 1963. Over the years, despite organizational problems, the AACC has become a working instrument of ecclesiastical cooperation and political influence as well as a public expression of the maturity that Protestant Christianity seeks. It has worked against formidable odds, not only because of the multiplicity and poverty of the local churches, but also because of the varying languages and governing styles inherited from their former colonial powers. Like the various national councils of churches, the AACC has depended heavily upon funds from abroad for its ecumenical projects. Still, these councils have become instruments for uniting the efforts of the churches and mission boards in their efforts to address the deep-seated needs of society as a whole.

It was during the 1970s that there emerged in African ecumenical circles the "moratorium" debate, calling for a cessation of sending and receiving money and missionary personnel from abroad for a period to allow time for the review of the best use of persons and money in response to the African churches' search for selfhood. John Gatu, then General Secretary of the Presbyterian Church of East Africa, first issued the call in 1971, arguing that "the time has come for the withdrawal of foreign missionaries from many parts of the third world, that the churches of the third world must be allowed to find their own identity, and that the continuation of the present missionary movement is a hindrance to this selfhood of the church." The proposal became a subject of heated debate in the World Council of Churches and subsequently at the All Africa Conference of Churches meeting in Lusaka, Zambia in 1975. However, most African churches would dissociate themselves from the AACC's moratorium resolution. Instead emphasis was placed on "partnership in mission" which would recognize that the sending and receiving of personnel and funds are joint responsibilities, and that traditional relationships, structures and attitudes that perpetuate dependence had to change for the sake of the selfhood of the churches.[604]

Meanwhile, there was emerging among the African churches a common sense of the need for an African theology that would address the distinctive needs of African nations as well as giving full expression to the positive elements in African culture. The idea of an Ecumenical Association of Third World Theologians (EATWOT) was inspired by young African theologians in conversation with Latin American and Asian church leaders. The organizational meeting of EATWOT took place in Dar es Salaam, Tanzania in 1976. In succeeding years, EATWOT offered challenging critiques of traditional European and American interpretations of Christian theology, and emphasized a theology supporting the common struggle for justice among the world's oppressed. Building upon EATWOT's initiative, an Ecumenical Association of African Theologians (EAAT) was founded in

1977, with offices in Yaounde, Cameroon. Out of its assemblies and consultations have emerged numerous publications on African Theology, emphasizing the indigenization of the gospel and the liberation of the people of Africa from the cultural and economic domination of the West.[605]

Despite and in some cases because of the crises which were gripping the African continent in the latter part of the 20th century, the Christian movement was experiencing astonishing growth. Whereas by 1970, it was estimated that the Christian population of Africa numbered some 117 million, by the year 2000 it was estimated that the number had reached some 335 million.[606] Truly it had become the fastest growing Christian community in the world, surpassing the number of Christians in North America, and outnumbering the total Muslim population on the African continent. The rapid growth of the churches has been both a boon and a challenge to African governments. The churches are the only independent organizations of any consequence functioning in most nations. Thus the churches are in a position to make a significant contribution to long-range nation-building. Conversely, at their best they can challenge the abuse of political power by corrupt government leadership.

AMERICAN PRESBYTERIANS UNDERGO CHANGES IN STRUCTURES FOR MISSION

The years between 1973 and 2000 saw numerous changes in the structures through which American Presbyterians engaged in the global Christian movement. In the **United Presbyterian Church, USA,** in 1973 the various program boards of the church were merged into **the Program Agency.** With the demise of the Commission on Ecumenical Mission and Relations, no longer was there a a separate world mission board. In its place, emphasis was placed on "mission in six continents." In the Program Agency, pressing domestic issues such as the civil rights movement and the Vietnam Wsr became the major foci of attention. Africa became a secondary concern, seen primarily as it related to the domestic racial situation.

In the **Presbyterian Church, U.S.,** after several years of preparation, in 1973 all program boards were moved to Atlanta and became part of a **General Executive Board**, later to become the **General Assembly Mission Board.** A **Division of International Mission** maintained the focus on the church's involvement in the global Christian movement; however, the resources available for global mission suffered a considerable reduction.

Nevertheless, several new programs were emerging that would focus on the desperate needs in Third World countries, as well as in situations of poverty in the United States. Within the UPCUSA, there came into being the **Self-Development of Peoples Program.** Responding to the demands of the civil rights movement that the poor be enabled to help themselves, grants were made to organizations formed by those living in poverty so that they could undertake self-help programs that in time would move them toward self-support. In time, such grants were also made to overseas self-development organizations.

Within the Presbyterian Church, U.S., in response to predictions of world-wide famine, the 1969 PCUS General Assembly declared that world hunger be given top priority in the mission planning of the church. An inter-board committee initiated a **Task Force on World Hunger**, and in 1971 a World Hunger office was established. As a result of a Consultation on World Hunger held in 1972, the World Hunger Program developed a five-fold emphasis: educating the church as to the root causes of hunger; engaging local churches in responding to hunger in their own communities: strengthening the church's response to global hunger through grants to programs of partner churches that addressed various aspects of the hunger problem; strengthening the church's witness in relation to U.S. government policies affecting the world's poorest nations; and encouraging changes in lifestyle that would reduce our consumption of the world's limited resources. Eventually the world hunger emphasis was picked up by other major denominations, including the UPCUSA, which began its hunger program in 1975. Increasingly the two Presbyterian denominations worked together in addressing world hunger and in 1981 the two programs were merged into the **Presbyterian Hunger Program.**

Through the years since its initiation, the Presbyterian Hunger Program and its predecessor programs have responded to specific needs and projects regardless of the nation in which the need or project was found. Hence American Presbyterians have become involved in programs and projects in sub-Saharan Africa where there was no previous mission involvement.[607] Much of its work has been done ecumenically, recognizing that the churches can address such deep-seated problems much more effectively by working together. Through **Church World Service,** an arm of the National Council of Churches, numerous hunger programs have been carried out in cooperation with National Christian Councils in Sub-Saharan Africa. Also, through **Bread for the World**, a Christian organization addressing public policy related to world hunger, American Presbyterians have exercised the "stewardship of their citizenship" on behalf of the world's poor, with a strong emphasis on the critical situation in Africa. Another lasting contribution of the Presbyterian Hunger Program has been the initiation of **presbytery partnerships**, linking individual U.S. presbyteries with denominations and presbyteries overseas, and enabling American Presbyterians to become more directly involved in the problems and issues facing people in poor nations. A number of such presbytery partnerships have developed in relation to partner churches in sub-Saharan Africa.

Through the years from 1973 to 1983, the UPCUSA and PCUS mission policy, planning and involvement drew closer together. When the two denominations finally were reunited at the historic 1983 General Assembly in Atlanta, to become the **Presbyterian Church (U.S.A.),** the two mission programs were merged. Though it would be four years before the two offices finally became one in 1987, moving from New York and Atlanta to Louisville, Kentucky, joint mission planning became a reality from the outset in the reunited church. Since that time, there have been several adjustments of mission structure. For several years, the world mission program was carried out through the **Global Mission Unit,** until at the present date there is a **Worldwide Ministries Division** within the **General Assembly Council**. The stated purpose of the Worldwide Ministries Division is "to empower the church in each place to share the transforming power of the gospel of Jesus Christ with all people through partnership and mutuality with the worldwide body of Christ." Within the Division's section on Ecumenical Partnership, there are two offices related to sub-Saharan Africa: a Central and West Africa office, and a Southern and East Africa office. It is through this structure that the Presbyterian Church (USA) now carries out Christian mission in the nations of sub-Saharan Africa.[608]

Surveying the involvement of American Presbyterians in sub-Saharan Africa during the past 28 years, one notes the following::

1) There has been continued diversification in missionary assignments to an increasing number of nations, in response to requests received from various partner churches.
2) There has been a decrease in the number of career missionaries, and an increase in the number of short-term and volunteer missionaries on special assignment.
3) There has been a decrease in the number of missionaries doing church-related evangelistic work, and an increase in the number related to various institutions, both educational and medical.
4) A number of missionaries have been appointed to non-traditional kinds of assignments, e.g. public health and environmental concerns.
5) There has been the beginning of a regional approach, with missionaries assigned to work in several countries and to bring resources to bear on specific needs in those countries, e.g. theological education, church development, public health.
6) Several mission support groups have emerged, working in covenant agreement with the General Assembly Council, each seeking to strengthen a particular aspect of the global mission enterprise; e.g. **Presbyterian Frontier Fellowship, Outreach Foundation, Medical Benevolence Foundation.**
7) Numerous efforts have been made toward mutuality in mission, seeking to enlist the leadership of partner churches in "Mission to the U.S.A."

An especially significant initiative taken by American Presbyterians has been the **Program for Evangelism and Church Growth in Africa.** Funded by the generous support of one Presbyterian elder, Alex Booth, as well as additional funds provided by churches contributing directly and through the Outreach Foundation, the program has funded three mission co-worker couples who have served as coordinators in Central and Western Africa, East Africa, and Southern Africa; built or repaired scores of churches, manses, schools, and seminaries in 17 African countries; trained church leaders in evangelism and special ministries to enable church growth; printed church school and other Christian materials; and supported national evangelists.[609] Also, the Presbyterian Frontier Fellowship has assisted partner churches in reaching unevangelized people groups in several African countries, including Sudan, Ethiopia, Kenya, Malawi, and Nigeria. Despite the critical situation in which the churches now find themselves, "in many places a new wave of renewal and hope has spread across the churches."[610]

Recognizing that sub-Saharan African had reached "a time of radical transformation", the 1994 PC(USA) General Assembly designated the following year (1994-1995) as "A Year with Africa."[611] Travel seminars were scheduled during that year to visit with partner churches in Ghana, Ethiopia, Madagascar, South Africa, Zimbabwe, Malawi and Namibia. Special attention was given to the critical situations in Zaire and Rwanda, Sudan and Ethiopia. Once again Africa had captured the attention of American Presbyterians as a critical focus of mission.

While there is "no turning back" to the patterns of mission which prevailed a century ago, there is profound gratitude for what has been accomplished by those who have gone before to lay the foundations for the "great reality of our time", the presence of Christ's Church in virtually every nation on earth, and the new opportunities for partnership in mission with the Christian community in sub-Saharan Africa.

B. AMERICAN PRESBYTERIAN INVOLVEMENT IN WEST AFRICA

During the period 1973-2000, American Presbyterians have been involved in the Christian movement in West Africa primarily in four nations: Cameroon, Equatorial Guinea, Ghana, and Nigeria.

PARTNERSHIP IN MISSION IN CAMEROON

The United Republic of Cameroon, with some 15 million people, had been the major mission field of the Presbyterian Church, U.S.A. (northern) since 1879. After gaining its independence in 1960-1961, it had combined the former French and British Cameroons, becoming the only African country to maintain officially two national languages, French and English. The French language and influence continued to predominate, since by far the larger area was the former French Cameroun. During the period 1973-2000, the country has gone through many changes. A one-party presidential system prevailed during the presidency of Ahmadou Ahidjo (1960-1982) and the early years of the presidency of Paul Biya (1982-1992). However, rising popular discontent in the early 1990s led to political reforms. In the nation's first multiparty elections in 1992 in which over 60 political parties participated, Biya was re-elected president. Biya has been re-elected in subsequent elections, though there have been increasing allegations of electoral fraud and corruption in the national government.

Early in 1994 a border dispute arose between Cameroon and Nigeria, after Nigerian troops invaded the petroleum-rich Bakassi Peninsula of Cameroon. The International Court of Justice agreed to resolve the border dispute, and the case has been broadened to include the entire 1044-mile frontier between the two countries, which has never been established using modern geographical methods. However, short skirmishes have sporadically broken out as each nation accuses the other of being the aggressor. As a consequence of the dispute, the All-Anglophone Conference (AAC) of English-speaking

African nations has threatened to push for a return to the two Federated French—and English-speaking states that existed before 1972.

Like other sub-Saharan countries, Cameroon has endured a series of economic crises. One of its major cash crops, cocoa, declined in value at least 30% on the world market in one year. Many government employees were not paid for several months, then had their salaries cut in half. The government then devalued the currency, which meant that overnight the purchasing power of one's money was cut in half. The impact of these developments have been felt in every aspect of the life of the people, including education and medical care.

Problems in the relationship between the *Eglise Presbyterienne Camerounaise (EPC)* and the United Presbyterian Church USA continued for several years into the 1970s. However, the exchange of church delegations led to agreements which enabled the continuation of UPC mission involvement. While the number of American Presbyterian workers in Cameroon has greatly diminished from the time in 1957 when some 123 missionaries served in this nation,[612] there has been continued involvement in the Christian movement in Cameroun in response to specific expressed needs of the Camerounian church, especially in relation to theological education, medical work, financial and administrative assistance.

In the 1970s, American Presbyterians joined the EPC in an extensive rehabilitation of the program and facilities of the Dager Seminary, which was producing most of the pastors serving the EPC. However, increasing emphasis was being placed on a higher level of theological education. The **Protestant Theological Faculty** in Yaounde, which came into being around the time of independence in 1960, was formed by several autonomous Protestant churches as a graduate institution of theological education. With a student body of over 150 plus some 10 doctoral candidates, the majority of the students are from Cameroon but many come from other French-speaking West African countries including Benin, Togo, Ivory Coast, and from Central African countries including Congo and Rwanda. A significant contribution to the institution was made through the service of American Presbyterian missionaries Drs. Paul and Ellenor Frelick from 1991 to 1996, with Mrs. Frelick serving as librarian and Dr. Frelick as professor of New Testament Theology.

The Frelicks testified to the courage of some church leaders:

> We celebrated communion with 800+ worshippers present at the French service which took a good two hours with a lot of singing. We are moved by the authenticity of worship, of vibrant hymn singing, of biblical attentiveness and faithful preaching. Some sermons with prophetic accent and courage have called the present government to account. Present conditions do not leave preachers free from harassment by authorities. So we do mean courage.[613]

Mrs. Frelick found the library "grossly insufficient." desperately needing recent theological works and periodicals. There were many structural needs as well: good cataloguing, good lighting, cleanliness, the paring down of outmoded books—most of all, a new library building. Through contacts in France, England and the Extra Commitment Opportunity Fund of the PC(USA), by 1993 a new library had been built, including an auditorium seating 400, conference rooms and ecumenical studies area. Among the library's recent acquisitions was a collection of the American Presbyterian mission magazine, *The Drum Call*, published for 45 years (1921-1966) as a record of the evangelistic, educational and medical work of the PCUSA mission, affording African theological students "inspiring and fascinating glimpses of Africans whose lives were totally changed as a result of the Good News."[614]

Through their experience in Cameroon, the Frelicks shared with the American church an "image of the church struggling to be faithful amid confusion and chaos"—a church often reflecting the degenerating situation of its nation, with unpaid salaries, lack of transparency in its management, energy often frittered by internecine and tribal battles; yet a church which often was ready to "stand up and be counted" and live out its faith. "It is only when the church models itself on God's kingdom come, that some hoped for transformation will come here as elsewhere."[615]

Medical work continued to call for the help of missionary co-workers. The Metet Hospital at Mbalmayo, south of the capital city of Yaounde, has had a long-standing place in the medical program begun by American Presbyterian missionaries. As a 140-bed surgical center performing over 1,200 surgical procedures a year, the hospital serves an area of some 75,000 people. "Patients may travel up to 100 kilometers for care at Metet, bypassing government hospitals that have no specialists and are not rated as well for surgery." Dr. Richard Freeman, who served as medical director at the Metet Hospital for some 25 years, upon retirement was decorated by the Camerounian Minister of Health for his service to the nation's medical needs. He had devoted a good part of his time to surgical training for young interns as part of their medical schooling, "looking to the future when Camerounian Christian doctors will be able to take over the work at Metet."

When a delegation from the PC(USA) visited Cameroon for a special anniversary observance at Metet, Dr. Evelyn Adams, M.D., at 82 years of age, traveled with the group. She spoke of the improvements which she observed since the years when she had served as the first woman doctor in Cameroon. She recalled the name she had been given many years before: *Bapetakudwa*—"the one who stayed when the others had gone away."[616]

Metet Hospital has been served by a succession of missionary doctors and specialists, not only from the PC(USA) but also from Cameroon, several European countries, as well as a Cameroon-trained Christian surgeon from neighboring Chad. Whenever possible, these have made their services available to the other hospitals that were the fruit of American Presbyterian medical mission work and are now part of the EPC medical program.

In addition, there has been a very significant contribution to enabling the EPC to develop a primary health care program. PC(USA) mission worker Dr. Dorothy Brewster-Lee writes:

I am currently working with an organization called *Association de Sante des Femmes Chretiennes* (Christian Women's Health Association.) I am acting as the health consultant to this group of Christian women who have decided to train other Christian women to conduct evangelism through community health projects. Without external funding these women have begun to disseminate their message of community health through love, collective work and prayer. [For our first training session] of the 42 church women's associations which applied, twelve have been selected to participate in this the first of three training workshops which will be held over the course of the year.[617]

Within the following year, the program had grown to include women from four different Protestant denominations, both English and French speaking, and one from the Catholic church. In response to the growing challenge of HIV transmission in Cameroon, the Association created an HIV/AIDS project that included an HIV prevention/education program and an AIDS support program. The program became a recipient of the 1995 PC(USA) Women's Birthday Offering.

Other mission co-workers engaged in a wide variety of activities at the invitation of the EPC. For example: Margaret Chase, who had served in Cameroon since 1952, served as chaplain for 700 students in three junior high and two senior iigh schools in Yaounde. Later the Younde Protestant Council of Churches decided that each church in Yaounde should be responsible for a chaplaincy presence in one secondary school and "Miss Chase will teach them." This became her primary activity until her retirement in 1990.[618]—Guy and Monique Bekaert who served for 20 years in Cameroon would write of wearing "many different hats: Church Projects Officer, Development Issues, Agricultural Mission, and West-Central Africa Coordinator for Projects of Evangelism and Church Growth in Africa (PECGA). "PECGA has sent me twice to Ghana to visit the Presbyterian Church and the Evangelical Presbyterian Church", and later to the troubled little country of Rwanda. Monique "continues her work in Acupressure with a strong patient demand."[619]—A short-termer, Brian Snyder, would write, "I was named business manager of the *College Unis D'Elat* [in Ebolowa]. This final surprise was sprung on me by the General Assembly of the *Eglise Presbyterienne Camerounaise* (EPC). The G.A. obviously was unaware that the only college course I ever failed was business math." His other responsibilities included English teacher and *secretair particulier* "which is just a tricky French way of saying third-in-command of the school."[620] As is true in mission partnership in many African countries, the tasks to be done often stretch the limits of the time and capabilities of the mission co-worker.

PARTNERSHIP IN MISSION IN EQUATORIAL GUINEA

The small postage-stamp-shaped nation between Cameroon and Gabon, with a population of less than half a million, had been a PCUSA mission field since 1865.[621] However, from early in its mission involvement, the American Presbyterian mission had faced formidable obstacles, first in the severe restrictions placed on their work by the Catholic-dominated Spanish colonial power (making it the only Spanish-speaking nation in Africa), then following independence in 1968 by the repressive regime of an atheist dictator, Francisco Macias Nguema. In 1979 Nguema was overthrown in a military coup, tried for treason, executed and replaced by another equally repressive ruler, Lt. Col. Teodoro Obiang Nguema (nephew of the former Nguema). Though the nation's alliance was shifted from the Soviet Union back to Spain, and multiparty elections were held during the 80s and 90s, the nation actually has been controlled by a supreme military council under President Nguema. The latest elections in 1999 have been condemned by international observers as fraudulent, with harassment, jailing, and alleged torture of political opponents.

A petroleum boom that began in 1996 has brought a sudden spurt of economic growth to this forgotten land that once was ranked among the world's poorest countries. However, the benefits of the new prosperity have been limited to the president's clan and little has been done to improve the education, health and welfare of the majority of the people.

The Presbyterian Reformed Church of Equatorial Guinea (IRPGE) is the fruit of the mission outreach of the Presbyterian Church U.S.A., the Methodist Church and the Worldwide Evangelization Crusade. While it is a relatively small denomination with less than 10,000 members, its influence has been significant as a counterforce to the overwhelming Catholic domination. The church has experienced the kind of repression well known to non-Roman Catholic churches under Spanish rule. Having experienced serious internal power struggles, there is recognition of the need for reconciliation, renewal, recommitment, and retraining. Within the past year, a brave Mission Specialist, the Rev. Diana Christine Wright, has been serving as an evangelist and church administrator in Equatorial Guinea. The PC(USA) Project for Evangelism and Church Growth in Africa has assisted the IRPGE with training for evangelism and with church construction.

PARTNERSHIP IN MISSION IN GHANA

The Republic of Ghana, with a population of over 18 million, had become a field for partnership in mission of both the United Presbyterian Church, U.S.A. (northern) and the Presbyterian Church, U.S. (southern) beginning in the 1960s. Following its independence in 1957, Ghana experienced a period of repeated coups that brought great political instability. When Flight Lieutenant Jerry Rawlings overthrew a military-controlled government in 1979, he inherited a severely troubled economy. Dedicated to uprooting corruption, Rawlings imposed an austerity plan that helped control inflation. Nevertheless, problems increased in the 1980s. Currency was devalued three times in order to stimulate exports, and despite fertile land and rainfall in southern Ghana, the nation suffered serious food shortages. Many educated professionals left the country. Several hundred thousand emigrated to Nigeria to find a place in that booming petroleum-rich economy, only to be forcefully repatriated when Nigeria's economy declined. Burdened by a large foreign debt, Ghana undertook an austerity program mandated by the International Monetary

Fund to control inflation and attract financial aid from the West. However, this only led to increased unemployment and a growing gap between the rich and the poor. Despite Rawlings' popularity with the people, his regime had to suppress several coup attempts. A referendum in April 1992 reestablished constitutional government, and Rawlings, running as a civilian, won the presidency in a multiparty election. He was reelected in 1996.

American Presbyterian involvement in Ghana has increased during the latter part of the 20th century. PCUS mission involvement had begun in 1968 with a missionary family serving under the National Christian Council of Ghana as the first full-time Protestant chaplain on the campus of the University College of Cape Coast. From this beginning emerged a Chaplaincy Program in various government institutions, including universities, hospitals, and prisons. Also, through the PCUS a partnership developed between Columbia Theological Seminary in Decatur, Georgia and Trinity Theological College in Accra. The experience of teaching at Trinity brought fresh insights to the Columbia professors into the dynamic of the Christian movement in Africa. 1977 saw the appointment of the first missionary from Africa to the PCUS, when the Rev. Dora Ofori-Owasu was sent by the Presbyterian Church of Ghana to Atlanta Presbytery. Later, the Presbyterian Church of Ghana would send one of the first long-term missionaries from one country of Africa to another, as the Rev. Alice Kyei-Anti served as a missionary to the women of the Church of Central Africa Presbyterian in Malawi. "Her deep faith has been an example to women and men alike and a bridge across the continent."[622] Also, Atlanta Presbytery entered into a partnership with the Evangelical Presbyterian Church of Ghana to undertake the Volta Dam Resettlement Program, assisting persons who were displaced by the building of the Volta River Dam and the lake which was formed covering a large inhabited area.

Following the reunion of northern and southern Presbyterians in 1983, the reunited PC(USA) became even more fully engaged in Ghana. At the invitation of the Presbyterian Church of Ghana (which by the end of the century had grown to some half a million constituents), American Presbyterian mission co-workers became involved in the Aframs Plains Development Project in the Eastern Region of Ghana. The project, centered at Tease, became an integrated comprehensive community development program including agricultural, medical and educational work. Robert and Nancy Crumpton, who were involved in the project from its inception, wrote of the numerous ways in which the project would help small farmers and villages in good development:

> The government has introduced tractors and mechanized farming and we want to introduce animal traction, which is between the tractors and manual work. We have plowed, planted and cultivated two maize fields plus a garden. The soil is fertile and loamy and the donkeys have little trouble pulling the farming implements. The donkeys are working part of every day hauling water, moving sand, stone and lumber to the next building site.[623]

> Sometime when we drive into the project it is hard to believe, but nice to see the house, the guard hut, the tractor shed, fuel room, donkey stables, the workers'

pit toilet and now under construction is the workshop. Every part of the work
is done by hand . . . . Every morning at 6:30 a.m. we meet under the acacia tree
for devotions and talk over the day's work and any problems a worker might
have. Recently, one of the workers prayed for the project and for the people
in the U.S.A. who donated the money for the project. He said that the people
in the U.S. didn't know their faces but sent money to them. He continued by
saying he did not know their faces either, but he knew their hearts.[624]

Another significant development project initiated by the Presbyterian Church of
Ghana has been the Northern Outreach Program (NOP) which has included a strong
evangelistic emphasis. Centered in Tamale, the program addresses the needs of those
peoples scattered across the dry semi-arid Sahel region of northern Ghana. While
agriculture, medicine and education are an integral part of the program, there is a major
emphasis on spreading the gospel to the people in northern Ghana, where Islam and
traditional religions are strong. Bill and Judi Young, who were involved in this project
for a number of years, would write:

> Our work here bears a relationship to harvesting. We seek to help the church
> be more effective in harvesting among the groups of people in the north. The
> literacy rate and the economic levels are much higher in the south, and the tribal
> fighting in the north has hampered educational efforts. Many of the village
> people still see no need for education, especially for girls . . . . The south has
> had exposure to the gospel for a much longer time. As far as the Presbyterian
> Church is concerned (and this is typical of most churches), the work in the
> south started some 168 years ago. Most work in the north started in the 1960s.
> People's lives are usually controlled by fear and are focused on how to deal with
> their fears. The gospel can bring the good news that Jesus can deal with their
> fears, that he is more powerful than any other gods or spirits or forces.[625]

The Northern Outreach Program also helps northerners in southern Ghana, as youth
from the drought-prone north migrate to southern cities to find work.

> The problem is, there is no work there either. With the currency having
> depreciated by half in the last six months the merchants only increase the prices
> to their dollar equivalent to maintain a profit margin. Robberies are increasing
> and tempers flaring. Meanwhile, scores of children, generally young girls,
> stand at every traffic light attempting to sell everything from toilet tissue to
> car parts . . . Being ethnic minorities does not help their situation or win them
> sympathy. Dr. Azumah [who is responsible for the Northern Outreach Program]
> challenged the congregation in Accra to treat their brothers and sisters from
> the north as humans, to understand their spiritual needs, and to support the
> NOP's ministries. Since most of the northerners provide domestic services to

the southerners, he really hit home when he told the congregation to at least allow their workers to go to church on Sundays!"[626]

Working with women from the north is an important part of the NOP ministry. Wendy Kelley has worked with a Women's Vocational Center in Accra, helping women gain life skills and run a batik-dyeing business that supports some of the ministries' activities. Mission Volunteer Barbara Mueller has worked in a similar Presbyterian Women's Vocational Institute in the rural town of Bogoro, creating a small sewing factory which produces "international quality" products under the label "Bogoro Maid."

The partnership with the Presbyterian Church of Ghana has also been a learning experience. Several PC(USA) International Volunteers have engaged in a year's experience of life in West Africa. Under the guidance of the Institute of Cross Cultural Studies in Tamale, these young people have lived in separate villages, learning the local language and "becoming familiar with the strange and wonderful rhythms of daily village life." One of them would write:

> I came across a quote recently by Richard Bohr, who said, "While we can't think ourselves into new ways of living, we can live ourselves into new ways of thinking."[627]

In many ways, the partnership with the Presbyterian churches of Ghana provides a foretaste of what Christian mission will be like in the 21st century.

PARTNERSHIP IN MISSION IN NIGERIA

American Presbyterian involvement in the Christian movement in the Federal Republic of Nigeria in the latter part of the twentieth century has been sporadic, due to the extremely unstable political situation. In this the most populous nation of sub-Saharan Africa, with a present population of some 114 million, its post-independence history has been dominated by military regimes which, under public pressure, have promised a transition to democratic rule but repeatedly disrupted the fulfilment of those promises. Finally, in May 1999, a democratically elected civilian president, Olusegun Obasanjo (a Christian), took office on a reform platform.

One of the most explosive issues greeting the new president is the tension that has plagued Nigeria for much of its modern history—relations between Muslims and Christians. Muslims account for approximately half the population, primarily in northern Nigeria. Christians account for approximately one-third of the population, primarily in southeastern Nigeria. Periodic clashes between Muslims and Christians, especially in northern Nigeria, have led to the burning of church buildings, as well as Christian schools and hospitals, and the killing and injuring of hundreds of Christians. Although the nation is officially prohibited from adopting a state religion, under the last military regime Nigeria joined the Organization of Islamic Countries, thus declaring itself a Muslim state. Calls by some Muslim leaders for the official adoption into the national constitution of *sharia* (Islamic law) have heightened tensions between Christian and Muslim communities. Christians are hopeful that the election of Obasanjo will ease tensions, particularly since he has appointed a Panel on Human Rights Abuses to examine alleged abuses occurring during the military dictatorships. The Project for Christian-Muslim Relations in Africa, of which the PC(USA) is a partner, has been working for better Christian-Muslim understanding in a number of African countries.

During the 1970s, oil money changed the face of Nigeria. While spectacular oil profits from its high production were dominating the economy, corruption grew with profits. Easy money encouraged the development of drug traffic for the American market. When the high tide of oil money ebbed in the 1980s, there was little left to mark its passing but the legacy of skyrocketing inflation, corruption and drug trafficing. The Christian community in Nigeria has sought to address the ethical issues related to Nigeria's social problems. At one point, a PCUS missionary couple was assigned to teach the Ethics of Development at the School of Religious Studies of the University of Ibadan, as well as being a consultant at the Institute of Church and Society. The Institute sought to monitor the government's petro-dollar supported development program and to ensure that human development was given higher priority.

The Presbyterian Church of Nigeria (PCN), though over 150 years old, represents only a small percentage of the total population, with a membership of about 120,000. It has focused its evangelism on the approximately 10 percent of the population that is animist. The Nigerian educational code requires that each student indicate a religious preference in public schools. PCN has seized the opportunity to send and support its own missionaries to teach those students who indicate a Christian preference. PC(USA) mission co-workers have served as consultants to support these efforts.

Because of the Muslim-dominated government, it has been difficult for Christian workers to receive visas for work in Nigeria. Mission co-workers Emory and Phyllis Van Gerpen were for a number of years the only PC(USA) missionaries in Nigeria, working with the Presbytery of the North, with a few small parishes scattered across northern Nigeria.

> Three years ago, the Presbytery of the North, of which Emory is the current Moderator, invited the General Assembly to hold their annual meeting in the predominantly Muslim north of Nigeria—something that has never been done before. The Assembly accepted the invitation; mostly, we presume, because at the time three years seemed too far away and nobody really worried much about it . . . . We planned for 450, knowing that some cannot come due to age, many are fearful, and others cannot afford the cost. Our theological college [of Northern Nigeria] was the venue . . . . Hosting the General Assembly had some very positive results. A very major point is that for the first time in its 147 year history, the General Assembly was held *outside* the traditional Presbyterian heartland. For many Nigerians, it was like going 'to

the mission field' (at a perceived risk to their very lives), to get a glimpse of the church's work there. We believe the experience has broadened the church's sense of mission.[628]

C. AMERICAN PRESBYTERIAN INVOLVEMENT IN CENTRAL AFRICA

During this period (1973-2000), American Presbyterians were involved in the Christian movement in Central Africa in the Democratic Republic of Congo and briefly in the tiny strife-torn nation of Rwanda.

PARTNERSHIP IN MISSION IN THE CONGO

The Democratic Republic of Congo (known from 1971 to 1997 as the Republic of Zaire), with a population of some 50 million, had been a field of mission for the Presbyterian Church in the United States (southern) since 1890. During the period from 1965 to 1997, the notoriously corrupt General Mobutu Sese Seko had complete control of the nation, making himself personally enormously wealthy at the expense of impoverishing the country. Reluctant to yield power but under pressure to democratize, he obstructed a supposed transition to a multiparty system in the 1990s.

However, his rule collapsed in the face of an insurgency led by Laurent Kabila, who headed a new regime from May 1997. Mobutu fled the country, dying shortly thereafter in exile in Morocco. The name Zaire was scrapped, returning the country to its previous name, the Congo. Political activity was suspended and elections deferred. Meanwhile, the Congo was descending into chaos as neighboring countries sent their armies across its borders seeking control over its rich natural resources. What ensued became known as the "great war of Central Africa", with armed forces from the nations north and east seeking to overthrow Kabila and those from the south supporting him. Only 40% of the Congo remained under the control of Kabila. Under international pressure, a cease-fire agreement was signed in August, 1999. However, tragically the long grinding war has continued with a horrendous loss of life, estimated to be more than 2.5 million, and some two million people displaced and unable to provide their own food.

Kabila, who had promised hope but brought increased misery, was assassinated in January 2001, and was succeeded by his son, Maj. Gen. Joseph Kabila. It remains to be seen whether the young Kabila will be able to bring any semblance of order into the chaos that is Congo today.

The history of Congo in the latter part of the 20th century is one of the most tragic stories in sub-Saharan Africa. As Mission Specialists Sue and Dr. William Sager write:

> Life in the Democratic Republic of Congo has been quite harsh and deprived
> for the past several years. Armies from six African neighbors, two refugee

groups and three Congo rebel groups are fighting each other over possession of the country's rich natural resources. None of the parties has interest in the plight of the Congolese people. The economy, roads, communications, schools, health facilities, etc. are in severe disarray and decay.[629]

Mission Co-workers Gwenda and Dr. John Fletcher add:

> The Congolese economy continues in a downward spiral. When we arrived six months ago, the exchange rate was six Congo Francs(CF) to the U.S. dollar. Today it is 30 CF to the U.S.dollar. At the moment, unemployment is probably less than the reported 90 percent, but only because large numbers of men and boys have joined the army. Unfortunately the army is only sporadically paid and the salary is very, very low.[630]

One of the primary effects of the poverty is hunger, especially for children. UNICEF estimates that in the Kasai region, where American Presbyterian work has been centered through the years, some 55 percent of child deaths are due to malnutrition. Other major health problems of the area such as malaria, tuberculosis and AIDS are exacerbated by weakness from malnutrition. Mission Specialists Haejung and Simon Park, who serve at the Christian Medical Institute of the Kasai (IMCK), write:

> When we first came here, we thought that people should have enough to eat since the growing season is so long and fruits seem to grow in the wild. Yet at the hospital we get about a hundred children a year with malnutrition so severe as to require hospitalization. And almost all the families are so poor they can't afford hospitalization. Seeing the stunted growth, vacant eyes, bloated stomachs, and low body weight, we can't help thinking about their future and that of this country.[631]

To confront these formidable odds, the force of mission co-workers in Zaire/Congo from the Presbyterian Church, U.S. and its successor the Presbyterian Church (USA) steadily declined over the past 28 years. Whereas in 1973 there had been a missionary force of 95 persons, by the year 2000 there were only ten. In fact, there were numerous times during these years when there were no American Presbyterian missionaries in the country, due to the dangerous political situation. Nevertheless, the PC(USA) continued its partnership in mission with the Presbyterian Community in Zaire/Congo and the Presbyterian Community in Kinshasa, building on the strong base established by its earlier missionary representatives.

The remarkable fact is that the Congolese Church continues its growth not only in numbers (estimated now at some two million members, making it among the largest of the 70 Protestant communities that form the Church of Christ in Congo) but also in witness and ministry.

They view this time of crisis as a time of great opportunity when Christians throughout Congo can share God's love and redemption in tangible, concrete ways. Government schools, hospitals, and training institutions have ceased to function, so the church has stepped in to fill the void. The number of children being orphaned by AIDS is rapidly rising, so the church is building orphanages. Refugees from ethnic violence are having to flee their homes, so the church welcomes them and receives them in the name of Christ. Families are suffering with extreme poverty, so the church sponsors self-development projects to teach marketable, viable ways to earn a living. They do this in partnership with you and other faithful Christians around the world.[632]

Chronic civil war and the devastated health care system have led to catastrophic health conditions throughout the Congo. In response, major emphasis in mission partnership during the post-independence years has been given to health care. The Good Shepherd Hospital, which is the base for the *Institut Medical Chretien du Kasai (IMCK)*, located in Tshikaji near the city of Kananga, was completed in 1975 through the PCUS Women's Birthday Offering. It has become a facility vastly superior to any other hospital in the Kasai region (an area the size of France), with departments of surgery, obstetrics/gynecology, pediatrics, ophthalmology, internal medicine, pathology, orthopedics, and community health; and training programs in nursing and laboratory work, as well as an intern/resident program for physicians in training and continuing education for all types of medical personnel.[633]

The many-faceted work at IMCK is reflected in the following excerpts from missionary correspondence:

In this "Year of the Child" we have been able to start a program targeting children, who are the most marginalized and vulnerable in this devastated economy, to ensure that they have access to good, affordable medical care . . . . Our tuberculosis treatment program is one of very few in the country that has not shut down because of war-related disruptions. It is essential that TB patients take their meds on an uninterrupted schedule, so we have pulled out all the stops to see that our program remains open in spite of difficulties, shortages, high prices and restricted mobility.[634]

HIV/AIDS is estimated by the World Health Organization to be present in 32 percent of the Kasai population.

There are at least 60,000 infected people in Kananga City alone who need or will need help with this horror of horrors. IMCK has the only clinic addressing the diagnosis and management of the disease.[635]

Dental care is a critical need in present-day Congo. To address this need, a Dental Clinic *(Clinique Dentaire)* has been initiated at IMCK, with the dual purpose of providing basic dental care and teaching dentistry to Congolese nurses. Dr. Knute Hernas describes his experience in this mission task:

> I work with a great bunch of guys and enjoy my work tremendously. Of particular interest are the trips we make out to the surrounding villages, for the dual purpose of providing dental care in remote areas and providing the nurses in our training program a regular experience in the type of dentistry which they in turn will be providing when they return to their own Health Zones. Seven of us pile into the Land Cruiser full of our gear and bodies and take off, along with two others on a motorcycle, for a two to four hour drive over washed-out roads and deep sand. We work pulling teeth and treating infections until mid-afternoon and then eat a locally prepared meal, finally getting home well after dark. It's a whole lot of fun, and our next trips will include spending the night.[636]

The critical health needs of women called for the special skills of a woman physician, Dr. Sue Makin.

> For a missionary trained in obstetrics/gynecology in the United States in the 1980s, many days are like living history lessons. The medical problems we see here have not been seen in the USA for 50 years. For example, a ruptured uterus from neglected labor in remote villages is a common occurrence. [637]

While missionary specialists would come and go, there were a few veteran missionaries who stayed through thick and thin. Such were mission co-workers Dr. Ralph and Mrs. Elsbeth Shannon, who completed their service as PC(USA) missionaries in 1997, having served in Congo for thirty-three years. In 1972, Dr. Shannon began ophthalmology work in Congo. Now IMCK has an eye department that serves far beyond the Kananga area. For five years prior to concluding their work Dr. Shannon served as director of IMCK.

> The primary goal as director was to keep the institute alive and functioning during those years of turmoil. We are most thankful that even with the collapse of so much of Zaire/Congo, by the grace of God, neither the hospital nor the training programs have ever had to close their doors. When we left Congo at the end of June 1997, we were able to leave in place a team of three capable Congolese—Dr. Mulaja Mukendi, interim director; Mr. Shamba Manenga, administrator; and Dr. Kasonga Lemba, legal representative—who are in charge of the direction and administration of this much-needed hospital and medical training facility.[638]

While IMCK has maintained a fairly steady flow of mission co-workers, other hospitals which had been established by PCUS medical missionaries had to continue on their own. Of the four other hospitals now managed by the Congolese Presbyterian Church, only Bulape and Lubondai have a doctor. Some did not make it. The hospital at Luebo, where Presbyterian missionaries had begun their work in 1891, "at present exists in name only, as there are no medicines, medical supplies, or functioning equipment." In contrast,

> Bulape is another former mission station, complete with a seminary, primary and secondary schools, a nursing school, and a hospital. The last missionaries left more than ten years ago, and Bulape is now entirely a Congolese institution. Unlike Luebo, however, they are proud to have continued to function and to have maintained a hospital with a good reputation. There is no question that they had to make adjustments and have managed with less, but the hospital has more than 90 percent occupancy in the midst of war and economic turmoil . . . . A mission hospital without missionary presence does not run like a North American institution, but it can find equilibrium and serve the people effectively. Praise God.[639]

The church's response to the health needs of the people of Congo is reaching beyond the church-related hospitals to the total health care program for the nation. Larry Sthreshley, who is based in Cameroon and serving as a community health consultant for West and Central Africa, writes of his experience in returning to Congo, where he had been raised as the son of missionaries:

> People were the poorest I have ever seen them. Malnutrition, even among adults, is common throughout the country. People I know that used to send their children to school or visit a health center when they were sick could not afford to do either. I was thankful that the visible presence of the church through its medical work gave people hope . . . .

> Most of my time was spent in helping the Programme de Sante Rurale (SANRU III) project get started. The project is a country-wide program to develop the decentralized health care system in rural areas. Phase I has $1 million funding from the U.S. Office of Foreign Disaster Assistance, to do mostly emergency relief work in 28 health zones. We were able to get a quick start on the project with an extra $150,000 grant from Presbyterian Disaster Assistance program for essential medicines. Phase II will be a much more comprehensive program that includes interventions for malaria, AIDS, emerging diseases, nutrition, water and sanitation, vaccinations, and health infrastructure support in 60 health zones . . . . Even though the project is funded by USAID and recognized by the Congo government as their health strategy, it is totally implemented through the church.[640]

The desperate situation of the Congo has most tragically affected children and youth. Bill and Ruth Metzel, who had spent their entire 42-year ministry in the Congo until their retirement in 1991, offered their services in 1999 as volunteers in mission to help meet the needs of children in crisis there. They returned to Mbuji Mayi, the capital city of the East Kasai Province, where they had spent a large part of their missionary service. There they found that, according to a UNICEF census, more than 4,000 street children were struggling to survive on their own. They worked with the churches in the city to get each church to commit to supplying food to centers for abandoned children. Ninety churches made such commitments, including "seven Protestant denominations, the Roman Catholics, the Kimbanguists and three mosques." Before they completed their service as volunteers in mission, a new center was opened in Mbujimayi, sponsored by the Presbyterian Church of the Congo.

> [It is] a center for young men, 15 years or older who have grown up as "abandoned children" and who find it extremely difficult to support themselves. Since October, Bill has gotten two of them out of prison, and one has tried to take his own life. We got a diamond company to plow and harrow two hectares of land ceded to the CPC. We bought two tents, some mats, lanterns, cooking pots. etc. and promised to supply the group of ten young men for the first four months, until their harvest in May. They were excited by the open, clean space and a spring about a mile away for bathing and drawing cooking water. Youth groups plan to help with sports and choral activities and there is a fine Christian director to help with the agriculture. The Lord is supplying others to give spiritual support.[641]

The PC(USA) partnership in mission with the church in Congo found expression in numerous ways in addition to mission personnel. A theological education study in 1976, led by Dr. Lamar Williamson, former Congo missionary and later theological professor at the Presbyterian School of Christian Education in Richmond, Virginia, laid the groundwork for the future training of ministers for the Congolese Church, both at Ndesha and at the Protestant University. It was called "the most important development in the life of the church."[642]—Presbytery partnerships made a significant contribution. Hanover Presbytery (Virginia) initiated "Project Waterhole", providing the equipment which would dig wells for 15 villages. Orange Presbytery (North Carolina) cooperated with the Presbyterian Community of Congo in planning and building a Public Health Center in Mbuji Mayi to combat the major killer diseases through both basic treatment and preventive education. The Presbytery of Eastern Virginia, through the leadership of a Congolese church leader called to serve within its bounds, embarked on a "partnership mission" with the Presbyterian Church in Kinshasa, which by 1993 would result in provision for six Health Clinic Centers and three new churches, as well as "many gifts, including a mimeograph machine, eye glasses, a guitar, youth choir robes, over 900 pounds of school materials and summer clothing, bicycles, and a pastor's robe. By the end of the year five more churches will be built. These new churches will also be used by our brothers and sisters as shelters, schools and places for emergency medical care."[643]

Ben and Betsy Hobgood, who had served previously in Congo and returned as volunteers in mission to be the PC(USA) Financial Representative in Kinshasa, wrote:

> Over a million dollars a year passes through the office where [Ben] works with Charlotte Mayandu, an able and talented Zairian accountant. This money from the United States goes to schools, health clinics, and churches in Kinshasa and in the Kasai, the center of Presbyterian work here. It also goes to the seminary at Ndesha and to that crown jewel of Presbyterian medical work, the Good Shepherd Hospital in Tshikaji.[644]

The true spirit of partnership in mission with the Christian community in Congo was well expressed by Bill and Sue Sager:

> I don't believe sending money, equipment, supplies and medicines, "mission presents", is principally what God expects of us. He would rather have disciples in "mission presence" here in this maelstrom of killing, plunder, disregard for human rights, ignorance, abject poverty, disease, illiteracy, and hunger we would all just as soon walk away from. The Congolese can't walk away. They need and ask for our continuing presence with them.[645]

PARTNERSHIP IN MISSION IN RWANDA

The tragedy of tiny Rwanda has captured the international news headlines in recent years. Yet very few know anything else about this country and its history. Rwanda is a beautiful, mountainous, and largely rural country located near the equator, at the edge of beautiful Lake Kivu, in the very heart of the African continent. It is a densely populated land of over 7 million people (the most densely populated nation in sub-Saharan Africa), with its people living mostly in contained compounds rather than typical African villages.

The bloodshed of the 1990s is rooted in centuries-long tensions and bitterness between two ethnic groups, the Hutus and the Tutsis. For centuries the minority (14 percent) Tutsis—very tall, narrow-featured, of Hamitic origin—ruled over the majority Hutus—shorter, more broad-featured, of Bantu origin. Even under German colonial occupation (1899-1916) and under the succeeding Belgian rule (1916-1962), a Tutsi feudal monarch continued in power. However, in 1959, a Hutu revolt overthrew the Tutsi government, and many were killed or forced into exile. Independence from Belgium came in 1962. In 1990, the Tutsi-dominated Rwandan Patriotic Front invaded the country from Uganda, and once again there was more death and displacement.

Then in April 1994, the presidents of both Rwanda and neighboring Burundi were killed in a suspicious plane crash as they returned from peace negotiations in Tanzania.

The horrors which erupted after that event placed this largely unknown nation in the front pages of the world's newspapers. The outbreak of political and ethnic violence unleashed by ethnic Hutu militants left over 800,000 Hutus and Tutsis dead, and over half of the surviving population displaced. The perpetrators of the genocide, driven out by a mainly Tutsi coalition force, gained control of desperately overcrowded refugee camps in neighboring Burundi, Tanzania and Zaire (now Congo).

Many of the Hutu refugees who fled the country when the Tutsis took over the government remained in hiding, especially in the Congo, fearful to return home. However, their presence just across the border was both an irritant and a threat to Tutsi survivors, who feared they might be organizing an invasion to continue the genocide. For that reason, Rwandan troops supported the efforts of Laurent Kabila to subdue the Congolese government forces in eastern Congo and to hunt down bands of Hutus in the process. However, when Kabila pressed his insurgency westward and finally deposed Mobutu and gained control of Congo, more than a million refugees returned home to Rwanda, fleeing what they feared was an impending purge of Hutus in Congo. Since that time, Rwanda has been plagued with outbursts of ethnic violence on the part of both Hutus and Tutsis. The repercussions of the genocide and ethnic violence continue and certainly will be felt throughout the region for years to come [646]

This tragic story belies the fact that the Christian movement had made significant progress in Rwanda, where an estimated 70% of the people are nominally Christian (mostly Roman Catholic). The first Protestant missionary intervention was by German Lutherans of the Bethel Evangelical Mission, who crossed the border from Tanzania in 1907. However, all German missionaries were expelled in May 1916 and Belgium refused to allow them to return after the First World War. Their work was continued in 1921 by the missionary arm of the Reformed Church of Belgium. When the Rwandan church became autonomous in 1959, it chose the Presbyterian form of government and became the Presbyterian Church of Rwanda (*Eglise Presbyterienne au Rwanda).*

It was in response to a request from the Rwandan church that in 1975 the Presbyterian Church, U.S. Division of International Mission appointed two educational missionaries, Mr. and Mrs.Edward Torsch, the husband to help start a program of adult literacy education, and the wife to work in family planning and community health. In 1978, through the Torsch's initiative, a project proposal came to the PCUS Task Force on World Hunger which read:

> Statistics point up the need for adult education. Rwanda has the highest population density of all African countries and a high population growth rate (2.8%) at which the population would double in 20 years, posing a threat of future starvation. Per capita income from all sources is only $70 per year. Soil is poor and eroded, and only the simplest of hand tools are used.

> Primary education is given in the Kinyarwanda language; secondary school and above are in French. Only 3000 places a year are open in secondary school,

which means that only about 1% of the population have a working knowledge of French. Primary education is available to about 50% of school-aged children. Also, Catholic and Protestant churches follow the practice of requiring literacy as a condition for church membership. Even though this means that up to half the population has had literacy instruction in Kinyarwanda, very few printed materials exist in that language, and many adults may be considered to have relapsed into illiteracy from disuse.[647]

The objective of the project was "to provide printed materials, written by Rwandais in the Kinyarwanda language, for adult education related to basic needs in the fields of Christian education, health and family education, vocational and agricultural education, and community education, and to develop through a pilot project an effective teaching program employing these materials." The carefully prepared proposal brought a positive response from the PCUS Task Force on World Hunger, as well as from the Presbytery of Middle Tennessee, which entered into a presbytery partnership with the Presbyterian Church of Rwanda. The well-conceived program progressed quietly over the next several years, even after missionary personnel were no longer provided.

However, the catastrophic events in 1994 brought Rwanda again to the center of attention of the Presbyterian Church (USA). The 1994 PC(USA) General Assembly adopted a resolution on Rwanda, expressing profound sorrow at the continuing bloodshed; appreciation to the governments of Tanzania, Burundi, Zaire and Uganda for receiving refugees; commendation to the World Council of Churches and the All Africa Conference of Churches for their efforts over the past years to establish dialogue among the various warring parties in Rwanda. The resolution also called on the United States to work through the United Nations and the Organization of African States to intensify diplomatic efforts; to the U.S. government to respond to the appeal of the UN High Commissioner on Refugees for humanitarian relief; to the US Attorney General to grant temporary protected status to nationals coming to the US from Rwanda and Burundi. Finally the resolution set aside Sunday, July 10 as a day of prayer for the Rwandan people and an appeal for Rwanda Relief; and directed the Worldwide Ministries Division to communicate to the Presbyterian Church of Rwanda our deep sorrow and continued commitment to pray for peace and reconciliation.[648]

In keeping with this General Assembly resolution, a delegation of three PC(USA) representatives visited Rwanda and the refugee camps in Zaire to deliver letters from the PC(USA) General Assembly to the General Secretary of the Presbyterian Church of Rwanda (in the Rwanda capital Kigali) and to the President of the Rwanda Church (who was among the refugees in Zaire). Also, the Presbyterian Disaster Assistance program provided funds for pastors and medical personnel from partner churches in Zaire to minister to the refugees from Rwanda who had flooded into Zaire after the massacres in their own country.[649] By 1998, Presbyterian Disaster Assistance had sent more than $1.4 million to assist in Rwanda's crisis; the Presbyterian Hunger Program had funded food canteens in various church schools; the Project for Evangelism and Church Growth in Africa had assisted with church reconstruction and with scholarships for seminary students; and a grant was made to the Protestant Council of Rwanda to help minister to refugees and displaced persons.

In 1997, Tim Emerick-Cayton, who with his wife Sher was serving as a mission specialist in Kenya, would report on his visit to Rwanda:

> After a weeklong visit to Rwanda, I am filled with a deep sense of grief and sadness for the country and its people. My most troubling experience during my brief stay was a visit to Ntarama Catholic Church, 30 kilometers south of the capital city of Kigali. When the mass killing of Tutsis and moderate Hutus began on April 6, 1994, thousands of people rushed to the church with what they could carry. Over the next nine days they camped in the sanctuary, Sunday school rooms, church offices, and surrounding compound. On April 15, however, a battalion of the national army surprised them and after surrounding the church, systematically killed with machetes, bullets, and clubs all 5,000 men, women, and children over the next six hours . . . .
>
> In the days that followed I was struck by the pain and fear visible in the faces of the Rwandan people. I easily concluded Rwanda is a country in shock, a country trying to come to terms with itself, care for its 250,000 orphaned children (some of whom are living in houses headed by 12- and 13-year-olds) and come to terms with the 150,000 prisoners, many falsely accused, being held in state prisons . . . .
>
> Our task now is to share [God's] love with others so that a tragedy such as this will never happen again. May God help us.[650]

Boniface Hitinara, a pastor in Kigali, would write to American Presbyterians:

> For us, we don't know where we are going, especially ordinary people. Now famine and other calamities are our common bread around the country. Is it the end of the world? Only God knows and we still believe in Him. What we can do is to pray. Also pray for us, the Rwandan people. I think we need not only goods but also God's power.[651]

D. AMERICAN PRESBYTERIAN INVOLVEMENT IN THE HORN OF AFRICA

In the period from 1973 to 2000, American Presbyterians continued their involvement in the Christian movement in the Horn of Africa which had been begun by the United Presbyterian Church of North America, in both the Sudan (in 1900) and Ethiopia (in 1919).

Both countries would experience overwhelming crises which would drastically affect the Christian movement and the involvement of the Presbyterian Church (USA) in it.

PARTNERSHIP IN MISSION IN THE SUDAN

The fragile peace which had been reached in 1972 between the Sudanese government and the southern rebel forces held together precariously until 1983. During this period, United Presbyterian missionaries resumed their work in the Sudan, in partnership with the Presbyterian Church of Sudan (PCOS) in the south, and the Sudan Presbyterian Evangelical Church (SPEC) in the north. It was a time of reconstruction and leadership training. Medical ministry was reopened in Nasir, Akobo and Ler. Also in 1974, at the request of the missionaries, the Khartoum authorities facilitated the education of Christian students in state primary schools by allowing Christian teachers to provide them religious instruction, and the missionary force participated in the training of teachers for this purpose.[652] By 1980 fifteen American Presbyterian missionaries were participating in a joint PCUS/PCUSA program "Affirm the Good News" (the first such joint mission program of the northern and southern churches), emphasizing evangelism and church planting, along with programs in agriculture and public health.[653]

However, there was still widespread discontent across the south based on the conviction that the government had not honored the 1972 peace agreement. Inhuman treatment of black southern Sudanese continued; their children were routinely denied access to public education; there was discrimination in medical services, housing, and employment. Though Colonel Gaafar Mohamed el-Nimeiri was re-elected for a third term as president in 1983, the regional problems in the south persisted. By sending more troops into the south against the emerging Sudan People's Liberation Army (SPLA), he alienated many in the north and reignited conflict in the south. He then caused additional unrest by replacing the penal code with strict Islamic law (*sharia*). By the end of 1983, civil war had broken out again. In March 1985, after a general strike because of severe economic problems, Nimeiri was ousted in a bloodless military coup.

The ensuing six years were chaotic, with coalition governments formed and deposed, strikes snd shortages persisting, inflation running rampant (Sudan incurred the highest national debt in Africa), north/south civil war becoming increasingly intense, and drought and famine gripping the country. Finally, in July 1989, the existing coalition government was overthrown in a military coup led by Islamic fundamentalist General Omar Hassan Ahmed el-Bashir, who established a 15-man revolutionary council with himself as head of state. Conditions continued to deteriorate in the 1990s, as the Bashir regime suppressed political opposition and stepped up the war against non-Muslim rebels in the south. Meanwhile, by the mid-1990s the SPLA, led by John Garang, a former officer in the Sudanese army, controlled most of southern Sudan and a number of important towns. However, the Sudanese government maintained control over Juba, a large city in the far south, and several key southern towns along the Nile and the main roads. Although several smaller rebel groups signed peace agreements with the government, the SPLA stated that it would accept nothing less than complete independence for southern Sudan.

The human cost of this chaotic situation is almost incomprehensible. In the Sudan's total population of some 25 million people, over 4.5 million southerners and easterners have been displaced fleeing the war, many fleeing across the border into neighboring Ethiopia, Uganda and Kenya. Over one and a half million people have died of hunger, disease, and exposure, as well as being casualties of the civil war. As the SPLA has pursued its goal and attacked government-held towns, the Sudanese army has bombed those towns held by the SPLA, resulting in widespread death and destruction.[654]

There are several major factors back of the government's aggressive policy. One is economic: the Sudanese government is fighting to keep the people and resources of the south within its control. Especially significant are the rich oil reserves in the south, now being exploited by a Canadian oil company. The Sudanese government's profits from this enterprise provide the funds needed for their continuing prosecution of the war.[655] More subtle but equally important is the government's determination to preserve and impose a fundamentalist Islamic state. While 70% of the total population is Muslim, mostly in the north, 19% are Christian, primarily in the south, where the crisis has led more and more people to turn from their traditional animist religion to the Christian faith.

> When militant Muslims took over Sudan in 1989, they drew up a plan for the total Islamization of Sudan. Though off schedule, that plan is obvious everywhere. Most of the seven million Africans in Sudan are non-Muslims, probably at least two-thirds are Christian, and the government has promoted many methods of pressure-Islamizing them.[656]

Beginning in 1990, the PC(USA) addressed the Sudan crisis at almost every ensuing General Assembly. Though it became increasingly difficult for American mission personnel to secure visas for service in Sudan, the small group of mission co-workers undertook a phenomenal task in their partnership in mission with the Sudanese church. As the crisis deepened, PC(USA) responded to the critical needs of some 400,000 refugees who were attacked in refugee camps in westernmost Ethiopia by Ethiopian rebel groups. As they fled westward across the Sudanese border, they were met by the Sudanese air force that bombed and strafed them. They made their way by night into their home areas in southern Sudan. Working with the Presbyterian Church of Sudan (PCOS), PC(USA) supported "Centers of Hope" which housed primary schools, women's work centers, and feeding centers both in southern Sudan and on the outskirts of major cities in the north where camps mushroomed among displaced southern Sudanese.[657] Later, a PC(USA) mission co-worker Mark Rasmussen would assist the PCOS leaders in exile in Nairobi, Kenya to establish a liaison and coordination office which would enable the scattered congregations in southern Sudan to stay in touch with each other, as well as with partner churches in the United States and Europe. His wife Caroline Kurtz would serve as an advocate for the women "who make up 80% of the Sudanese church membership, traveling in the south Sudan liberated areas, translating the hopes and aspirations of the villagers into project proposals that PC(USA) and other concerned denominations can participate in funding."[658]

Much primary evangelism took place among the refugees, and churches sprang up even without any trained pastoral leadership. In the hope of beginning to meet the critical need, PC(USA) mission co-workers assisted the PCOS in the struggle to prepare new leadership for the churches at the Giffen and Gereif Bible Schools, the new Sudan Theological College (later to be called the Nile Theological College) in Khartoum, and in supporting a number of Sudanese ministerial students at the St. Paul's United Theological College in Limuru, Kenya.[659] Also, a Theological Education by Extension Program reached prospective leaders who could not be reached in other ways. "It is an effective way to raise up leaders more quickly to keep pace with the growth until there is enough stability to begin a more sustainable training structure."[660]

The very existence of The Nile Theological College seemed a miracle. Founded in 1991 by the joint effort of the Sudan Presbyterian Evangelical Church (SPEC) and the Presbyterian Church of Sudan (PCOS), its purpose was to provide a baccalaureate degree for pastors and Christian educators. In 1993 the College.took a significant step toward indigenous leadership as it welcomed the Reverend Michael Chot as its Principal, following completion of his study at the Interdenominational Theological Center in Atlanta. In many ways the College expressed the very essence of what the Sudanese church could and should be.

> Within our walls we have students from many different tribes, backgrounds and disparate geographic locations. Some students are quite young, and some have been pastors or evangelists for a decade. Many different language groups are represented. In a country filled with often violent divisions, inside the walls of the College, all are united in praise to God, and in their desire to serve Him wholeheartedly. An Episcopal pastor and outgoing student body president said in his final address, "Here we are not Presbyterian and Episcopal, we are not northerners and southerners, we are not Dinka or Nuer or Shilluk or Anuak. Here we are the Church of Jesus Christ, and we are one in witness to the people of Sudan."[661]

Meanwhile, the situation in the south became even more confused and desperate. A major schism developed in the SPLA along tribal lines and conflict arose between the various rebel groups. Government forces blocked access for relief agencies to distribute supplies to large numbers of starving people both in the south and in refugee settlements in the north. The government accelerated efforts to relocate refugees from camps around Khartoum to desert areas in the south, without water or provisions. "The larger civil war and smaller factional conflicts displace hundreds of thousands of people, destroy harvests, raid cattle, pillage and burn villages, bomb civilian centers, and kill and wound countless people each year."[662]

The critical situation demanded close cooperation among the various Christian churches. The Sudan Council of Churches, located in Khartoum and including Protestant, Catholic and Orthodox bodies, undertook critical ministries among the displaced persons in camps around the city. However, since that Council was unable to reach people in the south, additional cooperative organizations were created. The New Sudan Council of Churches (NSCC) was formed to enable cooperation among the displaced Christians in the south and those who had fled to neighboring countries. Located at first in the city of Torit, it was forced to move its operations when government troops took that city in late 1992, and take up offices in Nairobi, Kenya. Led at first by missionaries Roger and Carolyn Schrock, in 1995 the NSCC General Assembly elected a Sudanese church leader, Dr. Haruun Ruun as its Executive Secretary. Dr. Ruun later would be honored by Human Rights Watch for his defense of human rights in Sudan, including the People-to-People reconciliation process among the ethnic tribes of southern Sudan; his leading role in opposing slavery and returning abducted women and children to their families; rebuilding villages destroyed in the conflict; restoring law and order to a chaotic region; and his courageous stand against oil exploration in southern Sudan.

To meet the critical needs of the suffering people living on the southern borders of Sudan as well as in refugee camps in Ethiopia, Kenya, Uganda, Zaire and the Central African Republic, the Association of Christian Resource Organizations Serving Sudan (ACROSS) was created to enable various Christian organizations from around the world to combine their resources. Also based in Nairobi, ACROSS reaches across the borders to carry out ministries of relief, agriculture, health, evangelism and education. "The churches which minister to these people move with them, in an attempt to continue the building of the Christian community among their people. The church structures which still exist are filled to overflowing with worshipers."[663] Mission Co-workers Bill Simmons and William Lowrey have provided critical leadership for the ACROSS program.

Virtually every program of the Presbyterian Church (USA) responded to the Sudan crisis in its own way. Working through the PC(USA) Washington Office and Bread for the World, American Presbyterian congregations and members wrote to their elected officials urging passage of the Horn of Africa Recovery and Food Security Act and support of the peacemaking process. The Presbyterian Hunger Program provided grants for seed for refugee farmers both in southern Sudan and in neighboring Ethiopia, and to support cattle vaccination and ox plough training.[664] The Refugee Resettlement Program worked with Presbyterian (USA) congregations in resettling Sudanese refugees in the United States, especially the "lost boys", orphans who had trekked hundreds of miles out of Sudan and Ethiopia into refugee camps in Kenya.[665] Shenango Presbytery (Pennsylvania) entered into partnership with the Sudanese Presbyterian Evangelical Church, providing donkey carts for much-needed transportation for churches and pastors. "Rev. Orozu is still smiling and telling all who listen how great God has been in providing these donkey carts through the churches in America."[666] The 1997 PC(USA) General Assembly approved an overture "to intensify and focus its efforts to work for peace and justice in the Sudan."[667]

An especially significant achievement of the PC{USA) mission involvement in the Sudan has been the bringing about of two very critical peace initiatives among the Nuer and Dinka ethnic groups as they suffer the oppression of the Sudanese government.[668]

> For many people, the fighting between the mostly Christian groups in the south was the most troubling, both because it made it easier for the government to fight a divided enemy and because the image of Christians fighting amongst themselves was not the witness that Christians were looking for. So for years the New Sudan Council of Churches has been working to get the two sides to talk to one another. Over the past couple of years, those efforts, encouraged by Mission Co-Worker the Rev. Bill Lowrey, have apparently borne fruit. In March 1999, leaders from the Nuer and from the Dinka factions met to work out details in agreements to stop the cycle of revenge that was dividing them. "Things had deteriorated to the point where people realized if they didn't figure out some way to get this together, they were just going to self-destruct," Mr. Lowrey said. By the time the leaders signed the agreement at Wunlit in March, major steps toward reconciliation had occurred, not least of which was the sense that anyone breaking the Dinka-Nuer Covenant would be answerable to the whole community. The pastor who led the closing prayer perhaps summed it up when he said, "This is the peace we have been calling for these many years."[669]

The effort to bring about peace among the various tribal groups in southern Sudan continues. In May 2000 an all-tribes peace-conference took place in the small village of Lelir. "Representatives from the Anuak, Dinka, Mule, Nuer and Taposa tribes were brought together by charter flights with the financial and logistical help of the New Sudan Council of Churches (NSCC). PC(USA) is a major funder of the NSCC Peace Department. The conference was a qualified success. All who attended agreed to stop the tribal raiding and worked hard to set up agreements on civilian rule and law."[670]

A crowning achievement of the work in which the PC(USA) participated in partnership with the Presbyterian Church of Sudan by the year 2000 was the completion and publication of the Nuer Bible.

> "The second-largest tribe in Sudan, the Nuer, are a majority of the Presbyterian Church," write Mission Co-workers William and Lois Anderson. "The New Testament had been published in the mid-sixties, bit it needed much updating. A team in Kenya recently finished the translation of the Old Testament and a revision of the New Testament. A number of us flew to Mading to celebrate. Mading is a small town in the swamps north of Nasir, the earliest mission among the Nuer. Since Nasir was captured by the government, Mading has become a center for the Nuer." [Mission Specialist Barry] Almy writes that he has taken several hundred copies for distribution to Nuer-speaking congregations on Ethiopia's border with Sudan.[671]

The year 2000 also marked the completion of a major work on the history of the church in the Sudan by veteran missionary Bill Anderson.

> The big book is called *Day of Devastation, Day of Contentment*. The title comes from a hymn written by MaryAlueel, a young Sudanese woman, which says, "Let us praise the Lord . . . in the day of devastation and in the day of contentment." She composed the hymn in a refugee camp where she was among 200,000 driven out of their homes by war. The devastation has been so terrible in Sudan that the archbishop who wrote a foreword said he could only write about the "day of devastation." Indeed, that has been the story in Sudan this year. To clear an area for exploitation of oil wells earlier this year, the Sudan army swept out Nuer, slaughtering thousands and sending tens of thousands into flight. The place is now being settled by Arabs. Days of devastation have continued and intensified. But there are also "days of contentment." In Khartoum, Matthew Othow, an engineer and a church elder, has for two years organized an evangelistic trip at Christmas, organizing a team to walk from village to village of the Shilluk people. They carry a generator and projector to show the Jesus film (in the Shilluk language) nightly. They had meetings in 32 different villages and towns in December and January. A pastor in the group baptized 1,053 new believers.[672]

The spirit of partnership in strife-torn Sudan has been well expressed by Mission Co-Worker Michael Parker:

> Life here is difficult, but there is much for which to be thankful, not least of which are the people themselves. They are a delight. They take everything in stride, and they have a wonderful sense of humor. Also, they have a great faith in God. Though a persecuted minority, the church is a growing, dynamic people. The West has much to give the Sudanese Church (education, organization, technology, money, etc.), but the Sudanese are giving us a powerful example of the kind of unconquerable faith that is slowly winning all of Africa for Christ.[673]

PARTNERSHIP IN MISSION IN ETHIOPIA

In the early 1970s, Emperor Haile Selassie continued to play a major role in international affairs, helping to mediate disputes between several warring African nations. However, he largely ignored urgent domestic problems: the great inequality in the distribution of wealth, rural under-development, corruption in government, rampant inflation, unemployment. Added to this, Ethiopia experienced a severe drought in the north from 1972 to 1975, resulting in the deaths of some 200,000 people.

By 1974, the critical situation erupted in strikes and demonstrations by students, workers and soldiers that culminated on September 12, 1974 with the deposition of

Haile Selassie[674] by members of the armed forces. Chief among the coup leaders was Major Mengistu Haile Mariam. A group called the Provisional Military Administrative Council, known as the Derg, was established to run the country, with Mengistu serving as chairman. Parliament was dissolved and the constitution suspended. The Derg issued a program for the establishment of a state-controlled socialist economy. In early 1975 all agricultural land in Ethiopia was nationalized, with much of it then parceled out in small plots to individuals.

At first, the overthrow of the monarchy and the creation of a so-called republic ushered in an era of political openness. In fact, the 1976 General Assembly of the United Presbyterian Church, U.S.A. issued a "Statement to the Provisional Military Government of Ethiopia", rejoicing in its action "to assist development of disadvantaged peoples of Ethiopia, and its commitment to religious freedom," though "saddened to hear of the arrest of Abuna Theophilus [of the Ethiopian Orthodox Church], who had addressed the 1973 General Assembly."[675] However, it soon became evident that Ethiopia was entering a period of strife and oppression which far exceeded its past sufferings. To begin with, ethnic groups that had been brought into the Ethiopian empire in the 19th and 20th centuries now stepped up their demands for self-determination. Several of these groups created guerrilla forces to fight for independence. The military government had to fight to keep control of Eritrea, Tigre and Ogaden, where Somalian troops were assisting local guerrillas. By the beginning of 1977 the Ethiopian People's Revolutionary Party (EPRP) had launched a systematic campaign to undermine the military regime.

Further, it became clear that Mengistu intended to consolidate his hold on power and establish a single-party Marxist state. Responding to the guerrilla warfare against his government, he initiated the "Red Terror" campaign. During 1977 and 1978 an estimated 100,000 people suspected of being enemies of the government were killed or disappeared. By early 1978 the Mengistu regime had secured military assistance from the USSR and Cuba, enabling it to regain control of most lost territories and drive its opponents underground.

The impact of these developments on the Christian movement was profound. The government took over most church institutions, including all the lands and wealth of the Ethiopian Orthodox Church. The central headquarters of the Mekane Yesus Church in Addis Ababa was seized to house the Ministry of Internal Security. At the Bethel Evangelical Secondary School in Dembi Dollo,the principal and several teachers were arrested; however, the government never succeeded in taking over the school. The government issued a "Declaration of Economic Policy" making it illegal for persons to receive a salary from two sources, making it very difficult for pastors to subsist on what the churches could pay. Some pastors were imprisoned, exiled or murdered. The crowning blow came as the government seized the ecumenical Christian radio station, "The Voice of the Gospel", and announced its nationalization as "The Radio Voice of the Revolution." The protests of churches and governments around the world went unheeded. It became necessary for most missionaries to leave the country, though a valiant few remained.[676]

Amid the confusion of protracted civil war, an even more severe famine arose in the north, including Eritrea, when the rains failed for three successive seasons. Massive emergency aid programs were mounted by many Western nations and churches. The Ethiopian government tried to alleviate the problem by resettling people from the north to the more fertile south. By 1986 more than 600.000 people had been forcibly resettled. During the 1980s an estimated one million Ethiopians died from starvation.

Despite famine and military defeats, Mengistu attempted to win popular support for his regime. In 1987 a new constitution was proclaimed and the People's Democratic Republic of Ethiopia declared, modeled after the Soviet system of government. The new constitution abolished the Derg and established a popularly elected national assembly. However, former Derg members remained in control, and the new assembly elected Mengistu as president. Meanwhile, despite its reorganization, the Mengistu government continued to be viewed by many as illegitimate, and opposition groups which had been driven underground a decade earlier emerged as better organized military organizations. Over the next two years, the Ethiopian army suffered an increasing number of defeats and its forces became demoralized. The Eritrean rebels regained control of most of Eritrea, and the Tigre rebels captured the entire Tigre region and began operations in surrounding regions. In the late 1980s, as the Cold War was subsiding, Ethiopia lost the support of the Soviet Union. Faced with both economic and military failure, the Ethiopian national assembly agreed to a mediation offer by former U.S. President Jimmy Carter and peace talks with the Eritrean rebels began in August 1989. However, rebel pressure increased steadily during early 1991. In May Mengistu fled the country and Tigre rebel forces occupied Addis Ababa, leaving some "50,000 retreating government soldiers in the city, hungry, homeless, discouraged and leaderless."[677] A period of breakdown in civil order ensued, with hundreds of thousands of refugees fleeing into neighboring countries and other regions inside Ethiopia. When it was announced that the United States had approved the transfer of power to the rebel forces, order began to be restored.

The rebel leadership established a transitional government made up of a number of political liberation fronts that had fought to topple the previous regime. The task ahead appeared formidable. In a 1994 election, the Ethiopian People's Revolutionary Democratic Front (EPRDF) won control of the government, and a new constitution granting special rights to different ethnic groups was adopted. The EPRDF has attempted to maintain order and implement democratic changes in cooperation with the many divided ethnic groups. However, many groups are critical of its growing human rights abuses, particularly against the Oromo people, who constitute some forty percent of the country's population and who the government fears will secede if given more freedom.

Meanwhile, periods of drought and famine have continued to leave a wake of pain and death. The government, non-governmental agencies, and the churches have continued to try to transform relief into development, but the immediate critical needs are so overwhelming that relief has become a way of life for many. Ironically, in the midst of famine conditions, in mid-1998 clashes broke out again between Ethiopia and Eritrea along their common border, which had not been precisely delineated when Eritrea became independent from Ethiopia in 1993. While both countries have appealed for millions of dollars for food aid to stave off famine, donor countries find it difficult to comprehend that at the same time huge amounts are being spent on arms by both countries. One diplomat has described this as "the stupidest war in Africa."

In the midst of this tumultuous and tragic situation, the Ethiopian Evangelical Church Mekane Yesus (EECMY), with which the Presbyterian Church (USA) works in partnership, has grown at a phenomenal rate. By 1994, the church had reached a membership of more than one million, having grown by 144,000 in 1992 alone. By the year 2000, EECMY membership had reached three million, and was growing at the rate of 200,000 per year, making it one of the fastest growing churches in the world. Among its nine synods are three which are the fruit of the missionary witness of American Presbyterians: the Western Wollega Bethel Synod, the Illubabor Bethel Synod, and more recently organized the Southwest Bethel Synod. It is within these synods that the PC(USA) continues its partnership in mission.

With the deposition of Mengistu in 1991, the door was opened for the return of mission co-workers. As the government gave back to the Mekane Yesus Church hundreds of confiscated church buildings, PC(USA) pitched in to help in the repair of reclaimed buildings. The Kaffa Bethel Presbytery requested the return of retired Presbyterian missionary Edward Pollock, who with his wife Dolly had been forced to leave their work in 1979. Under his guidance, the dilapidated mission compound at Gemeira (which had become the government headquarters in southwest Ethiopia during the Mengistu regime) was rebuilt so that it could be used as the presbytery headquarters, a training center for pastors and evangelists and guest quarters for visiting volunteer workers. With the assistance of volunteers from churches all over the United States, "Operation Return" rebuilt termite-infested buildings, restored the water and electric systems, and began the renovation of the Presbyterian clinic that had served the region for many years prior to 1979. Following a visit to the project, the Pollocks' pastor Earl S. Johnson, Jr. would write:

> What I found were people often living in abject poverty, some communities dwelling like living fossils in the stone age, all subject to the ravages of curable diseases like tetanus, pneumonia, fevers and viral infections. Nevertheless the Christians living there, in spite of battles they must also wage against tribal religions, powerful witch doctors and a popular belief in demonic possession, are still able to transcend all cultural barriers between themselves and us. They witness to their faith in Jesus Christ, as they tell their stories and sing their hymns of praise exuberantly to God, accompanied by homemade flutes, drums, string instruments and gourds filled with dried beans. Despite all the handicaps they have, and regardless of the fact that there are only 10 pastors to serve 70 congregations in a presbytery with more than 20,000 members, the churches are filled. All are people whose lives have been changed by the power of Jesus Christ and the presence of a loving church family.[678].

By 1998, the presbytery had grown to such an extent that it became the **Southwest Bethel Synod.** All this, as the result of work which had been begun only 45 years earlier through the efforts of pioneer American Presbyterian missionary Charles Haspels. Not long after this Christian community celebrated becoming a synod, another church was born, among the Surma people, through a partnership in mission between PC(USA) mission co-workers John and Gwen Haspels[679], physician Dr. Haile Tola, an Anuak pastor Keis Okwier, and a committed staff of young professionals of the Mekane Yesus Church. The Surma work had been initiated in 1970, as part of the Untouched Tribes Project to reach isolated tribes in Southwest Ethiopia. However, after 1974 the work had been thwarted by the Marxist government. Then in 1989, the government encouraged the EECMY to do a community development project among the Surma people. "There were to be five components: Roadbuilding—70-80 miles of it, Health Care, Safe Water Development, Agriculture, and Education. For us it would open the way to take the gospel to a very needy people."[680] Since its beginning, the project has been developing a holistic ministry to serve both the physical and spiritual needs of the Surma people. The founding of the Tulegit Church in 1998 marked a milestone in the work among the Surma people.

In Southwest Bethel Synod, mission specialist Caryl Weinberg has served as "health adviser", advising the staffs of two rural clinics, Gatcheb and Enja Clinics.

> Gatcheb is the clinic supported by the Presbyterian Church (USA) and the Medical Benevolence Foundation. It is located just outside of Mizan Teferi in the heart of rainforest and coffee country. The diseases seen most often there are malaria, diarrhea, and respiratory infections. It serves five peasant associations—village associations of about 14,000 people that are all rural and as far as a three- or four-hour walk away. Enja is higher up in the mountains in a cool area. It too serves five peasant associations of about 10,000 people. There is almost no malaria, but there is typhoid, and again many respiratory problems, and problems with deliveries. Both clinics are short of staff, medications, and some equipment. The workers are so good though, all hard-working and committed to serving the people of the area.[681]

In 1997 John and Anne Wheeler-Waddell[682] were invited to assist the Southwest Bethel Synod in setting up a training school for lay pastors, to help meet the critical need for leaders in the rapidly growing churches of that Synod. "The school will have a one-year course to better equip them for the work they are already doing. We are part of this new thing, so new that the building isn't built yet."[683] By the year 2000, they would write: "When we were invited four years ago to help start a Bible school in rural Ethiopia, our thoughts were on developing curricula, resourcing, teaching. Little did we anticipate that the bulk of support would be in overseeing construction, buying pots and pans, blankets and sheets, beds and chairs, *tef* by the quintel and goats on the hoof."[684] By the end of that year, the school building would be completed, its first class of 27 students completing their one-year course. It would bear the name, the Charles Haspels Bible School, named after one of the pioneer American Presbyterian missionaries to Ethiopia.

One of the byproducts of the EECMY's rapid growth has been a shortage of trained pastors and other leaders. Mission Co-worker Michael Weller wrote that in 1997 there were only 32 pastors to serve the **Western Wollega Bethel Synod**'s 227 congregations and 150,000 members. The Synod has been training both pastors and evangelists at the Gidada Bible School (GBS) in Dembi Dollo. In 1998 25 graduates were ordained, almost doubling the number of pastors in the synod. "Students at GBS are trained in the usual kind of seminary courses," writes Weller, "but a commitment to holistic ministry ensures they also get instruction in areas of community development, hygiene, and leadership. When they return to their homes in the countryside, they are prepared to serve their communities in ministry."[685]

With the Gidada Bible School as a base, the Western Wollega Bethel Synod (WWBS) has extended its witness into six new areas. Weller writes about working with one of these, "a community of people known as Majong. They are a small group of about 25 households who have come from an area southeast of Dembi Dollo and have settled nearby. Since they are traditionally a hunter/gatherer people and are unable to find enough food in the usual manner, the WWBS, using Presbyterian Hunger Program funds, has begun a project integrating development with discipleship. A man from the Oromo community has been selected to provide training in agricultural methods, animal care, beekeeping, and pottery work. He also gives Bible instruction and is a key person in discipleship of the new church." Rachel Weller, as health advisor for the WWBS, has given attention to a new rural clinic. "We have had three big immunization drives in cooperation with the local government. More than a thousand women and children participated. We hope to start some programs to get the communities more involved in their own health in the coming year."[686]

The Bethel Evangelical Secondary School (BESS) in Dembi Dollo has earned a reputation as one of the best secondary schools in Ethiopia, preparing leadership for church, community and nation. Mission co-workers amd mission specialists have taught in numerous fields, including Bible, agriculture, and English. Mission Co-Worker Jo Ann Griffith writes:

> Forty-two of forty-nine twelfth-grade graduates had a GPA of 3.0 or above on their matric, and so were assured of a place in the university in September. This acceptance means not only getting one's education at the expense of the government but also the promise of a job at the end. You can imagine that such an opportunity is a lifeline for young people in a developing country like Ethiopia. This annual record of academic excellence extends the reputation of BESS, bringing parents from farther distances to stand before the director's door."[687]

In neighboring **Illubabor Bethel Synod**, mission co-worker Brian Gilchrest has served as the social work advisor. His primary responsibilities have revolved around the Gore Bethel Home for Children, which is home to some 92 orphaned children from around the region.

At the opposite pole of EECMY/PC(USA) mission partnership is the work in **Addis Ababa.** Among those representing American Presbyterians in the capital city are Mission Co-workers Jim and Debbie Milley, who carry on a ministry among university students at three campuses. They report on the devastating effect which the Ethiopian/Eritrean war has had upon Ethiopian youth.

> In Ethiopia probably 100,000 young men—and probably about the same number of Eritrean young men—have died in their border war. We hear stories of forced conscription into the armed forces and employed people being pressured into giving financially toward the war effort. Ethiopian university students in Addis Ababa recently called all students to join in prayer in response to the war and other tragic events. Please join them in praying for the end of the war, and for rains to help quench the wildfires raging through several parts of Ethiopia and to help grow the food crops that can end the increasing famine in the country.[688]

A breakthrough in mission partnership took place in May 1998 as Jim Malley was ordained by the Ethiopian Evangelical Church Mekane Yesus to be a PC(USA) Minister of the Word and Sacrament.

Another significant mission partnership in Addis Ababa is the Yehiwot Berhan (Light of Life) Girls' School (formerly the American Mission Girls' School). Concerning her work at this school, Caroline Kurtz would write:

> YBS has one of the lowest student-teacher ratios of all public and private schools in Addis Ababa (even though teaching 60 girls in a class is difficult). About one fourth of the student body is Muslim,drawn by the school's reputation, agreeing to attend Bible classes and daily chapel. All this on tuition of $100 a year and small donations and grants from PCUSA from time to time! It is a credit to the fine Ethiopian administrative and teaching staff that so much can be done with so little resources![689]

Along with the demanding work in Ethiopia, PC(USA) has engaged in a regional approach to the needs of churches in East Africa. "Jack-of-all-trades" mission co-worker Mark Rasmussen traveled up and down the countries of East Africa, representing the Project of Evangelism and Church Growth in Africa in planning and building or rebuilding churches, schools and clinics in Sudan, Ethiopia, Kenya, Tanzania and Rwanda.

The future of Ethiopia at the turn of the 21st century remains very uncertain. Yet the faith which upholds the Christian community was well expressed by a statement adopted by the General Assembly of the Mekane Yesus Church in January 1993:

We are meeting at a critical moment in Ethiopian history. Eighteen years of brutal dictatorship are behind us and we thank God for the promise of freedom and peace. But we are uncertain about the future. Will it bring a flowering of democracy for all the Ethiopian people, or will it bring power and privilege for the few at the expense of the many? Of this we are certain, that all people are created by God with equal dignity, and that regardless of ethnic background, political leaning or religious belief, are endowed with basic human rights and freedoms. As the constitutional foundation for Ethiopia is laid, this is the moment to ensure that a just and democratic order is established."[690]

E. AMERICAN PRESBYTERIAN INVOLVEMENT IN EAST AFRICA

American Presbyterians continued their involvement in Kenya which had been begun by the United Presbyterian Church, U.S.A. in 1970, and entered into new partnerships in mission in two island nations off the coast of East Africa, Madagascar and Mauritius, in 1979.

PARTNERSHIP IN MISSION IN KENYA

After gaining its independence from Britain in 1963, politics in Kenya was dominated by Jomo Kenyatta, who served as Kenya's first president until his death in 1978. Kenyatta sought to unify the Kenyan people by appointing members of many different ethnic groups to government positions. Aided by a steady flow of foreign investment, largely from Britain, Kenya's economy flourished and the nation's economy became one of the fastest growing in post-colonial Africa.

Following Kenyatta's death in 1978, the vice-president Daniel arap Moi assumed the presidency. At first, Moi adopted a populist approach, seeking to build on Kenyatta's example. However, in the 1980s, Kenya's economic growth began to slow, it suffered several debilitating droughts and Moi's rule became increasingly authoritarian. In 1982 the Moi government altered the constitution to make Kenya officially a one-party state. Fueled by economic discontent, strong pressure for reform of the political system and an end to Moi's rule emerged from many sectors of Kenyan society by the end of the 1980s. Moi finally bowed to domestic and international pressure in December 1991 and agreed to legalize other political parties. Multiparty legislative and presidential elections were held in December 1992, but the opposition was split along ethnic lines, and Moi was reelected, his party, the Kenya African National Union (KANU) winning a majority of seats in the assembly.

Following the 1992 election, Moi's KANU party has become increasingly intolerant of any dissent and has been accused of widespread corruption and abuse of human rights. His administration has favored internationally funded development projects among the people of his own ethnic group, the Kalenjins. In the heavily-contested elections of

1997, Moi was re-elected to a fifth five-year term. Although the majority of Kenyans voted against him, once again the opposition was so divided that Moi received the largest number of votes. The National Council of Churches of Kenya (NCCK) urged citizens to accept the results, while working for peace with justice. Meanwhile, ethnic violence has continued as Moi's ethnic group, the Kalenjins, have committed atrocities against the Kikuyu in revenge for its strong vote against Moi. The country remains seriously divided, with many Kenyans complaining that they are tired of more than twenty years of corruption and mismanagement. Still, Kenya offers the safest refuge for those fleeing the political storms in surrounding countries; it is estimated that Kenya harbors some 800,000 refugees from Sudan, Ethiopia, Uganda, and Somalia.

Within and despite this context, the Christian movement has had a profound influence on the life of the people of Kenya. It is estimated that some 60% of the total population of appromately 25 million are Christian. The Presbyterian Church of East Africa (PCEA) has been the predominant church among the Kikuyu people, with a membership of some 110,000 in 22 presbyteries, which extend into Uganda and Tanzania. Founded by Scottish Presbyterian missionaries in 1891, the PCEA has had a strong role in education and health care, sponsoring some 275 primary schools, a number of secondary schools, and three hospitals, in addition to participating in the sponsorship of Daystar University and St. Paul's Theological College. The PCEA Pastoral Training Institute (later to become the Presbyterian College) has played a major role in the preparation of clergy for a growing church. PCEA also has provided significant leadership for the National Christian Council of Kenya (NCCK) and the All Africa Conference of Churches (AACC), both of which are based in Nairobi.

American Presbyterian partnership in mission with the PCEA has led to involvement especially in the fields of education and medicine. Dr. Marta Bennet writes of her experiences at Daystar University in Nairobi:

> The students in my class come from at least six different countries (Uganda, Burundi, Zaire, Ghana, Kenya, and the US), and we are all getting accustomed to each others' accents. Several are already pastors; they are eager learners, which is a treat, and I'm sure I'm learning at least as much from them . . . . In addition to teaching, I have just been formally asked if I would be willing to become the Director of Student Development, which would oversee all of student life outside the classroom (Campus Ministries, Dean of Student's office, Financial Aid, Sports, Residence Life, student government, career development, etc.) After lengthy discussion, I have agreed to take on the responsibility for the next two years, as the position and department are developed.[691]

The Pastoral Training Institute at Kikuyu, twenty minutes north of Nairobi, has called on the services of numerous mission co-workers. Anne Wheeler-Waddell, in addition to her teaching responsibilities, would serve as interim director of the Institute's

Theological Education Extension program. The Emerick-Caytons would write of Tim's responsibilities:

> The institute trains Presbyterian pastors in a three-year diploma course. Over the past year he has taught Systematic Theology, Old Testament Prophets, Pastoral Psychology, Pastoral Counseling, and Christian Ethics. In addition to his teaching responsibilities, he has been appointed by the Presbyterian Church of East Africa to serve as Assistant to the Nendeni (Mission) Board, which is responsible for Presbyterian mission and evangelism in Kenya, Tanzania, and Uganda. As if this is not enough, he has also been assigned to coordinate the development of a doctoral studies program at the Pastoral Institute, in cooperation with the San Francisco Theological Seminary, for pastors seeking additional professional training.[692]

Mission Volunteer Edward Danks, while serving as adjunct professor and library assistant at the Institute, would write:

> You may have noticed our change in name from the Pastoral Institute to the Presbyterian College. This is because our new entering class will follow a four-year bachelor of theology program instead of the three-year certificate course. Plans are also being formed to establish a business school, a media/communications school, a nursing school, etc. More and more, the Lord is using this institution to bear a strong impact on the Church and Kenya.[693]

In the central highlands of Kenya, Mission Volunteer Marian Strain would serve at the Presbyterian Teachers College at Rubate

> Rubate College's main goal is to prepare and send out Christian men and women who will instruct, guide, and nurture Christ's teaching in young children of Kenya. My responsibility in assisting Rubate to achieve this goal is to be a "tutor" or "lecturer" in teaching music theory, Western classical music appreciation, Christian education from an African perspective, and English composition.[694]

> God has opened up many new and exciting opportunities to serve since I came to Rubate, more than I could ever imagine. The Rubate staff ended the term with a staff fellowship and a surprise presentation for me—a Kenyan dress, accessories to go with it, and a sincere thank you for coming to Rubate. It is I who am grateful for the opportunity to serve Jesus Christ at Rubate.[695]

Probably the most lasting contribution of PC(USA) mission co-workers in Kenya has been made in the medical field. While several short-term and volunteer missionaries have served in other PCEA hospitals, outstanding work has been done by a remarkable medical missionary couple, Drs. Stan and Mia Topple at the Kikuyu Presbyterian Hospital. After 22 years of service at the Wilson Leprosy Center in Korea, in 1990 the Topples accepted the call to serve at the Kikuyu Hospital. Stan's gifts as an orthopedic surgeon and Mia's abilities as a dermatologist very soon became widely known and brought patients not only from other Kenyan hospitals but from surrounding countries. There soon emerged the vision of a Christian rehabilitation center.

> One reason that we were attracted to Kenya as a location for developing a Christian rehabilitation center was that this country serves as a hub for the region of East Africa. Since our arrival last year we have sensed Kenya to be an island in the political storms of this part of the continent. With the exception of Tanzania, the five countries touching our borders have been in various degrees of anarchy, famine, and destitution. This situation is reflected in the patients that have come into our care.

> The Anglican bishop of the long besieged Christian territory of Southern Sudan was under Stan's care for a disabling shoulder problem . . . . Two months ago an Ethiopian refugee who had fled with her family into the desert region of northeast Kenya received a bone-shattering gunshot wound to her thigh from raiding Somalian bandits. Flown here a couple of days later, she has been under Stan's care since . . . . Mia has encountered AIDS in several young adults from neighboring Uganda as well as Kenya . . . . Several days ago four young Somalian men were brought from their rebel ravaged homeland for care of gun shot limbs that were refusing to heal . . . . Here it is our privilege to show as well as tell the wonderful story of wholeness and salvation brought to all mankind through Jesus Christ the Son of God.[696]

Through the influence of the Topples and the assistance of the Medical Benevolence Foundation, a continuing flow of expatriate medical staff came from neighboring African nations, as well as from Korea, the United States and Europe, to serve at the Kikuyu Hospital.

> We thank God for some special people around us. For a young hospital chaplain coming from the Presbyterian C hurch in Tanzania.[697] . . . Dr. and Mrs. Yoo arrived from Korea to receive the baton for a three month period as we were departing in late June. They have been followed by Hal Forney (San Diego), Al Draper (West Virginia), and the David Minards (Omaha). We are privileged to see such quality of skill and compassion in these Christian professionals.[698] Dr. Jim York, who is a retired orthopaedist of the Presbyterian Church in Boca Raton, Florida, has been here with his wife for 10 weeks giving much needed help to the program. We have just had the departure of a plastic surgeon from Gainesville, Florida, who gave a full two weeks to children with cleft lip, cleft

palate and burn scar contractures as well as other deforming conditions. We have had Dr. David Webster, past President of Medical Benevolence Foundation and general surgeon, with his wife here for three weeks and now look forward to the arrival of a surgeon from Chapel Hill in the next week.[699] Others coming our way have included rotations of medical students from 5 different countries, Irish physical therapy students, a plastic surgeon and a Presbyterian layman from Oregon, and a maternity nurse from Atlanta . . . . Two former co-workers of days past, surgeon Dr. Yoo and prosthetist Mr. Choi, and their wives are now given to coming next year as missionaries to join with us in the work of the Kikuyu Orthopedic Rehabilitation Center.[700]

The dream of a Christian rehabilitation center continued to grow.

The Presbyterian Church of East Africa, the Medical Benevolence Foundation, churches and friends across the country share the vision to establish a facility by which we can say to thousands of those shackled by deformity, "Rise up and walk" in the name of Jesus.[701]

After years of fundraising by the Medical Benevolence Foundation, supporting churches and friends, word came in 1994 that the U.S. Agency for International Development grant that had been applied for establishing the center had been awarded "to the tune of 0.8 million dollars. This is a matching fund so that funds given to MBF will be matched 8 to 3 by the U.S. government."[702]

Construction was scheduled to begin in 1996, with the center to include a 30-bed hospital, nurses' residence, limb and brace shop, physical therapy section, staff quarters, training hostel and other components.

After the groundbreaking, the excitement spread as volunteers came from across the PC(USA) "to join hands with us in the building of the Rehabilitation Center and work of the Presbyterian Hospital of Kikuyu (painting, planting, renovating, laying walkways, joining in surgery and clinics, doing mural work on the ward, electrical, and cabinet work). We are caught up in a whirlwind of excited people who want to share their faith and expand their horizons. They have come—black and white, teenagers and eighty-three year olds, business women and pastors, Yankees and deep Southerners, schoolteachers and doctors—all bonding in the common Master . . . . The whole hospital compound was lifted by the joy and praise that swept over the pain, deformity, and suffering represented in its 200 beds."[703]

At last, on May 17, 1998, the dedication of the two-million-dollar Rehabilitation Center took place. As the dream became reality, the Topples prepared for their retirement in June.

Turning over responsibility is a breath-holding proposition . . . . There have been years of breaking ground, sowing seeds, and sweating. Now it is time for someone else to put their hand to the plow—someone of another culture, with a different value system, with different pressures, and of a different generation. In medicine we might compare it to cutting the umbilical cord. In family life it is comparable to waving good-bye to a just-married daughter. Yet as we run the relay race, how good it is to pass the baton to a fresh and faster runner. And so we want to "Let go and let God."[704]

The spirit of partnership in mission was well expressed by the Rev. Dr. Samuel Mwaniki, General Secretary of the Presbyterian Church of East Africa:

The church has been very much encouraged by its partners' participation and involvement. As partners, our primary factor is love for one another. Such a loving fellowship has a greater evangelistic power. It breaks out in compassion for the world; it yearns for the lost soul to save it and also to alleviate the material and physical needs of the poor, hungry, and oppressed.[705]

PARTNERSHIP IN MISSION IN MADAGASCAR

Lying in rhe Indian Ocean 300 miles east of Mozambique, Madagascar is the world's fourth-largest island and is almost as large in area as the state of Texas. Its isolation has made it home to a host of unique forms of wildlife and plants. Its people reflect successive waves of immigrants, not only from the continent of Africa, but also from Southeast Asia and Arab countries.

Although European explorers reached Madagascar as early as the 15th century, the island continued to be ruled by native kings and queens descended from the dominant tribal group. The French took over the country in 1896 and were in control until full independence was granted in 1960 as the Malagasy Republic. After a decade of political stability, Malagasy underwent serious unrest in the early 1970s. In 1975, martial law was imposed and a new one-party Marxist state, the Democratic Republic of Madagascar, was established. This socialist government continued into the late 1980s, at which time it began to move away from Marxism and the Soviet bloc. In the early 1990s, after massive anti-government demonstrations, a new unity government was formed and multiparty politics was formally permitted. Interparty struggle has continued. In 1997, Lt. Col. Didier Ratsiraka, who led the country during its Marxist regime, was reelected as president, professing himself a convert to free-market economics. Madagascar has become heavily dependent on international support as it struggles to rebuild its basically agricultural economy.

Though Christianity is now the predominant religion among the people of Madagascar (53% of the approximately 11 million population are professing Christians), Christians have undergone severe persecution at various times in the country's history. Catholic missionaries had been at work in Madagascar since the 17th century. The first Protestant missionaries arrived in 1818, from the London Missionary Society. However, during the reign of Queen Ranavalova I (1828-1861), who turned against Christianity, all Europeans were expelled, thousands of Christians were killed and many more were driven into exile. Still, the Christian community continued to grow and their numbers actually increased by the time missionaries were allowed to return in 1861. The baptism of a new queen, Ranavalona II, in 1869 resulted in a mass movement into the church. The next three decades saw the entrance of missionaries from numerous mission societies, both Catholic and Protestant, as well as from numerous European countries, especially France and Great Britain. A growing tension arose between French Catholics and English Protestant missions. After the French takeover of the country in 1896, Protestants were severely persecuted. Despite considerable anti-Christian propaganda under the more recent Marxist regime, the church has continued to grow, and there is now a fair degree of religious freedom in Madagascar.

The Presbyterian Church(USA)'s partner church in Madagascar is the Church of Jesus Christ of Madagascar (FJKM). This vibrant and growing church of nearly 1.5 million members was formed in 1968 by the union of three churches: the Church of Christ in Madagascar, established by the London Missionary Society in 1818; the Evangelical Church of Madagascar, begun by the Paris Evangelical Missionary Society in 1896; and the Friends Church of Madagascar, founded by British Friends in 1864. Constituting some two-thirds of all Madagascar's Protestants, FJKM participates in the operation of several hundred primary and secondary schools. The FJKM has four theological colleges. Beginning in 1979, the UPCUSA assisted in the area of theological education by contributing to the repair of buildings for student housing and by providing a mission co-worker to teach at one of the theological colleges. Other involvements in mission partnership have included training conferences for leaders in evangelism, evangelistic campaigns in rural areas where there are unevangelized villages, and the purchase of bicycles for several evangelists who otherwise would have to travel on foot. The PC(USA) also has supported two rehabilitation centers for homeless girls who might otherwise have been sent to prison.

More recently, the partnership has led to a new venture in mission, assisting the FJKM in a development program of community health and stewardship of the environment. Mission Specialists Dr. Dan Turk and Elizabeth Warlick Turk live in Ambositra, a town five hours south of the capital city Antananarivo, in the southern less-developed area of Madagascar. Working with the development department of FJKM, the Turks write:

> FJKM believes we are called to witness in word and to reach out to people in need. We are excited to be a part of their vision of serving Christ and the Malagasy people. Elizabeth works with the health program helping to design and implement a community health program that will involve training local community health workers. The main health problems facing the Malagasy people have simple solutions, such as washing hands, boiling water, or building latrines, but those solutions require people to change their habits, which is never easy. Dan works with the environmental program to promote sustainable development, especially in the area of reforestation. He concentrates mainly on fruit trees and trees native to Madagascar."[706]

In a situation where fewer than 50 percent of the rural population have access to safe drinking water and medical care is difficult to find, the Turks confront "the dilemma of development. How do we love and care for the pressing and immediate needs and also provide services that enable people to care for themselves? Too many handouts deprive people of their dignity and do not change the long-term conditions of poverty. It takes God's grace to help people in a way that they retain their God-given dignity."[707]

A beginning of the answer was seen in a village Ikiray, where FJKM began work in 1991.

> Faced with food shortages, poor access to medicines, inadequate veterinary care, and low income, Ikiray sought help from the church's development program. At first the local FJKM development unit (VOTETA) worked with the community to form a village association open to everyone. They then helped them address the needs they themselves identified. First was the need to organize communal rice storage. Later VOTETA helped train a villager to give animal vaccinations and obtain the vaccines. In 1998 a community health program identified high school youth alcohol consumption as a problem. The community built a basketball court and organized Sunday afternoon athletic activities limited to those without alcohol on their breath. Each of these projects has helped the community deal with its own problems. Within five months youth alcohol consumption had dropped drastically. Over the past decade, school attendance increased from 35 percent to more than 90 percent. But most important of all, the community believes it can continue to address whatever problems emerge.[708]

The Church of Jesus Christ of Madagascar well expresses its sense of mission for which it seeks partnership, in a statement which could apply to all the churches of Sub-Saharan Africa:

> In today's world, throughout Madagascar, communities of Christians have to face the harsh realities of everyday life: poverty, corruption, natural disasters. Their witness finds its strength in the word of God. Despite the material privations of most of its members, the FJKM counts on their faithfulness to achieve the following priorities: to increase efforts in evangelization, to become more involved in social action, to improve the living conditions of the people, to strengthen its present activities including lay training and the upkeep of its schools.[709]

PARTNERSHIP IN MISSION IN MAURITIUS

The islands that make up the tiny nation of Mauritius lie in the Indian Ocean 1,000 miles off the southeast coast of Africa and 550 miles beyond Madagascar. This island nation is smaller than the smallest of the U.S. states, Rhode Island. It is densely populated, with approximately 1.1 million people composed of an even more diverse population than neighboring Madagascar. The majority of its inhabitants are immigrants from India, but the ethnic mix includes Africans, Europeans and Chinese.

The islands were originally uninhabited and thus have no indigenous people. Although the Dutch were the first to settle the islands beginning in 1598, the French held it from 1715 to 1810 and the British from 1810 until independence was achieved in 1968. The ethnic diversity has worked against unity in the political sphere, and coalition governments have often been a necessity. Originally an important stop for ships on their way to India and the Far East, Mauritius was largely forgotten when the Suez Canal was completed. However, in more recent years it has become a popular tourist attraction. The tourist industry, along with recent industrial diversification has brought Mauritius considerable economic success; in comparison to its neighbor Madagascar where the percapita income is about $730, Mauritius enjoys a percapita income of approximately $10,000.

Regarding religion, Mauritius is unique among the nations of sub-Saharan Africa in that Hinduism is the principal religion, the professed faith of the majority Indian population. Christianity has the second largest constituency, with approximately 26% of the population, and Islam the third largest with about 15% of the population. The Roman Catholic Church constitutes the largest Christian community, having begun its evangelization of Mauritius in 1722. They are followed by the Anglicans who first entered Maruitius in 1810 and continue to be the largest portion of the non-Catholic Christian community. The Presbyterian Church of Mauritius is rooted in the mission work of the London Missionary Society (beginning its work in 1814) and the Church of Scotland (which began its work in 1837). The two missions were incorporated into one in 1875, and in 1979 the Presbyterian Church of Mauritius became autonomous. It is a small community with about 1,000 members in one English-speaking and four French-speaking parishes.

Mauritius is unusual in having a multi-religious council, the Mauritius Interreligious Committee, also known as World Fraternal Solidarity. It is composed of representatives of the various religious groups, including Hindu, Christian and Muslim. Its aim is the promotion of understanding and peace among Mauritians of various religious faiths.

It was into this multi-cultural situation that the UPCUSA was invited to participate as a partner in mission, along with partners from Canada, Scotland, France, Fiji, and Switzerland. The venture in which all would be engaged was the Formation Biblique et Theologique a Maurice (FBTM), a Theological Education by Extension program in which Roman Catholics, Anglicans and Presbyterians would cooperate. The objective which all shared was the establishment of a joint training program for the Christians of Mauritius, equipping them for witness and service in a multi-cultural society.

The experience of mission co-workers was one that expanded their own spiritual horizons. Joe and Becky Carle would write:

> We have enjoyed our five years living in Mauritius. We have made friends from
> all over the world. We have discovered the joy of living in a truly pluralistic

culture. We have come to know Hindus, Muslims and Christians from various denominations. Our children are fluent in French, English and Creole, but more important, they have made friends with children from very different backgrounds than our own.[710]

Brian and Liz Crosby, who arrived in Mauritius in 1982 to work in developing leadership within the Presbyterian Church of Mauritius, would soon find themselves involved in the program of FBTM, and in time Brian would become its director. Brian would write of a visit to one of the smaller islands, Rodrigues:

> Some 95% of Rodriguans are Roman Catholics, with handfuls of Anglicans, Adventists, Pentecostals and Muslims. We met yesterday with three of the four Catholic priests who work here (three Mauritians and one French) and, apart from enjoying their hospitality, were able to talk about FBTM and the possibility of establishing groups here to work on our introduction to the Bible course. Each of the priests was very aware of the need for much more biblical knowledge and understanding amongst his people as traditional popular piety comes more and more under strain in rapidly changing circumstances. As the majority of the population is illiterate, however, our work will have to concentrate on the educated leadership to begin with. Within the Anglican church there is a higher percentage of formally educated people and already a good number of them have expressed the desire to study the introduction to the Bible course in groups with their Catholic neighbors. And so we hope to come back to Rodrigues in two or three months to launch what will surely qualify as one of the remotest theological education programs on earth![711]

When the Crosbys completed their service in Mauritius in 1997, they would write: "Our tiny church in our tiny country—a mere dot in a vast ocean—knows that it is part of a great worldwide family of faith, and it is this family that will stay with us as we move on."[712]

F. AMERICAN PRESBYTERIAN INVOLVEMENT IN SOUTHERN AFRICA

Undoubtedly the area of sub-Saharan Africa in which American Presbyterians have become more fully involved in the latter part of the twentieth century has been southern Africa. This region has been the focus of much attention both in relation to General Assembly statements and actions, and in relation to mission partnerships through personnel and resources. In addition to those nations in which there had been involvement prior to 1973 (South Africa, beginning in 1960; Zimbabwe and Zambia, beginning in 1965; and Malawi in 1972), two other nations would claim the mission involvement of American Presbyterians: Lesotho and Mozambique, both beginning in 1975.

PARTNERSHIP IN MISSION IN SOUTH AFRICA

The eyes of the world have been focused on South Africa during the latter part of the twentieth century, as it has gone through the most important transformation in its history, a transformation which has had and will continue to have profound effect upon the future of the whole of Africa. As the South African government increasingly enforced its *apartheid* system, there developed increasing hostility on the part of the states surrounding South Africa. Angola and Mozambique achieved their independence from Portugal in 1975, and their new governments were strongly opposed to the South African government's policies. Liberation struggles were underway in Rhodesia and Namibia in the mid-1970s. Within South Africa, a Black Consciousness Movement (BCM) arose among black students, led by Stephen Biko, emphasizing black leadership and non-cooperation with the government. Biko's death at the hands of the police in 1977 only increased the resolve of these African youths, and many of the BCM participants would later play a crucial role in the liberation process. The 1970s also marked a new and revitalized phase of black trade unionism, and its growing power was demonstrated by a series of illegal boycotts and strikes. The dependence of the South African economy on black workers made this movement a powerful political and economic force in bringing about change.

A critical turning point was the confrontation between young protesters and South African police in the black township of Soweto, near Johannesburg, on June 16, 1976. Thousands of black high school students demonstrated against a government ruling that required certain subjects to be taught in Afrikaans, which was seen as the language of oppression. At least 575 people were killed, and rioting between police and students spread throughout the country. This led to a new phase in the liberation process, as black youth became deeply involved in the struggle, and many left the country to join the liberation movements.

Added to this was the growing international opposition to apartheid. The United Nations repeatedly took up the issue of South Africa's racial policies. By 1962, the UN voted sanctions against South Africa, and in 1966 voted to terminate South Africa's mandate over Southwest Africa (now Namibia), an action which South Africa ignored as it proceeded to integrate that territory into its own economy. In 1974 South Africa was suspended from the United Nations General Assembly, and by the 1980s UNGA resolutions referred to apartheid as a "crime against humanity." International financial institutions began to regard South Africa as unsafe for investment. This combined with increasing demands by churches and others for international sanctions led more than 200 U.S. companies to pull out of South Africa during the 1980s.

By the 1980s the psychological, financial and human costs of maintaining order were increasing as the cycle of repression, black violence and white counterviolence accelerated. Limited reforms were introduced, but the policy of limited reforms with continuing repression failed. Finally, in 1989, when F.W. de Klerk succeeded P.W. Botha as head of the National Party and later that year as president of South Africa, the process of dismantling apartheid was begun.

During this period up to 1989, the churches in South Africa were sharply divided regarding the South African government's policies. The Dutch Reformed churches in general supported the government's policy of apartheid, and sought scriptural or theological justification for it. In 1961, the largest Dutch Reformed Church (NGK) withdrew from the World Council of Churches, which had openly condemned apartheid. In 1978, the NGK severed relations with the Netherlands Reformed Church (Holland) over the latter's support of African liberation movements. The English-speaking churches for the most part officially opposed apartheid, although their protestations generally addressed the issue in measured tones. The most outspoken critics of the government were the South African Council of Churches (SACC), which in 1968 published a "Message to the people of South Africa", describing the policy of apartheid as anti-Christian; and the NGK break-away group, the Christian Institute of South Africa, which suffered increasing repression.

American Presbyterians made clear their stand in support of the liberation struggle. In 1978, the Presbyterian Church in the United States (PCUS) sent a delegation to Africa to meet with church leaders and missionaries in Zaire, Ghana, Nigeria, Rwanda, Lesotho, Mozambique, and finally in the Republic of South Africa. On the basis of that visit, the 1978 PCUS General Assembly sent messages to the South African Council of Churches and the Presbyterian Church of South Africa, "expressing encouragement and prayer in the matter of suppression of human rights of the black majority."[713] In 1980, the PCUS sent help to the SACC for ministries to relieve the suffering from political imprisonment and banishment. Aid was also sent to church-related centers in South Africa which helped black women employed by whites "to achieve a more humane existence and become aware of their rights."[714]

In the United Presbyterian Church in the U.S.A. (UPCUSA), the 1981 General Assembly issued a lengthy statement entitled "A Declaration of Conscience on South Africa and Namibia." The statement reaffirmed the position taken by previous General Assemblies in support of those victimized by the apartheid system and called upon the United States government and the church "to support all efforts to redress the injustices being imposed upon South Africa's blacks." The moderator of the UPCUSA General Assembly led a delegation to a historic Assembly of the Presbyterian Church of South Africa, which called upon that church to defy the laws of apartheid. The delegation also attended a historic meeting of Black Reformed Churches, which reaffirmed their position against apartheid.[715]

Included in the 1981 General Assembly statement was a resolution calling upon the Committee on Mission Responsibility through Investments "to continue to pursue all strategies, negotiations and stockholder resolutions that urge business or financial institutions to discontinue operations, investments and loans in South Africa." This would become a hotly contested issue in subsequent years, as church institutions and individuals questioned the impact of such a strategy upon their own investments in companies operating in South Africa. The 1983 uniting General Assembly of the PC(USA) adopted a resolution addressed to Citicorp on its loan activity in South Africa.[716] The 1988 General

Assembly received a lengthy report on the issue, and adopted an enabling action regarding "the phased, selective divestment of South-Africa related stocks."[717]

In 1989, the mood radically changed as South Africa President F.W. de Klerk expressed commitment to seeking new solutions to dismantle apartheid. On February 11, 1990, he released Nelson Mandela after 27 years of imprisonment, and the African National Congress (ANC) was recognized as a legal organization. By 1991, the legislation undergirding apartheid had been revoked, although there were few substantial changes in the conditions under which the black majority lived. On December 22, 1993, the end of "white only" rule in South Africa became law when parliament passed a bill enacting a transitional constitution and setting up a Transitional Executive Council. The first national elections allowing participation by all races were held in April 1994.

The 1995 PC(USA) General Assembly gave thanks for "the miracle in South Africa. After more than 300 years of official racism and decades of oppression under apartheid, South Africans of every race went to the polls and celebrated their new freedom by election of Nelson Mandela as state president. Now the hard realities of finding ways to restore even a minimum quality of life for three-fourths of the population have set in."[718]

The road ahead for the new government under Nelson Mandela would be a very difficult one. Although all apartheid legislation was repealed, South Africa remained a country of extreme contradictions. Mandela's government faced the challenge of restructuring the economy and redistributing economic benefits, providing housing and health care, and improving employment and educational opportunities. Yet the strong but gentle spirit of Mandela gave hope to those who had lost it, as he faced his former captors not with bitter vengefulness but with a spirit of forgiveness and a determination to move beyond the terrible history of which they had been a part.

That new spirit was movingly expressed in the setting up in 1996 of the Truth and Reconciliation Commission, chaired by the respected South African churchman, Archbishop Desmond Tutu. Seeking to move the country toward uncovering past atrocities without polarizing the society, the 17-member commission conducted hearings for the purpose of collecting and investigating reports of human rights' violations, considering amnesty for those who confessed their participation in such atrocities, and making recommendations for reparations. Though the commission endured much criticism from both sides, when it released its final report in 1998 condemning actions of all the major political organizations during the apartheid period, it was evident that the commission had blazed the trail for a new approach to achieving peace with justice and avoiding a period of violent vengeance.

During the six years from Mandela's election to the year 2000, South Africa has undergone further major changes. In late 1997 Mandela retired as ANC party leader and was replaced by executive deputy president Thabo Mbeki. In the 1999 legislative elections, the ANC won almost two-thirds of the seats in the legislature and selected Mbeki as South Africa's next president. Since 1996 there has been a struggle to develop a new constitution. A final version was approved by parliament in 1997, providing more autonomy for the provinces and allowing the possibility of a province controlled largely by Africaaners. The government faces monumental problems, with a rising crime rate, the highest incidence of AIDS in Africa, and the continuing challenge of overcoming the massive needs in areas such as housing, education, health care and economic development. Yet the spirit of a new South Africa prevails and is an inspiration not only to its own people but to oppressed people around the world.

The churches of South Africa have played an important role in the development of a nonracial democratic state in South Africa. In ways large and small, they have monitored the election process to help ensure free and fair elections; participated in post-election reconstruction and development; helped the nation break with the conflicts of the past and move toward reconciliation among the groups which have long been polarized. The PC(USA) has supported partner churches in these endeavors, providing resources for agricultural projects, cottage industries, job training programs, and ministries with children who are victims of apartheid and the AIDS epidemic. Also, assistance has been given in evangelism and church growth through the PC(USA) program established for this purpose.

A landmark event which dramatically expressed the changed situation took place in September 1999, when the Reformed Presbyterian Church in Southern Africa (RPCSA, a black denomination) and the Presbyterian Church of Southern Africa (PCSA, a predominantly white denomination) joined into one church, to be called the Uniting Presbyterian Church in Southern Africa (UPCSA). "It is important to note that they chose the term 'Uniting' rather than 'United', reflecting a clear intention to be joined in the future by the two other Presbyterian bodies in South Africa, the Evangelical Presbyterian Church and the Presbyterian Church of Africa." A PC(USA) delegation was present for the occasion, including representatives from the partnership presbyteries of Northern New England, New York City and Florida. Vernon S. Broyles, III, PC(USA) Director for Social Justice, described the scene:

> They gathered, hundreds of Presbyterian men and women, in two great clusters of humanity, down separate streets on either side of the huge Centenary Hall in New Brighton, the large "township" on the edge of Port Elizabeth, South Africa. And then they began to sing and move and dance toward a point of intersection near the hall. The marshals struggled to hold the crowds in some semblance of order as they followed the marching bands down the street, but when the two streams reached the intersection, they spilled together in one joyful mass, greeting, hugging, weeping, singing and praising God that these two Presbyterian denominations, one essentially White and the other essentially Black, were about to celebrate the unity which Jesus Christ gives, beyond every barrier of race and culture.[719]

The PC(USA) partnership in mission has been embodied in the presence of several mission co-workers, serving South African churches in various capacities and also serving as interpreters of the South African situation to churches in the United States. Mission

Specialist Doug Tilton has served since 1992 as an assistant in parliamentary advocacy with the South Africa Council of Churches.

> Recently the South African Parliament passed three key pieces of legislation, designed to protect fundamental rights guaranteed under the new democratic constitution, including broad rights of equality and access to information. A German journalist asked me, "So it's finished now? the transition to democracy is completed?" I knew what he meant. Most of the legal building blocks of South Africa's new democracy have now been put in place. Its constitution, hailed as one of the most enlightened in the world, has prompted a torrent of legislation during the past five years, much of it geared to replacing the laws and institutions of the apartheid era (1948-1994). In that sense, much has been accomplished . . . . However, my response [to the journalist] was, "No, the transition is just beginning." A 1999 report found that between 1991 and 1996, almost all of the increase in the income earned by black people in South Africa occurred among the wealthiest 10 percent of black households. The poorest 40 percent actually saw their income decline. White per capita income remained nine times that of blacks . . . . The challenge now is to ensure that people understand and are able to exercise their rights, that public officials honor them, and that government departments execute their responsibilities promptly and fairly.[720]

Mission Specialist Cynthia Easterday has served with African Enterprise, a program of the Uniting Presbyterian Church in Southern Africa.

> The ministry of African Enterprise (AE) has many facets in South Africa, all designed to address the changing and developing needs of a country continuing to adjust to a democratic way of life after several hundred years of white minority rule. One major area of concern is the youth. Caught on the cusp of change, the majority see little hope of a future due to limited education and skills combined with limited income opportunities and high unemployment. The country's change to a better life requires time—time the restlessness of youth can't accept. It's into this environment of uncertainty and outright despair that AE's youth evangelism team, the Foxfires, bring practical teachings, encouragement, challenge, truth, and hope to students in schools throughout the country.[721]

Mission Specialists the Rev. Dr. Kay-Robert Volkwijn and Desire Volkwijn work at a local level in the township of Guguletu, a suburb of Cape Town. They followed in the footsteps of the Rev. Sara Holben, who had served as Associate Pastor of the JL. Zwane Presbyterian Church, and Bob Schminkey, who had served as a consultant to the Presbytery on development and church partnerships. The Volkwijn's responsibilities range from getting various congregations serious about "reconciliation with justice", conducting workshops with various groups on racism, serving as an external examiner for the Stellenbosch Theology Seminary, and coordinating the Rainbow School which brings together students from different schools (black and coloured) in the Guguletu area.

> Apartheid in South Africa has been abolished; liberation and full franchise to all in South Africa have been established. But the churches now face a new challenge, namely the issue of justice. This is a daunting task, for the churches here, as elsewhere, have always dealt more easily with the Good Samaritan model than with the Lukan exhortation to preach release to the captives and to set at liberty those who are oppressed.[722]

Truly the miracle in South Africa has yet to be fully embodied in the lives of the majority of its people; yet the future is far brighter than ever before, and the church has a vital role to play in bringing about the fulfilment of that transformation.

PARTNERSHIP IN MISSION IN ZIMBABWE

The winds of change that were sweeping across Africa in the 1960s encountered a strong wall of resistance in Southern Rhodesia. Its partners in the Federation of Rhodesia and Nyasaland had been granted independence in 1964 as the black-governed nations of Zambia and Malawi. Ian Smith, Southern Rhodesia's prime minister, had unilaterally declared independence in 1965, without the approval of the British government or the African majority. Fifteen years of struggle and guerrilla warfare ensued. After 1976, the military wings of ZANU and ZAPU joined forces to create a more powerful liberation army, called the Patriotic Front (PF). After elections in that year, a moderate black leader, Methodist Bishop Abel Muzorewa, formed a coalition government and took office as prime minister. However, ZANU and ZAPU did not accept this arrangement, viewing Muzorewa as a puppet of the white government.

Finally in1980, the Rhodesia government accepted British and American mediation and signed the Lancaster House agreement allowing majority rule. In elections held that year, the Zimbabwe African National Union—Patriotic Front (ZANU-PF) decisively defeated the Zimbabwe African People's Union (ZAPU). Robert Mugabe was installed as prime minister, and the newly-independent nation was renamed Zimbabwe.

For the next ten years, Zimbabwe was officially a Marxist-Socialist state until the economic liberalization of the 1990s, following the end of the Cold War. The Mugabe government has stayed in power through several elections, despite threatening developments on its borders, with the civil war in Mozambique and the political conflict in South Africa. Although Zimbabwe has been known as a comparatively stable democracy, internal struggles for power, student unrest, charges of corruption and some continuing human rights violations have marred its political life. One of the major accomplishments since independence has been the substantial increase in primary and secondary education. Unfortunately, employment has not kept pace with education.

Although Zimbabwe possesses some mineral resources (especially chrome), agriculture is the backbone of its economy. In 1997, Mugabe announced the implementation of a promise that he had made soon after Zimbabwe had gained its independence, regarding land redistribution. About 1,500 white-owned commercial farms, comprising nearly half of Zimbabwe's total farmland, were designated to be seized without compensation and divided among landless blacks and those with only small landholdings, usually in the most infertile areas. (Approximately one percent of Zimbabwe's population own 90 percent of its fertile farmland.) Strong protests by white farmers and the international economic community led the government to announce that it would buy the farms with foreign aid money over a five-year period. However, the government has not yet succeeded in fulfiling this commitment, while black squatters have occupied more than 1,000 of the white-owned farms.

The crisis of land redistribution in Zimbabwe has been called the bellwether for other parts of Africa. "The issue of land redistribution remains to be resolved in several countries of Southern Africa and elsewhere. In neighboring South Africa, for example, blacks are hungry for land that they too claim was taken from their ancestors. The case is also true in Kenya where large farms are still owned by Kenyans of European heritage. The uniqueness of the Zimbabwe situation rests only in its use as a diversionary tactic to save a falling head of state."[723]

Within this nation of some ten million people, approximately 54% are professing Christians while 43% continue to practice traditional African religions. Zimbabwe is one of the African nations in which Protestants are in the majority in the Christian population, though no single denomination predominates. The fact that Zimbabwe's Protestant churches could host the eighth assembly of the World Council of Churches in December 1998 (the WCC's Jubilee Assembly) is indicative of the status that the churches have achieved in the life of this nation and the ecumenical world.

The Presbyterian Church (USA) is in partnership with the presbyteries of Mashonaland and Matebeleland of the South Africa-based Presbyterian Church of Southern Africa (PCSA) and the Harare Synod of the Malawi-based Church of Central Africa Presbyterian (CCAP). PC(USA) has been involved in Zimbabwe through numerous channels. The Presbyterian Hunger Program and the Self-Development of People Program have funded several drought-related and agricultural programs, including drought rehabilitation projects, school feeding programs, irrigation schemes, a dairy unit, a weavers training center, and a project for the disabled. Also, the PC(USA) has helped support the Zimbabwe Christian Council in some of its programs related to agriculture, health, and education.

However, the most significant ongoing mission partnership has been in relation to the Program for Evangelism and Church Growth in Africa (PECGA). With Zimbabwe's capital city Harare serving as a base, the missionary coordinator for the program has worked with church partners in Zimbabwe, Zambia, Malawi, Lesotho, Mozambique, as well as the islands of Madagascar and Mauritius, to help provide encouragement, vision, and resources for the equipping of the church to carry out its mission.

> In each case where the PC(USA) has helped train leaders or build churches, we have sought to be a catalyst, being careful not to do what the people can do for themselves. We often share the African proverb, "If you want me to help you, don't ask me to carry your load for you. You must first lift it to your knees, then I can help you get it to your head." You do your part in building your church and training your people, and we will help you get it to the place where you can carry it yourself. It is your church.[724]

It was mission co-workers David and Polly Miller who initiated the PECGA program in Southern Africa, first from their base in Maseru, Lesotho (where they were the first American Presbyterian missionaries assigned to serve in Southern Africa, beginning in 1977), then from 1988 from their base in Harare, Zimbabwe. Building on their 23 years of missionary experience in Zaire/Congo, then their 11 years in Lesotho, the Millers served as liaison to partner churches across Southern Africa, learning of their most pressing needs and offering to help in those projects which most urgently needed help for completion. As they approached retirement, the Millers would write:

> The PC(USA) Project of Evangelism, Church Growth, and Theological Education in Southern Africa has been a heart-warming and inspiring way to complete our years of service here in Africa. It has greatly encouraged and renewed the churches in Southern Africa during difficult years of suffering and conflict.[725]

In 1994, the mantle for the PECGA program in Southern Africa was passed on to Mission Co-Workers Bill and Nancy Warlick, who had initiated the program in Congo in the 1980s. Along with her other responsibilities, Nancy Warlick has become involved in the PCSA Presbytery of Zimbabwe's ministry with street children in Harare.

> Estimates from UNICEF indicate that approximately 15 million of the 100 million children worldwide who are living on the streets live in Africa. That number is likely to double over the next three or four years due to increased poverty, HIV-AIDS, breakdown of the family, war, and other problems. The Presbyterian program and ministry in Zimbabwe, Children in Crisis, continues to grow.[726]

Out of this ministry in Harare there has emerged the Mbuya Nehanda Training Centre and Farm in Melfort, about thirty miles from Harare, where some 120 children who have left the streets are living and going to a local primary school; also the Lovemore House in Harare, which provides a halfway house for those children who want to get off the streets and into a more stable environment.

Through the initiative of Nancy and fellow-workers, and funding provided by the PC(USA) Outreach Foundation, a "Frontline for Children" Conference was held in Harare in May-June, 2001, bringing together representatives of over 65 "children at risk" ministries from all over Zimbabwe "who work with street children, AIDS orphans, sexually-exploited and abused children, handicapped children, and the girl-child network, among others. The numbers of 'at risk' orphans and vulnerable children are increasing alarmingly in southern Africa . . . . A decision was made to form a national committee to lobby the government on behalf of 'children at risk' as well as other relevant institutions on the rights of these children . . . . At a time when the country of Zimbabwe is undergoing its worst economic and political challenges, this conference stands out as a clear reminder to all who attended that God cares for the vulnerable 'little ones' and wants them taken care of and helped. Our hope is a big one, to bring the needy, hurting children to Jesus."[727]

PARTNERSHIP IN MISSION IN ZAMBIA

Following Zambia's independence from British colonialism in 1964, Kenneth Kaunda became the leading architect of the new nation. In 1972 Zambia, following the lead of numerous other African nations, became a one-party state; however, its leadership remained moderate and generally pro-Western. In 1975, Zambia nationalized privately-held lands and other enterprises and claimed 51 percent of the country's rich copper mines. The completion of the rail link to Dar es Salaam, Tanzania in 1976 freed Zambia from its dependence on the Rhodesian and South African-controlled railway for the transport of its copper. The experiment in nationalization worked until severe droughts and falling copper prices caused the economy to collapse, leading to food riots.

President Kaunda opposed the white-dominated regimes in Rhodesia, as well as Namibia and South Africa. His assistance to liberation movements based in Zambia proved crucial to the establishment of a black majority government in Zimbabwe in 1980, and in South Africa in the early 1990s. Although Kaunda was reelected to a sixth presidential term in 1988, popular discontent with Zambia'a stagnant economy and his autocratic rule continued to grow. In 1990 an abortive coup shook the government, and the aging leader agreed to allow multiparty voting. The opposition Movement for Multiparty Democracy won the 1991 general election, and its presidential candidate, Frederick Chiluba, defeated Kaunda by a wide margin, bringing to an end his 27 years as Zambia's president. Kaunda stepped down from office peacefully, setting a new paradigm for African leaders in the 1990s. The economic troubles of Zambia have continued under President Chiluba, aggravated by the decreasing demand for copper on the world market. High rates of inflation and international agency-required austerity measures, such as the termination of government subsidies on the price of maize meal, its staple food, have led to strikes and riots. President Chiluba has sought to take measures to return Zambia to a free-market economy, though the demands of international and Western financial agencies have made it difficult for the majority of Zambia's people.

As in Zimbabwe, the majority of Zambia's people are Christian, constituting some 62% of the total population of over nine million. Also, as in Zimbabwe, Protestants constitute the majority of the Christian population. The United Church of Zambia, formed in 1965, is the largest Protestant church in Zambia. The Presbyterian Church (USA) relates to this church, as well as to two much smaller Presbyterian churches with branches in Zambia, The Church of Central Africa Presbyterian (CCAP) based in Malawi, and the Presbyterian Church of Southern Africa (PCSA), based in South Africa.

PC(USA) involvement in Zambia has been multi-faceted. During the Zimbabwe liberation war in the late 1970s, American Presbyterians made a significant contribution to relief work among the more than 60,000 Zimbabwe refugees who had taken refuge in camps in Zambia.—The Presbyterian Hunger Program has assisted with a program for young mothers which is supported by the Women's Work Department of the Council of Churches of Zambia, and also with a program for training volunteers at the Nambala Training Center.—The Project for Evangelism and Church Growth in Africa (PECGA) has given support to numerous endeavors: a new printing of hymnals; theological education by extension; church construction; theological seminary repairs and manse construction; provision of books and seminary scholarships; and the purchase of bicycles for ministers and evangelists.—Mission volunteers have served at Justo Mwale Theological College, which trains about fifteen ministers a year from five Presbyterian/Reformed denominations in central and southern Africa.—PC(USA) has continued to contribute resources and personnel for the Mindolo Ecumenical Foundation Center in Kitwe, Zambia, one of the strongest ecumenical institutions in the new Africa.—PC(USA) resources have funded the housing as well as the program of the ecumenical Kanyama Crisis Nursery in Lusaka. "A crisis nursery is a short-term 'safe home' for infants and young children under 5 who have been orphaned, abandoned or are in an urgent crisis situation. The children brought to the crisis nursery will find nurturing, temporary care while extended family or a foster adoptive family can be found and prepared. The crisis nursery is assisted by many local community members and organizations who participate in the support and activities of the nursery."[728]

A significant expression of partnership in mission was the work of Drs. Irma and Salvador de la Torre in transforming a rural hospital in the town of Mwandi to a modest but modern health center. After years of service in Haiti, the de la Torres responded to the call to service at this remote setting in Zambia.

> This village of Lozi-speaking Zambians is the site for the Mwandi Mission Hospital. Excitement can be heard throughout the village as a new foundation is being poured, a roof attached and "*Makuwas*," or white people, are around. The village people feel the excitement as they play an active role in the development of their community.

The past two years have been a period of improvement and great change for the community of Mwandi. Phase I, including the refurbishing of the existing hospital plan and organization of primary health care facilities, is complete. Phase II, the construction of a new surgical wing, and outpatient clinic and chapel, is underway. Phase III, a teaching-learning center to train and equip children and adults in health education, nutrition, and proper hygiene is in the near future. It's exciting to walk through the hospital compound and see men from the village employed, to talk with clinical officers about a recent conference they have attended, or to see an old patient, now comfortable, walking on a previously injured leg.

The project is underway, and you are a part of the excitement and success. The project is personally rewarding to a group of 16 Americans who spent three weeks of their summer to help out with painting buildings, repair and maintenance of the hospital, and the nearby Rural Health Care center of Masese. They have also been able to experience the excitement of watching a child enter the world, the thrill of seeing a crocodile slip into the river, and the love shown in the eyes of an African friend.[729]

PARTNERSHIP IN MISSION IN MALAWI

Following its independence from Britain in 1964, Malawi became a one-party state under the stern rule of President-for-life Hastings Kamuzu Banda. What his government described as "peace and calm" was experienced by many Malawians as repression, denial of human rights, detention without trial, exile, torture, and execution. Malawi's economy performed sluggishly, burdened by recurring drought, increasing foreign debt and by an influx of some 900,000 from wartorn Mozambique.[730] Banda's policy of cordiality toward South Africa brought serious criticism from the leaders of other black African countries, and his influence on continental African affairs was negative.

At last, change swept through Malawi, brought about largely by the leadership of the church. In March 1992, seven bishops of the Roman Catholic Church in Malawi issued a Lenten pastoral letter.

The letter is profound and moving, having at its heart the concern for the dignity of each person, however poor or powerless, as a child of God. Bringing the gospel to bear on societal problems in Malawi, it addresses issues as diverse as education, health care, economic structures and basic human freedoms, so long denied in Malawi. Among others, the Bishops call for a fair and impartial judiciary, an end to detention without trial, an end to censorship, the establishment of an independent press, freedom of association, and equal access to health care services and educational opportunities.[731]

Though the letter was banned and the bishops were arrested, publicly denounced and threatened with execution, soon other churches, including the Church of Central Africa Presbyterian (CCAP), joined in the call for a change in leadership and multiparty democracy.[732] President Banda finally was obliged to call for a referendum, and in June 1993, the people of Malawi voted almost 2 to 1 in favor of a new constitution providing for multiparty democracy. The first elections were held in May 1994, and Bakili Muluzi, leader of the United Democratic Front (UDF), defeated Banda for the presidency and formed a UDF-dominated government. In keeping with the new constitution, which established a human rights commission, Muluzi freed political prisoners and closed three prisons where tortures were reputed to have been practiced.

When Banda died in 1997, the general secretary of the CCAP Livingstonia Synod, Dr. Overtoun Mazunda, was asked to preach the sermon at the burial service, since Banda had been a member of the Presbyterian church.

> Dr. Mazunda had the unenviable task of trying to balance the truth (President Banda was known to have thrown his enemies to the crocodiles in the Shire River) with the Malawian tradition never to speak ill of the dead. His text was taken from II Samuel 1:17-26—David's lament over the deaths of Saul and Jonathan on Mount Gilboa. Dr. Mazunda delicately established that Banda had been ruthless (as Saul had been chasing all over Israel trying to kill David), yet proceeded to mourn and praise him for the good he had accomplished (even as David mourned Saul). This was a particularly poignant witness to the power of forgiveness in Jesus Christ, as it came from someone who had himself been on Banda's hit list.[733]

Despite this time of political oppression, the Christian community in Malawi is strong and growing, accounting for about 60% of the population of some 10 million. Among the Protestant population, by far the largest denomination is the Church of Central Africa Presbyterian (CCAP), with almost three million members, including its synods in neighboring Zimbabwe and Zambia. The church has grown until what had been three presbyteries now constitute three synods in Malawi: Livingstonia Synod in the north, Nkhoma Synod in the central region, and Blantyre Synod in the south. The CCAP is involved in a wide range of medical and educational work, growing out of the pioneer work of Scottish and Dutch missionaries. It supports five hospitals: Embangweni, Ekwendeni and Livingstonia Hospitals in the north; Nkhoma Hospital in the central region; and Mulanje Hospital in the south. The church is also involved in both primary and secondary education, including the Robert Laws Secondary School at Embangweni in Livingstonia Synod, Henry Henderson Institute Secondary School in Blantyre and a new Practical Learning for Living School at Domasi in Blantyre Synod. To address the shortage of ministers for this growing church, Zomba Theological College provides not only the traditional three-year course for ministers, but also an emergency two-year course for mature students wishing to enter the ministry, as well as a wives' school for women who will become pastors' wives. Other ministries of the CCAP include women's centers, youth and adult conference centers, a school for deaf children, child survival programs, self-development programs, and various forms of evangelistic outreach.

PC(USA) partnership in mission with the CCAP has led in recent years to a greater concentration of mission co-workers in Malawi than in any other country in sub-Saharan Africa. Numerous mission personnel have been reassigned to Malawi from nations which have been in political turmoil, such as Congo/Zaire and Ethiopia. Among them were Dr. and Mrs. Kenneth (Nancy) McGill, who had served for over 20 years in Congo and brought their rich experience and medical skill to the rural hospital at Embangweni in **Livingstonia Synod**. In 1989 they would write:

> A rural "bush" hospital has been transformed from darkness into light—glorious solar light. This happened within the last few years at Bulape in Zaire, and now it has happened again at Embangweni in Malawi. On February 1 the maternity ward had its first solar light at Embangweni, and the first baby was delivered by an adequate fluorescent light instead of a kerosene "railroad" lamp. Otis Rowe, PC(USA) missionary in southern Malawi who installed the system, named the baby girl "Delight." Now there are lights in all of the maternity department, including the room for the premature infants, who need constant watching and monitoring . . . .
>
> We pray that because of Presbyterians at home helping us to harness the power of the sun, the power of God's Son will shine even brighter at Embangweni.[734]

For a time, Dr. McGill served as the only physician and surgeon on the hospital staff—in fact, "the only qualified surgeon in the northern third of this country of 10 million people."[735] During Ken McGill's service as hospital director, the hospital supervised mobile clinics in ten outlying villages, with staff going out monthly to supervise the work of Malawian nurses and do minor surgery and dental extractions, seeing up to 200 patients a day. Emphasis was placed on education, immunizations, growth monitoring and ante-natal care. "It is very cost-effective medical care, with emphasis more on prevention than on cure of medical problems."[736] An effort was made to reach out to the traditional healers in the villages.

> Recently the traditional healers were invited to come to the hospital for a seminar on AIDS. The razor blades they use to make cuts on the skin that are part of their treatment can carry the virus from one person to another. Ten native healers were invited, but 24 came. And they indicated that they would be happy to come to other seminars if the hospital would plan them.[737]

The hospital had become progressively overcrowded, with an official bed capacity of 77 but a census running between 120 and 140 every day. Under the McGills' leadership and with resources provided by PC(USA) contributors, the hospital building was expanded to raise the bed capacity to 155, doubling the previous hospital size,

> . . . at a surprisingly low cost, about $50,000. And just as the buildings are nearing completion, a team of volunteers from the USA (organized by Medical Benevolence Foundation) have come to Malawi to paint at our hospital and at Mulanje Hospital in the southern part of Malawi. The funds for all of this work have been channeled through Medical Benevolence Foundation . . . . MBF also provided funds for the McGill's son, Jim, to come and oversee the construction projects. Not only has he done this with incredible efficiency, he has been able to construct covered walkways between each ward, build several needed staff houses, develop many shallow wells in the surrounding community, and catalyze the development of several 'fish farm ponds' in the area . . . . What a marvelous example of Christian stewardship and sharing we have seen here![738]

The McGill's work came to an end with retirement in June 1991, followed by Kenneth's untimely death in November 1991, after a brief battle with lymphatic cancer. However, the partnership in mission which the McGills had pioneered at Embangweni Hospital would be carried on by numerous PC(USA) mission co-workers in following years. Among them were Dr. and Mrs. Paul (Judy) Jewett, who had been reassigned to Malawi after serving in India. For a time, Dr. Jewett found himself the only physician on the hospital staff, though working with Malawian medical assistants and nurses. In time, reenforcements would come.

> Perhaps it is a reflection of God's sense of humor that our expatriate hospital staff is now made up of a former cardiologist (me), a very accomplished cardio-vascular surgeon who has just completed theological education at Princeton and been ordained (Dr. Don Mullen), and a family practitioner (Dr. Becky Loomis). We have been joined by a Scots nurse, Aileen Robson, and the promise of another nurse, of Irish descent, Sarah McCullough, coming in January. None of us could ever contribute what Ken and Nancy [McGill] have done . . . . But here we are, called to this time and place, and sustained by his Spirit and by your support, now shared also with the Church of Scotland and the Presbyterian Church of Ireland.[739]

In 1992, Mrs. Jewett experienced a serious medical problem which required surgery and extended hospitalization in the United States. Dr. Jewett would later comment:

> I don't need to deplore the high cost of medical care to those of you who experience it almost daily. Yet it is sobering to realize that Judy's medical costs for one illness would easily support our entire hospital budget here for a year

or more, caring for 4000 admissions a year, 500 operations, 800 deliveries, and extensive outreach community health plus three outlying primary health centers. Obviously we have evolved a health care system in the USA which has no place in most of the world, and which even we ourselves cannot afford.[740]

The problem of malnutrition became increasingly serious at Embangweni, as was true throughout Malawi, which is one of the world's ten poorest countries.

Malnutrition now replaces malaria as the most frequent admission diagnosis on our children's ward, and the leading cause of death. Children require a protein-rich diet to meet their growth needs, as we all know. If they are supplied calories with insufficient protein content, they become seriously ill . . . . It is said that 250 children out of every 1000 born to Malawian women die before those children reach five years of age. I suspect the dying fraction is even higher, based on innumerable family histories we obtain. Malnutrition is the underlying cause of most early childhood mortality in the developing world . . . .

You support mission hospitals which combat these malnutrition problems with "nutritional rehabilitation units (NRUs)," at hospitals and in outreach clinics throughout Africa . . . . Education is emphasized throughout. Lectures are given to mothers at under-fives clinics, emphasizing balanced diets from locally-available foods, improved agriculture, and child spacing. Non-governmental organizations (NGOs) contribute powerfully in support of these programs. Most notable are the United Nations World Food Programme, which supplies most of the food we use, and UNICEF, which supports the mobile clinics, training of community health workers, provides the immunization/growth charts for all the children, and even the scale to weigh them. In times of war and disaster, the United Nations High Commission on Refugees (UNHCR) provides life-giving support. But these NGOs, essential as they are, would be completely ineffective without the infrastructure we provide. Mission hospitals (and government health facilities) must provide the staff, the hospital care, and the transportation to conduct this whole program.[741]

As mission co-workers completed their terms of service, the need for replacements provided the opportunity for recruiting Malawian medical staff.

With the very effective recruiting efforts of Frank Dimmock, our mission co-worker in Mzuzu, the staffs of all our three Livingstonia Synod hospitals have been greatly strengthened with well trained Malawians. Embangweni Hospital has recruited Mr. Sanford Mbeya, a person who rose to the rank of "principal clinical superintendent" in the Malawian Ministry of Health before his recent retirement. His special interest is in obstetrics, and in surgical procedures, so his skills will greatly complement mine, which are primarily in medicine and pediatrics. He is a fine Christian (Seventh Day Adventist). Very importantly, his wife joins our hospital staff as a Senior Enrolled Nurse Midwife. Mr. Dimmock was also able to recruit a very top-flight person as our new hospital administrator, Mr. Nindi. He also just retired from Government of Malawi service, is a strong church person in the CCAP (Presbyterian), and brings along a wife who is also a Senior Enrolled Nurse Midwife! We are doubly pleased that very capable Malawian leadership, people not only skilled in their jobs but committed Christians, have chosen to come to mission hospitals and make contributions at a point in their lives when 10 or more very effective years of service can be expected.[742]

In time, a Malawian doctor would be added to the staff, Dr. Bagery Ngwira.

Dr. Bagery Ngwira's story illustrates how God works in the lives of each of us. He came to Embangweni first as a secondary school boarding student at Robert Laws Secondary School. During his time as a student he responded to the Lord's claim on his life. Then he became ill, was hospitalized at Embangweni Hospital, and decided he was being called to a career in medicine, with the desire to return and join the Embangweni Hospital staff. He was selected for training in medicine by the government of Malawi, and was sent to Great Britain for most of his training. During all these years of training he has never wavered in his desire to return to Embangweni.[743]

But the contribution of Malawian medical personnel was not limited to the highly trained. Take, for example, Mr. G. Chirwa, a Medical Assistant at Kalikumbi, where a Health Center was dedicated in November 1995.

Kalikumbi Health Center was dedicated with a huge celebration attended by all kinds of VIPs including the Minister of Health of Malawi. For the first time ever a large area of Northwestern Malawi has a trained nurse-midwife living in the community to do antenatal care and screening and deliveries—a tremendous need in a country where one out of thirty women dies of some complication of pregnancy or childbirth. Unknown to us, at the time of the dedication, the Medical Assistant (health care practitioner) at Kalikumbi had metastatic cancer. This man, Mr. G. Chirwa, was the person primarily responsible for mobilizing the community to build the new health center. He died this January, leaving behind him a legacy of health care and tireless work that has saved thousands of lives in the rural areas of Malawi, and because of the health center will save thousands more. With his encouragement the Kalikumbi people hand-molded and fired the bricks that built the health center; used their oxcarts to transport hundreds of cement tiles to make the roof; manually crushed rock to make the foundation, and helped with the actual building. Our Hospital and the community of Kalikumbi have suffered a great loss in the death of this dedicated Christian man, but he knew that he had completed a great task prior to his death and has gone to well-deserved rest and eternal reward.[744]

Yet, with the hospital and three health centers to serve, there was a continuing struggle to find adequate staff.

There simply are not enough trained health professionals in the country. The total pool of trained health workers is being depleted because of AIDS. At the same time, the need for health care because of AIDS is rapidly overwhelming such resources as are available. Every year the infection rate seems to rise. AIDS, together with its complications, has rapidly become the number one cause of illness and death among adults, and number two or three among children.[745]

Dr. Becky Loomis, a family doctor who joined the Embangweni Hospital staff in 1991 and in time would become Medical Officer in Charge, would reflect on her experience in Malawi as she approached the end of her term of service in 1998:

I am well but have been struggling with some burnout, which even chocolate chip cookies can't cure. However, I think I have found the cure—as of February 1, I handed over the Medical Officer In Charge job to Dr. Casimo Storniolo (energetic, enthusiastic, sense of humor still intact) and noticed I felt better immediately. Hearing about the struggles of so many medical personnel in other countries at [a Christian Medical and Dental Society Conference in Kenya], I was reminded of how relatively simple it is to work in Malawi. Some physicians have been repeatedly evacuated from dangerous places; others work in countries where they are not allowed to speak about Christianity; still others deal with corruption involving their own hospital staff or their own church ministers. I am reminded again of why Malawi is called "Africa for beginners," and reflect with chagrin on my ability to be incredibly comforted by the problems of others.[746]

While the Embangweni Hospital would be the focus of American Presbyterian involvement in Livingstonia Synod, mission co-workers would also be serving at the Robert Laws Secondary School in Embangweni and at the Ekwendeni Hospital. An especially significant work was being done by mission co-workers Frank and Nancy Dimmock, who were assigned to Livingstonia Synod in Malawi in 1992 after having served for six years in Lesotho.

> We have received our new assignment and we are so excited! The Presbyterian
> Church of Malawi has asked for someone to assess, develop and coordinate
> primary health care in their northern synod. The Church manages three hospitals
> in the area and the work will be developed out of those centers.[747]

> In PHC (Primary Health Care), Frank has been integrating village-based,
> income-generating activities and food security programs into child survival
> initiatives aimed at reducing malnutrition and infant mortality. He has been
> appointed to the CHAM (Christian Medical Association of Malawi) committees
> on PHC and planning, and on a national task force on orphans.[748]

In a conference between visiting PC(USA) staff persons and Dr. Mazunda, General
Secretary of Livingstonia Synod, "they concurred on the need for an evaluation of the
medical work of this Synod, and Frank was asked to conduct the evaluation and present
recommendations to a consultation of partner churches to be held in October/November."[749]
By December, 1993, the Dimmocks would report: "Frank completed the evaluation of
the Synod's health work and presented his report to a consultation of partner churches
in early November. As a result, he has been named Interim Medical Coordinator of the
Synod and has has been given the task of trying to implement the recommendations of
the consultation! His work is cut out for him for the next few years!"[750]

In his capacity as Interim Medical Coordinator for the Synod, Frank Dimmock
processed applications for job openings in the Synod's health programs. Through this
work, it was possible to staff the five CCAP hospitals with competent administrators,
clinical officers and primary health care people, as well as bringing about coordination
of the medical work of the various hospitals, health care centers and outpost clinics.

During the Dimmocks' furlough year in the United States, Frank completed course
work on a doctorate in public health at Tulane University, and upon their return to Malawi
in 1997 was given the responsibility of regional health consultant to PC(USA) partner
churches in seven countries of eastern and southern Africa, in addition to continuing to
serve the five hospitals in Malawi. While Frank was working in and out of Malawi, Nancy
Dimmock was devoting her time to ministry with the hundreds of orphans who filled the
streets of Malawi's cities—even adopting two of them into their own family.

Still other mission co-workers were serving in distinctive roles in Livingstonia
Synod. Mission Specialist Rev. Deborah Ann Chase served as clergy advisor to the synod
on women's issues. Out of her experience in Malawi, she would write about the wider
responsibility of American Christians to affect U.S. public policy:

> We must not close our eyes to the suffering of our brothers and sisters in Christ.
> Malawi's currency, the *kwacha*, has been devalued by 70 percent over the past
> two years. Only 57 percent of the people have access to clean drinking water.
> AIDS, malaria, cholera, and malnutrition daily take the lives of young and old
> alike. Desperately needed national debt relief from the global community seems

only a glimmer of hope on a distant horizon. As U.S. citizens and as members of the body of Christ, we must use our power to move our government and the multinational corporations to cancel Malawi's international debt. We will never be genuine partners with our friends in Malawi until we are willing to do our part to redistribute the wealth so that they may share in the abundance that God intends for all God's children.[751]

In **Nkhoma Synod** in central Malawi, a unique mission partnership was undertaken in the capital city Lilongwe. Following the end of President Banda's despotic rule, mission specialist Jim Cairns was assigned to work with the Public Affairs Committee (PAC) composed of Malawi church leaders, Moslem leaders, Law Society and members of the Alliance for Democracy.

PAC has firmly re-established itself as a major voice in public life here, perhaps most importantly through a statement we issued in the aftermath of civil service strikes in which we raised serious questions about the government's accountablility toward its citizens. We also held a series of roundtable forums in September that brought together politicians from all parties and other government officials at a regional level to discuss tolerance, reconciliation, accountability and transparency—the foundation of open, democratic government. These meetings offered a rare opportunity for opposing sides to speak honestly, but respectfully, with one another about the direction of the nation.

One of the deep-seated effects of thirty years of a very paternalistic, one-sided party state is an attitude of dependency and passivity. Perhaps our greatest challenge in civic education is to convince people that they have the right and the power to organize themselves and take control over their own lives. Citizens have claimed fully their right to speak openly, but need to gain confidence that they can act as well.[752]

PC(USA) mission co-workers in **Blantyre Synod** in southern Malawi have fulfilled a wide variety of functions. Veteran missionaries Wilma and Otis Rowe had served in Egypt and Cameroon before being assigned to Malawi in 1979. While living in the city of Blantyre, the Rowes carried out a distinctive work by serving mission hospitals throughout Malawi through planning, ordering, installing, maintaining and repairing the many types of hospital equipment. Writing from Embangweni in northern Malawi, the Rowes stated:

Two weeks and nine hospitals into a long work tour, the roads are "interesting" for this is the heart of rainy season. But after Cameroun, we never complain about Malawi's roads! Missions do at least 40% of the medical work in Malawi.

This particular trek's purpose, besides the usual repairs to generator engines, pumps, surgery lights, vacuum machines, refrigerators, etc., etc., is to service the oxygen concentrators, those life-saving devices given to all the hospitals by Denmark last year; and to check on solar electrical installations already done, and plan for some new ones.[753]

Mrs. Rowe made her special mission objective working with Social Clubs for the Disabled.

One of our hopes is to get Malawian women involved in this work on a continuing basis, as volunteers, so that it will survive after the foreign volunteers leave. One noteworthy success that we're thrilled about: Mabel Nkhoma is a young mother who grew up in a family with a polio-disabled sister. For the ten years the clubs have been going, Mabel has been a faithful, regular volunteer at the Chilomoni Club. Now, besides that, she has quietly started a small club for disabled persons in her neighborhood who cannot get to the Chilomoni one. With the meagerest of resources and no adequate place to meet, she does what she can for them, with love and respect.[754]

Also working out of the city of Blantyre but serving a regional ministry were Doug and Ruth Welch. The Welches came to Malawi in 1989 after serving in Zaire/Congo. While Ruth taught high school biology at the Henry Henderson Institute, Doug served as a consultant for the PC(USA) Presbyterian Hunger Program and the Self-Development of People Program in southern Africa. His travels took him to Mombasa, Kenya, to assist a group of women who were starting their own business of sewing and handcrafts; to Swaziland to work with local farmers as they expanded their agricultural production; to Chokwe, Mozambique, to assist displaced Presbyterian Church communities in starting a gardening and small animal husbandry program; to Bikita, Zimbabwe, where an indigenous church group sought help in developing an adequate water source in order to attain self-sufficiency through gardening.

I know that I personally have gained as I have traveled most of the southern Africa region. During these travels I have met so many people in so many different circumstances. I have interacted with church leaders and felt some of the vision which they have for their churches and their countries. I have visited in some very remote areas witnessing the struggles of the people and being with them as they work through the solutions to those struggles. I have been warmly welcomed in all situations and have been given the most gracious hospitality, a real outpouring of Christian spirit and African friendliness. For all these experiences I give thanks to God.[755]

Upon their return to Malawi after home assignment, Doug was invited to be the first Coordinator of a newly formed Projects Office for Blantyre Synod.

> Blantyre Synod has been involved in activities concerning the physical needs of people since the beginning of the mission work in the late 1800's. Over the years the specific types of activities have changed but the spirit has remained the same, to seek to preach the GOOD NEWS as it relates to both the spiritual and physical needs of the people it serves. People are the main focus of our attention in the Projects Office. "Development" to us means that process of change which people go through allowing them to become self sufficient. Our work has to do with sharing with others about their God given talents and encouraging them to use them to make the desired changes in their lives. We desire to be Christlike in our programs and our approach.[756]

Among the programs developed under Doug's leadership were the Child Survival Program, raising community awareness of the plight of the thousands of orphans that filled the streets of Malawi's cities and developing ways of ministering to them; the Functional Literacy Program which served adults who were unable to attend school as children, with over 30 centers of around 25 adults each; the 250-acre Naming'azi Demonstration Farm Training Center, an outreach program to subsistence farmers to move them from survival to sufficiency; relief programs following severe droughts that plagued southern Africa during the 1990s. When the Welches were preparing to leave Malawi in 1998 to serve on the staff of the PC(USA) Worldwide Ministries Division, they would write:

> Inner transformation of the individual is the first and foremost step for effective development to happen. In fact, that transformation is development. Thinking past oneself into the wider community provides a basis for people working together to make changes in their communities and their nation.[757]

Other American Presbyterian mission co-workers have been involved in a variety of services in Blantyre Synod: Robert and Edith Rasmussen as Associate Pastor at two of Blantyre's larger churches, St. Michael's and All Angels; Dorothy Crowell in primary health care, helping to establish a health care center at the remote Domasi Mission. Of particular significance has been the work at Zomba Theological College, which is the primary theological institution preparing ministers and evangelists for the rapidly-growing Church of Central Africa Presbyterian (CCAP). Among the mission co-workers serving there has been the Rev. Joseph M. Hopkins, who served as "seminary librarian, tutor (three courses), preacher (often two sermons per Sunday), pastor (hospital visits and funerals), and taxi driver (hauling everything from people and their parcels to sacks of maize and cement)."[758]

A distinctive contribution has been made by another missionary couple at Zomba Theological College, Dr. Joseph and Mrs. Hannah Kang. Dr. Kang explains:

> . . . the college is an ecumenical school. In addition to the students from five CCAP Synods (Blantyre, Nkhoma, and Livingstonia of Malawi, Harare of Zimbabwe, and Lusaka of Zambia), there are also students from the Diocese of Southern Malawi of the Anglican Church, and the Churches of Christ. For the new academic year we have received fifteen more students, and now I am teaching all the New Testament courses, including two extra Greek courses. I'm also teaching at the Department of Religious Studies of the University of Malawi. They launched a Bachelor's degree in Theology program this year in order to enhance the level of theological education in this country . . . . Hannah continues working both at the college library and the wives' school. Many in this community are marveling with joy at seeing the remarkable change of the library's system by her touch and care. We are very grateful for the fact that she had the experience of working at the San Francisco Theological Seminary library while I was studying there.[759]

With Joseph Hopkins' retirement, Dr. Kang was appointed as the new librarian.

> On much of the work I simply depend on Hannah and student librarians. Some contributions for expansion of the library came from Canada, Ireland and Holland. Although the projected amount of money is not secured, we decided to begin construction . . . . We pray that this $80,000 project will be finished without further delay to solve our current space problem.[760]

> With financial contributions made by partner churches our library extension is now under construction. Upon its completion ina few months we will be able to have ample space for books and reading. Right now, each day of the week is assigned for different classes because of limited space. Behind the library wings (right and left) we are building a multi-purpose hall, which will be used as a chapel as well as conference room.[761]

> The library extension of ZTC is at its final stage. We are going to have the dedication service before this year's graduation (July 1). Then we will have sufficient reading space for all of the students, along with a spacious multi-purpose hall which will be used as the chapel as well . . . . Promotion of academic standards and the increase in the number of students are the next projects for this college. The shortage of ministers is a pressing issue here and it is quite urgent that we expand the theological training institute. Your continuous prayers and support will help us accomplish all of these new projects.[762]

The extended library wings of ZTC were dedicated this past July 1 right after the commencement exercises when most of the board members were present. It was exciting especially for both of us to see it complete, not only because we are working for the library, but also because many of you had participated in this project financially. Our next project is to increase the number of students for theological training up to 200 by year 2000, and building a hostel and a dining hall and increasing the number of lecturers.[763]

During the year following the library's dedication, the ZTC principal, the Rev. Dr. H. Kamnkhawani, suffered a stroke and the ZTC board appointed Dr. Kang as the administrative caretaker. As the principal's condition deteriorated and he passed away, Dr. Kang was appointed interim principal with full responsibility for the adminstration of the College, a position which he would hold for the next two years. His tenure would bring numerous additional improvements in the College's facilities, as well as a significant increase in the student body. Also, a Continuing Education Program was developed for ordained ministers and church workers.

It was a highly demanding program, and was the first one in 19 years at the college. We were blessed to have Bruce and Ollie Gannaway here especially for the program. They made a great contribution to this new ministry, and our Malawian friends were so happy to see them in the classroom. We are very sure that they will be again remembered with many sweet memories by their friends in this country.[764]

During his tenure as Interim Principal, Dr. Kang became increasingly aware of the critical need for trained ministers to serve the CCAP churches:

According to reports I received from graduates of this college, one minister is serving an average of three congregations in Malawi. The size of each congregation is over 300 members. The situation is worse with CCAP and the Anglican Church in Zambia, which send students to our college for theological training. Churches are growing very rapidly in this country. This means that a lot more ministers should be produced by the college. It is therefore urgent for the college to expand both its programs and its facilities.[765]

I want to share with you the fact that in this country there are many young people who are eager for theological training to serve their growing churches. This year we allocated only four new students to each major Synod due to the limited housing. In Livingstonia Synod there were more than thirty applicants for the college, and they were pleading for more allocation. We ended up with seven new students from that particular Synod. It is really exciting to see that more younger students are coming to the college. Not only can they serve their church longer, but their academic performance will also be better.[766]

In addition to his teaching and administrative responsibilities, Dr. Kang took the lead in establishing a mission partnership between CCAP and the Presbyterian Church in the Republic of Korea.

> [Joseph] accompanied three Malawi church leaders to Korea in early September to attend the General Assembly meeting of the Presbyterian Church in the Republic of Korea. The Churches of Central Africa Presbyterian and the PROK have established a Mission Partnership relationship. During this visit of Malawi church leaders to Korea several mission projects, which would consolidate and strengthen this new relationship, were identified, and each side agreed to work together very closely, and to cooperate with each other for a fruitful relationship.[767]

Truly, the seven-year ministry of the Kangs in Malawi provides ample evidence of the truth of Jesus' words, "Well done, good and faithful servant; you have been faithful over a few things; I will put you in charge of many things." (Matthew 25:21)

The American Presbyterian partnership with the Presbyterian community in Malawi was a cause of continuing wonder and gratitude on the part of Malawian Christian leaders.

> I keep on wondering as to how Embangweni Station, a place so tiny and so remote, keeps on receiving such a large number of international visitors as contained in our visitors' book. It keeps me still wondering to note that most of our visitors travel all the way from the U.S.A. We are frequently visited by people from such states as Texas, California, Illinois, Indiana, Tennessee, Pennsylvania, New York, and Georgia just to mention a few.
>
> What is it that keeps these nice people flocking to Malawi in general and to Embangweni Station in particular? I think the most important reason behind their sacrifical visits to this part of the world is their belief "in the fellowship of all Christian believers." The Church to them is not fragmented by geographical, social, economic, or any other form of boundary. So, they come in order to make intercessory prayer concrete. For surely, when they leave, both visitors and hosts can better pray not only for each other but each other's Church as well. You are most welcome to our part of the world.—(Rev.) Lloyd Andrew Tembo, Head of Station—Embangweni, Malawi.[768]

PARTNERSHIP IN MISSION IN LESOTHO

The small, mountainous, landlocked country Lesotho is completely surrounded by the Republic of South Africa. This fact has had great influence on the country, both economically and politically. Since only about ten percent of its land is arable, it is extremely difficult for the country to feed its population and most of its food is imported from outside the country, through South Africa. Until very recently, thirty-eight percent of its men worked in South Africa, mostly in the mines, leaving women, children and the elderly to fend for themselves during a large part of the year.[769] The raising of sheep, goats, and cattle is the common occupation of those who remain at home. The political unrest in South Africa led to large numbers of refugees from that country seeking refuge in Lesotho, creating a heavy burden for both government and church. Known as one of the least developed and yet most highly educated countries of Sub-Saharan Africa, its major resources have been listed as "people, water, and scenery." In fact, one of its most profitable businesses is the Highlands Water Scheme for selling water to South Africa.

Since the 18th century, the area now known as Lesotho has been inhabited by the Sotho people, whose land was known as Basutoland. For protection against surrounding tribes, the Sotho king Moshoeshoe I sought the protection of Great Britain, and for almost a century, beginning in 1868, Lesotho was a kingdom under a British protectorate. It achieved independence in 1966. Since that time, it has experienced many changes in government. The first 20 years after independence were under the leadership of the prime minister elected at the time of independence, Chief Joseph Leabua Jonathan, a Roman Catholic and the leader of the Basutoland National Party (BNP).

However, in 1970, after the opposition Basotho Congress Party (BCP), predominantly Protestant, won a national election, Prime Minister Jonathan declared a state of emergency, nullified the elections, suspended the constitution, and undertook to govern the country by decree. The ensuing years were filled with political strife, imprisonment and execution of opponents, and pillaging of their villages. In 1986, Jonathan was overthrown by a military coup. Finally in 1993, after some 23 years of autocratic government, coups, sanctioned violence and neglect of basic human rights, elections were held in which the BCP won every seat and a new government and National Assembly were put in place. However, 18 months after free and fair elections took place, in August 1994, the Basotho king Letsie III announced that he was amending the constitution and dissolving the government, including the democratically elected parliament. The churches were the first to sound the alarm to the international community. This resulted in a tidal wave of protests. Finally, President Mugabe of Zimbabwe and President Mandela of South Africa interceded and the king backed down.[770]

Peace prevailed until 1998, when a multiparty election led to a power struggle. Members of the army joined the protestors, and troops from the Southern Africa Development Community (SADC) intervened to prevent a coup. As many Basotho people viewed the intervention as an invasion, rioting and looting swept the country, "turning three major towns into burned out skeletons."[771]. Finally the opposing parties worked out an agreement for new elections to be held within the next two years.

Within this tiny troubled nation of some two million people, approximately 90 percent claim Christianity as their faith, with the remaining ten percent continuing to practice traditional religions. The Lesotho Evangelical Church (LEC), which is the partner church of the Presbyterian Church (USA), is the oldest Christian denomination in the country, tracing its history to the arrival of Paris Missionary Society workers from the French

Huguenot Reformed Church in 1833. With a membership claiming approximately one quarter of the country's population, the LEC has been autonomous since 1964. It has a large commitment in the educational field, at both primary and secondary levels as well as in the area of teacher training. The church is strongly ecumenical, with membership in the Christian Council of Lesotho, the All Africa Conference of Churches, the World Council of Churches and the World Alliance of Reformed Churches. Through LEC's intiative, the Christian Council of Lesotho has developed the Thaba Khupa Ecumenical Farm Training Center, teaching students from across southern Africa appropriate farming techniques. During the years of political unrest, the Christian Council played a major role in assisting families affected by the political oppression.

The Catholic Church in Lesotho traces its origins to the arrival of French priests in 1862. With a membership of approximately one half the total population, the Catholic Church has had a strong influence on the political life of the country. During the political crisis of 1970, Prime Minister Jonathan, a Roman Catholic, ordered the imprisonment of opposition leaders, many of whom were members of the Lesotho Evangelical Church. However, in 1972, the Catholic Church itself joined the Christian Council of Lesotho, and in 1973, the Lesotho Ecumenical Association (with Catholic, Protestant and Anglican membership) launched an appeal for reconciliation between government and the opposition party. Although 17 members of the opposition Basotho Congress Party were convicted, the sentences were lighter than expected, giving hope that the Catholic/Protestant conflict underlying the political situation might be healed.[772]

American Presbyterian partnership in mission in Lesotho began in 1976, as PCUS missionaries David and Polly Miller were assigned to work with the Lesotho Evangelical Church, after having served for 23 years in Zaire/Congo. Their presence brought reassurance to the LEC leadership in a time of political repression and uncertainty, and provided an avenue for interpreting developments in Lesotho to the U.S. government and churches.[773] As the first American Presbyterian missionaries serving in southern Africa, they were profoundly available for service both in Lesotho and in neighboring nations of southern Africa. The 1977 Birthday Offering of the PCUS Women of the Church had been designated for "Evangelism in Southern Africa", providing the Millers with resources to assist Presbyterian-related churches throughout the region. Also, the Project of Evangelism and Church Growth in Africa, which had been initiated in Zaire/Congo, now would be implemented in southern Africa as well.

A focus of American Presbyterian involvement in Lesotho was Scott Hospital in Morija. First to serve there were Frank and Nancy Dimmock (1985-1991). With a speciality in Primary Health Care, Frank not only enabled the hospital to increase its outreach, but also worked on behalf of the Mission Hospital Association.

> Frank has been on a negotiations committee in which the Mission Hospitals'
> Association has been seeking more funding assistance from the government.
> (Many of the mission hospitals are on the verge of closing down due to severe
> financial problems.) After three years of intensive negotiations, there seems

to have been a breakthrough. They are considering paying the salaries of all health personnel regardless of whether they work for the government hospitals or mission hospitals. Pray with us that the Lesotho government will, in fact, do this. It will make all the difference in continued health coverage throughout the country, and will be cheaper, in the long run, than having to "pick up the pieces" after hospitals begin to close.[774]

Another priority for Frank was an infant mortality study for the entire country, to see what impact various health interventions, such as the national immunization program and community health care programs, had on early childhood mortality. While the Dimmocks would move on to Malawi in 1992, the impact of their work would continue to be felt in overall health care in Lesotho.

Another focus for American Presbyterian involvement in Lesotho has been the Morija Theological Seminary. After their effective service in Cameroon, Paul and Ellinor Frelick resumed their service in mission at the LEC Seminary in 1996.

> Morija, the village where we are now installed, serves as the dynamic center for the Lesotho Evangelical (Reformed) Church, our partner church, with a small headquarters building, an education office for over 450 schools nationwide, a book depot (bindery) and bookstore, an impressive printing establishment used by a variety of organizations, public and private, and five church-run schools. The famous national museum with archives is located here and on a hill off to one side, one of 13 national hospital establishments (2 managed by the church), a youth and ecumenical conference center, not to mention the seminary itself. [775]

The Frelicks continued the roles which they had fulfilled so effectively in Cameroon, "Ellenor seeking to build from a good basic library an expanded and updated collection in view of present and future generations of pastors and evangelists; Paul doing his thing in the classroom, small groups of students eager to prepare themselves for their ministries."[776] In addition to their regular work on the seminary campus, the Frelicks were called upon for a number of special tasks: the inauguration of the LEC's first refresher course for pastors, "two weeks of joyous coming together from mountain isolation to share experiences, explore new ideas and mine the riches of Morija seminary library full of books—a rare treasure trove for these pastors."[777]; a return visit to the Protestant Theological Faculty in Yaounde, Cameroon, where they had served for six years; and a visit to Madagascar to conduct library and theological workshops.

Out of their years of experience in mission in Africa, the Frelicks gained valuable insights into the situation prevailing in post-independence Africa:

> We wrestle with issues, both economic and cultural, which also impinge on present lifestyles in a larger Africa where so much need exists. A recent *Weekly*

Guardian article suggests that though Africa looks like "bleak house" to many, there are yet signs of hope. Though colonialism left its terrible legacy, and most present leaders fail any test of leadership in designing or pursuing visions of a noble future, a new generation is coming. If indeed they can believe in, pursue, and struggle for an agenda of progressive change, then we may see new signs for a positive future.

Let us pray and work for such transformation and become partners of a new Africa, asking our governments to bring to the winds of change fresh breaths of economic and political policy. We need not look only to Africa, but also to ourselves to nurture and support such change, which we have not done effectively to the present. Our myopic vision has not reached beyond our own boundaries to the larger world in which what happens in one place touches us all, for we have let our governments support the most monstrous and demonic African leaders. We must be compassionate for the present suffering poor while working to change the social, economic, and political powers that maintain and engender poverty . . . . Ours is a long-term witness to the fact that God's Kingdom does not come overnight but rather by day-to-day combat with the powers of oppression in our midst.[778]

PARTNERSHIP IN MISSION IN MOZAMBIQUE

In the 1993 Human Suffering Index produced by the Population Crisis Committee, Mozambique had the distinction of having the highest degree of suffering in the world. Only now is Mozambique beginning to recover from thirty years of war (fourteen of a war for independence and sixteen of civil war), followed by eight years of peace but overwhelming natural disasters.

Situated on the southeast coast of Africa, Mozambique is bisected from east to west by the Zambezi River. South of the Zambezi lies a semiarid savanna lowland. The north-central delta provinces are the most fertile and it is here that the bulk of Mozambique's racially mixed population lives. From the early 17th century, Portugal had occupied a wide swath of land from the Mozambican coast to the northern half of present-day Zimbabwe. Portugal maintained control of the region by ceding land grants to European colonists. This made their owners virtual lords of African fiefdoms, with nearly complete control over Mozambique labor and resources. Portugal controlled a prosperous trade in ivory and slaves. Under pressure from Great Britain, Portugal outlawed the slave trade in 1842, finally abolishing slavery altogether in 1878. In 1890, with the control of East Africa still unresolved, Britain threatened war against Portugal if its border demands were not met. Portugal conceded to most of Britain's demands, and in 1891 the frontiers of modern Mozambique were drawn. Portugal was left in control of the 1500-mile coastline with its numerous ports and trade stations, as well as the lowlands between the coast and the eastern highlands bordering Lake Malawi.

In the early 20th century, Portugal continued to allow private concession companies broad control of the colony. African workers were often forced to labor under brutal conditions, with extremely low (and sometimes no) wages, and with few political rights. In the south companies were given the right to recruit people and send them to work in the diamond and gold mines in South Africa. In 1932, Antonio de Oliveira Salazar began a long dictatorship of Portugal, and under his influence the Portuguese government established direct rule over Mozambique. Salazar ended the power of the private companies and in their place established a planned economy, by which Portugal controlled every aspect of the economy. Mozambican farmers were forced to grow crops such as cotton and rice for export, and very little consideration was given to the crops needed for subsistence. White settlement was encouraged, and the number of white settlers in the country grew from a few tens of thousands to nearly 200,000 by 1970.

Meanwhile, in 1962 a group of exiled Mozambicans led by Eduardo Mondlane met in Tanzania and formed the Front for the Liberation of Mozambique (FRELIMO). When FRELIMO launched a guerrilla war against Portuguese control of Mozambique, the Portuguese government, seeking to pacify the people, launched a major development program, building roads, schools and hospitals. Nevertheless, war with FRELIMO continued, even after Mondlane was assassinated in 1969. Only after Portugal underwent a revolution in 1974 did the colonial regime in Mozambique begin to crumble, and in July 1975 power was formally transferred to FRELIMO, and Mozambique became independent.

FRELIMO introduced a Marxist constitution that brought the economy under the control of the state. It supported the liberation movements in Southern Rhodesia and South Africa. In return, Southern Rhodesia and South Africa sponsored an anti-communist guerrilla movement in Mozambique, known as the Mozambique National Resistance (RENAMO). Many of RENAMO's forces were recruited at gunpoint, including young teenage children. Beginning in 1980 RENAMO targeted and destroyed government installations, industries, schools, and infrastructure. Within a short time the FRELIMO government controlled only a few cities, while RENAMO through terror tactics gained control over much of the country.

The sixteen years of civil war that ensued produced two million displaced persons within Mozambique and over one million refugees fleeing to neighboring countries. The death toll from the war exceeded six hundred thousand, including one hundred thousand defenseless civilians killed by RENAMO.[779] There was large-scale destruction of crops and collapse of the country's infrastructure. Several droughts also plagued the country during this period, adding to the miseries of war. Finally, in 1990 the government adopted a new constitution that disavowed Marxism, and in 1992 FRELIMO and RENAMO signed an accord that ended the civil war. In a multiparty election in 1994, FRELIMO won by a narrow margin, and Joaquim Chissano was elected president. Since 1994 the government has tried to rebuild the ravaged economy with the help of foreign aid. As refugees have returned to their homes and attempted to begin life anew, Mozambique remains among the poorest nations in the world.

Among Mozambique's estimated 19 million people, some 40% are Christian. The vast majority of these are part of the Roman Catholic Church, which traces its origins back to the arrival of Portuguese missionaries in the 16th century. In general, the Mozambican Catholic Church bears the marks of the church in Portugal, and until Mozambique gained its independence, the local Catholic hierarchy closely identified the interest of the church with those of the Portuguese state, sanctioning the colonial status quo and remaining silent in the face of injustices perpetrated in the name of "defense of Christian civilization." Only after Mozambique gained its independence in 1975 did the Catholic Church make an effort to adjust to the new situation.

The Protestant churches had been much more independent than the Catholic Church with respect to the colonial administration, without serving as any real or effective opposition. However, the Protestant emphasis on education served to train an African elite, thus indirectly promoting the idea of national emancipation. This explains the attachment of large numbers of Protestants to the liberation movement, as well as the repression and persecution which many of these churches and their leaders suffered prior to independence. Following independence, Mozambique's President Samora Machel declared that there would be no special privileges for any churches. A major move to reduce the influence of the churches was the nationalization of all educational, medical and social institutions. However, following the end of the civil war in 1992, the government asked churches to again participate in reconstruction of these institutions, as well as undertaking various aspects of social and development work.

The partner church of PC(USA) is the *Igreja Presbiteriana de Mocambique* (IPM), which traces its roots back to 1881 and the work of the Swiss Mission. Its churches originally were concentrated in the northwest, especially among the Tsonga and Shangaan peoples. However, in the years since the end of the civil war, IPM has expanded until there are congregations in all ten provinces of the country. PC(USA) has supported agricultural development projects to assist in the recovery of families devastated by war and drought. Assistance has also been given to the United Seminary at Ricatla in the form of building repairs and an occasional faculty member. New churches have been erected with the assistance of the Project for Evangelism and Church Growth in Africa. The largest concentration of unreached peoples in Africa, south of the equator, is located in Mozambique. With the assistance of the Presbyterian Frontier Fellowship and the Outreach Foundation, the gospel has continued to spread through the witness of many courageous Mozambicans.

Among the missionary personnel serving in Mozambique in recent years has been a courageous woman minister, the Rev. Ruth Minter. Actually she served as an "ecumenical appointment", supported by the Christian Church (Disciples of Christ) and the United Church of Christ, as well as the PC(USA). Her responsibilities were two-fold: serving as a Prrofessor of Ethics at the Ricatla United Seminary and as pastor of a local congregation. In 1991, while the country was still embroiled in civil war, Ms. Minter would write:

> Mozambique continues to be a country desperately in search of peace. For
> nearly ten years, RENAMO has disrupted the countryside. There is no family

untouched. Gaza Province, where Presbyterians have been strong, is one of the areas that has especially felt the effect of both war and drought in the past year. Families, churches, communities find themselves torn apart and scattered. "Dislocated" people crowd all the towns and cities. They are no longer in the countryside doing subsistence farming to feed their families—or to provide produce to feed the towns. Some have made their way to crowded centers where one of the over 100 non-governmental organizations in the country tries to feed, house and otherwise care for their needs. Others become additional members of already crowded households in towns or live on the street or in whatever rudimentary shelter they can. Partly because of the huge influx, even this capital city of Maputo finds itself short of food, short of buses, short of adequate water and sewer services, short of waste disposal services, and health and educational facilities struggle to keep up . . . . Some say Mozambique is the poorest country in the world now although I cannot verify that. But I do know that hunger and poverty are the rule even outside the war-weary rural zones. Please continue to support special offerings that can help ease the sorrow and death here.[780]

In the midst of the devastation brought about by thirty years of war, signs of hope would emerge through the work of the churches. In 1991, David and Polly Miller would write:

During these months, Dave was continuing his visits to the churches in Southern African countries on behalf of the PC(USA) project of Evangelism/ Church Growth/Theological Education. It is amazing how God is blessing the churches by your sharing with them through this project of our church. In Tete, Mozambique, in the middle of a huge suburb of mud and stick houses, caused by people running from the war, a new chapel is going up. The Christians make the brick, the project helps with cement and roofing.[781]

In 1993, the Millers would write:

After almost twenty years of war, how exciting and joyous to celebrate PEACE! Because of civil war in their country, the women of the Presbyterian Church of Mozambique had not been able to come together in a church-wide conference in many years. Recently, in Maputo, the capital city, the women came together to celebrate their 65th Anniversary! The theme of the conference was "ARISE, SHINE!"—that the glory may be His as we follow Him in these days of rebuilding! It was a wonderful time together in the Lord—a joyous time of song, speech and dance! Polly had been invited to attend, so brought greetings and a gift from the Presbyterian women of our own PC(USA). There were representatives from many churches and church councils in Africa and

Europe—over 500 in attendance and over 2,000 attending the closing service on Sunday.[782]

As Bill and Nancy Warlick succeeded the Millers as PC(USA) liaison mission co-workers in Southern Africa, they would report on numerous joyful and exciting events in the dedication of newly completed Presbyterian Church buildings in the Zobue area of Mozambique.

> On December 8, we were present at the four-hour, joyous dedication service of the Tchessa church sanctuary in Northern Mozambique. What a festive celebration! Seven choirs came from all over the area to sing and dance and to praise the Lord for what had been accomplished. The young governor of Tate province came with his wife and stayed for hours, thanking the Presbyterians for what they have done and are doing in the area. Dr. S. Chamango, General Secretary of the Presbyterian Church of Mozambique (IPM), drove for two days from Maputo with his wife and several church officials to attend the dedication and cut the ribbon to "officially" open the doors of the new church building. During the ceremony, Bill was asked to speak and to place on the wall words of appreciation and thanksgiving to God and to the PC(USA) for participation and support of this new church development.

The price paid by Mozambican Christians for their witness in the midst of sorrow and suffering was embodied in the story of one church leader:

> Few Mozambicans have suffered like Elder Yeretsani Kamangeni and his wife, who buried ten of their thirteen children between 1974 and 1995. Their family has been forced twice to flee their home and live in a refugee camp in nearby Malawi. Yet the elder is a radiant Christian. He has been instrumential in the rapid church growth that is taking place in the Zobue area. He is a very strong, joyful, and dedicated Presbyterian lay evangelist, living and working in the Ximpacho community. He helped and encouraged the people to build a permanent church sanctuary, which was dedicated on December 9. He is a modern-day Job.[783]

The spirit of the new Mozambique is well expressed in the words of the Rev. Amos Baltazar Zitha, President, Synodical Council, Presbyterian Church of Mozambique:

> For the second time in more than 14 years, the whole country celebrated Christmas in peace. It means a lot for a population where five out of eight families experienced the sadness of murder by war! We are leaving bad times behind and trying to build a new nation where harmony, tolerance, reconciliation, brotherhood, solidarity begin to have a place among all people.[784]

CONCLUSION

ANTICIPATING A NEW ERA

Standing on the threshold of the twenty-first century and looking back over the past two centuries, one cannot but marvel at the progress of the Christian movement in sub-Saharan Africa as well as the involvement of American Presbyterians in that movement. That involvement has been spearheaded by a noble army of witnesses, serving "in places and circumstances that fill us with wonder, awe, admiration, and inspiration."[785] They have served as pioneer evangelists in a then unknown continent; church organizers and builders; educators establishing institutions that would train future leaders; doctors and medical workers that would meet overwhelming health needs and establish hospitals and health systems that would pioneer the introduction of modern medicine; advocates for social justice that would speak to the principalities and powers on behalf of oppressed people; mediators in the relationships of church and government, as well as between rival factions within church and society; and the list could go on and on. True, they have been children of their age, sometimes revealing the limited vision of their times or even standing in the way of needed change. Yet all have been motivated by the message and spirit of Christ, and their very presence has communicated the steadfast love that motivated them to undertake such a mission.

Equally marvelous to behold is the emerging of such a remarkable Christian community within virtually every nation of sub-Saharan Africa, beginning with the members of local congregations and continuing through dedicated evangelists, pastors and lay leaders, to outstanding national leaders in church and society. For them the cost of discipleship often has been sacrifice, suffering and even death. Yet the sheer joy of their faith has set an example that humbles those of us from traditional Christian nations.

Along with this marveling at what God has wrought through the lives of individual Christians, we must also recognize the critical role of the church in our own nation, especially through its changing structures for mission. At times it has been the innovator, sending its representatives out in faith to places unknown, in the confidence that eventually the seed of the Gospel would bear fruit; initiating programs which had not previously been envisioned to meet particular needs. At other times it has been the encourager, standing behind its emissaries to give them advice and guidance in critical questions related to the national church. At times, it has sounded the call for justice, especially in its pronouncements against racial injustice and prejudice. Unfortunately, there have also been times when decisions, made without adequate understanding of the particular situation, have hindered rather than helped the advance of the church and the Christian movement. Yet in and through it all, American Presbyterians have remained faithful in their commitment to and support of the Christian mission in Africa.

The Christian movement in sub-Saharan Africa now stands on the threshold of the twenty-first century with tremendous hope as well as desperate need. In 1996 of the 600 million people in sub-Saharan Africa, roughly 60 percent claim the name Christian. They are organized in churches and ecumenical organizations that have a profound influence upon the life of their nations and the continent as a whole. The ecclesiastical, educational and medical institutions which had been initiated by missions are now under the governance of national churches, with leaders who for the most part reveal amazing competence in the face of overwhelming odds.

The human needs confronting the Christian movement are all too evident. Thirty-seven of sub-Saharan Africa's 48 countries are considered low income by the World Bank (an income of less than one dollar a day per person). One of every two children in sub-Saharan Africa is not in school. The total international debt for sub-Saharan Africa was $222 billion in 1998, or $370 for each man, woman, and child. The hunger and disease that rack the continent are all too evident in the account which has been given.

Wars continue to plague parts of Africa. As war broke out in the Democratic Republic of Congo in late 1998, many of the countries experiencing some degree of improvement found themselves embroiled in conflict both within their own borders and with other Africa countries. Troops from Angola, Chad, Namibia, Rwanda, Sudan, Uganda, and Zimbabwe have all been engaged in the war in Congo, leading some analysts to speak of Africa War I. The war in Sudan has continued with human casualties in enormous proportions. War continues between Ethiopia and Eritrea. There are some ten million refugees scattered across sub-Saharan Africa, with the largest camps holding 500,000 refugees. Up to six thousand refugees die each day from cholera and other public health diseases.

And yet, African leaders are now heralding the birth of an "African Renaissance", "a rebirth and renewal that is reshaping not only African societies but also Africa's relations with the rest of the world." There is a "positive wave of change rolling across the African continent, change that is marked by political and economic renewal and is setting the stage for the integration of Africa into the world economy and for new and mutually beneficial partnerships." There is "now more cause for optimism about Africa's future than at any time since the independence era of three decades ago."[786]

Dr. Setri Nyomi, coordinator of the October 1997 meeting of the seventh Assembly of the All Africa Conference of Churches, asserted at the opening ceremonies that "the next century will belong to Africa . . . . It will also be the century that will set in place the spiritual age—an era committed to God—an age centered in Africa." Archbishop Desmond Tutu sounded notes of realism and hope: "We are troubled, but not destroyed. I have full confidence in the future of Africa because it is the cradle of civilization and humanity, because God loves Africa."[787]

And what of the role of American Presbyterians in the Christian movement in sub-Saharan Africa at the outset of the twenty-first century? Through the several eras of mission traced in this study, we have seen progression from pioneer missionary work through church and institution building, then the training of national leadership and the passing of control from mission to church, and finally the concept of partnership in mission. Yet we have seen that partnership in mission is a many-splendored thing, which can be expressed in many different ways depending on the status of nation and church, as well as the particular gifts of the person in mission.

The critical question is, What is the degree of our commitment to the Christian mission in sub-Saharan Africa? At the 1999 PC(USA) General Assembly, a Commissioners' Resolution was adopted stating "That the General Assembly focus heightened attention, advocacy and compassionate response appropriate to the gravity and magnitude of the situation in Africa. These efforts will include resources of intercessory prayer, study and education, publicity, public policy advocacy, pastoral care and generous dedicated giving."[788]

Responding to this action, the Worldwide Ministries Division reported to the 2000 General Assembly:

1) Re Presbytery and Synod Partnerships with churches in Africa: Africa Area Offices have held three Presybtery Partnership Consultations for presbyteries with partnerships in Sudan, Malawi and Kenya. Plans are being made for representatives from presbyteries in partnership with churches in Congo, South Africa, Ethiopia and Ghana to engage in travel seminars to Africa.

2) Re Mission Personnel Support: 15 new mission personnel positions have opened. 79 long-term compensated mission personnel are serving in Sub-Saharan Africa—about 24% of the global total in that category. 20 are serving as long-term volunteers and 21 as short-term volunteers. In February 2000, the Worldwide Ministries Division sponsored an Africa-wide Personnel Retreat on the theme "Renewing the Vision: Mission in Christ's Way."

3) Re Financial Support: In 1999 the seven Global Service and Witness programs provided a total of $3,852,857 to mission in Sub-Saharan Africa.

The call to commitment to mission in Africa has been expressed most powerfully in a message to the Presbyterian Church (USA) from the participants in the All-Africa Mission Personnel Retreat held at Victoria Falls, Zimbabwe on February 6-10, 2000:

Greetings in the name of our Lord and Savior, Jesus Christ!

We are witnessing a wondrous outpouring of the Spirit of God across the continent of Africa. Christ's church is growing more rapidly in Africa than in any other region of the world, and African Christians are revitalizing our faith as we enter a new era. We celebrate the fact that Presbyterian mission has been an important part of the life of the Church in Africa for nearly 150 years.

At the same time, Africa is bleeding. Wars, natural disasters, and the AIDS pandemic have affected and claimed millions of lives. Economic exploitation has mired much of Sub-Saharan Africa in intractable poverty. Governments and paramilitary forces unaccountable to the people have perpetrated shocking violations of fundamental human rights.

We are outraged that Africa's suffering and the vibrant gifts of her people are so frequently ignored. As a nation, the USA has yet to acknowledge the true debt it owes to Africa. The industrialized world continues to plunder the natural resources of the continent, inventing new rationales to justify its actions. As a church, the PC(USA) has become increasingly absorbed in internal doctrinal disputes. It is time for us to reaffirm—and to demonstrate—that the mission of the church is doing mission.

Mission has many facets, therefore many talents must be harnessed. Some are blessed with a gift of prayer; we urge them to pray increasingly for peace and justice for the people of Africa. Others have a facility for writing, speaking, or organizing; we urge them to dedicate themselves to building strong and creative relationships with Africans and to ensuring that the concerns of Africans are increasingly heard in US public policy debates.

In particular, we call on all Presbyterians to get to know our sisters and brothers in Africa who, like you, are living in a fallen world of suffering and injustice. Listen to them. Encourage them. Pray for them. Find out what is happening on the continent. Learn about African initiatives in evangelism, education, health, and social and economic justice. Make use of the materials and expertise of Presbyterian agencies such as the Worldwide Ministries Division, the Presbyterian Peacemaking Program, Self-Development of People, and the PC(USA) Washington Office to assist you in advocacy for Africa. Commit yourselves to concrete ways in which you can support African endeavors.

And, dare we add, prayerfully consider joining that noble army of witnesses, that the world may know the Christ whom God has sent for the salvation of the world.

BIBLIOGRAPHY

DENOMINATIONAL RECORDS AND OFFICIAL PUBLICATIONS

PCUS Executive Committee of Foreign Missions Annual Report, in General Assembly Minutes, 1890-1949.

PCUS Board of World Missions Annual Report, in General Assembly Minutes, 1950-1973.

PCUS General Assembly Mission Board, in General Assembly Minutes, 1974-1983

PCUS *The Missionary* (1868-1911)

PCUS The Missionary Survey (1912-1924)

PCUS *The Presbyterian Survey* (1924-1995)

PCUSA Board of Foreign Missions Annual Report, in General Assembly Minutes, through 1958.

PCUSA *The Foreign Missionary* (1842-1886)

PCUSA *The Church at Home and Abroad* (1887-1894)

PCUSA *Assembly Herald* (1894-1918)

PCUSA *The Presbyterian Magazine* (1921-1933)

PCUSA *Presbyterian Life* (1948-1983)

PCUSA/BFM. *New frontiers for old*. NY, 1946. Articles by various authors.

PCUSA/BFM. *One world a-building*. NY, 1946. A selection of best stories submitted by missionaries.

PCUSA/BFM. *Report of the World Consultation, Lake Mohonk. NY, 1956.*

PCUSA/BFM. "That the world may believe". five-year program 1949-1953.

PCUSA/BFM. *This is our world mission.* Compiled by Charles Tudor Leber. NY: 1943.

PCUSA/BFM. *Unforgettable disciples.* NY: 1942. Sketches submitted by missionaries.

PCUSA/BFM. *We would be building.* NY: 1944. C.T. Leber, ed.

PCUSA/BFM. *Yearbook of prayer for missions.* NY, 1895-1958.

PC(USA) General Assembly Minutes, 1984-2000

PC(USA) General Assembly Council, *Mission Focus.*

PC(USA) *Missionary Yearbook for Prayer and Study,* 1983-2000

PC(USA) *Monday Morning*

PC(USA) *News Briefs.*

PC(USA) United Nations Office, *World Updates.*

PC(USA) Worldwide Ministries Division Information Sheets

UPCUSA Commission on Ecumenical Missions and Relations Annual Report, 1959-1971

UPCUSA Program Agency Annual Report, 1972-1983.

UPCUSA/COEMAR. "An Advisory Study". NY, 1962

UPCUSA/COEMAR. "Development and deployment of personnel". NY: 1968.

UPCUSA/COEMAR, *Mission yearbook for prayer and study.* 1958-2000.

UPCUSA/COEMAR. "Newly independent states." NY, 1965.

UPCUSA/COEMAR. *Together in mission.* NY:COEMAR, 1960.

UPCUSA/COEMAR. *A single new humanity.* NY, 1964.

UPNA General Assembly Minutes, 1898-1958

MISSION—GENERAL

Barnet, Richard J. & Ronald E. Muller, *Global reach: the power of the multinational corporations.* New York: Simon & Schuster, 1974.

Barrett, David B., editor. *World Christian encyclopedia: a comparative survey of churches and religions in the modern world, A.D. 1900-2000.* Nairobi, Oxford, New York: Oxford University Press, 1982.

Beckford, George L. *Persistent poverty: underdevelopment in plantation economies of the Third World.* New York: Oxford University Press, 1972

Black, Donald. *Merging mission and unity: a history of the Commission on Ecumenical Mission and Relations.* Philadelphia: Geneva Press, c. 1986

Black, Donald. "An Historical View of Developing Mission Policy." n.d.

Brown, Arthur Judson. *One hundred years: a history of the foreign missionary work of the* Presbyterian Church in the USA. NY: Fleming H. Revell Co., 1936.

Buhlmann, Walbert. *The coming of the third church: an analysis of the present and future of the church.* Maryknoll, NY: Orbis Books, 1977

Buhlmann, Walbert. *The church of the future: a model for the year 2001.* Maryknoll, NY: Orbis Books, 1986

Buhlmann, Walbert. *With eyes to see: church and world in the third millennium.* Maryknoll, NY: Orbis Books, 1990.

Christian Century

Crane, Sophie Montgomery. *A Legacy Remembered: A Century of Medical Missions.* Franklin, TN: Providence House Publishers, 1998.

Dictionary of the Ecumenical Movement, ed. by Nicholas Lossky, Jose Miguez Bonino, John Pobee, Tom Stransky, Geoffrey Wainwright, Pauline Webb. Geneva: WCC Publications, 1991.

Dodge, Ralph E. *The unpopular missionary.* Westwood, NJ: F.H. Revell Co., 1964

Elliott, Charles. *Patterns of poverty in the Third World.* New York: Praeger Publishers, 1975.

International Association for Mission Studies. Conference (6th: 1985: Harare, Zimbabwe). *Christian and human transformation: proceedings of the Sixth Conference of the International Association for Mission Studies*. F.J. Uerstraelen, ed. Gweru, Zimbabwe: Mambo Press, 1985

International Bulletin of Missionary Research.

International Review of Missions. World Council of Churches.

Jamison, Wallace N. *The United Presbyterian story: a centennial study, 1858-1958*. Pittsburgh: Geneva Press, 1958

Lappe, Frances Moore & Joseph Collins. *Food first: beyond the myth of scarcity*. Boston: Houghton Mifflin Co., 1977.

Latourette, Kenneth Scott. *A History of the Expansion of Christianity*, Vol. VII. *Advance Through Storm: A.D. 1914 and after, with concluding generalizations*. New York & London: Harper & Brothers publishers, 1945.

Latourette, Kenneth Scott. *Christianity in a Revolutionary Age*. Vol. V, *The Twentieth Century Outside Europe* New York & Evanston: Harper & Row, Publishers, 1962.

Loetscher, Lefferts A. *A Brief History of the Presbyterians* (4th ed.) Philadelphia: Westminster Press, 1983.

Presbyterian Outlook

Mutshi, The Rev. Morrisine Flennaugh and Stephen Bartlett, *African Americans in Mission: Serving the Presbyterian Church from 1833 to the Present*. Louisville, KY: Office of Global Awareness and Involvement, Worldwide Ministries Division, PC(USA), 2000.

Roy, The Rev. Dr. Andrew T. *Historical overview of the overseas mission policies of the United Presbyterian Church in the United States of America*. Compiled for the General Assembly Mission Council of the United Presbyterian Church in the United States of America. December 1977.

Rycroft, W. Stanley, *The ecumenical witness of the United Presbyterian Church in the U.S.A. NYC: COEMAR/UPCUSA, 1968*.

Scherer, James. *Gospel, Church, and Kingdom:Comparative Studies in World Mission Theology*. Minneapolis: Augsburg Publishing House, 1987.

Smith, John Coventry. *From colonialism to world community: the church's pilgrimage.* Philadelphia: The Geneva Press, 1982

Street, T. Watson. *On the growing edge of the church: new dimensions in world missions.* Richmond, VA: John Knox Press, 1965.

Street, T. Watson. *The story of Southern Presbyterians.* Richmond, VA: John Knox Press, 1960.

Taylor, Hugh Kerr, ed. *Foundations of world order: the foreign service of the Presbyterian Church, U.S., by a missionary from each field.* Richmond, VA: John Knox Press, 1941.

Thompson, Ernest T. *Presbyterians in the South.* 3 vols. Richmond: John Knox Press, 1973.

Vischer, Lukas, ed. *Church History in an Ecumenical Perspective. Papers and reports of an International Ecumenical Consultation held in Basle, October 12-17, 1981.* Bern: Evangelische Arbeitsstelle Oekumene Schweiz, 1982.

Vischer, Lukas, ed. *Towards a History of the Church in the Third World: The Issue of Periodisation. Papers and report of a Consultation on the Issue of Periodisation convened by the Working Commission on Church History of the Ecumenical Association of Third World Theologians* (July 17-21, 1983, Geneva). Bern: Evangelische Arbeitsstelle Oekumene Schweiz, 1985.

AFRICA–GENERAL

Ajayi, J.F.Ade and Michael Crowder, general editors. *Historical Atlas of Africa.* Cambridge, New York: Cambridge University Press, 1985.

Appiah-Kubi, Kofi and Sergio Torres, eds., *African Theology en Route: Papers from the Pan-African Conference of Third World Theologians,* December 1977, Accra, Ghana. Maryknoll, NY: Orbis, 1979.

Barrett, David B. *Schism and renewal in Africa: an analysis of six thousand contemporary religious movements.* Nairobi: Oxford University Press, 1968

Beetham, T.A. *Christianity and the New Africa.* New York, Washington, London: Frederick A. Praeger Publishers, 1967.

Berman, Edward H *African reactions to missionary education.* New York: Teachers College Press, teachers College, Columbia University, 1975

Collins, Robert O. *Americans in Africa: a preliminary guide to American missionary archives and.library manuscript collections on Africa*, by Robert Collins and Peter Duignan. Stanford, CA: Hoover Institution on War, Revolution, and Peace, Stanford University, 1963

Dougall, J.W.C. *Christians in the African Revolution*. Edinburgh: The St. Andrew Press, 1963.

Dubose, Hampton, *Memoirs of Rev. John Leighton Wilson, D.D.: Missionary to Africa and Secretary of Foreign Missions*. Richmond: Presbyterian Committee of Publication, 1895

Gatewood, Richard Duncan. *Some American Protestant contributions to the welfare of African countries in 1963*. New York: National Council of the Churches of Christ, 1964.

Gittings, James A *New nations and the United Presbyterians*. NY: COEMAR/UPCUSA, 1964.

Groves, Charles Pelham. *The planting of Christianity in Africa*. Vol. IV. London: Lutterworth Press, 1948-58.

Hastings, Adrian *A History of African Christianity (1950-1975)* Cambridge: Cambridge University Press, 1978

Hastings, Adrian. *African Christianity*. New York: Seabury Press, 1976.

Kalu, Ogbu U., ed. *African Church Historiography: An Ecumenical Perspective*. Papers presented at a Workshop on African Church History held at Nairobi, August 3-8, 1986. Bern: Evangelische Arbeitsstelle Oekumene Schweiz, 1988.

Kalu, Ogbu U., ed. *The history of Christianity in West Africa*. London, New York: Longman. 1980.

Kasonga, Kasongawa. *Toward revisioning Christian education in Africa: a critical reinterpretation of hope and imagination in light of African understanding of muoyo* Thesis (Ph.D.), Princeton Theological Seminary, 1988.

Kendall, R. Elliott *The end of an era: Africa and the missionary*. London: S.P.C.K., 1978.

Macartney, William M. *Dr. Aggrey, ambassador for Africa*. London: SCM Press, 1949

Mbiti, John S *The crisis of mission in Africa*. Mukono,Uganda Church Press, c. 1971.

Njoya, Timothy Murere. *Dynamics of change in African Christianity*. Thesis, Princeton Theological Seminary, 1976.

Peterson, Martha Jane. *God's fire: a personal journey*. Atlanta, GA: Office of Interpretation, PCUSA. 1984.

Pretorius, H.L., A.A. Odendaal, P.J. Robinson, G. van der Herwe, eds. *Reflections on mission in the African context: a handbook for missiology*. Bloemfontein: Pro Christo, 1987.

Rycroft, W. Stanley, *A factual study of sub-Saharan Africa*. NY: COEMAR/UPCUSA, 1962.

Rycroft, W. Stanley, *The ecumenical witness of the United Presbyterian Church in the U.S.A.*

Sanneh, Lamin. "Africa", in *Toward the 21st century in Christian mission*, ed. by James M. Phillips & Robert T. Coote. Grand Rapids, MI: Wm. B. Eerdmans Publishing Co., 1993.

Sanneh, Lamin, "Sprunt Lectures Explore Slavery, Missions", in *Focus: The Journal of Union Theological Seminary, Richmond, VA,* Summer 1999, p, 7,

Sanneh, Lamin. *West African Christianity: the religious impact*. Maryknoll, NY: Orbis Books, 1983

Schweitzer, Albert. *On the Edge of the Primeval Forest*. London: A. & C. Black, 1921.

Thomas, Winburn Townshed. *Africa and the United Presbyterians*. NY: COEMAR/ UPCUSA, 1960.

Trimingham, J. Spencer. *The Christian church and Islam in West Africa*. London: SCM Press, 1955.

Trimingham, J. Spencer. *The influence of Islam on Africa*. New York: Praeger, 1968.

Trimingham, J. Spencer. *Islam in East Africa: the report of a survey undertaken in 1961*. London: Edinburgh House Press, 1962

Uka, Emele Mba *Missionaries go home?: a sociological interpretation of an African response to Christian missions: a study in sociology of knowledge*. Berne, New York: Lang, c. 1989.

Utuk, Efiong Sam. *Africa and the making of ecumenical mission mandates 1900-1958*. Thesis (Ph.D.), Princeton Theological Seminary, 1988.

Wallerstein, Immanuel. *Africa: The Politics of Independence*. New York: Vintage Books, 1961.

Wallerstein, Immanuel. *Africa: The Politics of Unity.* New York: Vintage Books, 1967.

West Central Africa Regional Conference, Leopoldville, Congo, 1946. *Abundant life in changing Africa.* New York: Africa Committee of the Foreign Missions Conference of North America, 1946

Personal Correspondence:
  Brown, G. Thompson (mission board staff)
  Costen, Dr. James (President, Interdenominational Theological Centerd)
  Farrell, Hunter (mission board staff)
  Gannaway, Bruce (mission board staff)
  Goodpasture, Ken (mission professor)
  Hopkins, Paul (mission board staff)
  Pritchard, John.(mission board staff)

CAMEROON

Adams, Evelyn A., M.D. *First woman doctor to Cameroun*. Cincinnati, OH: Women's Society, Westwood First Presbyterian Church, 1988.

Akono, Samuel E. *Independence de 'eglise et crise financiere*. Traduit de l'anglais par Catherine Vittoz. Yaounde: Editions CLE, 1973

Anderson, Llewellyn Kennedy. *Bridge to Africa*. NY: PCUSA/BFM, 1952.

Anderson, L.K *Incidents and recollections of missionary service, 1926-65*. Unpublished memoirs, typescript.

Anderson, L.K. "West Africa". Ch. 15 in *The crisis decade: a history of the foreign missionary work of the Presbyterian Church in the U.S.A. 1937-1947.* New York: The Board of Foreign Missions of the Presbyterian Church in the U.S.A., 1950.

Anderson, L.K. "Cameroun Visit November 1968-February 1969".

Christiansen, Ruth *For the heart of Africa*. Minneapolis: Augsburg, 1956.

Drum Call. Official quarterly of the West Africa Mission of the Presbyterian Church in the USA. 1922-69.

Emerson, Frank Owen. *The farthest away man: autobiography of F.O. Emerson*. Edited by Vera Wolfe. Parkville, MO: Park College Press, 1965.

Greig, H. Wallace, M.D. "Annual Report of the Medical Department to the General Assembly at Metet, 1966."

Horner, Norman A. *The development of an indigenous Presbyterian Church in the French Cameroun during the decade 1938-1948*. M.A. dissertation, Hartford Seminary Foundation, 1950

Horner, Norman A *Protestant and Roman Catholic Missions among the Bantu of Cameroun: A Comparative Study*. Ph.D. Dissertation, Hartford Seminary Foundation, 1956.

Keller, Jean. "Founding ceremony of the General Assembly of the Cameroun Presbyterian Church": address by Rev. Jean Keller, 1957. 3p.

Kwast, Lloyd E *The Discipling of West Cameroun*. Grand Rapids, MI: Wm. Eerdmans, 1971.

Lehman, Anna McL . . . "Bekale Mindom of Africa". In *Unforgettable Disciples*. NY: PCUSA/BFM, 1942. pp. 159-163.

LeVine, Victor T. *The Cameroons, from mandate to independence*. Berkeley: University of California Press, 1964.

LeVine, Victor T. & Roger P. Nye, *Historical dictionary of Cameroun*. Metuchen, NJ: Scarecrow Press, 1974.

McNeill, Lois Johnson. *The Great Ngee: the life story of Silas Franklin Johnson, M.D.* Phila: UPCUSA/COEMAR, 1957.

Mokosso, Henry Teddy Efesoa *The United Presbyterian Mission Enterprise in Cameroun, 1879-1957*. Howard University, Washington, D.C., 1987. Ph.D. Dissertation.

Nassau, R.H. *My Ogowe*. New York: Neale Publishing Co., 1914.

Nyansako-ni-Nku, ed. *Journey in Faith: the story of the Presbyterian Church in Cameroon*. Silver Jubilee 1982. 177 p.

Nyansako-ni-Nku, ed. *The pioneers: a centenary picture book, 1886-1986*. Yaounde: Presbyterian Church in Cameroon, 1986

Palmer, Helen D. *Twenty-eight years in Africa*. NY: Carlton Press, 1985.

Parsons, E.C. *A life for Africa: Rev. Adolphus C. Good*. New York: Revell, 1900.

Peirce, Robert N. "The First Decade of the Cameroun Presbyterian Church." 1967.

Presbyterian Church of Cameroun. *Bulletin d'information de l'eglise Presbyterrienne camerounaise*. Yaounde, June 1960

PCUSA/BFM. *Now in Cameroun, West Africa*. NY: BFM, 1952. Pamphlet.

Reyburn, William David. *Out of the African night*. NY: Harper and Row, 1968.

Rowe, Anna Mae (Lovell). Newsletter concerning events that occurred at the General Assembly of the Cameroun Presbyterian Church, March 1964. 2p.

Tambi-Eyongetali and Robert Brain. *A history of the Cameroun*. Essex: Longmans, 1974.

Werner, Keller. *The history of the Presbyterian Church in West Cameroon A Survey of the general development of the Presbyterian Church in Cameroon up to 1960*. Victoria: Radio and Literature Dept. of the Presbyterian Church in West Cameroon, 1969.

Wheeler, William Reginald. *The words of God in an African forest: the story of an American Mission in West Africa*. New York, Chicago [etc.]: Fleming H. Revell, 1931.

Wilson, Frank Theodore. *Report of evaluation of schools related to Eglise Presbyterrienne Camerounaise, 1966*

Missionary Correspondence:
    Bekaert, Guy and Monique
    Brewster-Lee, Dr. Dorothy
    Frelick, Drs. Paul and Ellenor
    Mullen, Dr. and Mrs. Donald C.
    Snyder, Brian C.

Personal Correspondence:
    Adams, Evelyn A
    Horner, Norman A
    Peirce, Robert N.
    Pondi, Ambassador Paul
    Taylor, Marabelle

CONGO/ZAIRE

Almquist, Arden *Missionary, come back*. NY: World Publishing Co., 1970.

Anderson, Vernon A *Still led in triumph*. BWM/PCUS, 1959.

Bedinger, Robert Dabney. *Triumphs of the Gospel in the Belgian Congo*. Richmond, VA: Presbyterian Committee on Publication, 1920.

Board of World Missions, PCUS. *Nation in a hurry: PCUS at work in the Congo*. Nashville: BWM/PCUS, 1964.

Carpenter, George Wayland. *Highways for God in Congo: Commemorating seventy-five years of Protestant Missions 1878-1953*. Leopoldville: La Librairie Evangelique au Congo

Congo profile, 1965: a study of historical and socio-economic factors influencing the development of the church in the Democratic Republic of Congo. Ed. by Joseph M. Davis & L. Earl Griswold. NY: World Division of the Board of Missions, Methodist Church

Crane, William H. *Presbyterian work in the Congo: a historical study of the development of mission and church in the Kasai (1891-1959)*. Th.M. Thesis, Union Theological Seminary in Virginia, 1960.

Crawford, John R. *Protestant Missions in Congo, 1878-1969*. English edition printed in the United States by agreement with the Librairie Evangelique du Congo, Kinshasa. Dowdy, Homer E. *Out of the jaws of the lion*. NY: Harper & Row, 1965.

Four Presbyterian Pioneers in the Congo: Samuel N. Lapsley, William H. Shepherd, Maria Fearing, Lucy Gantt Sheppard. Various authors. Anniston, AL: First Presbyterian Church, 1965.

Hendrickson, Francis Harry. *A study of the reactions of selected Congo missionaries toward presumed criticism of missionary education in Africa. NY, 1964*. Thesis (Ed.D.), Columbia University. Microfilm, 1986 (UTS/NY)

Hochschild, Adam. *King Leopold's Ghost: A story of greed, terror and heroism in colonial Africa*. Boston, New York: Houghton Mifflin Company, 1998.

Irvine, Cecilia. *The Church of Christ in Zaire: a handbook of Protestant churches, missions and communities, 1878-1978*. Indianapolis: Dept. of Africa, DOM, Christian Church Disciples of Christ, 1978.

Kalb, Madeleine G. *The Congo cables: the cold war in Africa from Eisenhower to Kennedy.* New York: Macmillan, 1982.

Kellersberger, Julia Lake (Skinner). *God's ravens.* NY: Fleming H. Revell Co., 1941.

Kellersberger, Julia Lake (Skinner). *A life for the Congo: the story of Althea Brown Edmiston.* NY, London: Revell, 1947.

Kiantandu, Mavumi-sa Masakumunwa *A study of the contribution of American Presbyterians to the formation of the Church of Christ in Zaire with special reference to indigenization, 1891-1960.* Th.D. Dissertation, Union Theological Seminary in Virginia, 1983.

Kingsolver, Barbara. *The Poisonwood Bible.* New York: Harper Collins Publishers, 1998,

Longenecker, J. Hershey. *Memories of Congo.* Johnson City, TN: Royal Publishers, 1964

Makanzu Mairemilusa. *L'Histoire de l'Eglise du Christ au Zaire.* Kinshasa: Centre Protestant d'Editions et de Diffusion, 1973.

Markowitz, Marvin D. *Cross and sword: the political role of Christian missions in the Belgian Congo, 1908-1960.* Stanford, CA: Hoover Institute Press, 1973.

McGavran, Donald Anderson. *Zaire: midday in missions.* Valley Forge, PA: Judson Press, 1979.

McKinnon, Arch C. *Kapitene of the Congo Steamship Lapsley*; and
McKinnon, Fannie W. *Treasures of darkness.* Boston: Christopher Publishing House, 1968.

Morrison, John. *African Mission.* Nashville: Bradley Whitfield, 1979

Morrison, John. *Thomas T. Stixrud of Congo: beloved physician.* Nashville: BWM/PCUS, 1960.

Nelson, Robert Gilbert. *Congo crisis and Christian mission.* St. Louis: Bethany, 1961.

Nzongola-Ntalaja, ed. *The crisis in Zaire: myths and realities.* Trenton, NJ: Africa World Press, 1986.

Phipps, William E. *The Sheppards and Lapsley: Pioneer Presbyterians in the Congo* Louisville, KY: the Presbyterian Church (USA), 1991.

Phipps, William E. *William Sheppard: Congo's African American Livingstone*. Louisville, Geneva Press, 2002.

Pruitt, Virginia Gray. *New nation: new church. Congo: 1958-68.* (unpublished manuscript)

Rosevearre, Helen. *Give me the mountain: an autobiography*. Grand Rapids: Eerdmanns, 1966.

Ross, Charles. *The emergence of the Presbyterian Church in the Kasai, Congo*. M.A. Thesis, Fuller Theological Seminary, Pasadena, CA, 1967.

Rule, William. *Milestones in Mission*. 1991. (pre-publication manuscript)

Shaloff, Stanley. *Reform in Leopold's Congo*. Richmond, VA: John Knox, 1970

Slade, Ruth. *English-speaking missions in the Congo Independent State (1878-1908)*. Bruxelles: Academies Royales des Sciences Coloniales, 1959.

Slade, Ruth. *King Leopold's Congo: Aspects of the development of race relations in the Congo Independent State*. London, New York, Accra: Oxford University Press, 1962.

Tshihamba Mukoma Luendu. *The development of the ideology of authenticity as a pragmatic solution to the problem of cultural identity in Zaire*. Ph.D. Dissertation, Howard University, Washington, DC, May 1975.

Vass, Winifred Kellersberger. *Dr. Not Afraid: E.R. Kellersberger, M.D.* Austin, TX: Nortex Press, 1986.

Vass, Winifred K. and Lachlan C. *The Lapsley Saga*. Franklin, TN: Providence House Publishers, 1997.

Vinson, C.T. *William McCutchan Morrison, Twenty Years in Central Africa*. Richmond: Presbyterian Committee of Publication, 1921.

Wakuteka, Hany M. *Chemins d'edification d'une communaute Chretienne: l'Eglise Presbyterienne au Zaire*. Doctor of Ministry dissertation, Columbia Theological Seminary, 1983.

Weissman, Stephen R *American Foreign Policy in the Congo, 1960-1964*, Cornell University Press, 1974

Wharton, Ethel Taylor. *Led in triumph*. Nashville: PCUS/BWM, 1952.

Wharton, Edith Taylor. Pamphlet, "This is Congo". c. 1954

Missionary Correspondence:
    Fletcher, John and Glenda
    Hernas, Knute and Lynne
    Hobgood, Ben and Betsy
    Makin, Dr. Sue
    Metzel, Bill and Ruth
    Park, Haejung and Simon
    Sager, Sue and Bill
    Shannon, Drs. Ralph and Elsbeth
    Sthreshley, Larry

Personal Correspondence:
    Bobb, Donald F.
    Miller, David
    Rule, William

EQUATORIAL GUINEA

"Cameroun and Spanish Guinea, West Africa", 1959.

"Church Tourist Guide for Rio Muni". Undated paper.

Evangelical News. Rio Muni, Spanish Guinea, Feb-Oct, 1968.

Strange, Ray Powers, Jr. *Letters describing life and conditions in Spanish Equatorial Africa*, Apr. 18, 1961. 3 p

"Survey of Presbyterian Work in Rio Muni—1964-1965", n.d.

West Africa Mission, PCUSA. Benito Mission Station. Misc. reports, newsletters, etc. 1929-50

Personal Correspondence:
    Ainley, William W
    Envela-Makongo, Gustavo B.

Ruiz-Valera, Ramon
Strange, Mrs. Ray P., Jr. (Jane)

ETHIOPIA

Bakke, Johnny. *Christian ministry: patterns and functions within the Ethiopia Evangelical Church Mekane Yesus*. Oslo: Solum Forlag/Atlantic Highlands, NJ: Humanities Press. 1987.

Balisky, Lila W. "Theology in Song: Ethiopia's *Tesfaye Gabbiso"*, in *Missiology*, Vol. XXV, No. 4, October 1997, p.447f.

Birri, Debela. *History of the Evangelical Church Bethel, 1919 to 1947*. A dissertation presented to the faculty of the Lutheran School of Theology at Chicago, in partial fulfillment of the requirements for the degree of Doctor of Theology. May 1995.

Bockelman, Wilfred. *Ethiopia: where Lutheran is spelled "Mekane Yesus"*. Minneapolis: Augsburg, 1972.

Cotterell, F. Peter. *Born at midnight*. Chicago: Moody Press, 1973.

Davis, Raymond J. *Fire on the mountains: the story of a miracle—the church in Ethiopia*. Grand Rapids: Zondervan Publishing House, 1966.

Dortzbach, Karl. *Kidnapped*. NY: Harper & Row, 1975.

Ens, Anna H. "Have we finished the task?" May 1993.

Ethiopia Mission, UPNA Historical correspondence and papers relating to the Leffari Mahonnen Hospital and property with Ethiopian authorities, 1944-50.

Fairman, Edwin Batton *Ethiopian adventure: the story of Don and Lyda McClure*. Reprinted from Presbyterian Life, June 15, 1959. NY: COEMAR, 1959.

Henry, Emma Frances (Handy. *The river of life in Ethiopia*. Pittsburgh: WGMS/UPNA, 1952.

Jamison, Wallace Newlin. *The United Presbyterian story: a centennial study, 1858-1958*. Pittsburgh: Geneva Press, 1958.

Kissling, Carl J *May we introduce Ethiopia*. Phila: BFM, 1952.

"Facts from the foreign field: tragedy follows merrymaking in Sayo." From Christian Union Herald, Jan. 4, 1948.

Lambie, Thomas Alexander *Boot and saddle in Africa* Phila: Blakiston Co. Distributed by Fleming H. Revell Co.,New York, 1943

Lambie, T.A. *A doctor carries on.* NY: Revell, 1942.

Lambie, T.A. *A doctor's great commission.* NY: Revell, 1954.

Lambie, T.A. *A doctor without a country.* NY: Revell, 1939.

McClure, William Donald. *Red-headed, rash and religious: the story of a pioneer missionary.* Letters edited and compiled by Marion Fairman. Pittsburgh: Board of Christian Education of UPNA, 1954.

Pankhurst, Estelle Sylvia *Ethiopia, a cultural history.* Essex (Eng): Lalibela House, 1955.

Partee, Charles. *Adventure in Africa: The story of Don McClure, from Khartoum to Addis Ababa in five decades.* Grand Rapids, MI: Zondervan Publishing House, Ministry Resources Library, 1990.

Robertson, Elizabeth. Letter May 2, 1974 to Ruth Nichol. llp. Diary excerpts from Feb. 28-May 2, 1974.

Saeveras, Olav. *On church-mission relations in Ethiopia 1944-69: with special reference to the Evangelical Church Mekane Yesus and the Lutheran missions.* Lunde: Lunde Forlag og Bokhandel, 1974.

Solon, Gidada. *The other side of darkness, as told to and recorded by Ruth McCreery and Martha M. Vandevort.* Ed. by Marion Fairman. NY: Friendship Press, 1972.

Tippett, Alan Richard. *Peoples of southwest Ethiopia* South Pasadena, CKA: W. Carey Library, 1970.

Trimingham, John Spencer. *The Christian Church and missions in Ethiopia (including Eritrea and the Somalilands).* London, NY: World Dominion Press, 1950

Ullendorf, Edward. *The Ethiopians: an introduction to country and people.* London, NY: Oxford University Press, 1960.

UPNA/BFM. *Ethiopia, its land and people.* Phila: BFM,UPNA, 1954. 54p.

Missionary Correspondence:
>   Kurtz, Carolina
>   Rasmussen, Mark
>   Weinberg, Caryl
>   Weller, Michael and Rachel
>   Wheeler-Waddell, John and Anne

Personal Correspondence:
>   Endocatchew, Danny
>   Rankin, Dorothy L
>   Wilson, Ruth

GHANA

Adu-Andoh, Samuel. *The sacred in Ghana's struggle for justice and communal identity: the legacy of Kwame Nkrumah.* Thesis (Ph.D), Princeton Theological Seminary, 1986.

Assimens, J.H *Saints and social structures.* Tema, Ghana: Ghana Publishing Corporation, 1986.

UPCUSA/COEMAR. "A diary report: the Ghana study seminar, July 3-August 19, 1961."

Missionary Correspondence:
>   Crumpton, Robert and Nancy
>   Kelley, Wendy and Garvester
>   Nelson, Corey
>   Young, Bill and Judi

LESOTHO

Personal Correspondence:
>   Wagstaff, Leisa T.

KENYA

Capon, M.G. *Towards unity in Kenya: the story of cooperation between missions and churches in Kenya 1913-1947.* Nairobi: Christian Council of Kenya, 1962.

Mugambi, J.N.K. "A History of the Church in East Africa, with Special Reference to Kenya", in *Toward a History of the Church in the Third World: The Issue of Periodization*, Lukas Vischer, ed. Bern: Evangelische Arbeitsstelle Oekumene Schweitz, 1985.

Missionary Correspondence:
>Bennett, Dr. Marta
>Danks, Edward
>Emerick-Cayton, Tim and Sher
>Strain, Marion
>Topple, Drs. Mia and Stan

MALAWI

Pauw, Christoff Martin. *Mission and church in Malawi: the history of Nkhoma Synod of the Church of Central Africa, Presbyterian, 1889-1962*. Thesis (Th.D.) University of Stellenbosch, 1980.

Pons, Edwin S. *The Southern and Central Streams of Presbyterianism in Africa*. Johannesburg: The Presbyterdian Church of Southern Africa, 1982.

Sindima, Harvey Jeffery. *Malawian Churches and the struggle for life and personhood: crisis and rupture of Malawian thought and society*. Thesis (Ph.D.), Princeton Theological Seminary, 1987.

Weller, John C. *Mainstream Christianity to 1980 in Malawi, Zambia, and Zimbabwe*. Gweru: Mambo Press, 1984

Missionary Correspondence:
>Cairns, Jim
>Cameron-Gray, Mark and Betsy
>Dimmock, Frank and Nancy
>Hopkins, Joseph M.
>Jewett, Dr. Paul and Judy
>Kang, Hannah and Joseph
>Loomis, Dr. Becky
>McGill, Dr. Ken and Nancy
>Rowe, Wilma and Otis
>Stone, Dr. & Mrs. Frederic
>Welch, Doug and Ruth

MAURITIUS

Missionary Correspondence:
Carle, Joe and Becky
Crosby, Brian and Liz

MOZAMBIQUE

Missionary Correspondence:
Minter, Ruth B.

NIGERIA

Missionary Correspondence:
VanGerpen, Rev. and Mrs. Emory

SOUTH AFRICA

Maker, D.Alan. *The cost of apartheid for white South Africans*. Thesis (D.Min.), Princeton Theological Seminary, 1984.

Pons, Edwin S. *The Southern and Central Streams of Presbyterianism in Africa*. Johannesburg: The Presbyterdian Church of Southern Africa, 1982.

Stevens, Richard J. *Suffering as a key to social and political transformation in South Africa*. Thesis (Ph.D.) Princeton Theological Seminary, 1985.

SUDAN

The black book of the Sudan on the expulsion of the missionaries from Southern Sudan: an answer. Milano, Instituto Artigianelli, 1964.

Bode, Mary Ann. "Rain out of Season". Paper written in February 1966.

Crawford, Margaret B. *The Sudan: its land and people*. NY:COEMAR, 1952. 2nd ed., 1958.

Forsberg, Malcolm. *Last days on the Nile*. Philadelphia, New York: J.B. Lippincott Co., 1966.

Giffen, J. Kelly. *The Egyptian Sudan*. New York, Chicago, Toronto: Fleming H. Revell Co., 1905.

Lambie, Thomas Alexander. *A doctor without a country*. NY: Revell, 1939.

McCutchen, A. *The framework of Sudan's mass expulsion of missionaries. 1964.*

Open Door East Africa. *Profile of status of Christianity in Sudan. 1983*. Sudan Council of Churches

Partee, Charles. *Adventure in Africa: the story of Don McClure*. Grand Rapids, MI: Zondervan Publishing House, Ministry Resources Library, 1990.

Pillow, E. Verna. *A life of Faith (Story of Miss Faith Hamadain, 1910-1962)*. Malakal, Sudan: Spearhead Press, 1963.

Powell, James E. "Experiencing the cross: liturgy and mission", a paper prepared at the Interdenominational Theological Center, Atlanta, GA, 1989.

Shields, Reid Frampton. *Behind the garden of Allah*. Phila: UPNA/BFM, 1937.

Trimingham, John Spencer. *The Christian approach to Islam in the Sudan*. London, NY: Oxford University Press, 1948

Trimingham, John Spencer. *The Christian church in postwar Sudan*. London, NY: World Dominion Press, 1949.

Trimingham, John Spencer. *Islam in the Sudan*. London: F. Cass, 1965

UPNA. *May we introduce South Sudan*. Phil: UPNA/BFM, 1954.

Vandevort, Eleanor. *A leopard tamed: the story of an African pastor, his people and his problems*. NY: Harper & Row, 1968.

Missionary Correspondence:
    Almy, Barry
    Anderson, William and Lois.
    Healy, Mike and Billie
    Kurtz, Caroline
    McCormick, Betsy
    Parker, Michael

Rasmussen, Mark
Simmons, Bill and Willie

Personal Correspondence:
    Anderson, William A
    Bode, Mary Ann
    Chot, Michael.
    Farquhar, Marian
    Lowrey, William
    McLaughlin, S. Robb
    Philips, William H

ZAMBIA

Morris, Colin. *A Humanist in Africa.* Nashville: Abingdon, 1969.

ZIMBABWE

Missionary Correspondence:
    De la Torre, Drs. Irma and Salvador
    Miller, David and Polly
    Snyder, Bob and Bobbi
    Warlick, Bill and Nancy

ABBREVIATIONS AND ACRONYMS

AACC   All-Africa Conference of Churches

ABAKO   A political organization in Congo founded in 1954 for the "unification, preservation, perfection and expansion" of the Kongo culture.

ABCFM   American Board of Commissioners for Foreign Missions, an interdenominational mission board which came into being in 1810 and through which American Presbyterians engaged in foreign missions until the formation of the Presbyterian Board of Foreign Missions.in 1838.

ACROSS   Association of Christian Resource Organizations Serving Sudan

ANC   African National Congress (South Africa)

APCM   American Presbyterian Congo Mission.

BDC   *Bloc Democratique Camerounais*, a more moderate political party in Cameroun

BESS   Bethel Evangelical Secondary School, Ethiopia

BFM   Board of Foreign Missions, Presbyterian Church in the U.S.A

BWM   Board of World Missions, Presbyterian Church in the United States; formed in 1950, restructured into the Division of International Mission in 1972.

CCAP   Church of Central Africa Presbyterian

CCL   Christian Council of Lesotho

CCG   Christian Council of Ghana

CCM   Christian Council of Malawi

CCN   Christian Council of Nigeria

CCMO   Christian Council of Mozambique

CCZ   Christian Council of Zambia

CMS   Church Missionary Society of the Church of England.

COEMAR   Commission on Ecumenical Mission and Relations, Presbyterian Church in the U.S.A.; formed in 1958 and restructured into the Program Agency in 1972.

COPC   Cameroun Orthodox Presbyterian Church, which seceded from the Cameroun Presbyterian Church in 1967.

CPC   *Communaute Presbyterriene de Congo,* Presbyterian Community of Congo. During the Mobutu years, it was known as *Communaute Presbyterriene de Zaire (CPZ).*

CPK   *Communaute Presbyterriene de Kinshasa,* Presbyterian Community of Kinshasa

CRDA   Christian Relief and Development Association, Ethiopia

DIM   Division of International Mission, General Assembly Mission Board, Presbyterian Church in the United States; from 1972 to 1983.

EAAT   Ecumenical Association of African Theologians

EATWOT   Ecumenical Association of Third World Theologians

ECC   *Eglise du Christ Au Congo,* Church of Christ in Congo. During the Mobutu years, it was known as *Eglise du Christ Au Zaire (ECZ).*

ECFM   Executive Committee of Foreign Missions, Presbyterian Church in the United States; became the Board of World Missions in 1950.

ECOWAS   Economic Community of West African States
EEC   Ethiopian Evangelical Church, predecessor of the Ethiopian Evangelical Church Mekane Yesu

EECMY   Ethiopian Evangelical Church Mekane Yesus

EPC	*Eglise Presbyterienne Camerounaise,* Cameroun Presbyterian Church. For a brief period (1966-1970), the Presbyterian Church of Congo was referred to as the EPC.
EPCG	Evangelical Presbyterian Church of Ghana
EPCSA	Evangelical Presbyterian Church in South Africa
EPR	*Eglise Presbyterriene au Rwanda*, Presbyterian Church of Rwanda
EPRDF	Ethiopian People's Revolutionary Democratic Front
FJKM	Church of Jesus Christ in Madagascar
FLE	Front for Liberation of Eritrea
FPCM	Federation of the Protestant Churches in Madagascar
FPCMC	Federation of Protestant Churches and Missions in Cameroon
FRELIMO	Front for the Liberation of Mozambique
GBS	Gidada Bible School, Ethiopia
IMCK	*Institut Medical Chretien du Kasai,* Christian Medical School of Kasai, Congo.
IME	*Institut des Missions Evangeliques,* known in the U.S. as Cameroun Christian College.
IPM	*Igreja Presbiteriana de Mocambique,* Presbyterian Church of Mozambique
IRPGE	Presbyterian Reformed Church of Equatorial Guinea
KANU	Kenya African National Union
LEC	Lesotho Evangelical Church
MCP	Malawi Congress Party
MPL	*Mission Presbyterienne de Leopoldville,* American Presbyterian Mission in Leopoldville.

MPR   *Mouvement Populaire de la Revolution*, Mobutu's party which established absolute control of Zaire/Congo from 1966 to 1997.

NCCK   National Council of Churches of Kenya

NGK   *Nederduitse Gereformeerde Kirk,* Dutch Reformed Church (South Africa)

NOP   Northern Outreach Program, Ghana

NRAC   Northern Rhodesia African Congress (Zambia)

NSCC   New Sudan Council of Churches

OAU   Organization of African Unity

PCA   Presbyterian Church of Africa (South Africa)

PCEA   Presbyterian Church of East Africa

PCG   Presbyterian Church of Ghana

PCM   Presbyterian Church of Mauritius

PCN   Presbyterian Church of Nigeria

PCOS   Presbyterian Church of Sudan

PCR   Program to Combat Racism, World Council of Churches
Also, Protestant Council of Rwanda

PCSA   Presbyterian Church of Southern Africa

PCUS   Presbyterian Church in the United States (southern), which came into being in 1861 and which reunited with the United Presbyterian Church in the U.S.A. in 1983 to form the Presbyterian Church (USA).

PCUSA   Presbyterian Church in the U.S.A. (northern), which United with the United Presbyterian Church in North America in 1958 to form the United Presbyterian Church in the U.S.A.

PC(USA)   Presbyterian Church (USA), which came into being in 1983 upon the reunion of the United Presbyterian Church in the U.S.A. (northern) and the Presbyterian Church in the United States (southern).

PECGA	Program for Evangelism and Church Growth in Africa
PLF	Popular Liberation Force (Ethiopia)
RCA	Reformed Church in America
RDA	*Rassemblement Democratique Africain,* a pan-African movement seeking greater political rights for French-speaking Africans.
RENAMO	Mozambique National Resistance
RPCEG	Reformed Presbyterian Church of Equatorial Guinea
SACC	South African Council of Churches
SADC	Southern African Development Community
SANRU	*Programme de Sante Rurale,* Primary health care program, Zaire/Congo
SCC	Sudan Council of Churches
SPEC	Sudan Presbyterian Evangelical Church
SPLA	Sudan People's Liberation Army
UCCAR	United Church of Central Africa in Rhodesia (Zambia)
UCZ	United Church of Zambia
UNICEF	United Nations Children's Fund
UNIP	United National Independence Party (ZAMBIA)
UPC	*Union des Populations de Cameroun*, Camerounian branch of the RDA.
UPCSA	Uniting Presbyterian Church in Southern Africa
UPCUSA	United Presbyterian Church in the U.S.A., which came into being in 1958 with the merger of the United Presbyterian Church in North America and the Presbyterian Church in the U.S.A. and which united with the Presbyterian Church in the United States in 1983 to form the Presbyterian Church (USA).

UPNA   United Presbyterian Church in North America, which came into being in 1858 and which merged with the Presbyterian Church in the U.S.A. in 1958 to form the United Presbyterian Church in the U.S.A.

URCSA   Uniting Reformed Church in Southern Africa

USAID   United States Assistance in International Development Program

WCC   World Council of Churches

WMD   Worldwide Ministries Division, Presbyterian Church (USA)

YBS   Yehiwot Berhan Girls' School, Ethiopia

ZANU   Zimbabwe African National Union

ZAPU   Zimbabwe African People's Union

ZCC   Zlimbabwe Christian Council

LIST OF CHARTS

CHART I—Timeline of Mission Boards Preceding Presbyterian Church (USA)

CHART II—Independent Nations of Sub-Saharan Africa

CHART III—National Christian Councils in Sub-Saharan Africa

CHART IV—Presbyterian Church (USA) Partner Churches in Sub-Saharan Africa

CHART V—Statistics for Sub-Saharan Countries where PC(USA) has Partners in Mission

CHART I
TIMELINE OF MISSION BOARDS PRECEDING
PRESBYTERIAN CHURCH (USA)

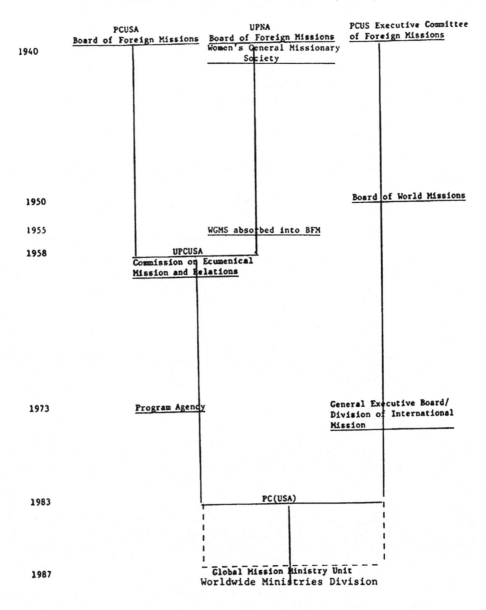

CHART II
INDEPENDENT NATIONS OF SUB-SAHARAN AFRICA

Nation Former	Colonial Power	Independence	Former Name
Angola	Portugal	1975	Angola
Benin	France (part of French West Africa)	1960	Dahomey
Botswana	British Protectorate	1966	Bechuanaland
Burkina Faso	France (part of French West	1960	Upper Volta
Burundi	Belgium	1962	part of Rwanda-Burundi
Cameroon	Germany; Britain and France	1960	Kamerun(Ger) Camerouns(Fr)
Cape Verde	Portugal	1975	Cape Verde
Central African Republic	France (part of French Equatorial Africa)	1960	Ubangi-Shari
Chad	France (part of French Equatorial Africa)	1960	Tchad
Comoros	France	1975	Comoro Islands
Congo, People's Republic	France (part of French Equatorial Africa)	1960	Middle Congo
Cote d'Ivoire	France	1960	Cote d'Ivoire (Ivory Coast)
Djibouti	France	1977	French Somaliland
Equatorial Guinea	Spain	1968	Spanish Guinea
Eritrea	Italy; Ethiopia	1991	Eritrea

Ethiopia	Independent; Italy (1936-1941)		
Gabon	France (part of French Equatorial Africa)	1960	Gabon
Gambia	Britain	1962	Gambia
Ghana	Britain	1957	Gold Coast
Guinea	France	1958	French Guinea
Guinea-Bissau	Portugal	1973	Portuguese Guinea
Kenya	Britain	1963	British East Africa
Lesotho	Britain	1966	Basutoland
Liberia	Independent		
Madagascar	France	1960	Madagascar
Malawi	Britain	1964	Nyasaland
Mali	France (part of French West Africa)	1960	French Sudan
Mauritania	France (part of French West Africa)	1960	Mauritania
Mauritius	Britain	1966	Mauritius
Mozambique	Portugal	1975	Macabique
Namibia	Germany; South Africa	1988	Southwest Africa
Niger	France (part of French West Africa)	1960	Niger
Nigeria	Britain	1960	Nigeria (Biafra seceded 1967-1970)

Rwanda	Belgium	1962	Part of Rwanda-Urundi
Sao Tome & Principe	Portugal	1975	Sao Tome & Principe
Senegal	France	1960	Senegal
Seychelles	Britain	1976	Seychelles Is.
Sierra Leone	Britain	1961	Sierra Leone
Somalia	Britain, Italy	1960	British & Italian Somaliland
South Africa	Independent		
Sudan	Britain/Egypt	1956	Sudan
Swaziland	Britain	1967	Swaziland
Tanzania	Germany; British trusteeship	1963	Tanganyika/Zanzibar
Togo	Germany: French trusteeship	1960	Togoland
Uganda	Britain	1962	Uganda
Zaire	Belgium (Katanga seceded 1960-1964)	1960	Belgian Congo
Zambia	Britain	1964	Northern Rhodesia
Zimbabwe	Britain	1980	Southern Rhodesia

(Rhodesia declared unilateral independence, 1965)

CHART III
NATIONAL CHRISTIAN COUNCILS IN
SUB-SAHARAN AFRICA

Nation	National Christian Council[1]	Established
Angola	Angolan Council of Evangelical Churches	1922
Botswana	Botswana Christian Council	1966
Burundi	Council of Churches of Burundi	1935
Cameroun	Federation of Protestant Churches and Missions in Cameroun	1970
Ethiopia	Christian Relief and Development Association	1973
Gambia	Christian Council of the Gambia	1963
Ghana	Christian Council of Ghana	1929
Kenya	National Council of Churches of Kenya	1943
Lesotho	Christian Council of Lesotho	1964
Madagascar	Federation of the Protestant Churches in Madagascar	1958
Malawi	Christian Council of Malawi	1939
Mozambique	Christian Council of Mozambique	1944
Namibia	Council of Churches of Namibia	1978
Nigeria	Christian Council of Nigeria	1930

---

[1] Technically, a Christian Council usually includes both churches and other Christian interdenominational and cooperative organizations. A Council of Churches is made up on representatives from the churches themselves.

Rwanda	Protestant Council of Rwanda	1935
Sierra Leone	United Christian Council of Sierra Leone	1924
South Africa	South African Council of Churches	1936
Sudan	Sudan Council of Churches	1965
	New Sudan Council of Churches	1990
Swaziland	Council of Swaziland Churches	1965
Tanzania	Christian Council of Tanzania	1936
Uganda	Uganda Joint Christian Council	1963
Zaire	Church of Christ in Zaire[2]	1970
Zambia	Christian Council of Zambia	1945
Zimbabwe	Zimbabwe Christian Council	1964

---

[2] The Church of Christ in Zaire was in reality an enforced ecumenism. In 1970 President Mobutu forced all the Protestant churches into a United Protestant Church, the *Eglise du Christ au Zaire* (ECZ), which is the only Protestant church that the government recognizes. The ECZ member churches (called *communautes*) maintain their previous ecclesiastic traditions, structures and fraternal ties.

CHART IV
PRESBYTERIAN CHURCH (USA) PARTNER
CHURCHES IN SUB-SAHARAN AFRICA
(from 2001 Mission Yearbook)

COUNTRY	PARTNER CHURCH(ES)	PC(USA) BEGAN INVOLVEMENT
Cameroon	Eglise Presbyterienne Camerounaise (EPC)	1879
Democratic Republic of Congo	Eglise du Christ au Congo (ECC) Presbyterian Community of Congo (CPC) Presbyterian Community of Kinshasa (CPK)	1891
Equatorial Guinea	Reformed Presbyterian Church of Equatorial Guinea (RPCEG)	1845
Ethiopia	Ethiopian Evangelical Church Mekane Yesus (EECMY)	1919
Ghana	Presbyterian Church of Ghana (PCG) Evangelical Presbyterian Church of Ghana (EPCG)	1964
Kenya	Presbyterian Church of East Africa ((PCEA)	1970
Lesotho	Lesotho Evangelical Church (LEC)	1975
Madagascar	Church of Jesus Christ in Madagascar (FJKM)	1979
Malawi	Church of Central Africa Presbyterian (CCAP)	1973
Mauritius	Presbyterian Church of Mauritius (PCM)	1979
Mozambique	Presbyterian Church of Mozambique (IPM)	1968
Nigeria	Presbyterian Church of Nigeria (PCN)	1964
Rwanda	Presbyterian Church of Rwanda (EPR)	1970
South Africa	Evangelical Presbyterian Church in South Africa (EPCSA)	1960

	Presbyterian Church of Africa (PCA)	
	Uniting Presbyterian Church in Southern Africa (UPCSA)	
	Uniting Reformed Church in Southern Africa (URCSA)	
Sudan	Presbyterian Church of Sudan (PCOS)	1900
	Sudan Presbyterian Evangelical Church ((SPEC)	
Zambia	United Church of Zambia (UCZ)	1965
Zimbabwe	Church of Central Africa Presbyterian (CCAP)	1965
	Presbyterian Church of Southern Africa ((PCSA)	

CHART V
STATISTICS FOR SUB-SAHARAN COUNTRIES
WHERE PC(USA) HAS PARTNERS IN MISSION
(from 2002 Mission Yearbook)

COUNTRY	POPULATION	% CHRISTIAN	LIFE EXPECTANCY
Cameroon	15,422,000	56%	54.8 yrs.
Democratic Republic of Congo	51,965,000	60%	48.7 yrs.
Equatorial Guinea	474,000	93%, predominantly Roman Catholic	53.5 yrs.
Ethiopia	64,117,000	45% Ethiopian Orthodox 11% Protestant	45.1 yrs.
Ghana	19,534,000	58%	57.4 yrs.
Kenya	30,340,000	60%	47.9 yrs
Lesotho	2,143,000	90%	50.8 yrs.
Madagascar	15,506,000	53%	54.9 yrs.
Malawi	10,386,000	60%	37.6 yrs.
Mauritius	1,179,000	26%	70.9 yrs.
Mozambique	19,105,000	40%	37.5 yrs.
Nigeria	123,338,000	42%	51.5 yrs.
Rwanda	7,600,000	70%	50.0 yrs.
South Africa	43,431,000	78%	51.1 yrs.
Sudan	35,080,000	19%	56.5 yrs.
Zambia	9,582,000	62%	37.2 yrs.
Zimbabwe	11,343,000	54%	37.8 yrs.

LIST OF MAPS

MAP I—Africa (c. 1987)

MAP II—West Africa (part 1)

MAP III—West Africa (part 2)

MAP IV—Central Africa

MAP V—The Horn of Africa

MAP VI—Southern Africa

MAP VII—American Presbyterian Mission Stations in Cameroon

MAP VIII—American Presbyterian Places of Work in Equatorial Guinea

MAP IX—American Presbyterian Mission Stations in Congo/Zaire

MAP X—American Presbyterian Mission Stations in the Sudan

MAP XI—American Presbyterian Mission Stations in Ethiopia

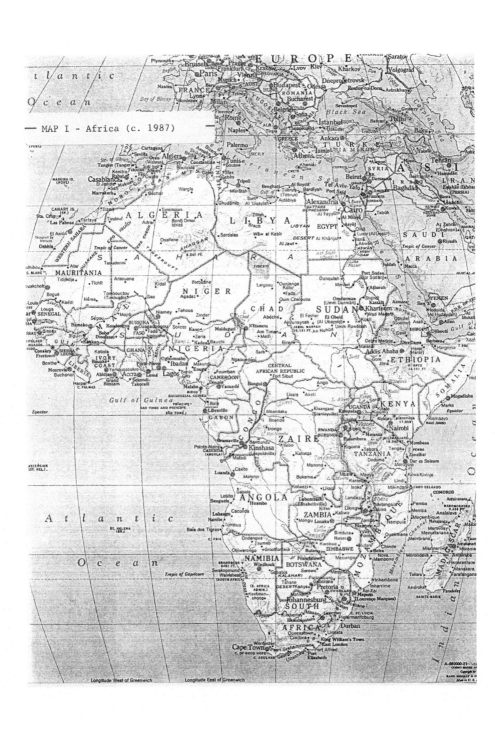

MAP I - Africa (c. 1987)

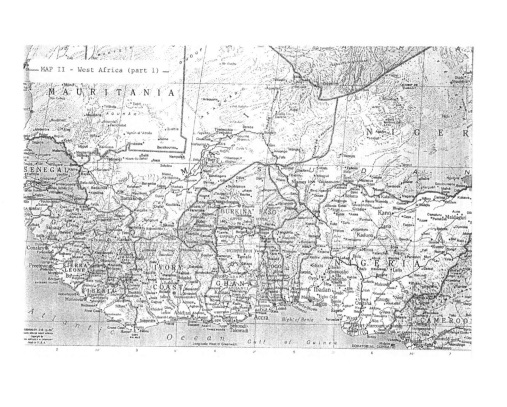

MAP II - West Africa (part 1) —

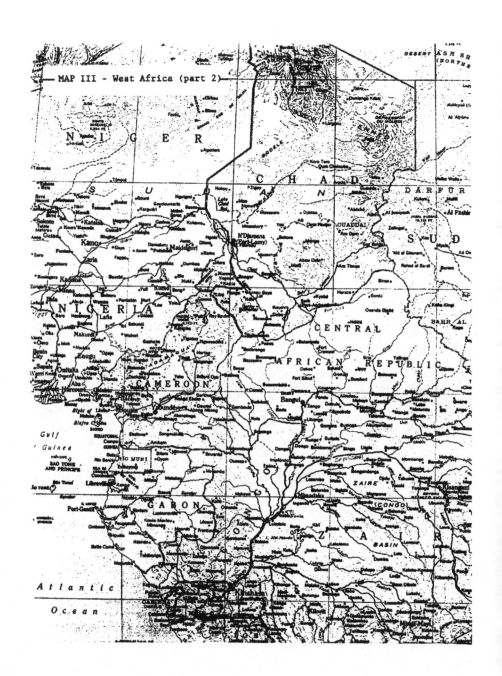

MAP III - West Africa (part 2)

— MAP IV - Central Africa —

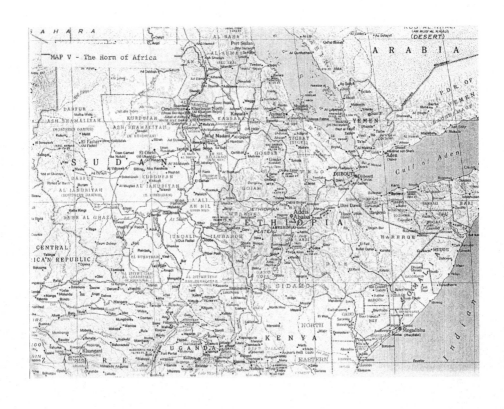

MAP V - The Horn of Africa

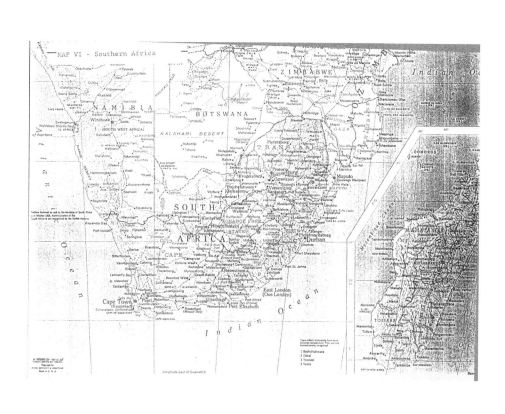

MAP VI - Southern Africa

MAP VII - American Presbyterian
Mission Stations in Cameroon

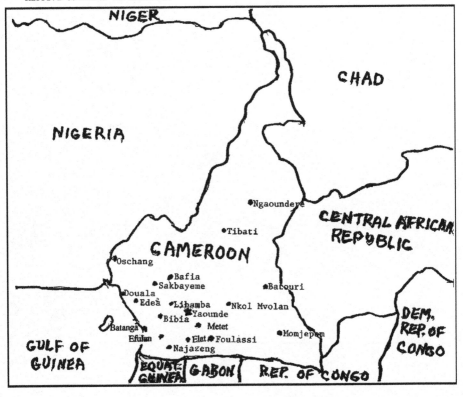

MAP VIII – American Presbyterian
— Places of Work in Equatorial Guinea —

MAP IX - American Presbyterian
Mission Stations in Congo/Zaire

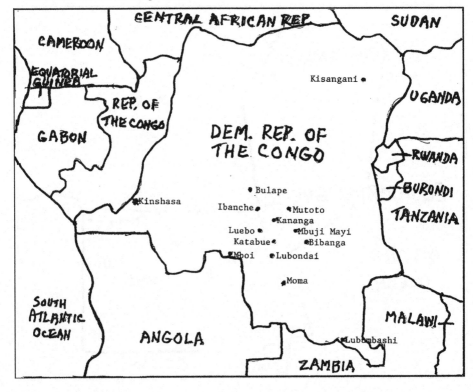

MAP X - American Presbyterian
Mission Stations in the Sudan

MAP XI – American Presbyterian
Mission Stations in Ethiopia

ENDNOTES

Introduction

1 See Chart I, "Timeline of Mission Boards preceding Presbyterian Church (U.S.A.)". The major chapter divisions for the latter part of this study correspond to the changes in structure within the mission agencies of the three churches. To a remarkable degree, these structural changes reflect the profound changes which were taking place in the overall context of mission.

2 Ogbu U. Kalu, "Doing Church History in Africa Today," *Church History in an Ecumenical Perspective*, p. 78

Chapter I

3 "The animus created among a number of southern tribes toward the French administration persisted long after forced labor had been abolished." Victor T. LeVine, *The Cameroons: from Mandate to Independence*, p. 104.

4 Minutes of the General Assembly, 1831, p. 332. Quoted in Arthur Judson Brown, *One Hundred Years*, p. 196.

5 Foreign Missionary Chronicle, Vol. I, p. 13. Quoted in Brown, p. 197

6 Green, *Presbyterian Missions*, p. 112. Quoted in Brown, p. 197.

7 Brown, p. 201.

8 Brown, p. 201.

9 Ernest Trice Thompson, *Presbyterians in the South*, Vol. I, p. 297.

10 *Missionary Herald*, XXXIII, Aug. 1837, p. 456. Quoted in paper, "John Leighton Wilson: Man of Vision, Man of Faith", by Martha Jane Peterson, p. 16.

11 Dr. Lamin Sanneh, a native of Gambia and professor of missions and world Christianity at Yale Divinity School, has stated that, while incipient racism affected the policies of the American Colonization Societies, there was at least one positive result of the settlement of former slaves from America in the African colonies. "The traditional pattern of Christian mission in the medieval [15th-17th centuries] period was to arrive in a strange land and ask to see the chief, the ruler, the king. The idea was you converted the king or the ruler, and then the rest of society would be christianized as a consequence. For three hundred years, this idea of mission was attempted in Africa without success. [In the 18th and 19th centuries, when] American blacks arrived in Africa, to christianize the continent, where would they begin? . . . . They said the victims of society—slaves, former slaves, those who were likely to be enslaved—would first be converted, redeemed, sanctified, educated. The example of these freed slaves would then

become so powerful that the rest of society would be converted. This was the model that transformed Africa." ("Sprunt Lectures Explore Slavery, Missions", in *Focus: the Journal of Union Theological Seminary, Richmond, VA,* Summer 1999, p. 7.

[12]   Wilson would serve in Gabon until 1852, when he was forced to return to the United States because of health. In 1853, he was elected one of the Secretaries of the Presbyterian Board of Foreign Missions, located in New York. With the outbreak of the Civil War in 1861, Wilson moved south to Columbia, South Carolina "to suffer with my people." He became Executive Secretary of the Committee on Foreign Missions of the newly-formed Presbyterian Church of the Confederate States of America (which following the war became the Presbyterian Church in the United States), preparing the ringing statement on world mission which was approved by the 1861 General Assembly of that church. In 1876, the headquarters of this Committee was moved from Columbia, S.C. to Baltimore, where Wilson continued to serve as Executive Secretary until his retirement in 1885. He passed away the following year. "Whenever, as is frequently done, the ringing missionary challenge of the 1861 General Assembly is repeated, Dr. J. Leighton Wilson speaks again to Presbyterians, reminding them that obedience to the Great Commission 'is the great end of her organization' and obedience to it 'the indispensable condition of her Lord's promised presence.'" E.T. Thompson, Vol. II, p. 306f. See also Hampton Dubose, *Memoirs of Rev. John Leighton Wilson, D.D.: Missionary to Africa and Secretary of Foreign Missions.* (Richmond: Presbyterian Committee of Publication, 1895)

[13]   The story of American Presbyterian work along the Ogowe River is told in the book *My Ogowe,* by one of the pioneer evangelistic/medical missionaries in that region, Dr. Robert H. Nassau, M.D., S.T.D. (New York: The Neale Publishing Co., 1914).

[14]   One of the stations turned over to the Paris Society was Kangwe, later called Lambarene. This would become famous as the center for the independent work of Dr. Albert Schweitzer, world-renowned surgeon, linguist, musician, theologian, New Testament scholar, philosopher and author. That story is told in Schweitzer's book, *The Forest Hospital of Lambarene.*

[15]   The story of American Presbyterian witness in Spanish Guinea (later to become Equatorial Guinea) will be pursued in the next chapter.

[16]   Relations with the German colonial government of Kamerun were better than with the French in Gabon, but still were not easy. "The government's conditions were that missionaries use the German language in schools, name representatives authorized to deal with the local administration, inform the government beforehand of land to be acquired and of buildings to be erected, and avoid conflicts with other missions." (Norman Horner, *Protestant and Roman Catholic Missions among the Bantu of Cameroun,* p. 39.) During the Bulu Wars (1898-1901) mission-government relations were strained as American Presbyterian missionaries felt that German efforts to quell the war were exceedingly cruel. Certain Presbyterian stations in Bulu country became a refuge for Africans fleeing from both German and African adversaries. The German Governor accused the missionaries of shielding natives against the colonial authorities, and advocated drastic action against the mission. Nevertheless, it was an American Presbyterian missionary, Dr. W.C. Johnston, who was able to arrange the treaty terms ending the war. (Horner, p. 40f.)

[17] The work of this outstanding pioneer missionary is told in the book by E.D. Parsons, *A Life for Africa: Rev. Adolphus C. Good.*

[18] Lois Johnson McNeill, *The Great Ngee: The Story of a Jungle Doctor*, p. 86.

[19] McNeill, p. 69.

[20] McNeill, p. 113f.

[21] McNeill, p. 98-102.

[22] The story of Dr. Johnson's remarkable life and work is told by his daughter, also later a missionary in Cameroun, Lois Johnson McNeill, in her book *The Great Ngee: the Story of a Jungle Doctor.*

[23] *The Drum Call*, January 1952, p. 3ff.

[24] Brown, p. 220.

[25] PCUSA General Assembly Minutes, 1914, p. 72.

[26] PCUSA General Assembly Minutes, 1914, p. 69.

[27] PCUSA General Assembly Minutes, 1914, p. 78.

[28] The German colonial government limited its work in education largely to schools to train staff to work in government administration, and "preferred to rely mostly on missions to carry out the general education of the people. By 1913, throughout the colony there were only four government schools, with 833 pupils, but there were 631 mission schools, with 49,000 pupils." Victor T. LeVine, *The Cameroons: from Mandate to Independence* p. 72.

[29] PCUSA General Assembly Minutes, 1914, p. 71.

[30] PCUSA General Assembly Minutes, 1914, p. 76.

[31] At this time the four missions working in Kamerun were the Gossner Mission (Norwegian), the Basel Mission (Swiss), the German Baptist Mission, and the American Presbyterian Mission. The Roman Catholics were invited to attend the meeting but declined.

[32] The change of geographic nomenclature from the colonial era to contemporary nationhood has been especially marked in the case of Congo. The country itself has borne the following names: Congo Free State (1885-1908); Belgian Congo (1908-1960); Republic of the Congo (1960-1964}; Democratic Republic of Congo (1964-1971); Republic of Zaire (1971-1998); and once again Democratic Republic of Congo (1998-present).

[33] Tshihamba, a Congolese Presbyterian minister, comments in his doctoral dissertation, "The Kimbanguist Movement was not only a protest, it was an affirmation of the cultural being of African people. Although Kimbangu, in the tradition of the Christian church, condemned many African customs—drinking, polygamy—he emphasized the worth of the black man, his genius and eventually his capacity of attending to his own destiny by recuperating his political power." Tshihamba Mukoma Kuendu, *The Development of the Ideology of Authenticity as a Pragmatic Solution to the Problem of Cultural Identity in Zaire* (1975), p. 129.

[34] PCUS General Assembly, 1865, p. 372.

[35] See E.T. Thompson, *Presbyterians in the South*, vol. 2, pp. 20, 94.

[36] Thompson, pp. 310ff.

[37] Ethel T. Wharton, *Led in Triumph*, p. 12. Mrs. Wharton's book is a primary resource for this section.

[38] The story of these pioneers is told in the book by William E. Phipps, *The Sheppards and Lapsley: Pioneers Presbyterians in the Congo.* Louisville, KY: The Presbyterian Church (USA), 1991. One of the presbyteries in Alabama now bears their names, "Sheppards and Lapsley".

[39] Roman Catholic missionary effort turned its interest to the Kasai in the same year, opening their first mission station at Mikilai near Luluabourg. See Kiantandu, *A Study of the Contribution of American Presbyterians to the Formation of the Church of Christ in Zaire with Special Reference to Indigenization, 1891-1960*, p. 50. Kiantandu's doctoral dissertation is an especially valuable resource for the period which it covers, presenting the history of the American Presbyterian Congo Mission and the church which grew out of its witness from a Congolese perspective.

[40] "This is Congo," pamphlet written by Ethel T. Wharton, missionary to Belgian Congo, c. 1954, p. 4.

[41] Between 1891 and 1906, Dr. Sheppard recruited seventeen African-American missionaries for the work in the Congo. Among those who responded to Sheppard's challenge was a remarkable woman, Maria Fearing. Volunteering for mission service at the age of fifty-six, the Executive Committee of Foreign Missions at first declined to send her. However, she offered to serve without compensation, using her personal savings for her own support. Within two years after her arrival in Congo, the Committee recognized the tremendous contribution which she was making in her service as a "mother" to orphaned and abandoned girls whom she brought into her own home in Luebo, and appointed her as a regular missionary under its care. When the first seven converts were baptized into Christ's church in 1895, three of them were girls under the care of Miss Fearing. Miss Fearing served in Congo for 21 years, with only one furlough to the United States during that time. A brief biography of Maria Fearing is found in the book, *Four Presbyterian Pioneers in Congo*, published by the First Presbyterian Church, Anniston, Alabama. Also included are biographies of Lapsley, William Sheppard and. Lucy Gantt Sheppard. More recently, the story of Miss Fearing and other African American missionaries is told in *African Americans in Mission: Serving the Presbyterian Church from 1833 to the Present,* by the Rev. Morrisine Flennaugh Mutshi and Stephen Bartlett.

[42] Kiantandu, p. 80. Another Congolese church leader, Tshihamba Mukoma Luendu, commented: "The Presbyterian Mission had known a rapid development because its work was based on the people who, because of slavery, wars and mistreatment from the colonial government and private companies, had nowhere else to turn. They had to turn to the mission where they could find shelter, food and a new direction, different from the traditional one . . . . While conversion can be considered as a factor, the misery accounted for the reason many joined the mission." Tshihamba, p. 93.

[43] Kiantandu, p. 86.

[44] In 1892, Dr. Sheppard had made an initial attempt to reach the Bakuba. After overcoming many difficulties he at last reached the presence of the king, who mistook him for a son lost in childhood and gave him a royal welcome. Unfortunately before sufficient reenforcements reached the field to take advantage of this opportunity, the king died and was succeeded by a monarch who prohibited foreigners from visiting his town. Bedinger, *Triumphs of the Gospel in the Belgian Congo*, p. 74f.

[45] It was Morrison who proposed that the APCM concentrate its work among the responsive Baluba and Bena Lulua, making use of their common trade language Tshiluba for future work. Later he would prepare the first grammar and dictionary of the Baluba-Lulua language, published by the American Tract Society in 1903. Morrison also translated considerable portions of Scripture into the Tshiluba language, and did the basic work on the Tshiluba Bible which, after Morrison's death in 1918, would be completed by Dr. T.C. Vinson. For a biography of this great missionary statesman, see C.T. Vinson, *William McCutchen Morrison: Twenty Years in Central Africa.*

[46] In 1904, while the Sheppards were on furlough in the United States, the mission station at Ibanche was destroyed by a Bakuba uprising. The Bakuba king, having suffered an affront by the colonial government, sent forth his fighting men "to drive out the white invader, be he trader, officer of the State or missionary." The mission station was rebuilt in early1905. Wharton, pp. 67ff.

    While on furlough, Dr. Sheppard was invited by the Royal Geographical Society of London to make a report of his research among the Bakuba people. As a result of his valuable discoveries, Dr. Sheppard was elected a fellow of the Royal Geographical Society.

[47] Ruth Slade, *English-speaking Missions in the Congo Independent State (1878-1908).* Quoted in Kiantandu, p. 101.

[48] Later a Congolese church leader would write, "From the days of the Congo Free State onward, the colonial administration relied on sheer military force for the accomplishment of the occupation of the country. The State organized a colonial force, the *Force Publique*, playing the role of the police and the army, composed mainly of undesirable elements of African societies. In its early stage, the *Force Publique* recruited its soldiers from groups of people considered either as criminals in the traditional system, the disinherited slaves, traitors to their own people or just Africans of good social standing but from a distant region. The idea behind this method of recruitment was to make sure that soldiers felt strangers among African people against whom they were to carry oppressive expeditions." Tshihamba, p. 76.

[49] William H. Crane, *Presbyterian Work in the Congo: a Historical Study of the Development of Mission and Church in the Kasai (1891-1959).* The full and fascinating account of this aspect of the work of the APCM is told in Stanley Shaloff's *Reform in Leopold's Congo* and in the more recent book by Adam Hockschild, *King Leopold's Ghost: A Story of Greed, Terror and Heroism in Colonial Africa.*

[50] Though the early missionaries did medical work of sorts by sharing what medicines they possessed, the first medical doctor, Dr. L.J. Coppedge, arrived in 1906. Being the only doctor within hundreds of miles, he served not only the African and missionary community, but also State and Company agents and the Roman Catholic missionary force. In 1911 King Albert of Belgium cited Dr. Coppedge "for devoted and distinguished service to his Majesty's subjects, both European and African." Later, other American Presbyterian missionaries would receive similar recognition as the Belgian Government acknowledged their service to the Colony. Wharton, p. 76f.

51   The first steamer met with disaster soon after its launching in 1901 in the treacherous whirlpools near the mouth of the Kasai River. A second Lapsley, larger and stronger than the first, docked at Luebo in Christmas Eve 1906, and would ply the Congo and its tributaries for the next 25 years, "bringing the Gospel to many who knew it not, and strength and encouragement to Christians scattered in the settlements along the river." Wharton, p. 67. The fascinating story of the steamer Lapsley is told in *The Lapsley Saga*, by Winifred K. and Lacklan C. Vass III, published by Providence House Publishers, Franklin, Tennessee, 1997.

52   The United Presbyterian Church of North America (UPNA) came into being in 1858, uniting two traditions of Scottish Presbyterians, the Covenanters and the Seceders. Their strength centered in the region surrounding Pittsburgh, Pennsylvania. The UPNA did a very significant work in the anti-slavery movement during and following the Civil War, working among black refugees who sought freedom behind Federal army lines in middle and east Tennessee. In time the church's work among blacks expanded to include churches and schools in Tennessee, Kentucky, Virginia, North Carolina, and Alabama. The church had a significant pioneer missionary work in Egypt (beginning in 1854), India and Pakistan (beginning in 1855), the Sudan (beginning in 1900), and Ethiopia (beginning in 1919). See Leffert A. Loetscher, *A Brief History of the Presbyterians*, pp. 150ff.

53   Tradition has it that Queen Candace of Merowe was converted by the preaching of her State Treasurer, the Ethiopian eunuch who had met Philip on the road from Jerusalem to Gaza (Acts 8:26-40), and that it was this witness which led to the conversion of many in the region of Nubia. See Reid F. Shields, *Behind the Garden of Allah*, p. 38f.

54   The story of the beginning of American Presbyterian work in the Sudan is told by Dr. Giffen in a book published in 1905, *The Egyptian Sudan*.

55   See Wallace M. Jamison, *The United Presbyterian Story: a Centennial Study, 1858-1958*, p. 179f.

56   Jamison, p. 182.

57   Shields, p. 110.

58   Trimingham (1948), p. 22.

59   Trimingham, *The Christian Church in Postwar Sudan* (1949), p. 8.

60   Trimingham (1948), pp. 29-36.

61   Jamison, p. 183.

62   UPNA General Assembly Minutes, 1914, p. 747f.

63   UPNA General Assembly Minutes, 1914, p. 748.

64   The sailboat was later succeeded by a motorboat, then a launch called "The Erskine" and a small barge christened "The Evangel." The account of these early decades of American Presbyterian witness in the Sudan is told in the book by Reid Frampton Shields, *Behind the Garden of Allah*.

65   Trimingham comments, "This advance of Christianity into a region which might easily have become a sphere for the further penetration of Islamic influence into Central Africa is highly important from the strategical point of view since it vitally affects the influence and relative position of the two faiths." Trimingham (1949), p. 19.

Chapter II

66   Dr. Evelyn Adams recalls how, on December 26, 1914, the Germans attacked Batanga Station and more than 1000 Batanga people crowded into the station area. "Some of the people were taken prisoner and many ran away. A British ship took as many as it could to Victoria but the sea was left black with people who could not get on board. Many died at Victoria but also many returned when the fighting was over. May 9th became a day of Thanksgiving which is observed every year, a day of thanksgiving when the people returned to Batanga and a revival began which greatly added to the church membership." (Personal correspondence from. Dr. Evelyn Adams.)

67   McNeill, p. 141.

68   There was great suspicion among Protestant missionaries that the French government at first did all within its power to hinder Protestant work and to favor Roman Catholic missionary efforts. As one Presbyterian Board Secretary put it, "It is apparent that our erstwhile ally, the Republic of France, is not so favorable to Protestant missions as our enemy Germany." Yet following initial difficulties, the American missionaries enjoyed generally satisfactory relations with the French administration. Horner, p. 81ff.

69   The church at Elat would become at one point the largest Presbyterian church in the world, with a membership of some 15,000 members. The *Drum Call* (October 1950, p. 3ff.) would recall the memorable Sunday in 1915 when some 6000 people gathered for the baptism of 608 new church members. "In the depths of the world-wide depression [the Bulu Christians] decided to raise funds to build their largest church", dedicated in 1933. See William D. Reyburn, *Out of the African Night*, p. 86.

70   Foulassi was an administrative post established by the new French colonial government. It was located in the area of the Yebekolo people, and was considered cannibal country. See McNeill, ch. 22, "A Clinic for the Yebekolo."

71   The story of the Bulu evangelist, Evina Zambo, who began the Christian witness at Bafia, is told in L.K. Anderson's *Incidents and Recollections of Missionary Service*, p. 42ff. Also, the fascinating story of the building of the church at Bafia is told in the book *Bridge to Africa*, by L.K. Anderson and W. Sherman Skinner.

72   The Basel Mission continued its work in the British Cameroons, work which later produced the English-speaking Presbyterian Church of Cameroon.

73   Statistics and other information regarding the situation of American Presbyterian work in 1940 is drawn from the General Assembly minutes of the Presbyterian Church, U.S.A, 1940. The station at Benito in Spanish Guinea was considered part of the West Africa Mission during this period. However, we shall reserve consideration of this work until the next section of this chapter.

74   Information regarding American Presbyterian work in West Africa up to 1936 has been gleaned primarily from the monumental work by Arthur Judson Brown, *One Hundred Years: A History of the Foreign Missionary Work of the Presbyterian Church in the USA*, published in 1936. Brown's work relies extensively upon the book by W. Reginald Wheeler, *The Words of God in an African Forest: the Story of an American Mission in West Africa*, published in 1931. Also helpful has been Groves, *The Planting of Christianity in Africa*, Vol. 4, p. 38 et al.

75 The work of the Rev. Frank D. Emerson is described in his autobiography, *The Farthest Away Man*.

76 "Churches are grouped according to Mission Stations. In 1938 they were entirely dependent upon their stations for distribution of literature, payment of salaries, conducting of conferences and institutes, and the assignment of all lay Bible readers and teachers. Since the missionary was *de facto* director of the station, he inevitably supervised all these church affairs." The situation was further exacerbated by the fact that the French colonial government conceived of the African Church solely in terms of the Mission. All communications were directed to the missionary in charge, and all African pastors were considered Mission employees. "In many cases, the local [colonial] administrator scarcely knew who they were, and made little effort to find out." Horner, *The Development of an Indigenous Presbyterian Church in the French Cameroun*, p. 25f.

An effort was made to bridge this difficult gap between Mission and Church by the organizing in 1938 of a Joint Conference of missionaries and nationals, composed of selected representatives from the evangelistic, educational and medical departments of the work. Designed to serve as a clearing house for the discussion of church, school and hospital problems, the conference had no power of decision, but it did help to clarify issues and facilitate proper disposition by the groups concerned. Horner, *op. cit.,* p. 33f.

77 Henry Teddy Mokosso, *The United Presbyterian Mission Enterprise in Cameroun, 1879-1957*, p. 54. Mokosso, a Camerounian, completed this doctoral dissertation at Howard University in 1987.

78 Wheeler, p. 168. The teachers of the vernacular schools were always considered to be the companions of the village catechists, and in the case of the small villages, the two jobs were often performed by the same individual. Horner, p. 34.

79 Brown, p. 227.

80 Brown, p. 228.

81 The scourge of sleeping sickness was an especially serious threat. In 1936 an epidemic occurred in the region of Nkol Mvolan and hundreds died. The hospital at Nkol Mvolan was closed for years by the colonial government to prevent people coming from non-infected areas into that region. (Personal correspondence from Dr. Evelyn Adams)

82 From *African Clearings*, by Jean Kenyon MacKenzie; qouted in Wheeler, p. 169.

83 The press was initiated through a memorial gift in tribute to Dr. A.W. Halsey, Secretary of the Board of Foreign Missions of the PCUSA, whose visit to West Africa in 1905 made a lasting impression upon the future planning for mission in Cameroun. McNeill, p. 96ff.

84 PCUSA General Assembly Minutes, 1940, BFM Report, p. 100, 107.

85 PCUSA General Assembly Minutes, 1942, BFM Report, p. 123f.

86 PCUSA General Assembly Minutes, 1940, BFM Report, p. 124.

87 Dr. W.M. Morrison, quoted in Wharton, p. 86.

88 Mutoto, meaning "star", was the African name of Bertha Stebbins (Mrs. William M.) Morrison, who had died in service in 1910.

89 Lusambo, on the Sankuru River, was sought primarily as a transport station where the steamer Lapsley could dock the whole year round.

90 "Bulape" was the Bakuba name given to Mrs. Annie Katherine Taylor Rochester. When the new station was occupied in 1915, it was named Bulape "to perpetuate the memory of Mrs. A.A. Rochester, a colored missionary of high ability who died at Mutoto on May 14, 1914, after eight years of efficient and consecrated service." Mutschi, p. 20.

91 Wharton, pp. 90ff.

92 Kiantandu, p. 184.

93 Bedinger p.124.

94 Wharton, p. 114

95 Wharton, p. 96.

96 Bedinger, p. 180f. Most Protestant missionaries in this period saw the Roman Catholic missionary effort in terms of "the peril of Romanism." It was described as "destructive to morals", "destructive to education", and "destructive to freedom of government." (Bedinger, p. 176-180) However, William Morrison advised an attitude of consideration and friendship: "We should recognize at the beginning that both Protestant and Roman Catholic missionaries are in the same work of establishing the kingdom of our Lord Jesus Christ among the Congo people. We desire to be open minded and charitable toward all who come in the name of Jesus Christ." (Vinson, p. 135. Quoted in Kiantandu, p. 214.)

97 Wharton, p. 121f.

98 Kiantandu, p. 223.

99 Wharton, p. 130.

100 Adrian Hastings, one of the leading authorities on African Christianity, comments: "All the Christian Mission societies working in Africa in 1925 were very hesitant to organize autonomous churches . . . . The reason was the growth of institutions. The very development of increasingly complex institutions appeared to justify this attitude. Who could run all these things in the foreseeable future except white men?" Adrian Hastings, *African Christianity*, p. 6f.

101 One of the three pastors ordained in 1916, Kachunga, had "proven a disappointment." After his conversion, he had shown an aptitude for translation work and became the helper of Dr. Morrison in the completion of the Dictionary and Grammar of the Baluba-Lulua language, even accompanying Dr. Morrison to America for this purpose. Though "unusually intelligent and a strong preacher", he was "very proud" and, soon after his ordination as a pastor, developed "a spirit of insubordination to Mission authority, which unhappily affected a number of evangelists." The "Kachunga rebellion", as it was called, was seen as a threat to the work of the mission. Kachunga was censured by the mission and reduced to the rank of an ordinary evangelist. However, instead of creating another branch of the church as happened in numerous other places in Africa during this period, Kachunga accepted his disgrace and requested that he be permitted to return to his boyhood home to labor without pay until "he had retrieved his mistake." Bedinger commented, "His experience will doubtless have a salutary effect on the entire Church." See Bedinger, p. 126f.; also Kiantandu, p. 187f.

102 Kiantandu, p. 238.

103 Kiantandu, p. 248ff.

104 Crane, p. 103.

105 Kiantandu, p. 275f.

106 Crane, p. 90.

107 Kiantandu, p. 255. See also Wharton, p. 105f.

108 Crane, p. 85. Crane refers to this as the "heroic age" of the APCM's history, "even more so than the age of the pioneers." More adult missionary deaths were recorded during this period than during any other period of the Mission's history.

109 However, APCM refused to cooperate with sister missions in a Union Normal School, saying that "we do not believe the time is propitious: that the trend of the native at the present time is toward commercialism and material advantages to be gained from it, and that the present missionary force and restricted budget are insufficient." APCM Minutes, 1937, p. 13. Quoted in Kiantandu, p. 331.

110 Crane, p. 82. Ross comments, "These smaller tribes had languages different from Tshiluba, they were much more traditional in their views and less influenced by the entrance of Europeans. Therefore, churches in these areas have remained relatively small. Perhaps one of the reasons is to be found in the paucity of leaders from these tribes, since all evangelism was accomplished by members of the Baluba and Lulua tribes who were much more advanced and open to the Gospel." Charles Ross, *The Emergence of the Presbyterian Church in the Kasai, Congo*, p. 60.

111 Wharton, p. 157.

112 Jamison, p. 181.

113 UPNA General Assembly Minutes, 1940, p. 63.

114 Jamison, p. 184.

115 UPNA General Assembly Minutes, 1935, p. 967.

116 UPNA General Assembly Minutes, 1939, p. 1007.

117 See I Kings 10:1-13; II Chronicles 9:1-12. A fourteenth-century Ethiopian document, "The Glory of Kings", tells how the Queen of Sheba visited Solomon, returned home pregnant with his child who became Menelik I of Ethiopia, founder of the Solomonic dynasty; further, how Menelik later visited his father and carried off the Ark of the Covenant which he bore back to Axum, the ancient capital of Ethiopia. See Hastings, *A History of African Christianity 1950-1975*, p. 36.

118 A fundamental question which each Protestant mission had to face was the relationship to the Ethiopian Orthodox Church. Actually, few entered Ethiopia with the idea of competition. "They came to stimulate the people to an awareness of the truths of Christ and the Bible, truths which would give them a reality in Christian living. This spiritual awakening might help the Ethiopic Church to regain its vitality." (Kissling, *May We Introduce Ethiopia*, p. 27) However, Ethiopians who came under the influence of Protestant witness adopted an outlook on Christian faith and worship quite different from that of the national Church, and eventually found themselves in such disharmony with the traditional church that they felt it necessary to form their own congregations. Added to this, as we shall see, was the persecution which the Orthodox Church at first leveled against the Protestant witness.

119 That Ethiopia was not only an ancient African kingdom but also an ancient Christian kingdom and church has been of immense importance in shaping the aspirations of many African

Christians. "Ethiopianism" affirms the values of authentic African culture and history over against indiscriminate Europeanization. Many indigenous churches both in Africa and among African-Americans in the United States have taken into their names either "Ethiopia" or another ancient name for this kingdom "Abyssinia." The Rastafarian movement, found particularly among young Caribbean black men, has taken its name from one of the titles for the Ethiopian emperor Haile Selassie, "Ras Tafari." See Hastings, *African Christianity*, p. 40.

[120] Ullendorf, *The Ethiopians: An Introduction to Country and People*, p. 33.

[121] Krapf was deeply struck by the enormous number of Oromo (Galla) in Ethiopia and believed that their conversion would be the clue to converting Eastern Africa. This made an indelible impression on Protestant missions in nearby Kenya. In 1844, Krapf pioneered for CMS in Kenya, and in 1860 led a Methodist mission into Ethiopia with the aim of "reaching the Gallas." After his martyrdom, the effort was abandoned; yet in following years, missions working in central Kenya built chains of mission stations to the north trying to reach the fabled Galla people. (From personal correspondence of Dr. William B. Anderson.)

[122] The story of Dr. Lambie's ministry is told in several autobiographical works, *A Doctor without a Country* (1939}, *A Doctor Carries On* (1942), *Boot and Saddle in Africa* (1943), and *A Doctor's Great Commission* (1954). Soon after beginning the work in Addis Ababa, Dr. Lambie, dissatisfied with the reluctance of his home board to sanction an advance into new territory, organized the Abyssinian Frontier Mission, which in 1927 merged with the Sudan Interior Mission (Latourette, *A History of the Expansion of Christianity*, Vol. VII, p. 260).

Chapter III

[123] Quoted in C.P. Groves, *The Planting of Christianity in Africa, Volume Four, 1914-1954*, p. 5. Aggrey was one of the most prominent African Christian leaders in the 1920s. Twenty years of study in America had been followed by travel throughout Africa. "A magnetic orator, a man of endless energy, humour and balance, he was the black world's ideal ambassador to the white, the white world's ideal ambassador to the black." (Adrian Hastings, *African Christianity*, p. 8). For further information regarding Aggrey, see William M. Macartney, *Dr. Aggrey, Ambassador for Africa*.

[124] Quoted in Groves, p. 254. By contrast to the First World War, many more in the African military ranks were at least nominally Christian—indeed, some sixty per cent has been estimated. "We were one company of men in a far country but we knew that we needed the help of God and that He was near us." *Ibid.*, p. 256.

[125] J.F.A. Ajayi, *Historical Atlas of Africa*, p. 67f. The writer is indebted to this work for much of the above summary of the impact of World War II on Africa.

[126] The most thorough work in this regard has been done by David Barrett, and appears in the monumental work which he has edited, *World Christian Encyclopedia*, published in 1982.

[127] The above figures appear in Groves, p. 245.

[128] PCUSA General Assembly Minutes, 1940, Board of Foreign Missions (BFM) Report, p. 97.

[129] Dr. Reyburn tells the heartrending story of the arrival of a huge order of medical supplies at the Camerounian harbor of Kribi in 1941, having made its way across the perilous Atlantic,

only to be dropped into the sea in the offloading from the ship. "She was gone, sunk to the bottom, and down with her went the lives of many." Reyburn, p. 101ff.

130 PCUSA General Assembly Minutes, 1946, BFM Report, p. 63.

131 PCUSA General Assembly Minutes, 1941, BFM Report, p. 111.

132 Reyburn, p. 101.

133 PCUSA General Assembly Minutes, 1941, BFM Report, p. 109.

134 The tremendous task of translating the Old Testament was primarily the work of Dr. A.C. Good, "with his constant helper Ndo at his side." However, there were some missionaries who doubted the value of this work, "hinting that the polygamous practices of the Old Testament characters corresponded too closely with the conditions actually existing in West Africa to make it safe for free distribution among a people whose customs were incompatible with Christian principles." PCUSA General Assembly minutes, 1941, BFM report, p. 108.

The choice of the Bulu vernacular as the language for the Bible and other Christian literature for the larger part of the West Africa Mission's work did not meet with universal approval. There were frequent protests from disgruntled tribes who considered their own vernaculars slighted, especially in areas where there had been strong traditional rivalry with the Bulu people. See Horner, *The Development of an Indigenous Presbyterian Church in the French Cameroun*, p. 40f.

135 Reyburn, p. 119.

136 PCUSA General Assembly Minutes, 1942, BFM Report, p. 118. The Bassa New Testament and Psalms were first published in 1950, and the entire Bible in Bassa was published in 1969.

137 PCUSA General Assembly Minutes, 1942, BFM Report, p. 122.

138 PCUSA General Assembly Minutes, 1940, BFM Report, p. 99. In time, Presbyterian missionary Ronald B. Brook was able to do a significant work among the pygmies and translated portions of the Scriptures into their language. Evelyn A. Adams, *Forst Woman Doctor to Cameroun*, p. 56.

139 PCUSA General Assembly Minutes, 1943, BFM Report, p. 16.

140 Full details regarding developments in church-mission relationships during this period are given in the final chapter of Horner's *The Development of an Indigenous Presbyterian Church*, Chapter V, "The Final Steps Toward Autonomy."

141 PCUSA General Assembly Minutes, 1942, BFM Report, p. 120.

142 Assale, a former government medical assistant, later left the UPC and became Minister of Finance in the pre-independence government, then Prime Minister in the government of President Ahiojo in 1960. Um Nyobe, formerly a teacher in a mission school, had gone to France for study and there became involved in the independence movement encouraged by the French Communist party. He continued as a UPC leader and while in hiding with guerrilla forces in the forest was assassinated in 1958.

143 The American Presbyterian missionaries were more cautious and diplomatic. At the height of the rebellion in 1955, the Mission appointed a special task force known as the "Special Committee on Present Day Problems." Its report included the following: "This committee feels that, as a Mission, and as individual missionaries, our primary responsibility to our African brothers has been in the past, and remains today, that of preaching Jesus Christ and presenting

Him as the final answer to all problems. It is felt that it would be unwise for us to discuss or to present to our African friends a consideration of such secondary issues as communism, nationalism and other present day problems, without making clear their relation to Jesus Christ Himself." Mokosso, p. 272f. Nevertheless, the Presbyterian Mission and Church came under severe criticism from the French colonial government "for fostering and aiding the revolutionaries", since most of the leaders of the independence movement were Protestant.

144   Anderson gives a graphic description of the guerrilla fighters: they were "huge men all dressed in jungle outfits, camouflaged khaki, high boots, steel helmets, with grenades hanging from their belts, large knives strapped to their legs and vicious looking automatic rifles slung over their shoulders. They were everywhere, in the streets, in the shops, as well as truck loads on the move hither and yon." Still they could do little to deter the guerrillas: "The *maquizards* as the terrorists were called struck almost nightly at some unprotected village, burning, killing and taking with them all edible supplies and livestock. They camped out in the forest in groups of three or four. By the use of drums and other signals they gathered forces to attack some chosen village or town at a pre-determined time, and dispersed again carrying their new provisions with them." Anderson, *Incidents and Recollections of Missionary Service*, p. 96.

145   Material for this section on political developments is drawn primarily from Chapter VI, "Ferment of Party Politics—1945—1955", of LeVine's *The Camerouns: from Mandate to Independence.*

146   The Roman Catholic Church encouraged a Christian labor union within its own constituency, with a view to safeguarding its interests against possible Communist domination. The feasibility of Protestant Christian trade unions was discussed among mission groups, but did not materialize. Therefore, many mission employees joined secular labor unions. Horner, *The Development of an Indigenous Presbyterian Church*, p. 59.

147   Mokosso, p. 88f.

148   Mokosso, p. 148-154. Mokosso makes a strong case for considerable racial prejudice among some American Presbyterian missionaries during this period.

149   The catechists class was usually much larger, composed of "mature men who had already served several years as catechists, and were chosen by their mission stations as giving marked promise of leadership ability." The usual course was two years, "after which they received a certificate, and then returned to their home stations, often on foot, for a larger assignment." The theological class was usually made up of younger men with a more advanced education, who pursued a three-year course of study. "They maintained a social distance from the catechists toward whom their superior education gave them a kind of disdain." Horner, *op. cit.* p. 103f.

150   PCUSA General Assembly Minutes, 1945, BFM Report, p. 20.

151   PCUSA Board of Foreign Missions, Report of Deputation, p. 4; quoted in Morosso, p. 232.

152   In commenting on the revised curriculum, Horner wrote, "This curriculum has much to commend it at the point of integrating the Cameroun Church with the traditions of Protestant Christianity throughout the world. But it is woefully lacking in preparation for African ministers to cope with their own environment. Moreover, the pre-seminary training of the students is also lacking in the social sciences. This is especially serious in a time of nationalistic ambitions and

seething unrest, social upheaval through urbanization and detribalization." Beginning in 1954, the seminary course was extended to four years, allowing for wider variety in the curriculum. Horner, *Protestant and Roman Catholic Missions among the Bantu of Cameroun*, p. 185.

153 Report of Dager Biblical Seminary to the Board of Foreign Missions, PCUSA, 1956. Another result of the 1945 Mission Board Deputation was the decision to separate the catechists' department from the seminary, and establish a school for catechists in each of the three presbyteries. The plan was carried out with mixed results: "The new presbyterial certificate given at the completion of two years' study did not seem to carry the prestige of the old Dager Seminary certificate." Horner, *The Development of an Indigenous Presbyterian Church*, p. 129ff.

154 PCUSA General Assembly Minutes, 1946, BFM Report, p. 64.

155 PCUSA General Assembly Minutes, 1946, BFM Report, p. 66.

156 PCUSA General Assembly Minutes, 1951, BFM Report, p. 83.

157 PCUSA General Assembly Minutes, 1956, BFM Report, p. 61.

158 Actually during its early years the Institut included only those levels which in the American educational system would correspond to High School. It was after 1960 that courses were added leading to the Bachelor degree, which in the French educational system is preparatory to a university education. For a period of time, IME was the only such school in Cameroun. (Personal correspondence from Dr. Robert N. Peirce, who served as Directeur of IME from 1951 until 1962. I am indebted to Dr. Peirce for other details regarding these early years of IME.)

159 Anderson, *Incidents*, p. 106.

160 PCUSA General Assembly Minutes, 1947, BFM Report, p. 62.

161 Mokosso writes, "By educating their converts, the Presbyterian missionaries helped to create a Western educated class which rivalled and in some respects comprised an elite separate from the traditional elite in the African social order." Mokosso, p. 288.

162 The Rev. Camille Chazeaud, a French Reformed minister who joined the American Presbyterian Mission, was the founder of this school which "was to become an important nursery for future educators and government leaders." The school hymn, composed by the students under Chazeaud's supervision, would later become the national anthem of the United Republic of Cameroun. See L.K. Anderson, *Incidents*, p. 18.

163 Mokosso comments, "The Frank James Industrial School was one of the outstanding ventures of Presbyterian missionary education. The purpose of the school was to produce skilled workmen of sterling Christian character. The school began earnestly in 1908 with two Bulu boys being taught carpentry under roughly constructed sheds. To the carpentry and tailoring classes were added shoemaking, tanning, general machine, garage and blacksmithing, agriculture, manufacture of rattan furniture, ivory works, pith helmets, hats and caps, mechanical drawing, and masonry." Mokosso, p. 46.

164 In her memoirs, Dr. Evelyn A. Adams describes the training given to prepare medical assistants: an eight-week course in Pharmacology, Medicine, Physical Diagnosis, and Anatomy was required for a fourth-class medical assistant; after three years of service, an additional eight-week session in Pediatrics, Obstetrics, Preventive Medicine, and Laboratory prepared a person for third-class; After three more years, eight weeks training in Surgery, Advanced Medicine, Gynecology, and Therapeutics led to second-class status; three years later, after

passing examinations, one was eligible to become a first-class medical assistant. Only one period of training and examination was required for those preparing for nursing. See *First Woman Doctor to Cameroun*, p. 22.

165 Horner, *Protestant and Roman Catholic Missions*, p. 343.

166 PCUSA General Assembly Minutes, BFM Report, p. 61f.

167 Helen D. Palmer tells the story of her work among the lepers at Ndjazeng in her autobiography, *Twenty-eight Years in Africa*.

168 Reyburn writes, "Kan Mo Chung, an amputee from the Presbyterian Hospital in Taegu, Korea, came to the Cameroun and set up the limb shop. He taught six Africans to make artificial arms and legs from the special lightweight woods which were supplied by the leprosy patients at Ndjazeng. Mr. Chung's work was an immediate success." Reyburn, p. 157.

169 Horner, *Protestant and Roman Catholic Missions*, p. 339. In 1955, Dr. George Thorne, veteran medical missionary at Central Hospital, was recognized by the French colonial government with the French Legion of Honor; then later with a similar tribute by the Cameroun government. Reyburn, p. 165ff.

170 UPCUSA General Assembly Minutes, 1958, BFM Report, p. 71f.

171 "The chief missionary drive . . . continued toward the interior and the smaller villages, to the unfortunate, perhaps ruinous, neglect of work in large and important centers like Yaounde." Horner, *The Development of an Indigenous Presbyterian Church*, p. 61.

172 PCUSA General Assembly Minutes, 1946, BFM Report, p. 65.

173 Horner, *The Development of an Indigenous Presbyterian Church*, pp. 64-68.

174 Mokosso comments, "Generally the missionary impact was greater upon young people than upon the older generation . . . Having acquired the skills to read and write, the youths saw themselves as heirs of the white man's civilization which they believed placed them above other people. They spoke disparagingly of the customs and traditions of their society and hailed the new era of Christianity and Western civilization as a blessing from God." Mokosso, p. 109f.

175 Mokosso comments, "Although the break in relations between the Presbyterian Mission and the Ngoumba occurred in 1934, the grievances of the Ngoumba against the Presbyterians on the one hand, and against the Bulu on the other, were deeper and long standing . . . . The Ngoumba and the Bulu were traditional rivals and enemies in the trade on the coast in the pre-colonial era. Far too often the Bulu raided the Ngoumba, carrying away booty and marriageable girls." Mokosso, p. 58-63.

176 PCUSA General Assembly Minutes, 1951, BFM Report, p. 80.

177 Report of the Dager Seminary Conference, pp. 3-4; quoted in Mokosso, p. 265.

178 Mokosso comments, "Apparently the Africans were suspicious of the change of terminology from missionary to 'fraternal worker.' To most of them it was neo-colonialism in the church. Pessimists of the change compared it with wolves putting on sheep's clothing. Most Africans did not believe that the missionaries, especially the older and conservative ones, would reconcile with the reality of the independence of the church." Mokosso, p. 276.

179 Mokosso, p. 266. Also, Andrew T. Roy, *Historical Overview of the Overseas Mission Policies of the UPCUSA*, p. 29f.

180 PCUSA General Assembly Minutes, 1955, BFM Report, p. 63f.

[181]   Anderson recalled: "As soon as roads leading South and North were open and relatively safe, with temporary bridges rebuilt, I received permission to make trips of investigation to find out how our little primary schools and chapels had fared. It was utter destruction in many of the areas I visited. Tall watch towers, now deserted, had been built by the army to protect some of the villages that escaped, but in most cases it was desolation after desolation, nothing but charred remains of what formerly had been a thriving village of several hundred inhabitants. There were no remains of either schools or chapels, except a few torn leaves from Bibles, hymn books or exercise books from the schools, no chickens, goats or sheep anywhere to be seen, not a soul would answer my echoing call." Anderson, *Incidents*, p. 96f.

[182]   The murder of Presbyterian missionary Lucia Cozzens on October 13, 1949 by an unknown intruder was never solved, though there was suspicion of UPC involvement, since Mrs. Cozzens was involved in preparing materials for a forthcoming mission from the United Nations concerning the French Trusteeship of Cameroun. (Personal correspondence from Dr. Evelyn Adams.) See *The Drum Call*, April 1950, which is in memorium of Mrs. Cozzens.

[183]   Anderson was called to the office of the Secretary General of the territory of Cameroun. "He was an old associate and a real friend over the years of our residence in Cameroun. Rather apologetically he explained that at a cabinet meeting that morning serious consideration was given to the proposal to have all the Presbyterian missionaries deported from the territory because of their subversive activities, aiding and abetting the anti-colonial guerrilla forces . . . . He assured the cabinet he would report to me these suspicions of the Government and request the Mission to refrain from anything that might be interpreted as aid to the guerrillas." Anderson, *Incidents*, p. 98f.

[184]   A Long-Range Study conducted by the Board of Foreign Missions in September 1956 made this assessment: "The political situation in the Cameroun, as in all Africa, is in a very real sense the determinative factor in the future of mission work there. Many leaders of the independence movements, perhaps most of them, are either Christians or at least the products of Christian institutions . . . . Independence movements in most countries are the outgrowth of the very systems of education and Christian training which the Missions have engendered in those countries. We have not ourselves to *blame* for this; we should rejoice in the fact; but we stand in judgment if, in the light of these changing conditions which we ourselves have helped to create, we are not able to adjust our perspectives and find equitable and just solutions for the problems which arise from it."

[185]   Mary Hunter, "Cameroun General Assembly", *The Drum Call*, April 37, 1958, p. 6; quoted in Mokosso, p. 277f. L.K. Anderson gives a graphic description of certain events at this first EPC General Assembly. In his sermon Dr. Eugene Carson Blake, Stated Clerk of the PCUSA, chose as his text Galatians 5:13: "For you were called to freedom, only do not use your freedom as an opportunity for the flesh, but through love be servants one of another." Anderson writes, "Every time Dr. Blake spoke of 'freedom' there would be a shout from the masses of people surrounding the platform." French authorities at the ceremony "were very much disturbed by Dr. Blake's address which, they felt, had incited the populace to riot against the Government by encouraging them to strike for 'freedom'." Later a French translation of the sermon, along with a visit of Dr. Blake and Mr. Anderson to the French High Commissioner, assured the authorities

that the sermon was intended to encourage church members to take seriously the responsibilities which went with their new-found freedom in the church Anderson, *Incidents*, p. 104f.

[186] From the statistical report of the Board of Foreign Missions, in the PCUSA General Assembly Minutes, 1957. Statistics reported in the BFM Long-range Study of September 1956 indicated that all Protestants in Cameroun numbered 336,170 or 11% of the total population, as compared to 16% being Roman Catholic.

[187] Quoted in UPCUSA General Assembly Minutes, 1958, final report of the Board of Foreign Missions, p. 74.

[188] PCUSA General Assembly Minutes, 1948, BFM Report, p. 79.

[189] PCUSA General Assembly Minutes, 1950, BFM Report, p. 66.

[190] PCUSA General Assembly Minutes, 1951, BFM Report, p. 81.

[191] PCUSA General Assembly Minutes, 1952, BFM Report, p. 64.

[192] PCUSA General Assembly Minutes, 1953, BFM Report, p. 62.

[193] One reason given for the Spanish colonial government's restrictive measures against the American Presbyterian work was the fact that the missionaries employed the Bulu language in their preaching and teaching. Bulu, one of the languages of people living across the border in French Cameroun, was foreign to the people of the interior of Spanish Guinea who spoke Ntumu and Okak. Doubtless this raised suspicion among the Spanish authorities that people living in the interior might become more sympathetic with the French than with the Spanish.

[194] Among the places where churches had been established at this point were six coastal churches with full sessions: Corisco, established in 1856; Bolondo (formerly Benito), the oldest Presbyterian church in continental West Africa; Bata, the capital city and major port; Handje, Pienta Mbonda, and Myuma. Along the east-west highway were churches at Mongo, 38 miles east of Bata, where the first church among the interior Ntumu people was established in 1933, and which in turn became the mother church of some 30 chapels among the Ntumu and Okak tribes; Ebabiyin, in the upper northeast corner of Rio Muni, location of the largest Presbyterian Church in Rio Muni with over 430 members; Bidjabijan and Mbeme. On the north-south highway was the church at Adjabasi. The only other Protestant work in Rio Muni was carried out by the Worldwide Evangelization Crusade (WEC) of Great Britain, begun in 1933. The American Presbyterian work was strongest along the borders with Cameroun and Gabon, while the WEC work was concentrated in southern Rio Muni. See paper, "Church Tourist Guide for Rio Muni."

[195] While no official medical work was permitted in Rio Muni, the Central Hospital in Elat, Cameroun was of tremendous service to those from the churches and villages of Rio Muni needing medical help. Also, most of the few ministerial candidates received their theological training at the Dager Seminary in Cameroun.

[196] At the stations where there was no resident physician, the Government withheld subsidies, which meant a loss of considerable income for the work. PCUS Foreign Mission Annual Report 1941, p. 20. Dr. William Rule tells vividly the story of his grueling experience during the war years, when he spent less than half the year at the hospital in Lubondai and most of the year traveling from mission station to mission station to give "the illusion that all work responsibilities [at all the mission hospitals] were being adequately covered." Dr. William Rule's personal memoirs, *Milestones in Mission*, pp. 118ff.

197   The colonial government recognized medical helpers in three categories. Those with the least training were called *aide-infirmiers*, or nurse's aides. Beyond this there were several organized schools with a three-year course plus a two-year period of practical application which awarded a diploma of *infirmier diplome*, equivalent to a registered nurse. The highest category at this time, which was discontinued after independence, was assistant medical or medical assistant. After independence, the medical assistants were giving further schooling in Europe and returned to Congo as physicians. Rule, p. 169.

198   Dr. Kellersberger had initiated the medical work at Bibanga in the early years following the beginning of that mission station in 1917. The Edna Kellersberger Memorial Hospital at Bibanga stood as a tribute to his deceased first wife. Rule, p. 166.

199   Crane, p. 55. During this period there were 24 cases of sleeping sickness among Presbyterian missionaries and their families, a larger number than in all the previous fifty years. Rule, p. 118.

200   "Helping One Another," *Congo Mission News*, October 1940, p. 2. Quoted in Kiantandu, p. 370f.

201   Kiantandu, p. 374f.

202   Crane, p. 84.

203   By 1945 the Protestant church in Africa numbered about 2,131,000 communicants (with almost 20% of them in the Belgian Congo) and the Catholic Church almost 4,613,000 (with more than 40% of them in the Belgian Congo). Kiantandu, p. 401.

204   Crane, p. 83.

205   The significant role of the evangelists in the remarkable growth of the Kasai Church was well expressed by John Morrison in 1941: "What shall be said of our native evangelists, whose faithful service had made so much of this possible? Today there are 1,048 of them, many of them receiving no financial aid, and others receiving but a few cents a month from their equally poor parishioners. Year after year, they have voluntarily given back a portion of their meager salary that the work might not be hampered by lack of funds . . . . The world will never know the full story of the sacrifice of these men and women. Laboring in these outlying posts, mostly in tribes other than their own, some of them persecuted by the Roman Catholic priests, others compelled by the very nature of their task to incur the hostility of the heathen chiefs and proponents of fetishism, they have nevertheless more than anyone else been responsible for the success accomplished in that tremendous growth . . . . Many of them, now in the twilight of life, have spent the vigor of their youth in tramping over the hills and dales of the Kasai, inspired by the living truth in their hearts. Now old and gray, they are still in the service, sterling examples of Paul's statement, 'I have fought a good fight . . . . I have kept the faith.'" John Morrison, in Foundations of World Order (1941).

206   Crane, p. 91. The Tshiluba word for "Protestant" was "Mission", while the word for "Catholic" was "Father" or "Priest." Missionaries were often called *tatu*, father, or *mamu*, mother, and were expected to provide answers to the "children's" questions and respond to their material needs. "African adherents of both communions were proud of the names, because they distinguished them from the followers of banned Kimbanguists and other religious bodies. The banned groups had no 'fathers' to protect them or speak for them to the government or trade companies." Kiantandu, p. 383.

207 PCUS Foreign Mission Annual Report 1940, p. 10.

208 Crane, p. 88.

209 Groves, IV:195; 245; quoted in Kiantandu, p. 401.

210 In 1952 it was estimated that five holding companies controlled about 70% of all Congo business, and that the State held strong interest in all five. Rule, p. 211.

211 Kiantandu, p. 404f. Quotations are from Marvin D. Markowitz, *Cross and sword: the political role of Christian Missions in the Belgian Congo, 1908-1960.* (1973)

212 *Congo Mission News*, April 1946, p. 1. Quoted in Kiantandu, p. 407. Needless to say, Roman Catholic authorities in the Congo were not happy with this decision. Bishop Jean de Hemptinne, Vicar Apostolic of Katanga and an unflinching opponent of Protestant missionary work, believed that there was an "identity between the political programme of the American missions and the political programme of Moscow . . . . Protestantism gnaws at the principle of authority wherever it can. With Belgian money principles are spread which will end by undermining the authority of the Belgians in the Congo. That is certainly one of the greatest mistakes which can be committed at this time." Adrian Hastings, *A History of African Christianity*, p. 63f.

213 PCUS Foreign Mission Annual Report, 1949, p. 10. The PCUS Executive Committee of Foreign Missions began in 1948 to require a full year's study in Belgium of all its appointees to the Congo.

214 Crane, p. 124.

215 Crane, p. 126.

216 Crane, p. 127

217 Crane, p. 133.

218 Crane, p. 144.

219 Crane observed that, as the Mission entered this new epoch in educational work, "it threatened to relegate the Church to a position of obscurity and irrelevance in the emerging new Congo. The great clamor from every side was for more and better schools, . . . and the Church was virtually forgotten by many missionaries and Congolese alike." Crane, pp. 112-113. Kiantandu observed, "So far their Program of Progress had brought secular schools instead of indigenization in the church." Kiantandu, p. 445.

220 Those coming in greatest numbers to find work and to make permanent settlements were the Baluba, whom from the first showed an extraordinary receptivity to advantages the Europeans brought. This intrusion of Baluba into Lulua territory would later prove to be a major factor in precipitating the Baluba-Lulua wars of 1959-1962. Virginia Pruitt, *Congo, 1958-1968: New Nation, New Church*, (1969).

221 Crane, p. 115

222 Crane, p. 117.

223 The development of work at Luluabourg also marked the beginning of a change in the relationship of the APCM with Roman Catholics. In 1948, when the Mission requested that the State grant it an additional ten hectares of land to expand its activities in and around Luluabourg, the Colonial Council hesitated. However, Father Van Wing, a Belgian missionary and representative of Catholic interests in the Colonial Council, spoke out in their support.

Van Wing's support for the APCM request was seen as a significant improvement in Catholic-Protestant relations. Kiantandu, p. 422.

[224] APCM Minutes, 1947, p. 18. Quoted in Kiantandu, p. 416.

[225] In 1951 a Congolese elder, was confirmed as a half-time assistant to the Bible Revision Committee, "submitting his suggestions to members of the committee." APCM Minutes, 1951, p. 19. Quoted in Kiantandu, p. 437.

[226] APCM Minutes, 1948, p. 44. Quoted in Kiantandu, p. 430.

[227] APCM Minutes, 1948, p. 45. Quoted in Kiantandu, p. 433.

[228] Crane, p 150f.

[229] Kiantandu, p. 439.

[230] Kiantandu, p. 440.

[231] PCUS World Missions Annual Report, 1952, p. 8.

[232] The PCUS Executive Committee of Foreign Missions was restructured in 1950, taking the new name Board of World Missions.

[233] Vernon A. Anderson, *Still Led in Triumph* (1959), p. 6.

[234] Minutes of the APCM Conference, September 1952; quoted in Kiantandu, pp. 450-452. The APCM meeting of 1953 devoted an entire day to meeting with five African delegates sent by the Synod. The minutes reported: "The Mission appreciates the fine spirit of these men and the valuable contribution that they made to the discussions." Kiantandu comments, "Missionaries learned from this integrated meeting that they had been underestimating the creativity and imagination of Africans." Kiantandu, p. 457.

[235] Darby Fulton, "Africa Comes of Age," *Presbyterian Survey*, January 1953, p. 13. Quoted in Kiantandu, p. 455.

[236] World Missions Annual Report, 1953, p. 39. The whole Protestant Church in the Belgian Congo at this point had approximately 600,000 adult members and 270,000 inquirers with 315 local pastors. Foreign missionaries numbered 1,700. The Catholic Church had 245 local priests for more than three million communicants. Kiantandu comments, "So, both Protestant and Catholic Churches still depended heavily on missionary pastors and priests." Kiantandu, p 455.

A serious problem in mission relations occurred when, in 1950, Seventh Day Adventist missionaries arrived in the area of the Kasai that, according to the comity agreement established by the Congo Protestant Council, was to be served by the APCM. "The ensuing confusion and hostility generated division in some areas of the church. Only when the Adventists left their mission during the upheaval of independence did the church regain stabilization." Ross, p. 47.

[237] World Missions Report, 1953, p. 7.

[238] Hastings, p. 91.

[239] Tshihamba comments, "ABAKO was only a secular expression of what Kimbanguism had been expressing religiously." Tshihamba, p. 145.

[240] "Lulua-Freres in operation presented for the first time since the subjugation of the people to colonization, the true cultural and political expression of a large African group in the Kasai." Tshihamba, p. 152.

[241] Anderson, p. 23f.

[242] Kiantandu, p. 463

243 Tshisungu Daniel was often called the "Dwight L. Moody" of the Congo. An evangelist of extraordinary power, he conducted evangelistic services not only among Protestant churches all across the Kasai, but in principal cities throughout the Congo, as well as in other African countries. Dr. William Rule later would comment, "I feel sure there is no other person who has led as many people to Christ throughout a ministry under the Presbyterian Church in Congo as has Daniel Moody Tshisungu." See Dr. William Rule's personal memoirs, *Milestones in Mission* (1991), p.103f.

244 Some Catholic leaders were strongly opposed to the trends toward nationalism. A Catholic paper, the *Courrier d'Afrique*, stated that "the Bible has had a subversive influence in Africa." Protestants were held responsible for nationalistic feelings, because they were the ones who gave the Bible to the people. Protestants denied the charges of subversion. In the Congo Mission News, January 1954, appeared an article stating that "indeed the Bible awakens in those who read it an awareness of injustice and a passion for righteousness which has an inevitable impact on the politics of any existing human society." Kiantandu, p. 461f.

245 APCM Minutes, 1954, p. 10. Quoted in Kiantandu, p. 469.

246 Anderson, p. 29.

247 Anderson contended that there were "probably half as many more Tshiluba-speaking Christians . . . scattered through other parts of the Congo where they are a strong and influential part of their community and of the churches which they attend." Anderson, p. 48. The total Protestant community at this point numbered approximately 1,500,000, with 576 ordained pastors, almost 20,000 village evangelists, about 4,000 certified school teachers and more than 700 medical assistants. Along with the Catholic population, the total Christian constituency in the Belgian Congo was estimated at approximately 45 percent of the population. Pruitt, p. 6.

248 PCUS World Missions Annual Report, 1957, p. 8f.

249 Anderson, p. 52.

250 PCUS World Missions Annual Report, 1957, p. 36.

251 A Muslim Ethiopian wrote a letter to the Ethiopian Minister in London in September 1936, stating: "When I saw the wholesale massacre of Christian Ethiopians by Christian Italians, I stood and thanked God that he had not made me a Christian; yet I knew that the sin did not lie with Christ." Estelle Sylvia Pankhurst, *Ethiopia, a Cultural History*, p. 540.

252 Latourette comments, "The Roman Catholic Church bestirred itself to take advantage of the opportunity presented by the altered political situation . . . . The purpose was cherished of bringing the Abyssinian Church into obedience to Rome . . . . It sought to control the Abyssinian Church and to separate it from its connexion with the Coptic Church in Egypt; it endeavoured to replace non-Italian with Italian missionaries, whether Roman Catholic or Protestant." Latourette, *A History of the Expansion of Christianity*, Vol. VII, p. 260.

253 UPNA General Assembly Minutes, 1940, p. 37.

254 Kissling, p. 10. The story which follows is taken largely from this pamphlet.

255 The story of the remarkable life and ministry of Gidada Solon is told in his own words in the book, *The Other Side of Darkness*, as told to and recorded by Ruth McCreery and Martha M. Vandevort. Gidada traveled from village to village through the forests and mountains of

western Ethiopia by mule. "My mule seemed to understand the rider was blind. When she came to a protruding stump or a low-hanging branch, she would go around it . . . . She always paused when [we] met someone on the path just in case [we] wanted to talk! And as she went past a house she would turn her head in toward the house, expecting her rider would want to go in! I remembered that it was Balaam's ass that saw the angel of the Lord in the path when her rider could not see him, and I was happy that my mule knew how the work of the Lord had to be carried out, by speaking to one person after the other about our Christ." Gidada, p. 83.

[256] Gidada, p. 34.

[257] Bakke, *Christian Ministry: Patterns and Functions within the Ethiopia Evangelical Church Mekane Yesus*, p. 136.

[258] UPNA General Assembly Minutes, 1940, p. 63.

[259] UPNA General Assembly Minutes, 1942, p. 665.

[260] Quotations in this paragraph are from Bakke, p. 139f.

[261] UPNA General Assembly minutes, 1944, p. 124; 1945, p. 474.

[262] Kissling, p. 18

[263] "Thus for the first time in the history of United Presbyterian foreign missionary effort an indigenous Church, sponsored by a United Presbyterian Mission, is no longer an integral part of our denomination." UPNA General Assembly Minutes, 1947, p. 1250.

[264] The above information on mission and church is combined from Kissling, p. 20; and Trimingham, The Christian Church and Missions in Ethiopia, p. 37f.

[265] UPNA General Assembly Minutes, 1950, p. 954.

[266] Bakke, p. 120. Another significant political development at this point was the decision regarding the fate of Eritrea. The United Nations was called upon in 1950 to settle the status of Eritrea, which had been a part of Italy's old empire. There were those who supported Ethiopia's claim for its total amalgamation, those who proposed a federal relationship with Ethiopia, and those who wanted it to remain autonomous. Finally in 1952 Eritrea was assigned to Ethiopia within a federal constitution (later repudiated by Haile Selassie), setting up a situation that would become the source of untold misery for both parties in years to come. See Hastings, A history of African Christianity, 1950-1975, p. 10.

[267] UPNA General Assembly Minutes, 1952, p. 203.

[268] UPNA General Assembly Minutes, 1955, p. 1456.

[269] Bakke, p. 130.

[270] Bakke, p. 135

[271] General Assembly Minutes, 1943, p. 1103. "Most of the members of this rather remarkable church are of Egyptian, Syrian or Ethiopian origin and of Christian birth, and racially are almost as foreign to the Sudan as are their missionary colleagues, though the common tongue of Arabic binds all except the Ethiopians into a kinship with their non-Christian Sudanese brethren." *International Review of Missions*, Vol. 33, p. 45.

[272] UPNA General Assembly Minutes, 1942, p. 373.

[273] The impact of Western education upon the peoples of southern Sudan was profound. "The isolation from which the Southern Sudanese peoples have suffered is now a thing of the past . . . . Special problems arise as a result of contact with the West, which varies so

considerably, not only between different tribes, but within the same tribe. The young go to the mission school and acquire a changed outlook on life to that of their parents . . . . To enable the Southerner to resist tendencies leading towards disintegration of tribal life and assimilate the new without dislocation of soul is the primary aim of both mission and government working together in partnership, but what the outcome of this vast process of change will be depends primarily upon the Christian Church." Trimingham (1949), p. 14.

274 UPNA General Assembly Minutes, 1946, p. 881.

275 UPNA General Assembly Minutes, 1945, p. 473.

276 Crawford, p. 74.

277 From "A History of the Murle Church," letter written by Albert G. Roode, M.D. to John Atiel, Sudanese student at the Moffat School of Bible at Kijabe, Kenya, January 1990.

278 Winburn Thomas, *Africa and the United Presbyterians*, p. 22.

279 Trimingham (1949), p. 23.

280 The Reformed Church in America was considering union with the United Presbyterian Church of North America at the time. They were especially attracted by the vision of the Anuak Project, and therefore assigned their first missionaries to Akobo. (Personal correspondence from Dr. Wm. B. Anderson)

281 Eleanor Vandevort, in *A Leopard Tamed*, tells the story of Kuac, the first ministerial student from the Nuer tribe to attend Bishop Gwynne College (p. 60ff.). This poignant story wrestles with the encounter between African traditional culture and Christian faith.

282 From a letter of Don McClure, quoted in Partee, *Adventure in Africa: The Story of Don McClure*, p. 144.

283 Partee, p. 151.

284 Don McClure was among those who had a strong conviction about the urgency of the missionary task, along with the primary importance of the development of national Christian leadership: "I keep insisting that the white man's time in Africa is short. Therefore I believe we must crash ahead with our evangelistic task and get out while we still possess the gratitude of African people. If we overstay our welcome, they will kick us out with their curses ringing in our ears. However, most missionaries expect to be here a long time." Partee, p. 179.

285 UPNA General Assembly Minutes, 1948, p. 178. However, Dr. William B. Anderson comments that Bible translation work was "the one very great failing of the mission." Citing several examples of persons who were "set aside" but then heaped with many other duties, he states, "The mission woke up very late to fulfilling this need." (Personal correspondence from Dr. Anderson.)

286 UPNA General Assembly Minutes, 1947, p. 1249.

287 UPNA General Assembly Minutes, 1953, p. 628.

288 Trimingham (1949), p. 25.

289 Jamison, p. 185.

290 UPNA General Assembly Minutes, 1953, p. 628.

291 Dr. Anderson comments, "The hostels were started mostly for the Nuba Mountains (an African part of North Sudan) came to Khartoum. Through these, the Presbyterian Church became involved in working among Nuba, a ministry the mission itself never opened." (Personal correspondence from Dr. Wm. B. Anderson.)

292 Thomas, p. 23.

293 After prayerful consideration, most Protestant missions agreed, and discussed how to work most effectively with the government. Roman Catholics at first refused, saying the school property belonged to the Pope. However, they eventually were compelled to comply. "1957 marked the end of missions owning any schools, except for evangelist and pastoral training." (Personal correspondence from Dr. Wm. B. Anderson.)

294 See Malcolm Forsberg, *Last Days on the Nile*, p. 156ff.

Chapter IV

295 See Chart II.

296 Among the many books providing analysis of the economic impact of neo-colonialism, see George L. Beckford, *Persistent poverty: underdevelopment in plantation economies of the Third World* (1976); Charles Elliott, *Patterns of poverty in the Third World: a study of social and economic stratification* (1975). Regarding the role of multinational corporations in the Third World, see Richard J. Barnet & Ronald E. Muller, *Global Reach: the power of the multinational corporations* (1974). The effect of neo-colonialism on hunger in the Third World is well presented in *Food first: beyond the myth of scarcity*, by Frances Moore Lappe & Joseph Collins (1977).

297 For the following summary, the writer is especially indebted to T.A. Beetham, *Christianity and the New Africa* (1967).

298 From J.S. Trimingham, *The Christian Church and Islam in West Africa* (1955), p. 40. Quoted in Beetham, p. 83.

299 From A. Luthuli, *Let my people go* (1962), p. 154. Quoted in Beetham, p. 87.

300 From A. Aluko, *Christianity and Communism* (1964), p. 68. Quoted in Beetham, p. 88.

301 From J.S. Trimingham, *A history of Islam in West Africa* (1962), p. 229. Quoted in Beetham, p. 80f.

302 Beetham, p. 85.

303 Beetham, p. 85.

304 *National Catholic Almanac 1962*, p. 363. Quoted in Rycroft, *A factual study of sub-Saharan Africa*, p. 100, 109.

305 *World Christian Handbook 1962*. Quoted in Rycroft, op. cit., p. 110.

306 Bouffard, Adrien. *Propagation of the Faith*, 1958. Quoted in Rycroft, op. cit., p. 100f.

307 Beetham, p. 52.

308 Quoted in Beetham, p. 30.

309 Beetham, p. 32.

310 African theologian John Mbiti comments, "The scandal of division in Protestant mission Churches has set an example to African converts. This is made worse by the fact that missionaries who brought and propagated divided Christianity, are (or were) proud of their denominational founders, traditions and brand of Christianity. This gives the impression that Church divisions do not matter. The logic, from the African point of view, is that since missionaries belong to so many denominations, why should Africans not have their own

Churches, founded and led by fellow African Christians? . . . One of the things that sparks off separatism from mission Churches is the control that missionaries exercise over their African converts and congregations . . . . Thus missionary paternalism and over-domination have led many African Christians to seek local independence and sever their organizational ties with missionary-led churches." John Mbiti, *African Religions and Philosophy*, p. 233.

[311]   See Chart III

[312]   A native of Nigeria, Francis Akani Ibiam was the first African student at the medical school of the University of St. Andrews, Scotland; became a missionary doctor, founding the Abiriba hospital and later directing the Church of Scotland mission hospital in Itu; was president of the Christian Council of Nigeria; served on the standing committee of the International Missionary Council; was a speaker at the New Delhi Assembly of the World Council of Churches in 1961, then a president of the WCC 1961-1968. Great Britain appointed him as the first indigenous governor of Eastern Nigeria in 1960. In the Biafra War, he sided with his people of Eastern Nigeria and consequently had to go into exile in Switzerland until he was received back with honor in Nigeria. In protest against British government support of the central Nigerian government against Biafra, in 1967 he renounced the knighthood that Great Britian had bestowed on him. (From "Ibiam, Francis Akanu" by John S. Pobee, in *Dictionary of the Ecumenical Movement*, p. 495).

[313]   Quoted in W. Stanley Rycroft, *The ecumenical witness of the United Presbyterian Church in the U.S.A.*, p. 120.

[314]   A native of South Africa, Dr. M'Timkulu had been senior lecturer in education at the Fort Hare University in South Africa, and had held a number of responsible positions on public bodies.

[315]   Dr. Marsh later would be called to serve as the first Director of the AACC Ecumenical Program for Emergency Action in Africa, serving on the AACC staff from 1965 through 1969. In 1973, Marsh was elected moderator of the General Assembly of the United Presbyterian Church, U.S.A.

[316]   Ibid., p. 131.

[317]   John S. Pobee, "Africa", in *Dictionary of the Ecumenical Movement*, p. 10. Much of the information in the above section has been drawn from this article.

[318]   The movement toward merger of American Presbyterian denominations in the 1950s had included the Presbyterian Church, U.S. However, while the PCUS General Assembly in 1954 approved the plan for union, the necessary number of presbyteries did not approve. When the three-way union did not materialize, the two General Assemblies of the PCUSA and the UPNA proceeded to prepare a plan to unite those two churches.

[319]   Annual Report, Board of Foreign Missions, PCUSA, 1957; p. 7.

[320]   The UPNA Women's General Missionary Society had merged with the UPNA Board of Foreign Missions in 1955.

[321]   Annual Report of the Board of Foreign Missions, PCUSA, 1958, p. 8.

[322]   Annual Report of the Commission on Ecumenical Mission and Relations, UPCUSA, 1959, p. 9.

[323]   John Coventry Smith, *From Colonialism to World Community: The Church's Pilgrimage* (1982), p. 174.

324   Ibid., p. 58.

325   Ibid. A report on this historic visit appears in an article in Presbyterian Life, December 1, 1960, pp. 19ff. The opening sentences are enlightening:

> Counsellor M.S. Cooper, Assistant Stated Clerk of the Liberian Presbyterian Church, was midway in his reading of an impressive list of needs for the denomination. Four members of a delegation from the United Presbyterian Church U.S.A. had just enjoyed their first African meal and were listening attentively. The blazing sun made its oppressive presence felt through the walls and the roof of the Todee Mission School. Suddenly, Dr. Cooper interrupted his address: "There's a fly biting you, brother." The Moderator of the Liberian Church, Dr. J.J. Mends Cole, reached over and expertly swatted an outsized fly on the person of Dr. Edler G. Hawkins, head of the visiting group of churchmen.
>
> In this incident can be seen a parable applicable to the entire recent visit of the United Presbyterian delegation to West Africa. Whenever we were about to become preoccupied with traditional church needs, the dramatic qualities of a changing continent stung us awake; moreover, the gracious African people were constantly prepared to provide every comfort, from swatting flies to affording refreshment for visitors unaccustomed to the superheated climate.

326   Donald Black, who had been General Secretary of the UPNA Board of Foreign Missions and who became the Associate General Secretary of COEMAR, later recalled, "The forces that were pushing toward merging mission and unity were evident in the PCUSA, but they were scarcely felt in the UPNA. The latter denomination had established overseas synods in all its mission fields except Ethiopia, and that church was not developed enough to be involved in the ecumenical movement. The problem for the UPNA was to get overseas church organizations to accept autonomy. The PCUSA, on the other hand, was dealing with some churches of considerable sophistication and the pressure in those situations involved participation in church mergers and membership in ecumenical organizations." *Merging Mission and Unity* (1986), p. 21.

327   1962 Annual Report, Board of World Missions, PCUS, p. 5.

328   Ibid

329   T. Watson Street, *The Story of Southern Presbyterians*, (1960), p. 123. Dr. Street's mission theology is spelled out in his book, *On the Growing Edge of the Church: New Dimensions in World Missions* (1965).

330   The nation was given this title with the achievement of complete independence and unity in 1972. In this section, the term "Cameroun" is used for the former French colony until the year 1972, and from that point the term "Cameroon" is used. However, in the case of the national church, the term continues to be *Eglise Presbyterienne Camerounaise,* since it was within the bounds of the former French territory.

[331] In 1958, the French colonies in Western and Central Africa, from west to east, were Senegal, French Guinea, Mauritania, French Sudan, Ivory Coast, Upper Volta, Niger, Dahomey, French Equatorial Africa, and French Cameroun. In 1960, all would attain independence, while maintaining close ties with the French Community. Eventually French Guinea would become Guinea, French Sudan would become Mali, Upper Volta would become Burkina Faso, Dahomey would become Benin, French Cameroun would become the Republic of Cameroun, and French Equatorial Africa would be divided into Chad, the Central African Republic, the People's Republic of Congo, and Gabon.

[332] The story is told in detail in LeVine's *The Cameroons, from mandate to independence*.

[333] Rayburn, p. 167.

[334] Palmer, p. 130.

[335] Latourette, p. 484.

[336] The Catholic Church strenuously opposed activities of the UPC, accusing them of being communist. In retaliation, UPC followers systematically attacked and destroyed Catholic missions. An added complication occurred when a Catholic bishop was accused of being implicated in a plot against the head of state, along with a UPC leader, and both were sentenced to death. The UPC leader later was executed, but the bishop's sentence eventually was commuted to life imprisonment. Relations between the state and the Catholic Church, which traditionally was more conservative than the Protestants and actively supported a major political rival as head of state, deteriorated during this period. *World Christian Encyclopedia*, p. 209.

[337] Palmer, p. 138.

[338] News release from Presbyterian Office of Information, Dec. 30, 1959.

[339] Minutes of the General Assembly of UPCUSA, 1961, COEMAR Report, p. 90. On a visit back to Cameroun after Independence, Mr. George Anker had the joy of meeting some of his former students at *Ecole Camille Chazeaud*. One of them said to him, "Doesn't it make you proud to know that now so many of your former students are in high chairs?" (Palmer, p. 139)

[340] Rayburn, p. 167.

[341] These UPCUSA fraternal workers included 13 doctors, 15 nurses, 6 technical workers, 25 educators, 2 agricultural workers, and some 62 in evangelistic and general missionary work. 106 were from the United States, 16 from Switzerland, France and Italy, and one Australian doctor. In post-war Africa, European missions often found themselves in financial difficulty and thus their missionaries often would ally themselves with an American mission.

The population of Cameroun at this point was approximately 3,142,000. Of this number, approximately 478,000 were Roman Catholics, and 326,300 were Protestants. (UPCUSA Office of Information news release, December 30, 1959.)

[342] Minutes of the UPCUSA General Assembly, 1959, COEMAR Report, p. 91.

[343] Ibid. p. 93.

[344] Ibid.

[345] Ibid. The remarks of the UPCUSA Moderator, Eugene Carson Blake, and the COEMAR General Secretary, Charles Leber, at the ceremony declaring the independence of the EPC (December 11, 1957) had given the EPC church leadership the impression that they would be given immediate authority over all the resources and personnel of the UPCUSA in Cameroun.

"They promised the church the moon. They [the EPC] were now in charge; the missionaries were to work under their directions; the properties would be turned over to the church. They were to be in charge of all administration, etc. etc. And they [the UPCUSA leaders] were believed. After all, they were the two highest officials of our church who had come to tell them the facts!" (Personal correspondence from Paul Hopkins, January 11, 1998)

346   Ibid., p. 94.

347   Minutes of the UPCUSA General Assembly, COEMAR Report, 1961, p. 93.

348   Minutes of the UPCUSA General Assembly, COEMAR Report, 1960, p. 92.

349   Reyburn, p. 27.

350   Minutes of the UPCUSA General Assembly, COEMAR Report, 1961, p. 90.

351   Minutes of the UPCUSA General Assembly, COEMAR Report, 1963, p. 33.

352   Reyburn, p. 29.

353   Gittings, p. 21.

354   An excellent article concerning the state of medical work at this time is "Mission and Medicine in Cameroun", by Steven and Mary Spencer, appearing in *Presbyterian Life*, June 1, 1961, p. 10f.

355   Pamphlet, "Mission Through Medicine: Nkol Mvolan, Cameroun", COEMAR, c. 1962.

356   Adams, *First Woman Doctor to Cameroun*, p. 48. On January 1, 1964, Dr. Adams was honored by the Cameroun government, which presented her with the medal "*Merite Camerounaise*". Several years later, she received a second medal, presented to those who had served 25 years or more in Cameroun.

357   A 1959 report states, "Seventy percent of primary schools [in Cameroun] are still Church or Mission controlled. Before World War II, over half of these were Protestant. Now, Roman Catholic school enrollment is twice the Protestant and even exceeds that of the government schools, thus practically assuring Catholic dominance in the next generation." Typed COEMAR report, dated February 16-17, 1959.

358   Typed Report of Simon Ngo'o, Director, Camille Chazeaud Normal School, c. 1963.

359   Gittings, p. 71.

360   Report "Re: Capital Funds for Education Projects in Cameroun", from Mary Hunter to Dr. John Weir, Sept. 18, 1963.

361   Minutes of the UPCUSA General Assembly, 1960, COEMAR report, p. 95.

362   Minutes of the UPCUSA General Assembly, 1959, COEMAR report, p. 90.

363   Reyburn, "Africanization and African Studies," *Practical Anthropology*, Vol. 6, No. 3, May-June 1962, p. 97; quoted in Rycroft, p. 108.

364   The 1960 COEMAR report rejoiced in this development that gave a Protestant interpretation of current issues, "after long leaving unchallenged a splendid Roman Catholic paper, which week after week has spoken out about issues on which Protestants have remained silent." Minutes of UPCUSA General Assembly, 1960, COEMAR report, p. 95.

365   Minutes of UPCUSA General Assembly, 1959, COEMAR report, p. 91f. In subsequent years, Camerounian church youth would participate in such work camps in other parts of Africa.

366   Minutes of UPCUSA General Assembly, 1961, COEMAR report, p. 92f.

367   Minutes of UPCUSA General Assembly, 1964, COEMAR report, p. 72.

368 Minutes of UPCUSA General Assembly, 1965, COEMAR report, p. 79. John Coventry Smith, COEMAR General Secretary, in his book From Colonialism to World Community, acknowledged that Cameroun was one of "the most difficult areas" in the transition to the new church-to-church relationship. p. 152.

369 Ibid.

370 Minutes of the UPCUSA General Assembly, 1966, COEMAR report, p. 11.

371 Translation of Joseph C. Oban Eteme's letter of February 1, 1966 to the Secretary of the Commission of Ecumenical Mission and Relation.

372 Adams, p. 51.

373 A careful analysis of the Church division is given in a report prepared by Dr. L.K. Anderson, retired veteran missionary to Cameroun, who was invited to return for a visit from November 1968 to February 1969. Several quotations from that report provide valuable insights into the reasons for the division and the results of it:

> The division . . . is between those who maintain that they are guardians of the faith once delivered to the saints of Cameroun by the old missionaries, together with the strict moral code adopted years ago to curb practices of primitive Africa, and the younger graduates of our theological schools, particularly those who have continued their studies in Europe, particularly in France. As long as South Cameroun, dominated by the Bulu tribe, remained more or less isolated through lack of communication with the areas evangelized first by the German Basil Mission and later by the Paris Evangelical Missions Society, there was no problem . . . . Now, with a united Cameroun and free communication between all parts of the Republic, other theological and behavioral influences have flooded in upon this isolated community.

> Over twenty years ago, we were conscious of the fact that our African associates were shocked to discover that the German and French trained African pastors drank beer or wine and used tobacco . . . . When something so basic to their belief and conduct is suddenly discovered to be condoned by a church group, that Church naturally becomes suspect. Not only moral but theological decadence is implied . . . .

> Complicating the situation is the fact that the younger generation is wont to lapse into French, when debates arise in the judicatories, a language not too well understood by the older Bulu-trained men. This causes no end of frustration and, perhaps, a feeling of inferiority, by those who by their very seniority ought to be demanding respect and obedience . . . .

> The influence of former missionary, Paul Moore, who for a short time taught in Dager Seminary, and is now allied with the Carl McIntyre organization, has been considerable in nurturing a dispensational Biblical interpretation which

colors much of what is being written in the literature he is now providing the Separatist Group. ("Cameroun Visit November 1968-February 1969", L.K. Anderson, p. 2f.)

[374] Ibid., p. 4.

[375] Ibid. p. 6.

[376] Ibid., p. 7.

[377] Ibid., p. 6.

[378] William DuVal, COEMAR's Regional Secretary for Africa and Europe, presented a report to the Commission dated June 11, 1964, following a visit to Cameroun. His report and recommendations reflect the decisions later made by COEMAR:

> In fact, because of our concern that existing work not suffer from lack of funds, I said that we would be making no further transfers to the church until the General Council drew up a scheme for recovering as much of the funds as possible, and a program for re-establishing the cash position of the credit balances in each account . . . .
>
> Although there is an indication of how much cash is missing, the EPC does not have a precise picture of what balances should be on the books for each project, and what that actual relationship is to the cash portion . . . .
>
> The EPC also recognizes that there is presently no African they can call upon to handle the Church's Treasury. It was agreed that a European accountant, with French language and training in French bookkeeping should be sought . . .
>
> I suggested that it was also an hypocrisy for the EPC to be related to cooperative or union work only through UPCUSA funds. If the EPC believes in cooperative relations with its sister churches in Cameroun, it should make its own contributions to such efforts—for its own sake and for the comprehension of its congregations. So beginning in 1965 UPCUSA contributions to Union Work will go direct—EPC will make its own contributions. (William K. DuVal report, dated June 11, 1964, to all fraternal workers, executive staff, and COEMAR board members)
>
> Paul Hopkins, who succeeded William DuVal as Regional Secretary for Africa, makes an astute observation: "The African understanding of money became the operating system of finance . . . . In the African extended family system, when one member has money in his pocket, he is expected to share it when needed. And it always is needed in African society. So the treasurer was doling out funds from the church to extended family members . . . . It just was used for purposes other than church projects but not dishonestly!"

Hopkins also adds, "In the providence of God, at the same time I came on the desk, Albert Nyemb was elected General Secretary of the EPC . . . . We talked about the problems openly and honestly and saw them to a large degree in the same way. He worked as best he could to cleanup the administration . . . . I could not have asked for a better partner to work with." (Personal Correspondence from Paul A. Hopkins, January 11, 1998)

379   Reyburn, p. 164f.
380   Paper, "Administrative Council for Medical Work in the Cameroun", c. 1965.
381   Ibid.
382   Ibid.
383   Ibid.
384   Paper, "Annual Report of the Medical Department to the General Assembly at Metet, 1966", prepared by H. Wallace Greig, M.D.
385   Ibid.
386   Paper, "Report of Evaluation of Schools Related to Cameroun Presbyterian Church", c. 1966, pp. 119-121.
387   Minutes of the UPCUSA General Assembly, 1961, COEMAR Report, p. 93.
388   Minutes of the UPCUSA General Assembly, 1965, COEMAR Report, p. 81f.
389   Roy, p. 36.
390   Statistical reports in UPCUSA General Assembly reports for 1967 and 1972.
391   Minutes of UPCUSA General Assembly, 1967, COEMAR Report, p. 82.
392   Robert N. Peirce, "The First Decade of the Cameroun Presbyterian Church", p. 6.
393   Ibid.
394   Minutes of the UPCUSA General Assembly, 1967, COEMAR Report, p. 8.
395   L.K. Anderson, p. 7.
396   The Drum Call, November 1969, "Kaat Nyambe I Nlo", by R. Peirce, p. 16f.
397   Adams, p. 57.
398   The Drum Call, November 1969, "Evangelism in Depth for Cameroun", p. 25f.
399   World Christian Encyclopedia, p. 210.
400   The Drum Call, November 1969, p. 32.
401   From 1961 COEMAR Report, p. 94f. and material prepared by Mrs. Strange for mission packet on Equatorial Guinea, p. 2.
402   At this point, Spanish Guinea with a total area of about 10,800 square miles, had a population of approximately 212,000. (UPCUSA General Assembly Minutes, 1963, COEMAR Report, p. 33).
403   UPCUSA General Assembly Minutes, 1966, COEMAR Report, p. 12.
404   UPCUSA General Assembly Minutes, 1960, COEMAR Report, p. 95f.
405   Paper, "Cameroun and Spanish Guinea, West Africa", dated February 16-17, 1959.
406   UPCUSA General Assembly Minutes, 1960, COEMAR Report, p. 96.
407   UPCUSA General Assembly Minutes, 1961, COEMAR Report, p. 95.
408   UPCUSA General Assembly Minutes, 1964, COEMAR Report, p. 73.
409   Paper, "Survey of Presbyterian Work in Rio Muni—1964-1965", p. 2.

410   UPCUSA General Assembly Minutes, 1966, COEMAR Report, p. 13.

411   Mrs. Roy Strange, material prepared for packet on Equatorial Guinea, p. 3.

412   Paper, "Church Tourist Guide for Rio Muni", p. 3.

413   UPCUSA General Assembly Minutes, 1965, COEMAR Report, p. 83.

414   Dr. Llobell could not come to Rio Muni until the summer of 1967, when he would finish his
       Spanish military service. Paper, "Survey of Presbyterian Work in Rio Muni—1964-1965", p. 2

415   UPCUSA General Assembly Minutes, 1966, COEMAR Report, p. 13.

416   Letter from William W. Ainley and Gustavo Envela, January 15,1999. In 1969, Rev. Envela
       was appointed Ambassador to the United Nations by President Macias Nguema. However, in
       1970 because of the oppressive Macias regime, Rev. Envela became a political refugee in the
       United States, where he has continued to live.

417   Paper, "Survey of Presbyterian Work in Rio Muni—1964-1965", p. 5.

418   Howard W. French, "Oil Profits Trickle Up or Out of Africa's Forgotten Land," The New York
       Times, February 15, 1998.

419   World Christian Encyclopedia, p. 282.

420   Undated letter from files of Presbyterian Department of History, Philadelphia. While the appeal
       from Mr. Nchama expressed the yearning of the Rio Muni Church for renewed cooperation
       with the American Church, it needs to be recognized that Mr. Nchama himself was part of
       the problem that the church faced. Being related to the family of President Macias, he ruled
       the church in much the same manner as Macias ruled the government, forcing any who
       objected out of the church and leading numerous church leaders to flee the country. (Personal
       correspondence from Paul A. Hopkins, January 11, 1998)

421   Donald Black, Merging mission and unity, p. 58.

422   Donald Black, "An Historical View of Developing Mission Policy", no date.

423   James Gittings, New Nations and the United Presbyterians, 1964, p. 50f.

424   Hastings, History of African Christianity, 86f.

425   Latourette, Christianity in a Revolutionary Age, Vol. V, p. 492f.

426   World Christian Encyclopedia, p. 323.

427   Latourette, op. cit., p. 491f.

428   James Scherer, Gospel, Church, and Kingdom, p. 99ff.

429   Hastings, op. cit., p. 179.

430   Gittings, op. cit., p. 50.

431   Ibid.

432   Article by Rev. & Mrs. Harry F. Peterson in brochure of PCUS Board of World

433   Latourette, op. cit., p. 489

434   Gittings, op. cit., p. 47.

435   COEMAR did locate a missionary couple in Kano, Northern Nigeria, to work with the
       struggling Christian community in evangelism. (Personal correspondence from Paul Hopkins,
       January 30, 1998)

436   General Assembly World Mission Report, 1959, p. 36.

437   Wallerstein comments, "As of this point and in the wake of the Congo crisis, the United States
       actively entered the African political scene. Before that time, it had been a major bystander,

scarcely more important than the U.S.S.R., and active only as a counterbalance to potential long-range Soviet influence. The U.S. had the reputation of mild anticolonialism and sympathy for African aspirations. But after 1960, the United States came bit by bit to play a role as large as, often far larger than, that of the former colonial powers." Wallerstein, p. 44.

438   1959 World Missions Report, p. 27.

439   1959 World Missions Report, p. 28.

440   1959 World Missions Report, p. 29.

441   CPC Minutes, 1958, p. 3. Quoted in Kiantandu, p. 486.

442   Quoted in Crawford, p. 15.

443   1958 World Missions Report, p. 30

444   1958 World Missions Report, p. 31. It was during this period that one of the members of the APCM, the Rev. William H. (Hank) Crane, was called to serve as Africa Secretary for the World Student Christian Federation, traveling across Africa and meeting with students to help them strengthen their witness on and off campus.

445   1958 World Missions Report, p. 35

446   1958 World Missions Report, p. 28

447   1958 World Missions Report, p. 8.

448   1958 World Missions Report, p. 27.

449   At this point the Synod, made up of ten presbyteries, was composed almost entirely of Congolese pastors and elders, with evangelistic missionaries holding membership but outnumbered fifteen to one. The one exception to complete autonomy was that the Mission held veto power over actions of the Presbytery or Synod "which might have been deemed unwise." The Mission rarely exercised this prerogative, "but the arrangement stood as a symbolic intrusion upon the complete freedom of the Congolese Church in self-government." 1959 World Missions Report, p. 9.

450   Kiantandu, p. 505.

451   Wm. Crane, p. 167

452   1958 World Missions Report, p. 9.

453   Six weeks earlier, the Belgian government had promulgated a *loi fundamentale* to serve as a temporary governing instrument until the Congolese should fashion their own constitution. The temporary government was fashioned after that of Belgium, providing for a Prime Minister and a Chief of State and leaving a door open for the Belgian hope that the Congo might accept the Belgian king as its Chief of State. "Thus, on June 30 King Baudouin and all of his royal retinue arrived in Leopoldville to surrender and transfer the reins of government into the hands of the Congolese. With much pomp and ceremony he made his speech of transfer, and Joseph Kasavubu, preferred by the Congolese as their indigenous Chief of State, declared his acceptance with the same pomp and dignity." Rule, p. 244.

454   1960 World Missions Report, p. 8

455   1960 World Missions Report, p. 9. On July 10, most of the APCM missionaries were gathered at Luluabourg and many spent that night resting on the ground at the airport. Three missionary pilots, Mark Poole, John Davis and John Miller, in the small mission planes had collected people from all the mission stations. Christian Congolese women, knowing that missionary

families were at the airport without food or shelter, prepared hot food and brought it that evening. A handful of missionaries of various denominations remained in Leopoldville, among them Rev. Alex McCutchen, the sole remaining representative of the APCM. (Rule, p. 246.)

[456] 1960 World Mission Report, p. 9. Kiantandu comments, "Their leaving was a shock to the Africans. They began to return after one month, but their action did affect the church-mission relationship. While almost all Protestant missionaries fled, most of the Roman Catholic missionaries stayed. All the missionaries who talked to me recognized that it was a mistake to leave." Kiantandu, p. 524.

[457] 1960 World Mission Report, p. 33.

[458] Virginia Pruitt, *Congo: 1958-1968: New Nation, New Church*, p. 13. This unpublished monograph has been very helpful in preparing the account of this period.

[459] Pruitt, p. 13

[460] Pruitt, p. 17

[461] 1962 World Missions Report, p. 62

[462] 1960 World Missions Report, p. 37.

[463] 1963 World Missions Report, p. 23

[464] 1963 World Missions Report, p. 24. The three synods were formed to correspond to the three geographical divisions which the government had imposed on the Kasai at this point: one for the Lulua, another for the Baluba, and a third for a number of smaller tribes—Bakuba, Bakete, Basala and others.

[465] Dr. Rule served for five years (1956-1961) as Medical Secretary of the Congo Protestant Council. See Rule, p. 215-218. During this period the U.S. Christian Medical Society rendered an invaluable service, recruiting doctors for the "Operation Doctor" program, and shipping thousands of dollars worth of medicines and hospital materials for doctors in the interior. Rule, p. 288.

[466] Pruitt, p. 56

[467] Medical missionary Dr. Mark Poole had pioneered in missionary aviation in the Congo in the 50s, using his privately owned plane for visiting bush dispensaries. The Mission for some years declined to become involved. However, by 1960, the advantages of the use of small planes had been amply demonstrated by Dr. Poole, by the Missionary Aviation Fellowship then operating in other parts of the Congo, and by other convinced APCM pilots. Pruitt, p. 53.

[468] 1962 World Missions Report, p. 68

[469] Pruitt, p. 53

[470] 1962 World Missions Report, p. 64

[471] 1963 World Missions Report, p. 18.

[472] The approach of rebel forces and stories of atrocities committed by rebels on missionaries and Congolese Christian leaders led the APCM, gathered in Luluabourg in August 1964, to consider whether they should evacuate. However, recognizing that the total missionary evacuation of 1960 appeared in retrospect to have been too precipitate, the mission arrived at this statement: "The intention of the Mission shall be to continue its work in the Congo regardless of what government is in control. As long as we are permitted to remain by the authorities, and as

long as our presence does not prejudice the safety of our Congolese brethren or of the Congo Church, we shall stay. It is realized that the following of such a policy may lead to dangers or hardships, but we rely on the promises of God and on His protection and guidance." Pruitt, p. 48.

[473] 1964 World Missions Report, p. 20

[474] 1964 World Missions Report, p. 21

[475] 1964 World Missions Report, p. 23

[476] 1964 World Missions Report, p. 23

[477] The full story of the medical work during this period is found in Sophie Montgomery Crane's book, *A Legacy Remembered: A Century of Medical Missions*, Part III.

[478] 1965 World Missions Report, p. 21

[479] 1965 World Missions Report, p. 22. Kiantandu comments that most of the other missions working in the Congo eventually followed the example of the APCM in merging their work into their related churches. Kiantandu, p. 523.

[480] 1965 World Missions Report, p. 27

[481] Pruitt, p. 54.

[482] 1967 World Missions Report, p. 11

[483] Rule p. 350f.

[484] It must be acknowledged that, beginning with the meeting of the Congo Protestant Council in 1958, Congolese delegates had declared with one voice that they were not pleased with the denominational labels of their mother missions. Wm. Crane comments, "The denominational divisions of Baptists, Methodists, Presbyterians, Congregationalists, etc., are a part of the history of the Western church; they did not grow out of the history of the African church. To burden the African churches with these divisions is to place a yoke on their necks that they should not have to bear. As one layman told me after the Luluabourg Laymen's Conference [in 1959], "If we are going to give up our tribal labels to become the New Tribe of the Church, we don't want your tribal labels in exchange!" Wm. Crane, p. 204

[485] A number of church leaders remained very supportive of Mobutu's regime for years to come. The Rev. Tshihamba Mukoma Luendu, a Zairois Presbyterian minister, in his doctoral dissertation submitted in 1975 to the Faculty of the Graduate School of Howard University, *The Development of the Ideology of Authenticity as a Pragmatic Solution to the Problem of Cultural Identity in Zaire*, states: "In the Mobutu model, an African government effectively uses its power and authority to initiate change through political education, a one-party system, and a cultural ideology. Most important, the Mobutu model is explicit on the choice of the direction the nation can take. In the case of Zaire, Authenticity has dictated "*la voie africane du Zaire*", as against the importation or imitation of an alien culture, whether the matter of concern is related to family life, religion, economy or national unity . . . . The Mobutu model, using no less power and authority than the ones used to destroy African culture, hopes to restore the lost human dignity through the re-establishment of the Zairian cultural identity. This way, African culture becomes *the culture* through which foreign elements can be adapted to the Zairian environment and social context." Tshihamba dissertation, p. 2f.

[486] 1966 World Missions Report, p. 12.

[487] 1966 World Missions Report, p. 21

[488] Pruitt, p. 61

[489] Pruitt, p. 61

[490] Pruitt, p. 62

[491] Pruitt, p. 63

[492] "This is Zaire", published by the Board of World Missions, n.d. 1971?

[493] Pruitt, p. 67

[494] Pruitt, p. 67

[495] Pruitt, p. 67

[496] Pruitt, p. 72

[497] Pruitt, p. 98

[498] 1967 World Missions Report, p. 13

[499] "CPZ/CCZ: Church—God's Gift of Love", p. 8

[500] Ibid.

[501] Pruitt, p. 81

[502] Minutes of the Board of World Missions, July 1969, p. 110

[503] Minutes of the Board of World Missions, July 1969, p. 11

[504] From "A personal report of the day of integration in Luluabourg: March 15, 1970". No author identified.

[505] 1970 World Mission Report, p. 3

[506] From a paper, "American Presbyterian Congo Mission and the Presbyterian Church in Congo, 1891-1969", presented at the Service of Integration, March 15, 1970. No author identified.

[507] From a report, "CPZ/CCZ: Church—God's Gift of Love." No author identified. p. 2.

[508] Teams of ministers from the organized churches were sent out to train the village ministers who often "have never had any training beyond 5th grade grammar school, and the ideal is for them to receive four-day institutes every month until they can attend a regular school." Ibid, p. 4.

[509] Pruitt, p. 99

[510] Forsburg, p. 206f.

[511] Forsberg, p. 153.

[512] Minutes of the General Assembly of the UPCUSA, 1965, Part II, Report of COEMAR, p. 85f.

[513] Forsberg, p. 168.

[514] Ibid., p. 209.

[515] Ibid., p. 213.

[516] Actually, this was the successor to the Northern Sudan Christian Council; however, it was broader in membership and stronger in the responsibilities given to it.

[517] Margaret B. Crawford, *The Sudan: its land and people* (1958), p. 72.

[518] Ibid.

[519] Ibid., p. 76.

[520] Minutes of the General Assembly of the UPCUSA, 1959, Part II, Report of COEMAR, p.81.

521 Crawford, p. 73.

522 Ibid., p. 96.

523 Ibid.

524 Ibid., p. 97.

525 Ibid.

526 Ibid., p. 101.

527 Ibid.

528 James E. Powell, "Experiencing the Cross: liturgy and mission"; a paper prepared at Interdenominational Theological Center, Atlanta, 1989; p. 24.

529 Charles Partee, *Adventure in Africa: the story of Don McClure, from Khartoum to Addis Ababa in five decades*. (1990), p. 350.

530 Ibid., p. 358f.

531 Ibid., p. 360. Partee gives a vivid description of this harrowing experience in his book, pp. 360-365.

532 Ibid., p. 366

533 Ibid., p. 367.

534 Ibid., p. 371.

535 Minutes of the General Assembly of UPCUSA, 1967, COEMAR Report, p. 13.

536 Ibid.

537 Minutes of the General Assembly of UPCUSA, 1967, COEMAR Report, p. 12.

538 Mary Ann Bode, *Rain out of Season* (February 1966), p. 6.

539 Partee, p. 345.

540 Ibid., p. 350. During this period, the American Presbyterian missionary force in Ethiopia jumped to a record number of 97, thanks to the relocation of missionaries from southern Sudan.

541 Letter from William B. Anderson to Dr. Glenn Reed, July 8, 1964, p. 3.

542 Gidada Solon, *The Other Side of Darkness*, p. 111.

543 Latourette, *Christianity in a Revolutionary Age*, Volume V, p. 286f.

544 Debela Birri, p. 264.

545 Minutes of the General Assembly of the UPCUSA, Part II, Ninth Annual Report of the COEMAR, May 18-24, 1967, p. 9. Quoted in Debela Birri, p. 265.

546 The term "Mekane Yesus" literally means "dwelling place of Jesus." It is significant that this term was chosen, rather than one that would identify the churches as distinctly Lutheran. As we shall see, this opened the way for churches that were the fruit of other denominational missionary witness to become part of the Mekane Yesus Church.

547 Paul Hopkins, COEMAR's Area Secretary for Africa, indicates that the Evangelical Church Bethel was supportive from the outset of the goal of a United Evangelical Church, but that the struggle was with the Mission, which had wanted to keep the fruit of its work in a separate denomination, even though its financial support for the Evangelical Church Bethel was very limited. (Conversation with Paul Hopkins)

548 Debela Birri, p. 287. Debela Birri comments, "Bethel was severely incapacitated by lack of trained leadership on equal footing with Mekane Yesus and lack of internal unity. Furthermore, whereas the Lutheran Missions rallied around Mekane Yesus in providing financial support

and trained leadership, the American Mission stood far away and watched as the Bethel struggled to survive. The neighboring Western Synod of the Ethiopian Evangelical Church Mekane Yesus was seen growing and prospering, and many of the Bethel Congregations joined the Western Synod. The outreach program that the Qellem Synod started in Gidami, Sayo Badda and Dapo Gacho was turned over to the Western Synod of the Ethiopian Evangelical Church Mekane Yesus due to lack of funds. These and similar reasons led the leaders of the Qellem Synod of the Ethiopian Evangelical Church Bethel to question its relationship with the American Mission with regard to the work of the Church. This was discussed at the meeting of the Executive Committee of Qellem Synod on December 15, 1973 and a Study Committee was appointed to find a Mission or a Church or any organization that would help the Church to fully carry on her mission in that part of the country." Debela Birri, p. 282f.

Also, Bakke comments: "Unity did not mean uniformity; considerable differences existed. This was only to be expected since the congregations came from different traditional and missionary backgrounds. The concepts of leadership in the various traditional cultures were somewhat different from area to area." Bakke, p. 107.

[549]   Debela Birri is the author of the dissertation on a history of the Evangelical Church Bethel, to whom the present writer is deeply indebted for much of the information in this section.

[550]   Harold Kurtz, "Church Ordains 10 Pastors, *Ethio-Echo* Vol. 8, No. 2 (1971): 1-2. Quoted in Debela Birri, p. 246.

[551]   Gidada, p. 31.

[552]   See Debela Birri, pp. 253-255.

[553]   Debela Birri, p. 257.

[554]   Debela implies that the "Renewal Meeting" had been engineered by the missionary who was responsible for the evangelistic work of Sayo Station, and that this precipitated the ensuing division. Ibid., p. 258

[555]   Ibid., p. 259.

[556]   Ibid. Debela Birri was among the leaders of the Youth Association during this time. It marked a point at which the leadership of the church was passing into the hands of a younger, better educated generation.

[557]   Minutes of the General Assembly of the UPCUSA, Part II, Ninth Annual Report of COEMAR, 1967, p. 8. This was the last year in which separate field reports and statistics appeared in the UPCUSA General Assembly minutes. From this point, statistics and other information regarding specific mission endeavors become difficult to ascertain.

[558]   In 1967, it was reported that there were 97 missionaries in the American Presbyterian Mission, nearly twice as many as the number at the beginning of this period. Only ten of these were working in the new tribal areas, four of whom had been secunded by the Reformed Church in America. The educational work at this point included central primary schools at Sayo, Ghimeera, and Maji; The Matthews School for the Blind in Sayo; and the Annie Campbell George Memorial Girls' Boarding School in Addis Ababa. The medical work included the Jean R. Orr Memorial Hospital at Sayo, and clinics at Maji, Ghimeera and Pokwo.

[559]   The project was also known as the Forgotten Tribes Mission (see Partee, p. 376f.), and as the Ilubabor-Kefa Project.

560   Donald Black, Merging mission and unity: a history of the Commission on Ecumenical Mission and Relations (1986), p. 158. According to Partee, the tribes to be included in the project were the Nuers in Ethiopia; the Masongos, estimated at between 20,000 and 30,000 people; the Shakkos, with between 15,000 and 20,000 people; the Mochas, with 40,000 to 50,000; the Teshenas, estimated at 100,000 people; the Tid-Termas, with approximately 20,000; and the Gulebs, "perhaps the least known and most inaccessible of all the tribes of western Ethiopia" (Partee, p. 377). While the Anuak work actually had been begun in 1951, it was administered as one of the tribal groups in the project. COEMAR commissioned a study of the tribal peoples of southwest Ethiopia, which was carried out by Alan Tippett; see his book, Peoples of Southwest Ethiopia (1970). It was estimated that there were twenty or more tribal groups in this area, numbering as many as a million people.

     Black, who was serving as COEMAR's Associate General Secretary, admits that the Untouched Tribes Project was not given high priority by COEMAR. "The Mission in Ethiopia had presented a good plan for expanding into new areas, but there was no new money to provide for it. The increases in giving were tapering off, and increased costs were absorbing all the new money. When the General Mission Budget was being presented to the General Assembly [apparently in 1961], the Missionary Advisory Delegate from Ethiopia asked where this new program was included. The reply that it was not possible to include it caused a stir among the commissioners. A motion was later presented from the floor that made the project acceptable for extra giving, over and above the regular budget. The motion was approved with enthusiasm." Black, p. 157.

561   Harold Kurtz, in *The Presbyterian Layman*, January/February 1996, page 13.

562   Missionaries resented the fact that those who were chosen by COEMAR were not the established leaders of the Ethiopian Church, but rather younger leaders who were fluent in English. "This put the administration of the church in the hands of those less qualified. This effort from New York to 'micromanage' the situation in Ethiopia, channeling all funds through the church, has led to power struggles in the Ethiopian church, especially over money and property." (Paper prepared by retired mission personnel who had served in Ethiopia, February 14, 1997, p. 2)

563   Abuna Theophilus was one of the presidents of the World Council of Churches from 1954 to 1961.

564   As the youth caravan was in the planning stage, Don McClure commented, "Recently the commission wanted to send a caravan to Ethiopia. The team was to be composed of youngsters sixteen to nineteen years old with their adult advisers. The board proposed to fly them to Ethiopia for a week at Pokwo, a week in Ghimeera, and two weeks in Addis Ababa, helping us with anything that needed to be done. I cannot imagine a bunch of kids like that doing anything worthwhile out here in one week. They would cause us more trouble in feeding and sleeping them than they could possibly contribute. I don't know what I would give them to do, unless it was hoeing corn, and I am sure the Anuaks can do it better." Partee, p. 376.

565   Bakke, p. 251ff. A new musical creativity emerged out of the *Mulu Wongel* movement, combining original Christian lyrics with authentic Ethiopian melodies. These songs were a major factor in the spiritual dynamics that sustained the Ethiopian church through the 17

difficult years following the Marxist revolution that began in 1974. See "Theology in Song: Ethiopia's Tesfaye Gabbiso", by Lila W. Balisky, in *Missiology*, Vol. XXV, No. 4, October 1997, p. 447ff.

[566] "A History of the Church in East Africa, with Special Reference to Kenya", by J.N.K. Mugambi, in *Toward a History of the Church in the Third World: The Issue of Periodization*, p. 40.

[567] Ibid., p. 47

[568] Ibid., p. 49.

[569] Latourette, *Christianity in a Revolutionary Age*, vol. 5, p. 476.

[570] Donald Black acknowledges that COEMAR ran into problems in this regard: "The new outreach into Africa was not without its mistakes. Since we were dealing directly with churches, we did not take the time to communicate with other churches [i.e. mission agencies] and explain our plans. We established relations with the Presbyterian Church of East Africa but we strained relations with the Church of Scotland whose missionaries had helped in the founding of that church." Donald Black, *Merging mission and unity: a history of the Commission on Ecumenical Missions and Relations*, p., 59.

[571] Gittings, p. 45.

[572] Gittings, p. 46.

[573] 1954 General Assembly Minutes, pp. 187f

[574] The Sharpeville massacre took place as a result of a demonstration against the Pass Laws, which required every African over sixteen to carry a "reference book" indicating their racial status. Though the large crowd was non-violent, the South African police began firing into them, and 69 people were killed and 180 were wounded. Nine days later some 30,000 Africans marched to the center of Cape Town, staging a massive but peaceful challenge to the government. That same day, March 30, 1960, the government declared a state of emergency, arresting hundreds of leaders of the African National Congress and the Pan-Africanist Congress, and banning both organizations forever. Thus organized legal African opposition came to an end and over the next years the structures of oppression grew steadily more formidable. Hastings, p. 136f.

[575] 1960 General Assembly Minutes, pp. 352f.

[576] 1965 General Assembly Minutes, pp. 402ff.

[577] General Assembly Minutes, pp. 328ff.

[578] 1969 General Assembly Minutes, pp. It was at the 1969 General Assembly in San Antonio that James Forman confronted the commissioners with the demand for reparations to the black American community for the injustices of slavery and oppression. This prepared the Assembly to look seriously at the problem of racism in Southern Africa as well. The World Council of Churches Executive Committee would meet shortly afterward in Canterbury to initiate the Program to Combat Racism.

[579] By 1970, there were over 3,000 such churches in South Africa, with over four million adherents. The first such bodies were identified with the Ethiopian movement emphasizing African independence. "They arose from a wide variety of causes, not all of them operating in any one body: rebellion against white control, desire to create a distinctive African expression of Christianity, impatience with imported forms of worship, personal ambitions of individual

leaders, appeal to the emotions, and confidence in faith healing." (Latourette, *Christianity in a Revolutionary Age*, Vol. V, p. 457) Black denominations in the United States have also played an important role in South Africa, the most important being the African Methodist Episcopal (AME) Church.

580   In February 1972, the Catholic hierarchy under the leadership of Archbishop Denis Hurley issued a "Call to Conscience" which "was probably the best spelt-out major statement on justice in South Africa to come at any time from any ecclesiastical source." (Hastings, p. 205). However, it suffered from a weakness common among the English-speaking white churches, i.e. inability to cooperate intimately with black people or to apply liberal theory effectively to the political reality.

581   The African National Congress (ANC) was a multiracial organization formed in South Africa in 1912 to extend the franchise to the whole population and to end all racial discrimination. Originally non-violent, it was supported by the Organization of African Unity as a movement aimed at introducing majority rule in South Africa. The ANC was banned by the South African government in 1960, at which point it moved its headquarters to Mozambique and developed its military wing to engage in sabotage and guerrilla training. In 1990 the ban on the ANC was lifted, its imprisoned leaders were released, and talks began between the government and the ANC. In 1994, the ANC was victorious in the first non-racial elections, and ANC leader Nelson Mandela became South Africa's president.

582   Article on Z.K. Matthews in *Dictionary of the Ecumenical Movement*, p. 665f.; also article on Cottesloe Consultation, ibid., p. 230f. Later Matthews became Africa Secretary of the WCC's Division of Inter-Church Aid, Refugee and World Service. He was a key figure in the formation of the All Africa Conference of Churches in 1963. In 1966 he became Botswana's ambassador to Washington and permanent representative at the UN.

583   Hastings, *History of African Christianity*, 1950-1975, p. 28f.

584   Ibid., p. 93f.

585   Black, p. 58.

586   Ibid., p. 133.

587   Dr. John Coventry Smith, COEMAR's Executive Secretary, was a member of the WCC Executive Committee from 1969 to 1975. He served for two years as a member of the Committee for the Program to Combat Racism. See Smith, *From Colonialism to World Christianity*, p. 300ff.

588   The WCC contributed $200,000 from its reserves to start the fund. However, from that point the fund was supported by voluntary contributions only.

589   "Programme to Combat Racism", *Dictionary of the Ecumenical Movement*, p. 825ff.

590   Hastings, p. 215ff.

591   Ibid., p. 16.

592   Ibid., p. 133.

593   Hastings, p. 188. Kaunda's strong churchmanship was recognized by his being asked to address the World Council of Churches at Uppsala in 1968. Kaunda's letters to his close missionary friend and colleague, Colin Morris, have been published in the book, *A Humanist in Africa* (Abingdon, 1969).

594   Latourette, *Christianity in a Revolutionary Age*, Vol. V, p. 462.

595   This separated a portion of the Presbyterian Church in Zambia from the Presbyterian Church in Nyasaland (Malawi), to which they had hitherto belonged. Hastings, p. 161.

596   Hastings, p. 162.

597   Hastings, p. 125.

598   Hastings, p. 131.

599   The attitude of Banda's government toward Jehovah's Witnesses was even more intolerant than that of the government of Zambia. "First in 1967 and then almost continuously from 1972 the Witnesses were harried with mounting brutality by the Malawi Congress Party and its tough boys in the Youth League. They were denied legal protection, excluded from all employment, their homes were burnt, and dozens were murdered. After a vain attempt to find refuge in Zambia some 36,000 fled . . . to Mozambique, where their apolitical attitudes were just what the Portuguese authorities liked to see in Africans." (Hastings, p. 195f.)

600   Edwin S. Pons, *The Southern and Central Streams of Presbyterianism in Africa*, p. 9. This is a valuable resource for the study of the origins of the Presbyterian Church of South Africa (PCSA) and the Church of Central Africa Presbyterian (CCAP).

601   Ibid., p. 10.

Chapter V

602   Article in *Presbyterian (USA) News Briefs*, October 8, 1999, p. 14.

603   The United Nations has estimated that, of the 36 million people in the world living with HIV/AIDS in the year 2000, over 25 million of them are in Africa. Also, of the 13 million children aged 14 or younger who have been orphaned by AIDS, 12 million of them were from sub-Saharan Africa. About half of all 15 year olds in those African countries most affected by AIDS will eventually die of the disease even if the rates of infection drop substantially in the next few years. However, if infection rates remain high, the odds are that more than two-thirds of the 15 year olds will die from AIDS in some countries. The most seriously affected countries include Botswana, Kenya, Malawi, Mozambique, Namibia, Rwanda, South Africa, Zambia and Zimbabwe. About 85% of AIDS deaths world-wide took place in Sub-Saharan Africa. See "Africa" by Yenwith K. Whitney, in *World Updates,* Summer 2000, issued by the Presbyterian (USA) United Nations Office. See also "AIDS in South Africa: Why the churches matter" by Sarah Ruden, in *The Christian Century*, May 17, 2000; "The Plague Years", NEWSWEEK, January 17, 2000.

604   See article "Moratorium" in *Dictionary of the Ecumenical Movement*, p. 702f.

605   See articles "Ecumenical Association of Third-World Theologians" and "Ecumenical Association of African Theologians", in *Dictionary of the Ecumenical Movement*, p. 322f. A major work produced by EATWOT regarding African theology is *African Theology en Route*, edited by Kofi Appiah-Kubi and Sergio Torres, published by Orbis Press, 1979. The EATWOT Historical Commission has produced a book, *African Church Historiography: An Ecumenical Perspective*, edited by Ogbu U. Kalu, published by the Swiss Protestant Ecumenical Office, 1986.

606   See "Status of Global Mission: 2000", prepared by David B. Barrett, in *International Bulletin of Missionary Research*, January 2000, p. 25

607 Between its inception in 1971 and its merger with the UPCUSA World Hunger Program, the PCUS World Hunger Program made grants to 45 programs of partner churches in 17 African nations, totaling over $821,000.

The 1984 General Assembly adopted a resolution on the Food Crisis in Africa, urging congregations and governing bodies to study and sign a "Covenant of Compassion in Response to Famine in Africa." See 1984 PC(USA) General Assembly Minutes, Part I, p. 377f.

608 See Chart IV for a list of partner churches with which the Presbyterian Church (USA) is working in sub-Saharan Africa. Also Chart V for comparative statistics of population, percentage of Christians, and life expectancy in countries where PC(USA) has partners in mission.

609 The Program for Evangelism and Church Growth in Africa was initiated by mission co-worker Bill Warlick. Beginning in Zaire, the program gradually expanded until it was carried out in all the countries where the PC(USA) was involved in partnership in mission.

610 PC(USA) General Assembly Minutes, 1991, Part I, page 633.

611 PC(USA) General Assembly Minutes, 1994, Part I, page 241f.

612 An American Presbyterian surgeon visiting Cameroon in 1992 would write, "It is interesting that the people in the grassroots of the EPC in all areas of Cameroon feel like we have deserted them. 'Where are all your people? We are your children. Why have you deserted us? Parents do not desert their children—ever!' We said it was necessary for us to 'let them fly' on their own and be partners with them, and these people in the trenches tell us it has not worked. They cannot understand why mission giving in our churches is drying up. Yes, these people plead for more direct relationships between them and the churches in our country." Mission Correspondence from Dr. and Mrs. Donald C. Mullen, June 3, 1992.

613 Missionary Correspondence from the Frelicks, October 1991.

614 Missionary Correspondence from the Frelicks, April/May 1993

615 Missionary Correspondence from the Frelicks, January 1994.

616 *Mission Focus*, April 1990, published by the PC(USA) General Assembly Council.

617 Missionary Correspondence from Dr. Dorothy Brewster-Lee, November 1994.

618 Mission Briefs in *Presbyterian Survey*, July-August 1989,

619 Missionary Correspondence from Guy and Monique Bekaert, January 1995.

620 Missionary Correspondence from Brian C. Snyder, Oct. 8, 1996.

621 American Presbyterian missionaries had first come to the tiny island of Corisco off the coast of Spanish Guinea in 1850, but it was 1865 before the first missionary was stationed on the mainland of what is now Equatorial Guinea.

622 2000 Mission Yearbook for Prayer and Study, p. 28.

623 Missionary Correspondence from Robert and Nancy Crumpton, July 29, 1991

624 Missionary Correspondence from Robert and Nancy Crumpton, February 18, 1992

625 Missionary Correspondence from Bill and Judi Young, November 1996.

626 Missionary Correspondence from Wendy and Garvester Kelley, January 2000.

627 Missionary Correspondence from Corey Nelson, November 1995.

628 Missionary Correspondence from the Rev. & Mrs. Emory VanGerpen, December 1993.

629 Missionary Correspondence from Sue and Bill Sager, April 8, 2000

630 Missionary Correspondence from John and Gwenda Fletcher, January 2000

[631] Missionary Correspondence from Haejung and Simon Park, November 1999. The 1993 PC(USA) General Assembly adopted a resolution "On Praying for the People of Zaire", in light of the increased violence and oppression initiated by Mobutu; who forcably displaced more than 350,000 Kasaians from the mineral-rich Shaba region, creating a serious refugee problem in the Kasai. The Good Shepherd Hospital took leadership in providing medical care for these internal refugees. See 1993 General Assembly Minutes. pp. 937-938. Also, the 1997 General Assembly issued "A Call to Prayer for Congo/Zaire", p. 443f.

[632] Missionary Correspondence from John and Gwenda Fletcher, February 1999. An account of the church situation up to 1983 is given in Sophie Montgomery Crane's *A Legacy Remembered*, p. 300f. In the early 1970s, the government nationalized all church schools and prohibited the teaching of religion. This later proved unworkable, and the schools were returned to the churches. However, the churches were not equipped to maintain an effective school system on their own. The few educational missionaries who remained were given teaching assignments but had neither the authority nor the responsibility to uphold standards. The unfortunate deterioration of the church-related school system has continued to the present.

[633] A superb detailed description of the medical work of IMCK as well as other mission-founded hospitals is given in Crane, op. cit., pp. 305-345. While Mrs. Crane's account describes the work up to 1983, this account focuses on the situation in the 1990s.

[634] Missionary Correspondence from John and Gwenda Fletcher, January 2000.

[635] Missionary Correspondence from Bill and Sue Sager, March 4, 2001.

[636] Missionary Correspondence from Knute and Lynn Hernas, Summer 1996.

[637] Missionary Correspondence from Sue Makin, M.D., June 24, 1995. Dr. Makin would serve three terms in the Congo, both at IMCK and as an ob/gyn consultant at other hospitals in the Kasai.

[638] Missionary Correspondence from Ralph and Elsbeth Shannon, January 1998. Rather than retiring, Dr. Shannon accepted an itinerating ophthalmologist position with the Christian Blind Mission, filling four-month assignments in various countries in Africa. In addition to improving the effectiveness of the ophthalmology departments in hospitals with new or developing eye programs and doing surgery, he would conduct in-service training. The Shannons' first assignment was Rwanda.

[639] Missionary Correspondence from Haejung & Simon Park, November 2000.

[640] Missionary Correspondence from Larry Sthreshley, May 15, 2001. The SANRU program, initiated in the early 1980s as a nationwide program of primary health care, was organized and subsidized by USAID in cooperation with the Department of Health of the Zairian government and the Protestant churches of Zaire. PCUS medical missionary Dr. John Miller served as a consultant in planning and setting up the program. IMCK, along with the Bulape and Bibanga Hospitals, was designated a Regional Reference Hospital. IMCK was put in charge of a "health zone" consisting of 150,000 people. Responsibilities included supervision of 23 city and rural health posts, training of health workers, updating of skills through refresher courses, and provision of a constant supply of basic medicines. See Crane, p. 323.

[641] Missionary Correspondence from Ruth and Bill Metzel, February 18, 2000.

[642] 1976 PCUS General Assembly Minutes, p. 420.

[643] *Currents of the Presbytery of Eastern Virginia*, Winter Issue 1997, p. 4.

[644] Missionary Correspondence from Ben and Betsy Hobgood, May 1995.

[645] Missionary Correspondence from Bill and Sue Sager, March 4, 2001.

[646] A report appearing in the 1995 PC(USA) General Assembly Minutes commented: "It was yet one more blot in a dark history of colonial exploitation by Belgium. The Belgians instituted an apartheid-like system, with cards that identified people by race and tribe. The Belgians ruled through the Tutsi minority . . . . The church which has often ministered within particular tribal and community contexts, has encountered its own difficulties in trying to be an agent for reconciliation. The churches are reaching out for help in rebuilding their people and nation, both physically and psychologically." 1995 PC(USA) General Assembly Minutes, p. 450.

[647] Project proposal submitted to the PCUS Task Force on World Hunger.

[648] 1994 PC(USA) General Assembly Minutes, p. 334f.

[649] 1995 PC(USA) General Assembly Minutes, p. 309.

[650] "Rwanda: Country in Shock", by Tim Emerick-Cayton, in *Monday Morning*, Dec. 8, 1997, p. 5ff.

[651] Flyer produced by the Worldwide Ministries Division, no date.

[652] 1979 UPCUSA General Assembly Minutes, p. 348f.

[653] 1980 PCUS General Assembly Minutes, p. 450.

[654] In December 1992, the United Nations condemned the government of Sudan for "gross and flagrant violations of human rights." The 1993 PC(USA) General Assembly approved a Commissioner's Resolution "Expressing Concern for the People of Sudan." 1993 PC(USA) General Assembly Minutes, p. 938. United States military support for the government of Sudan in the 1980s caused the southern and eastern Sudanese to call on US groups to become stronger advocates for human rights in Sudan. 1994 PC(USA) General Assembly Minutes, p. 304.

[655] Veteran missionary William Anderson writes, "In June [2000], the government quietly cleared out tens of thousands of Nuer and Dinka tribesmen 500 miles south of Khartoum to make a path for a large, thousand-mile oil pipeline to the sea. Since most of the oil is located in southern Sudan, the southern Sudanese are being displaced so the government can have access to it." 2001 Mission Yearbook for Prayer and Study, p. 48.

[656] Mission Co-worker William Anderson, in 2001 Mission Yearbook for Prayer and Study, p. 48.

[657] The government repeatedly destroyed these "illegal" settlements, forcing thousands to flee and find other temporary shelter. 1992 PC(USA) General Assembly Minutes, p. 737.

[658] Missionary Correspondence from Mark Rasmussen and Caroline Kurtz, February 15, 1996.

[659] 1992 PC(USA) General Assembly Minutes, p. 592.

[660] 1999 Mission Yearbook for Prayer and Study, p. 51.

[661] Missionary Correspondence from Mike and Billie Healy, December 21, 1993.

[662] 1996 PC(USA) General Assembly Minutes, p. 571.

[663] Missionary Correspondence from Bill and Willie Simmons, Spring 1995.

[664] 1992 PC(USA) General Assembly Minutes, p. 636.

665   1995 PC(USA) General Assembly Minutes, p. 328. Both government and rebel forces imposed conscription upon these children, compelling them to undergo military training and then sending them into battle, where thousands were killed. 1995 GA Minutes, p. 454. Also, there was strong evidence that government forces participated in the abduction, sale and trafficking of southern Sudanese children, continuing the practice of slave trade which has prevailed in parts of the Arab world. 1996 PC(USA) General Assembly Minutes, p. 571.

666   Missionary Correspondence from Betsy McCormick and Barry Almy, September 1996.

667   1997 PC(USA) General Assembly Minutes, p. 721.

668   1999 PC(USA) General Assembly Minutes, p. 788.

669   2000 Mission Yearbook for Prayer and Study, p. 49.

670   Missionary Correspondence from Mark Rasmussen and Caroline Kurtz, August 2000.

671   2001 Mission Yearbook for Prayer and Study, p. 49.

672   Missionary Correspondence from Bill and Lois Anderson, June 5, 2000.

673   Missionary Correspondence from Michael Parker, November 23, 1995.

674   Haile Selassie died the following year, 1975, at age 83, in a small apartment in his former palace in Addis Ababa, bringing to a tragic end his 45-year reign and the centuries-old imperial lineage of Ethiopia.

675   1976 UPCUSA General Assembly Minutes, p. 569.

676   UPCUSA General Assembly Minutes: 1978, p. 315; 1979; p. 348f.; 1980, p. 251; 1981, p. 322; 1982, p. 355. Most American Presbyterian missionaries were reassigned to other African countries, including Cameroon, Malawi, and Zambia.

677   Missionary Correspondence from Mark Rasmussen and Caroline Kurtz, May 23, 1991.

678   "Operation Return: Ethiopia", by Earl. S. Johnson Jr., in *The Presbyterian Outlook*, March 13, 1995, p. 10.

679   John and Gwen Haspels, both children of missionaries, had extensive experience in pioneer work in both Ethiopia and the Sudan.

680   "Have We Finished the Task?", paper by Anna H. Ens, May 1993, p. 1. Miss Ens served as a missionary teacher in Ethiopia from 1952 to 1973.

681   Missionary Correspondence from Caryl Weinberg, Fall 1998.

682   The Wheeler-Waddells had served effectively at the Pastoral Training Institute of the Presbyterian Church of East Africa in Kikuyu, Kenya from 1991 to 1996.

683   Missionary Correspondence from John and Anne Wheeler-Waddell, March 1997.

684   Missionary Correspondence from John and Anne Wheeler-Waddell, July 2000.

685   *1999 Mission Yearbook for Prayer and Study*, p. 30.

686   Missionary Correspondence from Michael and Rachel Weller, June 1999.

687   2000 Mission Yearbook for Prayer and Study, p. 34.

688   2001 Mission Yearbook for Prayer and Study, p. 33.

689   Missionary Correspondence from Caroline Kurtz, March 10, 1994.

690   Ethiopia information sheet produced by the PC(USA) Worldwide Ministries Division.

691   Missionary Correspondence from Dr. Marta Bennett, February 9, 1995.

692   Missionary Correspondence from Tim and Sher Emerick-Cayton, February 1998.

693   Missionary Correspondence from the Rev. Edward Danks, Advent/Christmas 1999.

694 Missionary Correspondence from Marion Strain, June 1999.

695 Missionary Correspondence from Marion Strain, December 1999.

696 Missionary Correspondence from Mia and Stan Topple, June 1991.

697 Missionary Correspondence from Mia and Stan Topple, Christmas 1992.

698 Missionary Correspondence from Mia and Stan Topple, November 1993.

699 Missionary Correspondence from Mia and Stan Topple, April 1994.

700 Missionary Correspondence from Mia and Stan Topple, November 1994.

701 Missionary Correspondence from Mia and Stan Topple, November 1993.

702 Missionary Correspondence from Mia and Stan Topple, November 1994.

703 Missionary Correspondence from Mia and Stan Topple, July 1997.

704 Missionary Correspondence from Stan and Mia Topple, May 1998. Though retired, the Topples continue to return to spend some time each year as "emeritus missionaries" at Kikuyu.

705 Kenya information sheet produced by the PC(USA) Worldwide Ministries Division.

706 1999 Mission Yearbook for Prayer & Study, p. 37.

707 2000 Mission Yearbook for Prayer & Study, p. 42.

708 2001 Mission Yearbook for Prayer & Study, p. 42.

709 Madagascar Information Sheet produced by the PC(USA) Worldwide Ministries Division.

710 Missionary Correspondence from Joe & Becky Carle, Easter 1991.

711 Missionary Correspondence from Brian and Liz Crosby, August 1991.

712 Missionary Correspondence from Brian and Liz Crosby, January 1997.

713 1978 PCUS General Assembly Minutes, p. 442f.

714 1980 PCUS General Assembly Minutes, p. 450.

715 1981 UPCUSA General Assembly Minutes, p. 247-253. Also, 1982 UPCUSA General Assembly Minutes, p. 355.

716 1983 PC(USA) General Assembly Minutes, p. 175.

717 1988 PC(USA) General Assembly Minutes, p. 229f. The 1989 General Assembly received a report on South Africa divestment policy implementation. 1989 GA Minutes, p. 448f. Also, the 1991 General Assembly received a report entitled, "The Dividends of Hope: An Evanluation of Divestment for South Africa." 1991 GA Minutes, p. 728ff.

718 1995 PC(USA) General Assembly Minutes, p. 453.

719 Vernon S. Broyles, III, "The Churches of South Africa: Bearers of Hope for the Future", *NEWS BRIEFS*, November 5, 1999.

720 2001 Mission Yearbook for Prayer & Study, p. 46f.

721 2000 Mission Yearbook for Prayer & Study, p. 47.

722 2001 Mission Yearbook for Prayer & Study, p. 47.

723 "Africa", by Yenwith K. Whitney, in *World Updates*, Spring 2000, p. 1f.

724 Missionary Correspondence from Bob and Bobbi Snyder, August 2001.

725 Missionary Correspondence from Polly and David Miller, Christmas 1993. The theological education dimension of PECGA was added during the course of its development, as the critical need for leadership training became increasingly evident.

726 2000 Mission Yearbook for Prayer and Study, p. 51.

727 Missionary Correspondence from Nancy Warlick, June 30, 2001.

728 Missionary Correspondence from Bill and Nancy Warlick, October 1999.

729 Missionary Correspondence from Irma and Salvador de la Torre, October 1992.

730 The 1992 PC(USA) Women's Birthday Offering provided funding to assist the Church of Central Africa Presbyterian (CCAP) in a program to rehabilitate refugee children from Mozambique. 1992 PC(USA) General Assembly Minutes, p. 593. Also, through Church World Service, PC(USA) World Service sent relief assistance to CCAP and the Christian Council of Malawi. Malawi's traditional route to the sea through neighboring Mozambique was all but closed due to that country's protracted civil war.

731 Missionary Correspondence from Mark & Betsy Cameron-Gray, March 22, 1992.

732 A Commissioner's Resolution was adopted by the 1992 PC(USA) General Assembly concerning the political oppression in Malawi and in support of the CCAP in speaking out concerning the pain and suffering of its people. 1992 PC(USA)/GA Minutes, p. 926.

733 1999 Mission Yearbook for Prayer and Study, p. 40. Dr. Mazunda had earned his doctorate at Columbia Theological Seminary in Decatur, Georgia. During his stay in the United States, he visited numerous churches and made many friends. His influence undoubtedly greatly increased the interest of American Presbyterians in the Christian movement in Malawi.

734 "And There was Light, And It Was Good!", by Ken and Nancy McGill, *Presbyterian Survey*, September 1989, p. 36f.

735 Missionary Correspondence from Paul & Judy Jewett, March 17, 1991.

736 Missionary Correspondence from Paul & Judy Jewett, April 1991.

737 "Mission Briefs," *Presbyterian Survey*, November 1990.

738 Missionary Correspondence from Paul and Judy Jewett, July 19, 1991.

739 Missionary Correspondence from Paul and Judy Jewett, October 1991.

740 Missionary Correspondence from Paul and Judy Jewett, February 21, 1993.

741 Missionary Correspondence from Paul and Judy Jewett, December 10, 1995.

742 Missionary Correspondence from Paul and Judy Jewett, July 19, 1994

743 Missionary Correspondence from Paul and Judy Jewett, September 10, 1996.

744 Missionary Correspondence from Dr. Becky Loomis, Spring 1996.

745 Missionary Correspondence from Paul and Judy Jewett, September 10, 1996.

746 Missionary Correspondence from Dr. Betty Loomis, February 1998.

747 Missionary Correspondence from Frank and Nancy Dimmock, May 1992.

748 Missionary Correspondence from Frank and Nancy Dimmock, May 1993.

749 Missionary Correspondence from Frank and Nancy Dimmock, May 1993.

750 Missionary Correspondence from Frank and Nancy Dimmock, December 1993.

751 2001 Mission Yearbook for Prayer and Study, p. 41.

752 Missionary Correspondence from Jim Cairns, Christmas 1995

753 Missionary Correspondence from Wilma and Otis Rowe, February 1991.

754 Missionary Correspondence from Wilma and Otis Rowe, Christmas 1991

755 Missionary Correspondence from Doug and Ruth Welch, December 1992.

756 Missionary Correspondence from Doug and Ruth Welch, February 1993.

757 Missionary Correspondence from Ruth and Doug Welch, November 1997.

758 Missionary Correspondence from Joseph M. Hopkins, November 1991.

[759] Missionary Correspondence from Hannah and Joseph Kang, November 21, 1991.

[760] Missionary Correspondence from Hannah and Joseph Kang, November 20, 1992.

[761] Missionary Correspondence from Hannah and Joseph Kang, March 15, 1993.

[762] Missionary Correspondence from Hannah and Joseph Kang, Spring/Summer 1994.

[763] Missionary Correspondence from Hannah and Joseph Kang, Fall/Winter 1994

[764] Missionary Correspondence from Hannah and Joseph Kang, Fall/Winter 1996. Bruce and Ollie Gannaway had served in Egypt, Kenya, Malawi, and Ghana, and later as staff persons with the PCUS and PC(USA) mission boards.

[765] Missionary Correspondence from Hannah and Joseph Kang, Spring/Summer 1996.

[766] Missionary Correspondence from Hannah and Joseph Kang, March 1997.

[767] Missionary Correspondence from Hannah and Joseph Kang, Fall/Winter 1996.

[768] Quoted in Missionary Correspondence from Dr. and Mrs. Frederic Stone, October 1993.

[769] In 1997 the South African gold mines began to close down, due to the fall of the price of gold on the world market. "Only five of thirty mines remain profitable. Of those 150,000 Basotho miners formerly employed, only 70,000 remain at work; the remainder were sent home to eke out a bare existence with their families." Missionary Correspondence from Ellenor and Paul Frelick, October 1997.

[770] 1995 PC(USA) General Assembly Minutes, p. 450. The GA Minutes read, "The Mountain Kingdom's march toward freedom and democracy is back on track and the people of Lesotho have a much deeper respect for voting rights and what it takes to secure them."

[771] Missionary Correspondence from Ellenor and Paul Frelick, November 1999.

[772] "It is deeply saddening that Roman Catholics and PC(USA) partner the Lesotho Evangelical Church tend to split politically, reflecting cancerous distrust that goes back more than forty years. We ask your prayers that our partners will help to build a national consensus crossing confessional lines for a more representative democracy so that the Sesotho greeting, *khotso* ('peace'), may become God's benediction, a living reality in this beautiful land." Ellenor and Paul Frelick, in *2000 Mission Yearbook for Prayer & Study*, p. 39.

[773] The 1979 PCUS General Assembly instructed the denomination's Mission Board "to monitor the situation in Lesotho and keep the courts of the church informed about future developments there." In turn, the General Assembly Mission Board adopted a resolution "express[ing] its compassion for its brothers and sisters in Christ in Lesotho who are being persecuted because of their faith", "deplor[ing] the injustice that is being perpetrated by the government of Lesotho that is dehumanizing;" and "call[ing] upon the government of the United States to stop all support for the government inside Lesotho and governments outside Lesotho that are the supporters of the violations of human rights." The resolution was delivered in person to the Lesotho Evangelical Church and the government of Lesotho by the moderator of the 1979 PCUS General Assembly, Dr. Albert C. Winn.

[774] Missionary Correspondence from Nancy and Frank Dimmock, February 1991.

[775] Missionary Correspondence from Paul and Ellenor Frelick, October/November 1996.

[776] Ibid.

[777] Missionary Correspondence from Paul and Ellenor Frelick, November 1999.

[778] Missionary Correspondence from Ellenor and Paul Frelick, October 1997.

779   In an article in *The Christian Century* of August 22-29, 1990, p. 756f., Jeffrey Phillips recounts: "Over the years the Swiss Reformed Church has been one of the leading international partners of the Mozambican church. I was told that one Swiss missionary doctor had been serving in the bush since 1964 despite political changes and obvious dangers. The next morning word reached us that this very physician, Rene Gagnaux, had been ambushed by RENAMO soldiers, shot twice, his dead body left along the road, and his Toyota Landcruiser burned. He had been on his way to treat victims of RENAMO brutality. For the next week I prayed every evening with grieving Christian sisters and brothers at the Central Presbyterian Church. At the funeral Pastor Isaiah Fundzamo [said]: 'Christians should be used to deaths like that of Rene Gagnaux because they are similar to Jesus' death—a death on behalf of others.' The next day the national legislature made Gagnaux posthumously a citizen of Mozambique."

780   Missionary Correspondence from Ruth B. Minter, Lent 1991.

781   Missionary Correspondence from Dave & Polly Miller, April 1991.

782   Missionary Correspondence from David & Polly Miller, October 1993.

783   Missionary Correspondence from Bill and Nancy Warlick, February 1997

784   Mission Information sheet prepared by Worldwide Ministries Division, c. 1994.

Conclusion

785   2001 Mission Yearbook for Prayer and Study, p. 28.

786   1999 Mission Yearbook for Prayer and Study, p. 27.

787   Ibid.

788   1999 PC(USA) General Assembly Minutes, p. 680.

Made in the USA
Monee, IL
05 July 2022

99081608R00233